教育部高校工商管理类教学指导委员会双语教学推荐教材

BUSINESS
ADMINISTRATION
CLASSICS

工商管理经典教材·会计与财务系列

Business Administration Classics

中级会计学

（第12版）

Intermediate Accounting (Twelfth Edition)

唐纳德·E·基索（Donald E.Kieso）
杰里·J·韦安特（Jerry J. Weygandt）　著
特里·D·沃菲尔德（Terry D. Warfield）
饶菁　崔学刚　改编

中国人民大学出版社
·北京·

教育部高校工商管理类教学指导委员会双语教学推荐教材

工商管理经典教材·会计与财务系列

编委会

总　序

随着我国加入WTO，越来越多的国内企业参与到国际竞争中来，用国际上通用的语言思考、工作、交流的能力也越来越受到重视。这样一种能力也成为我国各类人才参与竞争的一种有效工具。国家教育机构、各类院校以及一些主要的教材出版单位一直在思考，如何顺应这一发展潮流，推动各层次人员通过学习来获取这种能力。双语教学就是这种背景下的一种尝试。

双语教学在我国主要指汉语和国际通用的英语教学。事实上，双语教学在我国教育界已经不是一个陌生的词汇了，以双语教学为主的科研课题也已列入国家"十五"规划的重点课题。但从另一方面来看，双语教学从其诞生的那天起就被包围在人们的赞成与反对声中。如今，依然是有人赞成有人反对，但不论是赞成居多还是反对占上，双语教学的规模和影响都在原有的基础上不断扩大，且呈大发展之势。一些率先进行双语教学的院校在实践中积累了经验，不断加以改进；一些待进入者也在模仿中学习，并静待时机成熟时加入这一行列。由于我国长期缺乏讲第二语言（包括英语）的环境，开展双语教学面临特殊的困难，因此，选用合适的教材就成为双语教学成功与否的一个重要问题。我们认为，双语教学从一开始就应该使用原版的各类学科的教材，而不是由本土教师自编的教材，从而可以避免中国式英语问题，保证语言的原汁原味。各院校除应执行国家颁布的教学大纲和课程标准外，还应根据双语教学的特点和需要，适当调整教学课时的设置，合理选择优秀的、合适的双语教材。

顺应这样一种大的教育发展趋势，中国人民大学出版社同众多国际知名的大出版公司，如麦格劳-希尔出版公司、培生教育出版公司等合作，面向大学本科生层次，遴选了一批国外最优秀的管理类原版教材，涉及专业基础课，人力资源管理、市场营销及国际化管理等专业方向课，并广泛听取有着丰富的双语一线教学经验的教师的建议和意见，对原版教材进行了适当的改编，删减了一些不适合我国国情和不适合教学的内容；另一方面，根据教育部对双语教学教材篇幅合理、定价低的要求，我们更是努力区别于目前市场上形形色色的各类英文版、英文影印版的大部头，将目标受众锁定在大学本科生层次。本套教材尤其突出了以下一些特点：

● 保持英文原版教材的特色。本套双语教材根据国内教学实际需要，对原书进行了一定的改编，主要是删减了一些不适合教学以及不符合我国国情的内容，但在体系结构和内容特色方面都保持了原版教材的风貌。专家们的认真改编和审定，使本套教材既保持了学术上的完整性，又贴近中国实际；既方便教师教学，又方便学生理解和掌握。

● 突出管理类专业教材的实用性。本套教材既强调学术的基础性，又兼顾应用的广泛性；既侧重让学生掌握基本的理论知识、专业术语和专业表达方式，又考虑到教材和管理实践的紧密结合，有助于学生形成专业的思维能力，培养实际的管理技能。

● 体系经过精心组织。本套教材在体系架构上充分考虑到当前我国在本科教育阶段推广双语教学的进度安排，首先针对那些课程内容国际化程度较高的学科进行双语教材开发，在其专业模块内精心选择各专业教材。这种安排既有利于我国教师摸索双语教学的经验，使得双语教学贴近现实教学的需要；也有利于我们收集关于双语教学教材的建议，更好地推出后续的双语教材及教辅材料。

● 篇幅合理，价格相对较低。为适应国内双语教学内容和课时上的实际需要，本套教材进行了一定的删减和改编，使总体篇幅更为合理；而采取低定价，则充分考虑到了学生实际的购买能力，从而使本套教材得以真正走近广大读者。

● 提供强大的教学支持。依托国际大出版公司的力量，本套教材为教师提供了配套的教辅材料，如教师手册、PowerPoint讲义、试题库等，并配有内容极为丰富的网络资源，从而使教学更为便利。

本套教材是在双语教学教材出版方面的一种尝试。我们在选书、改编及出版的过程中得到了国内许多高校的专家、教师的支持和指导，在此深表谢意。同时，为使我们后续推出的教材更适于教学，我们也真诚地期待广大读者提出宝贵的意见和建议。需要说明的是，尽管我们在改编的过程中已加以注意，但由于各教材的作者所处的政治、经济和文化背景不同，书中内容仍可能有不妥之处，望读者在阅读时注意比较和甄别。

徐二明

中国人民大学商学院

主持人语

（一）

2006年9月，中国人民大学出版社的编辑与我们联系，探讨筹划出版一套会计学系列英文原版教材，我们立即表示愿意合作。

在谈论我国改革开放伟大事业时有一个常被提到的故事：20世纪70年代后期，西方发达国家和我国港澳台地区的企业家、投资人来到中国大陆寻求商机和洽谈合作，总是有两种职业人才相伴，那就是律师和会计师。律师帮助企业家、投资人探究资本的安全性和发展的法制环境，会计师则帮助企业家、投资人分析合作者的财务状况和潜在的投资获利前景。所以，改革开放初期首先面世的相关规范，就是“三资企业法规”和“三资企业会计制度”。

一个显然的事实是，法律不可能国际化（甚至在一个主权国家之内，也存在着地区间的立法差异）。而会计，则一直在朝着成为“国际商业语言”的方向发展。资产负债表、利润表、现金流量表、股东权益变动表等作为会计语言的载体，在全世界的企业家、金融家、资本市场交易者之间，都是基本一致或相似的通用交流工具；而财务报告的编制者和审计者，都在遵循着促成大家得以相互理解、逐渐走向趋同的会计和审计专业规则。

相应地，我国改革开放20多年来，在国际交流的知识融会中，与国际接轨最快的领域当属商学各学科知识，其中会计学更是走在前面。大学会计专业教学在积极采用翻译教材的同时，很早就尝试采用英文原版教材，让广大师生受益匪浅。近年来国内出版的会计类英文版教科书越来越多，几乎没有漏掉大家公认的好书。而在出版时间方面，有些教材在中国出版的影印版和翻译版，甚至与其在母国的原版实现了同步，这使得我们在接受新知识方面几乎不存在时间差。可见，知识领域是没有不可逾越的语言界限的。

不过，我们也注意到，目前我国国内已经出版的众多会计专业英文版教科书，对院校教育的主角——教师和学生——来说，存在着两个严重的弱项：一是多而不成体系，分别看，每本都不错，可是怎么配套呢？要知道，一桌盛宴不能只是道道好菜一股脑儿端上来，还得有荤素冷热搭配才行；二是篇幅厚重、价格吓人，动辄半百元以上，别说多数学生买不起，就连教师们在书店也常常因囊中羞涩而犹豫再三，拿起又放下。

所以，我们很愿意与中国人民大学出版社的编辑一起，针对上述两个弱项来有意识地组织这套英文版改编教材。

（二）

工作的第一步是组织团队。接受邀请的团队成员都是在院校教学一线的青年教师，分别来自中国人民大学、北京大学、厦门大学、北京师范大学、对外经济贸易大学、北京工商大学、北方工业大学、北京语言大学等。他们都拥有博士学位；英文功底都非常好；都已经在教学中采用英文原版教材，从而深有体会；都在海内外核心期刊发表过学术论文；主持和参加的科学研究课题都得到国家自然科学基金、国家社会科学基金、国家博士后科学基金和教育部专项研究基金的有力支持。他们是会计教育和学术研究的“少壮派”：其中两位获得2007年“教育部新世纪优秀人才支持计划”研究项目资助，三位曾留学美国，四位入选“首届全国会计学术带头人后备人才”。

第二步是选书。结合当前中国院校会计学专业培养学生的课程设置，在国际著名教育出版公司推荐的基础上，改编团队成员与中国人民大学出版社的编辑一起，选择能够配套成体系的英文教科书。然后请各位改编者提出意向，向国外版权公司提交改编方案，申请版权合同。目前选定的丛书都是在美国院校会计教育中享有盛誉的教科书，作者均为欧美会计、财务学界的知名学者和专业人士。其中有几本已经在国内出版多次翻译版，为会计界人士所熟悉。

应该提到的一点是，这套丛书并不是封闭的，还计划继续增加新书（如信息系统、内部控制、会计理论、公司财务理论等），以不断充实和完善丛书体系。

第三步是确定改编原则。篇幅要缩小，但是力求改编后尽量保持全书结构的完整，主要是删除章后习题和附录，以及与我国实际情况相差较远、教学中不涉及的部分章节，使得改编后的书适合我国教学的实践。为了方便院校老师教学和学生学习，在教材之外，还计划在中国人民大学出版社网站（www.crup.com.cn）上提供中英文对照的目录和术语表、教学辅助资料、习题、案例、英文PPT等，供老师们免费下载；对于删除的完整章节，有兴趣的读者也可以上网免费下载。

随着我国教育改革的深入发展，我国各大学的商学院都越来越重视双语教学，选择反映国外最新教学研究成果的英文原版教材，已经成为普遍要求。为此我们希望，这套丛书能为院校的同仁提供帮助，同时也欢迎提出批评指正意见和改进建议。

王立彦（北京大学光华管理学院）
耿建新（中国人民大学商学院）

改编者前言

在教育部的大力倡导下，财经和管理类专业的双语教学和全英语教学已经在我国各大高校逐步开展起来。一些较早开展双语教学的院校积累了丰富的经验，同时也发现了教学过程中存在的一些问题，因此对教材提出了更高的要求。国外的原版教材是为国外教学量身定做的，普遍篇幅较大，侧重于描述性讲解，辅助材料繁杂，尤其是许多内容针对性太强，与所在国的法律结构和经济文化背景结合过于紧密，显然不适合国内教学采用，成为制约国内双语教学发展的瓶颈。因此，对国外原版教材进行本土化的精简改编，使之变成更加适用的双语教材，已经迫在眉睫。

财务会计作为会计的一个独立分支，通过编制和对外披露企业的财务报告，向包括企业外部和内部的会计信息使用者提供他们所需的有关企业财务状况、经营成果和现金流量的信息，供他们做出明智的决策。在财务会计教学中，中级会计学是联系初级会计学和高级会计学的桥梁，它涵盖了大部分的会计专业词汇，因此成为许多高校开展会计双语教学的首选课程。鉴于此，中国人民大学出版社和改编者在筛选教材时反复斟酌，选取了美国最畅销的中级会计学教材之一——由基索、韦安特和沃菲尔德三位教授编写的《中级会计学》。该书在美国的会计教学和实务界影响深远，是改编者在美国攻读会计学硕士时教授选用的教材，至今已经是第 12 版了。

第 12 版继续保持了一贯的特色，即会计学的课堂教学与真实的会计环境、实务操作紧密结合。在此基础上，作者更加强调时效性，并增加了真实案例讲解和会计的国际化视野，使之成为中级财务会计教学的经典教材。

从严格的意义上说，我们的改编应是删编。因为原版书过于厚重，内容相对较丰富，很多关于美国特色情况的介绍过于冗长，所以对中国学生而言，无论在经济承受能力方面，还是在学习接受程度方面都面临较大压力。因此，删除书中无伤大雅的枝节内容，保留其原汁原味的特色，不失为一举多得的明智选择。

我们删减的原则如下：

1. 在不影响全书可读性、完整性和实用性的前提下，把我们认为对中国学生而言可能相对冗余的内容删除（如原书第 20 章和第 21 章）。

2. 删除在其他会计学教学中会涉及的重复性内容（如原书第 6 章）。

3. 删除各章后的附录、练习题和案例分析题，将这些内容放在网上，读者如果对这些删除的内容感兴趣，也可上网免费下载。

删减后，全书内容如下：

第 1 章至第 3 章主要介绍会计准则、财务报告的基本原则和会计信息系统；

第 4 章至第 5 章主要介绍财务报告中的三大报表：资产负债表、利润表和现金流量表；

第 6 章至第 11 章分章节详细介绍各资产类科目；

第 12 章至第 13 章详细介绍各负债类科目；

第 14 章详细介绍所有者权益类科目；

第 15 章详细介绍债权投资和股权投资；

第 16 章主要介绍收入的确认；

第 17 章主要介绍所得税的计算；

第 18 章涉及会计政策、会计估计变更和会计差错更正；

第 19 章介绍现金流量表的编制；

第 20 章涉及详细披露的原理和实践操作。

本书可以作为大学会计、财务管理本科专业或其他经济管理本科专业全英语教学或双语教学的教材，也可作为 MBA 学生的财务会计教材。

为方便老师教学和学生学习，中国人民大学出版社网站 www. crup. com. cn 上为老师提供了丰富的原版教辅资源，如 PPT 演示文稿、教师指导手册、习题解答、题库等，老师可上网注册并经人大出版社确认后免费下载；另外还为广大读者提供了原版书中被删除的习题、部分整体章节，中英文对照的术语表，中英文对照的原版书目录等，有兴趣的读者可上网直接下载。同时，我们还会根据读者的实际需求不断更新和丰富网上的内容。

我们建议，教师在使用本教材时，根据学生的学习目的、学习能力、英文功底、学习时间要求等，有所取舍，如针对会计专业学生，可以详细讲述，并从网上下载已删除内容作为补充。

本书的改编过程得到了北京大学国际会计与财务研究中心主任、博士生导师王立彦教授的悉心指导，在此深表谢意！中国人民大学出版社的陈永凤编辑在教材改编过程中也给予了我们极大的帮助。

当然，对原书的删编难免有不当及疏漏之处，恳请各位会计同仁和读者多多指教。

CONTENTS

C H A P T E R O N E

FINANCIAL ACCOUNTING AND ACCOUNTING STANDARDS

The Size of the New York Phone Book, If Necessary

Enron, **Global Crossing**, **Kmart**, **WorldCom**, **Williams Cos.**, and **Xerox** are all companies that the Securities and Exchange Commission (SEC) recently scrutinized because of accounting issues. Share prices of all these companies have declined substantially. Investors punish any company whose quality of earnings is in doubt.

The unfortunate part of accounting scandals is that we all pay. For example, Enron's market capitalization totaled $80 billion before disclosure of its accounting irregularities. Today, it is bankrupt. Employees lost their pension money and investors their savings. Further, the entire stock market caught "Enronitis," a distrust of accounting that has led to substantial declines in the overall stock market. At one point, at least 10 congressional committees were inquiring into corporate governance issues, and Congress introduced over 30 Enron-related bills that addressed matters such as regulation of derivative securities, auditor–client conflicts, and development of an oversight body to regulate the accounting profession.

Companies have also taken steps to respond to the many investor concerns about the completeness and reliability of the accounting numbers. Many companies now expand the financial disclosures in their annual reports. For example, **General Electric**'s CEO Jeffrey Immelt stated, "I want people to think about GE as we think of GE—as a transparent company." He noted that GE's annual report will be "the size of New York City's phone book, if necessary" to provide the information needed to help investors and creditors make the proper investing decisions.

We believe that meaningful reform will come out of these recent investigations into sloppy or fraudulent accounting. Although many consider the United States to have the finest financial reporting system in the world, we must do better. As former chair of the FASB Ed Jenkins remarked recently, "If anything positive results . . . it may be that [these accounting issues] serve as an indelible reminder to all that transparent financial reporting does matter and that lack of transparency imposes significant costs on all who participate [in our markets]."

Learning Objectives

After studying this chapter, you should be able to:

1 Identify the major financial statements and other means of financial reporting.
2 Explain how accounting assists in the efficient use of scarce resources.
3 Describe some of the challenges facing accounting.
4 Identify the objectives of financial reporting.
5 Explain the need for accounting standards.
6 Identify the major policy-setting bodies and their role in the standard-setting process.
7 Explain the meaning of generally accepted accounting principles.
8 Describe the impact of user groups on the standard-setting process.
9 Understand issues related to ethics and financial accounting.

PREVIEW OF CHAPTER 1

As our opening story indicates, companies must provide relevant and reliable information so that our capital markets work efficiently. This chapter explains the environment of financial reporting and the many factors affecting it, as follows.

FINANCIAL ACCOUNTING AND ACCOUNTING STANDARDS

- **FINANCIAL STATEMENTS AND FINANCIAL REPORTING**
  - Accounting and capital allocation
  - Challenges
  - Objectives
  - Need to develop standards
- **PARTIES INVOLVED IN STANDARD SETTING**
  - Securities and Exchange Commission
  - American Institute of CPAs
  - Financial Accounting Standards Board
  - Governmental Accounting Standards Board
  - Changing Role of the AICPA
- **GENERALLY ACCEPTED ACCOUNTING PRINCIPLES**
- **ISSUES IN FINANCIAL REPORTING**
  - Political environment
  - Expectations gap
  - International accounting standards
  - Ethics

FINANCIAL STATEMENTS AND FINANCIAL REPORTING

The essential characteristics of accounting are: (1) the identification, measurement, and communication of financial information about (2) economic entities to (3) interested parties. **Financial accounting** is the process that culminates in the preparation of financial reports on the enterprise for use by both internal and external parties. Users of these financial reports include investors, creditors, managers, unions, and government agencies. In contrast, **managerial accounting** is the process of identifying, measuring, analyzing, and communicating financial information needed by management to plan, control, and evaluate a company's operations.

OBJECTIVE 1
Identify the major financial statements and other means of financial reporting.

Financial statements are the principal means through which a company communicates its financial information to those outside it. These statements provide a company's history quantified in money terms. The **financial statements** most frequently provided are (1) the balance sheet, (2) the income statement, (3) the statement of cash flows, and (4) the statement of owners' or stockholders' equity. Note disclosures are an integral part of each financial statement.

Some financial information is better provided, or can be provided only, by means of **financial reporting** other than formal financial statements. Examples include the president's letter or supplementary schedules in the corporate annual report, prospectuses, reports filed with government agencies, news releases, management's forecasts, and social or environmental impact statements. Companies may need to provide such information because of authoritative pronouncement, regulatory rule, or custom. Or they may supply it because management wishes to disclose it voluntarily.

In this textbook, we focus on the development of two types of financial information: (1) the basic financial statements and (2) related disclosures.

Accounting and Capital Allocation

OBJECTIVE 2
Explain how accounting assists in the efficient use of scarce resources.

Resources are limited. As a result, people try to conserve them and ensure that they are used effectively. Efficient use of resources often determines whether a business thrives. This fact places a substantial burden on the accounting profession.

Accountants must measure performance accurately and fairly on a timely basis, so that the right managers and companies are able to attract investment capital. For example, relevant and reliable financial information allows investors and creditors to compare the income and assets employed by such companies as **IBM, McDonald's, Microsoft,** and **Ford.** Because these users can assess the relative return and risks associated with investment opportunities, they channel resources more effectively. Illustration 1-1 shows how this process of capital allocation works.

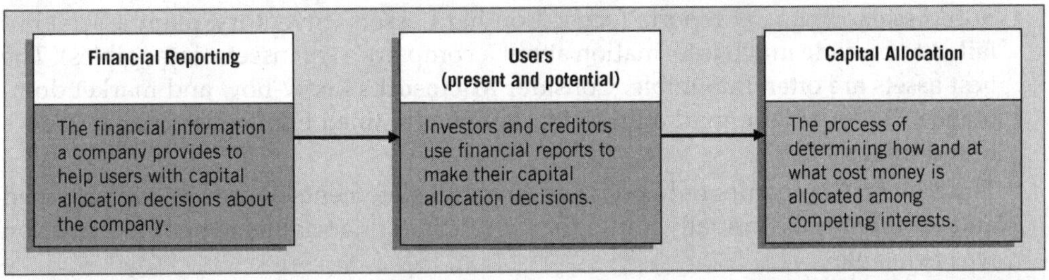

ILLUSTRATION 1-1
Capital Allocation Process

An effective process of capital allocation is critical to a healthy economy. It promotes productivity, encourages innovation, and provides an efficient and liquid market for buying and selling securities and obtaining and granting credit.[1] As we indicated in our opening story, unreliable and irrelevant information leads to poor capital allocation, which adversely affects the securities markets.

IT'S NOT THE ECONOMY, ANYMORE, STUPID

WHAT DO THE NUMBERS MEAN?

It's not the economy anymore. It's the accounting. That's what many investors seem to be saying these days. As indicated in our opening story, even the slightest hint of any accounting irregularity at a company leads to a subsequent pounding of the company's stock price. For example, recent editions of the *Wall Street Journal* had the following headlines related to accounting and its effects on the economy.

- Stocks take a beating as accounting woes spread beyond **Enron**.
- Once hot **Krispy Kreme** ousts its CEO amid accounting woes.
- **Nortel** unveils new accounting flubs.
- Accounting woes at **AIG** take their toll on insurers' shares.
- Bank stocks fall as investors take issue with **PNC**'s accounting.

It now has become clear that investors must trust the accounting numbers or they will abandon the market and put their resources elsewhere. With investor uncertainty, the cost of capital increases for companies who need additional resources. In short, relevant and reliable financial information is necessary for markets to be efficient.

[1]AICPA Special Committee on Financial Reporting, "Improving Business Reporting—A Customer Focus," *Journal of Accountancy*, Supplement (October 1994).

The Challenges Facing Financial Accounting

OBJECTIVE 3
Describe some of the challenges facing accounting.

Much is right about financial reporting in the United States. We presently have the most liquid, deep, secure, and efficient public capital markets of any country at any time in history. One reason for this success is that our financial statements and related disclosures capture and organize financial information in a useful and reliable fashion. However, much still needs to be done. For example, if we move to the year 2020 and look back at financial reporting today, we might read the following:

- **Nonfinancial Measurements.** Financial reports failed to provide some key performance measures widely used by management, such as customer satisfaction indexes, backlog information, and reject rates on goods purchased.
- **Forward-looking Information.** Financial reports failed to provide forward-looking information needed by present and potential investors and creditors. One individual noted that financial statements in 2005 should have started with the phrase, "Once upon a time," to signify their use of historical cost and accumulation of past events.
- **Soft Assets.** Financial reports focused on hard assets (inventory, plant assets) but failed to provide much information about a company's soft assets (intangibles). The best assets are often intangible. Consider **Microsoft**'s know-how and market dominance, **Dell**'s unique marketing setup and well-trained employees, and **J. Crew**'s brand image.
- **Timeliness.** Companies only prepared financial statements quarterly, and provided audited financials annually. Little to no real-time financial statement information was available.

We believe each of these challenges must be met for the accounting profession to provide the type of information needed for an efficient capital allocation process. We are confident that changes will occur, based on these positive signs:

INTERNATIONAL INSIGHT

The objectives of financial reporting differ across nations. Traditionally, the primary objective of accounting in many continental European nations and in Japan was conformity with the law. In contrast, Canada, the U.K., the Netherlands, and many other nations share the U.S. view that the primary objective is to provide information for investors.

- Already some companies voluntarily disclose information deemed relevant to investors. Often such information is nonfinancial. For example, regional banking companies, such as **BankOne Corp.**, **Fifth Third Bancorp**, and **Sun Trust Banks**, now include data on loan growth, credit quality, fee income, operating efficiency, capital management, and management strategy.
- Initially, companies used the World Wide Web to provide limited financial data. Now most companies publish their annual reports in several formats on the Web. The most innovative companies offer sections of their annual reports in a format that the user can readily manipulate, such as in an Excel spreadsheet format. Companies also format their financial reports using extensible business reporting language (XBRL), which permits quicker and lower cost access to companies' financial information.
- More accounting standards now require the recording or disclosing of fair value information. For example, companies either record investments in stocks and bonds, debt obligations, and derivatives at fair value or companies show information related to fair values in the notes to the financial statements.

Changes in these directions will enhance the relevance of financial reporting and provide useful information to financial statement readers.

Objectives of Financial Reporting

OBJECTIVE 4
Identify the objectives of financial reporting.

To establish a foundation for financial accounting and reporting, the accounting profession identified a set of **objectives of financial reporting by business enterprises**. Financial reporting should provide information that:

1 Is useful to present and potential investors and creditors and other users **in making rational investment, credit, and similar decisions**. The information should be comprehensible to those who have a **reasonable understanding** of business and economic activities and are willing to study the information with reasonable diligence.

2 Helps present and potential investors, creditors, and other users **assess the amounts, timing, and uncertainty of prospective cash receipts** from dividends or interest and the proceeds from the sale, redemption, or maturity of securities or loans. Since investors' and creditors' cash flows are related to enterprise cash flows, financial reporting should provide information to help investors, creditors, and others assess the amounts, timing, and uncertainty of prospective net cash inflows to the related enterprise.

3 **Clearly portrays the economic resources of an enterprise, the claims to those resources** (obligations of the enterprise to transfer resources to other entities and owners' equity), and the effects of transactions, events, and circumstances that change its resources and claims to those resources.[2]

In brief, the objectives of financial reporting are to provide information that is (1) useful in investment and credit decisions, (2) useful in assessing cash flow prospects, and (3) about company resources, claims to those resources, and changes in them.

The emphasis on "assessing cash flow prospects" does not mean that the cash basis is preferred over the accrual basis of accounting. That is not the case. Information based on **accrual accounting generally better indicates a company's present and continuing ability to generate favorable cash flows** than does information limited to the financial effects of cash receipts and payments.[3]

Recall from your first accounting course the objective of **accrual-basis accounting**: It ensures that a company records events that change its financial statements in the periods in which the events occur, rather than only in the periods in which it receives or pays cash. Using the accrual basis to determine net income means that a company recognizes revenues when it earns them rather than when it receives cash. Similarly, it recognizes expenses when it incurs them rather than when it pays them. Under accrual accounting, a company generally recognizes revenues when it makes sales. The company can then relate the revenues to the economic environment of the period in which they occurred. Over the long run, trends in revenues and expenses are generally more meaningful than trends in cash receipts and disbursements.

The Need to Develop Standards

OBJECTIVE 5
Explain the need for accounting standards.

The main controversy in setting accounting standards is, "Whose rules should we play by, and what should they be?" The answer is not immediately clear. Users of financial accounting statements have both coinciding and conflicting needs for information of various types. To meet these needs, and to satisfy the fiduciary[4] reporting responsibility of management, companies prepare a single set of **general-purpose financial statements.** Users expect these statements to present fairly, clearly, and completely the company's financial operations.

The accounting profession has attempted to develop a set of standards that are generally accepted and universally practiced. Otherwise, each enterprise would have to develop its own standards. Further, readers of financial statements would have to familiarize themselves with every company's peculiar accounting and

[2] "Objectives of Financial Reporting by Business Enterprises," *Statement of Financial Accounting Concepts No. 1* (Stamford, Conn.: FASB, November 1978), pars. 5–8.

[3] *SFAC No. 1*, p. iv. As used here, *cash flow* means "cash generated and used in operations." The term *cash flows* also frequently means cash obtained by borrowing and used to repay borrowing, cash used for investments in resources and obtained from the disposal of investments, and cash contributed by or distributed to owners.

[4] Management's fiduciary responsibility is to manage assets with care and trust.

reporting practices. It would be almost impossible to prepare statements that could be compared.

This common set of standards and procedures is called **generally accepted accounting principles (GAAP)**. The term "generally accepted" means either that an authoritative accounting rule-making body has established a principle of reporting in a given area or that over time a given practice has been accepted as appropriate because of its universal application.[5] Although principles and practices continue to provoke both debate and criticism, most members of the financial community recognize them as the standards that over time have proven to be most useful. We present a more extensive discussion of what constitutes GAAP later in this chapter.

PARTIES INVOLVED IN STANDARD SETTING

OBJECTIVE 6
Identify the major policy-setting bodies and their role in the standard-setting process.

Four organizations are instrumental in the development of financial accounting standards (GAAP) in the United States:

1. Securities and Exchange Commission (SEC)
2. American Institute of Certified Public Accountants (AICPA)
3. Financial Accounting Standards Board (FASB)
4. Government Accounting Standards Board (GASB)

Securities and Exchange Commission (SEC)

INTERNATIONAL INSIGHT

The International Organization of Securities Commissions (IOSCO), established in 1987, consists of more than 100 securities regulatory agencies or securities exchanges from all over the world. Collectively, its members represent a substantial proportion of the world's capital markets. The SEC is a member of IOSCO.

External financial reporting and auditing developed in tandem with the growth of the industrial economy and its capital markets. However, when the stock market crashed in 1929 and the nation's economy plunged into the Great Depression, there were calls for increased government regulation of business generally, and especially financial institutions and the stock market.

As a result of these events, the federal government established the **Securities and Exchange Commission (SEC)** to help develop and standardize financial information presented to stockholders. The SEC is a federal agency. It administers the Securities Exchange Act of 1934 and several other acts. Most companies that issue securities to the public or are listed on a stock exchange are required to file audited financial statements with the SEC. In addition, the SEC has broad powers to prescribe, in whatever detail it desires, the accounting practices and standards to be employed by companies that fall within its jurisdiction. The SEC currently exercises oversight over 12,000 companies that are listed on the major exchanges (e.g., the New York Stock Exchange and the Nasdaq).

Public/Private Partnership

At the time the SEC was created, no group—public or private—issued accounting standards. The SEC encouraged the creation of a private standard-setting body because it believed that the private sector had the appropriate resources and talent to achieve this daunting task. As a result, accounting standards have developed in the private sector either through the American Institute of Certified Public Accountants (AICPA) or the Financial Accounting Standards Board (FASB).

The SEC has affirmed its support for the FASB by indicating that financial statements conforming to standards set by the FASB are presumed to have substantial authoritative support. In short, the **SEC requires registrants to adhere to GAAP**. In addition, the SEC indicated in its reports to Congress that "it continues to believe that the initiative for establishing and improving accounting standards should remain in the private sector, subject to Commission oversight."

[5]The terms *principles* and *standards* are used interchangeably in practice and throughout this textbook.

SEC Oversight

The SEC's partnership with the private sector works well. The SEC acts with remarkable restraint in the area of developing accounting standards. Generally, **the SEC relies on the FASB to develop accounting standards.**

The SEC's involvement in the development of accounting standards varies. In some cases, the SEC rejects a standard proposed by the private sector. In other cases, the SEC prods the private sector into taking quicker action on certain reporting problems, such as accounting for investments in debt and equity securities and the reporting of derivative instruments. In still other situations, the SEC communicates problems to the FASB, responds to FASB exposure drafts, and provides the FASB with counsel and advice upon request.

The SEC's mandate is to establish accounting principles. The private sector, therefore, must listen carefully to the views of the SEC. In some sense the private sector is the formulator and the implementor of the standards.[6] However, when the private sector fails to address accounting problems as quickly as the SEC would like, the partnership between the SEC and the private sector can be strained. This occurred in the recent deliberations on the accounting for business combinations and intangible assets, and concerns over the accounting for off-balance sheet special-purpose entities, highlighted in the failure of **Enron**.

Enforcement

As we indicated earlier, companies listed on a stock exchange must submit their financial statements to the SEC. If the SEC believes that an accounting or disclosure irregularity exists regarding the form or content of the financial statements, it sends a deficiency letter to the company. Companies usually resolve these deficiency letters quickly. However, if disagreement continues, the SEC may issue a "stop order," which prevents the registrant from issuing or trading securities on the exchanges. The Department of Justice may also file criminal charges for violations of certain laws. The SEC process, private sector initiatives, and civil and criminal litigation help to ensure the integrity of financial reporting for public companies.

INTERNATIONAL INSIGHT

Nations also differ in the degree to which they developed national standards and consistent accounting practices. One indicator of the level of a nation's accounting is the nature of the accounting profession within the country. For example, the Netherlands, the U.K., Canada, and the U.S. established professional accounting bodies in the nineteenth century. In contrast, Hong Kong, Singapore, and Korea established similar bodies only in the last half century.

American Institute of Certified Public Accountants (AICPA)

The **American Institute of Certified Public Accountants (AICPA)**, which is the national professional organization of practicing Certified Public Accountants (CPAs), has been an important contributor to the development of GAAP. Various committees and boards established since the founding of the AICPA have contributed to this effort.

Committee on Accounting Procedure

At the urging of the SEC, the AICPA appointed the Committee on Accounting Procedure in 1939. The **Committee on Accounting Procedure (CAP)**, composed of practicing CPAs, issued 51 **Accounting Research Bulletins** during the years 1939 to 1959. These bulletins dealt with a variety of accounting problems. But this problem-by-problem approach failed to provide the needed structured body of accounting principles. In response, in 1959 the AICPA created the Accounting Principles Board.

---

[6]One writer described the relationship of the FASB and SEC and the development of financial reporting standards using the analogy of a pearl. The pearl (a financial reporting standard) "is formed by the reaction of certain oysters (FASB) to an irritant (the SEC)—usually a grain of sand—that becomes embedded inside the shell. The oyster coats this grain with layers of nacre, and ultimately a pearl is formed. The pearl is a joint result of the irritant (SEC) and oyster (FASB); without both, it cannot be created." John C. Burton, "Government Regulation of Accounting and Information," *Journal of Accountancy* (June 1982).

Accounting Principles Board

The major purposes of the **Accounting Principles Board (APB)** were to (1) advance the written expression of accounting principles, (2) determine appropriate practices, and (3) narrow the areas of difference and inconsistency in practice. To achieve these objectives, the APB's mission was twofold: to develop an overall conceptual framework to assist in the resolution of problems as they become evident and to substantively research individual issues before the AICPA issued pronouncements. The Board's 18 to 21 members, selected primarily from public accounting, also included representatives from industry and academia. The Board's official pronouncements, called **APB Opinions**, were intended to be based mainly on research studies and be supported by reasons and analysis. Between its inception in 1959 and its dissolution in 1973, the APB issued 31 opinions.

Unfortunately, the APB came under fire early, charged with lack of productivity and failing to act promptly to correct alleged accounting abuses. Later the APB tackled numerous thorny accounting issues, only to meet a buzz saw of opposition from industry and CPA firms. It also ran into occasional governmental interference. In 1971 the accounting profession's leaders, anxious to avoid governmental rule-making, appointed a Study Group on Establishment of Accounting Principles. Commonly known as the **Wheat Committee** for its chair Francis Wheat, this group examined the organization and operation of the APB and determined the necessary changes to attain better results. The Study Group submitted its recommendations to the AICPA Council in the spring of 1972. The AICPA Council adopted the recommendations in total, and implemented them by early 1973.

Financial Accounting Standards Board (FASB)

The Wheat Committee's recommendations resulted in the demise of the APB and the creation of a new standard-setting structure composed of three organizations—the Financial Accounting Foundation (FAF), the Financial Accounting Standards Board (FASB), and the Financial Accounting Standards Advisory Council (FASAC). The **Financial Accounting Foundation** selects the members of the FASB and the Advisory Council, funds their activities, and generally oversees the FASB's activities.

The major operating organization in this three-part structure is the **Financial Accounting Standards Board (FASB)**. Its mission is to establish and improve standards of financial accounting and reporting for the guidance and education of the public, which includes issuers, auditors, and users of financial information. The expectations of success and support for the new FASB relied on several significant differences between it and its predecessor, the APB:

1. **Smaller Membership.** The FASB consists of seven members, replacing the relatively large 18-member APB.
2. **Full-time, Remunerated Membership.** FASB members are well-paid, full-time members appointed for renewable 5-year terms. The APB members volunteered their part-time work.
3. **Greater Autonomy.** The APB was a senior committee of the AICPA. The FASB is not part of any single professional organization. It is appointed by and answerable only to the Financial Accounting Foundation.
4. **Increased Independence.** APB members retained their private positions with firms, companies, or institutions. FASB members must sever all such ties.
5. **Broader Representation.** All APB members were required to be CPAs and members of the AICPA. Currently, it is not necessary to be a CPA to be a member of the FASB.

INTERNATIONAL INSIGHT

The U.S. legal system is based on English common law, whereby the government generally allows professionals to make the rules. The private sector, therefore, develops these rules (standards). Conversely, some countries follow codified law, which leads to government-run accounting systems.

In addition to research help from its own staff, the FASB relies on the expertise of various task force groups formed for various projects and on the **Financial Accounting Standards Advisory Council (FASAC)**. FASAC consults with the FASB on major policy and technical issues and also helps select task force members.

Due Process

In establishing financial accounting standards, the FASB relies on two basic premises: (1) The FASB should be responsive to the needs and viewpoints of the entire economic community, not just the public accounting profession. (2) It should operate in full view of the public through a "due process" system that gives interested persons ample opportunity to make their views known. To ensure the achievement of these goals, the FASB follows specific steps to develop a typical FASB Statement of Financial Accounting Standards, as Illustration 1-2 shows.

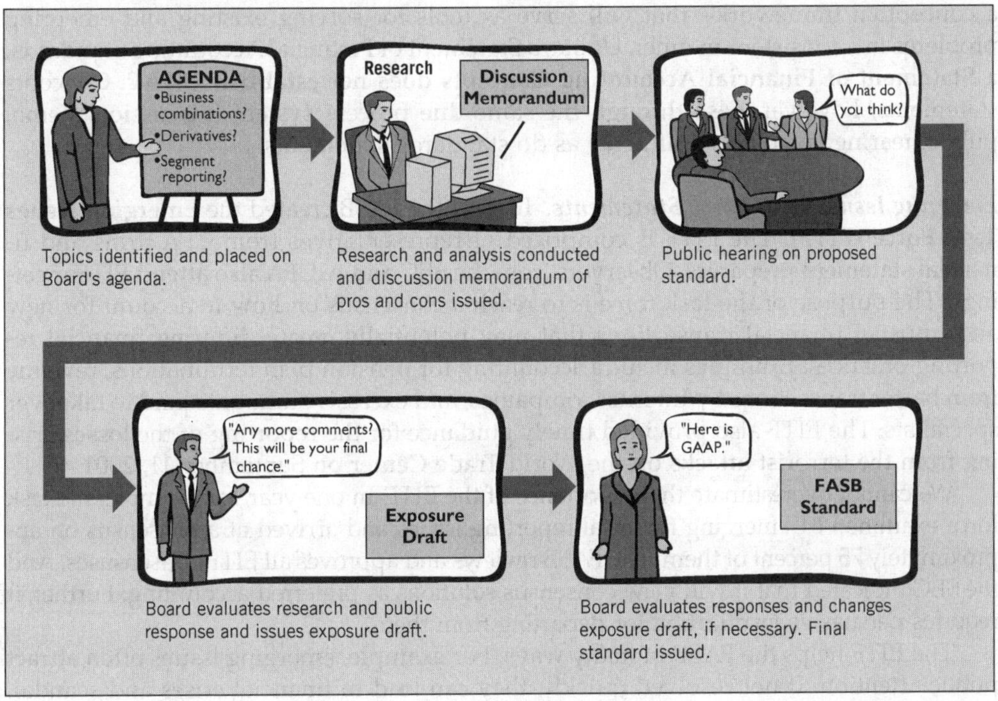

ILLUSTRATION 1-2
The Due Process System of the FASB

The passage of a new FASB **Standards Statement** requires the support of four of the seven Board members. FASB Statements are considered GAAP and thereby binding in practice. All ARBs and APB Opinions implemented by 1973 (when the FASB formed) continue to be effective until amended or superseded by FASB pronouncements. In recognition of possible misconceptions of the term "principles," the FASB uses the term **financial accounting standards** in its pronouncements.

Types of Pronouncements

The FASB issues three major types of pronouncements:

1 Standards, Interpretations, and Staff Positions.
2 Financial Accounting Concepts.
3 Emerging Issues Task Force Statements.

Standards, Interpretation, and Staff Positions. Financial accounting **standards** issued by the FASB are considered generally accepted accounting principles. In addition, the FASB also issues **interpretations** that modify or extend existing standards. Interpretations have the same authority, and require the same votes for passage, as standards. The APB also issued interpretations of APB Opinions. Both types of interpretations are now considered authoritative for purposes of determining GAAP. Finally, the FASB issues staff positions, which provide interpretive guidance and also minor amendments to standards and interpretations. These staff positions have the same authority as standards and interpretations. The Board also has issued FASB Technical Bulletins, which

provide timely guidance on selected issues; staff positions are now used in lieu of technical bulletins. Since replacing the APB, the FASB has issued 154 standards, 47 interpretations, and over 30 staff positions. (See list at the back of the book.)

Financial Accounting Concepts. As part of a long-range effort to move away from the problem-by-problem approach, the FASB in November 1978 issued the first in a series of **Statements of Financial Accounting Concepts** as part of its conceptual framework project. (See list at the back of the book.) The series sets forth fundamental objectives and concepts that the Board uses in developing future standards of financial accounting and reporting. The Board intends to form a cohesive set of interrelated concepts—a conceptual framework—that will serve as tools for solving existing and emerging problems in a consistent manner. Unlike a Statement of Financial Accounting Standards, **a Statement of Financial Accounting Concepts does not establish GAAP**. Concepts statements, however, pass through the same due process system (discussion memo, public hearing, exposure draft, etc.) as do standards statements.

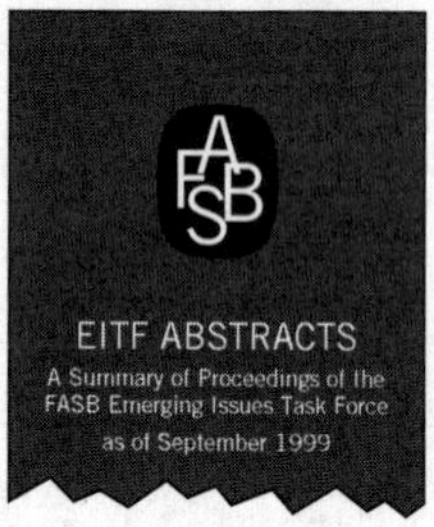

Emerging Issues Task Force Statements. In 1984 the FASB created the **Emerging Issues Task Force (EITF)**. The EITF is comprised of representatives from CPA firms and financial statement preparers. Observers from the SEC and AICPA also attend EITF meetings. The purpose of the task force is to reach a consensus on how to account for new and unusual financial transactions that may potentially create differing financial reporting practices. Examples include accounting for pension plan terminations, revenue from barter transactions by Internet companies, and excessive amounts paid to takeover specialists. The EITF also provided timely guidance for the reporting of the losses arising from the terrorist attacks on the World Trade Center on September 11, 2001.

We cannot overestimate the importance of the EITF. In one year, for example, the task force examined 61 emerging financial reporting issues and arrived at a consensus on approximately 75 percent of them. The FASB reviews and approves all EITF consensuses. And the SEC indicated that it will view consensus solutions as preferred accounting. Further, it requires persuasive justification for departing from them.

The EITF helps the FASB in many ways. For example, emerging issues often attract public attention. If not resolved quickly, they can lead to financial crises and scandal. They can also undercut public confidence in current reporting practices. The next step, possible governmental intervention, would threaten the continuance of standard setting in the private sector. The EITF identifies controversial accounting problems as they arise. The EITF determines whether it can quickly resolve them, or whether to involve the FASB in solving them. In essence, it becomes a "problem filter" for the FASB. Thus, the FASB will hopefully work on more pervasive long-term problems, while the EITF deals with short-term emerging issues.

Governmental Accounting Standards Board (GASB)

Financial statements prepared by state and local governments are not comparable with financial reports prepared by private business organizations. The lack of comparability was highlighted in the 1970s when a number of large cities such as New York and Cleveland faced potential bankruptcy. As result, the **Governmental Accounting Standards Board (GASB)** came into being.

The operational structure of the GASB is similar to that of the FASB. That is, it has an advisory council called the Governmental Accounting Standards Advisory Council (GASAC), and has its own technical staff and task forces to assist its work.

The creation of the GASB was controversial. Many believe that there should be only one standard-setting body—the FASB. It was hoped that dividing standard-setting between the GASB, which deals with state and local government reporting, and the FASB, which addresses reporting for all other entities, would not lead to conflict. Since we are primarily concerned with financial reports prepared by profit-seeking organizations, this textbook focuses on standards issued by the FASB. Illustration 1-3 shows the current formal organizational structure for the development of financial reporting standards.

ILLUSTRATION 1-3
Organizational Structure for Setting Accounting Standards

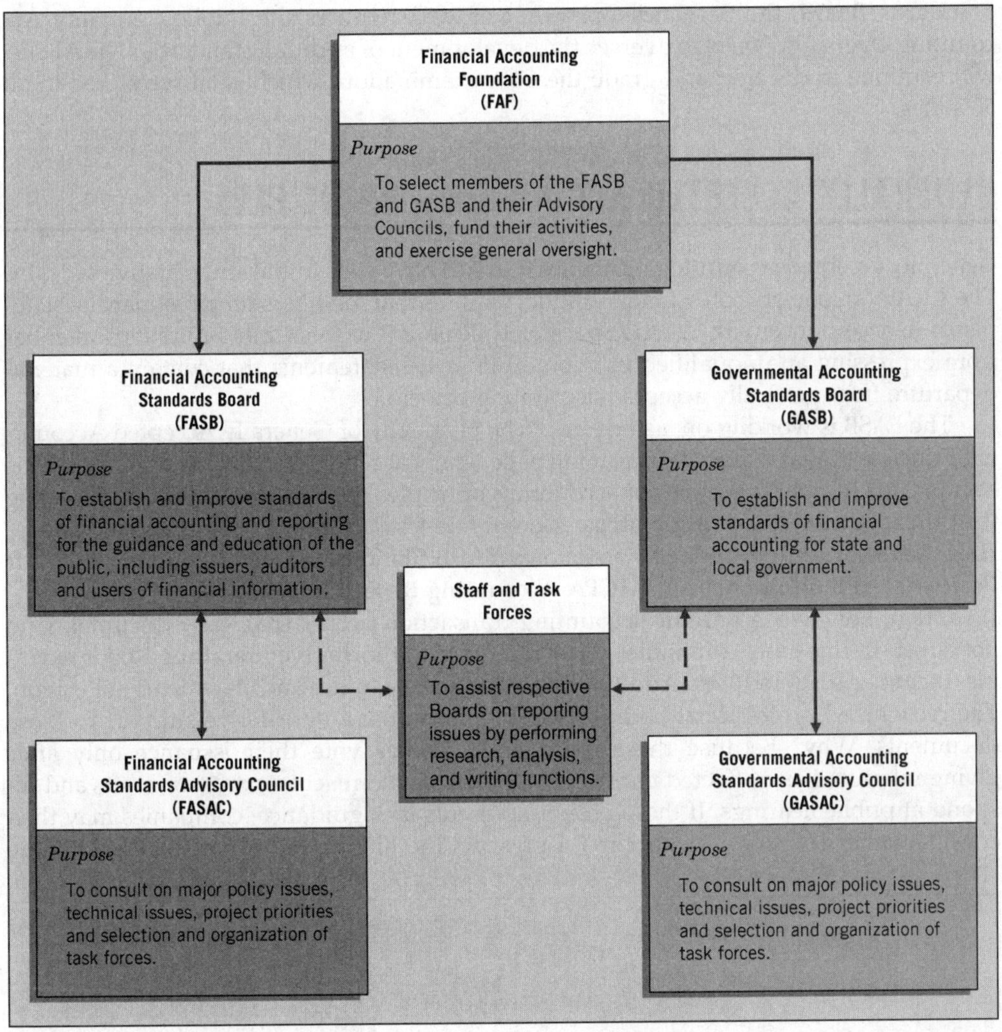

Changing Role of the AICPA

For several decades the AICPA provided leadership in developing accounting principles and rules. More than any other organization, it regulated the accounting profession, and developed and enforced accounting practice. When the FASB replaced the Accounting Principles Board, the AICPA established the **Accounting Standards Executive Committee (AcSEC)** as the committee authorized to speak for the AICPA in the area of financial accounting and reporting. It does so through various written communications:

Audit and Accounting Guides summarize the accounting practices of specific industries and provide specific guidance on matters not addressed by the FASB. Examples are accounting for casinos, airlines, colleges and universities, banks, insurance companies, and many others.

Statements of Position (SOP) provide guidance on financial reporting topics until the FASB sets standards on the issue in question. SOPs may update, revise, and clarify audit and accounting guides or provide free-standing guidance.

Practice Bulletins indicate AcSEC's views on narrow financial reporting issues not considered by the FASB.

Recently, the role of the AICPA in standard-setting has diminished. The FASB and the AICPA agree that, after a transition period, the AICPA and AcSEC no longer will issue authoritative accounting guidance for public companies. Furthermore, while the AICPA has been the leader in developing auditing standards through its **Auditing**

Standards Board, the Sarbanes-Oxley Act of 2002 requires the Public Company Accounting Oversight Board to oversee the development of auditing standards. The AICPA will continue to develop and grade the CPA examination, which is administered in all 50 states.

GENERALLY ACCEPTED ACCOUNTING PRINCIPLES

OBJECTIVE 7
Explain the meaning of generally accepted accounting principles.

Generally accepted accounting principles (GAAP) have substantial authoritative support. The AICPA's Code of Professional Conduct requires that members prepare financial statements in accordance with GAAP. Specifically, Rule 203 of this Code prohibits a member from expressing an unqualified opinion on financial statements that contain a material departure from generally accepted accounting principles.

The FASB is working on a standard, "The Hierarchy of Generally Accepted Accounting Principles," that defines the meaning of generally accepted accounting principles. This standard identifies the sources of accounting principles and the framework for selecting the principles to be used in the preparation of financial statements. The standard categorizes the major sources of GAAP as follows: **FASB Standards, Interpretations, and Staff Positions**; **APB Opinions**; and **AICPA Accounting Research Bulletins.**[7]

Often, however, a specific accounting transaction occurs that these documents do not cover. In this case, companies must use other authoritative literature. Major examples include AICPA Industry Auditing and Accounting Guides and Statements of Position. The recognized professional bodies provide substantial authoritative support to these documents. Why? Because these professional bodies vote their issuance only after giving interested and affected parties the opportunity to react to exposure drafts and respond at public hearings. If these pronouncements lack guidance, companies may then consider other sources. Illustration 1-4 presents the hierarchy of these sources.[8] If the

ILLUSTRATION 1-4
The House of GAAP

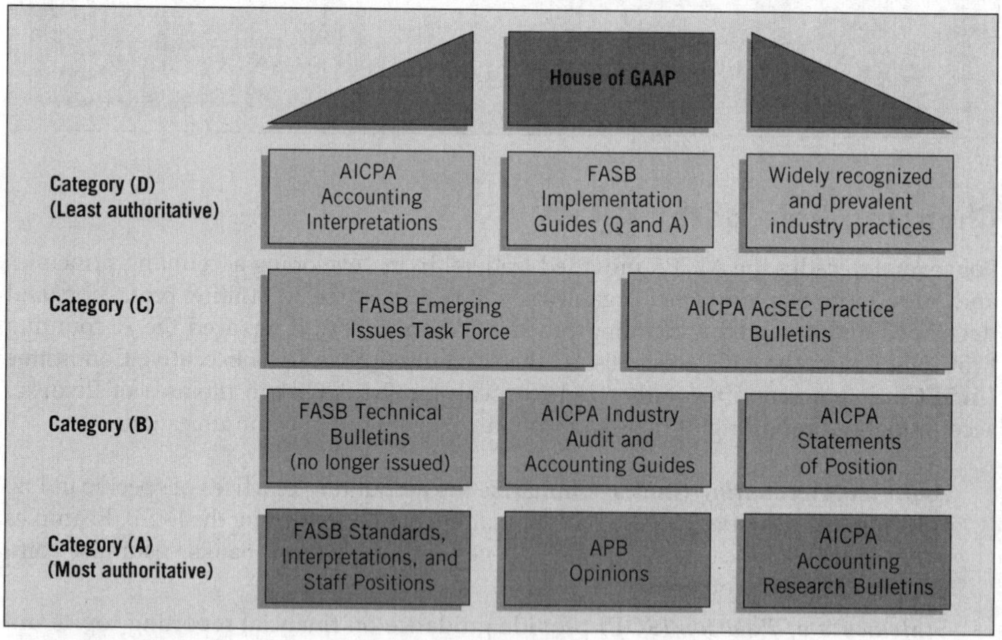

[7]The auditing literature presented the GAAP hierarchy prior to the issuance of this standard. The FASB decided that the GAAP hierarchy should be directed specifically to the company because it is the company (not the auditor) that is responsible for selecting the accounting principles for financial statements. As a result, the GAAP hierarchy should reside in the accounting literature, not the auditing literature. "The Hierarchy of Generally Accepted Accounting Principles," *Proposed Statement of Financial Accounting Standards* (Norwalk, Conn.: FASB, April 28, 2005.)

[8]See for example, Douglas Sauter, "Remodeling the House of GAAP," *Journal of Accountancy* (July 1991), pp. 30–37.

accounting treatment of an event is not specified by a Category A pronouncement, then Categories B through D should be investigated. If there is a conflict between pronouncements in B through D, companies should follow the higher category. For example, B is higher than C.

If none of these pronouncements addresses the event, companies seek support from other accounting literature. Examples include FASB Concepts Statements, International Accounting Standards, and accounting articles.[9]

WHAT DO THE NUMBERS MEAN?

YOU HAVE TO STEP BACK

Should the accounting profession have principles-based standards or rules-based standards? Critics of the profession today say that over the past three decades, standard-setters have moved away from broad accounting principles aimed at ensuring that companies' financial statements are fairly presented.

Instead, these critics say, standard-setters have moved toward drafting voluminous rules that, if technically followed in "check-box" fashion, may shield auditors and companies from legal liability. That has resulted in companies creating complex capital structures that comply with GAAP but hide billions of dollars of debt and other obligations. To add fuel to the fire, the chief accountant of the enforcement division of the SEC recently noted, "One can violate SEC laws and still comply with GAAP."

In short, what he is saying is that it is not enough just to check the boxes. You then have to step back and determine whether the *overall impression* created by GAAP financial statements fairly portrays the underlying economics of the company. It is a tough standard, but one that auditors and corporate management should strive to achieve.

Sources: Adapted from S. Liesman, "SEC Accounting Cop's Warning: Playing by the Rules May Not Head Off Fraud Issues," *Wall Street Journal* (February 12, 2002), p. C7. See also "Study Pursuant to Section 108(d) of the Sarbanes-Oxley Act of 2002 on the Adoption by the United States Financial Reporting System of a Principles-Based Accounting System," *SEC* (July 25, 2003).

ISSUES IN FINANCIAL REPORTING

Since the implementation of an accounting standard may affect many interests, much discussion often occurs about who should develop these standards and to whom they should apply. We discuss some of the major issues below.

Standard Setting in a Political Environment

User groups are possibly the most powerful force influencing the development of accounting standards. User groups consist of those most interested in or affected by accounting standards, rules, and procedures. Like lobbyists in our state and national capitals, user groups play a significant role. **Accounting standards are as much a product**

[9]A reasonable question to ask is, "Why is one set of documents more authoritative than others?" There are two explanations. First, at the time the AICPA or FASB developed a standard, the SEC recognized these organizations as the appropriate body to establish accounting principles. Second, in most cases, a document is more authoritative if, before the document is issued, its contents are (a) debated in a public forum, (b) exposed in writing to the public for comment, and (c) approved by the Board.

Existing GAAP comprises over 2,000 pronouncements. Recently the FASB has started a project to codify all these pronouncements into one major document. Everything in this document will be considered authoritative. Any material excluded would be considered non-authoritative.

of political action as they are of careful logic or empirical findings. User groups may want particular economic events accounted for or reported in a particular way, and they fight hard to get what they want. They know that the most effective way to influence the standards is to participate in the formulation of these standards or to try to influence or persuade the formulator of them.

OBJECTIVE 8
Describe the impact of user groups on the standard-setting process.

These user groups often target the FASB, to pressure it to influence changes in the existing standards and the development of new ones.[10] In fact, these pressures have been multiplying. Some influential groups demand that the accounting profession act more quickly and decisively to solve its problems. Other groups resist such action, preferring to implement change more slowly, if at all. Illustration 1-5 shows the various user groups that apply pressure.

ILLUSTRATION 1-5
User Groups that Influence the Formulation of Accounting Standards

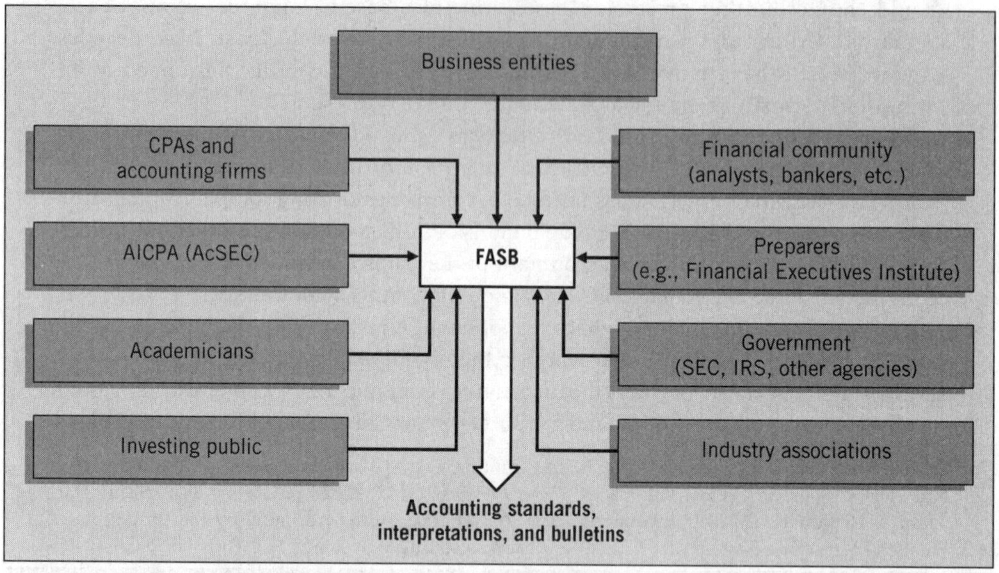

Should there be politics in setting standards for financial accounting and reporting? Why not? We have politics at home; at school; at the fraternity, sorority, and dormitory; at the office; at church, temple, and mosque. Politics is everywhere. Standard setting is part of the real world, and it cannot escape politics and political pressures.

WHAT DO THE NUMBERS MEAN?

THE ECONOMIC CONSEQUENCES OF GOODWILL

Investors generally ignore an accounting change, except when it substantially affects net income. Recently issued goodwill rules are one such change. Under previous GAAP, companies with goodwill charged it to revenues over time. Under new rules, companies no longer have to write off this cost. The effect on the bottom line for some companies is substantial. For example, assuming no goodwill amortization, **International Paper** estimates an income increase of 21 percent, **Johnson Controls** 16 percent, and **Pepsi Bottling Group** 30 percent.

Some believe this change will increase their stock's attractiveness. Others argue that it should have no effect because the write-off is a mere bookkeeping charge. Still others argue that the change has no effect on cash flows, but that investors will perceive the company to be more profitable, and therefore a good buy in the marketplace. In short, the numbers have consequences. What do you think?

[10]FASB board members acknowledged that they undertook many of the Board's projects, such as "Accounting for Contingencies," "Accounting for Pensions," "Statement of Cash Flows," and "Accounting for Derivatives," due to political pressure.

That is not to say that politics in standard setting is a negative force. Considering the **economic consequences**[11] of many accounting standards, special interest groups should vocalize their reactions to proposed standards. What the Board should *not* do is issue pronouncements that are primarily politically motivated. While paying attention to its constituencies, the Board should base its standards on sound research and a conceptual framework that has its foundation in economic reality.

The Expectations Gap

Accounting scandals at companies like **Enron**, **Cendant**, **Sunbeam**, **Rite-Aid**, **Xerox**, and **WorldCom** have attracted the attention of Congress. In 2002, it enacted legislation—the **Sarbanes-Oxley Act**. The new law increases the resources for the SEC to combat fraud and curb poor reporting practices.[12] And the SEC has increased its policing efforts, approving new auditor independence rules and materiality guidelines for financial reporting. In addition, the Sarbanes-Oxley Act introduces sweeping changes to the institutional structure of the accounting profession. The following are some of the key provisions of the legislation.

- Establishes an oversight board, the **Public Company Accounting Oversight Board (PCAOB)**, for accounting practices. The PCAOB has oversight and enforcement authority and establishes auditing, quality control, and independence standards and rules.
- Implements stronger independence rules for auditors. Audit partners, for example, are required to rotate every five years and auditors are prohibited from offering certain types of consulting services to corporate clients.
- Requires CEOs and CFOs to personally certify that financial statements and disclosures are accurate and complete and requires CEOs and CFOs to forfeit bonuses and profits when there is an accounting restatement.
- Requires audit committees to be comprised of independent members and members with financial expertise.
- Requires codes of ethics for senior financial officers.

In addition, Section 404 of the Sarbanes-Oxley Act requires public companies to attest to the effectiveness of their internal controls over financial reporting. **Internal controls** are a system of checks and balances designed to prevent and detect fraud and errors. Most companies have these systems in place, but many have never completely documented them. Companies are finding that it is a costly process but perhaps badly needed. Already intense examination of internal controls has found lingering problems in the way companies operate. Recently, 424 companies reported deficiencies in internal control.[13] Many problems involved closing the books, revenue recognition deficiencies, reconciling accounts, or dealing with inventory. **SunTrust Bank**, for example, fired three officers after discovering errors in how the company calculates its allowance for bad debts. And **Visteon**, a car parts supplier, said it found problems recording and managing receivables from its largest customer, **Ford Motor**.

Will these changes be enough? The **expectations gap**—what the public thinks accountants *should* do and what accountants think they *can* do—is difficult to close. Due

---

[11]*Economic consequences* means the impact of accounting reports on the wealth positions of issuers and users of financial information, and the decision-making behavior resulting from that impact. The resulting behavior of these individuals and groups could have detrimental financial effects on the providers of the financial information. See Stephen A. Zeff, "The Rise of 'Economic Consequences'," *Journal of Accountancy* (December 1978), pp. 56–63. We extend appreciation to Professor Zeff for his insights on this chapter.

[12]*Sarbanes-Oxley Act of 2002*, H. R. Rep. No. 107-610 (2002).

[13]Leah Townsend, "Internal Control Deficiency Disclosures—Interim Alert," *Yellow Card—Interim Trend Alert* (April 12, 2005), Glass, Lewis & Co., LLC.

to the number of fraudulent reporting cases, some question whether the profession is doing enough. Although the profession can argue rightfully that accounting cannot be responsible for every financial catastrophe, it must continue to strive to meet the needs of society. However, efforts to meet these needs will become more costly to society. The development of a highly transparent, clear, and reliable system will require considerable resources.

International Accounting Standards

INTERNATIONAL INSIGHT

Foreign accounting firms that provide an audit report for a U.S.-listed company are subject to the authority of the accounting oversight board (mandated by the Sarbanes-Oxley Act).

Former Secretary of the Treasury Lawrence Summers indicated that the single most important innovation shaping the capital markets was the idea of generally accepted accounting principles. He went on to say that we need something similar internationally.

We believe that the Secretary is right. Relevant and reliable financial information is a necessity for viable capital markets. Unfortunately, companies outside the United States often prepare financial statements using standards different from U.S. GAAP. As a result, international companies such as **Coca-Cola**, **Microsoft**, and **IBM** have to develop financial information in different ways. Beyond the additional costs these companies incur, users of the financial statements often must understand at least two sets of GAAP. (Understanding one set is hard enough!) It is not surprising therefore that there is a growing demand for one set of high-quality international standards.

Presently, there are two sets of standards accepted for international use—U.S. GAAP and the International Financial Reporting Standards (IFRS) issued by the London-based **International Accounting Standards Board (IASB)**. As you will learn, there are many similarities between U.S. and IASB standards.

U.S. companies that list overseas are still permitted to use U.S. GAAP. Conversely foreign companies listed on our exchanges are required to reconcile their financial information to U.S. GAAP. The reason for the reconciliation is that U.S. GAAP is more extensive and detailed than the IASB standards.

Already 90 countries use IFRS, and the European Union now requires all listed companies in Europe (over 7,000 companies) to use it. The FASB and the IASB are now working hard to find common ground related to existing and proposed standards. Both parties recognize that global markets will best be served if only one set of GAAP is used. The task will not be easy, but the environment is conducive to convergence of the two systems. As Mary Barth, a member of the IASB noted, "There is still a lot to do, but I would never have dreamed we would be working as closely with the FASB as we do today."

Throughout the textbook, we provide in the margins international insights to help you understand the international reporting environment.

Ethics in the Environment of Financial Accounting

OBJECTIVE 9
Understand issues related to ethics and financial accounting.

Robert Sack, a noted commentator on the subject of accounting ethics, observed, "Based on my experience, new graduates tend to be idealistic . . . thank goodness for that! Still it is very dangerous to think that your armor is all in place and say to yourself, 'I would have never given in to that.' The pressures don't explode on us; they build, and we often don't recognize them until they have us."

These observations are particularly appropriate for anyone entering the business world. In accounting, as in other areas of business, we frequently encounter ethical dilemmas. Some of these dilemmas are simple and easy to resolve. However, many are not, requiring difficult choices among allowable alternatives.

Companies that concentrate on "maximizing the bottom line," "facing the challenges of competition," and "stressing short-term results" place accountants in an environment of conflict and pressure. Basic questions such as, "Is this way of communicating financial information good or bad?" "Is it right or wrong?" "What should I do in the circumstance?" cannot always be answered by simply adhering to GAAP or following the rules of the profession. Technical competence is not enough when encountering ethical decisions.

Doing the right thing is not always easy or obvious. The pressures "to bend the rules," "to play the game," "to just ignore it" can be considerable. For example, "Will my decision affect my job performance negatively?", "Will my superiors be upset?", "Will my colleagues be unhappy with me?" are often questions business people face in making a tough ethical decision. The decision is more difficult because there is no comprehensive ethical system to provide guidelines.

wiley.com/college/kieso

Expanded Discussion of Ethical Issues in Financial Reporting

Time, job, client, personal, and peer pressures can complicate the process of ethical sensitivity and selection among alternatives. Throughout this textbook, **we present ethical considerations to help sensitize you** to the type of situations you may encounter in the performance of your professional responsibility.

HERE COME THE POLITICS

WHAT DO THE NUMBERS MEAN?

Given the many recent accounting scandals mentioned so far in the text, it is not surprising that both political parties are working to ensure that corporate management be ethical. President Bush, for example, announced a set of proposals to crack down on unethical behavior by corporate officials, expanding the offenses subject to criminal and civil penalties. And both the SEC and the Justice Department are to get more funding to combat financial fraud. At the same time, Democrats in Congress have pushed for more corporate-reform initiatives. So it is not surprising that both houses in Congress passed the Sarbanes-Oxley Act of 2002 with almost unanimous support and the president quickly signed it into law.

One thing is certain: Recent financial reporting undermined consumer confidence in corporate America and the capital markets. Because these issues hurt the U.S. economy, we can expect politicians to continue to seek solutions.

Conclusion

Bob Herz, FASB chairman, believes that there are three fundamental considerations the FASB must keep in mind in its standard-setting activities: (1) improvement in financial reporting, (2) simplification of the accounting literature and the standard-setting process, and (3) international convergence. These are notable objectives, and the Board is making good progress on all three dimensions. Issues such as off-balance-sheet financing, measurement of fair values, enhanced criteria for revenue recognition, and stock option accounting are examples of where the Board has exerted leadership. Improvements in financial reporting should follow.

Also, the Board is making it easier to understand what GAAP is. Presently GAAP is contained in a number of different documents. The lack of a single source makes it difficult to access and understand generally accepted principles. The Board is embarked on a long-term project ("the codification") that will compile GAAP in one document. This codification will organize existing GAAP by accounting topic regardless of its source (FASB Statements, APB Opinions, and so on). The codified standards will then be considered to be GAAP and to be authoritative, and all other literature will be considered non-authoritative.

Finally, international convergence is underway. Some projects already are completed and differences eliminated. Many more are on the drawing board. The crisis caused in the capital markets due to accounting irregularities of companies like **Enron**, **Krispy Kreme**, **Fannie Mae**, **Xerox**, and a host of others has caused the profession to reexamine its processes and standards. At present, we believe that the profession is reacting responsibly to remedy identified shortcomings.

QUESTIONS

1. Differentiate broadly between financial accounting and managerial accounting.
2. Differentiate between "financial statements" and "financial reporting."
3. How does accounting help the capital allocation process?
4. What are some of the major challenges facing the accounting profession?
5. What are the major objectives of financial reporting?
6. Of what value is a common set of standards in financial accounting and reporting?
7. What is the likely limitation of "general-purpose financial statements"?
8. In what way is the Securities and Exchange Commission concerned about and supportive of accounting principles and standards?
9. What was the Committee on Accounting Procedure, and what were its accomplishments and failings?
10. For what purposes did the AICPA in 1959 create the Accounting Principles Board?
11. Distinguish among Accounting Research Bulletins, Opinions of the Accounting Principles Board, and Statements of the Financial Accounting Standards Board.
12. If you had to explain or define "generally accepted accounting principles or standards," what essential characteristics would you include in your explanation?
13. In what ways was it felt that the statements issued by the Financial Accounting Standards Board would carry greater weight than the opinions issued by the Accounting Principles Board?
14. How are FASB discussion memoranda and FASB exposure drafts related to FASB "statements"?
15. Distinguish between FASB "statements of financial accounting standards" and FASB "statements of financial accounting concepts."
16. What is Rule 203 of the Code of Professional Conduct?
17. Rank from the most authoritative to the least authoritative, the following three items: FASB Technical Bulletins, AICPA Practice Bulletins, and FASB Standards.
18. The chairman of the FASB at one time noted that "the flow of standards can only be slowed if (1) producers focus less on quarterly earnings per share and tax benefits and more on quality products, and (2) accountants and lawyers rely less on rules and law and more on professional judgment and conduct." Explain his comment.
19. What is the purpose of FASB Staff Positions?
20. Explain the role of the Emerging Issues Task Force in establishing generally accepted accounting principles.
21. What is the purpose of the Governmental Accounting Standards Board?
22. What are some possible reasons why another organization, such as the Governmental Accounting Standards Board, should not issue financial reporting standards?
23. What are the sources of pressure that change and influence the development of accounting principles and standards?
24. Some individuals have indicated that the FASB must be cognizant of the economic consequences of its pronouncements. What is meant by "economic consequences"? What dangers exist if politics play too much of a role in the development of financial reporting standards?
25. If you were given complete authority in the matter, how would you propose that accounting principles or standards should be developed and enforced?
26. One writer recently noted that 99.4 percent of all companies prepare statements that are in accordance with GAAP. Why then is there such concern about fraudulent financial reporting?
27. What is the "expectations gap"? What is the profession doing to try to close this gap?
28. The Sarbanes-Oxley Act was enacted to combat fraud and curb poor reporting practices. What are some key provisions of this legislation?
29. A number of foreign countries have reporting standards that differ from those in the United States. What are some of the main reasons why reporting standards are often different among countries?
30. Why would it be advantageous for U.S. GAAP and International GAAP to be the same?
31. How are financial accountants challenged in their work to make ethical decisions? Is technical mastery of GAAP not sufficient to the practice of financial accounting?

CHAPTER TWO

CONCEPTUAL FRAMEWORK UNDERLYING FINANCIAL ACCOUNTING

Show Me the Earnings!

The growth of new-economy business on the Internet has led to the development of new measures of performance. When **Priceline.com** splashed on the dot-com scene, it touted steady growth in a measure called "unique offers by users" to explain its heady stock price. To draw investors to its stock, **Drugstore.com** focused on the number of "unique customers" at its website. After all, new businesses call for new performance measures, right?

Not necessarily. In fact, these indicators failed to show any consistent relationship between profits and website visits. Eventually, as the graphs below show, the profits never materialized, and stock prices fell. The lesson here: Although the new economy may require some new measures, investors need to be careful not to forget the reliable traditional ones.[1]

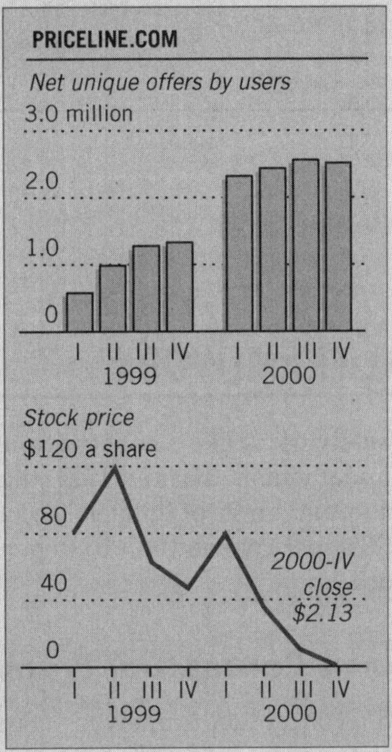

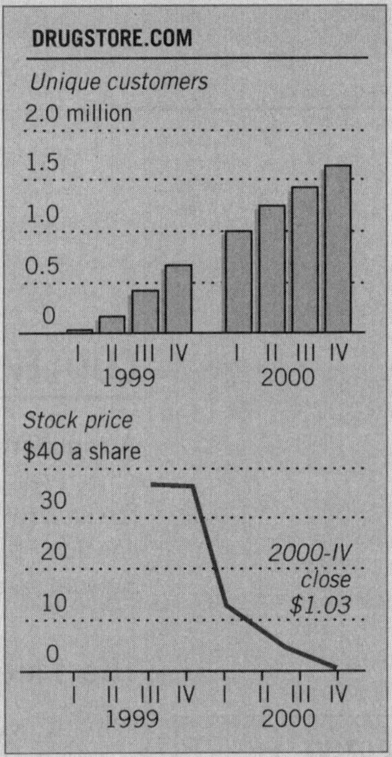

[1]Story and graphs adapted from Gretchen Morgenson, "How Did They Value Stocks? Count the Absurd Ways," *New York Times* (March 18, 2001), section 3, p. 1.

Learning Objectives

After studying this chapter, you should be able to:

1. Describe the usefulness of a conceptual framework.
2. Describe the FASB's efforts to construct a conceptual framework.
3. Understand the objectives of financial reporting.
4. Identify the qualitative characteristics of accounting information.
5. Define the basic elements of financial statements.
6. Describe the basic assumptions of accounting.
7. Explain the application of the basic principles of accounting.
8. Describe the impact that constraints have on reporting accounting information.

PREVIEW OF CHAPTER 2

As our opening story indicates, users of financial statements need relevant and reliable information. To help develop this type of financial information, financial accounting and reporting relies on a conceptual framework. In this chapter, we discuss the basic concepts underlying the conceptual framework, as follows.

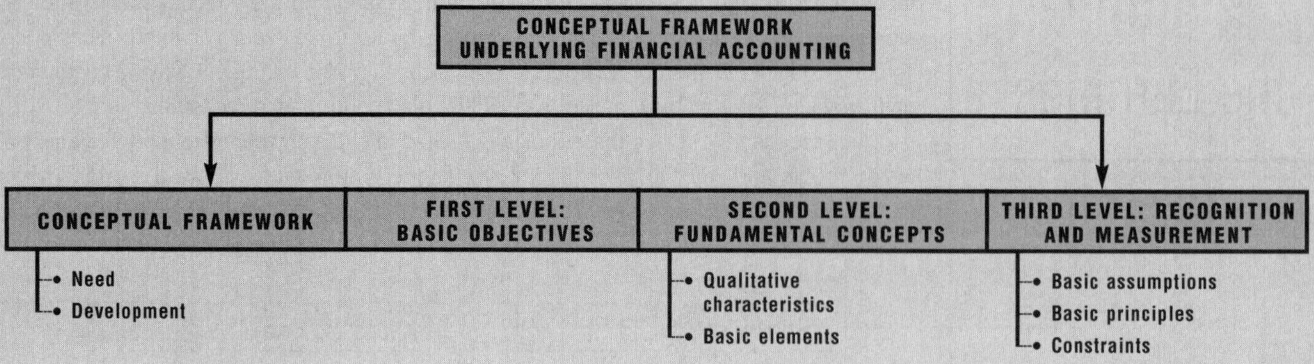

CONCEPTUAL FRAMEWORK

A **conceptual framework** is like a **constitution**: It is "a coherent system of interrelated objectives and fundamentals that can lead to consistent standards and that prescribes the nature, function, and limits of financial accounting and financial statements."[2] Many consider the FASB's real contribution to depend on the quality and utility of the conceptual framework.

The Need for a Conceptual Framework

OBJECTIVE 1
Describe the usefulness of a conceptual framework.

Why do we need a conceptual framework? First, to be useful, standard setting should build on and relate to an established body of concepts and objectives. A soundly developed conceptual framework thus enables the FASB to issue more useful and consistent standards over time. **A coherent set of standards and rules should result.** The framework should increase financial statement users' understanding of and confidence in financial reporting. It should enhance comparability among companies' financial statements.

Second, the profession should be able to more quickly solve new and emerging **practical problems by referring to an existing framework of basic theory**. For example, **Sunshine Mining** (a silver-mining company) sold two issues of bonds. It can redeem them either with $1,000 in cash or with 50 ounces of silver, whichever is worth

[2] "Conceptual Framework for Financial Accounting and Reporting: Elements of Financial Statements and Their Measurement," *FASB Discussion Memorandum* (Stamford, Conn.: FASB, 1976), page 1 of the "Scope and Implications of the Conceptual Framework Project" section. For an excellent discussion of the functions of the conceptual framework, see Reed K. Storey and Sylvia Storey, Special Report, "The Framework of Financial Accounting and Concepts" (Norwalk, Conn.: FASB, 1998), pp. 85–88.

more at maturity. Both bond issues have a stated interest rate of 8.5 percent. At what amounts should Sunshine or the buyers of the bonds record them? What is the amount of the premium or discount on the bonds? And how should Sunshine amortize this amount, if the bond redemption payments are to be made in silver (the future value of which is unknown at the date of issuance?) Consider that Sunshine cannot know, at the date of issuance, the value of future silver bond redemption payments.

It is difficult, if not impossible, for the FASB to prescribe the proper accounting treatment quickly for situations like this. Practicing accountants, however, must resolve such problems on a daily basis. How? Though good judgment and with the help of a universally accepted conceptual framework, practitioners can quickly focus on an acceptable treatment.

WHAT'S YOUR PRINCIPLE?

WHAT DO THE NUMBERS MEAN?

The need for a conceptual framework is highlighted by recent accounting scandals such as those at **Enron**, **Healthsouth**, and other companies. To restore public confidence in the financial reporting process, Congress passed the Sarbanes-Oxley Act of 2002 ("SOX"). One of the provisions of SOX is a requirement for the Securities and Exchange Commission (SEC) to evaluate the usefulness of "principles-based" accounting standards relative to the current set of accounting standards (which many argue are too "rules-based").

Some have suggested a move toward principles-based standards because they believe that companies exploited the detailed provisions in rules-based standards to manage accounting reports, rather than report the economic substance of transactions. For example, many of the off-balance-sheet arrangements of Enron avoided transparent reporting by barely achieving 3 percent outside equity ownership, a requirement in an obscure accounting standard interpretation. Enron's financial engineers were able to structure transactions to achieve a desired accounting treatment, even if that accounting treatment did not reflect the transaction's true nature.

In 2003 the SEC issued a report recommending that accounting standard setters move away from a rules-based approach toward a more principles-based approach ("Study Pursuant to Section 108(d) . . ."). If the profession adopts this approach, accounting standards will be more conceptual in nature, and the financial reporting objective of each standard will be more clearly stated. Top management's financial reporting responsibility will shift from demonstrating compliance with rules to demonstrating that a company has attained financial reporting objectives.

Source: "Study Pursuant to Section 108(d) of the Sarbanes-Oxley Act of 2002 on the Adoption by the United States Financial Reporting System of a Principles-Based Accounting System," *www.sec.gov/news/studies/principlesbasedstand.htm.*

Development of a Conceptual Framework

OBJECTIVE 2
Describe the FASB's efforts to construct a conceptual framework.

Over the years, numerous organizations developed and published their own conceptual frameworks, but no single framework was universally accepted and relied on in practice. In 1976 the FASB began to develop a conceptual framework that would be a basis for setting accounting standards and for resolving financial reporting controversies. The FASB has since issued six Statements of Financial Accounting Concepts that relate to financial reporting for business exterprises.[3] They are as follows.

[3]The FASB also issued a Statement of Financial Accounting Concepts that relates to nonbusiness organizations: "Objectives of Financial Reporting by Nonbusiness Organizations," *Statement of Financial Accounting Concepts No. 4* (December 1980).

INTERNATIONAL INSIGHT

The IASB has also issued a conceptual framework. The FASB and the IASB have agreed on a joint project to develop a common conceptual framework–one that converges and improves upon the existing frameworks of the two boards.

1 *SFAC No. 1*, "Objectives of Financial Reporting by Business Enterprises," presents the goals and purposes of accounting.

2 *SFAC No. 2*, "Qualitative Characteristics of Accounting Information," examines the characteristics that make accounting information useful.

3 *SFAC No. 3*, "Elements of Financial Statements of Business Enterprises," provides definitions of items in financial statements, such as assets, liabilities, revenues, and expenses.

4 *SFAC No. 5*, "Recognition and Measurement in Financial Statements of Business Enterprises," sets forth fundamental recognition and measurement criteria and guidance on what information should be formally incorporated into financial statements and when.

5 *SFAC No. 6*, "Elements of Financial Statements," replaces *SFAC No. 3* and expands its scope to include not-for-profit organizations.

6 *SFAC No. 7*, "Using Cash Flow Information and Present Value in Accounting Measurements," provides a framework for using expected future cash flows and present values as a basis for measurement.

Illustration 2-1 provides an overview of the conceptual framework.[4] The first level lists the **objectives**—that is, the goals and purposes of accounting. Ideally, accounting standards developed according to a conceptual framework will result in more useful accounting reports.

ILLUSTRATION 2-1
Conceptual Framework for Financial Reporting

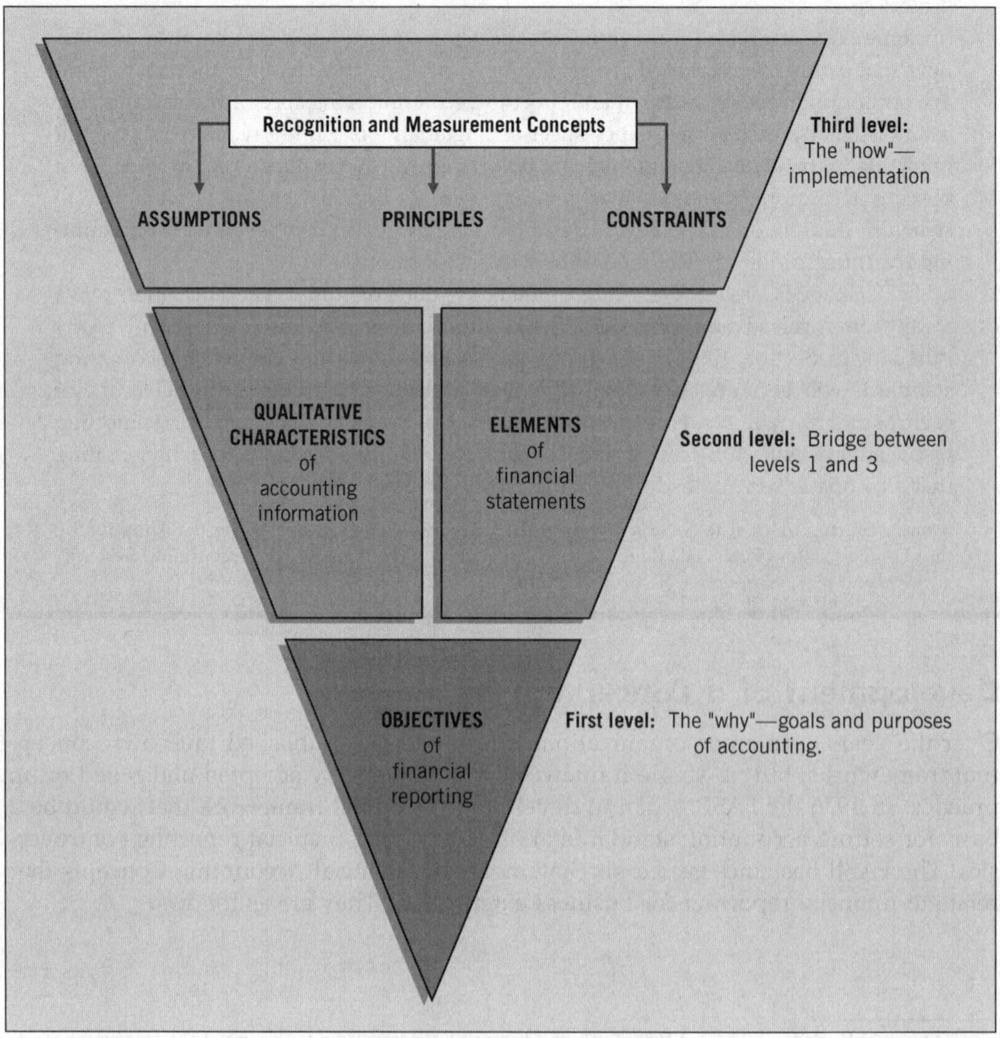

[4]Adapted from William C. Norby, *The Financial Analysts Journal* (March–April 1982), p. 22.

The second level provides the **qualitative characteristics** that make accounting information useful and the **elements** of financial statements (assets, liabilities, and so on). The third level identifies the **recognition and measurement concepts** used in establishing and applying accounting standards. These concepts include assumptions, principles, and constraints that describe the present reporting environment. We examine these three levels of the conceptual framework next.

FIRST LEVEL: BASIC OBJECTIVES

OBJECTIVE 3
Understand the objectives of financial reporting.

As we discussed in Chapter 1, the **objectives of financial reporting** are to provide information that is: (1) useful to those making investment and credit decisions, who have a reasonable understanding of business and economic activities; (2) helpful to present and potential investors, creditors, and other users in assessing the amounts, timing, and uncertainty of future cash flows; and (3) about economic resources, the claims to those resources, and the changes in them.

The objectives, therefore, broadly concern information that is useful to investor and creditor decisions. That concern narrows to the investors' and creditors' interest in receiving cash from their investments in, or loans to, business enterprises. Finally, the objectives focus on the financial statements, which provide information useful in assessing future cash flows. This approach is referred to as **decision usefulness**.

To provide information to decision makers, companies prepare general-purpose financial statements. These statements provide the most useful information possible at the least cost. However, users do need reasonable knowledge of business and financial accounting matters to understand the information contained in financial statements. This point is important. It means that financial statement preparers assume a level of competence on the part of users. This assumption impacts the way and the extent to which companies report information.

INTERNATIONAL INSIGHT

In Switzerland, Germany, Korea, and other nations, the primary providers of capital to companies are large banks. Creditors maintain very close ties to companies and can obtain information directly from them. Creditors do not need to rely on publicly available information, and financial information focuses on creditor protection. This process of capital allocation, however, is changing. It is likely that the need for publicly available information will change as well.

SECOND LEVEL: FUNDAMENTAL CONCEPTS

The objectives (first level) focus on the goals and purposes of accounting. Later, we will discuss the ways these goals and purposes are implemented (third level). What, then, is the purpose of the second level? The second level provides conceptual building blocks that explain the qualitative characteristics of accounting information and define the elements of financial statements. That is, the second level forms a bridge between the **why** of accounting (the objectives) and the **how** of accounting (recognition and measurement).

Qualitative Characteristics of Accounting Information

OBJECTIVE 4
Identify the qualitative characteristics of accounting information.

Should companies like **Walt Disney** or **Kellogg's** provide information in their financial statements on how much it costs them to acquire their assets (historical cost basis) or how much the assets are currently worth (fair-value basis)? Should **PepsiCo** combine and show as one company the four main segments of its business, or should it report PepsiCo Beverages, Frito Lay, Quaker Foods, and PepsiCo International as four separate segments?

How does a company choose an acceptable accounting method, the amount and types of information to disclose, and the format in which to present it? The answer: By determining **which alternative provides the most useful information for decision-making purposes (decision usefulness)**. The FASB identified the **qualitative characteristics** of accounting information that distinguish better (more useful) information from inferior (less useful) information for decision-making purposes.[5] In addition, the

[5] "Qualitative Characteristics of Accounting Information," *Statement of Financial Accounting Concepts No. 2* (Stamford, Conn.: FASB, May 1980).

FASB identified certain constraints (cost-benefit and materiality) as part of the conceptual framework (discussed later in the chapter). As Illustration 2-2 shows, the characteristics may be viewed as a hierarchy.

ILLUSTRATION 2-2
Hierarchy of Accounting Qualities

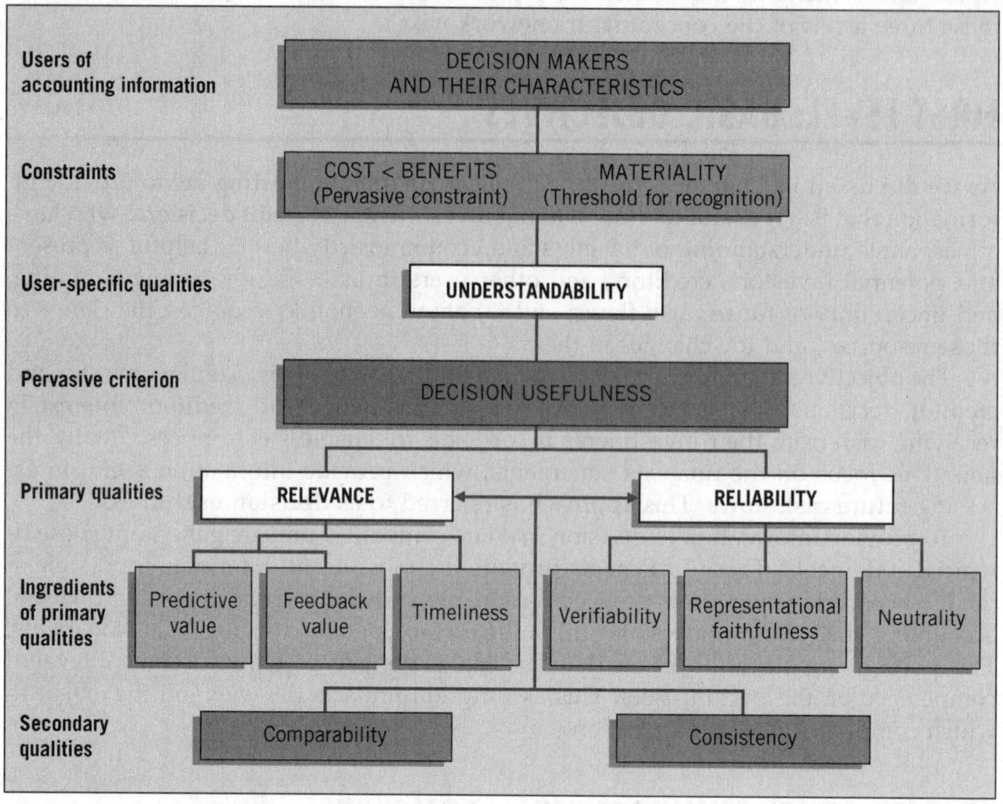

Decision Makers (Users) and Understandability

Decision makers vary widely in the types of decisions they make, how they make decisions, the information they already possess or can obtain from other sources, and their ability to process the information. For information to be useful, there must be a connection (linkage) between these users and the decisions they make. This link, **understandability**, is the quality of information that lets reasonably informed users see its significance.

For example, assume that **IBM Corp.** issues a three-months' report that shows interim earnings way down. This interim report provides relevant and reliable information for decision-making purposes. Now say that some users, upon reading the report, decide to sell their stock. Other users, however, do not understand the report's content and significance. They are surprised when IBM declares a smaller year-end dividend and the value of the stock declines. Thus, although IBM presented highly relevant and reliable information, it was useless to those who did not understand it.

Primary Qualities: Relevance and Reliability

Relevance and reliability are the two primary qualities that make accounting information useful for decision making. As stated in FASB *Concepts Statement No. 2*, "the qualities that distinguish 'better' (more useful) information from 'inferior' (less useful) information are primarily the qualities of relevance and reliability, with some other characteristics that those qualities imply."[6]

[6]Ibid., par. 15.

Relevance. To be relevant, accounting information must be capable of making a difference in a decision.[7] Information with no bearing on a decision is irrelevant. Relevant information helps users predict the ultimate outcome of past, present, and future events. That is, it has **predictive value**. Relevant information also helps users confirm or correct prior expectations; it has **feedback value**. For example, when **UPS (United Parcel Service)** issues an interim report, the information in it is relevant because it provides both a basis for forecasting annual earnings and feedback on past performance.

Finally, relevant information is available to decision makers before it loses its capacity to influence their decisions. It has **timeliness**. If UPS waited to report its interim results until six months after the end of the period, the information would be much less useful for decision-making purposes. **For information to be relevant, it needs predictive or feedback value, presented on a timely basis.**

Reliability. Accounting information is reliable to the extent that **it is verifiable, is a faithful representation, and is reasonably free of error and bias**. Reliability is a necessity, because most users have neither the time nor the expertise to evaluate the factual content of the information.

Verifiability occurs when independent measurers, using the same methods, obtain similar results. For example, would several independent auditors reach the same conclusion about a set of financial statements? If not, then the statements are not verifiable. Auditors could not render an opinion on such statements.

Representational faithfulness means that the numbers and descriptions match what really existed or happened. If **General Motors'** income statement reports sales of $225 billion when it had sales of $193.5 billion, then the statement fails to faithfully represent the proper sales amount.

Neutrality means that a company cannot select information to favor one set of interested parties over another. Unbiased information must be the overriding consideration. For example, in the notes to financial statements, tobacco companies such as **R. J. Reynolds** should not suppress information about the numerous lawsuits that have been filed because of tobacco-related health concerns—even though such disclosure is damaging to the company.

Neutrality in standard setting has come under increasing attack. Some argue that the FASB should not issue standards that cause undesirable economic effects on an industry or company. We disagree. Standards must be free from bias, or we will no longer have credible financial statements. Without credible financial statements, individuals will no longer use this information. An analogy demonstrates the point: In the United States, many individuals bet on boxing matches because such contests are assumed not to be fixed. But nobody bets on wrestling matches. Why? Because the public assumes that wrestling matches are rigged. If financial information is biased (rigged), the public will lose confidence and no longer use it.

Secondary Qualities: Comparability and Consistency

Information about a company is more useful if decision makers can compare it with similar information about another company and with similar information about the same company at other points in time. The first of these qualities is **comparability**, and the second is **consistency**.

Comparability. Information that is measured and reported in a similar manner for different companies is considered comparable. Comparability enables users to identify the real similarities and differences in economic events between companies.

For example, the accounting for pensions in the United States differs from that in Japan. In the United States, companies record pension cost as incurred. In Japan, companies record little or no charge to income for these costs. As a result, it is difficult to compare and evaluate the financial results of **General Motors** or **Ford** to Japanese competitors.

[7]Ibid., par. 47.

Also, resource allocation decisions involve evaluating alternatives. A valid evaluation can be made only if comparable information is available.

Consistency. When a company applies the same accounting treatment to similar events, from period to period, the company shows consistent use of accounting standards. The idea of consistency does not mean, however, that companies cannot switch from one accounting method to another. A company *can* change methods, but it must first demonstrate that the newly adopted method is preferable to the old. If approved, the company must then disclose the nature and effect of the accounting change, as well as the justification for it, in the financial statements for the period in which it made the change.[8] When a change in accounting principles occurs, the auditor refers to it in an explanatory paragraph of the audit report. This paragraph identifies the nature of the change and refers the reader to the note in the financial statements that discusses the change in detail.[9]

WHAT DO THE NUMBERS MEAN?

YOU MAY NEED A MAP

Beyond touting nonfinancial measures to investors (see opening story), many companies increasingly promote the performance of their companies through the reporting of various "pro-forma" earnings measures. A recent survey of newswire reports found 36 instances of the reporting of pro-forma measures in just a three-day period.

Pro-forma measures are standard measures (such as earnings) that companies adjust, usually for one-time or nonrecurring items. For example, companies usually adjust earnings for the effects of an extraordinary item. Such adjustments make the numbers more comparable to numbers reported in periods without the unusual item.

However, rather than increasing comparability, it appears that some companies use pro-forma reporting to accentuate the positive in their results. Examples include **Yahoo Inc.** and **Cisco**, which define pro-forma income after adding back payroll tax expense. **Level 8 Systems** transformed an operating loss into a pro-forma profit by adding back expenses for depreciation and amortization of intangible assets.

Lynn Turner, former Chief Accountant at the SEC, calls such earnings measures EBS—"Everything but Bad Stuff." To provide investors a more complete picture of company profitability, not the story preferred by management, the SEC issued Regulation G (REG G). REG G requires companies to reconcile non-GAAP financial measures to GAAP, thereby giving investors a roadmap to analyze adjustments companies make to their GAAP numbers to arrive at pro-forma results.

Sources: Adapted from Gretchen Morgenson, "How Did They Value Stocks? Count the Absurd Ways," *New York Times* (March 18, 2001), section 3, p. 1; and Gretchen Morgenson, "Expert Advice: Focus on Profit," *New York Times* (March 18, 2001), section 3, p. 14. See also SEC Regulation G, "Conditions for Use of Non-GAAP Financial Measures, "Release No. 33–8176 (March 28, 2003).

Basic Elements

OBJECTIVE 5
Define the basic elements of financial statements.

An important aspect of developing any theoretical structure is the body of **basic elements** or definitions to be included in it. Accounting uses many terms with distinctive and specific meanings. These terms constitute the language of business or the jargon of accounting.

---

[8]Surveys indicate that users highly value consistency. They note that a change tends to destroy the comparability of data before and after the change. Some companies assist users to understand the pre- and post-change data. Generally, however, users say they lose the ability to analyze over time. It is hoped that the new standard on accounting changes will improve the comparability of the data before and after the change.

[9]"Reports on Audited Financial Statements," *Statement on Auditing Standards No. 58* (New York: AICPA, April 1988), par. 34.

One such term is **asset**. Is it merely something we own? Or is an asset something we have the right to use, as in the case of leased equipment? Or is it anything of value used by a company to generate revenues—in which case, should we also consider the managers of a company as an asset?

As this example illustrates, it seems necessary, therefore, to develop basic definitions for the elements of financial statements. *Concepts Statement No. 6* defines the ten interrelated elements that most directly relate to measuring the performance and financial status of a business enterprise. We list them here for review and information purposes; you need not memorize these definitions at this point. We will explain and examine each of these elements in more detail in subsequent chapters.

ELEMENTS OF FINANCIAL STATEMENTS

ASSETS. Probable future economic benefits obtained or controlled by a particular entity as a result of past transactions or events.

LIABILITIES. Probable future sacrifices of economic benefits arising from present obligations of a particular entity to transfer assets or provide services to other entities in the future as a result of past transactions or events.

EQUITY. Residual interest in the assets of an entity that remains after deducting its liabilities. In a business enterprise, the equity is the ownership interest.

INVESTMENTS BY OWNERS. Increases in net assets of a particular enterprise resulting from transfers to it from other entities of something of value to obtain or increase ownership interests (or equity) in it. Assets are most commonly received as investments by owners, but that which is received may also include services or satisfaction or conversion of liabilities of the enterprise.

DISTRIBUTIONS TO OWNERS. Decreases in net assets of a particular enterprise resulting from transferring assets, rendering services, or incurring liabilities by the enterprise to owners. Distributions to owners decrease ownership interests (or equity) in an enterprise.

COMPREHENSIVE INCOME. Change in equity (net assets) of an entity during a period from transactions and other events and circumstances from nonowner sources. It includes all changes in equity during a period except those resulting from investments by owners and distributions to owners.

REVENUES. Inflows or other enhancements of assets of an entity or settlement of its liabilities (or a combination of both) during a period from delivering or producing goods, rendering services, or other activities that constitute the entity's ongoing major or central operations.

EXPENSES. Outflows or other using up of assets or incurrences of liabilities (or a combination of both) during a period from delivering or producing goods, rendering services, or carrying out other activities that constitute the entity's ongoing major or central operations.

GAINS. Increases in equity (net assets) from peripheral or incidental transactions of an entity and from all other transactions and other events and circumstances affecting the entity during a period except those that result from revenues or investments by owners.

LOSSES. Decreases in equity (net assets) from peripheral or incidental transactions of an entity and from all other transactions and other events and circumstances affecting the entity during a period except those that result from expenses or distributions to owners.[10]

[10] "Elements of Financial Statements," *Statement of Financial Accounting Concepts No. 6* (Stamford, Conn.: FASB, December 1985), pp. ix and x.

The FASB classifies the elements into two distinct groups. The first group of three elements—assets, liabilities, and equity—describes amounts of resources and claims to resources at a **moment in time**. The other seven elements describe transactions, events, and circumstances that affect a company during a **period of time**. The first class, affected by elements of the second class, provides at any time the cumulative result of all changes. This interaction is referred to as "articulation." That is, key figures in one financial statement correspond to balances in another.

THIRD LEVEL: RECOGNITION AND MEASUREMENT CONCEPTS

The third level of the framework consists of concepts that implement the basic objectives of level one. These concepts explain how companies should recognize, measure, and report financial elements and events. The FASB sets forth most of these in its *Statement of Financial Accounting Concepts No. 5,* "Recognition and Measurement in Financial Statements of Business Enterprises." According to *SFAC No. 5,* to be recognized, an item (event or transaction) must meet the definition of an "element of financial statements" as defined in *SFAC No. 6* and must be measurable. Most aspects of current practice follow these recognition and measurement concepts.

The accounting profession continues to use the concepts in *SFAC No. 5* as operational guidelines. Here, we identify the concepts as basic assumptions, principles, and constraints. Not everyone uses this classification system, so focus your attention more on **understanding the concepts** than on how we classify and organize them. These concepts serve as guidelines in responding to controversial financial reporting issues.

Basic Assumptions

OBJECTIVE 6
Describe the basic assumptions of accounting.

Four basic **assumptions** underlie the financial accounting structure: (1) **economic entity**, (2) **going concern**, (3) **monetary unit**, and (4) **periodicity**. We'll look at each in turn.

Economic Entity Assumption

The **economic entity assumption means that economic activity can be identified with a particular unit of accountability**. In other words, a company keeps its activity separate and distinct from its owners and any other business unit. At the most basic level, the economic entity assumption dictates that **Panera Bread Company** record the company's financial activities separate from those of its owners and managers. Equally important, financial statement users need to be able to distinguish the activities and elements of different companies, such as **General Motors**, **Ford**, and **DaimlerChrysler**. If users could not distinguish the activities of different companies, how would they know which company financially outperformed the other?

The entity concept does not apply solely to the segregation of activities among competing companies, such as **Best Buy** and **Circuit City**. An individual, department, division, or an entire industry could be considered a separate entity if we choose to define it in this manner. Thus, **the entity concept does not necessarily refer to a legal entity**. A parent and its subsidiaries are separate **legal** entities, but merging their activities for accounting and reporting purposes does not violate the **economic entity** assumption.[11]

[11]The concept of the entity is changing. For example, defining the "outer edges" of companies is now harder. Public companies often consist of multiple public subsidiaries, each with joint ventures, licensing arrangements, and other affiliations. Increasingly, companies form and dissolve joint ventures or customer-supplier relationships in a matter of months or weeks. These "virtual companies" raise accounting issues about how to account for the entity. See Steven H. Wallman, "The Future of Accounting and Disclosure in an Evolving World: The Need for Dramatic Change," *Accounting Horizons* (September 1995).

WHOSE COMPANY IS IT?

The importance of the entity assumption is illustrated by scandals involving **W. R. Grace** and, more recently, **Adelphia**. In both cases, senior company employees entered into transactions that blurred the line between the employee's financial interests and those of the company. At Adelphia, among many other self-dealings, the company guaranteed over $2 billion of loans to the founding family. W. R. Grace used company funds to pay for an apartment and chef for the company chairman. As a result of these transactions, these insiders benefitted at the expense of shareholders. Additionally, the financial statements failed to disclose the transactions. Such disclosure would have allowed shareholders to sort out the impact of the employee transactions on company results.

WHAT DO THE NUMBERS MEAN?

Going Concern Assumption

Most accounting methods rely on the **going concern assumption—that the company will have a long life**. Despite numerous business failures, most companies have a fairly high continuance rate. As a rule, we expect companies to last long enough to fulfill their objectives and commitments.

This assumption has significant implications. The historical cost principle would be of limited usefulness if we assume eventual liquidation. Under a liquidation approach, for example, a company would better state asset values at net realizable value (sales price less costs of disposal) than at acquisition cost. **Depreciation and amortization policies are justifiable and appropriate only if we assume some permanence to the company.** If a company adopts the liquidation approach, the current/non-current classification of assets and liabilities loses much of its significance. Labeling anything a fixed or long-term asset would be difficult to justify. Indeed, listing liabilities on the basis of priority in liquidation would be more reasonable.

The going concern assumption applies in most business situations. **Only where liquidation appears imminent is the assumption inapplicable.** In these cases a total revaluation of assets and liabilities can provide information that closely approximates the company's net realizable value. You will learn more about accounting problems related to a company in liquidation in advanced accounting courses.

INTERNATIONAL INSIGHT

Due to their experiences with persistent inflation, several South American countries produce "constant-currency" financial reports. Typically, companies in these countries use a general price-level index to adjust for the effects of inflation.

Monetary Unit Assumption

The **monetary unit assumption** means that money is the common denominator of economic activity and provides an appropriate basis for accounting measurement and analysis. That is, the monetary unit is the most effective means of expressing to interested parties changes in capital and exchanges of goods and services. **The monetary unit is relevant, simple, universally available, understandable, and useful.** Application of this assumption depends on the even more basic assumption that quantitative data are useful in communicating economic information and in making rational economic decisions.

In the United States, accounting ignores price-level changes (inflation and deflation) and assumes that the unit of measure—the dollar—remains reasonably stable. We therefore use the monetary unit assumption to justify adding 1980 dollars to 2007 dollars without any adjustment. The FASB in *SFAC No. 5* indicated that it expects the dollar, unadjusted for inflation or deflation, to continue to be used to measure items recognized in financial statements. Only if circumstances change dramatically (such as if the United States experiences high inflation similar to that in many South American countries) will the FASB again consider "inflation accounting."

wiley.com/college/kieso

Accounting for Changing Prices

Periodicity Assumption

To measure the results of a company's activity accurately, we would need to wait until it liquidates. Decision makers, however, cannot wait that long for such information.

Users need to know a company's performance and economic status on a timely basis so that they can evaluate and compare firms, and take appropriate actions. Therefore, companies must report information periodically.

The **periodicity** (or **time period**) **assumption** implies that a company can divide its economic activities into artificial time periods. These time periods vary, but the most common are monthly, quarterly, and yearly.

The shorter the time period, the more difficult it is to determine the proper net income for the period. A month's results usually prove less reliable than a quarter's results, and a quarter's results are likely to be less reliable than a year's results. Investors desire and demand that a company quickly process and disseminate information. Yet the quicker a company releases the information, the more likely the information will include errors. **This phenomenon provides an interesting example of the trade-off between relevance and reliability in preparing financial data.**

The problem of defining the time period becomes more serious as product cycles shorten and products become obsolete more quickly. Many believe that, given technology advances, companies need to provide more online, real-time financial information to ensure the availability of relevant information.

Basic Principles of Accounting

OBJECTIVE 7
Explain the application of the basic principles of accounting.

We generally use four basic **principles of accounting** to record transactions: (1) historical cost, (2) revenue recognition, (3) matching, and (4) full disclosure. Again, we look at each in turn.

Historical Cost Principle

GAAP requires that companies account for and report most assets and liabilities on the basis of acquisition price. This is often referred to as the **historical cost principle**. Cost has an important advantage over other valuations: **it is reliable**. To illustrate this advantage, consider the problems if companies select current selling price instead. Companies might have difficulty establishing a value for unsold items. Every member of the accounting department might value the assets differently. Further, how often would it be necessary to establish sales value? All companies close their accounts at least annually. Some compute their net income every month. These companies would have to place a sales value on every asset each time they wished to determine income. Critics raise similar objections against current cost (replacement cost, present value of future cash flows) and any other basis of valuation **except historical cost**.

What about liabilities? Do companies account for them on a cost basis? Yes, they do. Companies issue liabilities, such as bonds, notes, and accounts payable, in exchange for assets, or perhaps services, for an agreed-upon price. **This price, established by the exchange transaction, is the "cost" of the liability.** A company uses this amount to record the liability in the accounts and report it in financial statements.

In general, users prefer historical cost because it provides them with a reliable benchmark for measuring historical trends. However, **fair value information** may be more useful for certain types of assets and liabilities and in certain industries. For example, companies report many financial instruments, including derivatives, at fair value, and inventories at lower of cost or market. Certain industries, such as brokerage houses and mutual funds, prepare their basic financial statements on a fair value basis.

At initial acquisition, historical cost equals fair value. In subsequent periods, as market and economic conditions change, historical cost and fair value often diverge. As a result, fair value measures or estimates often provide more relevant information about the expected future cash flows related to the asset or liability. For example, when long-lived assets decline in value, a fair value measure determines any impairment loss.

The FASB now appears to support greater use of fair value measurements in the financial statements. The Board believes that fair value information is more relevant to users than historical cost. Fair value measurement, it is argued, provides better insight into the value of a company's asset and liabilities (its financial position) and provides a better basis for assessing future cash flow prospects.

The FASB is developing a standard on "Fair Value Measurements," which provides guidance on how to measure fair value. This standard applies to both financial and nonfinancial assets that are measured at fair value. As a result, we should now have increased consistency and comparability when fair value measurements are used in the financial statements and related notes. Such consistency and comparability is very much needed in light of controversies using fair values at companies like **Enron** (valuation of energy contracts) and **J. P. Morgan** (valuation of its bond portfolio). In addition, this new standard clarifies and incorporates the guidance in *Concepts Statement 7*, "Using Cash Flow Information and Present Value in Accounting Measurements," for using present value techniques to estimate future cash flows, and it provides enhanced disclosure of fair value information.[12]

As we indicated above, we presently have a "mixed-attribute" system that permits the use of historical cost, fair value, and other valuation bases. Although the historical cost principle continues to be the primary basis for valuation, recording and reporting of fair value information is increasing.

Revenue Recognition Principle

A crucial question for many companies is when to recognize revenue. Revenue recognition generally occurs (1) when **realized** or **realizable** and (2) when **earned**. This approach has often been referred to as the **revenue recognition principle.**

A company **realizes** revenues when it exchanges products (goods or services), merchandise, or other assets for cash or claims to cash. Revenues are realizable when assets received or held are readily convertible into cash or claims to cash. Assets are readily convertible when they are salable or interchangeable in an active market at readily determinable prices without significant additional cost.

In addition to the first test (realized or realizable), a company delays recognition of revenues until earned. Revenues are considered **earned** when the company substantially accomplishes what it must do to be entitled to the benefits represented by the revenues.[13] Generally, an objective test, such as a sale, indicates the point at which a company recognizes revenue. The sale provides an objective and verifiable measure of revenue—the sales price. Any basis for revenue recognition short of actual sale opens the door to wide variations in practice. **Recognition at the time of sale provides a uniform and reasonable test.**

However, as Illustration 2-3 shows, exceptions to the rule exist. We discuss these exceptions in the following sections.

During Production. A company can recognize revenue **before** it completes the job in certain long-term construction contracts. In this method, a company recognizes revenue periodically, based on the percentage of the job it has completed. Although technically a transfer of ownership has not occurred, the earning process is considered substantially completed at various stages of construction. If it is not possible to obtain dependable estimates of cost and progress, then a company delays revenue recognition until it completes the job.

At End of Production. At times, a company may recognize revenue **after completion of the production cycle but before the sale takes place**. This occurs if products or other assets are salable in an active market at readily determinable prices without significant

[12]"Fair Value Measurement," *Proposed Statement of Financial Accounting Standards* (Norwalk, Conn.: FASB, October 21, 2005).

[13]"Recognition and Measurement in Financial Statements of Business Enterprises," *Statement of Financial Accounting Concepts No. 5* (Stamford, Conn.: FASB, December 1984), par. 83(a) and (b).

ILLUSTRATION 2-3
Timing of Revenue Recognition

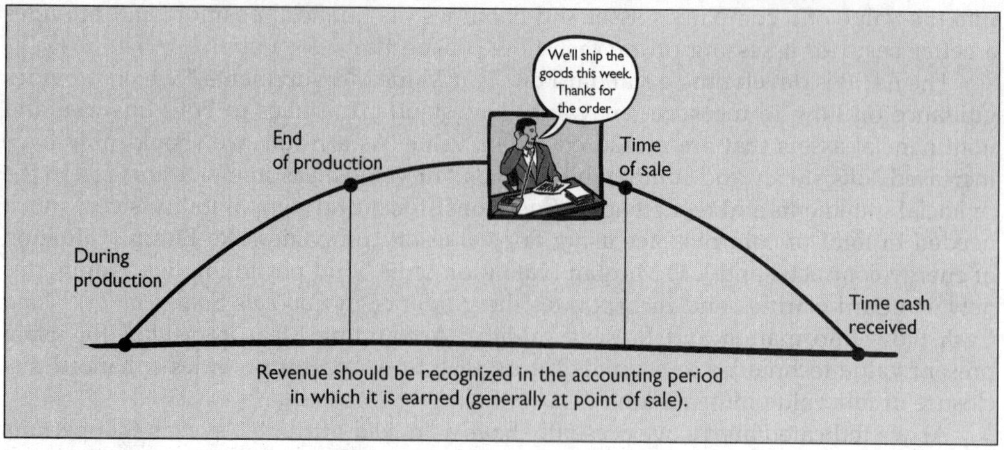

additional cost. An example is the mining of certain minerals. Once a company mines the mineral, a ready market at a quoted price exists. The same holds true for some agricultural products.

Upon Receipt of Cash. **Receipt of cash is another basis for revenue recognition.** Companies use the cash-basis approach only when collection is uncertain at the time of sale.

One form of the cash basis is the **installment-sales method**. Here, a company requires payment in periodic installments over a long period of time. Its most common use is in retail, such as for farm and home equipment and furnishings. Companies frequently justify the installment-sales method based on the high risk of not collecting an account receivable. In some instances, this reasoning may be valid. Generally, though, if a sale has been completed, the company should recognize the sale; if bad debts are expected, the company should record them as separate estimates.

To summarize, a company records revenue in the period when realized or realizable and when earned. Normally, this is the date of sale. But circumstances may dictate application of the percentage-of-completion approach, the end-of-production approach, or the receipt-of-cash approach.

NO TAKE-BACKS!

WHAT DO THE NUMBERS MEAN?

Investors in **Lucent Technologies** got an unpleasant surprise when the SEC forced the company to restate its financial results. What happened? Lucent violated one of the fundamental criteria for revenue recognition—the "no take-back" rule. This rule holds that a company should not book revenue on inventory that it shipped if the customer can return it at some point in the future. In this particular case, Lucent agreed to take back shipped inventory from its distributors if they could not sell the items to their customers.

Lucent recorded the sales on the shipped goods, which helped it report continued sales growth. However, Lucent's distributors did indeed return many of those shipped goods. The restatement erased $679 million in revenues, turning an operating profit into a loss. In response, Lucent's stock price declined $1.31 per share or 8.5 percent. Lucent has since changed its policy. It now records inventory as sold only when the final customer buys the equipment, not when Lucent ships the inventory to the distributor.

The lesson for investors: Review a company's revenue recognition policy for indications that revenues may be overstated due to generous return provisions for inventory. And remember, no take-backs!

Source: Adapted from S. Young, "Lucent Slashes First Quarter Outlook, Erases Revenue from Latest Quarter," *Wall Street Journal Online Edition* (December 22, 2000).

Matching Principle

In recognizing expenses, the approach is "Let the expense follow the revenues." Companies recognize expenses not when they pay wages or make a product, but when the work (service) or the product actually contributes to revenue. Thus, companies tie expense recognition to revenue recognition. This practice is referred to as the **matching principle**, because it dictates that **efforts (expenses) be matched with accomplishment (revenues) whenever it is reasonable and practicable to do so.**

Some costs, however, are difficult to associate with revenue. As a result, some other approach must be developed. Often, companies use a "rational and systematic" allocation policy that will approximate the matching principle. This type of expense recognition involves assumptions about the benefits that a company receives as well as the cost associated with those benefits. For example, a company like **Intel** or **Motorola** allocates the cost of a long-lived asset over all of the accounting periods during which it uses the asset because the asset contributes to the generation of revenue throughout its useful life.

HOLLYWOOD ACCOUNTING

WHAT DO THE NUMBERS MEAN?

Hollywood accounting illustrates that the problem of expense recognition is as complex as that of revenue recognition. Following then-existing GAAP standards, major motion picture studios capitalized advertising and marketing costs, and then amortized these costs against revenues over the life of the film. As a result, many investors suggested that the studios overstated their profit numbers. Under a new GAAP standard, the studios must now amortize these costs over no more than three months. In many cases, the studios have to expense them immediately.

Similarly, the studios often allocated the costs related to abandoned projects to overhead, thus spreading them out over the lives of the successful projects. Not anymore. The studios must now expense these costs as incurred.

Here is a rough estimate of the amounts of capitalized advertising costs some major studios charged off in response to the change in GAAP.

Studio (Parent Company)	Capitalized Advertising (in millions)
Columbia Tri-Star (Sony)	$200
Paramount (Viacom)	200
20th Century Fox (News Corp)	150

The more conservative approach results from a stricter application of the definitions of assets and expenses. While many argue that advertising and marketing costs have future service potential, difficulty in reliably measuring these benefits suggests they are not assets. Therefore, a very short amortization period or immediate write-off is justified. Under these new guidelines, investors will have more reliable measures for assessing the performance of companies in this industry.

Companies charge some costs to the current period as expenses (or losses) simply because they cannot determine a connection with revenue. Examples of these types of costs are officers' salaries and other administrative expenses.

Costs are generally classified into two groups: **product costs** and **period costs. Product costs**, such as material, labor, and overhead, attach to the product. Companies carry these costs into future periods if they recognize the revenue from the product in subsequent periods. **Period costs**, such as officers' salaries and other administrative expenses, attach to the period. Companies charge off such costs in the immediate period, even though benefits associated with these costs may occur in the future. Why? Because companies cannot determine a direct relationship between period costs and revenue. Illustration 2-4 summarizes these expense recognition procedures.

ILLUSTRATION 2-4
Expense Recognition

Type of Cost	Relationship	Recognition
Product costs: • Material • Labor • Overhead	Direct relationship between cost and revenue.	Recognize in period of revenue (matching).
Period costs: • Salaries • Administrative costs	No direct relationship between cost and revenue.	Expense as incurred.

As indicated in the discussion of Hollywood accounting, there is some debate about the conceptual validity of the matching principle. A major concern is that matching permits companies to defer certain costs and treat them as assets on the balance sheet. In fact, these costs may not have future benefits. If abused, this principle permits the balance sheet to become a "dumping ground" for unmatched costs. In addition, there appears to be no objective definition of "systematic and rational."

Full Disclosure Principle

In deciding what information to report, companies follow the general practice of providing information that is of sufficient importance to influence the judgment and decisions of an informed user. Often referred to as the **full disclosure principle**, it recognizes that the nature and amount of information included in financial reports reflects a series of judgmental trade-offs. These trade-offs strive for (1) sufficient detail to disclose matters that **make a difference** to users, yet (2) sufficient condensation to make the **information understandable**, keeping in mind costs of preparing and using it.

Users find information about financial position, income, cash flows, and investments in one of three places: (1) within the main body of financial statements, (2) in the notes to those statements, or (3) as supplementary information.

As discussed in Chapter 1, the **financial statements** are the balance sheet, income statement, statement of cash flows, and statement of owners' equity. They are a structured means of communicating financial information. To be recognized in the main body of financial statements, **an item should meet the definition of a basic element, be measurable with sufficient certainty, and be relevant and reliable.**[14]

Disclosure is not a substitute for proper accounting. As a former chief accountant of the SEC noted, "Good disclosure does not cure bad accounting any more than an adjective or adverb can be used without, or in place of, a noun or verb." Thus, for example, cash-basis accounting for cost of goods sold is misleading, even if a company discloses accrual-basis amounts in the notes to the financial statements.

The **notes to financial statements** generally amplify or explain the items presented in the main body of the statements. If the main body of the financial statements gives an incomplete picture of the performance and position of the company, the notes should provide the additional information needed. Information in the notes does not have to be quantifiable, nor does it need to qualify as an element. Notes can be partially or totally narrative. Examples of notes include descriptions of the accounting policies and methods used in measuring the elements reported in the statements, explanations of uncertainties and contingencies, and statistics and details too voluminous for inclusion in the statements. The notes can be essential to understanding the company's performance and position.

Supplementary information may include details or amounts that present a different perspective from that adopted in the financial statements. It may be quantifiable information that is high in relevance but low in reliability. For example, oil and gas companies typically provide information on proven reserves as well as the related discounted cash flows.

[14]*SFAC No. 5*, par. 63.

Supplementary information may also include management's explanation of the financial information and its discussion of the significance of that information. For example, many business combinations have produced financing arrangements that demand new accounting and reporting practices and principles. In each of these situations, the same problem must be faced: making sure the company presents enough information to ensure that the **reasonably prudent investor** will not be misled.

We discuss the content, arrangement, and display of financial statements, along with other facets of full disclosure, in Chapters 4, 5, and 20.

Constraints

OBJECTIVE 8
Describe the impact that constraints have on reporting accounting information.

In providing information with the qualitative characteristics that make it useful, companies must consider two overriding factors that limit (constrain) the reporting. These **constraints** are: (1) the **cost-benefit relationship** and (2) **materiality**. We also review two other less-dominant yet important constraints that are part of the reporting environment: **industry practices** and **conservatism**.

Cost-Benefit Relationship

Too often, users assume that information is free. But preparers and providers of accounting information know that it is not. Therefore, companies must consider the **cost-benefit relationship**: They must weigh the costs of providing the information against the benefits that can be derived from using it. Standard-setting bodies and governmental agencies use cost-benefit analysis before making final their informational requirements. In order to justify requiring a particular measurement or disclosure, the benefits perceived to be derived from it must exceed the costs perceived to be associated with it.

A corporate executive made the following remark to the FASB about a proposed standard: "In all my years in the financial arena, I have never seen such an absolutely ridiculous proposal. . . . To dignify these 'actuarial' estimates by recording them as assets and liabilities would be virtually unthinkable except for the fact that the FASB has done equally stupid things in the past. . . . For God's sake, use common sense just this once."[15] Although extreme, this remark indicates the frustration expressed by members of the business community about standard setting, and whether the benefits of a given standard exceed the costs.

The difficulty in cost-benefit analysis is that the costs and especially the benefits are not always evident or measurable. The costs are of several kinds: costs of collecting and processing, of disseminating, of auditing, of potential litigation, of disclosure to competitors, and of analysis and interpretation. Benefits to preparers may include greater management control and access to capital at a lower cost. Users may receive better information for allocation of resources, tax assessment, and rate regulation. As noted earlier, benefits are generally more difficult to quantify than are costs.

The recent implementation of the provisions of the Sarbanes-Oxley Act of 2002 illustrates the challenges in assessing costs and benefits of standards. One study estimated the increased costs of complying with the new internal-control standards related to the financial reporting process to be an average of $7.8 million per company. However, the study concluded that "...quantifying the benefits of improved more reliable financial reporting is not fully possible."[16]

Despite the difficulty in assessing the costs and benefits of its standards, the FASB attempts to determine that each proposed standard will fill a significant need and that the costs imposed to meet the standard are justified in relation to overall benefits of

[15] "Decision-Usefulness: The Overriding Objective," *FASB Viewpoints* (October 19, 1983), p. 4.

[16] Charles Rivers and Associates, "Sarbanes-Oxley Section 404: Costs and Remediation of Deficiencies" letter from Deloitte and Touche, Ernst and Young, KPMG, and Pricewaterhouse-Coopers to the SEC (April 11, 2005).

the resulting information. In addition, the Board seeks input on costs and benefits as part of its due process.[17]

Materiality

The **materiality** constraint concerns an item's impact on a company's overall financial operations. An item is *material* if its inclusion or omission would influence or change the judgment of a reasonable person.[18] It is *immaterial,* and therefore irrelevant, if it would have no impact on a decision maker. In short, **it must make a difference** or a company need not disclose it.

The point involved here is of **relative size and importance**. If the amount involved is significant when compared with the other revenues and expenses, assets and liabilities, or net income of the company, sound and acceptable standards should be followed in reporting it. If the amount is so small that it is unimportant when compared with other items, applying a particular standard may be considered of less importance.

It is difficult to provide firm guidelines in judging when a given item is or is not material. Materiality varies both with relative amount and with relative importance. For example, the two sets of numbers presented below illustrate relative size.

ILLUSTRATION 2-5
Materiality Comparison

	Company A	Company B
Sales	$10,000,000	$100,000
Costs and expenses	9,000,000	90,000
Income from operations	$ 1,000,000	$ 10,000
Unusual gain	$ 20,000	$ 5,000

During the period in question, the revenues and expenses, and therefore the net incomes of Company A and Company B, are proportional. Each reported an unusual gain. In looking at the abbreviated income figures for Company A, it appears insignificant whether the amount of the unusual gain is set out separately or merged with the regular operating income. The gain is only 2 percent of the net income. If merged, it would not seriously distort the net income figure. Company B has had an unusual gain of only $5,000. However, it is relatively much more significant than the larger gain realized by A. For Company B, an item of $5,000 amounts to 50 percent of its income from operations. Obviously, the inclusion of such an item in ordinary operating income would affect the amount of that income materially. Thus we see the importance of the **relative size** of an item in determining its materiality.

Companies and their auditors generally adopt the rule of thumb that anything under 5 percent of net income is considered immaterial. However, the SEC indicates that a company may use this percentage for an initial assessment of materiality, but it must also consider other factors.[19] For example, companies can no longer fail to record items in order to meet consensus analysts' earnings numbers, preserve a positive earnings trend, convert a loss to a profit or vice versa, increase management compensation, or hide an illegal transaction like a bribe. In other words, **companies must consider both quantitative and qualitative factors in determining whether an item is material.**

---

[17]For example, as part of its project on "Share-Based Payment," *SFAS No. 123R,* the Board conducted a field study and surveyed commercial software providers to collect information on the costs of measuring the fair values of share-based compensation arrangements.

[18]*SFAC No. 2,* par. 132, sets forth the essence of materiality: "The omission or misstatement of an item in a financial report is material if, in the light of surrounding circumstances, the magnitude of the item is such that it is probable that the judgment of a reasonable person relying upon the report would have been changed or influenced by the inclusion or correction of the item." The auditing profession also adopted this same concept of materiality. See "Audit Risk and Materiality in Conducting an Audit," *Statement on Auditing Standards No. 47* (New York: AICPA, 1983), par. 6.

[19]"Materiality," *SEC Staff Accounting Bulletin No. 99* (Washington, D.C.: SEC, 1999).

The SEC also indicated that in determining materiality, companies must consider each misstatement separately and the aggregate effect of all misstatements. For example, at one time, **General Dynamics** disclosed that its Resources Group improved its earnings by $5.8 million. At the same time, it disclosed that one of its other subsidiaries had taken write-offs of $6.7 million. Although both numbers exceeded the $2.5 million that General Dynamics as a whole earned for the year, the company disclosed neither as unusual because it considered the net effect on earnings as immaterial. **This practice is prohibited** because each item must be considered separately. In addition, even though an individual item may be immaterial, it may be considered material when added to other immaterial items. Companies must disclose such items.

Materiality factors in a great many internal accounting decisions, too. Examples of such judgments that companies must make include: the amount of classification required in a subsidiary expense ledger, the degree of accuracy required in prorating expenses among the departments of a company, and the extent to which adjustments should be made for accrued and deferred items. Only by **the exercise of good judgment and professional expertise** can reasonable and appropriate answers be found, which is the materiality constraint sensibly applied.

LIVING IN A MATERIAL WORLD

WHAT DO THE NUMBERS MEAN?

The first line of defense for many companies caught "cooking the books" had been to argue that a questionable accounting item is immaterial. That defense has not been working so well lately, in the wake of recent accounting meltdowns at **Enron** and **Global Crossing** and the tougher rules on materiality issued by the SEC (*SAB 99*).

For example, the SEC alleged in a case against **Sunbeam** that the company racked up so many immaterial adjustments that they added up to a material misstatement that misled investors about the company's financial position. More recently, the SEC called for a number of companies, such as **Jack in the Box**, **McDonalds**, and **AIG**, to restate prior financial statements for the effects of incorrect accounting. In some cases, the restatements did not meet traditional materiality thresholds. Don Nicholaisen, SEC Chief Accountant, observed that whether the amount is material or not-material, some transactions appear to be "flat out intended to mislead investors." In essence he is saying that any wrong accounting for a transaction can represent important information to the users of financial statements.

Responding to new concerns about materiality, blue-chip companies such as **IBM** and **General Electric** are providing expanded disclosures of transactions that used to fall below the materiality radar. As a result, some good may yet come from the recent accounting failures.

Source: Adapted from K. Brown and J. Weil, "A Lot More Information Is 'Material' After Enron," *Wall Street Journal Online Edition* (February 22, 2002); S. D. Jones and R. Gibson, "Restaurants Serve Up Restatements," *Wall Street Journal* (January 26, 2005), p. C3; and R. McTauge, "Nicholaisen Says Restatement Needed When Deal Lacks Business Purpose," *Securities Regulation & Law Reporter* (May 9, 2005).

Industry Practices

Another practical consideration is **industry practices. The peculiar nature of some industries and business concerns** sometimes requires departure from basic theory. For example, public-utility companies report noncurrent assets first on the balance sheet to highlight the industry's capital-intensive nature. Agricultural companies often report crops at market value because it is costly to develop accurate cost figures on individual crops.

Such variations from basic theory are infrequent, yet they do exist. Whenever we find what appears to be a violation of basic accounting theory, we should determine whether some peculiarity of the industry explains the violation before we criticize the procedures followed.

Conservatism

Few conventions in accounting are as misunderstood as the constraint of conservatism. **Conservatism** means **when in doubt, choose the solution that will be least likely to overstate assets and income.** Note that the conservatism convention does not urge that net assets or net income be *understated*. Unfortunately, some interpret conservatism to mean just that.

All that conservatism does, properly applied, is provide a reasonable guide in difficult situations: Refrain from overstatement of net income and net assets. Examples of conservatism in accounting are the use of the lower-of-cost-or-market approach in valuing inventories, and the rule that companies recognize accrued net losses on firm purchase commitments for goods for inventory. When in doubt, it is better to understate than overstate net income and net assets. Of course, if no doubt exists, there is no need to apply this constraint.

Summary of the Structure

Illustration 2-6 presents the conceptual framework discussed in this chapter. It is similar to Illustration 2-1, except that it provides additional information for each level. We cannot overemphasize the usefulness of this conceptual framework in helping to understand many of the problem areas that we examine in later chapters.

ILLUSTRATION 2-6
Conceptual Framework for Financial Reporting

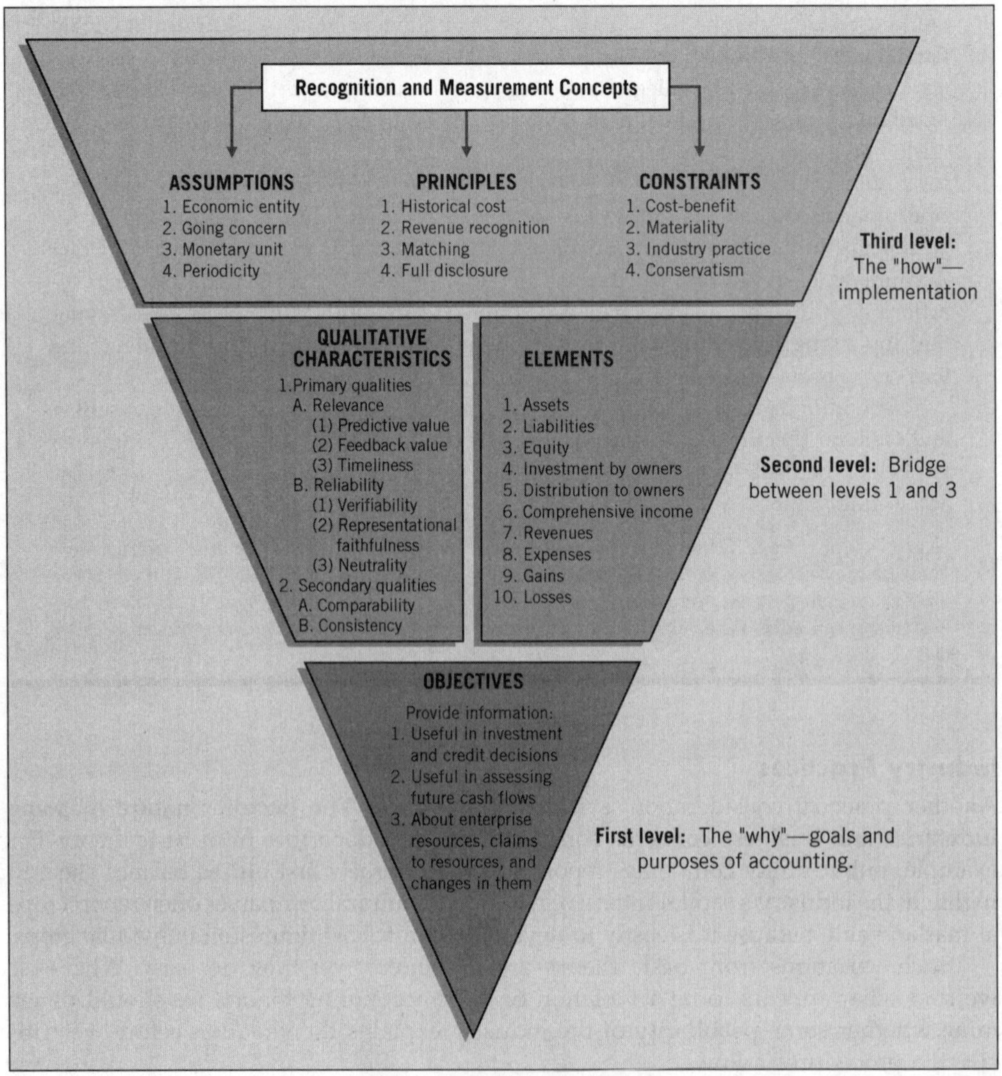

QUESTIONS

1. What is a conceptual framework? Why is a conceptual framework necessary in financial accounting?
2. What are the primary objectives of financial reporting as indicated in *Statement of Financial Accounting Concepts No. 1?*
3. What is meant by the term "qualitative characteristics of accounting information"?
4. Briefly describe the two primary qualities of useful accounting information.
5. According to the FASB conceptual framework, the objectives of financial reporting for business enterprises are based on the needs of the users of financial statements. Explain the level of sophistication that the Board assumes about the users of financial statements.
6. What is the distinction between comparability and consistency?
7. Why is it necessary to develop a definitional framework for the basic elements of accounting?
8. Expenses, losses, and distributions to owners are all decreases in net assets. What are the distinctions among them?
9. Revenues, gains, and investments by owners are all increases in net assets. What are the distinctions among them?
10. What are the four basic assumptions that underlie the financial accounting structure?
11. The life of a business is divided into specific time periods, usually a year, to measure results of operations for each such time period and to portray financial conditions at the end of each period.
    (a) This practice is based on the accounting assumption that the life of the business consists of a series of time periods and that it is possible to measure accurately the results of operations for each period. Comment on the validity and necessity of this assumption.
    (b) What has been the effect of this practice on accounting? What is its relation to the accrual system? What influence has it had on accounting entries and methodology?
12. What is the basic accounting problem created by the monetary unit assumption when there is significant inflation? What appears to be the FASB position on a stable monetary unit?
13. The chairman of the board of directors of the company for which you are chief accountant has told you that he has little use for accounting figures based on cost. He believes that replacement values are of far more significance to the board of directors than "out-of-date costs." Present some arguments to convince him that accounting data should still be based on cost.
14. When is revenue generally recognized? Why has that date been chosen as the point at which to recognize the revenue resulting from the entire producing and selling process?
15. Magnus Eatery operates a catering service specializing in business luncheons for large corporations. Magnus requires customers to place their orders 2 weeks in advance of the scheduled events. Magnus bills its customers on the tenth day of the month following the date of service and requires that payment be made within 30 days of the billing date. Conceptually, when should Magnus recognize revenue related to its catering service?
16. What is the difference between realized and realizable? Give an example of where the concept of realizable is used to recognize revenue.
17. What is the justification for the following deviations from recognizing revenue at the time of sale?
    (a) Installment sales method of recognizing revenue.
    (b) Recognition of revenue at completion of production for certain agricultural products.
    (c) The percentage-of-completion basis in long-term construction contracts.
18. Jane Hull Company paid $135,000 for a machine in 2007. The Accumulated Depreciation account has a balance of $46,500 at the present time. The company could sell the machine today for $150,000. The company president believes that the company has a "right to this gain." What does the president mean by this statement? Do you agree?
19. Three expense recognition methods (associating cause and effect, systematic and rational allocation, and immediate recognition) were discussed in the text under the matching principle. Indicate the basic nature of each of these types of expenses and give two examples of each.
20. *Statement of Financial Accounting Concepts No. 5* identifies four characteristics that an item must have before it is recognized in the financial statements. What are these four characteristics?
21. Briefly describe the types of information concerning financial position, income, and cash flows that might be provided: (a) within the main body of the financial statements, (b) in the notes to the financial statements, or (c) as supplementary information.
22. In January 2008, Alan Jackson Inc. doubled the amount of its outstanding stock by selling on the market an additional 10,000 shares to finance an expansion of the business. You propose that this information be shown by a footnote on the balance sheet as of December 31, 2007. The president objects, claiming that this sale took place after December 31, 2007, and, therefore, should not be shown. Explain your position.

23. Describe the two major constraints inherent in the presentation of accounting information.

24. What are some of the costs of providing accounting information? What are some of the benefits of accounting information? Describe the cost-benefit factors that should be considered when new accounting standards are being proposed.

25. How are materiality (and immateriality) related to the proper presentation of financial statements? What factors and measures should be considered in assessing the materiality of a misstatement in the presentation of a financial statement?

26. The treasurer of Joan Osborne Co. has heard that conservatism is a doctrine that is followed in accounting and, therefore, proposes that several policies be followed that are conservative in nature. State your opinion with respect to each of the policies listed below.

(a) The company gives a 2-year warranty to its customers on all products sold. The estimated warranty costs incurred from this year's sales should be entered as an expense this year instead of an expense in the period in the future when the warranty is made good.

(b) When sales are made on account, there is always uncertainty about whether the accounts are collectible. Therefore, the treasurer recommends recording the sale when the cash is received from the customers.

(c) A personal liability lawsuit is pending against the company. The treasurer believes there is an even chance that the company will lose the suit and have to pay damages of $200,000 to $300,000. The treasurer recommends that a loss be recorded and a liability created in the amount of $300,000.

(d) The inventory should be valued at "cost or market, whichever is lower" because the losses from price declines should be recognized in the accounts in the period in which the price decline takes place.

CHAPTER THREE

THE ACCOUNTING INFORMATION SYSTEM

Needed: A Reliable Information System

Maintaining a set of accounting records is not optional. The **Internal Revenue Service (IRS)** requires that businesses prepare and retain a set of records and documents that can be audited. The Foreign Corrupt Practices Act (federal legislation) requires public companies to ". . . make and keep books, records, and accounts, which, in reasonable detail, accurately and fairly reflect the transactions and dispositions of the assets. . . ." But beyond these two reasons, a company that fails to keep an accurate record of its business transactions may lose revenue and is more likely to operate inefficiently.

Consider, for example, the **Long Island Railroad (LIRR)**, once one of the nation's busiest commuter lines. The LIRR lost money because of poor recordkeeping. It forgot to bill some customers, mistakenly paid some payables twice, and neglected to record redemptions of bonds. **FFP Marketing**, which operates convenience stores in 11 states, provides another example. The SEC forced it to restate earnings when an audit uncovered faulty bookkeeping for its credit card accounts and fuel payables.

Inefficient accounting also cost the **City of Cleveland**, Ohio. An audit discovered over 313 examples of dysfunctional accounting, costing taxpayers over $1.3 million. Its poor accounting system resulted in the Cleveland treasurer's ignorance of available cash, which led to missed investment opportunities. Further, delayed recording of pension payments created the false impression of $13 million in the city coffers.

Even the use of computers is no assurance of accuracy and efficiency. "The conversion to a new system called MasterNet fouled up data processing records to the extent that **Bank of America** was frequently unable to produce or deliver customer statements on a timely basis," said an executive at one of the country's largest banks.

Although these situations may occur only rarely in large organizations, they illustrate the point: Companies must properly maintain accounts and detailed records or face unnecessary costs. The SEC suspended trading in FFP Marketing's stock until it corrected the errors and re-issued financial statements. The City of Cleveland's municipal bond rating took a hit because of its poor accounting practices.

Learning Objectives

After studying this chapter, you should be able to:

1 Understand basic accounting terminology.

2 Explain double-entry rules.

3 Identify steps in the accounting cycle.

4 Record transactions in journals, post to ledger accounts, and prepare a trial balance.

5 Explain the reasons for preparing adjusting entries.

6 Prepare financial statements from the adjusted trial balance.

7 Prepare closing entries.

8 Explain how to adjust inventory accounts at year-end.

PREVIEW OF CHAPTER 3

As the opening story indicates, a reliable information system is a necessity for all companies. The purpose of this chapter is to explain and illustrate the features of an accounting information system. The content and organization of this chapter are as follows.

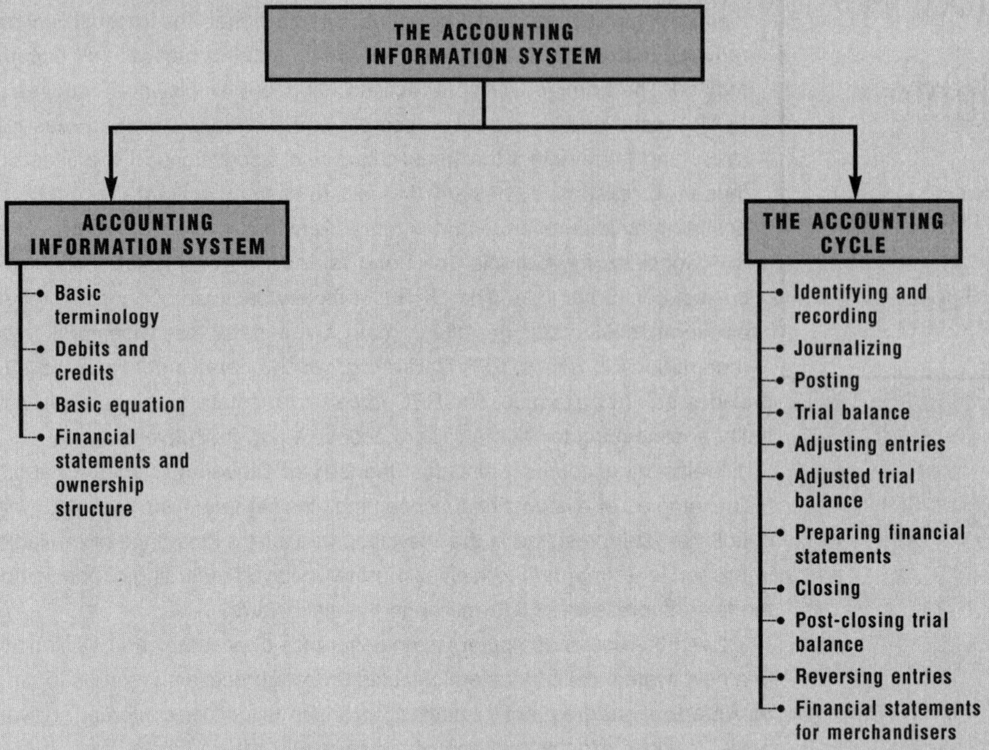

ACCOUNTING INFORMATION SYSTEM

An **accounting information system** collects and processes transaction data and then disseminates the financial information to interested parties. Accounting information systems vary widely from one business to another. Various factors shape these systems: the nature of the business and the transactions in which it engages, the size of the firm, the volume of data to be handled, and the informational demands that management and others require.

As we discussed in Chapters 1 and 2, in response to the requirements of the Sarbanes-Oxley Act of 2002, companies are placing a renewed focus on their accounting systems to ensure relevant and reliable information is reported in financial statements.[1] A good accounting information system helps management answer such questions as:

How much and what kind of debt is outstanding?

Were our sales higher this period than last?

What assets do we have?

What were our cash inflows and outflows?

[1]One study of first compliance with the internal-control testing provisions of the Sarbanes-Oxley Act documented material weaknesses for about 13 percent of companies reporting in 2004 and 2005. L. Townsend, "Internal Control Deficiency Disclosures–Interim Alert," *Yellow Card–Interim Trend Alert* (April 12, 2005) Glass, Lewis & Co., LLC.

Did we make a profit last period?
Are any of our product lines or divisions operating at a loss?
Can we safely increase our dividends to stockholders?
Is our rate of return on net assets increasing?

Management can answer many other questions with the data provided by an efficient accounting system. A well-devised accounting information system benefits every type of company.

Basic Terminology

Financial accounting rests on a set of concepts (discussed in Chapters 1 and 2) for identifying, recording, classifying, and interpreting transactions and other events relating to enterprises. You therefore need to understand the **basic terminology employed in collecting accounting data.**

OBJECTIVE 1
Understand basic accounting terminology.

BASIC TERMINOLOGY

EVENT. A happening of consequence. An event generally is the source or cause of changes in assets, liabilities, and equity. Events may be external or internal.

TRANSACTION. An **external event** involving a transfer or exchange between two or more entities.

ACCOUNT. A systematic arrangement that shows the effect of transactions and other events on a specific element (asset, liability, and so on). Companies keep a separate account for each asset, liability, revenue, and expense, and for capital (owners' equity).

REAL AND NOMINAL ACCOUNTS. Real (permanent) **accounts** are asset, liability, and equity accounts; they appear on the balance sheet. **Nominal** (temporary) **accounts** are revenue, expense, and dividend accounts; except for dividends, they appear on the income statement. Companies periodically close nominal accounts; they do not close real accounts.

LEDGER. The book (or computer printouts) containing the accounts. A **general ledger** is a collection of all the asset, liability, owners' equity, revenue, and expense accounts. A **subsidiary ledger** contains the details related to a given general ledger account.

JOURNAL. The "book of original entry" where the company initially records transactions and selected other events. Various amounts are transferred from the book of original entry, the journal, to the ledger.

POSTING. The process of transferring the essential facts and figures from the book of original entry to the ledger accounts.

TRIAL BALANCE. The list of all open accounts in the ledger and their balances. The trial balance taken immediately after all adjustments have been posted is called an **adjusted trial balance.** A trial balance taken immediately after closing entries have been posted is called a **post-closing** or **after-closing trial balance**. Companies may prepare a trial balance at any time.

ADJUSTING ENTRIES. Entries made at the end of an accounting period to bring all accounts up to date on an accrual basis, so that the company can prepare correct financial statements.

FINANCIAL STATEMENTS. Statements that reflect the collection, tabulation, and final summarization of the accounting data. Four statements are involved: (1) The **balance sheet** shows the financial condition of the enterprise at the end of a period.

(2) The **income statement** measures the results of operations during the period. (3) The **statement of cash flows** reports the cash provided and used by operating, investing, and financing activities during the period. (4) The **statement of retained earnings** reconciles the balance of the retained earnings account from the beginning to the end of the period.

CLOSING ENTRIES. The formal process by which the enterprise reduces all nominal accounts to zero and determines and transfers the net income or net loss to an owners' equity account. Also known as "closing the ledger," "closing the books," or merely "closing."

OBJECTIVE 2
Explain double-entry rules.

Debits and Credits

The terms **debit** (Dr.) and **credit** (Cr.) mean left and right, respectively. These terms do not mean increase or decrease, but instead describe *where* a company makes entries in the recording process. That is, when a company enters an amount on the left side of an account, it **debits** the account. When it makes an entry on the right side, it **credits** the account. When comparing the totals of the two sides, an account shows a **debit balance** if the total of the debit amounts exceeds the credits. An account shows a **credit balance** if the credit amounts exceed the debits.

The positioning of debits on the left and credits on the right is simply an accounting custom. We could function just as well if we reversed the sides. However, the United States adopted the custom, now the rule, of having debits on the left side of an account and credits on the right side, similar to the custom of driving on the right-hand side of the road. This rule applies to all accounts.

The equality of debits and credits provides the basis for the double-entry system of recording transactions (sometimes referred to as double-entry bookkeeping). Under the universally used **double-entry accounting** system, a company records the dual (two-sided) effect of each transaction in appropriate accounts. This system provides a logical method for recording transactions. It also offers a means of proving the accuracy of the recorded amounts. If a company records every transaction with equal debits and credits, then the sum of all the debits to the accounts must equal the sum of all the credits.

Illustration 3-1 presents the basic guidelines for an accounting system. Increases to all asset and expense accounts occur on the left (or debit side) and decreases on the

ILLUSTRATION 3-1
Double-entry (Debit and Credit) Accounting System

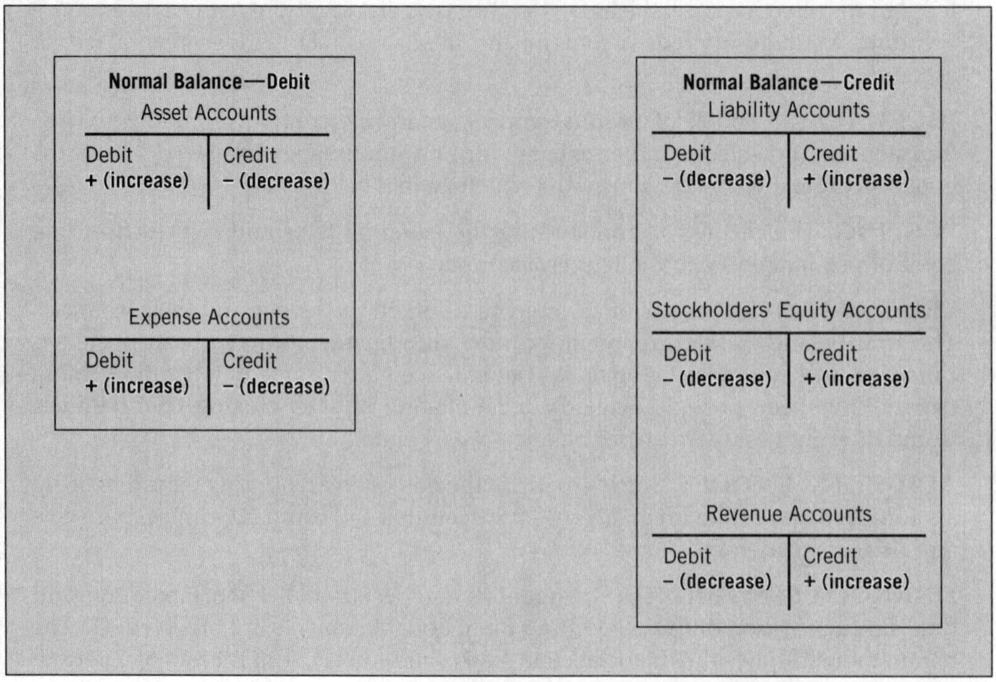

right (or credit side). Conversely, increases to all liability and revenue accounts occur on the right (or credit side) and decreases on the left (or debit side). A company increases stockholders' equity accounts, such as Common Stock and Retained Earnings, on the credit side, but increases Dividends on the debit side.

Basic Equation

In a double-entry system, for every debit there must be a credit, and vice versa. This leads us, then, to the basic equation in accounting (Illustration 3-2).

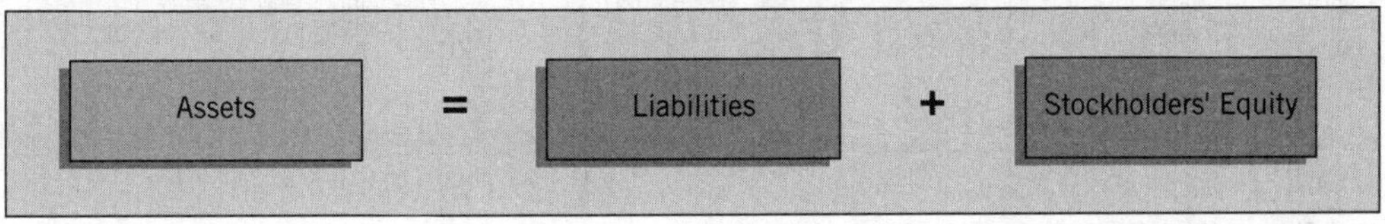

ILLUSTRATION 3-2
The Basic Accounting Equation

Illustration 3-3 expands this equation to show the accounts that make up stockholders' equity. The figure also shows the debit/credit rules and effects on each type of account. Study this diagram carefully. It will help you understand the fundamentals of the double-entry system. Like the basic equation, the expanded basic equation must also balance (total debits equal total credits).

ILLUSTRATION 3-3
Expanded Basic Equation and Debit/Credit Rules and Effects

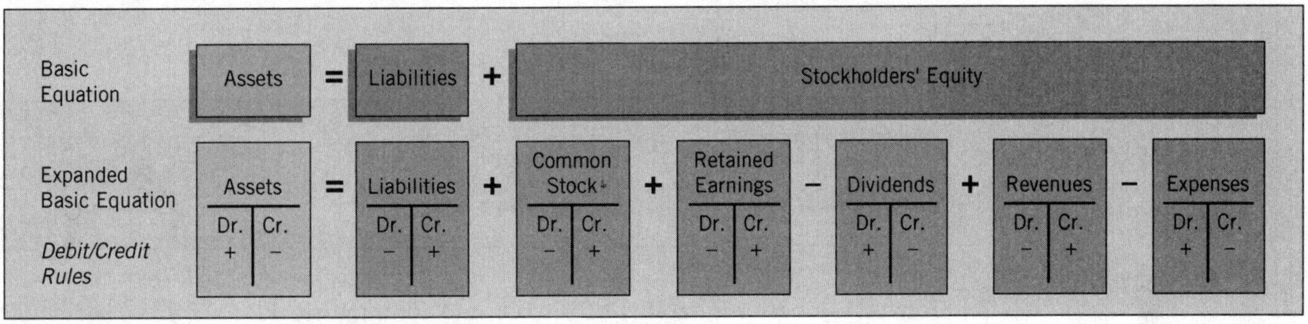

Every time a transaction occurs, the elements of the equation change. However, the basic equality remains. To illustrate, consider the following eight different transactions for Perez Inc.

1 Owners invest $40,000 in exchange for common stock.

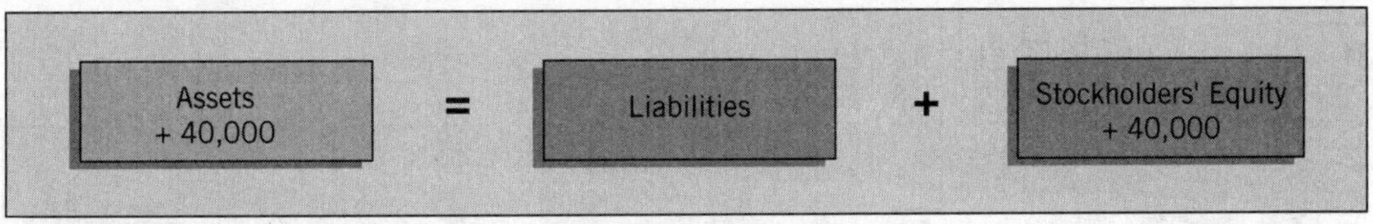

2 Disburse $600 cash for secretarial wages.

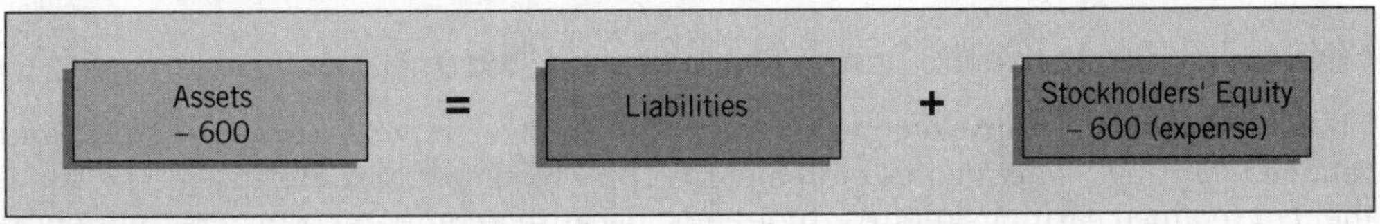

3 Purchase office equipment priced at $5,200, giving a 10 percent promissory note in exchange.

Assets		Liabilities		Stockholders' Equity
+ 5,200	=	+5,200	+	

4 Receive $4,000 cash for services rendered.

Assets		Liabilities		Stockholders' Equity
+ 4,000	=		+	+ 4,000 (revenue)

5 Pay off a short-term liability of $7,000.

Assets		Liabilities		Stockholders' Equity
− 7,000	=	− 7,000	+	

6 Declare a cash dividend of $5,000.

Assets		Liabilities		Stockholders' Equity
	=	+ 5,000	+	− 5,000

7 Convert a long-term liability of $80,000 into common stock.

Assets		Liabilities		Stockholders' Equity
	=	− 80,000	+	+ 80,000

8 Pay cash of $16,000 for a delivery van.

Assets		Liabilities		Stockholders' Equity
−16,000 +16,000	=		+	

Financial Statements and Ownership Structure

The stockholders' equity section of the balance sheet reports common stock and retained earnings. The income statement reports revenues and expenses. The statement of retained earnings reports dividends. Because a company transfers dividends, revenues, and expenses to retained earnings at the end of the period, a change in any one of these three items affects stockholders' equity. Illustration 3-4 shows the stockholders' equity relationships.

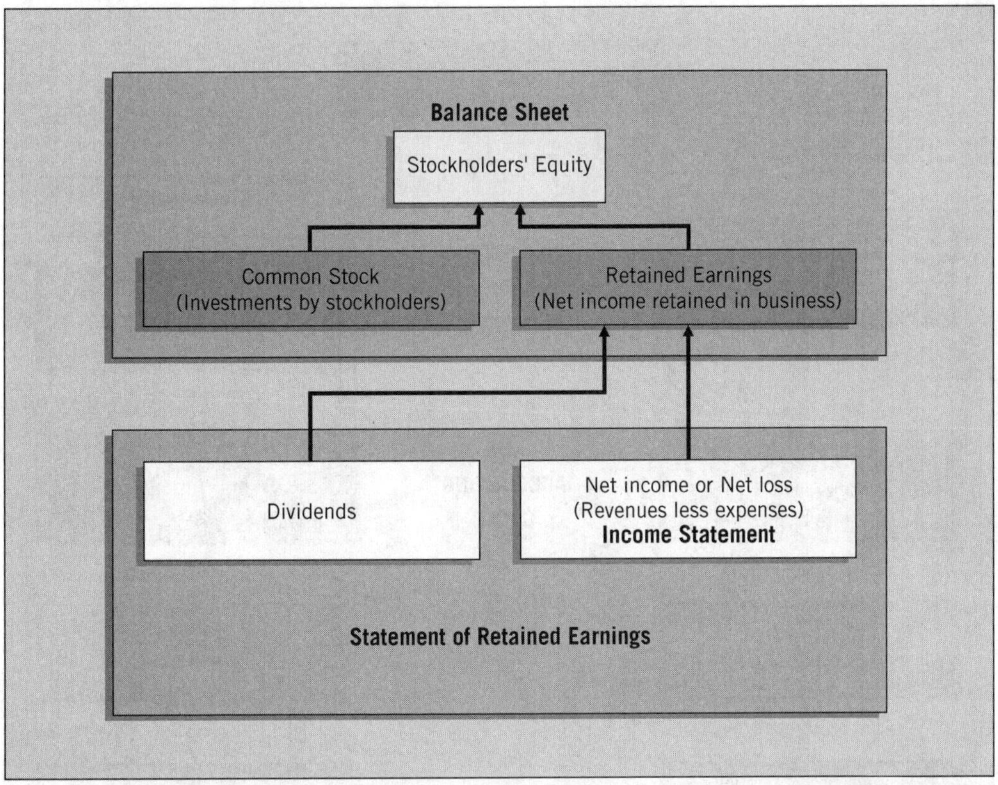

ILLUSTRATION 3-4
Financial Statements and Ownership Structure

The enterprise's ownership structure dictates the types of accounts that are part of or affect the equity section. A corporation commonly uses Common Stock, Additional Paid-in Capital, Dividends, and Retained Earnings accounts. A proprietorship or a partnership uses a Capital account and a Drawing account: A Capital account indicates the owner's or owners' investment in the company. A Drawing account tracks withdrawals by the owner(s).

Illustration 3-5 summarizes and relates the transactions affecting owners' equity to the nominal (temporary) and real (permanent) classifications and to the types of business ownership.

ILLUSTRATION 3-5
Effects of Transactions on Owners' Equity Accounts

		Ownership Structure			
		Proprietorships and Partnerships		Corporations	
Transactions Affecting Owners' Equity	Impact on Owners' Equity	Nominal (Temporary) Accounts	Real (Permanent) Accounts	Nominal (Temporary) Accounts	Real (Permanent) Accounts
Investment by owner(s)	Increase		Capital		Common Stock and related accounts
Revenues earned Expenses incurred Withdrawal by owner(s)	Increase Decrease Decrease	Revenue Expense Drawing	Capital	Revenue Expense Dividends	Retained Earnings

THE ACCOUNTING CYCLE

OBJECTIVE 3
Identify steps in the accounting cycle.

Illustration 3-6 shows the steps in the **accounting cycle**. An enterprise normally uses these accounting procedures to record transactions and prepare financial statements.

ILLUSTRATION 3-6
The Accounting Cycle

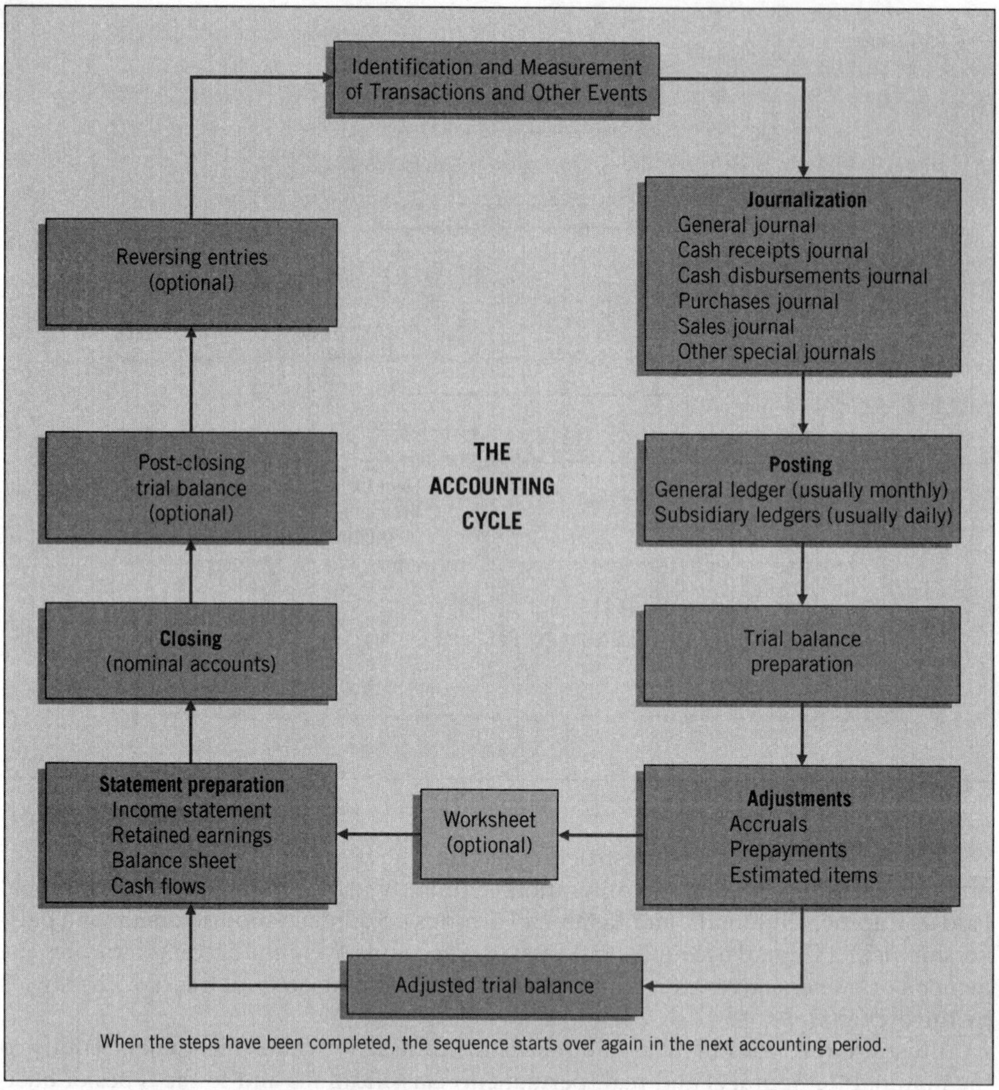

wiley.com/college/kieso

Accounting Cycle Tutorial

Identifying and Recording Transactions and Other Events

The first step in the accounting cycle is analysis of transactions and selected other events. The first problem is to determine what to record. Although GAAP provides guidelines, no simple rules exist that state which events a company should record. Although changes in a company's personnel or managerial policies may be important, the company should not record these items in the accounts. On the other hand, a company should record all cash sales or purchases—no matter how small.

The concepts we presented in Chapter 2 determine what to recognize in the accounts. An item should be recognized in the financial statements if it is an element, is measurable, and is relevant and reliable. Consider human resources. **R. G. Barry & Co.** at one time reported as supplemental data total assets of $14,055,926, including $986,094 for "Net investments in human resources." **AT&T** and **ExxonMobil Company** also experimented with human resource accounting. Should we value employees for balance sheet and income statement purposes? Certainly skilled employees are an important asset (highly relevant), but the problems of determining their value and measuring it reliably have not yet been solved. Consequently, human resources are not recorded. Perhaps when measurement techniques become more sophisticated and accepted, such information will be presented, if only in supplemental form.

UNDERLYING CONCEPTS

Assets are probable economic benefits controlled by a particular entity as a result of a past transaction or event. Do human resources of a company meet this definition?

The FASB uses the phrase "transactions and other events and circumstances that affect a business enterprise" to describe the sources or causes of changes in an entity's assets, liabilities, and equity.[2] Events are of two types: (1) **External events** involve interaction between an entity and its environment, such as a transaction with another entity, a change in the price of a good or service that an entity buys or sells, a flood or earthquake, or an improvement in technology by a competitor. (2) **Internal events** occur within an entity, such as using buildings and machinery in operations, or transferring or consuming raw materials in production processes.

Many events have both external and internal elements. For example, hiring an employee, which involves an exchange of salary for labor, is an external event. Using the services of labor is part of production, an internal event. Further, an entity may initiate and control events, such as the purchase of merchandise or use of a machine. Or, events may be beyond its control, such as an interest rate change, theft, or a tax hike.

Transactions are types of external events. They may be an exchange between two entities where each receives and sacrifices value, such as purchases and sales of goods or services. Or, transactions may be transfers in one direction only. For example, an entity may incur a liability without directly receiving value in exchange, such as charitable contributions. Other examples include investments by owners, distributions to owners, payment of taxes, gifts, casualty losses, and thefts.

In short, an enterprise records as many events as possible that affect its financial position. As discussed earlier in the case of human resources, it omits some events because of tradition and others because of complicated measurement problems. Recently, however, the accounting profession shows more receptiveness to accepting the challenge of measuring and reporting events previously viewed as too complex and immeasurable.

Journalizing

A company records in **accounts** those transactions and events that affect its assets, liabilities, and equities. The **general ledger** contains all the asset, liability, stockholders' equity, revenue, and expense accounts. A **T-account** (see Illustration 3-3) shows the effect of transactions on particular asset, liability, equity, revenue, and expense accounts.

OBJECTIVE 4
Record transactions in journals, post to ledger accounts, and prepare a trial balance.

In practice, companies do not record transactions and selected other events originally in the ledger. A transaction affects two or more accounts, each of which is on a different page in the ledger. Therefore, in order to have a complete record of each transaction or other event in one place, a company uses a **journal** (also called "the book of original entry"). In its simplest form, a **general journal** chronologically lists transactions and other events, expressed in terms of debits and credits to accounts.

Illustration 3-7 depicts the technique of journalizing, using the first two transactions for Softbyte, Inc. These transactions were:

September 1 Stockholders invested $15,000 cash in the corporation in exchange for shares of stock.

Purchased computer equipment for $7,000 cash.

The J1 indicates these two entries are on the first page of the general journal.

ILLUSTRATION 3-7
Technique of Journalizing

GENERAL JOURNAL J1

Date	Account Titles and Explanation	Ref.	Debit	Credit
2007				
Sept. 1	Cash		15,000	
	Common Stock			15,000
	(Issued shares of stock for cash)			
1	Computer Equipment		7,000	
	Cash			7,000
	(Purchased equipment for cash)			

[2]"Elements of Financial Statements of Business Enterprises," *Statement of Financial Accounting Concepts No. 6* (Stamford, Conn.: FASB, 1985), pp. 259–260.

Each **general journal entry** consists of four parts: (1) the accounts and amounts to be debited (Dr.), (2) the accounts and amounts to be credited (Cr.), (3) a date, and (4) an explanation. A company enters debits first, followed by the credits (slightly indented). The explanation begins below the name of the last account to be credited and may take one or more lines. A company completes the "Ref." column at the time it posts the accounts.

Expanded Discussion of Special Journals

In some cases, a company uses **special journals** in addition to the general journal. Special journals summarize transactions possessing a common characteristic (e.g., cash receipts, sales, purchases, cash payments). As a result, using them reduces bookkeeping time.

Posting

The procedure of transferring journal entries to the ledger accounts is called **posting**. Posting involves the following steps.

1 In the ledger, enter in the appropriate columns of the debited account(s) the date, journal page, and debit amount shown in the journal.

2 In the reference column of the journal, write the account number to which the debit amount was posted.

3 In the ledger, enter in the appropriate columns of the credited account(s) the date, journal page, and credit amount shown in the journal.

4 In the reference column of the journal, write the account number to which the credit amount was posted.

Illustration 3-8 diagrams these four steps, using the first journal entry of Softbyte, Inc. The illustration shows the general ledger accounts in **standard account form**. Some

ILLUSTRATION 3-8
Posting a Journal Entry

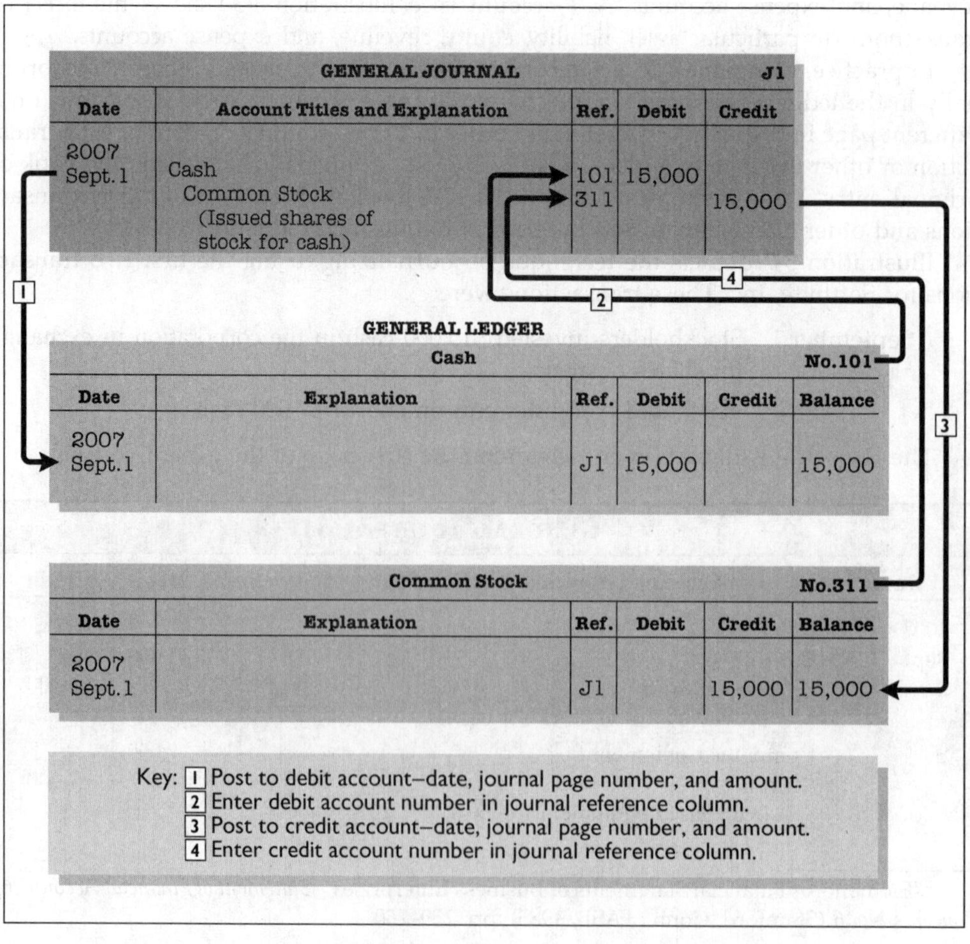

companies call this form the **three-column form of account** because it has three money columns—debit, credit, and balance. The balance in the account is determined after each transaction. The explanation space and reference columns provide special information about the transaction. The boxed numbers indicate the sequence of the steps.

The numbers in the "Ref." column of the general journal refer to the ledger accounts to which a company posts the respective items. For example, the "101" placed in the column to the right of "Cash" indicates that the company posted this $15,000 item to Account No. 101 in the ledger.

The posting of the general journal is completed when a company records all of the posting reference numbers opposite the account titles in the journal. Thus the number in the posting reference column serves two purposes: (1) It indicates the ledger account number of the account involved. (2) It indicates the completion of posting for the particular item. Each company selects its own numbering system for its ledger accounts. Many begin numbering with asset accounts and then follow with liabilities, owners' equity, revenue, and expense accounts, in that order.

The ledger accounts in Illustration 3-8 show the accounts after completion of the posting process. The reference J1 (General Journal, page 1) indicates the source of the data transferred to the ledger account.

Expanded Example. To show an expanded example of the basic steps in the recording process, we use the October transactions of Pioneer Advertising Agency Inc. Pioneer's accounting period is a month. Illustrations 3-9 through 3-18 show the journal entry and posting of each transaction. For simplicity, we use a T-account form instead of the standard account form. Study the transaction analyses carefully.

The purpose of transaction analysis is (1) to identify the type of account involved, and (2) to determine whether a debit or a credit is required. You should always perform this type of analysis before preparing a journal entry. Doing so will help you understand the journal entries discussed in this chapter as well as more complex journal entries in later chapters. Keep in mind that every journal entry affects one or more of the following items: assets, liabilities, stockholders' equity, revenues, or expenses.

1 October 1: Stockholders invest $100,000 cash in an advertising venture to be known as Pioneer Advertising Agency Inc.

ILLUSTRATION 3-9
Investment of Cash by Stockholders

Journal Entry

Oct. 1	Cash	101	100,000	
	Common Stock	311		100,000
	(Issued shares of stock for cash)			

Posting

Cash 101	
Oct. 1, 100,000	

Common Stock 311	
	Oct. 1, 100,000

2 October 1: Pioneer Advertising purchases office equipment costing $50,000 by signing a 3-month, 12%, $50,000 note payable.

ILLUSTRATION 3-10
Purchase of Office Equipment

Journal Entry

Oct. 1	Office Equipment	157	50,000	
	Notes Payable	200		50,000
	(Issued 3-month, 12% note for office equipment)			

Posting

Office Equipment 157	
Oct. 1, 50,000	

Notes Payable 200	
	Oct. 1, 50,000

3 October 2: Pioneer Advertising receives a $12,000 cash advance from R. Knox, a client, for advertising services that are expected to be completed by December 31.

ILLUSTRATION 3-11
Receipt of Cash for Future Service

Journal Entry

Oct. 2	Cash	101	12,000	
	Unearned Service Revenue	209		12,000
	(Received cash from R. Knox for future service)			

Posting

Cash 101	
Oct. 1 100,000	
2 12,000	

Unearned Service Revenue 209	
	Oct. 2 12,000

4 October 3: Pioneer Advertising pays $9,000 office rent, in cash, for October.

ILLUSTRATION 3-12
Payment of Monthly Rent

Journal Entry

Oct. 3	Rent Expense	729	9,000	
	Cash	101		9,000
	(Paid October rent)			

Posting

Cash 101	
Oct. 1 100,000	Oct. 3 9,000
2 12,000	

Rent Expense 729	
Oct. 3 9,000	

5 October 4: Pioneer Advertising pays $6,000 for a one-year insurance policy that will expire next year on September 30.

ILLUSTRATION 3-13
Payment for Insurance

Journal Entry

Oct. 4	Prepaid Insurance	130	6,000	
	Cash	101		6,000
	(Paid one-year policy; effective date October 1)			

Posting

Cash 101	
Oct. 1 100,000	Oct. 3 9,000
2 12,000	4 6,000

Prepaid Insurance 130	
Oct. 4 6,000	

6 October 5: Pioneer Advertising purchases, for $25,000 on account, an estimated 3-month supply of advertising materials from Aero Supply.

ILLUSTRATION 3-14
Purchase of Supplies on Account

Journal Entry

Oct. 5	Advertising Supplies	126	25,000	
	Accounts Payable	201		25,000
	(Purchased supplies on account from Aero Supply)			

Posting

Advertising Supplies 126	
Oct. 5 25,000	

Accounts Payable 201	
	Oct. 5 25,000

7 October 9: Pioneer Advertising signs a contract with a local newspaper for advertising inserts (flyers) to be distributed starting the last Sunday in November. Pioneer will start work on the content of the flyers in November. Payment of $7,000 is due following delivery of the Sunday papers containing the flyers.

ILLUSTRATION 3-15
Signing a Contract

A business transaction has not occurred. There is only an agreement between Pioneer Advertising and the newspaper for the services to be provided in November. Therefore, no journal entry is necessary in October.

8 October 20: Pioneer Advertising's board of directors declares and pays a $5,000 cash dividend to stockholders.

ILLUSTRATION 3-16
Declaration and Payment of Dividend by Corporation

Journal Entry

Oct. 20	Dividends	332	5,000	
	Cash	101		5,000
	(Declared and paid a cash dividend)			

Posting

Cash	101		Dividends	332
Oct. 1 100,000	Oct. 3 9,000		Oct. 20 5,000	
2 12,000	4 6,000			
	20 5,000			

9 October 26: Pioneer Advertising pays employee salaries in cash. Employees are paid once a month, every four weeks. The total payroll is $10,000 per week, or $2,000 per day. In October, the pay period began on Monday, October 1. As a result, the pay period ended on Friday, October 26, with salaries of $40,000 being paid.

ILLUSTRATION 3-17
Payment of Salaries

Journal Entry

Oct. 26	Salaries Expense	726	40,000	
	Cash	101		40,000
	(Paid salaries to date)			

Posting

Cash	101		Salaries Expense	726
Oct. 1 100,000	Oct. 3 9,000		Oct. 26 40,000	
2 12,000	4 6,000			
	20 5,000			
	26 40,000			

10 October 31: Pioneer Advertising receives $28,000 in cash and bills Copa Company $72,000 for advertising services of $100,000 provided in October. (See Illustration 3-18.)

Journal Entry

Oct. 31	Cash	101	28,000	
	Accounts Receivable	112	72,000	
	Service Revenue	400		100,000
	(Recognize revenue for services provided)			

Posting

Cash			101
Oct. 1	100,000	Oct. 3	9,000
2	12,000	4	6,000
31	28,000	20	5,000
		26	40,000

Accounts Receivable			112
Oct. 31	72,000		

Service Revenue			400
		Oct. 31	100,000

ILLUSTRATION 3-18
Recognize Revenue for Services Provided

Trial Balance

A **trial balance** lists accounts and their balances at a given time. A company usually prepares a trial balance at the end of an accounting period. The trial balance lists the accounts in the order in which they appear in the ledger, with debit balances listed in the left column and credit balances in the right column. The totals of the two columns must agree.

The trial balance proves the mathematical equality of debits and credits after posting. Under the double-entry system this equality occurs when the sum of the debit account balances equals the sum of the credit account balances. A trial balance also uncovers errors in journalizing and posting. In addition, it is useful in the preparation of financial statements. The procedures for preparing a trial balance consist of:

1 Listing the account titles and their balances.
2 Totaling the debit and credit columns.
3 Proving the equality of the two columns.

For example, Illustration 3-19 presents the trial balance prepared from the ledger of Pioneer Advertising Agency Inc. Note that the total debits ($287,000) equal the total credits ($287,000). A trial balance also often shows account numbers to the left of the account titles.

ILLUSTRATION 3-19
Trial Balance (Unadjusted)

PIONEER ADVERTISING AGENCY INC.
TRIAL BALANCE
OCTOBER 31, 2007

	Debit	Credit
Cash	$ 80,000	
Accounts Receivable	72,000	
Advertising Supplies	25,000	
Prepaid Insurance	6,000	
Office Equipment	50,000	
Notes Payable		$ 50,000
Accounts Payable		25,000
Unearned Service Revenue		12,000
Common Stock		100,000
Dividends	5,000	
Service Revenue		100,000
Salaries Expense	40,000	
Rent Expense	9,000	
	$287,000	$287,000

A trial balance does not prove that a company recorded all transactions or that the ledger is correct. Numerous errors may exist even though the trial balance columns agree. For example, the trial balance may balance even when a company (1) fails to journalize a transaction, (2) omits posting a correct journal entry, (3) posts a journal entry twice, (4) uses incorrect accounts in journalizing or posting, or (5) makes offsetting errors in recording the amount of a transaction. In other words, as long as a company posts equal debits and credits, even to the wrong account or in the wrong amount, the total debits will equal the total credits.

Adjusting Entries

OBJECTIVE 5
Explain the reasons for preparing adjusting entries.

In order for a company, like **McDonald's**, to record revenues in the period in which it earns them, and to recognize expenses in the period in which it incurs them, McDonald's makes **adjusting entries** at the end of the accounting period. In short, adjustments ensure that McDonald's follows the revenue recognition and matching principles.

The use of adjusting entries makes it possible to report on the balance sheet the appropriate assets, liabilities, and owners' equity at the statement date. Adjusting entries also make it possible to report on the income statement the proper revenues and expenses for the period. However, the trial balance—the first pulling together of the transaction data—may not contain up-to-date and complete data. This occurs for the following reasons.

1 Some events are not journalized daily because it is not expedient. Examples are the consumption of supplies and the earning of wages by employees.

2 Some costs are not journalized during the accounting period because these costs expire with the passage of time rather than as a result of recurring daily transactions. Examples of such costs are building and equipment deterioration and rent and insurance.

3 Some items may be unrecorded. An example is a utility service bill that will not be received until the next accounting period.

Adjusting entries are required every time a company, such as **Coca-Cola**, prepares financial statements. At that time, Coca-Cola must analyze each account in the trial balance to determine whether it is complete and up-to-date for financial statement purposes. The analysis requires a thorough understanding of Coca-Cola's operations and the interrelationship of accounts. Because of this involved process, usually a skilled accountant prepares the adjusting entries. In gathering the adjustment data, Coca-Cola may need to make inventory counts of supplies and repair parts. Further, it may prepare supporting schedules of insurance policies, rental agreements, and other contractual commitments. Companies often prepare adjustments after the balance sheet date. However, they date the entries as of the balance sheet date.

Types of Adjusting Entries

Adjusting entries are classified as either prepayments or accruals. Each of these classes has two subcategories, as Illustration 3-20 shows.

ILLUSTRATION 3-20
Classes of Adjusting Entries

Prepayments	Accruals
1. **Prepaid Expenses.** Expenses paid in cash and recorded as assets before they are used or consumed.	3. **Accrued Revenues.** Revenues earned but not yet received in cash or recorded.
2. **Unearned Revenues.** Revenues received in cash and recorded as liabilities before they are earned.	4. **Accrued Expenses.** Expenses incurred but not yet paid in cash or recorded.

We review specific examples and explanations of each type of adjustment in subsequent sections. We base each example on the October 31 trial balance of Pioneer Advertising Agency Inc. (Illustration 3-19). We assume that Pioneer uses an accounting period of one month. Thus, Pioneer will make monthly adjusting entries, dated October 31.

Adjusting Entries for Prepayments

As we indicated earlier, prepayments are either prepaid expenses or unearned revenues. Adjusting entries for prepayments, required at the statement date, record the portion of the prepayment that represents the **expense incurred or the revenue earned** in the current accounting period.

If a company does not make an adjustment for these prepayments, the asset and liability are overstated, and the related expense and revenue are understated. For example, in Pioneer's trial balance (Illustration 3-19), the balance in the asset Advertising Supplies shows only supplies purchased. This balance is overstated; the related expense account, Supplies Expense, is understated because the cost of supplies used has not been recognized. Thus the adjusting entry for prepayments will decrease a balance sheet account and increase an income statement account. Illustration 3-21 shows the effects of adjusting entries for prepayments.

ILLUSTRATION 3-21
Adjusting Entries for Prepayments

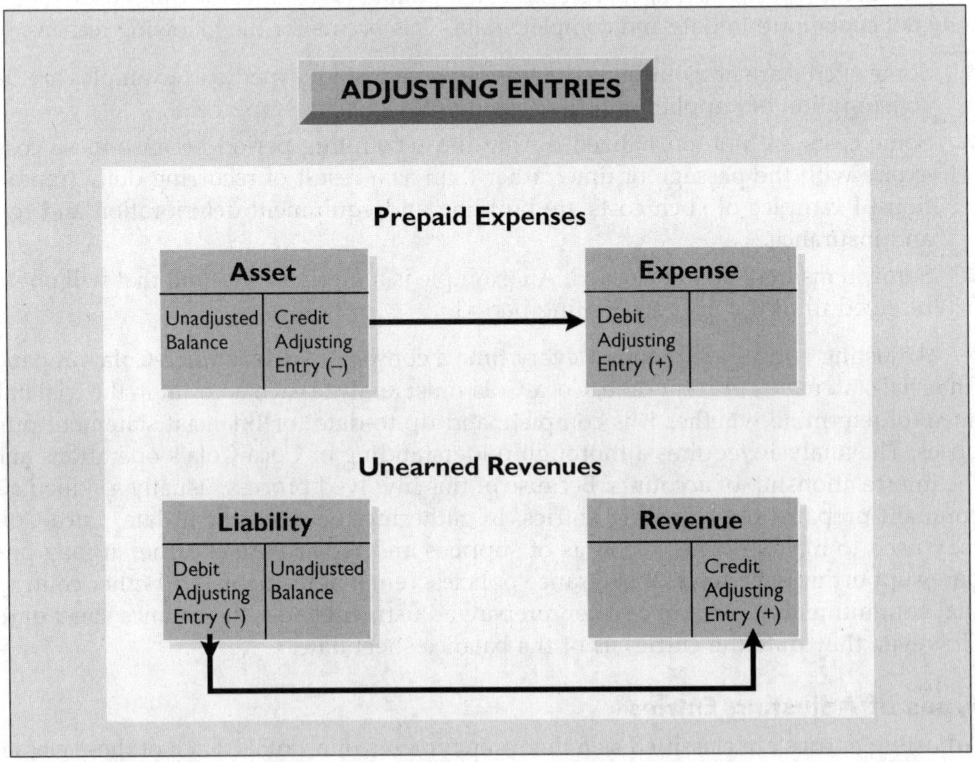

Prepaid Expenses. Assets paid for and recorded before a company, uses them are called **prepaid expenses.** When a company incurs a cost, it debits an asset account to show the service or benefit it will receive in the future. Prepayments often occur in regard to insurance, supplies, advertising, and rent. In addition, companies make prepayments when purchasing buildings and equipment.

Prepaid expenses expire either with the passage of time (e.g., rent and insurance) or **through use and consumption** (e.g., supplies). The expiration of these costs does not require daily recurring entries, an unnecessary and impractical task. Accordingly, a company, like **Walgreens**, usually postpones the recognition of such cost expirations until it prepares financial statements. At each statement date, Walgreens makes adjusting entries to record the expenses that apply to the current accounting period and to show the unexpired costs in the asset accounts.

As was shown above, prior to adjustment, assets are overstated and expenses are understated. Thus, the prepaid expense adjusting entry results in a debit to an expense account and a credit to an asset account.

Supplies

Oct. 5

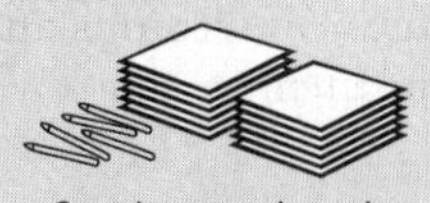

Supplies purchased; record asset

Oct. 31

Supplies used; record supplies expense

Supplies. A business enterprise may use several different types of supplies. For example, a CPA firm will use office supplies such as stationery, envelopes, and accounting paper. An advertising firm will stock advertising supplies such as graph paper, video film, and poster paper. Supplies are generally debited to an asset account when they are acquired. Recognition of supplies used is generally deferred until the adjustment process. At that time, a physical inventory (count) of supplies is taken. The difference between the balance in the Supplies (asset) account and the cost of supplies on hand represents the supplies used (expense) for the period.

For example, Pioneer (see Illustration 3-19) purchased advertising supplies costing $25,000 on October 5. Pioneer therefore debited the asset Advertising Supplies. This account shows a balance of $25,000 in the October 31 trial balance. An inventory count at the close of business on October 31 reveals that $10,000 of supplies are still on hand. Thus, the cost of supplies used is $15,000 ($25,000 − $10,000). Pioneer makes the following adjusting entry.

Oct. 31		
Advertising Supplies Expense	15,000	
Advertising Supplies		15,000
(To record supplies used)		

A	=	L +	SE
			−15,000
−15,000			

Cash Flows
no effect

After Pioneer posts the adjusting entry, the two supplies accounts in T-account form show the following.

ILLUSTRATION 3-22
Supplies Accounts after Adjustment

Advertising Supplies				Advertising Supplies Expense		
10/ 5	25,000	10/31	Adj. 15,000	10/31	Adj. 15,000	
10/31	Bal. 10,000					

The asset account Advertising Supplies now shows a balance of $10,000, which equals the cost of supplies on hand at the statement date. In addition, Advertising Supplies Expense shows a balance of $15,000, which equals the cost of supplies used in October. **Without an adjusting entry, October expenses are understated and net income overstated by $15,000. Moreover, both assets and owners' equity are overstated by $15,000 on the October 31 balance sheet.**

Insurance

Oct. 4

Insurance purchased; record asset

Insurance Policy			
Oct $500	Nov $500	Dec $500	Jan $500
Feb $500	March $500	April $500	May $500
June $500	July $500	Aug $500	Sept $500
I YEAR $6,000			

Oct. 31
Insurance expired; record insurance expense

Insurance. Most companies maintain fire and theft insurance on merchandise and equipment, personal liability insurance for accidents suffered by customers, and automobile insurance on company cars and trucks. The extent of protection against loss determines the cost of the insurance (the amount of the premium to be paid.) The insurance policy specifies the term and coverage. The minimum term usually covers one year, but three- to five-year terms are available and may offer lower annual premiums. A company usually debits insurance premiums to the asset account Prepaid Insurance when paid. At the financial statement date, it then debits Insurance Expense and credits Prepaid Insurance for the cost that expired during the period.

For example, on October 4, Pioneer paid $6,000 for a one-year fire insurance policy, beginning October 1. Pioneer debited the cost of the premium to Prepaid Insurance at that time. This account still shows a balance of $6,000 in the October 31 trial balance. An analysis of the policy reveals that $500 ($6,000 ÷ 12) of insurance expires each month. Thus, Pioneer makes the following adjusting entry.

Oct. 31		
Insurance Expense	500	
Prepaid Insurance		500
(To record insurance expired)		

A	=	L +	SE
			−500
−500			

Cash Flows
no effect

After Pioneer posts the adjusting entry, the insurance-related accounts show:

ILLUSTRATION 3-23
Insurance Accounts after Adjustment

Prepaid Insurance				Insurance Expense		
10/ 4	6,000	10/31	Adj. 500	10/31	Adj. 500	
10/31	Bal. 5,500					

The asset Prepaid Insurance shows a balance of $5,500, which represents the unexpired cost for the remaining 11 months of coverage. At the same time, the balance in Insurance Expense equals the insurance cost that expired in October. **Without an adjusting entry, October expenses are understated by $500 and net income overstated by $500. Moreover, both assets and owners' equity also are overstated by $500 on the October 31 balance sheet.**

Depreciation. Companies, like **Caterpillar** or **Boeing**, typically own various productive facilities, such as buildings, equipment, and motor vehicles. These assets provide a service for a number of years. The term of service is commonly referred to as the **useful life** of the asset. Because Caterpillar, for example, expects an asset such as a building to provide service for many years, Caterpillar records the building as an asset, rather than an expense, in the year the building is acquired. Caterpillar records such assets at cost, as required by the historical cost principle.

According to the matching principle, Caterpillar should report a portion of the cost of a long-lived asset as an expense during each period of the asset's useful life. The process of **depreciation** allocates the cost of an asset to expense over its useful life in a rational and systematic manner.

Depreciation

Oct. 1

Office equipment purchased; record asset ($50,000)

Office Equipment			
Oct $400	Nov $400	Dec $400	Jan $400
Feb $400	March $400	April $400	May $400
June $400	July $400	Aug $400	Sept $400
Depreciation = $4,800/year			

Oct. 31
Depreciation recognized; record depreciation expense

Need for depreciation adjustment. Generally accepted accounting principles (GAAP) view the acquisition of productive facilities as a long-term prepayment for services. The need for making periodic adjusting entries for depreciation is, therefore, the same as we described for other prepaid expenses. That is, a company recognizes the expired cost (expense) during the period and reports the unexpired cost (asset) at the end of the period. The primary causes of depreciation of a productive facility are actual use, deterioration due to the elements, and obsolescence. For example, at the time Caterpillar acquires an asset, the effects of these factors cannot be known with certainty. Therefore, Caterpillar must estimate them. **Thus, depreciation is an estimate rather than a factual measurement of the expired cost.**

To estimate depreciation expense, Caterpillar often divides the cost of the asset by its useful life. For example, if Caterpillar purchases equipment for $10,000 and expects its useful life to be 10 years, Caterpillar records annual depreciation of $1,000.

In the case of Pioneer Advertising, it estimates depreciation on its office equipment to be $4,800 a year (cost $50,000 less salvage value $2,000 divided by useful life of 10 years), or $400 per month. Accordingly, Pioneer recognizes depreciation for October by the following adjusting entry.

A	=	L	+	SE
				−400
−400				

Cash Flows
no effect

	Debit	Credit
Oct. 31		
Depreciation Expense	400	
Accumulated Depreciation—Office Equipment		400
(To record monthly depreciation)		

After Pioneer posts the adjusting entry, the accounts show the following.

ILLUSTRATION 3-24
Accounts after Adjustment for Depreciation

Office Equipment			
10/1	50,000		

Accumulated Depreciation—Office Equipment				Depreciation Expense		
		10/31	Adj. 400	10/31	Adj. 400	

The balance in the accumulated depreciation account will increase $400 each month. Therefore, after journalizing and posting the adjusting entry at November 30, the balance will be $800.

Statement presentation. Accumulated Depreciation—Office Equipment is a contra asset account. A **contra asset account** offsets an asset account on the balance sheet. This means that the accumulated depreciation account offsets the Office Equipment account on the balance sheet. Its normal balance is a credit. Pioneer uses this account instead of crediting Office Equipment in order to disclose both the original cost of the equipment and the total expired cost to date. In the balance sheet, Pioneer deducts Accumulated Depreciation—Office Equipment from the related asset account as follows.

Office equipment	$50,000	
Less: Accumulated depreciation—office equipment	400	$49,600

ILLUSTRATION 3-25
Balance Sheet Presentation of Accumulated Depreciation

The **book value** of any depreciable asset is the difference between its cost and its related accumulated depreciation. In Illustration 3-25, the book value of the equipment at the balance sheet date is $49,600. Note that the asset's book value generally differs from its market value because depreciation is not a matter of valuation but rather a means of cost allocation.

Note also that depreciation expense identifies that portion of the asset's cost that expired in October. As in the case of other prepaid adjustments, without this adjusting entry, total assets, total owners' equity, and net income are overstated, and depreciation expense is understated.

A company records depreciation expense for each piece of equipment, such as delivery or store equipment, and for all buildings. A company also establishes related accumulated depreciation accounts for the above, such as Accumulated Depreciation—Delivery Equipment; Accumulated Depreciation—Store Equipment; and Accumulated Depreciation—Buildings.

Unearned Revenues. Revenues received in cash and recorded as liabilities before a company earns them are called **unearned revenues**. Such items as rent, magazine subscriptions, and customer deposits for future service may result in unearned revenues. Airlines, such as **Northwest**, **American**, and **Southwest**, treat receipts from the sale of tickets as unearned revenue until they provide the flight service. Tuition received prior to the start of a semester is another example of unearned revenue. Unearned revenues are the opposite of prepaid expenses. Indeed, unearned revenue on the books of one company is likely to be a prepayment on the books of the company that made the advance payment. For example, if we assume identical accounting periods, a landlord will have unearned rent revenue when a tenant has prepaid rent.

When a company, such as **Intel**, receives payment for services to be provided in a future accounting period, it credits an unearned revenue (a liability) account to recognize the obligation that exists. It subsequently earns the revenues through rendering service to a customer. However, making daily recurring entries to record this revenue is impractical. Therefore, Intel delays recognition of earned revenue until the adjustment process. Then Intel makes an adjusting entry to record the revenue that it earned and to show the liability that remains. In the typical case, liabilities are overstated and revenues are understated prior to adjustment. **Thus, the adjusting entry for unearned revenues results in a debit (decrease) to a liability account and a credit (increase) to a revenue account.**

For example, Pioneer Advertising received $12,000 on October 2 from R. Knox for advertising services expected to be completed by December 31. Pioneer credited the payment to Unearned Service Revenue. This account shows a balance of $12,000 in the October 31 trial balance. Analysis reveals that Pioneer earned $4,000 of these services in October. Thus, Pioneer makes the following adjusting entry.

A	=	L	+	SE
		−4,000		
				+4,000

Cash Flows
no effect

Oct. 31		
Unearned Service Revenue	4,000	
Service Revenue		4,000
(To record revenue for services provided)		

After Pioneer posts the adjusting entry, the accounts show the following.

ILLUSTRATION 3-26
Service Revenue Accounts after Prepayments Adjustment

Unearned Service Revenue				Service Revenue	
10/31 Adj.	4,000	10/ 2	12,000	10/31	Bal. 100,000
				31	Adj. 4,000
		10/31 Bal.	8,000		

The liability Unearned Service Revenue now shows a balance of $8,000, which represents the remaining advertising services expected to be performed in the future. At the same time, Service Revenue shows total revenue earned in October of $104,000. **Without this adjustment, revenues and net income are understated by $4,000 in the income statement. Moreover, liabilities are overstated and owners' equity are understated by $4,000 on the October 31 balance sheet.**

Adjusting Entries for Accruals

The second category of adjusting entries is accruals. Companies make adjusting entries for accruals to record unrecognized revenues earned and expenses incurred in the current accounting period. Without an accrual adjustment, the revenue account (and the related asset account) or the expense account (and the related liability account) are understated. Thus, the adjusting entry for accruals **will increase both a balance sheet and an income statement account**. Illustration 3-27 shows adjusting entries for accruals.

ILLUSTRATION 3-27
Adjusting Entries for Accruals

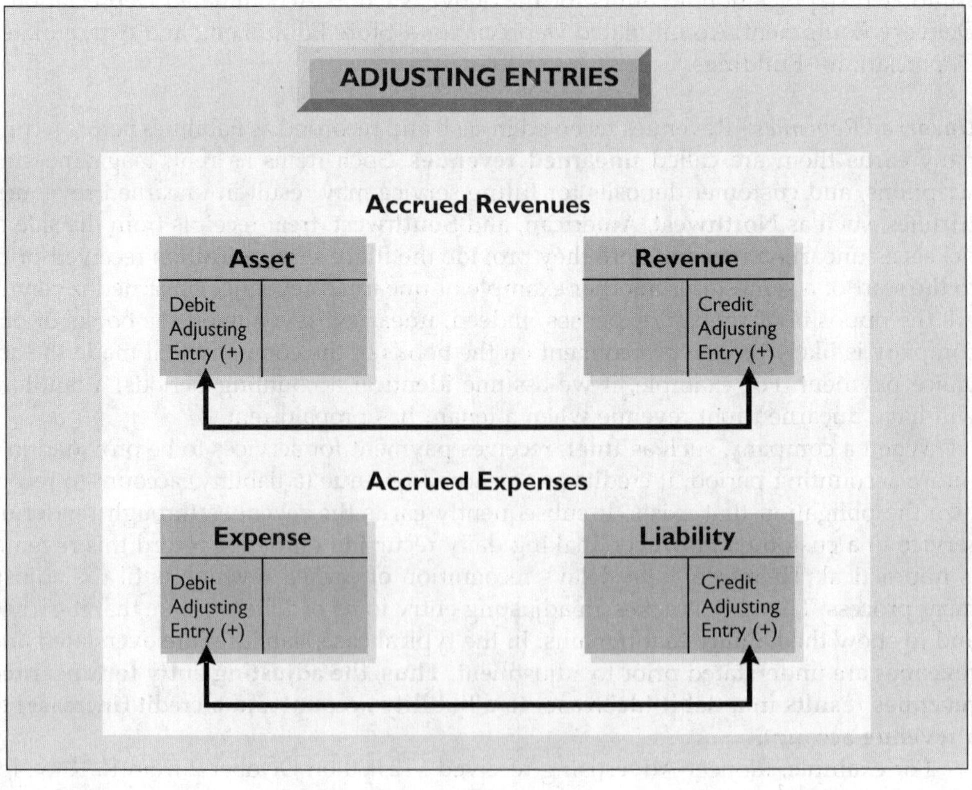

Accrued Revenues. Revenues earned but not yet received in cash or recorded at the statement date are **accrued revenues**. A company accrues revenues with the passing of time, as in the case of interest revenue and rent revenue. Because interest and rent do not involve daily transactions, these items are often unrecorded at the statement date. Or accrued revenues may result from unbilled or uncollected services that a company performed, as in the case of commissions and fees. A company does not record commissions or fees daily, because only a portion of the total service has been provided.

An adjusting entry shows the receivable that exists at the balance sheet date and records the revenue that a company earned during the period. Prior to adjustment both assets and revenues are understated. Accordingly, **an adjusting entry** for accrued revenues results in a debit (increase) to an asset account and a credit (increase) to a revenue account.

In October Pioneer earned $2,000 for advertising services that it did not bill to clients before October 31. Pioneer therefore did not yet record these services. Thus, Pioneer makes the following adjusting entry.

Oct. 31		
Accounts Receivable	2,000	
Service Revenue		2,000
(To record revenue for services provided)		

A	=	L	+	SE
+2,000				
				+2,000

Cash Flows
no effect

After Pioneer posts the adjusting entry, the accounts show the following.

ILLUSTRATION 3-28
Receivable and Revenue Accounts after Accrual Adjustment

Accounts Receivable				Service Revenue	
10/31	72,000			10/31	100,000
31	Adj. 2,000			31	4,000
				31	Adj. 2,000
10/31	Bal. 74,000			10/31	Bal. 106,000

The asset Accounts Receivable shows that clients owe $74,000 at the balance sheet date. The balance of $106,000 in Service Revenue represents the total revenue earned during the month ($100,000 + $4,000 + $2,000). **Without an adjusting entry, assets and owners' equity on the balance sheet, and revenues and net income on the income statement, are understated.**

Accrued Expenses. Expenses incurred but not yet paid or recorded at the statement date are called **accrued expenses,** such as interest, rent, taxes, and salaries. Accrued expenses result from the same causes as accrued revenues. In fact, an accrued expense on the books of one company is an accrued revenue to another company. For example, the $2,000 accrual of service revenue by Pioneer is an accrued expense to the client that received the service.

Adjustments for accrued expenses record the obligations that exist at the balance sheet date and recognize the expenses that apply to the current accounting period. Prior to adjustment, both liabilities and expenses are understated. Therefore, the adjusting entry for accrued expenses results in a debit (increase) to an expense account and a credit (increase) to a liability account.

Accrued Interest. Pioneer signed a three-month note payable in the amount of $50,000 on October 1. The note requires interest at an annual rate of 12 percent. Three factors determine the amount of the interest accumulation: (1) the face value of the note; (2) the interest rate, which is always expressed as an annual rate; and (3) the length of time the note is outstanding. The total interest due on Pioneer's $50,000 note at its due date three months hence is $1,500 ($50,000 × 12% × 3/12), or $500 for one month. Illustration 3-29 shows the formula for computing interest and its application to Pioneer. Note that the formula expresses the time period as a fraction of a year.

ILLUSTRATION 3-29
Formula for Computing Interest

Face Value of Note	×	Annual Interest Rate	×	Time in Terms of One Year	=	Interest
$50,000	×	12%	×	1/12	=	$500

Pioneer makes the accrued expense adjusting entry at October 31 as follows.

A	=	L	+	SE
				−500
		+500		

Cash Flows
no effect

	Oct. 31		
Interest Expense		500	
Interest Payable			500
(To record interest on notes payable)			

After Pioneer posts this adjusting entry, the accounts show the following.

ILLUSTRATION 3-30
Interest Accounts after Adjustment

Interest Expense			Interest Payable	
10/31	500		10/31	500

Interest Expense shows the interest charges applicable to the month of October. Interest Payable shows the amount of interest owed at the statement date. Pioneer will not pay this amount until the note comes due at the end of three months. Why does Pioneer use the Interest Payable account instead of crediting Notes Payable? By recording interest payable separately, Pioneer discloses the two types of obligations (interest and principal) in the accounts and statements. **Without this adjusting entry, both liabilities and interest expense are understated, and both net income and owners' equity are overstated.**

Accrued Salaries. Companies pay for some types of expenses, such as employee salaries and commissions, after the services have been performed. For example, Pioneer last paid salaries on October 26. It will not pay salaries again until November 23. However, as shown in the calendar below, three working days remain in October (October 29–31).

At October 31, the salaries for these days represent an accrued expense and a related liability to Pioneer. The employees receive total salaries of $10,000 for a five-day work week, or $2,000 per day. Thus, accrued salaries at October 31 are $6,000 ($2,000 × 3). Pioneers makes the adjusting entry as follows.

	Oct. 31		
Salaries Expense		6,000	
Salaries Payable			6,000
(To record accrued salaries)			

A	=	L	+	SE
				−6,000
		+6,000		

Cash Flows
no effect

After Pioneer posts this adjusting entry, the accounts show the following.

ILLUSTRATION 3-31
Salary Accounts after Adjustment

Salaries Expense			Salaries Payable		
10/26	40,000			10/31	Adj. 6,000
31	Adj. 6,000				
10/31	Bal. 46,000				

After this adjustment, the balance in Salaries Expense of \$46,000 (23 days × \$2,000) is the actual salary expense for October. The balance in Salaries Payable of \$6,000 is the amount of the liability for salaries owed as of October 31. **Without the \$6,000 adjustment for salaries, both Pioneer's expenses and liabilities are understated by \$6,000.**

Pioneer pays salaries every four weeks. Consequently, the next payday is November 23, when it will again pay total salaries of \$40,000. The payment consists of \$6,000 of salaries payable at October 31 plus \$34,000 of salaries expense for November (17 working days as shown in the November calendar × \$2,000). Therefore, Pioneer makes the following entry on November 23.

	Nov. 23		
Salaries Payable		6,000	
Salaries Expense		34,000	
Cash			40,000
(To record November 23 payroll)			

A	=	L	+	SE
		−6,000		
				−34,000
−40,000				

Cash Flows
−40,000

This entry eliminates the liability for Salaries Payable that Pioneer recorded in the October 31 adjusting entry. This entry also records the proper amount of Salaries Expense for the period between November 1 and November 23.

AM I COVERED?

Rather than purchasing insurance to cover casualty losses and other obligations, some companies "self-insure." That is, a company decides to pay for any possible claims, as they arise, out of its own resources. The company also purchases an insurance policy to cover losses that exceed certain amounts.

For example, **Almost Family, Inc.**, a healthcare services company, has a self-insured employee health-benefit program. However, Almost Family ran into accounting problems when it failed to record an accrual of the liability for benefits not covered by its back-up insurance policy. This led to restatement of Almost Family's fiscal results for the accrual of the benefit expense.

WHAT DO THE NUMBERS MEAN?

Bad Debts

Oct. 31
Uncollectible accounts; record bad debt expense

Bad Debts. Proper matching of revenues and expenses dictates recording bad debts as an expense of the period in which a company earned revenue instead of the period in which the company writes off the accounts or notes. The proper valuation of the receivable balance also requires recognition of uncollectible receivables. Proper matching and valuation require an adjusting entry.

At the end of each period, a company, such as **General Mills**, estimates the amount of receivables that will later prove to be uncollectible. General Mills bases the estimate on various factors: the amount of bad debts it experienced in past years, general economic conditions, how long the receivables are past due, and other factors that indicate the extent of uncollectibility. To illustrate, assume that, based on past experience, Pioneer reasonably estimates a bad debt expense for the month of $1,600. It makes the adjusting entry for bad debts as follows.

A	= L	+ SE
−1,600		−1,600

Oct. 31		
Bad Debt Expense	1,600	
Allowance for Doubtful Accounts		1,600
(To record monthly bad debt expense)		

After Pioneer posts the adjusting entry, the accounts show the following.

ILLUSTRATION 3-32
Accounts after Adjustment for Bad Debt Expense

Accounts Receivable

10/ 1	72,000		
31	Adj. 2,000		

Allowance for Doubtful Accounts

		10/31	Adj. 1,600

Bad Debt Expense

10/31	Adj. 1,600		

A company often expresses bad debts as a percentage of the revenue on account for the period. Or a company may compute bad debts by adjusting the Allowance for Doubtful Accounts to a certain percentage of the trade accounts receivable and trade notes receivable at the end of the period.

Adjusted Trial Balance

After journalizing and posting all adjusting entries, Pioneer prepares another trial balance from its ledger accounts. This trial balance is called an **adjusted trial balance**. It shows the balance of all accounts, including those adjusted, at the end of the accounting period. The adjusted trial balance thus shows the effects of all financial events that occurred during the accounting period.

ILLUSTRATION 3-33
Adjusted Trial Balance

PIONEER ADVERTISING AGENCY INC.
ADJUSTED TRIAL BALANCE
OCTOBER 31, 2007

	Debit	Credit
Cash	$ 80,000	
Accounts Receivable	74,000	
Allowance for Doubtful Accounts		$ 1,600
Advertising Supplies	10,000	
Prepaid Insurance	5,500	
Office Equipment	50,000	
Accumulated Depreciation—Office Equipment		400
Notes Payable		50,000
Accounts Payable		25,000
Interest Payable		500
Unearned Service Revenue		8,000
Salaries Payable		6,000
Common Stock		100,000
Dividends	5,000	
Service Revenue		106,000
Salaries Expense	46,000	
Advertising Supplies Expense	15,000	
Rent Expense	9,000	
Insurance Expense	500	
Interest Expense	500	
Depreciation Expense	400	
Bad Debt Expense	1,600	
	$297,500	$297,500

Preparing Financial Statements

OBJECTIVE 6
Prepare financial statements from the adjusted trial balance.

Pioneer can prepare financial statements directly from the adjusted trial balance. Illustrations 3-34 and 3-35 show the interrelationships of data in the adjusted trial balance and the financial statements.

PIONEER ADVERTISING AGENCY INC.
Adjusted Trial Balance
October 31, 2007

Account	Debit	Credit
Cash	$80,000	
Accounts Receivable	74,000	
Allowance for Doubtful Accounts		1,600
Advertising Supplies	10,000	
Prepaid Insurance	5,500	
Office Equipment	50,000	
Accumulated Depreciation—Office Equipment		$ 400
Notes Payable		50,000
Accounts Payable		25,000
Unearned Service Revenue		8,000
Salaries Payable		6,000
Interest Payable		500
Common Stock		100,000
Retained Earnings		–0–
Dividends	5,000	
Service Revenue		106,000
Salaries Expense	46,000	
Advertising Supplies Expense	15,000	
Rent Expense	9,000	
Insurance Expense	500	
Interest Expense	500	
Depreciation Expense	400	
Bad Debt Expense	1,600	
	$297,500	$297,500

PIONEER ADVERTISING AGENCY INC.
Income Statement
For the Month Ended October 31, 2007

Revenues		
Service Revenue		$106,000
Expenses		
Salaries expense	$46,000	
Advertising supplies expense	15,000	
Rent expense	9,000	
Insurance expense	500	
Interest expense	500	
Depreciation expense	400	
Bad Debt expense	1,600	
Total expenses		73,000
Net income		$ 33,000

PIONEER ADVERTISING AGENCY INC.
Retained Earnings Statement
For the Month Ended October 31, 2007

Retained earnings, October 1	–0–
Add: Net income	33,000
	33,000
Less: Dividends	5,000
Retained earnings, October 31	$28,000

To balance sheet

ILLUSTRATION 3-34
Preparation of the Income Statement and Retained Earnings Statement from the Adjusted Trial Balance

As Illustration 3-34 shows, Pioneer begins preparation of the income statement from the revenue and expense accounts. It derives the retained earnings statement from the retained earnings and dividends accounts and the net income (or net loss) shown in the income statement. As Illustration 3-35 shows, Pioneer then prepares the balance sheet from the asset and liability accounts, the common stock account, and the ending retained earnings balance as reported in the retained earnings statement.

PIONEER ADVERTISING AGENCY INC.
Adjusted Trial Balance
October 31, 2007

Account	Debit	Credit
Cash	$80,000	
Accounts Receivable	74,000	
Allowance for Doubtful Accounts		1,600
Advertising Supplies	10,000	
Prepaid Insurance	5,500	
Office Equipment	50,000	
Accumulated Depreciation—Office Equipment		$ 400
Notes Payable		50,000
Accounts Payable		25,000
Unearned Service Revenue		8,000
Salaries Payable		6,000
Interest Payable		500
Common Stock		100,000
Retained Earnings		-0-
Dividends	5,000	
Service Revenue		106,000
Salaries Expense	46,000	
Advertising Supplies Expense	15,000	
Rent Expense	9,000	
Insurance Expense	500	
Interest Expense	500	
Depreciation Expense	400	
Bad Debt Expense	1,600	
	$297,500	$297,500

PIONEER ADVERTISING AGENCY INC.
Balance Sheet
October 31, 2007

Assets		
Cash		$80,000
Accounts receivable	$74,000	
Less: Allowance	1,600	72,400
Advertising supplies		10,000
Prepaid insurance		5,500
Office equipment	$50,000	
Less: Accumulated depreciation	400	49,600
Total assets		$217,500
Liabilities and Stockholders' Equity		
Liabilities		
Notes payable		$ 50,000
Accounts payable		25,000
Unearned service revenue		8,000
Salaries payable		6,000
Interest payable		500
Total liabilities		89,500
Stockholders' equity		
Common stock		100,000
Retained earnings		28,000
Total liabilities and stockholders' equity		$217,500

Balance at Oct. 31 from Retained Earnings Statement in Illustration 3-34

ILLUSTRATION 3-35
Preparation of the Balance Sheet from the Adjusted Trial Balance

WHAT DO THE NUMBERS MEAN?

24/7 ACCOUNTING

To achieve the vision of "24/7 accounting," a company must be able to update revenue, income, and balance sheet numbers every day within the quarter and publish them on the Internet. Such real-time reporting responds to the demand for more timely financial information made available to all investors—not just to analysts with access to company management.

Two obstacles typically stand in the way of 24/7 accounting: having the necessary accounting systems to close the books on a daily basis, and reliability concerns associated with unaudited real-time data. Only a few companies have the necessary accounting capabilties. **Cisco Systems**, which pioneered the concept of the 24-hour close, is one such company.

Closing

OBJECTIVE 7
Prepare closing entries.

Basic Process

The **closing process** reduces the balance of nominal (temporary) accounts to zero in order to prepare the accounts for the next period's transactions. In the closing process Pioneer transfers all of the revenue and expense account balances (income statement items) to a clearing or suspense account called Income Summary. The Income Summary account matches revenues and expenses.

Pioneer uses this clearing account only at the end of each accounting period. The account represents the net income or net loss for the period. It then transfers the net result of this matching (the net income or net loss) to an owners' equity account. (For a corporation, the owners' equity account is retained earnings; for proprietorships and partnerships, it is a capital account.) Companies post all such **closing entries** to the appropriate general ledger accounts.

Closing Entries

In practice, companies generally prepare closing entries only at the end of a company's annual accounting period. However, to illustrate the journalizing and posting of closing entries, we will assume that Pioneer Advertising Agency Inc. closes its books monthly. Illustration 3-36 shows the closing entries at October 31.

ILLUSTRATION 3-36
Closing Entries Journalized

GENERAL JOURNAL			J3
Date	**Account Titles and Explanation**	**Debit**	**Credit**
	Closing Entries		
	(1)		
Oct. 31	Service Revenue	106,000	
	Income Summary		106,000
	(To close revenue account)		
	(2)		
31	Income Summary	73,000	
	Advertising Supplies Expense		15,000
	Depreciation Expense		400
	Insurance Expense		500
	Salaries Expense		46,000
	Rent Expense		9,000
	Interest Expense		500
	Bad Debt Expense		1,600
	(To close expense accounts)		
	(3)		
31	Income Summary	33,000	
	Retained Earnings		33,000
	(To close net income to retained earnings)		
	(4)		
31	Retained Earnings	5,000	
	Dividends		5,000
	(To close dividends to retained earnings)		

A couple of cautions about preparing closing entries: (1) Avoid unintentionally doubling the revenue and expense balances rather than zeroing them. (2) Do not close Dividends through the Income Summary account. **Dividends are not expenses, and they are not a factor in determining net income.**

Posting Closing Entries

Illustration 3-37 shows the posting of closing entries and the ruling of accounts. All temporary accounts have zero balances after posting the closing entries. In addition, note that the balance in Retained Earnings represents the accumulated undistributed earnings of Pioneer at the end of the accounting period. Pioneer reports this amount in the balance sheet as the ending amount reported on the retained earnings statement. As noted above, **Pioneer uses the Income Summary account only in closing.** It does not journalize and post entries to this account during the year.

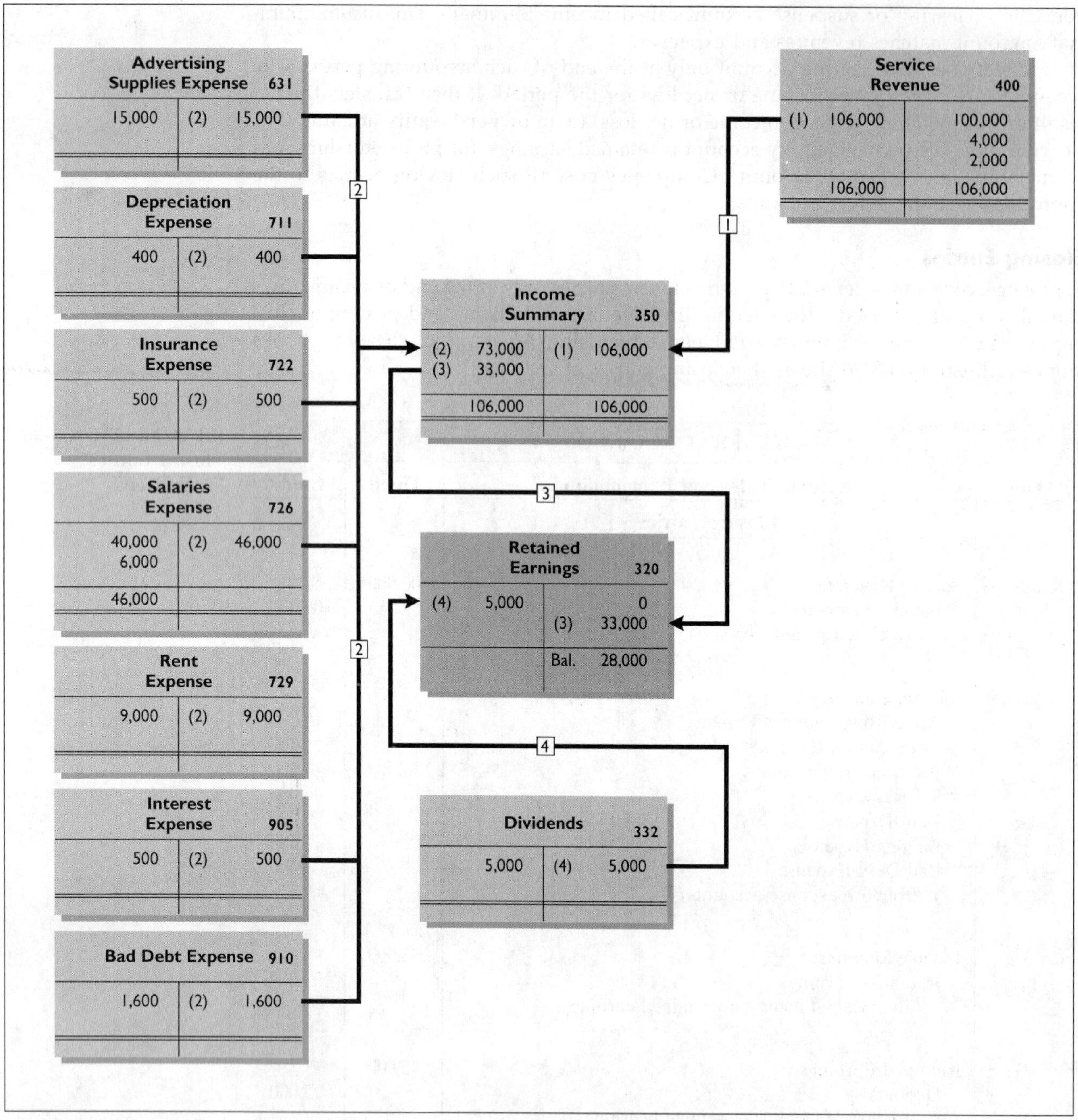

ILLUSTRATION 3-37
Posting of Closing Entries

As part of the closing process, Pioneer totals, balances, and double-rules the **temporary accounts**—revenues, expenses, and dividends—as shown in T-account form in Illustration 3-37. It does not close the **permanent accounts**—assets, liabilities, and stockholders' equity (Common Stock and Retained Earnings). Instead, the preparer draws a single rule beneath the current-period entries, and enters beneath the single rules the account balance to be carried forward to the next period. (For example, see Retained Earnings.)

After the closing process, each income statement account and the dividend account are balanced out to zero and are ready for use in the next accounting period.

Post-Closing Trial Balance

Recall that a trial balance is prepared after entering the regular transactions of the period, and that a second trial balance (the adjusted trial balance) occurs after posting the adjusting entries. A company may take a third trial balance after posting the closing entries.

The trial balance after closing, called the **post-closing trial balance**, consists only of asset, liability, and owners' equity accounts—the real accounts.

Reversing Entries

After preparing the financial statements and closing the books, a company may reverse some of the adjusting entries before recording the regular transactions of the next period. Such entries are called **reversing entries**. A company makes a reversing entry at the beginning of the next accounting period; this entry is the exact opposite of the related adjusting entry made in the previous period. Making reversing entries is an optional step in the accounting cycle that a company may perform at the beginning of the next accounting period.

The Accounting Cycle Summarized

A summary of the steps in the accounting cycle shows a logical sequence of the accounting procedures used during a fiscal period:

1. Enter the transactions of the period in appropriate journals.
2. Post from the journals to the ledger (or ledgers).
3. Take an unadjusted trial balance (trial balance).
4. Prepare adjusting journal entries and post to the ledger(s).
5. Take a trial balance after adjusting (adjusted trial balance).
6. Prepare the financial statements from the second trial balance.
7. Prepare closing journal entries and post to the ledger(s).
8. Take a trial balance after closing (post-closing trial balance).
9. Prepare reversing entries (optional) and post to the ledger(s).

A company normally completes all of these steps in every fiscal period.

STATEMENTS, PLEASE

WHAT DO THE NUMBERS MEAN?

The use of a worksheet at the end of each month or quarter enables a company to prepare interim financial statements even though it closes the books only at the end of each year. For example, assume that **Google** closes its books on December 31, but it wants monthly financial statements. To do this, at the end of January, Google prepares an adjusted trial balance to supply the information needed for statements for January.

At the end of February, it uses a worksheet again. Note that because Google did not close the accounts at the end of January, the income statement taken from the adjusted trial balance on February 28 will present the net income for two months. If Google wants an income statement for only the month of February, the company obtains it by subtracting the items in the January income statement from the corresponding items in the income statement for the two months of January and February.

If Google executes such a process daily, it can realize "24/7 accounting".

Financial Statements for a Merchandising Company

Pioneer Advertising Agency Inc. is a service company. A detailed set of financial statements is now shown for a merchandising company, Uptown Cabinet Corp. The financial statements on the next two pages are prepared from the adjusted trial balance.

Income Statement

The income statement for Uptown is self-explanatory. The income statement classifies amounts into such categories as gross profit on sales, income from operations, income before taxes, and net income. Although earnings per share information is required to be shown on the face of the income statement for a corporation, we omit this item here; it will be discussed more fully later in the text. *(For homework problems, do not present earnings per share information unless required to do so).*

ILLUSTRATION 3-38
An Income Statement

UPTOWN CABINET CORP.
INCOME STATEMENT
FOR THE YEAR ENDED DECEMBER 31, 2007

Net sales			$400,000
Cost of goods sold			316,000
Gross profit on sales			84,000
Selling expenses			
Sales salaries expense		$20,000	
Traveling expense		8,000	
Advertising expense		2,200	
Total selling expenses		30,200	
Administrative expenses			
Salaries, office and general	$19,000		
Depreciation expense—furniture and equipment	6,700		
Property tax expense	5,300		
Rent expense	4,300		
Bad debt expense	1,000		
Telephone and Internet expense	600		
Insurance expense	360		
Total administrative expenses		37,260	
Total selling and administrative expenses			67,460
Income from operations			16,540
Other revenues and gains			
Interest revenue			800
			17,340
Other expenses and losses			
Interest expense			1,700
Income before income taxes			15,640
Income taxes			3,440
Net income			$ 12,200

Statement of Retained Earnings

A corporation may retain the net income earned in the business, or it may distribute it to stockholders by payment of dividends. In the illustration, Uptown added the net income earned during the year to the balance of retained earnings on January 1, thereby increasing the balance of retained earnings. Deducting dividends of $2,000 results in the ending retained earnings balance of $26,400 on December 31.

ILLUSTRATION 3-39
A Statement of Retained Earnings

UPTOWN CABINET CORP.
STATEMENT OF RETAINED EARNINGS
FOR THE YEAR ENDED DECEMBER 31, 2007

Retained earnings, January 1	$16,200
Add: Net income	12,200
	28,400
Less: Dividends	2,000
Retained earnings, December 31	$26,400

Balance Sheet

The balance sheet for Uptown is a classified balance sheet. Interest receivable, prepaid insurance, and prepaid rent expense are included as current assets. Uptown considers these assets current because they will be converted into cash or used by the business within a relatively short period of time. Uptown deducts the amount of Allowance for Doubtful Accounts from the total of accounts, notes, and interest receivable because it estimates that only $54,800 of $57,800 will be collected in cash.

In the property, plant, and equipment section, Uptown deducts the accumulated depreciation from the cost of the furniture and equipment. The difference represents the book or carrying value of the furniture and equipment.

The balance sheet shows property tax payable as a current liability because it is an obligation that is payable within a year. The balance sheet also shows other short-term liabilities such as accounts payable.

The bonds payable, due in 2015, are long-term liabilities. As a result, the balance sheet shows the account in a separate section. (The company paid interest on the bonds on December 31.)

Because Uptown is a corporation, the capital section of the balance sheet, called the stockholders' equity section in the illustration, differs somewhat from the capital section for a proprietorship. Total stockholders' equity consists of the common stock, which is the original investment by stockholders, and the earnings retained in the business. *For homework purposes, unless instructed otherwise, prepare an unclassified balance sheet.*

ILLUSTRATION 3-40
A Balance Sheet

UPTOWN CABINET CORP.
BALANCE SHEET
AS OF DECEMBER 31, 2007

Assets			
Current assets			
Cash			$ 1,200
Notes receivable	$16,000		
Accounts receivable	41,000		
Interest receivable	800	$57,800	
Less: Allowance for doubtful accounts		3,000	54,800
Merchandise inventory			40,000
Prepaid insurance			540
Prepaid rent expense			500
Total current assets			97,040
Property, plant, and equipment			
Furniture and equipment		67,000	
Less: Accumulated depreciation		18,700	
Total property, plant, and equipment			48,300
Total assets			$145,340
Liabilities and Stockholders' Equity			
Current liabilities			
Notes payable			$ 20,000
Accounts payable			13,500
Property tax payable			2,000
Income tax payable			3,440
Total current liabilities			38,940
Long-term liabilities			
Bonds payable, due June 30, 2015			30,000
Total liabilities			68,940
Stockholders' equity			
Common stock, $5.00 par value, issued and outstanding, 10,000 shares		$50,000	
Retained earnings		26,400	
Total stockholders' equity			76,400
Total liabilities and stockholders' equity			$145,340

Closing Entries

Uptown makes closing entries as follows.

General Journal
December 31, 2007

Interest Revenue	800	
Sales	400,000	
Income Summary		400,800
(To close revenues to Income Summary)		
Income Summary	388,600	
Cost of Goods Sold		316,000
Sales Salaries Expense		20,000
Traveling Expense		8,000
Advertising Expense		2,200
Salaries, Office and General		19,000
Depreciation Expense—Furniture and Equipment		6,700
Rent Expense		4,300
Property Tax Expense		5,300
Bad Debt Expense		1,000
Telephone and Internet Expense		600
Insurance Expense		360
Interest Expense		1,700
Income Tax Expense		3,440
(To close expenses to Income Summary)		
Income Summary	12,200	
Retained Earnings		12,200
(To close Income Summary to Retained Earnings)		
Retained Earnings	2,000	
Dividends		2,000
(To close Dividends to Retained Earnings)		

Inventory and Cost of Goods Sold

OBJECTIVE 8
Explain how to adjust inventory accounts at year-end.

Because Uptown is a merchandising company, it has inventory. Companies with inventory generally use a **perpetual inventory system.** With such a system, a company records the cost of the inventory purchased and sold directly in the Inventory account as the purchases and sales occur. Therefore, the balance in the Inventory account should represent the ending inventory amount, and no adjusting entries are needed. To ensure this accuracy, a physical count of the items in inventory is performed on an annual basis.

With the perpetual inventory system, because the company debits purchases directly to the Inventory account, it does not use a Purchases account. However, the company does use a Cost of Goods Sold account to accumulate the issuances from inventory. That is, when inventory is sold, the company credits the cost of the sold goods to Inventory and debits Cost of Goods Sold. In closing the accounts, the company credits Cost of Goods Sold and debits Income Summary.

With a **periodic inventory system**, a company uses a Purchases account to record purchases of inventory during the period. Here, the Inventory account remains **unchanged** during the period. The Inventory account represents the beginning inventory amount throughout the period. Then, at the end of the accounting period the company must adjust the inventory account by **closing out the beginning inventory amount** and **recording the ending inventory amount**. A company determines the ending inventory by physically counting the items on hand and valuing them at cost or at the lower-of-cost-or-market. Under the periodic inventory system, a company therefore determines the cost of goods sold by adding the beginning inventory together with net purchases and deducting the ending inventory.

To illustrate how to compute cost of goods sold with a periodic inventory system, assume that Collegiate Apparel Shop begins with an inventory of $30,000. It records purchases of $200,000, transportation-in of $6,000, purchase returns and allowances of $1,000, and purchase discounts of $3,000. The ending inventory is $26,000. Collegiate computes cost of goods sold as shown in Illustration 3-41.

Beginning inventory			$ 30,000
Purchases		$200,000	
Less: Purchase returns and allowances	$1,000		
Purchase discounts	3,000	4,000	
Net purchases		196,000	
Plus: Transportation-in		6,000	
Cost of goods purchased			202,000
Cost of goods available for sale			232,000
Less: Ending inventory			26,000
Cost of goods sold			$206,000

ILLUSTRATION 3-41
Computation of Cost of Goods Sold under Periodic Inventory System

Cost of goods sold will be the same amount whether a company uses the perpetual or periodic method.

QUESTIONS

1. Give an example of a transaction that results in:
   (a) A decrease in an asset and a decrease in a liability.
   (b) A decrease in one asset and an increase in another asset.
   (c) A decrease in one liability and an increase in another liability.
2. Do the following events represent business transactions? Explain your answer in each case.
   (a) A computer is purchased on account.
   (b) A customer returns merchandise and is given credit on account.
   (c) A prospective employee is interviewed.
   (d) The owner of the business withdraws cash from the business for personal use.
   (e) Merchandise is ordered for delivery next month.
3. Name the accounts debited and credited for each of the following transactions.
   (a) Billing a customer for work done.
   (b) Receipt of cash from customer on account.
   (c) Purchase of office supplies on account.
   (d) Purchase of 15 gallons of gasoline for the delivery truck.
4. Why are revenue and expense accounts called temporary or nominal accounts?
5. Omar Morena, a fellow student, contends that the double-entry system means that each transaction must be recorded twice. Is Omar correct? Explain.
6. Is it necessary that a trial balance be taken periodically? What purpose does it serve?
7. Indicate whether each of the items below is a real or nominal account and whether it appears in the balance sheet or the income statement.
   (a) Prepaid Rent.
   (b) Salaries and Wages Payable.
   (c) Merchandise Inventory.
   (d) Accumulated Depreciation.
   (e) Office Equipment.
   (f) Service Revenue.
   (g) Office Salaries Expense.
   (h) Supplies on Hand.
8. Employees are paid every Saturday for the preceding work week. If a balance sheet is prepared on Wednesday, December 31, what does the amount of wages earned during the first three days of the week (12/29, 12/30, 12/31) represent? Explain.
9. (a) How do the components of revenues and expenses differ between a merchandising company and a service enterprise? (b) Explain the income measurement process of a merchandising company.
10. What is the purpose of the Cost of Goods Sold account? (Assume a periodic inventory system.)
11. Under a perpetual system, what is the purpose of the Cost of Goods Sold account?
12. If the $3,900 cost of a new microcomputer and printer purchased for office use were recorded as a debit to Purchases, what would be the effect of the error on the balance sheet and income statement in the period in which the error was made?
13. What differences are there between the trial balance before closing and the trial balance after closing with respect to the following accounts?
    (a) Accounts Payable.
    (b) Expense accounts.
    (c) Revenue accounts.
    (d) Retained Earnings account.

(e) Cash.

14. What are adjusting entries and why are they necessary?

15. What are closing entries and why are they necessary?

16. John Damon, maintenance supervisor for Red Sox Insurance Co., has purchased a riding lawnmower and accessories to be used in maintaining the grounds around corporate headquarters. He has sent the following information to the accounting department.

Cost of mower and accessories	$3,000	Date purchased	7/1/07
Estimated useful life	5 yrs	Monthly salary of groundskeeper	$1,100
		Estimated annual fuel cost	$150

Compute the amount of depreciation expense (related to the mower and accessories) that should be reported on Red Sox's December 31, 2007, income statement. Assume straight-line depreciation.

17. Selanne Enterprises made the following entry on December 31, 2007.

Interest Expense	10,000	
Interest Payable		10,000
(To record interest expense due on loan from Anaheim National Bank.)		

What entry would Anaheim National Bank make regarding its outstanding loan to Selanne Enterprises? Explain why this must be the case.

CHAPTER FOUR

INCOME STATEMENT AND RELATED INFORMATION

Which Income Number?

Recently, 40 percent of the companies in the Standards and Poor's 500 provided investors a choice in reported income numbers. In addition to income measured according to generally accepted accounting principles (GAAP), companies also reported an income measure that they adjusted for certain items. Companies make these adjustments because they believe the items are not representative of operating results. In some cases these adjustments are quite large. As we show in the following table, in a recent quarter the reporting of such "pro forma" income measures put a very different spin on operating results. In some cases (**JDS-Uniphase**, **PMC-Sierra**, and **Yahoo**), a loss under GAAP measurement rules became an operating profit after pro forma adjustments.

Company	Earnings Per Share Pro Forma	Earnings Per Share GAAP	Company	Earnings Per Share Pro Forma	Earnings Per Share GAAP
JDS-Uniphase	$0.14	−$1.13	**PMC-Sierra**	0.02	−0.38
Checkfree	0.04	−1.17	**Qualcomm**	0.29	0.18
Amazon.com	−0.22	−0.66	**Yahoo**	0.01	−0.02

Characteristic of pro forma reporting practices is Amazon.com. It adjusted for items such as stock-based compensation, amortization of goodwill and intangibles, impairment charges, and equity in losses of investees. All of these adjustments make pro forma earnings higher than GAAP income. In its earnings announcement, Amazon defended its pro forma reporting, saying that it gives better insight into the fundamental operations of the business.

So what's wrong with focusing investors on the fundamentals of the business? According to Ed Jenkins, former chair of the FASB, one problem is that there are no standards for the reporting of pro forma numbers. As a result, investors will have a hard time comparing Amazon's pro forma measure with that reported by another company, which has a different idea of what is fundamental to its business. Also, there is concern that companies may use pro forma reporting to deflect investor attention from bad news. In response, the SEC issued Regulation G, which requires companies to reconcile non-GAAP financial measures to GAAP. This regulation provides investors with a roadmap to analyze adjustments companies make to their GAAP numbers to arrive at pro forma results.[1]

[1]Story adapted from David Henry, "The Numbers Game," *Business Week* (May 14, 2001), pp. 100–110. See also SEC Regulation G, "Conditions for Use of Non-GAAP Financial Measures," *Release No. 33-8176* (March 28, 2003).

Learning Objectives

After studying this chapter, you should be able to:

1. Understand the uses and limitations of an income statement.
2. Prepare a single-step income statement.
3. Prepare a multiple-step income statement.
4. Explain how to report irregular items.
5. Explain intraperiod tax allocation.
6. Identify where to report earnings per share information.
7. Prepare a retained earnings statement.
8. Explain how to report other comprehensive income.

PREVIEW OF CHAPTER 4

As we indicate in the opening story, investors need complete and comparable information on income and its components to assess company profitability correctly. In this chapter we examine the many different types of revenues, expenses, gains, and losses that affect the income statement and related information, as follows.

INCOME STATEMENT AND RELATED INFORMATION

- **INCOME STATEMENT**
  - Usefulness
  - Limitations
  - Quality of earnings
- **FORMAT OF THE INCOME STATEMENT**
  - Elements
  - Single-step
  - Multiple-step
  - Condensed income statements
- **REPORTING IRREGULAR ITEMS**
  - Discontinued operations
  - Extraordinary items
  - Unusual gains and losses
  - Changes in accounting principle
  - Changes in estimates
  - Corrections of errors
- **SPECIAL REPORTING ISSUES**
  - Intraperiod tax allocation
  - Earnings per share
  - Retained earnings statement
  - Comprehensive income

INCOME STATEMENT

OBJECTIVE 1
Understand the uses and limitations of an income statement.

The **income statement** is the report that measures the success of company operations for a given period of time. (It is also often called the statement of income or statement of earnings.[2]) The business and investment community uses the income statement to determine profitability, investment value, and creditworthiness. It provides investors and creditors with information that helps them predict the **amounts, timing, and uncertainty of future cash flows.**

Usefulness of the Income Statement

The income statement helps users of financial statements predict future cash flows in a number of ways. For example, investors and creditors use the income statement information to:

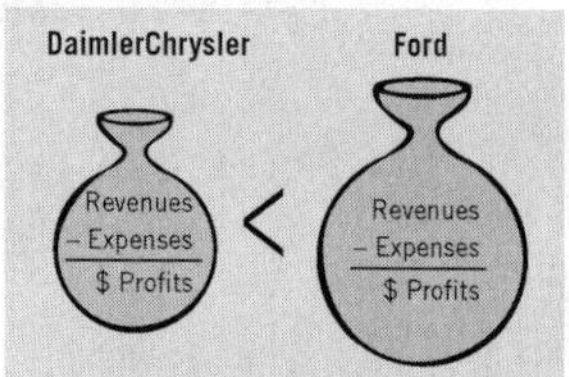

Which company did better last year?

1 **Evaluate the past performance of the company.** Examining revenues and expenses indicates how the company performed and allows comparison of its performance to its competitors. For example, analysts use the income data provided by **DaimlerChrysler** to compare its performance to that of **Ford**.

2 **Provide a basis for predicting future performance.** Information about past performance helps to determine important trends that, if continued, provide

[2] *Accounting Trends and Techniques—2004* (New York: AICPA) indicates that out of 600 companies surveyed, 242 used the term *income* in the title of income statements, 261 used *operations* (many companies had net losses), and 90 used *earnings*.

information about future performance. For example, **General Electric** at one time reported consistent increases in revenues. Obviously past success does not necessarily translate into future success. However, analysts can better predict future revenues, and hence earnings and cash flows, if a reasonable correlation exists between past and future performance.

Hmm....Where am I headed?

3 **Help assess the risk or uncertainty of achieving future cash flows.** Information on the various components of income—revenues, expenses, gains, and losses—highlights the relationships among them. It also helps to assess the risk of not achieving a particular level of cash flows in the future. For example, investors and creditors often segregate **IBM**'s operating performance from other nonrecurring sources of income because IBM primarily generates revenues and cash through its operations. Thus, results from continuing operations usually have greater significance for predicting future performance than do results from nonrecurring activities and events.

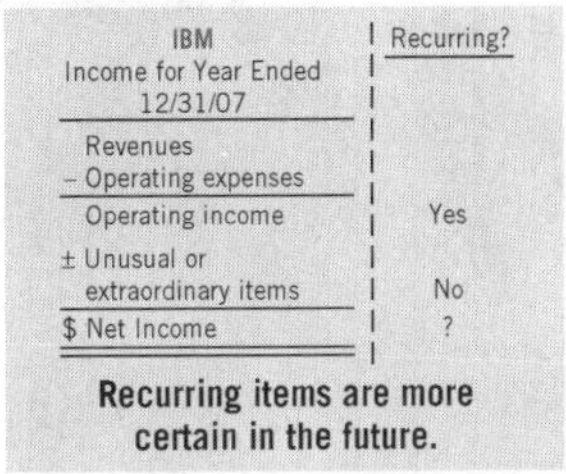

Recurring items are more certain in the future.

In summary, information in the income statement—revenues, expenses, gains, and losses—helps users evaluate past performance. It also provides insights into the likelihood of achieving a particular level of cash flows in the future.

Limitations of the Income Statement

Because net income is an estimate and reflects a number of assumptions, income statement users need to be aware of certain limitations associated with its information. Some of these limitations include:

You left something out!

1 **Companies omit items from the income statement that they cannot measure reliably.** Current practice prohibits recognition of certain items from the determination of income even though the effects of these items can arguably affect the company's performance. For example, a company may not record unrealized gains and losses on certain investment securities in income when there is uncertainty that it will ever realize the changes in value. In addition, more and more companies, like **Cisco Systems** and **Microsoft**, experience increases in value due to brand recognition, customer service, and product quality. A common framework for identifying and reporting these types of values is still lacking.

Hmm... Is the income the same?

2 **Income numbers are affected by the accounting methods employed.** One company may depreciate its plant assets on an accelerated basis; another chooses straight-line depreciation. Assuming all other factors are equal, the first company will report lower income. In effect, we are comparing apples to oranges.

3 **Income measurement involves judgment.** For example, one company in good faith may estimate the useful life of an asset to be 20 years while another company uses a 15-year estimate for the same type of asset. Similarly, some companies may make optimistic estimates of future warranty returns and bad debt write-offs, which results in lower expense and higher income.

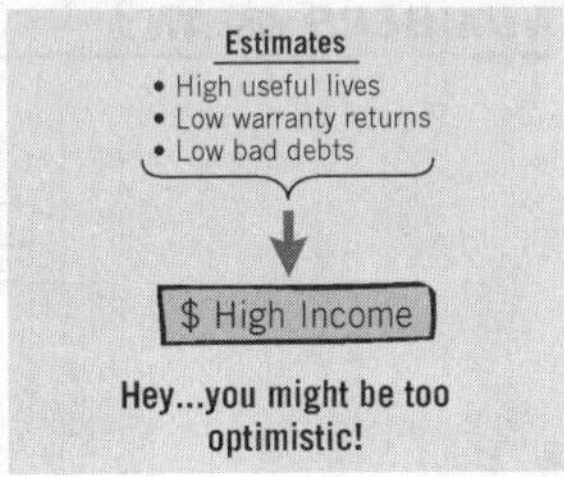

Hey...you might be too optimistic!

In summary, several limitations of the income statement reduce the usefulness of its information for predicting the amounts, timing, and uncertainty of future cash flows.

Quality of Earnings

So far, our discussion has highlighted the importance of information in the income statement for investment and credit decisions, including the evaluation of the company and its managers.[3] Companies try to meet or beat Wall Street expectations so that the

[3]In support of the usefulness of income information, accounting researchers have documented an association between the market prices of companies and reported income. See W. H. Beaver, "Perspectives on Recent Capital Markets Research," *The Accounting Review* (April 2002), pp. 453–474.

market price of their stock and the value of management's stock options increase. As a result, companies have incentives to manage income to meet earnings targets or to make earnings look less risky.

Recently, the SEC has expressed concern that the motivations to meet earnings targets may override good business practices. This erodes the quality of earnings and the quality of financial reporting. As indicated by one SEC chairman, "Managing may be giving way to manipulation; integrity may be losing out to illusion."[4] As a result, the SEC has started to take decisive action to prevent the practice of earnings management.

What is **earnings management**? It is often defined as the planned timing of revenues, expenses, gains, and losses to smooth out bumps in earnings. In most cases, companies use earnings management to increase income in the current year at the expense of income in future years. For example, they prematurely recognize sales (i.e., before earned) in order to boost earnings. As one commentator noted, ". . . it's like popping a cork in [opening] a bottle of wine before it is ready."

Companies also use earnings management to decrease current earnings in order to increase income in the future. The classic case is the use of "cookie jar" reserves. Companies establish these reserves by using unrealistic assumptions to estimate liabilities for such items as loan losses, restructuring charges, and warranty returns. The companies then reduce these reserves in the future to increase reported income in the future.

Such earnings management negatively affects the **quality of earnings** if it distorts the information in a way that is less useful for predicting future earnings and cash flows. Markets rely on trust. The bond between shareholders and the company must remain strong. Investors or others losing faith in the numbers reported in the financial statements will damage U.S. capital markets. As we mentioned in the opening story, we need heightened scrutiny of income measurement and reporting to ensure the quality of earnings and investors' confidence in the income statement.

WHAT DO THE NUMBERS MEAN?

MANAGE UP, MANAGE DOWN

Managing earnings up or down adversely affects the quality of earnings. For example, **W. R. Grace** managed earnings down by taking excess "cookie jar" reserves in good earnings years. During the early 1990s, Grace was growing fast, with profits increasing 30 percent annually. Analysts' targets had Grace growing 24 percent each year. Worried about meeting these growth expectations, Grace began stashing away excess profits in an all-purpose reserve (a "cookie jar"). In 1995, when profits fell below expectations, Grace wanted to reduce this reserve and so increase income. The SEC objected, noting this violated generally accepted accounting principles.

More recently, **MicroStrategy** managed earnings up by booking revenue for future software upgrades, even though it had not yet delivered them. And **Rent-Way, Inc.** managed its earnings up by understating some $65 million in expenses relating to such items as automobile maintenance and insurance payments.

Does the market value accounting quality? Apparently so: The stock of each of these companies took a beating in the marketplace when the earnings management practices came to light. For example, Rent-Way's stock price plummeted from above $25 per share to below $10 per share when it announced restatements for its improper expense accounting. So, whether managing earnings up or down, companies had better be prepared to pay the price for poor accounting quality.

[4] A. Levitt, "The Numbers Game." Remarks to NYU Center for Law and Business, September 28, 1998 (Securities and Exchange Commission, 1998).

FORMAT OF THE INCOME STATEMENT

Elements of the Income Statement

Net income results from revenue, expense, gain, and loss transactions. The income statement summarizes these transactions. This method of income measurement, the **transaction approach**, focuses on the income-related activities that have occurred during the period.[5] The statement can further classify income by customer, product line, or function or by operating and nonoperating, continuing and discontinued, and regular and irregular categories.[6] The following lists more formal definitions of income-related items, referred to as the major elements of the income statement.

ELEMENTS OF FINANCIAL STATEMENTS

REVENUES. Inflows or other enhancements of assets of an entity or settlements of its liabilities during a period from delivering or producing goods, rendering services, or other activities that constitute the entity's ongoing major or central operations.

EXPENSES. Outflows or other using-up of assets or incurrences of liabilities during a period from delivering or producing goods, rendering services, or carrying out other activities that constitute the entity's ongoing major or central operations.

GAINS. Increases in equity (net assets) from peripheral or incidental transactions of an entity except those that result from revenues or investments by owners.

LOSSES. Decreases in equity (net assets) from peripheral or incidental transactions of an entity except those that result from expenses or distributions to owners.[7]

Revenues take many forms, such as sales, fees, interest, dividends, and rents. Expenses also take many forms, such as cost of goods sold, depreciation, interest, rent, salaries and wages, and taxes. Gains and losses also are of many types, resulting from the sale of investments or plant assets, settlement of liabilities, write-offs of assets due to impairments or casualty.

The distinction between revenues and gains, and between expenses and losses, depend to a great extent on the typical activities of the company. For example, when **McDonald's** sells a hamburger, it records the selling price as revenue. However, when McDonald's sells land, it records any excess of the selling price over the book value as a gain. This difference in treatment results because the sale of the hamburger is part of McDonald's regular operations. The sale of land is not.

INTERNATIONAL INSIGHT

Companies in some nations prepare financial reporting on the same basis as tax returns. In such cases, companies have incentives to *minimize* reported income.

[5]The most common alternative to the transaction approach is the **capital maintenance approach** to income measurement. Under this approach, a company determines income for the period based on the change in equity, after adjusting for capital contributions (e.g., investments by owners) or distributions (e.g., dividends). The main drawback associated with the capital maintenance approach is that the components of income are not evident in its measurement. The Internal Revenue Service uses the capital maintenance approach to identify unreported income and refers to this approach as the "net worth check."

[6]The term "irregular" encompasses transactions and other events that are derived from developments outside the normal operations of the business.

[7]"Elements of Financial Statements," *Statement of Financial Accounting Concepts No. 6* (Stamford, Conn.: FASB, 1985), pars. 78–89.

We cannot overemphasize the importance of reporting these elements. Most decision makers find the *parts* of a financial statement to be more useful than the whole. As we indicated earlier, investors and creditors are interested in predicting the amounts, timing, and uncertainty of future income and cash flows. Having income statement elements shown in some detail and in comparison with prior years' data allows decision makers to better assess future income and cash flows.

Single-Step Income Statements

OBJECTIVE 2
Prepare a single-step income statement.

In reporting revenues, gains, expenses, and losses, companies often use a format known as the **single-step income statement.** The single-step statement consists of just two groupings: revenues and expenses. Expenses are deducted from revenues to arrive at net income or loss, hence the expression "single-step." Frequently companies report income tax separately as the last item before net income to indicate its relationship to income before income tax. Illustration 4-1 shows the single-step income statement of Dan Deines Company.

ILLUSTRATION 4-1
Single-Step Income Statement

DAN DEINES COMPANY
INCOME STATEMENT
FOR THE YEAR ENDED DECEMBER 31, 2007

Revenues	
Net sales	$2,972,413
Dividend revenue	98,500
Rental revenue	72,910
Total revenues	3,143,823
Expenses	
Cost of goods sold	1,982,541
Selling expenses	453,028
Administrative expenses	350,771
Interest expense	126,060
Income tax expense	66,934
Total expenses	2,979,334
Net income	$ 164,489
Earnings per common share	$1.74

Companies that use the single-step income statement in financial reporting typically do so because of its simplicity. In recent years, though, the multiple-step form has gained popularity.[8]

The primary advantage of the single-step format lies in its simple presentation and the absence of any implication that one type of revenue or expense item has priority over another. This format thus eliminates potential classification problems.

Multiple-Step Income Statements

OBJECTIVE 3
Prepare a multiple-step income statement.

Some contend that including other important revenue and expense classifications makes the income statement more useful. These further classifications include:

1 A separation of operating and nonoperating activities of the company. For example, companies often present income from operations followed by sections entitled "Other revenues and gains" and "Other expenses and losses." These other categories include such transactions as interest revenue and expense, gains or losses from sales of long-term assets, and dividends received.

[8]*Accounting Trends and Techniques—2004* (New York: AICPA). Of the 600 companies surveyed by the AICPA, 467 employed the multiple-step form, and 133 employed the single-step income statement format. This is a reversal from 1983, when 314 used the single-step form and 286 used the multiple-step form.

2 A classification of expenses by functions, such as merchandising (cost of goods sold), selling, and administration. This permits immediate comparison with costs of previous years and with other departments in the same year.

Companies use a **multiple-step income statement** to recognize these additional relationships. This statement separates operating transactions from nonoperating transactions, and matches costs and expenses with related revenues. It highlights certain intermediate components of income that analysts use to compute ratios for assessing the performance of the company.

Intermediate Components of the Income Statement

When a company uses a multiple-step income statement, it may prepare some or all of the following sections or subsections.

INCOME STATEMENT SECTIONS

1 OPERATING SECTION. A report of the revenues and expenses of the company's principal operations.
- (a) **Sales or Revenue Section.** A subsection presenting sales, discounts, allowances, returns, and other related information. Its purpose is to arrive at the net amount of sales revenue.
- (b) **Cost of Goods Sold Section.** A subsection that shows the cost of goods that were sold to produce the sales.
- (c) **Selling Expenses.** A subsection that lists expenses resulting from the company's efforts to make sales.
- (d) **Administrative or General Expenses.** A subsection reporting expenses of general administration.

2 NONOPERATING SECTION. A report of revenues and expenses resulting from secondary or auxiliary activities of the company. In addition, special gains and losses that are infrequent or unusual, but not both, are normally reported in this section. Generally these items break down into two main subsections:
- (a) **Other Revenues and Gains.** A list of the revenues earned or gains incurred, generally net of related expenses, from nonoperating transactions.
- (b) **Other Expenses and Losses.** A list of the expenses or losses incurred, generally net of any related incomes, from nonoperating transactions.

3 INCOME TAX. A short section reporting federal and state taxes levied on income from continuing operations.

4 DISCONTINUED OPERATIONS. Material gains or losses resulting from the disposition of a segment of the business.

5 EXTRAORDINARY ITEMS. Unusual and infrequent material gains and losses.

6 EARNINGS PER SHARE.

Although the content of the operating section is always the same, the organization of the material can differ. The breakdown above uses a **natural expense classification**. Manufacturing concerns and merchandising companies in the wholesale trade commonly use this. Another classification of operating expenses, recommended for retail stores, uses a **functional expense classification** of administrative, occupancy, publicity, buying, and selling expenses.

Usually, financial statements provided to external users have less detail than internal management reports. Internal reports include more expense categories—usually grouped along lines of responsibility. This detail allows top management to judge staff performance. Irregular transactions such as discontinued operations and extraordinary items are reported separately, following income from continuing operations.

Dan Deines Company's statement of income illustrates the multiple-step income statement. This statement, shown in Illustration 4-2, includes items 1, 2, 3, and 6

ILLUSTRATION 4-2
Multiple-Step Income Statement

wiley.com/college/kieso

Income Statements for Real Companies

DAN DEINES COMPANY
INCOME STATEMENT
FOR THE YEAR ENDED DECEMBER 31, 2007

Sales Revenue			
Sales			$3,053,081
Less: Sales discounts		$ 24,241	
Sales returns and allowances		56,427	80,668
Net sales revenue			2,972,413
Cost of Goods Sold			
Merchandise inventory, Jan. 1, 2007		461,219	
Purchases	$1,989,693		
Less: Purchase discounts	19,270		
Net purchases	1,970,423		
Freight and transportation-in	40,612	2,011,035	
Total merchandise available for sale		2,472,254	
Less: Merchandise inventory, Dec. 31, 2007		489,713	
Cost of goods sold			1,982,541
Gross profit on sales			989,872
Operating Expenses			
Selling expenses			
Sales salaries and commissions	202,644		
Sales office salaries	59,200		
Travel and entertainment	48,940		
Advertising expense	38,315		
Freight and transportation-out	41,209		
Shipping supplies and expense	24,712		
Postage and stationery	16,788		
Depreciation of sales equipment	9,005		
Telephone and Internet expense	12,215	453,028	
Administrative expenses			
Officers' salaries	186,000		
Office salaries	61,200		
Legal and professional services	23,721		
Utilities expense	23,275		
Insurance expense	17,029		
Depreciation of building	18,059		
Depreciation of office equipment	16,000		
Stationery, supplies, and postage	2,875		
Miscellaneous office expenses	2,612	350,771	803,799
Income from operations			186,073
Other Revenues and Gains			
Dividend revenue		98,500	
Rental revenue		72,910	171,410
			357,483
Other Expenses and Losses			
Interest on bonds and notes			126,060
Income before income tax			231,423
Income tax			66,934
Net income for the year			$ 164,489
Earnings per common share			$1.74

from the list.[9] Note that in arriving at net income, the statement presents three subtotals of note:

1 Net sales revenue
2 Gross profit on sales
3 Income from operations

The disclosure of net sales revenue is useful because Deines reports regular revenues as a separate item. It discloses irregular or incidental revenues elsewhere in the income statement. As a result, analysts can more easily understand and assess trends in revenue from continuing operations.

Similarly, the reporting of gross profit provides a useful number for evaluating performance and predicting future earnings. Statement readers may study the trend in gross profits to determine how successfully a company uses its resources. They also may use that information to understand how competitive pressure affected profit margins.

Finally, disclosing income from operations highlights the difference between regular and irregular or incidental activities. This disclosure helps users recognize that incidental or irregular activities are unlikely to continue at the same level. Furthermore, disclosure of operating earnings may assist in comparing different companies and assessing operating efficiencies.

Condensed Income Statements

In some cases a single income statement cannot possibly present all the desired expense detail. To solve this problem, a company includes only the totals of expense groups in the statement of income. It then also prepares supplementary schedules to support the totals. This format may thus reduce the income statement itself to a few lines on a single sheet. For this reason, readers who wish to study all the reported data on operations must give their attention to the supporting schedules. For example, consider the income statement shown in Illustration 4-3 for Dan Deines Company. This statement is a condensed version of the more detailed multiple-step statement presented earlier. It is more representative of the type found in practice.

ILLUSTRATION 4-3
Condensed Income Statement

DAN DEINES COMPANY
INCOME STATEMENT
FOR THE YEAR ENDED DECEMBER 31, 2007

Net sales		$2,972,413
Cost of goods sold		1,982,541
Gross profit		989,872
Selling expenses (see Note D)	$453,028	
Administrative expenses	350,771	803,799
Income from operations		186,073
Other revenues and gains		171,410
		357,483
Other expenses and losses		126,060
Income before income tax		231,423
Income tax		66,934
Net income for the year		$ 164,489
Earnings per share		$1.74

Illustration 4-4 shows an example of a supporting schedule, cross-referenced as Note D and detailing the selling expenses.

[9]Companies must include *earnings per share* or *net loss per share* on the face of the income statement.

ILLUSTRATION 4-4
Sample Supporting Schedule

Note D: Selling expenses	
Sales salaries and commissions	$202,644
Sales office salaries	59,200
Travel and entertainment	48,940
Advertising expense	38,315
Freight and transportation-out	41,209
Shipping supplies and expense	24,712
Postage and stationery	16,788
Depreciation of sales equipment	9,005
Telephone and Internet expense	12,215
Total selling expenses	$453,028

How much detail should a company include in the income statement? On the one hand, a company wants to present a simple, summarized statement so that readers can readily discover important factors. On the other hand, it wants to disclose the results of all activities and to provide more than just a skeleton report. As we showed above, the income statement always includes certain basic elements, but companies can present them in various formats.

REPORTING IRREGULAR ITEMS

OBJECTIVE 4
Explain how to report irregular items.

As the use of a multiple-step or condensed income statement illustrates, GAAP allows flexibility in the presentation of the components of income. However, the FASB developed specific guidelines in two important areas: what to include in income and how to report certain unusual or irregular items.

What should be included in net income has been a controversy for many years. For example, should companies report irregular gains and losses, and corrections of revenues and expenses of prior years, as part of retained earnings? Or should companies first present them in the income statement and then carry them to retained earnings?

This issue is extremely important because the number and magnitude of irregular items are substantial. For example, Illustration 4-5 identifies the most common types and number of irregular items reported in a survey of 600 large companies. Notice that more than one-third of the surveyed firms reported restructuring charges, which often contain write-offs and other one-time items. About 20 percent of the surveyed firms reported either an extraordinary item or a discontinued operation charge. And many companies had two or more accounting changes in 2003.[10]

ILLUSTRATION 4-5
Number of Irregular Items Reported in a Recent Year by 600 Large Companies

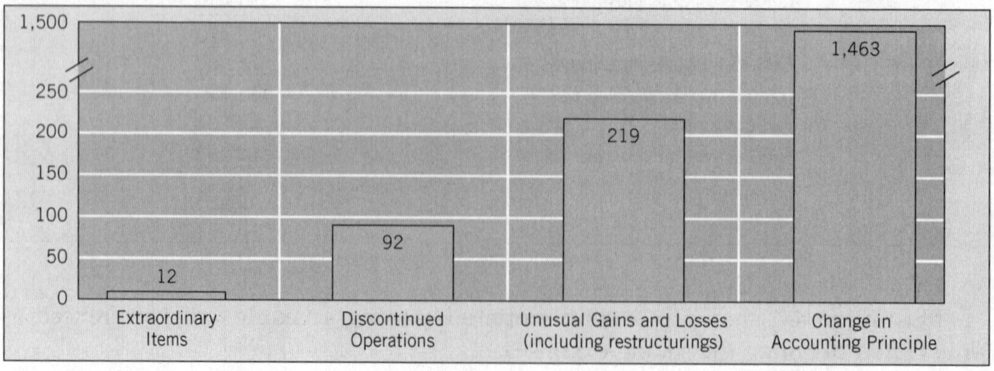

[10]*Accounting Trends and Techniques—2004* (New York: AICPA).

As our opening story discusses, we need consistent and comparable income reporting practices to avoid "promotional" information reported by companies. Developing a framework for reporting irregular items is important to ensure reliable income information.[11]

Some users advocate a **current operating performance approach** to income reporting. These analysts argue that the most useful income measure reflects only regular and recurring revenue and expense elements. Irregular items do not reflect a company's future earning power.

In contrast, others warn that a focus on operating income potentially misses important information about a company's performance. Any gain or loss experienced by the company, whether directly or indirectly related to operations, contributes to its long-run profitability. As one analyst notes, "write-offs matter. . . . They speak to the volatility of (past) earnings."[12] As a result, analysts can use some nonoperating items to assess the riskiness of future earnings. Furthermore, determining which items are operating and which are irregular requires judgment. This might lead to differences in the treatment of irregular items and to possible manipulation of income measures.

ARE ONE-TIME CHARGES BUGGING YOU?

WHAT DO THE NUMBERS MEAN?

Which number—net income or income from operations—should an analyst use in evaluating companies that have unusual items? Some argue that operating income better represents what will happen in the future. Others note that special items are often no longer special. For example, one study noted that in 2001, companies in the Standard & Poor's 500 index wrote off items totaling $165 billion—more than in the prior five years combined.

A study by Multex.com and the *Wall Street Journal* indicated that analysts should not ignore these charges. Based on data for companies taking unusual charges from 1996–2001, the study documented that companies reporting the largest unusual charges had more negative stock price performance following the charge, compared to companies with smaller charges. Thus, rather than signaling the end of bad times, these unusual charges indicated poorer future earnings.

In fact, some analysts use these charges to weed out stocks that may be headed for a fall. Following the "cockroach theory," any charge indicating a problem raises the probability of more problems. Thus, investors should be wary of the increasing use of restructuring and other one-time charges, which may bury expenses that signal future performance declines.

Source: Adapted from J. Weil and S. Liesman, "Stock Gurus Disregard Most Big Write-offs, But They Often Hold Vital Clues to Outlook," *Wall Street Journal Online* (December 31, 2001).

INTERNATIONAL INSIGHT

In many countries the "modified all-inclusive" income statement approach does not parallel that of the U.S. For example, companies in these countries take some gains and losses directly to owners' equity accounts instead of reporting them on the income statement.

So, what to do? The accounting profession has **adopted a modified all-inclusive concept and requires application of this approach in practice**. This approach indicates that companies record most items, including irregular ones, as part of net income.[13] In addition, companies are required to highlight irregular items in the financial statements so that users can better determine the long-run earning power of the company.

[11]The FASB and other international accounting standard setters continue to study the best way to report income. See *Reporting Financial Performance: A Proposed Approach* (Norwalk, Conn.: FASB, September 1999).

[12]D. McDermott, "Latest Profit Data Stir Old Debate Between Net and Operating Income," *Wall Street Journal* (May 3, 1999).

[13]The FASB issued a statement of concepts that offers some guidance on this topic—"Recognition and Measurement in Financial Statements of Business Enterprises," *Statement of Financial Accounting Concepts No. 5* (Stamford, Conn.: FASB, 1984).

Irregular items fall into six general categories, which we discuss in the following sections:

1. Discontinued operations.
2. Extraordinary items.
3. Unusual gains and losses.
4. Changes in accounting principle.
5. Changes in estimates.
6. Corrections of errors.

Discontinued Operations

As Illustration 4-5 shows, one of **the most common types of irregular items is discontinued operations. A discontinued operation** occurs when two things happen: (a) a company eliminates the results of operations and cash flows of a *component* from its ongoing operations, and (b) there is no significant continuing involvement in that component after the disposal transaction.

To illustrate a **component, S. C. Johnson** manufactures and sells consumer products. It has several product groups, each with different product lines and brands. For S. C. Johnson, a product group is the lowest level at which it can clearly distinguish the operations and cash flows from the rest of the company's operations. Therefore each product group is a component of the company. If a component were disposed of, S. C. Johnson would classify it as a discontinued operation.

Here is another example. Assume that Softso Inc. has experienced losses with certain brands in its beauty-care products group. As a result, Softso decides to sell that part of its business. It will discontinue any continuing involvement in the product group after the sale. In this case, Softso eliminates the operations and the cash flows of the product group from its ongoing operations, and reports it as a discontinued operation.

On the other hand, assume Softso decides to remain in the beauty-care business but will discontinue the brands that experienced losses. Because Softso cannot differentiate the cash flows from the brands from the cash flows of the product group as a whole, it cannot consider the brands a component. Softso does not classify any gain or loss on the sale of the brands as a discontinued operation.

Companies report as discontinued operations (in a separate income statement category) the gain or loss from **disposal of a component of a business.** In addition, companies report the **results of operations of a component that has been or will be disposed of** separately from continuing operations. Companies show the effects of discontinued operations net of tax as a separate category, after continuing operations but before extraordinary items.[14]

To illustrate, Multiplex Products, Inc., a highly diversified company, decides to discontinue its electronics division. During the current year, the electronics division lost $300,000 (net of tax). Multiplex sold the division at the end of the year at a loss of $500,000 (net of tax). Multiplex shows the information on the current year's income statement as follows.

ILLUSTRATION 4-6
Income Statement Presentation of Discontinued Operations

Income from continuing operations		$20,000,000
Discontinued operations		
Loss from operation of discontinued electronics division (net of tax)	$300,000	
Loss from disposal of electronics division (net of tax)	500,000	800,000
Net income		$19,200,000

[14] "Accounting for the Impairment or Disposal of Long-Lived Assets," *Statement of Financial Accounting Standards No. 144* (Norwalk, Conn.: FASB, 2001), par. 4. This standard requires discontinued-operation reporting, even though the assets disposed of (i.e., component of the business) do not meet the definition of a business segment.

Companies use the phrase **"Income from continuing operations"** only when gains or losses on discontinued operations occur.

Extraordinary Items

Extraordinary items are nonrecurring **material** items that differ significantly from a company's typical business activities. The criteria for extraordinary items are as follows.

> Extraordinary items are events and transactions that are distinguished by their unusual nature **and** by the infrequency of their occurrence. Classifying an event or transaction as an extraordinary item requires meeting **both** of the following criteria:
>
> (a) **Unusual Nature.** The underlying event or transaction should possess a high degree of abnormality and be of a type clearly unrelated to, or only incidentally related to, the ordinary and typical activities of the company, taking into account the environment in which it operates.
>
> (b) **Infrequency of Occurrence.** The underlying event or transaction should be of a type that the company does not reasonably expect to recur in the foreseeable future, taking into account the environment in which the company operates.[15]

For further clarification, the following gains and losses are **not extraordinary items**.

(a) Write-down or write-off of receivables, inventories, equipment leased to others, deferred research and development costs, or other intangible assets.

(b) Gains or losses from exchange or translation of foreign currencies, including those relating to major devaluations and revaluations.

(c) Gains or losses on disposal of a component of an entity (reported as a discontinued operation).

(d) Other gains or losses from sale or abandonment of property, plant, or equipment used in the business.

(e) Effects of a strike, including those against competitors and major suppliers.

(f) Adjustment of accruals on long-term contracts.[16]

The above items are not considered extraordinary "because they are usual in nature and may be expected to recur as a consequence of customary and continuing business activities."

Only rarely does an event or transaction clearly meet the criteria for an extraordinary item.[17] For example, a company classifies gains or losses such as (a) and (d) above as extraordinary if they **resulted directly from a major casualty** (such as an earthquake), **an expropriation**, or a **prohibition under a newly enacted law or regulation**. Such circumstances clearly meet the criteria of unusual and infrequent. For example, **Weyerhaeuser Company** (forest and lumber) incurred an extraordinary item (an approximate $36 million loss) as a result of volcanic activity at Mount St. Helens. The eruption destroyed standing timber, logs, buildings, equipment, and transportation systems covering 68,000 acres.

In determining whether an item is extraordinary, **a company must consider the environment in which it operates**. The environment includes such factors as industry characteristics, geographic location, and the nature and extent of governmental regulations. Thus, the FASB accords extraordinary item treatment to the loss from hail damages to a tobacco grower's crops if hailstorm damage in its locality is rare. On the other hand, frost damage to a citrus grower's crop in Florida does not qualify as extraordinary because frost damage normally occurs there every three or four years.

INTERNATIONAL INSIGHT

Classification of items as extraordinary differs across nations. Even in countries with similar criteria for identifying extraordinary items, they are not interpreted identically. Thus, what is extraordinary in the U.S. is not necessarily extraordinary elsewhere.

[15]"Reporting the Results of Operations," *Opinions of the Accounting Principles Board No. 30* (New York: AICPA, 1973), par. 20.

[16]Ibid., par. 23, as amended by "Accounting for the Impairment or Disposal of Long-lived Assets," *Statement of Financial Accounting Standards No. 144* (Norwalk, Conn.: FASB, 2001).

[17]*Accounting Trends and Techniques—2004* (New York: AICPA) indicates that just 12 of the 600 companies surveyed reported an extraordinary item.

Similarly, when a company sells the only significant security investment it has ever owned, the gain or loss meets the criteria of an extraordinary item. Another company, however, that has a portfolio of securities acquired for investment purposes would not report such a sales as an extraordinary item. Sale of such securities is part of its ordinary and typical activities.[18]

In addition, considerable judgment must be exercised in determining whether to report an item as extraordinary. For example, the government condemned the forestlands of some paper companies to preserve state or national parks or forests. Is such an event extraordinary, or is it part of a paper company's normal operations? Such determination is not easy. Much depends on the frequency of previous condemnations, the expectation of future condemnations, materiality, and the like.[19]

WHAT DO THE NUMBERS MEAN?

EXTRAORDINARY TIMES

No recent event better illustrates the difficulties of determining whether a transaction meets the definition of extraordinary than the financial impacts of the terrorist attack on the World Trade Center on September 11, 2001.

To many, this event, which resulted in the tragic loss of lives, jobs, and in some cases, entire businesses, clearly meets the criteria for unusual and infrequent. For example, in the wake of the terrorist attack that destroyed the World Trade Center and turned much of lower Manhattan including Wall Street into a war zone, airlines, insurance companies, and other businesses recorded major losses due to property damage, business disruption, and suspension of airline travel and of securities trading.

But, to the surprise of many, the FASB did not permit extraordinary item reporting for losses arising from the terrorist attacks. The reason? After much deliberation, the Emerging Issues Task Force (EITF) of the FASB decided that measurement of the possible loss was too difficult. Take the airline industry as an example: What portion of the airlines' losses after September 11 was related to the terrorist attack, and what portion was due to the ongoing recession? Also, the FASB did not want companies to use the attack as a reason for reporting as extraordinary some losses that had little direct relationship to the attack. Indeed, energy company **AES** and shoe retailer **Footstar**, who both were experiencing profit pressure before 9/11, put some of the blame for their poor performance on the attack.

Source: Julie Creswell, "Bad News Bearers Shift the Blame," *Fortune* (October 15, 2001), p. 44.

Companies must show extraordinary items net of taxes in a separate section in the income statement, usually just before net income. After listing the usual revenues, expenses, and income taxes, the remainder of the statement shows the following.

ILLUSTRATION 4-7
Income Statement Placement of Extraordinary Items

Income before extraordinary items
Extraordinary items (less applicable income tax of $__________)
Net income

[18]Debt extinguishments had been the most common reason for companies reporting extraordinary items. The FASB has now eliminated extraordinary item treatment for these gains and losses, unless they are both unusual and infrequent in nature ("Rescission of FASB Statements No. 4, 44, and 64 and Technical Corrections," *Statement of Financial Accounting Standards No. 145* (Norwalk, Conn.: FASB, 2002). Thus, reporting an extraordinary item is likely to become a rare event in the future.

[19]Because assessing the materiality of individual items requires judgment, determining what is extraordinary is difficult. However, in making materiality judgments, companies should consider extraordinary items individually, and not in the aggregate. "Reporting the Results of Operations," op. cit., par. 24.

For example, Illustration 4-8 shows how **Keystone Consolidated Industries** reported an extraordinary loss.

ILLUSTRATION 4-8
Income Statement Presentation of Extraordinary Items

Keystone Consolidated Industries, Inc.

Income before extraordinary item	$11,638,000
Extraordinary item—flood loss (Note E)	1,216,000
Net income	$10,422,000

Note E: **Extraordinary Item.** The Keystone Steel and Wire Division's Steel Works experienced a flash flood on June 22. The extraordinary item represents the estimated cost, net of related income taxes of $1,279,000, to restore the steel works to full operation.

Unusual Gains and Losses

Because of the restrictive criteria for extraordinary items, financial statement users must carefully examine the financial statements for items that are **unusual or infrequent but not both**. Recall that companies cannot consider items such as write-downs of inventories and transaction gains and losses from fluctuation of foreign exchange as extraordinary items. Thus, companies sometimes show these items with their normal recurring revenues and expenses. If not material in amount, companies combine these with other items in the income statement. If material, companies must disclose them separately, and report them **above** "Income (loss) before extraordinary items."

For example, **PepsiCo, Inc.** presented an unusual charge in its income statement, as Illustration 4-9 shows.

ILLUSTRATION 4-9
Income Statement Presentation of Unusual Charges

PEPSICO

PepsiCo, Inc.
(in millions)

Net sales	$20,917
Costs and expenses, net	
Cost of sales	8,525
Selling, general, and administrative expenses	9,241
Amortization of intangible assets	199
Unusual items (Note 2)	290
Operating income	$ 2,662

Note 2 (Restructuring Charge)

Dispose and write down assets	$183
Improve productivity	94
Strengthen the international bottler structure	13
Net loss	$290

The net charge to strengthen the international bottler structure includes proceeds of $87 million associated with a settlement related to a previous Venezuelan bottler agreement, which were partially offset by related costs.

Restructuring charges, like the one PepsiCo reported, have been common in recent years (see also Illustration 4-5). A **restructuring charge** relates to a major reorganization of company affairs, such as costs associated with employee layoffs, plant closing costs, write-offs of assets, and so on. A company should not report a restructuring charge as an extraordinary item, because these write-offs are part of a company's ordinary and typical activities.

Companies tend to **report unusual items in a separate section just above "Income from operations before income taxes" and "Extraordinary items,"** especially when there are multiple unusual items. For example, when **General Electric Company** experienced multiple unusual items in one year, it reported them in a separate "Unusual items" section of the income statement below "Income before unusual items and income taxes." When preparing a multiple-step income statement for homework purposes, you should report unusual gains and losses in the "Other revenues and gains" or "Other expenses and losses" section unless you are instructed to prepare a separate unusual items section.[20]

In dealing with events that are either unusual or nonrecurring but not both, the profession attempted to prevent a practice that many believed was misleading. Companies often reported such transactions on a net-of-tax basis and prominently displayed the earnings per share effect of these items. Although not captioned "Extraordinary items," companies presented them in the same manner. Some had referred to these as "first cousins" to extraordinary items.

As a consequence, the Board specifically **prohibited a net-of-tax treatment for such items**, to ensure that users of financial statements can easily differentiate extraordinary items—reported net of tax—from material items that are unusual or infrequent, but not both.

Changes in Accounting Principle

UNDERLYING CONCEPTS

Companies can change principles, but they must demonstrate that the newly adopted principle is preferable to the old one. Such changes result in lost consistency from period to period.

Changes in accounting occur frequently in practice, because important events or conditions may be in dispute or uncertain at the statement date. One type of accounting change results when a company adopts a different accounting principle. Changes in accounting principle include a change in the method of inventory pricing from FIFO to average cost, or a change in accounting for construction contracts from the percentage-of-completion to the completed-contract method.[21]

A company recognizes a change in accounting principle by making a **retrospective adjustment** to the financial statements. Such an adjustment recasts the prior years' statements on a basis consistent with the newly adopted principle. The company records the cumulative effect of the change for prior periods as an adjustment to beginning retained earnings of the earliest year presented.

To illustrate, Gaubert Inc. decided in March 2007 to change from FIFO to weighted-average inventory pricing. Gaubert's income before taxes, using the new weighted-average method in 2007, is $30,000. Illustration 4-10 presents the pretax income data for 2005 and 2006 for this example.

ILLUSTRATION 4-10
Calculation of a Change in Accounting Principle

Year	FIFO	Weighted-Average Method	Excess of FIFO over Weighted-Average Method
2005	$40,000	$35,000	$5,000
2006	30,000	27,000	3,000
Total			$8,000

[20] Many companies report "one-time items." However, some companies take restructuring charges practically every year. **Citicorp** (now **Citigroup**) took restructuring charges six years in a row, between 1988 and 1993; **Eastman Kodak Co.** did so five out of six years in 1989 to 1994. Research indicates that the market discounts the earnings of companies that report a series of "nonrecurring" items. Such evidence supports the contention that these elements reduce the quality of earnings. J. Elliott and D. Hanna, "Repeated Accounting Write-offs and the Information Content of Earnings," *Journal of Accounting Research* (Supplement, 1996).

[21] "Accounting Changes and Error Corrections," *Statement of Financial Accounting Standards No. 154* (Norwalk, Conn.: FASB, 2005). In Chapter 18, we examine in greater detail the problems related to accounting changes.

Illustration 4-11 shows the information Gaubert presented in its comparative income statements, based on a 30 percent tax rate.

ILLUSTRATION 4-11
Income Statement Presentation of a Change in Accounting Principle

	2007	2006	2005
Income before taxes	$30,000	$27,000	$35,000
Income tax	9,000	8,100	10,500
Net income	$21,000	$18,900	$24,500

Thus, under the retrospective approach, the company recasts the prior years' income numbers under the newly adopted method. This approach thus preserves comparability across years.

Changes in Estimates

Estimates are inherent in the accounting process. For example, companies estimate useful lives and salvage values of depreciable assets, uncollectible receivables, inventory obsolescence, and the number of periods expected to benefit from a particular expenditure. Not infrequently, due to time, circumstances, or new information, even estimates originally made in good faith must be changed. A company accounts for such **changes in estimates** in the period of change if they affect only that period, or in the period of change and future periods if the change affects both.

To illustrate a change in estimate that affects only the period of change, assume that DuPage Materials Corp. consistently estimated its bad debt expense at 1 percent of credit sales. In 2006 however, DuPage determines that it must revise upward the estimate of bad debts for the current year's credit sales to 2 percent, or double the prior years' percentage. The 2 percent rate is necessary to reduce accounts receivable to net realizable value. Using 2 percent results in a bad debt charge of $240,000, or double the amount using the 1 percent estimate for prior years, DuPage records the provision at December 31, 2006, as follows.

Bad Debt Expense	240,000	
Allowance for Doubtful Accounts		240,000

DuPage includes the entire change in estimate in 2006 income because the change does not affect future periods. **Companies do not handle changes in estimate retrospectively.** That is, such changes are not carried back to adjust prior years. (We examine changes in estimate that affect both the current and future periods in greater detail in Chapter 18.) **Changes in estimate are not considered errors or extraordinary items.**

Corrections of Errors

Errors occur as a result of mathematical mistakes, mistakes in the application of accounting principles, or oversight or misuse of facts that existed at the time financial statements were prepared. In recent years, many companies have corrected for errors in their financial statements. For example, one consulting group noted that error-driven restatements were up 28 percent (to 414 restatements) in 2004.[22] The most common errors involved improper reporting of revenue, accounting for stock options, allowances for receivables, inventories, restructurings, and loss contingencies.

Companies must correct errors by making proper entries in the accounts and reporting the corrections in the financial statements. Corrections of errors are treated as **prior period adjustments,** similar to changes in accounting principles. Companies record a correction of an error in the year in which it is discovered. They report the

[22] Carrie Johnson, "Restatements Up 28% in 2004," *Washingtonpost.com* (January 20, 2005), p. E 04.

error in the financial statements as an adjustment to the beginning balance of retained earnings. If a company prepares comparative financial statements, it should restate the prior statements for the effects of the error.

To illustrate, in 2008, Hillsboro Co. determined that it incorrectly overstated its accounts receivable and sales revenue by $100,000 in 2007. In 2008, Hillboro makes the following entry to correct for this error (ignore income taxes).

Retained Earnings	100,000	
Accounts Receivable		100,000

UNDERLYING CONCEPTS

The AICPA Special Committee on Financial Reporting indicates a company's core activities—usual and recurring events—provide the best historical data from which users determine trends and relationships and make their predictions about the future. Therefore, companies should separately display the effects of core and non-core activities.

Retained Earnings is debited because sales revenue, and therefore net income, was overstated in a prior period. Accounts Receivable is credited to reduce this overstated balance to the correct amount.

Summary of Irregular Items

The public accounting profession now tends to accept a modified all-inclusive income concept instead of the current operating performance concept. Except for changes in accounting principle and error corrections, which are charged or credited directly to retained earnings, companies close all other irregular gains or losses or nonrecurring items to Income Summary and include them in the income statement.

Of these irregular items, companies classify **discontinued operations of a component** of a business as a separate item in the income statement, after "Income from continuing operations." Companies show the **unusual, material, nonrecurring items** that significantly differ from the typical or customary business activities in a separate

ILLUSTRATION 4-12
Summary of Irregular Items in the Income Statement

Type of Situation[a]	Criteria	Examples	Placement on Income Statement
Discontinued operations	Disposal of a component of a business for which the company can clearly distinguish operations and cash flows from the rest of the company's operations.	Sale by diversified company of major division that represents only activities in electronics industry. Food distributor that sells wholesale to supermarket chains and through fast-food restaurants decides to discontinue the division that sells to one of two classes of customers.	Show in separate section after continuing operations but before extraordinary items. (Shown net of tax.)
Extraordinary items	Material, and both unusual and infrequent (nonrecurring).	Gains or losses resulting from casualties, an expropriation, or a prohibition under a new law.	Show in separate section entitled "Extraordinary items." (Shown net of tax.)
Unusual gains or losses, not considered extraordinary	Material; character typical of the customary business activities; unusual or infrequent but not both.	Write-downs of receivables, inventories; adjustments of accrued contract prices; gains or losses from fluctuations of foreign exchange; gains or losses from sales of assets used in business.	Show in separate section above income before extraordinary items. Often reported in "Other revenues and gains" or "Other expenses and losses" section. (Not shown net of tax.)
Changes in principle	Change from one generally accepted principle to another.	Change in the basis of inventory pricing from FIFO to average cost.	Recast prior years' income statements on the same basis as the newly adopted principle.
Changes in estimates	Normal, recurring corrections and adjustments.	Changes in the realizability of receivables and inventories; changes in estimated lives of equipment, intangible assets; changes in estimated liability for warranty costs, income taxes, and salary payments.	Show change only in the affected accounts. (Not shown net of tax.)
Corrections of errors	Mistake, misuse of facts.	Error in reporting revenue.	Restate prior years' income statements to correct for error.

[a]This summary provides only the general rules to be followed in accounting for the various situations described above. Exceptions do exist in some of these situations.

"Extraordinary items" section below "Discontinued operations." They separately disclose other items of a material amount that are of an **unusual or nonrecurring** nature and are **not considered extraordinary**.

Because of the numerous intermediate income figures created by the reporting of these irregular items, readers must carefully evaluate earnings information reported by the financial press. Illustration 4-12 summarizes the basic concepts that we previously discussed. Although simplified, the chart provides a useful framework for determining the treatment of special items affecting the income statement.

SPECIAL REPORTING ISSUES

Intraperiod Tax Allocation

OBJECTIVE 5
Explain intraperiod tax allocation.

Companies report irregular items (except for unusual gains and losses) on the income statement or statement of retained earnings net of tax. This procedure is called **intraperiod tax allocation**, that is, allocation within a period. It relates the income tax expense (sometimes referred to as the income tax provision) of the fiscal period to the **specific items** that give rise to the amount of the tax provision.

Intraperiod tax allocation helps financial statement users better understand the impact of income taxes on the various components of net income. For example, readers of financial statements will understand how much income tax expense relates to "income from continuing operations" and how much relates to certain irregular transactions and events. This approach should help users to better predict the amount, timing, and uncertainty of future cash flows. In addition, intraperiod tax allocation discourages statement readers from using pretax measures of performance when evaluating financial results, and thereby recognizes that income tax expense is a real cost.

Companies use intraperiod tax allocation on the income statement for the following items: (1) income from continuing operations, (2) discontinued operations, and (3) extraordinary items. The general concept is **"let the tax follow the income."**

To compute the income tax expense attributable to "Income from continuing operations," a company would find the income tax expense related to both the revenue and expense transactions used in determining this income. (In this computation, the company does not consider the tax consequences of items excluded from the determination of "Income from continuing operations.") Companies then associate a separate tax effect with each irregular item (e.g., discontinued operations and extraordinary items). Here we look in more detail at calculation of intraperiod tax allocation for extraordinary gains and losses.

Extraordinary Gains

In applying the concept of intraperiod tax allocation, assume that Schindler Co. has income before income tax and extraordinary item of $250,000. It has an extraordinary gain of $100,000 from a condemnation settlement received on one its properties. Assuming a 30 percent income tax rate, Schindler presents the following information on the income statement.

Income before income tax and extraordinary item		$250,000
Income tax		75,000
Income before extraordinary item		175,000
Extraordinary gain—condemnation settlement	$100,000	
Less: Applicable income tax	30,000	70,000
Net income		$245,000

ILLUSTRATION 4-13
Intraperiod Tax Allocation, Extraordinary Gain

Schindler determines the income tax of $75,000 ($250,000 × 30%) attributable to "Income before income tax and extraordinary item" from revenue and expense transactions related to this income. Schindler omits the tax consequences of items excluded from the determination of "Income before income tax and extraordinary item." The company shows a separate tax effect of $30,000 as "Extraordinary gain—condemnation settlement."

Extraordinary Losses

To illustrate the reporting of an extraordinary loss, assume that Schindler Co. has income before income tax and extraordinary item of $250,000. It suffers an extraordinary loss from a major casualty of $100,000. Assuming a 30 percent tax rate, Schindler presents the income tax on the income statement as shown in Illustration 4-14. In this case, the loss provides a positive tax benefit of $30,000. Schindler, therefore, subtracts it from the $100,000 loss.

ILLUSTRATION 4-14
Intraperiod Tax Allocation, Extraordinary Loss

Income before income tax and extraordinary item		$250,000
Income tax		75,000
Income before extraordinary item		175,000
Extraordinary item—loss from casualty	$100,000	
Less: Applicable income tax reduction	30,000	70,000
Net income		$105,000

Companies may also report the tax effect of an extraordinary item by means of a note disclosure, as illustrated below.

ILLUSTRATION 4-15
Note Disclosure of Intraperiod Tax Allocation

Income before income tax and extraordinary item	$250,000
Income tax	75,000
Income before extraordinary item	175,000
Extraordinary item, less applicable income tax reduction (Note 1)	70,000
Net income	$105,000

Note 1: During the year the Company suffered a major casualty loss of $70,000, net of applicable income tax reduction of $30,000.

Earnings per Share

OBJECTIVE 6
Identify where to report earnings per share information.

A company customarily sums up the results of its operations in one important figure: net income. However, the financial world has widely accepted an even more distilled and compact figure as the most significant business indicator—**earnings per share** (EPS).

The computation of earnings per share is usually straightforward. **Earnings per share is net income minus preferred dividends (income available to common stockholders), divided by the weighted average of common shares outstanding.**[23]

To illustrate, assume that Lancer, Inc. reports net income of $350,000. It declares and pays preferred dividends of $50,000 for the year. The weighted average number of common shares outstanding during the year is 100,000 shares. Lancer computes earnings per share of $3, as shown in Illustration 4-16.

ILLUSTRATION 4-16
Equation Illustrating Computation of Earnings per Share

$$\frac{\text{Net Income} - \text{Preferred Dividends}}{\text{Weighted Average of Common Shares Outstanding}} = \text{Earnings per Share}$$

$$\frac{\$350{,}000 - \$50{,}000}{100{,}000} = \$3$$

[23]In calculating earnings per share, companies deduct preferred dividends from net income if the dividends are declared or if they are cumulative though not declared.

Note that EPS measures the number of dollars earned by each share of common stock. It does not represent the dollar amount paid to stockholders in the form of dividends.

Prospectuses, proxy material, and annual reports to stockholders commonly use the "net income per share" or "earnings per share" ratio. The financial press, statistical services like Standard & Poor's, and Wall Street securities analysts also highlight EPS. Because of its importance, **companies must disclose earnings per share on the face of the income statement**. A company that reports a discontinued operation or an extraordinary item must report per share amounts for these line items either on the face of the income statement or in the notes to the financial statements.[24]

To illustrate, consider the income statement for Poquito Industries Inc. shown in Illustration 4-17. Notice the order in which Poquito shows the data, with per share information at the bottom. Assume that the company had 100,000 shares outstanding for the entire year. The Poquito income statement, as Illustration 4-17 shows, is highly condensed. Poquito would need to describe items such as "Unusual charge," "Discontinued operations," and "Extraordinary item" fully and appropriately in the statement or related notes.

ILLUSTRATION 4-17
Income Statement

POQUITO INDUSTRIES INC.
INCOME STATEMENT
FOR THE YEAR ENDED DECEMBER 31, 2007

Sales revenue		$1,420,000
Cost of goods sold		600,000
Gross profit		820,000
Selling and administrative expenses		320,000
Income from operations		500,000
Other revenues and gains		
Interest revenue		10,000
Other expenses and losses		
Loss on disposal of part of Textile Division	$ (5,000)	
Unusual charge—loss on sale of investments	(45,000)	(50,000)
Income from continuing operations before income tax		460,000
Income tax		184,000
Income from continuing operations		276,000
Discontinued operations		
Income from operations of Pizza Division, less applicable income tax of $24,800	54,000	
Loss on disposal of Pizza Division, less applicable income tax of $41,000	(90,000)	(36,000)
Income before extraordinary item		240,000
Extraordinary item—loss from earthquake, less applicable income tax of $23,000		(45,000)
Net income		$ 195,000
Per share of common stock		
Income from continuing operations		$2.76
Income from operations of discontinued division, net of tax		0.54
Loss on disposal of discontinued operation, net of tax		(0.90)
Income before extraordinary item		2.40
Extraordinary loss, net of tax		(0.45)
Net income		$1.95

Many corporations have simple capital structures that include only common stock. For these companies, a presentation such as "Earnings per common share" is appropriate on the income statement. In many instances, however, companies' earnings per

[24]"Earnings Per Share," *Statement of Financial Accounting Standards No. 128* (Norwalk, Conn.: FASB, 1996).

share are subject to dilution (reduction) in the future because existing contingencies permit the issuance of additional common shares.[25]

In summary, the simplicity and availability of EPS figures lead to their widespread use. Because of the importance that the public, even the well-informed public, attaches to earnings per share, companies must make the EPS figure as meaningful as possible.

Retained Earnings Statement

OBJECTIVE 7
Prepare a retained earnings statement.

Net income increases retained earnings. A net loss decreases retained earnings. Both cash and stock dividends decrease retained earnings. Changes in accounting principles (generally) and prior period adjustments may increase or decrease retained earnings. Companies charge or credit these adjustments (net of tax) to the opening balance of retained earnings. This excludes the adjustments from the determination of net income for the current period.

Companies may show retained earnings information in different ways. For example, some companies prepare a separate retained earnings statement, as Illustration 4-18 shows.

ILLUSTRATION 4-18
Retained Earnings Statement

TIGER WOODS INC.
RETAINED EARNINGS STATEMENT
FOR THE YEAR ENDED DECEMBER 31, 2007

Retained earnings, January 1, as reported		$1,050,000
Correction for understatement of net income in prior period (inventory error)		50,000
Retained earnings, January 1, as adjusted		1,100,000
Add: Net income		360,000
		1,460,000
Less: Cash dividends	$100,000	
Stock dividends	200,000	300,000
Retained earnings, December 31		$1,160,000

The reconciliation of the beginning to the ending balance in retained earnings provides information about why net assets increased or decreased during the year. The association of dividend distributions with net income for the period indicates what management is doing with earnings: It may be "plowing back" into the business part or all of the earnings, distributing all current income, or distributing current income plus the accumulated earnings of prior years.[26]

Restrictions of Retained Earnings

Companies often restrict retained earnings to comply with contractual requirements, board of directors' policy, or current necessity. Generally, companies disclose in the notes to the financial statements the amounts of restricted retained earnings. In some cases, companies transfer the amount of retained earnings restricted to an account titled **Appropriated Retained Earnings**. The retained earnings section may therefore report two separate amounts—(1) retained earnings free (unrestricted) and (2) retained earnings appropriated (restricted). The total of these two amounts equals the total retained earnings.

[25] Ibid.

[26] *Accounting Trends and Techniques—2004* (New York: AICPA) indicates that most companies (593 of 600 surveyed) present changes in retained earnings either within the statement of stockholders' equity (586 firms) or in a separate statement of retained earnings. Only 2 of the 600 companies prepare a combined statement of income and retained earnings.

Comprehensive Income

Companies generally include in income all revenues, expenses, and gains and losses recognized during the period. These items are classified within the income statement so that financial statement readers can better understand the significance of various components of net income. Changes in accounting principles and corrections of errors are excluded from the calculation of net income because their effects relate to prior periods.

In recent years, there is increased use of fair values for measuring assets and liabilities. Furthermore, possible reporting of gains and losses related to changes in fair value have placed a strain on income reporting. Because fair values are continually changing, some argue that recognizing these gains and losses in net income is misleading. The FASB agrees and has identified a limited number of transactions that should be recorded directly to stockholders equity. One example is unrealized gains and losses on available-for-sale securities.[27] These gains and losses are excluded from net income, thereby reducing volatility in net income due to fluctuations in fair value. At the same time disclosure of the potential gain or loss is provided.

Companies include these items that bypass the income statement in a measure called comprehensive income. **Comprehensive income** includes all changes in equity during a period *except* those resulting from investments by owners and distributions to owners. Comprehensive income, therefore, includes the following: all revenues and gains, expenses and losses reported in net income, and all gains and losses that bypass net income but affect stockholders' equity. These items—non-owner changes in equity that bypass the income statement—are referred to as **other comprehensive income**.

OBJECTIVE 8
Explain how to report other comprehensive income.

The FASB decided that companies must display the components of other comprehensive income in one of three ways: **(1) a second income statement; (2) a combined statement of comprehensive income; or (3) as a part of the statement of stockholders' equity.**[28] Regardless of the format used, companies must add net income to other comprehensive income to arrive at comprehensive income. Companies are not required to report earnings per share information related to comprehensive income.[29]

To illustrate, assume that V. Gill Inc. reports the following information for 2007: sales revenue $800,000; cost of goods sold $600,000; operating expenses $90,000; and an unrealized holding gain on available-for-sale securities of $30,000, net of tax.

Second Income Statement

Illustration 4-19 shows the two-income statement format based on the above information for V. Gill. Reporting comprehensive income in a separate statement indicates that the gains and losses identified as other comprehensive income have the same status as traditional gains and losses. Placing net income as the starting point in the comprehensive income statement highlights the relationship of the statement to the traditional income statement.

---

[27]We further discuss available-for-sale securities in Chapter 15. Additional examples of other comprehensive items are translation gains and losses on foreign currency, excess of additional pension liability over unrecognized prior service cost, and unrealized gains and losses on certain hedging transactions.

[28]"Reporting Comprehensive Income," *Statement of Financial Accounting Standards No. 130* (Norwalk, Conn.: FASB, June 1997). *Accounting Trends and Techniques—2004* (New York: AICPA) indicates that for the 600 companies surveyed, 580 report comprehensive income. Most companies (488 of 580) include comprehensive income as part of the statement of stockholders' equity.

[29]A company must display the components of other comprehensive income either (1) net of related tax effects, or (2) before related tax effects, with one amount shown for the aggregate amount of tax related to the total amount of other comprehensive income. Both alternatives must show each component of other comprehensive income, net of related taxes either in the face of the statement or in the notes.

ILLUSTRATION 4-19
Two-Statement Format: Comprehensive Income

V. GILL INC.
INCOME STATEMENT
FOR THE YEAR ENDED DECEMBER 31, 2007

Sales revenue	$800,000
Cost of goods sold	600,000
Gross profit	200,000
Operating expenses	90,000
Net income	$110,000

V. GILL INC.
COMPREHENSIVE INCOME STATEMENT
FOR THE YEAR ENDED DECEMBER 31, 2007

Net income	$110,000
Other comprehensive income	
Unrealized holding gain, net of tax	30,000
Comprehensive income	$140,000

Combined Statement of Comprehensive Income

The second approach to reporting other comprehensive income provides a **combined statement** of comprehensive income. In this approach, the traditional net income is a subtotal, with total comprehensive income shown as a final total. The combined statement has the advantage of not requiring the creation of a new financial statement. However, burying net income as a subtotal on the statement is a disadvantage.

Statement of Stockholders' Equity

A third approach reports other comprehensive income items in a **statement of stockholders' equity** (often referred to as statement of changes in stockholders' equity). This statement reports the changes in each stockholder's equity account and in total stockholders' equity during the year. Companies often prepare **in columnar form** the statement of stockholders' equity. In this format, they use columns for each account and for total stockholders' equity.

To illustrate, assume the same information for V. Gill. The company had the following stockholder equity account balances at the beginning of 2007: Common Stock $300,000; Retained Earnings $50,000; and Accumulated Other Comprehensive Income $60,000. No changes in the Common Stock account occurred during the year. Illustration 4-20 shows a statement of stockholders' equity for V. Gill.

ILLUSTRATION 4-20
Presentation of Comprehensive Income Items in Stockholders' Equity Statement

V. GILL INC.
STATEMENT OF STOCKHOLDERS' EQUITY
FOR THE YEAR ENDED DECEMBER 31, 2007

	Total	Comprehensive Income	Retained Earnings	Accumulated Other Comprehensive Income	Common Stock
Beginning balance	$410,000		$ 50,000	$60,000	$300,000
Comprehensive income					
Net income	110,000	$110,000	110,000		
Other comprehensive income					
Unrealized holding gain, net of tax	30,000	30,000		30,000	
Comprehensive income		$140,000			
Ending balance	$550,000		$160,000	$90,000	$300,000

Most companies use the statement of stockholders' equity approach to provide information related to other comprehensive income. Because many companies already provide a statement of stockholders' equity, adding additional columns to display information related to comprehensive income is not costly.

Examples of Comprehensive Income Reporting

Balance Sheet Presentation

Regardless of the display format used, V. Gill reports the **accumulated other comprehensive income** of $90,000 in the stockholders' equity section of the balance sheet as follows.

ILLUSTRATION 4-21
Presentation of Accumulated Other Comprehensive Income in the Balance Sheet

V. GILL INC.
BALANCE SHEET
AS OF DECEMBER 31, 2007
(STOCKHOLDERS' EQUITY SECTION)

Stockholders' equity	
Common stock	$300,000
Retained earnings	160,000
Accumulated other comprehensive income	90,000
Total stockholders' equity	$550,000

By providing information on the components of comprehensive income, as well as accumulated other comprehensive income, the company communicates information about all changes in net assets.[30] With this information, users will better understand the quality of the company's earnings.

QUESTIONS

1. What kinds of questions about future cash flows do investors and creditors attempt to answer with information in the income statement?
2. How can information based on past transactions be used to predict future cash flows?
3. Identify at least two situations in which important changes in value are not reported in the income statement.
4. Identify at least two situations in which application of different accounting methods or accounting estimates results in difficulties in comparing companies.
5. Explain the transaction approach to measuring income. Why is the transaction approach to income measurement preferable to other ways of measuring income?
6. What is earnings management?
7. How can earnings management affect the quality of earnings?
8. Why should caution be exercised in the use of the income figure derived in an income statement? What are the objectives of generally accepted accounting principles in their application to the income statement?
9. A *Wall Street Journal* article noted that **MicroStrategy** reported higher income than its competitors by using a more aggressive policy for recognizing revenue on future upgrades to its products. Some contend that MicroStrategy's quality of earnings is low. What does the term "quality of earnings" mean?
10. What is the major distinction (a) between revenues and gains and (b) between expenses and losses?
11. What are the advantages and disadvantages of the single-step income statement?
12. What is the basis for distinguishing between operating and nonoperating items?
13. Distinguish between the modified all-inclusive income statement and the current operating performance income statement. According to present generally accepted accounting principles, which is recommended? Explain.
14. How should correction of errors be reported in the financial statements?
15. Discuss the appropriate treatment in the financial statements of each of the following.
    (a) An amount of $113,000 realized in excess of the cash surrender value of an insurance policy on the life of one of the founders of the company who died during the year.
    (b) A profit-sharing bonus to employees computed as a percentage of net income.
    (c) Additional depreciation on factory machinery because

of an error in computing depreciation for the previous year.

(d) Rent received from subletting a portion of the office space.

(e) A patent infringement suit, brought 2 years ago against the company by another company, was settled this year by a cash payment of $725,000.

(f) A reduction in the Allowance for Doubtful Accounts balance, because the account appears to be considerably in excess of the probable loss from uncollectible receivables.

16. Indicate where the following items would ordinarily appear on the financial statements of Allepo, Inc. for the year 2007.

(a) The service life of certain equipment was changed from 8 to 5 years. If a 5-year life had been used previously, additional depreciation of $425,000 would have been charged.

(b) In 2007 a flood destroyed a warehouse that had a book value of $1,600,000. Floods are rare in this locality.

(c) In 2007 the company wrote off $1,000,000 of inventory that was considered obsolete.

(d) An income tax refund related to the 2004 tax year was received.

(e) In 2004, a supply warehouse with an expected useful life of 7 years was erroneously expensed.

(f) Allepo, Inc. changed from weighted-average to FIFO inventory pricing.

17. Give the section of a multiple-step income statement in which each of the following is shown.

(a) Loss on inventory write-down.

(b) Loss from strike.

(c) Bad debt expense.

(d) Loss on disposal of a component of the business.

(e) Gain on sale of machinery.

(f) Interest revenue.

(g) Depreciation expense.

(h) Material write-offs of notes receivable.

18. Barry Bonds Land Development, Inc. purchased land for $70,000 and spent $30,000 developing it. It then sold the land for $160,000. Tom Glavine Manufacturing purchased land for a future plant site for $100,000. Due to a change in plans, Glavine later sold the land for $160,000. Should these two companies report the land sales, both at gains of $60,000, in a similar manner?

19. You run into Rex Grossman at a party and begin discussing financial statements. Rex says, "I prefer the single-step income statement because the multiple-step format generally overstates income." How should you respond to Rex?

20. Federov Corporation has eight expense accounts in its general ledger which could be classified as selling expenses. Should Federov report these eight expenses separately in its income statement or simply report one total amount for selling expenses?

21. Jose DeLeon Investments reported an unusual gain from the sale of certain assets in its 2007 income statement. How does intraperiod tax allocation affect the reporting of this unusual gain?

22. What effect does intraperiod tax allocation have on reported net income?

23. Letterman Company computed earnings per share as follows.

$$\frac{\text{Net income}}{\text{Common shares outstanding at year-end}}$$

Letterman has a simple capital structure. What possible errors might the company have made in the computation? Explain.

24. Maria Shriver Corporation reported 2007 earnings per share of $7.21. In 2008, Maria Shriver reported earnings per share as follows.

On income before extraordinary item	$6.40
On extraordinary item	1.88
On net income	$8.28

Is the increase in earnings per share from $7.21 to $8.28 a favorable trend?

25. What is meant by "tax allocation within a period"? What is the justification for such practice?

26. When does tax allocation within a period become necessary? How should this allocation be handled?

27. During 2007, Natsume Sozeki Company earned income of $1,000,000 before income taxes and realized a gain of $450,000 on a government-forced condemnation sale of a division plant facility. The income is subject to income taxation at the rate of 34%. The gain on the sale of the plant is taxed at 30%. Proper accounting suggests that the unusual gain be reported as an extraordinary item. Illustrate an appropriate presentation of these items in the income statement.

28. On January 30, 2006, a suit was filed against Pierogi Corporation under the Environmental Protection Act. On August 6, 2007, Pierogi Corporation agreed to settle the action and pay $920,000 in damages to certain current and former employees. How should this settlement be reported in the 2007 financial statements? Discuss.

29. Tiger Paper Company decided to close two small pulp mills in Conway, New Hampshire, and Corvallis, Oregon. Would these closings be reported in a separate section entitled "Discontinued operations after income from continuing operations"? Discuss.

30. What major types of items are reported in the retained earnings statement?

31. Generally accepted accounting principles usually require the use of accrual accounting to "fairly present" income. If the cash receipts and disbursements method of accounting will "clearly reflect" taxable income, why does this method not usually also "fairly present" income?

32. State some of the more serious problems encountered in seeking to achieve the ideal measurement of periodic net income. Explain what accountants do as a practical alternative.

33. What is meant by the terms *elements* and *items* as they relate to the income statement? Why might items have to be disclosed in the income statement?

34. What are the three ways that other comprehensive income may be displayed (reported)?

35. How should the disposal of a component of a business be disclosed in the income statement?

C H A P T E R F I V E

BALANCE SHEET AND STATEMENT OF CASH FLOWS

"There Ought to Be a Law"

As one manager noted, "There ought to be a law that before you can buy a stock, you must be able to read a balance sheet." We agree, and the same can be said for a statement of cash flows.

Krispy Kreme Doughnuts provides an example of how stunning earnings growth can hide real problems. Not long ago the doughnut maker was a glamour stock with a 60 percent earnings per share growth rate and a price-earnings ratio around 70. Seven months later its stock price had dropped 72 percent. What happened? Stockholders alleged that Krispy Kreme may have been inflating its revenues and not taking enough bad debt expense (which inflated both assets and income). In addition, Krispy Kreme's operating cash flow was negative. Most financially sound companies throw off positive cash flow.

Here are additional examples of how one rating agency rated the earnings quality of some companies, using some key balance sheet and statement of cash flow measurements.

Earnings-Quality Winners	Company	Earnings-Quality Indicators
	Avon Products	Strong cash flow
	Capital One Financial	Conservatively capitalized
	Ecolab	Good management of working capital
	Timberland	Minimal off-balance-sheet commitments

Earnings-Quality Losers	Company	Earnings-Quality Indicators
	Ford Motor	High debt and underfunded pension plan
	Kroger	High goodwill and debt
	Ryder System	Negative free cash flow
	Teco Energy	Selling assets to meet liquidity needs

Just as a deteriorating balance sheet and statement of cash flows warn of earnings declines (and falling stock prices), improving balance sheet and cash flow information is a leading indicator of improved earnings.[1]

[1]Adapted from Gretchen Morgenson, "How Did They Value Stocks? Count the Absurd Ways," *New York Times on the Web* (March 18, 2001), and from K. Badanhausen, J. Gage, C. Hall, and M. Ozanian, "Beyond Balance Sheet: Earnings Quality," *Forbes.com* (January 28, 2005).

Learning Objectives

After studying this chapter, you should be able to:

1. Explain the uses and limitations of a balance sheet.
2. Identify the major classifications of the balance sheet.
3. Prepare a classified balance sheet using the report and account formats.
4. Determine which balance sheet information requires supplemental disclosure.
5. Describe the major disclosure techniques for the balance sheet.
6. Indicate the purpose of the statement of cash flows.
7. Identify the content of the statement of cash flows.
8. Prepare a statement of cash flows.
9. Understand the usefulness of the statement of cash flows.

PREVIEW OF CHAPTER 5

Readers of the financial statements sometimes ignore important information in the balance sheet and statement of cash flows. As our opening story shows, analyzing these financial statements helps investors avoid surprises in earnings. In this chapter we examine the many different types of assets, liabilities, and stockholders' equity items that affect the balance sheet and the statement of cash flows. The content and organization of the chapter are as follows.

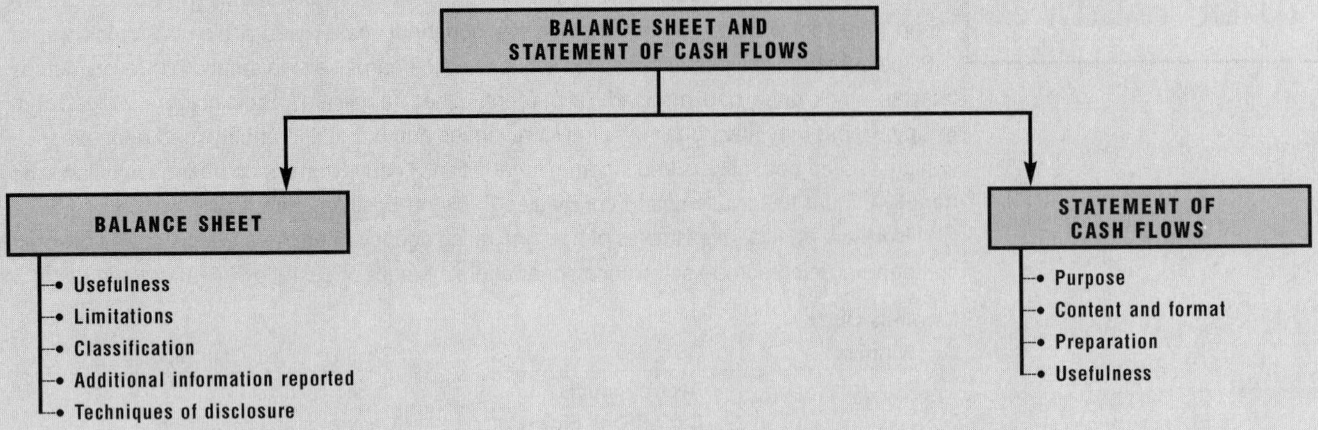

SECTION 1 BALANCE SHEET

OBJECTIVE 1
Explain the uses and limitations of a balance sheet.

The **balance sheet**, sometimes referred to as the **statement of financial position**, reports the assets, liabilities, and stockholders' equity of a business enterprise at a specific date. This financial statement provides information about the nature and amounts of investments in enterprise resources, obligations to creditors, and the owners' equity in net resources.[2] It therefore helps in predicting the amounts, timing, and uncertainty of future cash flows.

USEFULNESS OF THE BALANCE SHEET

By providing information on assets, liabilities, and stockholders' equity, the balance sheet provides a basis for computing rates of return and evaluating the capital structure of the enterprise. As our opening story indicates, analysts also use information in the balance sheet to assess a company's risk[3] and future cash flows. In this regard,

[2]*Accounting Trends and Techniques—2004* (New York: AICPA) indicates that approximately 96 percent of the companies surveyed used the term "balance sheet." The term "statement of financial position" is used infrequently, although it is conceptually appealing.

[3]Risk conveys the unpredictability of future events, transactions, circumstances, and results of the company.

analysts use the balance sheet to assess a company's liquidity, solvency, and financial flexibility.

Liquidity describes "the amount of time that is expected to elapse until an asset is realized or otherwise converted into cash or until a liability has to be paid."[4] Creditors are interested in short-term liquidity ratios, such as the ratio of cash (or near cash) to short-term liabilities. These ratios indicate whether a company, like **Amazon**, will have the resources to pay its current and maturing obligations. Similarly, stockholders assess liquidity to evaluate the possibility of future cash dividends or the buyback of shares. In general, the greater Amazon's liquidity, the lower its risk of failure.

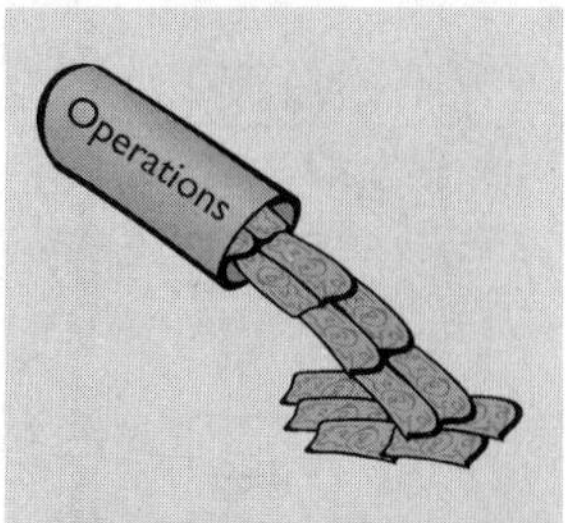

How quickly will my assets convert to cash?

Solvency refers to the ability of a company to pay its debts as they mature. For example, when a company carries a high level of long-term debt relative to assets, it has lower solvency than a similar company with a low level of long-term debt. Companies with higher debt are relatively more risky because they will need more of their assets to meet their fixed obligations (interest and principal payments).

We are drowning in a sea of debt!

Liquidity and solvency affect a company's **financial flexibility,** which measures the "ability of an enterprise to take effective actions to alter the amounts and timing of cash flows so it can respond to unexpected needs and opportunities."[5] For example, a company may become so loaded with debt—so financially inflexible—that it has little or no sources of cash to finance expansion or to pay off maturing debt. A company with a high degree of financial flexibility is better able to survive bad times, to recover from unexpected setbacks, and to take advantage of profitable and unexpected investment opportunities. Generally, the greater an enterprise's financial flexibility, the lower its risk of failure.

GROUNDED

WHAT DO THE NUMBERS MEAN?

The terrorist attacks of September 11, 2001, showed how vulnerable the major airlines are to falling demand for their services. Since that infamous date, major airlines have reduced capacity and slashed jobs to avoid bankruptcy. **United Airlines**, the second largest U.S. air carrier, **Northwest Airlines**, the fourth largest U.S. carrier, **US Airways**, the seventh largest U.S. carrier, and several smaller competitors have filed for bankruptcy.

Here are some statements made in a recent annual report of **Delta Airlines**, whose auditors have noted that there is substantial doubt about the company's ability to continue as a going concern.

> "If we are unsuccessful in further reducing our operating costs...we will need to restructure our costs under Chapter 11 of the U.S. Bankruptcy Code.... We have substantial liquidity needs and there is no assurance that we will be able to obtain the necessary financing to meet those needs on acceptable terms, if at all."

The financial distress related to the airline industry was not an insider's secret. The airlines' balance sheets clearly revealed their financial inflexibility and low liquidity even before September 11. For example, major airlines such as **Braniff**, **Continental**, **Eastern**, **Midway**, and **America West** declared bankruptcy before September 11.

Conversely, some airlines have done well. In 2004, **Southwest Airlines** recorded its 32nd consecutive year of profitability.

[4]"Reporting Income, Cash Flows, and Financial Position of Business Enterprises," *Proposed Statement of Financial Accounting Concepts* (Stamford, Conn.: FASB, 1981), par. 29.

[5]"Reporting Income, Cash Flows, and Financial Position of Business Enterprises," *Proposed Statement of Financial Accounting Concepts* (Stamford, Conn.: FASB, 1981), par. 25.

Hmm... I wonder if they will pay me back?

LIMITATIONS OF THE BALANCE SHEET

Some of the major limitations of the balance sheet are:

1 Most assets and liabilities are reported at **historical cost**. As a result, the information provided in the balance sheet has high reliability. But it is often criticized for not reporting a more relevant fair value. For example, **Georgia-Pacific** owns timber and other assets that may appreciate in value after purchase. Yet, Georgia-Pacific reports any increase only if and when it sells the assets.

2 Companies use **judgments and estimates** to determine many of the items reported in the balance sheet. For example, in its balance sheet, **Dell** estimates the amount of receivables that it will collect, the useful life of its warehouses, and the number of computers that will be returned under warranty.

3 The balance sheet necessarily **omits many items that are of financial value** but that a company cannot record objectively. For example, the knowledge and skill of **Intel** employees in developing new computer chips are arguably the company's most significant asset. However, because Intel cannot reliably measure the value of its employees and other intangible assets (such as customer base, research superiority, and reputation), it does not recognize these items in the balance sheet. Similarly, many other liabilities are reported in an "off-balance-sheet" manner, if at all.

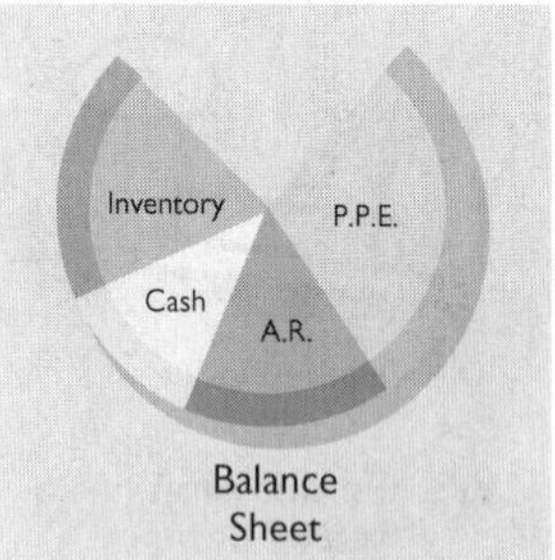

Hey....we left out the value of the employees!

The recent bankruptcy of the seventh-largest U.S. company, **Enron**, highlights the omission of important items in the balance sheet. In Enron's case, it failed to disclose certain off-balance-sheet financing obligations in its main financial statements.[6]

CLASSIFICATION IN THE BALANCE SHEET

OBJECTIVE 2
Identify the major classifications of the balance sheet.

Balance sheet accounts are **classified**. That is, balance sheets group together similar items to arrive at significant subtotals. Furthermore, the material is arranged so that important relationships are shown.

The FASB has often noted that the parts and subsections of financial statements can be more informative than the whole. Therefore, the FASB discourages the reporting of summary accounts alone (total assets, net assets, total liabilities, etc.). Instead, companies should report and classify individual items in sufficient detail to permit users to assess the amounts, timing, and uncertainty of future cash flows. Such classification also makes it easier for users to evaluate the company's liquidity and financial flexibility, profitability, and risk.

To classify items in financial statements, companies group those items with similar characteristics and separate items with different characteristics.[7] For example, companies should report separately:

1 Assets that differ in their **type or expected function** in the company's central operations or other activities. For example, **IBM** reports merchandise inventories separately from property, plant, and equipment.

2 Assets and liabilities with **different implications for the company's financial flexibility**. For example, a company that uses assets in its operations, like **Walgreens**, should report those assets separately from assets held for investment and assets subject to restrictions, such as leased equipment.

3 Assets and liabilities with **different general liquidity characteristics**. For example, **Boeing Company** reports cash separately from inventories.

[6]We discuss several of these omitted items (such as leases and other off-balance-sheet arrangements) in later chapters. See Wayne Upton, Jr., Special Report: *Business and Financial Reporting, Challenges from the New Economy* (Norwalk, Conn.: FASB, 2001).

[7]"Reporting Income, Cash Flows, and Financial Positions of Business Enterprises," *Proposed Statement of Financial Accounting Concepts* (Stamford, Conn.: FASB, 1981), par. 51.

The three general classes of items included in the balance sheet are assets, liabilities, and equity. We defined them in Chapter 2 as follows.

ELEMENTS OF THE BALANCE SHEET

1 *ASSETS.* Probable future economic benefits obtained or controlled by a particular entity as a result of past transactions or events.

2 *LIABILITIES.* Probable future sacrifices of economic benefits arising from present obligations of a particular entity to transfer assets or provide services to other entities in the future as a result of past transactions or events.

3 *EQUITY.* Residual interest in the assets of an entity that remains after deducting its liabilities. In a business enterprise, the equity is the ownership interest.[8]

Companies then further divide these items into several subclassifications. Illustration 5-1 indicates the general format of balance sheet presentation.

ILLUSTRATION 5-1
Balance Sheet Classifications

Assets	Liabilities and Owners' Equity
Current assets	Current liabilities
Long-term investments	Long-term debt
Property, plant, and equipment	Owners' equity
Intangible assets	Capital stock
Other assets	Additional paid-in capital
	Retained earnings

A company may classify the balance sheet in some other manner, but you usually see little departure from these major subdivisions in practice. A proprietorship or partnership does present the classifications within the owners' equity section a little differently, as we will show later in the chapter.

Current Assets

Current assets are cash and other assets a company expects to convert into cash, sell, or consume either in one year or in the operating cycle, whichever is longer. The operating cycle is the average time between when a company acquires materials and supplies and when it receives cash for sales of the product (for which it acquired the materials and supplies). The cycle operates from cash through inventory, production, receivables, and back to cash. When several operating cycles occur within one year, a company uses the one-year period. If the operating cycle is more than one year, a company uses the longer period.

Current assets are presented in the balance sheet in order of liquidity. The five major items found in the current assets section, and their bases of valuation, are shown in Illustration 5-2.

ILLUSTRATION 5-2
Current Assets and Basis of Valuation

Item	Basis of Valuation
Cash and cash equivalents	Fair value
Short-term investments	Generally, fair value
Receivables	Estimated amount collectible
Inventories	Lower of cost or market
Prepaid expenses	Cost

[8]"Elements of Financial Statements of Business Enterprises," *Statement of Financial Accounting Concepts No. 6* (Stamford, Conn.: FASB, 1985), paras. 25, 35 and 49.

A company does not report these five items as current assets if it does not expect to realize them in one year or in the operating cycle, whichever is longer. For example, a company excludes cash restricted for purposes other than payment of current obligations or for use in current operations from the current assets section. **Generally, if a company expects to convert an asset into cash or to use it to pay a current liability within a year or the operating cycle, whichever is longer, it classifies the asset as current.**

This rule, however, is subject to interpretation. A company classifies an investment in common stock as either a current asset or a noncurrent asset depending on management's intent. When it has small holdings of common stocks or bonds that it will hold long-term, it should not classify them as current.

Although a current asset is well defined, certain theoretical problems also develop. For example, how is including prepaid expenses in the current assets section justified? The rationale is that if a company did not pay these items in advance, it would instead need to use other current assets during the operating cycle. If we follow this logic to its ultimate conclusion, however, any asset previously purchased saves the use of current assets during the operating cycle and would be considered current.

Another problem occurs in the current-asset definition when a company consumes plant assets during the operating cycle. Conceptually, it seems that a company should place an amount equal to the current depreciation charge on the plant assets in the current assets section, because it will consume them in the next operating cycle. However, this conceptual problem is ignored. This example illustrates that the formal distinction made between some current and noncurrent assets is somewhat arbitrary.

Cash

Cash is generally considered to consist of currency and demand deposits (monies available on demand at a financial institution.) **Cash equivalents** are short-term highly liquid investments that will mature within three months or less. Most companies use the caption "Cash and cash equivalents," and they indicate that this amount approximates fair value.

A company must disclose any restrictions or commitments related to the availability of cash. As an example, see the excerpt from the annual report of **Alterra Healthcare Corp.** in Illustration 5-3.

ILLUSTRATION 5-3
Balance Sheet Presentation of Restricted Cash

Alterra
AGING WITH CHOICE

Alterra Healthcare Corp.

Current assets	
Cash	$18,728,000
Restricted cash and investments (Note 7)	7,191,000

Note 7: Restricted Cash and Investments. Restricted cash and investments consist of certificates of deposit restricted as collateral for lease arrangements and debt service with interest rates ranging from 4.0% to 5.5%.

Alterra Healthcare restricted cash to meet an obligation due currently. Therefore, Alterra included this restricted cash under current assets.

If a company restricts cash for purposes other than current obligations, it excludes the cash from current assets. Illustration 5-4 shows an example of this, excerpted from the annual report of **Owens Corning, Inc.**

ILLUSTRATION 5-4
Balance Sheet Presentation of Current and Noncurrent Restricted Cash

Owens Corning, Inc.
(in millions)

Current assets	
Cash and cash equivalents	$ 70
Restricted securities—Fibreboard—current portion (Note 23)	900
Other assets	
Restricted securities—Fibreboard (Note 23)	938

Note 23 (in part). The Insurance Settlement funds are held in and invested by the Fibreboard Settlement Trust (the "Trust") and are available to satisfy Fibreboard's pending and future asbestos related liabilities. . . . The assets of the Trust are comprised of cash and marketable securities (collectively, the "Trust Assets") and are reflected on Owens Corning's consolidated balance sheet as restricted assets. These assets are reflected as current assets or other assets, with each category denoted "Restricted securities—Fibreboard."

Short-Term Investments

Companies group investments in debt and equity securities into three separate portfolios for valuation and reporting purposes:

Held-to-maturity: Debt securities that a company has the positive intent and ability to hold to maturity.

Trading: Debt and equity securities bought and held primarily for sale in the near term to generate income on short-term price differences.

Available-for-sale: Debt and equity securities not classified as held-to-maturity or trading securities.

A company should report trading securities (whether debt or equity) as current assets. It classifies individual held-to-maturity and available-for-sale securities as current or noncurrent depending on the circumstances. It should report held-to-maturity securities at amortized cost. All trading and available-for-sale securities are reported at fair value.[9]

For example, see Illustration 5-5, which is an excerpt from the annual report of **Intuit Inc.** with respect to its available-for-sale investments.

ILLUSTRATION 5-5
Balance Sheet Presentation of Investments in Securities

Intuit Inc.
(in thousands)

Assets	
Cash and cash equivalents	$ 170,043
Short-term investments (Note 2)	1,036,758

Note 2 (in part). The following schedule summarizes the estimated fair value of our short-term investments (all available-for-sale):

Corporate notes	$ 50,471
Municipal bonds	931,374
U.S. government securities	54,913

[9] "Accounting for Certain Investments in Debt and Equity Securities," *Statement of Financial Accounting Standards No. 115* (Norwalk, Conn.: FASB, 1993).

Receivables

A company should clearly identify any anticipated loss due to uncollectibles, the amount and nature of any nontrade receivables, and any receivables used as collateral. Major categories of receivables should be shown in the balance sheet or the related notes. For receivables arising from unusual transactions (such as sale of property, or a loan to affiliates or employees), companies should separately classify these as long-term, unless collection is expected within one year. **Mack Trucks, Inc.** reported its receivables as shown in Illustration 5-6.

ILLUSTRATION 5-6
Balance Sheet Presentation of Receivables

Mack Trucks, Inc.

Current assets	
Trade receivables	
Accounts receivable	$102,212,000
Affiliated companies	1,157,000
Installment notes and contracts	625,000
Total	103,994,000
Less: Allowance for uncollectible accounts	8,194,000
Trade receivables—net	95,800,000
Receivables from unconsolidated financial subsidiaries	22,106,000

UNDERLYING CONCEPTS

The lower-of-cost-or-market valuation reflects the use of *conservatism* in accounting.

Inventories

To present inventories properly, a company discloses the basis of valuation (e.g., lower-of-cost-or-market) and the method of pricing (e.g., FIFO or LIFO). A manufacturing concern (like **Abbott Laboratories**, shown in Illustration 5-7) also indicates the stage of completion of the inventories.

ILLUSTRATION 5-7
Balance Sheet Presentation of Inventories, Showing Stage of Completion

Abbott Laboratories
(in thousands)

Current assets	
Inventories	
Finished products	$ 772,478
Work in process	338,818
Materials	384,148
Total inventories	1,495,444

Note 1 (in part): Inventories. Inventories are stated at the lower of cost (first-in, first-out basis) or market.

Weyerhaeuser Company, a forestry company and lumber manufacturer with several finished-goods product lines, reported its inventory as shown in Illustration 5-8.

Weyerhaeuser Company

Current assets	
Inventories—at FIFO lower of cost or market	
Logs and chips	$ 68,471,000
Lumber, plywood and panels	86,741,000
Pulp, newsprint and paper	47,377,000
Containerboard, paperboard, containers and cartons	59,682,000
Other products	161,717,000
Total product inventories	423,988,000
Materials and supplies	175,540,000

ILLUSTRATION 5-8
Balance Sheet Presentation of Inventories, Showing Product Lines

Prepaid Expenses

A company includes prepaid expenses in current assets if it will receive benefits (usually services) within one year or the operating cycle, whichever is longer.[10] As we discussed earlier, these items are current assets because if they had not already been paid, they would require the use of cash during the next year or the operating cycle. A company reports prepaid expenses at the amount of the unexpired or unconsumed cost.

A common example is the prepayment for an insurance policy. A company classifies it as a prepaid expense because the payment precedes the receipt of the benefit of coverage. Other common prepaid expenses include prepaid rent, advertising, taxes, and office or operating supplies. **Knight Ridder, Inc.**, for example, listed its prepaid expenses in current assets as shown in Illustration 5-9.

Knight Ridder, Inc.
(in thousands)

Current assets	
Cash, including short-term cash investments of $7,001	$ 41,661
Accounts receivable, net of allowances of $20,238	416,498
Inventories	52,786
Prepaids	30,767
Other current assets	34,382

ILLUSTRATION 5-9
Balance Sheet Presentation of Prepaid Expenses

Noncurrent Assets

Noncurrent assets are those not meeting the definition of current assets. They include a variety of items, as we discuss in the following sections.

Long-Term Investments

Long-term investments, often referred to simply as investments, normally consist of one of four types:

1 Investments in securities, such as bonds, common stock, or long-term notes.
2 Investments in tangible fixed assets not currently used in operations, such as land held for speculation.

[10] *Accounting Trends and Techniques—2004* (New York: AICPA) in its survey of 600 annual reports identified 351 companies that reported prepaid expenses.

3 Investments set aside in special funds such as a sinking fund, pension fund, or plant expansion fund. This includes the cash surrender value of life insurance.

4 Investments in nonconsolidated subsidiaries or affiliated companies.

Companies expect to hold long-term investments for many years. They usually present them on the balance sheet just below "Current assets," in a separate section called "Investments." Realize that many securities classified as long-term investments are, in fact, readily marketable. But a company does not include them as current assets unless it intends to convert them to cash in the short-term—that is, within a year or in the operating cycle, whichever is longer. As indicated earlier, securities classified as available-for-sale are reported at fair value, and held-to-maturity securities are reported at amortized cost.

Motorola, Inc. reported its investments section, located between "Property, plant, and equipment" and "Other assets," as shown in Illustration 5-10.

ILLUSTRATION 5-10
Balance Sheet Presentation of Long-Term Investments

Motorola, Inc.
(in millions)

Investments	
Equity investments	$ 872
Other investments	2,567
Fair value adjustment to available-for-sale securities	2,487
Total	$5,926

Property, Plant, and Equipment

Property, plant, and equipment are tangible long-lived assets used in the regular operations of the business. These assets consist of physical property such as land, buildings, machinery, furniture, tools, and wasting resources (timberland, minerals). With the exception of land, a company either depreciates (e.g., buildings) or depletes (e.g., timberlands or oil reserves) these assets.

Mattel, Inc. presented its property, plant, and equipment in its balance sheet as shown in Illustration 5-11.

ILLUSTRATION 5-11
Balance Sheet Presentation of Property, Plant, and Equipment

Mattel, Inc.

Property, plant, and equipment	
Land	$ 32,793,000
Buildings	257,430,000
Machinery and equipment	564,244,000
Capitalized leases	23,271,000
Leasehold improvements	74,988,000
	952,726,000
Less: Accumulated depreciation	472,986,000
	479,740,000
Tools, dies and molds, net	168,092,000
Property, plant, and equipment, net	647,832,000

A company discloses the basis it uses to value property, plant, and equipment; any liens against the properties; and accumulated depreciation–usually in the notes to the statements.

Intangible Assets

Intangible assets lack physical substance and are not financial instruments. They include patents, copyrights, franchises, goodwill, trademarks, trade names, and customer lists. A company writes off (amortizes) limited-life intangible assets over their useful lives. It periodically assesses indefinite-life intangibles (such as goodwill) for impairment. Intangibles can represent significant economic resources, yet financial analysts often ignore them, because valuation is difficult.

PepsiCo, Inc. reported intangible assets in its balance sheet as shown in Illustration 5-12.

ILLUSTRATION 5-12
Balance Sheet Presentation of Intangible Assets

PEPSICO

PepsiCo, Inc.
(in millions)

Intangible assets	
Goodwill	$3,374
Trademarks	1,320
Other identifiable intangibles	147
Total intangibles	$4,841

Other Assets

The items included in the section "Other assets" vary widely in practice. Some include items such as long-term prepaid expenses, prepaid pension cost, and noncurrent receivables. Other items that might be included are assets in special funds, deferred income taxes, property held for sale, and restricted cash or securities. A company should limit this section to include only unusual items sufficiently different from assets included in specific categories.

Liabilities

Similar to assets, companies classify liabilities as current or long-term.

Current Liabilities

Current liabilities are the obligations that a company reasonably expects to liquidate either through the use of current assets or the creation of other current liabilities. This concept includes:

1. Payables resulting from the acquisition of goods and services: accounts payable, wages payable, taxes payable, and so on.
2. Collections received in advance for the delivery of goods or performance of services, such as unearned rent revenue or unearned subscriptions revenue.
3. Other liabilities whose liquidation will take place within the operating cycle, such as the portion of long-term bonds to be paid in the current period or short-term obligations arising from purchase of equipment.

At times, a liability that is payable within the next year is not included in the current liabilities section. This occurs either when the company expects to refinance the debt through another long-term issue[11] or to retire the debt out of noncurrent assets. This approach is used because liquidation does not result from the use of current assets or the creation of other current liabilities.

Companies do not report current liabilities in any consistent order. In general, though, companies most commonly list notes payable, accounts payable, or short-term

[11]"Classification of Short-term Obligations Expected to Be Refinanced," *Statement of Financial Accounting Standards No. 6* (Stamford, Conn.: FASB, 1975).

debt as the first item. Income taxes payable, current maturities of long-term debt, or other current liabilities are commonly listed last. For example, see **Halliburton Company**'s current liabilities section in Illustration 5-13.

ILLUSTRATION 5-13
Balance Sheet Presentation of Current Liabilities

Halliburton Company
(in millions)

Current liabilities	
Short-term notes payable	$1,570
Accounts payable	782
Accrued employee compensation and benefits	267
Unearned revenues	386
Income taxes payable	113
Accrued special charges	6
Current maturities of long-term debt	8
Other current liabilities	694
Total current liabilities	3,826

Current liabilities include such items as trade and nontrade notes and accounts payable, advances received from customers, and current maturities of long-term debt. If the amounts are material, companies classify income taxes and other accrued items separately. A company should fully describe in the notes any information about a secured liability—for example, stock held as collateral on notes payable—to identify the assets providing the security.

The excess of total current assets over total current liabilities is referred to as **working capital** (sometimes called **net working capital**). Working capital represents the net amount of a company's relatively liquid resources. That is, it is the liquidity buffer available to meet the financial demands of the operating cycle.

Companies seldom disclose an amount for working capital on the balance sheet. But bankers and other creditors compute it as an indicator of the short-run liquidity of a company. To determine the actual liquidity and availability of working capital to meet current obligations, however, requires analysis of the composition of the current assets and their nearness to cash.

WHAT DO THE NUMBERS MEAN?

"SHOW ME THE ASSETS!"

Recently, concerned about the liquidity and solvency of many dot-com companies, creditors have demanded more assurance that these companies can pay their bills when due. A key indicator for creditors is the amount of working capital. For example, when a report predicted that **Amazon.com**'s working capital would turn negative, the company's vendors began to explore steps that would ensure that Amazon would pay them.

Some vendors have demanded that their dot-com customers sign notes stating that the goods shipped to them serve as collateral for the transaction. Other vendors began shipping goods on consignment—an arrangement whereby the vendor retains ownership of the goods until a third party buys and pays for them.

Such creditor protection measures arise from creditors' concerns about dot-coms' lack of tangible assets that they can convert to cash to meet short-term obligations. For example, the primary asset for many dot-coms is its customer list. However, these lists have little resale value because privacy agreements prohibit sharing the customer information.

With fewer hard assets that they can convert to cash, a dot-com can experience a severe credit squeeze as vendors curtail shipments or take other measures to limit their financial risk. Such actions can further erode the company's liquidity and financial flexibility.

Long-Term Liabilities

Long-term liabilities are obligations that a company does not reasonably expect to liquidate within the normal operating cycle. Instead, it expects to pay them at some date beyond that time. Bonds payable, notes payable, some deferred income tax amounts, lease obligations, and pension obligations are the most common examples. **Companies classify long-term liabilities that mature within the current operating cycle as current liabilities if payment of the obligation requires the use of current assets.**

Generally, long-term liabilities are of three types:

1. Obligations arising from specific financing situations, such as the issuance of bonds, long-term lease obligations, and long-term notes payable.
2. Obligations arising from the ordinary operations of the company, such as pension obligations and deferred income tax liabilities.
3. Obligations that depend on the occurrence or non-occurrence of one or more future events to confirm the amount payable, or the payee, or the date payable, such as service or product warranties and other contingencies.

Companies generally provide a great deal of supplementary disclosure for long-term liabilities, because most long-term debt is subject to various covenants and restrictions for the protection of lenders.[12]

It is desirable to report any premium or discount separately as an addition to or subtraction from the bonds payable. Companies frequently describe the terms of all long-term liability agreements (including maturity date or dates, rates of interest, nature of obligation, and any security pledged to support the debt) in notes to the financial statements. Illustration 5-14 provides an example of this, taken from an excerpt from **The Great Atlantic & Pacific Tea Company**'s financials.

The Great Atlantic & Pacific Tea Company, Inc.

Total current liabilities	$978,109,000
Long-term debt (See note)	254,312,000
Obligations under capital leases	252,618,000
Deferred income taxes	57,167,000
Other non-current liabilities	127,321,000
Note: Indebtedness. Debt consists of:	
9.5% senior notes, due in annual installments of $10,000,000	$ 40,000,000
Mortgages and other notes due through 2011 (average interest rate of 9.9%)	107,604,000
Bank borrowings at 9.7%	67,225,000
Commercial paper at 9.4%	100,102,000
	314,931,000
Less: Current portion	(60,619,000)
Total long-term debt	$254,312,000

ILLUSTRATION 5-14
Balance Sheet Presentation of Long-Term Debt

[12]Companies usually explain the pertinent rights and privileges of the various securities (both debt and equity) outstanding in the notes to the financial statements. Examples of information that companies should disclose are dividend and liquidation preferences, participation rights, call prices and dates, conversion or exercise prices or rates and pertinent dates, sinking fund requirements, unusual voting rights, and significant terms of contracts to issue additional shares. "Disclosure of Information about Capital Structure," *Statement of Financial Accounting Standards No. 129* (Norwalk: FASB, 1997), par. 4.

Owners' Equity

The **owners' equity (stockholders' equity)** section is one of the most difficult sections to prepare and understand. This is due to the complexity of capital stock agreements and the various restrictions on stockholders' equity imposed by state corporation laws, liability agreements, and boards of directors. Companies usually divide the section into three parts:

STOCKHOLDERS' EQUITY SECTION

1. *CAPITAL STOCK.* The par or stated value of the shares issued.
2. *ADDITIONAL PAID-IN CAPITAL.* The excess of amounts paid in over the par or stated value.
3. *RETAINED EARNINGS.* The corporation's undistributed earnings.

For capital stock, companies must disclose the par value and the authorized, issued, and outstanding share amounts. A company usually presents the additional paid-in capital in one amount, although subtotals are informative if the sources of additional capital are varied and material. The retained earnings amount may be divided between the **unappropriated** (the amount that is usually available for dividend distribution) and **restricted** (e.g., by bond indentures or other loan agreements) amounts. In addition, companies show any capital stock reacquired (treasury stock) as a reduction of stockholders' equity.

Illustration 5-15 presents an example of the stockholders' equity section from **Quanex Corporation**.

ILLUSTRATION 5-15
Balance Sheet Presentation of Stockholders' Equity

Quanex Corporation
(in thousands)

Stockholders' equity (Note 12):	
Preferred stock, no par value, 1,000,000 shares authorized; 345,000 issued and outstanding	$ 86,250
Common stock, $0.50 par value, 25,000,000 shares authorized; 13,638,005 shares issued and outstanding	6,819
Additional paid-in capital	87,260
Retained earnings	57,263
	$237,592

The ownership or stockholders' equity accounts in a corporation differ considerably from those in a partnership or proprietorship. Partners show separately their permanent capital accounts and the balance in their temporary accounts (drawing accounts). Proprietorships ordinarily use a single capital account that handles all of the owner's equity transactions.

OBJECTIVE 3
Prepare a classified balance sheet using the report and account formats.

Balance Sheet Format

One common arrangement that companies use in presenting a classified balance sheet is the **account form**. It lists assets, by sections, on the left side, and liabilities and stockholders' equity, by sections, on the right side. The main disadvantage is the need for a sufficiently wide space in which to present the items side by side. Often, the account form requires two facing pages.

To avoid this disadvantage, the **report form** lists the sections one above the other, on the same page. See, for example, Illustration 5-16, which lists assets, followed by liabilities and stockholders' equity directly below, on the same page.[13]

ILLUSTRATION 5-16
Classified Report Form Balance Sheet

SCIENTIFIC PRODUCTS, INC.
BALANCE SHEET
DECEMBER 31, 2006

Assets			
Current assets			
Cash		$ 42,485	
Available-for-sale securities—at fair value		28,250	
Accounts receivable	$165,824		
Less: Allowance for doubtful accounts	1,850	163,974	
Notes receivable		23,000	
Inventories—at average cost		489,713	
Supplies on hand		9,780	
Prepaid expenses		16,252	
Total current assets			$ 773,454
Long-term investments			
Investments in Warren Co.			87,500
Property, plant, and equipment			
Land—at cost		125,000	
Buildings—at cost	975,800		
Less: Accumulated depreciation	341,200	634,600	
Total property, plant, and equipment			759,600
Intangible assets			
Goodwill			100,000
Total assets			$1,720,554
Liabilities and Stockholders' Equity			
Current liabilities			
Notes payable to banks		$ 50,000	
Accounts payable		197,532	
Accrued interest on notes payable		500	
Income taxes payable		62,520	
Accrued salaries, wages, and other liabilities		9,500	
Deposits received from customers		420	
Total current liabilities			$ 320,472
Long-term debt			
Twenty-year 12% debentures, due January 1, 2016			500,000
Total liabilities			820,472
Stockholders' equity			
Paid in on capital stock			
Preferred, 7%, cumulative			
Authorized, issued, and outstanding, 30,000 shares of $10 par value	$300,000		
Common—			
Authorized, 500,000 shares of $1 par value; issued and outstanding, 400,000 shares	400,000		
Additional paid-in capital	37,500	737,500	
Retained earnings		162,582	
Total stockholders' equity			900,082
Total liabilities and stockholders' equity			$1,720,554

UNDERLYING CONCEPTS

The presentation of balance sheet information meets one of the objectives of financial reporting—to provide information about enterprise resources, claims to resources, and changes in them.

[13] *Accounting Trends and Techniques—2004* (New York: AICPA) indicates that all of the 600 companies surveyed use either the "report form" (506) or the "account form" (94), sometimes collectively referred to as the "customary form."

Infrequently, companies use other balance sheet formats. For example, companies sometimes deduct current liabilities from current assets to arrive at working capital. Or, they deduct all liabilities from all assets.

WHAT DO THE NUMBERS MEAN?

WARNING SIGNALS

Analysts use balance sheet information in models designed to predict financial distress. Researcher E. I. Altman pioneered a bankruptcy-prediction model that derives a "Z-score" by combining balance sheet and income measures in the following equation.

$$Z = \frac{\text{Working capital}}{\text{Total assets}} \times 1.2 + \frac{\text{Retained earnings}}{\text{Total assets}} \times 1.4 + \frac{\text{EBIT}}{\text{Total assets}} \times 3.3 + \frac{\text{Sales}}{\text{Total assets}} \times 0.99 + \frac{\text{MV equity}}{\text{Total liabilities}} \times 0.6$$

Following extensive testing, Altman found that companies with Z-scores above 3.0 are unlikely to fail. Those with Z-scores below 1.81 are very likely to fail.

Altman developed the original model for publicly held manufacturing companies. He and others have modified the model to apply to companies in various industries, emerging companies, and companies not traded in public markets.

At one time, the use of Z-scores was virtually unheard of among practicing accountants. Today, auditors, management consultants, and courts of law use this measure to help evaluate the overall financial position and trends of a firm. In addition, banks use Z-scores for loan evaluation. While a low score does not guarantee bankruptcy, the model has been proven accurate in many situations.

Source: Adapted from E. I. Altman and E. Hotchkiss, *Corporate Financial Distress and Bankruptcy*, 3rd edition (New York: John Wiley and Sons, 2005).

wiley.com/college/kieso

Presentation of Balance Sheet Formats for Various Real Companies

ADDITIONAL INFORMATION REPORTED

OBJECTIVE 4
Determine which balance sheet information requires supplemental disclosure.

The balance sheet is not complete if a company simply lists the assets, liabilities, and owners' equity accounts. It still needs to provide important supplemental information. This may be information not presented elsewhere in the statement, or it may elaborate on items in the balance sheet. There are normally four types of information that are supplemental to account titles and amounts presented in the balance sheet. They are listed below.

SUPPLEMENTAL BALANCE SHEET INFORMATION

1. *CONTINGENCIES.* Material events that have an uncertain outcome.
2. *ACCOUNTING POLICIES.* Explanations of the valuation methods used or the basic assumptions made concerning inventory valuations, depreciation methods, investments in subsidiaries, etc.
3. *CONTRACTUAL SITUATIONS.* Explanations of certain restrictions or covenants attached to specific assets or, more likely, to liabilities.
4. *FAIR VALUES.* Disclosures of fair values, particularly for financial instruments.

Contingencies

A **contingency** is an existing situation involving uncertainty as to possible gain (gain contingency) or loss (loss contingency) that will ultimately be resolved when one or more future events occur or fail to occur. In short, contingencies are material events with an uncertain future. Examples of gain contingencies are tax operating-loss carry-forwards or company litigation against another party. Typical loss contingencies relate to litigation, environmental issues, possible tax assessments, or government investigations. We examine the accounting and reporting requirements involving contingencies more fully in Chapter 12.

UNDERLYING CONCEPTS

The basis for including additional information should meet the *full disclosure* principle. That is, the information should be of sufficient importance to influence the judgment of an informed user.

Accounting Policies

APB Opinion No. 22 recommends disclosure for all significant accounting principles and methods that involve selection from among alternatives or those that are peculiar to a given industry.[14] For instance, companies can compute inventories under several cost flow assumptions (e.g., LIFO and FIFO), depreciate plant and equipment under several accepted methods (e.g., double-declining balance and straight-line), and carry investments at different valuations (e.g., cost, equity, and fair value). Sophisticated users of financial statements know of these possibilities and examine the statements closely to determine the methods used.

Companies must also disclose information about the nature of their operations, the use of estimates in preparing financial statements, certain significant estimates, and vulnerabilities due to certain concentrations.[15] Illustration 5-17 shows an example of such a disclosure.

ILLUSTRATION 5-17
Balance Sheet Disclosure of Significant Risks and Uncertainties

Chesapeake Corporation

Risks and Uncertainties. Chesapeake operates in three business segments which offer a diversity of products over a broad geographic base. The Company is not dependent on any single customer, group of customers, market, geographic area or supplier of materials, labor or services. Financial statements include, where necessary, amounts based on the judgments and estimates of management. These estimates include allowances for bad debts, accruals for landfill closing costs, environmental remediation costs, loss contingencies for litigation, self-insured medical and workers' compensation insurance and determinations of discount and other rate assumptions for pensions and postretirement benefit expenses.

Disclosure of significant accounting principles and methods and of risks and uncertainties is particularly useful if given in a separate **Summary of Significant Accounting Policies** preceding the notes to the financial statements or as the initial note.

Contractual Situations

Companies should disclose contractual situations, if significant, in the notes to the financial statements. For example, they must clearly state the essential provisions of lease contracts, pension obligations, and stock option plans in the notes. Analysts want to know not only the amount of the liabilities, but also how the different contractual provisions affect the company at present and in the future.

[14]"Disclosure of Accounting Policies," *Opinions of the Accounting Principles Board No. 22* (New York: AICPA, 1972).

[15]"Disclosure of Certain Significant Risks and Uncertainties," *Statement of Position 94-6* (New York: AICPA, 1994).

Companies must disclose the following commitments if the amounts are material: commitments related to obligations to maintain working capital, to limit the payment of dividends, to restrict the use of assets, and to require the maintenance of certain financial ratios. Management must exercise considerable judgment to determine whether omission of such information is misleading. The rule in this situation is, "When in doubt, disclose." It is better to disclose a little too much information than not enough.

WHAT DO THE NUMBERS MEAN?

WHAT ABOUT YOUR COMMITMENTS?

Many of the recent accounting scandals related to the nondisclosure of significant contractual obligations. In response, the SEC has mandated that companies disclose contractual obligations in a tabular summary in the management discussion and analysis section of the company's annual report.

Presented below, as an example, is a disclosure from **The Procter & Gamble Company**.

Contractual Commitments, as of June 30, 2004 ($ in millions)

	Total	Less Than 1 Year	1–3 Years	3–5 Years	After 5 Years
Recorded liabilities					
Total debt	$20,399	$ 8,229	$3,954	$1,935	$ 6,281
Capital leases	252	30	46	169	7
Wella domination and profit transfer agreement	1,106	1,106	–	–	–
Other					
Interest payments relating to long-term debt	7,587	715	1,202	874	4,796
Operating leases	920	186	284	185	265
Minimum pension funding[1]	702	237	465	–	–
Purchase obligations[2]	5,471	1,640	1,334	955	1,542
Total contractual commitments	$36,437	$12,143	$7,285	$4,118	$12,891

[1]Represents future pension payments to comply with local funding requirements. The projected payments beyond fiscal year 2007 are not currently determinable.

[2]The amounts indicated in this line primarily reflect future contractual payments under various take-or-pay arrangements entered into as part of the normal course of business.

Fair Values

As we discussed in Chapter 2, companies use historical cost as the primary valuation basis in financial statements. However, fair value information may be more useful for certain types of assets and liabilities. This is particularly so in the case of financial instruments.

Financial instruments are defined as cash, an ownership interest, or a contractual right to receive or obligation to deliver cash or another financial instrument. Such contractual rights to receive cash or other financial instruments are assets. Contractual obligations to pay are liabilities. Cash, investments, accounts receivable, and payables are examples of financial instruments.

Financial instruments are increasing both in use and variety. As a consequence of the increasing use, companies must disclose both the carrying value and the estimated fair values of their financial instruments. For example, **YUM! Brands Inc.**, a franchiser of restaurants such as Pizza Hut and Taco Bell, provides extensive disclosures of the fair value of its financial instrument assets and liabilities, as shown in Illustration 5-18. We provide more extensive discussion of financial instrument accounting and reporting in Chapters 6, 13, and 15.

YUM! Brands Inc.

The carrying amounts and fair values of our other financial instruments subject to fair value disclosures are as follows:

	Carrying Amount	Fair Value
Debt		
Short-term borrowings and long-term debt, excluding capital leases and the derivative instrument adjustments	$ 1,925	$ 2,181
Debt-related derivative instruments		
Open contracts in a net asset position	31	31
Lease guarantees	8	37
Guarantees of supporting financial arrangements of certain franchisees, unconsolidated affiliates and other third parties	8	10
Letters of credit	–	3

We estimated the fair value of debt, debt-related derivative instruments, foreign currency-related derivative instruments, guarantees and letters of credit using market quotes and calculations based on market rates.

ILLUSTRATION 5-18
Disclosure of Financial Instrument Fair Values

TECHNIQUES OF DISCLOSURE

OBJECTIVE 5
Describe the major disclosure techniques for the balance sheet.

Companies should disclose as completely as possible the effect of various contingencies on financial condition, the methods of valuing assets and liabilities, and the company's contracts and agreements. To disclose this pertinent information, companies may use parenthetical explanations, notes, cross reference and contra items, and supporting schedules.

Parenthetical Explanations

Companies often provide additional information by parenthetical explanations following the item. For example, Illustration 5-19 shows a parenthetical explanation of the number of shares issued by **Ford Motor Company** on the balance sheet under Stockholders' Equity.

Ford Motor Company

Stockholders' Equity (in millions)

Common stock, par value $0.01 per share (1,837 million shares issued) $18

ILLUSTRATION 5-19
Parenthetical Disclosure of Shares Issued—Ford Motor Company

This additional pertinent balance sheet information adds clarity and completeness. It has an advantage over a note because it brings the additional information into the body of the statement where readers will less likely overlook it. Companies, however, should avoid lengthy parenthetical explanations, which might be distracting.

UNDERLYING CONCEPTS

The user-specific quality of *understandability* requires accountants to be careful in describing transactions and events.

Notes

Companies use notes if they cannot conveniently show additional explanations as parenthetical explanations. Illustration 5-20 shows how **International Paper Company** reported its inventory costing methods in its accompanying notes.

ILLUSTRATION 5-20
Note Disclosure

International Paper Company

(Note 11)

Inventories by major category were (millions):

Raw materials	$ 371
Finished pulp, paper and packaging products	1,796
Finished lumber and panel products	184
Operating supplies	351
Other	16
Total inventories	$2,718

The last-in, first-out inventory method is used to value most of International Paper's U.S. inventories. Approximately 70% of total raw materials and finished products inventories were valued using this method. If the first-in, first-out method had been used, it would have increased total inventories balances by approximately $170 million.

Companies commonly use notes to disclose the following: the existence and amount of any preferred stock dividends in arrears, the terms of or obligations imposed by purchase commitments, special financial arrangements and instruments, depreciation policies, any changes in the application of accounting principles, and the existence of contingencies.

Notes therefore must present all essential facts as completely and succinctly as possible. Careless wording may mislead rather than aid readers. Notes should add to the total information made available in the financial statements, not raise unanswered questions or contradict other portions of the statements. The following notes illustrate the presentation of such information.

ILLUSTRATION 5-21
More Note Disclosures

Alberto-Culver Company

Note 3: Long-Term Debt. Various borrowing arrangements impose restrictions on such items as total debt, working capital, dividend payments, treasury stock purchases and interest expense. The company was in compliance with these arrangements and $68 million of consolidated retained earnings was not restricted as to the payment of dividends and purchases of treasury stock.

Consolidated Papers, Inc.

Note 7: Commitments. The company had capital expenditure purchase commitments outstanding of approximately $17 million.

Willamette Industries, Inc.

Note 4: Property, Plant, and Equipment (partial): The company changed its accounting estimates relating to depreciation. The estimated service lives for most machinery and equipment were extended five years. The change was based upon a study performed by the company's engineering department, comparisons to typical industry practices, and the effect of the company's extensive capital investments which have resulted in a mix of assets with longer productive lives due to technological advances. As a result of the change, net income was increased $51,900, or $0.46 per diluted share.

Cross-Reference and Contra Items

Companies "cross-reference" a direct relationship between an asset and a liability on the balance sheet. For example, as shown in Illustration 5-22, on December 31, 2006, a company might show the following entries—one listed among the current assets, and the other listed among the current liabilities.

ILLUSTRATION 5-22
Cross-Referencing and Contra Items

Current Assets (in part)	
Cash on deposit with sinking fund trustee for redemption of bonds payable—see Current liabilities	$800,000

Current Liabilities (in part)	
Bonds payable to be redeemed in 2007—see Current assets	$2,300,000

This cross-reference points out that the company will redeem $2,300,000 of bonds payable currently, for which it has only set aside $800,000. Therefore, it needs additional cash from unrestricted cash, from sales of investments, from profits, or from some other source. Alternatively, the company can show the same information parenthetically.

Another common procedure is to establish contra or adjunct accounts. A **contra account** on a balance sheet reduces either an asset, liability, or owners' equity account. Examples include Accumulated Depreciation and Discount on Bonds Payable. Contra accounts provide some flexibility in presenting the financial information. With the use of the Accumulated Depreciation account, for example, a reader of the statement can see the original cost of the asset as well as the depreciation to date.

An **adjunct account**, on the other hand, increases either an asset, liability, or owners' equity account. An example is Premium on Bonds Payable, which, when added to the Bonds Payable account, describes the total bond liability of the company.

Supporting Schedules

Often a company needs a separate schedule to present more detailed information about certain assets or liabilities, as follows.

ILLUSTRATION 5-23
Disclosure through Use of Supporting Schedules

Property, plant, and equipment	
Land, buildings, equipment, and other fixed assets—net (see Schedule 3)	$643,300

SCHEDULE 3
LAND, BUILDINGS, EQUIPMENT, AND OTHER FIXED ASSETS

	Total	Land	Buildings	Equip.	Other Fixed Assets
Balance January 1, 2007	$740,000	$46,000	$358,000	$260,000	$76,000
Additions in 2007	161,200		120,000	38,000	3,200
	901,200	46,000	478,000	298,000	79,200
Assets retired or sold in 2007	31,700			27,000	4,700
Balance December 31, 2007	869,500	46,000	478,000	271,000	74,500
Depreciation taken to January 1, 2007	196,000		102,000	78,000	16,000
Depreciation taken in 2007	56,000		28,000	24,000	4,000
	252,000		130,000	102,000	20,000
Depreciation on assets retired in 2007	25,800			22,000	3,800
Depreciation accumulated December 31, 2007	226,200		130,000	80,000	16,200
Book value of assets	$643,300	$46,000	$348,000	$191,000	$58,300

Terminology

INTERNATIONAL INSIGHT

Internationally, accounting terminology is a problem. Confusion arises even between nations that share a language. For example, U.S. investors normally think of "stock" as "equity" or "ownership"; to the British, "stocks" means inventory. In the United States "fixed assets" generally refers to "property, plant, and equipment"; in Britain the category includes more items.

The account titles in the general ledger do not necessarily represent the best terminology for balance sheet purposes. Companies often use brief account titles and include technical terms that only accountants understand. But many persons unacquainted with accounting terminology examine balance sheets. Thus, balance sheets should contain descriptions that readers will generally understand and clearly interpret.

For example, companies have used the term "reserve" in differing ways: to describe amounts deducted from assets (contra accounts such as accumulated depreciation and allowance for doubtful accounts), as a part of the title of contingent or estimated liabilities, and to describe an appropriation of retained earnings. Because of the different meanings attached to this term, misinterpretation often resulted from its use. Therefore, the profession has recommended that companies use the word **reserve** only to describe an appropriation of retained earnings. The use of the term in this narrower sense—to describe appropriated retained earnings—has resulted in a better understanding of its significance when it appears in a balance sheet. However, the term "appropriated" appears more logical, and we encourage its use.

For years the profession has recommended that the use of the word **surplus** be discontinued in balance sheet presentations of owners' equity. The use of the terms *capital surplus, paid-in surplus,* and *earned surplus* is confusing. Although condemned by the profession, these terms appear all too frequently in current financial statements.

SECTION 2 | *STATEMENT OF CASH FLOWS*

Chapter 2 indicated that one of the three basic objectives of financial reporting is "assessing the amounts, timing, and uncertainty of cash flows." The three financial statements we have looked at so far—the income statement, the statement of stockholders' equity, and the balance sheet—each present some information about the cash flows of an enterprise during a period. But they do so to a limited extent. For instance, the income statement provides information about resources provided by operations, but not exactly cash. The statement of stockholders' equity shows the amount of cash used to pay dividends or purchase treasury stock. Comparative balance sheets might show what assets the company has acquired or disposed of and what liabilities it has incurred or liquidated.

UNDERLYING CONCEPTS

The statement of cash flows meets one of the objectives of financial reporting—to help assess the amounts, timing, and uncertainty of future cash flows.

However, none of these statements presents a detailed summary of all the cash inflows and outflows, or the sources and uses of cash during the period. To fill this need, the FASB requires the **statement of cash flows** (also called the **cash flow statement**).[16]

PURPOSE OF THE STATEMENT OF CASH FLOWS

OBJECTIVE 6
Indicate the purpose of the statement of cash flows.

The primary purpose of a statement of cash flows is to provide relevant information about the cash receipts and cash payments of an enterprise during a period. To achieve this purpose, the statement of cash flows reports the following: (1) the cash effects of operations during a period, (2) investing transactions, (3) financing transactions, and (4) the net increase or decrease in cash during the period.[17]

Reporting the sources, uses, and net increase or decrease in cash helps investors, creditors, and others know what is happening to a company's most liquid resource. Be-

[16]"Statement of Cash Flows," *Statement of Financial Accounting Standards No. 95* (Stamford, Conn.: FASB, 1987).

[17]The FASB recommends the basis as "cash and cash equivalents." **Cash equivalents** are liquid investments that mature within three months or less.

cause most individuals maintain a checkbook and prepare a tax return on a cash basis, they can comprehend the information reported in the statement of cash flows, such as causes and effects of cash inflows and outflows and the net change in cash.

The statement of cash flows provides answers to the following simple but important questions:

1 Where did the cash come from during the period?

2 What was the cash used for during the period?

3 What was the change in the cash balance during the period?

WATCH THAT CASH FLOW

WHAT DO THE NUMBERS MEAN?

Investors usually focus on net income measured on an accrual basis. However, information on cash flows can be important for assessing a company's liquidity, financial flexibility, and overall financial performance. The graph below shows **W. T. Grant**'s financial performance over 7 years.

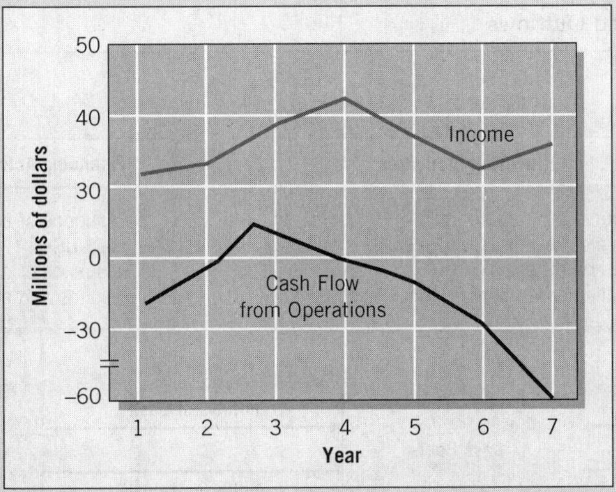

Although W. T. Grant showed consistent profits and even some periods of earnings growth, its cash flow began to "go south" starting in about year 3. The company filed for bankruptcy shortly after year 7. Financial statement readers who studied the company's cash flows would have found an early-warning signal of W. T. Grant's problems.

CONTENT AND FORMAT OF THE STATEMENT OF CASH FLOWS

OBJECTIVE 7
Identify the content of the statement of cash flows.

Companies classify cash receipts and cash payments during a period into three different activities in the statement of cash flows—operating, investing, and financing activities, defined as follows.

1 **Operating activities** involve the cash effects of transactions that enter into the determination of net income.

2 **Investing activities** include making and collecting loans and acquiring and disposing of investments (both debt and equity) and property, plant, and equipment.

3 **Financing activities** involve liability and owners' equity items. They include (a) obtaining resources from owners and providing them with a return on their investment, and (b) borrowing money from creditors and repaying the amounts borrowed.

Illustration 5-24 shows the basic format of the statement of cash flows.

ILLUSTRATION 5-24
Basic Format of Cash Flow Statement

Statement of Cash Flows

Cash flows from operating activities	$XXX
Cash flows from investing activities	XXX
Cash flows from financing activities	XXX
Net increase (decrease) in cash	XXX
Cash at beginning of year	XXX
Cash at end of year	$XXX

Illustration 5-25 graphs the inflows and outflows of cash classified by activity.

ILLUSTRATION 5-25 Cash Inflows and Outflows

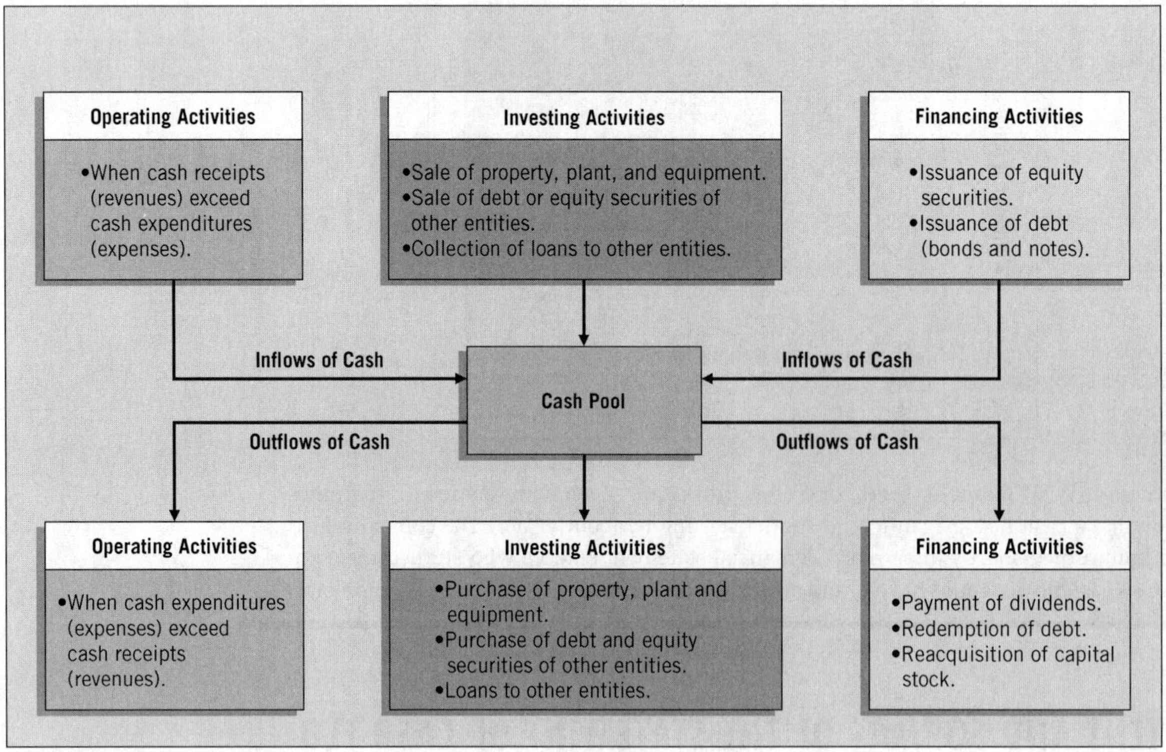

The statement's value is that it helps users evaluate liquidity, solvency, and financial flexibility. As we indicated earlier in the chapter, **liquidity** refers to the "nearness to cash" of assets and liabilities. **Solvency** is the firm's ability to pay its debts as they mature. **Financial flexibility** is a company's ability to respond and adapt to financial adversity and unexpected needs and opportunities.

We have devoted Chapter 19 entirely to the preparation and content of the statement of cash flows. The intervening chapters will cover several elements and complex topics that affect the content of a typical statement of cash flows. The presentation in this chapter is introductory—a reminder of the existence of the statement of cash flows and its usefulness.

PREPARATION OF THE STATEMENT OF CASH FLOWS

OBJECTIVE 8
Prepare a statement of cash flows.

Companies obtain the information to prepare the statement of cash flows from several sources: (1) comparative balance sheets, (2) the current income statement, and (3) selected transaction data. Preparing the statement of cash flows from these sources involves four steps:

1 Determine the cash provided by or used in operating activities.
2 Determine the cash provided by or used in investing and financing activities.
3 Determine the change (increase or decrease) in cash during the period.
4 Reconcile the change in cash with the beginning and the ending cash balances.

The following simple example demonstrates how companies apply these steps in preparing a statement of cash flows.

On January 1, 2007, in its first year of operations, Telemarketing Inc. issued 50,000 shares of $1 par value common stock for $50,000 cash. The company rented its office space, furniture, and telecommunications equipment and performed marketing services throughout the first year. In June 2007 the company purchased land for $15,000. Illustration 5-26 shows the company's comparative balance sheets at the beginning and end of 2007.

INTERNATIONAL INSIGHT

Not all countries require statements of cash flows. Some countries require a statement reporting sources and applications of "funds" (often defined as working capital). Others have no requirement for either cash or funds flow statements.

ILLUSTRATION 5-26 Comparative Balance Sheets

TELEMARKETING INC.
BALANCE SHEETS

Assets	Dec. 31, 2007	Jan. 1, 2007	Increase/Decrease
Cash	$31,000	$–0–	$31,000 Increase
Accounts receivable	41,000	–0–	41,000 Increase
Land	15,000	–0–	15,000 Increase
Total	$87,000	$–0–	
Liabilities and Stockholders' Equity			
Accounts payable	$12,000	$–0–	12,000 Increase
Common stock	50,000	–0–	50,000 Increase
Retained earnings	25,000	–0–	25,000 Increase
Total	$87,000	$–0–	

Illustration 5-27 presents the income statement and additional information.

ILLUSTRATION 5-27
Income Statement Data

TELEMARKETING INC.
INCOME STATEMENT
FOR THE YEAR ENDED DECEMBER 31, 2007

Revenues	$172,000
Operating expenses	120,000
Income before income tax	52,000
Income tax	13,000
Net income	$ 39,000

Additional information:
Dividends of $14,000 were paid during the year.

Cash provided by operating activities is the excess of cash receipts over cash payments from operating activities. Companies determine this amount by converting net income on an accrual basis to a cash basis. To do so, they add to or deduct from net income those items in the income statement that do not affect cash. This procedure requires that a company analyze not only the current year's income statement but also the comparative balance sheets and selected transaction data.

Analysis of Telemarketing's comparative balance sheets reveals two items that will affect the computation of net cash provided by operating activities:

1. The increase in accounts receivable reflects a noncash increase of $41,000 in revenues.
2. The increase in accounts payable reflects a noncash increase of $12,000 in expenses.

Therefore, to arrive at cash provided by operations, Telemarketing Inc. deducts from net income the increase in accounts receivable ($41,000), and it adds back to net income the increase in accounts payable ($12,000). As a result of these adjustments, the company determines cash provided by operations to be $10,000, computed as shown in Illustration 5-28.

ILLUSTRATION 5-28
Computation of Net Cash Provided by Operations

Net income		$39,000
Adjustments to reconcile net income to net cash provided by operating activities:		
Increase in accounts receivable	$(41,000)	
Increase in accounts payable	12,000	(29,000)
Net cash provided by operating activities		$10,000

INTERNATIONAL INSIGHT

International Accounting Standard 7 requires a statement of cash flows. Both international standards and U.S. GAAP specify that the cash flows must be classified as operating, investing, or financing.

Telemarketing Inc.'s only investing activity was the land purchase. It had two financing activities: (1) the increase of $50,000 in common stock resulting from the issuance of 50,000 shares for cash, and (2) the payment of $14,000 cash in dividends. Illustration 5-29 presents Telemarketing Inc.'s statement of cash flows for 2007.

ILLUSTRATION 5-29 Statement of Cash Flows

TELEMARKETING INC.
STATEMENT OF CASH FLOWS
FOR THE YEAR ENDED DECEMBER 31, 2007

Cash flows from operating activities		
Net income		$39,000
Adjustments to reconcile net income to net cash provided by operating activities:		
Increase in accounts receivable	$(41,000)	
Increase in accounts payable	12,000	(29,000)
Net cash provided by operating activities		10,000
Cash flows from investing activities		
Purchase of land	(15,000)	
Net cash used by investing activities		(15,000)
Cash flows from financing activities		
Issuance of common stock	50,000	
Payment of cash dividends	(14,000)	
Net cash provided by financing activities		36,000
Net increase in cash		31,000
Cash at beginning of year		–0–
Cash at end of year		$31,000

The increase in cash of $31,000 reported in the statement of cash flows agrees with the increase of $31,000 in cash calculated from the comparative balance sheets.

Not all of a company's significant activities involve cash. Examples of significant noncash activities are:

1. Issuance of common stock to purchase assets.
2. Conversion of bonds into common stock.
3. Issuance of debt to purchase assets.
4. Exchanges of long-lived assets.

Significant financing and investing activities that do not affect cash are not reported in the body of the statement of cash flows. Rather, these activities are reported in either a separate schedule at the bottom of the statement of cash flows or in separate notes to the financial statements. Such reporting of these noncash activities satisfies the full disclosure principle. *In solving homework assignments, you should present significant noncash activities in a separate schedule at the bottom of the statement of cash flows.*

Illustration 5-30 shows an example of a comprehensive statement of cash flows. Note that the company purchased equipment through the issuance of $50,000 of bonds, which is a significant noncash transaction.

ILLUSTRATION 5-30
Comprehensive Statement of Cash Flows

NESTOR COMPANY
STATEMENT OF CASH FLOWS
FOR THE YEAR ENDED DECEMBER 31, 2007

Cash flows from operating activities		
Net income		$320,750
Adjustments to reconcile net income to net cash provided by operating activities:		
Depreciation expense	$88,400	
Amortization of intangibles	16,300	
Gain on sale of plant assets	(8,700)	
Increase in accounts receivable (net)	(11,000)	
Decrease in inventory	15,500	
Decrease in accounts payable	(9,500)	91,000
Net cash provided by operating activities		411,750
Cash flows from investing activities		
Sale of plant assets	90,500	
Purchase of equipment	(182,500)	
Purchase of land	(70,000)	
Net cash used by investing activities		(162,000)
Cash flows from financing activities		
Payment of cash dividend	(19,800)	
Issuance of common stock	100,000	
Redemption of bonds	(50,000)	
Net cash provided by financing activities		30,200
Net increase in cash		279,950
Cash at beginning of year		135,000
Cash at end of year		$414,950
Noncash investing and financing activities		
Purchase of equipment through issuance of $50,000 of bonds		

Additional Disclosures of Cash Flow Reporting

USEFULNESS OF THE STATEMENT OF CASH FLOWS

OBJECTIVE 9
Understand the usefulness of the statement of cash flows.

"Happiness is a positive cash flow" is certainly true. Although net income provides a long-term measure of a company's success or failure, cash is the lifeblood of a company. Without cash, a company will not survive. For small and newly developing companies, cash flow is the single most important element for survival. Even medium and large companies must control cash flow.

Creditors examine the cash flow statement carefully because they are concerned about being paid. They begin their examination by finding net cash provided by operating activities. A high amount indicates that a company is able to generate sufficient cash from operations to pay its bills without further borrowing. Conversely, a low or negative amount of net cash provided by operating activities indicates that a company may have to borrow or issue equity securities to acquire sufficient cash to pay its bills. Consequently, creditors look for answers to the following questions in the company's cash flow statements.

1. How successful is the company in generating net cash provided by operating activities?
2. What are the trends in net cash flow provided by operating activities over time?
3. What are the major reasons for the positive or negative net cash provided by operating activities?

You should recognize that companies can fail even though they report net income. The difference between net income and net cash provided by operating activities can be substantial. Companies such as **W. T. Grant Company** and **Prime Motor Inn**, for example, reported high net income numbers but negative net cash provided by operating activities. Eventually both companies filed for bankruptcy.

In addition, substantial increases in receivables and/or inventory can explain the difference between positive net income and negative net cash provided by operating activities. For example, in its first year of operations Hu Inc. reported a net income of $80,000. Its net cash provided by operating activities, however, was a negative $95,000, as shown in Illustration 5-31.

ILLUSTRATION 5-31
Negative Net Cash Provided by Operating Activities

HU INC.
NET CASH FLOW FROM OPERATING ACTIVITIES

Cash flows from operating activities		
Net income		$ 80,000
Adjustments to reconcile net income to net cash provided by operating activities:		
Increase in receivables	$ (75,000)	
Increase in inventories	(100,000)	(175,000)
Net cash provided by operating activities		$(95,000)

Hu could easily experience a "cash crunch" because it has its cash tied up in receivables and inventory. If Hu encounters problems in collecting receivables, or if inventory moves slowly or becomes obsolete, its creditors may have difficulty collecting on their loans.

WHAT DO THE NUMBERS MEAN?

CASH IS KING?

Analysts increasingly use cash-flow-based measures of income, such as cash flow provided by operations, instead of or in addition to net income. The reason for the change is that they have been losing faith in accrual-accounting-based net income numbers.

Sadly, these days even cash flow from operations isn't always what it seems to be. For example, in 2002 **WorldCom, Inc.** disclosed that it had improperly capitalized expenses: It moved $3.8 billion of cash outflows from the "Cash from operating activities" section of the cash flow statement to the "Investing activities" section, thereby greatly enhancing cash provided by operating activities.

Similarly, in 2002 **Dynegy, Inc.** restated its cash flow statement for 2001. In doing so, the company removed $300 million tied to its complex natural gas trading operation from operating cash flow and instead put that amount into the financing section—a drop of 37 percent in cash flow from operations.

Source: Henny Sender, "Sadly, These Days Even Cash Flow Isn't Always What It Seems To Be," *Wall Street Journal Online* (May 8, 2002).

Financial Liquidity

Readers of financial statements often assess liquidity by using the **current cash debt coverage ratio**. It indicates whether the company can pay off its current liabilities from its operations in a given year. Illustration 5-32 shows the formula for this ratio.

$$\frac{\text{Net Cash Provided by Operating Activities}}{\text{Average Current Liabilities}} = \text{Current Cash Debt Coverage Ratio}$$

ILLUSTRATION 5-32
Formula for Current Cash Debt Coverage Ratio

The higher the current cash debt coverage ratio, the less likely a company will have liquidity problems. For example, a ratio near 1:1 is good: It indicates that the company can meet all of its current obligations from internally generated cash flow.

Financial Flexibility

The **cash debt coverage ratio** provides information on financial flexibility. It indicates a company's ability to repay its liabilities from net cash provided by operating activities, without having to liquidate the assets employed in its operations. Illustration 5-33 shows the formula for this ratio. (Notice its similarity to the current cash debt coverage ratio. However, because it uses average total liabilities in place of average current liabilities, it takes a somewhat longer-range view.)

$$\frac{\text{Net Cash Provided by Operating Activities}}{\text{Average Total Liabilities}} = \text{Cash Debt Coverage Ratio}$$

ILLUSTRATION 5-33
Formula for Cash Debt Coverage Ratio

The higher this ratio, the less likely the company will experience difficulty in meeting its obligations as they come due. It signals whether the company can pay its debts and survive if external sources of funds become limited or too expensive.

Free Cash Flow

A more sophisticated way to examine a company's financial flexibility is to develop a free cash flow analysis. **Free cash flow** is the amount of discretionary cash flow a company has for purchasing additional investments, retiring its debt, purchasing treasury stock, or simply adding to its liquidity. Financial statement users calculate free cash flow as net cash provided by operating activities less capital expenditures and dividends. Obviously, the greater the amount of free cash flow, the greater the company's amount of financial flexibility.

Questions that a free cash flow analysis answers are:

1 Is the company able to pay its dividends without resorting to external financing?

2 If business operations decline, will the company be able to maintain its needed capital investment?

3 What is the amount of discretionary cash flow that can be used for additional investment, retirement of debt, purchase of treasury stock, or addition to liquidity?

Illustration 5-34 is a free cash flow analysis using the cash flow statement for Nestor Company (shown in Illustration 5-30).

ILLUSTRATION 5-34
Free Cash Flow Computation

NESTOR COMPANY FREE CASH FLOW ANALYSIS	
Net cash provided by operating activities	$411,750
Less: Capital expenditures	(252,500)
Dividends	(19,800)
Free cash flow	$139,450

This analysis shows that Nestor has a positive, and substantial, net cash provided by operating activities of $411,750. Nestor's statement of cash flows reports that the company purchased equipment of $182,500 and land of $70,000 for total capital spending of $252,500.

In a free cash flow analysis, we first deduct capital spending, to indicate it is the least discretionary expenditure a company generally makes. (Without continued efforts to maintain and expand facilities, it is unlikely that Nestor can continue to maintain its competitive position.) We then deduct dividends. Although a company *can* cut its dividend, it usually will do so only in **a financial emergency**. The amount resulting after these deductions is the company's free cash flow. Nestor has more than sufficient cash flow to meet its dividend payment and therefore has satisfactory financial flexibility.

As you can see from looking back at Illustration 5-30, Nestor used its free cash flow to redeem bonds and add to its liquidity. If it finds additional investments that are profitable, it can increase its spending without putting its dividend or basic capital spending in jeopardy. Companies that have strong financial flexibility can take advantage of profitable investments even in tough times. In addition, strong financial flexibility frees companies from worry about survival in poor economic times. In fact, those with strong financial flexibility often fare better in a poor economy because they can take advantage of opportunities that other companies cannot.

QUESTIONS

1. How does information from the balance sheet help users of the financial statements?

2. What is meant by solvency? What information in the balance sheet can be used to assess a company's solvency?

3. A recent financial magazine indicated that the airline industry has poor financial flexibility. What is meant by financial flexibility, and why is it important?

4. Discuss at least two situations in which estimates could affect the usefulness of information in the balance sheet.

5. Safin Company reported an increase in inventories in the past year. Discuss the effect of this change on the current ratio (current assets ÷ current liabilities). What does this tell a statement user about Safin Company's liquidity?

6. What is meant by liquidity? Rank the following assets from one to five in order of liquidity.

(a) Goodwill.

(b) Inventories.

(c) Buildings.

(d) Short-term investments.

(e) Accounts receivable.

7. What are the major limitations of the balance sheet as a source of information?

8. Discuss at least two items that are important to the value of companies like **Intel** or **IBM** but that are not recorded in their balance sheets. What are some reasons why these items are not recorded in the balance sheet?

9. How does separating current assets from property, plant, and equipment in the balance sheet help analysts?

10. In its December 31, 2007, balance sheet Oakley Corporation reported as an asset, "Net notes and accounts receivable, $7,100,000." What other disclosures are necessary?

11. Should available-for-sale securities always be reported as a current asset? Explain.

12. What is the relationship between current assets and current liabilities?

13. The New York Knicks, Inc. sold 10,000 season tickets at $2,000 each. By December 31, 2007, 18 of the 40 home games had been played. What amount should be reported as a current liability at December 31, 2007?

14. What is working capital? How does working capital relate to the operating cycle?

15. In what section of the balance sheet should the following items appear, and what balance sheet terminology would you use?

(a) Treasury stock (recorded at cost).

(b) Checking account at bank.

(c) Land (held as an investment).

(d) Sinking fund.

(e) Unamortized premium on bonds payable.

(f) Copyrights.

(g) Pension fund assets.

(h) Premium on capital stock.

(i) Long-term investments (pledged against bank loans payable).

16. Where should the following items be shown on the balance sheet, if shown at all?

(a) Allowance for doubtful accounts receivable.

(b) Merchandise held on consignment.

(c) Advances received on sales contract.

(d) Cash surrender value of life insurance.

(e) Land.

(f) Merchandise out on consignment.

(g) Franchises.

(h) Accumulated depreciation of plant and equipment.

(i) Materials in transit—purchased f.o.b. destination.

17. State the generally accepted accounting principle applicable to the balance sheet valuation of each of the following assets.

(a) Trade accounts receivable.

(b) Land.

(c) Inventories.

(d) Trading securities (common stock of other companies).

(e) Prepaid expenses.

18. Refer to the definition of assets on page 173. Discuss how a leased building might qualify as an asset of the lessee (tenant) under this definition.

19. Christine Agazzi says, "Retained earnings should be reported as an asset, since it is earnings which are reinvested in the business." How would you respond to Agazzi?

20. The creditors of Nick Anderson Company agree to accept promissory notes for the amount of its indebtedness with a proviso that two-thirds of the annual profits must be applied to their liquidation. How should these notes be reported on the balance sheet of the issuing company? Give a reason for your answer.

21. What are some of the techniques of disclosure for the balance sheet?

22. What is a "Summary of Significant Accounting Policies"?

23. What types of contractual obligations must be disclosed in great detail in the notes to the balance sheet? Why do you think these detailed provisions should be disclosed?

24. What is the profession's recommendation in regard to the use of the term "surplus"? Explain.

25. What is the purpose of a statement of cash flows? How does it differ from a balance sheet and an income statement?

26. The net income for the year for Won Long, Inc. is $750,000, but the statement of cash flows reports that the cash provided by operating activities is $640,000. What might account for the difference?

27. Net income for the year for Jenkins, Inc. was $750,000, but the statement of cash flows reports that cash provided by operating activities was $860,000. What might account for the difference?

28. Differentiate between operating activities, investing activities, and financing activities.

29. Each of the following items must be considered in preparing a statement of cash flows. Indicate where each item is to be reported in the statement, if at all. Assume that net income is reported as $90,000.

(a) Accounts receivable increased from $32,000 to $39,000 from the beginning to the end of the year.

(b) During the year, 10,000 shares of preferred stock with a par value of $100 a share were issued at $115 per share.

(c) Depreciation expense amounted to $14,000, and bond premium amortization amounted to $5,000.

(d) Land increased from $10,000 to $30,000.

30. Marker Co. has net cash provided by operating activities of $900,000. Its average current liabilities for the period are $1,000,000, and its average total liabilities are $1,500,000. Comment on the company's liquidity and financial flexibility, given this information.

31. Net income for the year for Hatfield, Inc. was $750,000, but the statement of cash flows reports that cash provided by operating activities was $860,000. Hatfield also reported capital expenditures of $75,000 and paid dividends in the amount of $20,000. Compute Hatfield's free cash flow.

32. What is the purpose of a free cash flow analysis?

C H A P T E R S I X

CASH AND RECEIVABLES

No-Tell Nortel

Recently, **Nortel** announced that its net income for 2003 was really half what it originally reported. In addition, the company had understated net income for 2002. How could this happen? One reason: It appears that Nortel set up "cookie jar" reserves, using the allowance for doubtful accounts as the cookie jar. As the following chart shows, in 2002 Nortel overestimated the amount of bad debt expense (with a sizable allowance for doubtful accounts). Then, in 2003 Nortel slashed the amount of bad debt expense, even though the total money owed by customers remained nearly unchanged. In 2002, its allowance was 19 percent of receivables compared to 10 percent in 2003—quite a difference.

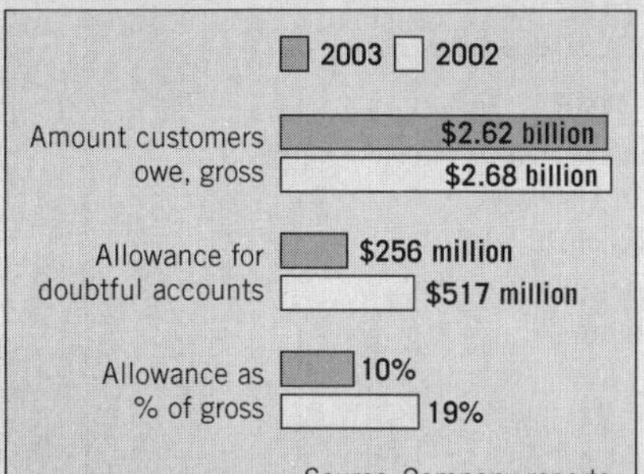

Source: Company reports

It is difficult to determine if the allowance was too high in 2002 or too low in 2003, or both. Whatever the case, the use of the allowance cookie jar permitted Nortel to report higher operating margins and net income in 2003.

This analysis suggests the importance of looking carefully at the amount of bad debt expense reported in annual reports. Sometimes companies use it to artificially *decrease* income. Others understate bad debt expense to *increase* income. For example, analysts have noted that many large hospitals, such as **Tenet Healthcare** and **HCA**, may be facing increasing uncollectible accounts that are presently not fully reflected in their balance sheets.

Adapted from J. Weil, "At Nortel, Warning Signs Existed Months Ago, *Wall Street Journal* (May 18, 2004), p. C3; and B. McLean, "Reality Checkup," *Fortune* (January 12, 2004), p. 140.

Learning Objectives

After studying this chapter, you should be able to:

1. Identify items considered as cash.
2. Indicate how to report cash and related items.
3. Define receivables and identify the different types of receivables.
4. Explain accounting issues related to recognition of accounts receivable.
5. Explain accounting issues related to valuation of accounts receivable.
6. Explain accounting issues related to recognition of notes receivable.
7. Explain accounting issues related to valuation of notes receivable.
8. Explain accounting issues related to disposition of accounts and notes receivable.
9. Describe how to report and analyze receivables.

PREVIEW OF CHAPTER 6

As our opening story indicates, estimating the collectibility of accounts receivable has important implications for accurate reporting of operating profits, net income, and assets. In this chapter we discuss cash and receivables—two assets that are important to companies as diverse as **Nortel** and **Tenet Healthcare**. The content and organization of the chapter are as follows.

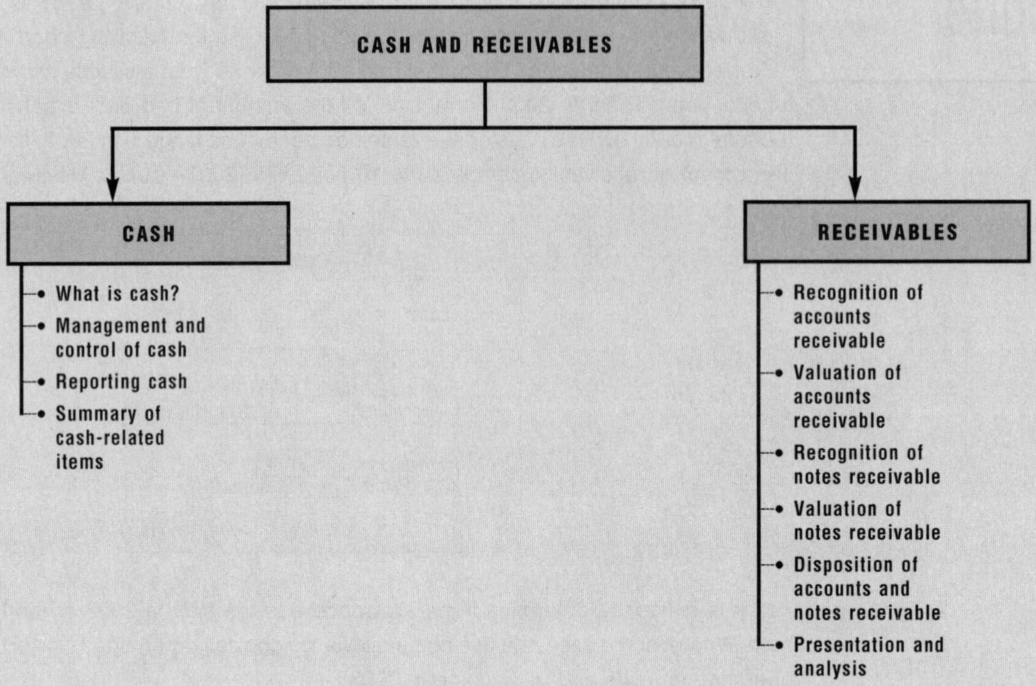

SECTION 1 | *CASH*

WHAT IS CASH?

OBJECTIVE 1
Identify items considered cash.

Cash, the most liquid of assets, is the standard medium of exchange and the basis for measuring and accounting for all other items. Companies generally classify cash as a current asset. Cash consists of coin, currency, and available funds on deposit at the bank. Negotiable instruments such as money orders, certified checks, cashier's checks, personal checks, and bank drafts are also viewed as cash. What about savings accounts? Banks do have the legal right to demand notice before withdrawal. But, because banks rarely demand prior notice, savings accounts nevertheless are considered cash.

Some negotiable instruments provide small investors with an opportunity to earn interest. These items, more appropriately classified as temporary investments than as cash, include money market funds, money market savings certificates, certificates of deposit (CDs), and similar types of deposits and "short-term paper."[1] These securities usually contain restrictions or penalties on their conversion to cash. Money market funds that provide checking account privileges, however, are usually classified as cash.

Certain items present classification problems: Companies treat **postdated checks and I.O.U.s** as receivables. They also treat **travel advances** as receivables if collected from employees or deducted from their salaries. Otherwise, companies classify the travel advance as a prepaid expense. **Postage stamps on hand** are classified as part of office supplies inventory or as a prepaid expense. Because **petty cash funds and change funds are used** to meet current operating expenses and liquidate current liabilities, companies include these funds in current assets as cash.

MANAGEMENT AND CONTROL OF CASH

Cash is the asset most susceptible to improper diversion and use. Management faces two problems in accounting for cash transactions: (1) to establish proper controls to prevent any unauthorized transactions by officers or employees, and (2) to provide information necessary to properly manage cash on hand and cash transactions. Yet even with sophisticated control devices, errors can and do happen. For example, the *Wall Street Journal* ran a story entitled "A $7.8 Million Error Has a Happy Ending for a Horrified Bank." The story described how **Manufacturers Hanover Trust Co.** mistakenly overpaid about $7.8 million in cash dividends to its stockholders. (As implied in the headline, most stockholders returned the monies.)

To safeguard cash and to ensure the accuracy of the accounting records for cash, companies need effective **internal control** over cash. Provisions of the Sarbanes-Oxley Act of 2002 call for enhanced efforts to increase the quality of internal control (for cash and other assets). Such efforts are expected to result in improved financial reporting.

However, the increasing volume of transactions conducted with the swipe of a debit or credit card presents new challenges to the effort to maintain control over liquid assets. As one writer noted, "In 5,000 years there have been only four times that we have changed the way we pay—there was barter to coinage; coins to paper; paper to checks; and then cards. Just since 1995, the amount of stuff that American consumers buy using plastic has increased 430 percent."[2] In 2003, for the first time, Americans bought more using cards than cash.[3] In addition, electronic commerce conducted over the Internet continues to grow.

---

[1]A variety of "short-term paper" is available for investment. For example, **certificates of deposit** (CDs) represent formal evidence of indebtedness, issued by a bank, subject to withdrawal under the specific terms of the instrument. Issued in $1,000 to $100,000 denominations, they have maturities anywhere from 7 days to 10 years and generally pay interest at the short-term interest rate in effect at the date of issuance.

Banks and savings and loan associations issue **money-market savings certificates** in denominations of $10,000 or more for 6-month periods (6 to 48 months). The interest rate is tied to the 26-week Treasury bill rate.

In **money-market funds**, a variation of the mutual fund, the mix of Treasury bills and commercial paper making up the fund's portfolio determines the yield. Most money-market funds require an initial minimum investment of $1,000; many allow withdrawal by check or wire transfer.

Treasury bills are U.S. government obligations generally issued with 4-, 13-, and 26-week maturities; they are sold in $10,000 denominations at weekly government auctions.

Commercial paper is a short-term note issued by corporations with good credit ratings. Often issued in $5,000 and $10,000 denominations, these notes generally yield a higher rate than Treasury bills.

[2]K. Brooker, "Just One Word: Plastic," *Fortune* (February 23, 2004), p. 130.

[3]Ibid, p. 132. Non-U.S. consumers are even bigger users of digital cash than U.S. consumers. For example, non-check payments in Japan and Europe comprise over 70 percent of all payment transactions. U.S. consumers' continued use of checks and cash for payment raises fraud concerns, though, as duplication technology makes it easier to forge checks and currency.

Each of these trends contributes to the shift from cold cash to digital cash, and poses new challenges for the control of cash.

REPORTING CASH

OBJECTIVE 2
Indicate how to report cash and related items.

Although the reporting of cash is relatively straightforward, a number of issues merit special attention. These issues relate to the reporting of:

1. Restricted cash.
2. Bank overdrafts.
3. Cash equivalents.

Restricted Cash

Petty cash, payroll, and dividend funds are examples of cash set aside for a particular purpose. In most situations, these fund balances are not material. Therefore, companies do not segregate them from cash in the financial statements. When material in amount, companies segregate **restricted cash** from "regular" cash for reporting purposes. Companies classify restricted cash either in the current assets or in the long-term assets section, depending on the date of availability or disbursement. Classification in the current section is appropriate if using the cash for payment of existing or maturing obligations (within a year or the operating cycle, whichever is longer). On the other hand, companies show the restricted cash in the long-term section of the balance sheet if holding the cash for a longer period of time.

Cash classified in the long-term section is frequently set aside for plant expansion, retirement of long-term debt or, in the case of **International Thoroughbred Breeders**, for entry fee deposits.

ILLUSTRATION 6-1
Disclosure of Restricted Cash

International Thoroughbred Breeders

Restricted cash and investments (See Note) $3,730,000

Note: Restricted Cash. At year-end, the Company had approximately $3,730,000, which was classified as restricted cash and investments. These funds are primarily cash received from horsemen for nomination and entry fees to be applied to upcoming racing meets, purse winnings held in trust for horsemen, and amounts held for unclaimed ticketholder winnings.

Banks and other lending institutions often require customers to maintain minimum cash balances in checking or savings accounts. The SEC defines these minimum balances, called **compensating balances**, as "that portion of any demand deposit (or any time deposit or certificate of deposit) maintained by a corporation which constitutes support for existing borrowing arrangements of the corporation with a lending institution. Such arrangements would include both outstanding borrowings and the assurance of future credit availability."[4]

[4] *Accounting Series Release No. 148*, "Amendments to Regulations S-X and Related Interpretations and Guidelines Regarding the Disclosure of Compensating Balances and Short-Term Borrowing Arrangements," Securities and Exchange Commission (November 13, 1973). The SEC defines 15 percent of liquid assets (current cash balances, whether restricted or not, plus marketable securities) as being material, thereby requiring additional reporting.

To avoid misleading investors about the amount of cash available to meet recurring obligations, the SEC recommends that companies state separately **legally restricted deposits** held as compensating balances against **short-term** borrowing arrangements among the "Cash and cash equivalent items" in current assets. Companies should classify separately restricted deposits held as compensating balances against **long-term** borrowing arrangements as noncurrent assets in either the investments or other assets sections, using a caption such as "Cash on deposit maintained as compensating balance." In cases where compensating balance arrangements exist without agreements that restrict the use of cash amounts shown on the balance sheet, companies should describe the arrangements and the amounts involved in the notes.

INTERNATIONAL INSIGHT

Among other potential restrictions, companies need to determine whether any of the cash in accounts outside the U.S. is restricted by regulations against exportation of currency.

Bank Overdrafts

Bank overdrafts occur when a company writes a check for more than the amount in its cash account. Companies should report bank overdrafts in the current liabilities section, adding them to the amount reported as accounts payable. If material, companies should disclose these items separately, either on the face of the balance sheet or in the related notes.[5]

Bank overdrafts are generally not offset against the cash account. A major exception is when available cash is present in another account in the same bank on which the overdraft occurred. Offsetting in this case is required.

Cash Equivalents

A current classification that has become popular is "Cash and cash equivalents."[6] **Cash equivalents** are short-term, highly liquid investments that are both (a) readily convertible to known amounts of cash, and (b) so near their maturity that they present insignificant risk of changes in interest rates. Generally, only investments with original maturities of three months or less qualify under these definitions. Examples of cash equivalents are Treasury bills, commercial paper, and money market funds. Some companies combine cash with temporary investments on the balance sheet. In these cases, they describe the amount of the temporary investments either parenthetically or in the notes.

wiley.com/college/kieso

Additional Disclosures of Restricted Cash

SUMMARY OF CASH-RELATED ITEMS

Cash and cash equivalents include the medium of exchange and most negotiable instruments. If the item cannot be quickly converted to coin or currency, a company separately classifies it as an investment, receivable, or prepaid expense. Companies segregate and classify cash that is unavailable for payment of currently maturing liabilities in the long-term assets section. Illustration 6-2 summarizes the classification of cash-related items.

[5]Bank overdrafts usually occur because of a simple oversight by the company writing the check. Banks often expect companies to have overdrafts from time to time and therefore negotiate a fee as payment for this possible occurrence. However, at one time, **E. F. Hutton** (a large brokerage firm) began intentionally overdrawing its accounts by astronomical amounts—on some days exceeding $1 billion—thus obtaining interest-free loans that it could invest. Because the amounts were so large and fees were not negotiated in advance, E. F. Hutton came under criminal investigation for its actions.

[6]*Accounting Trends and Techniques—2004*, indicates that approximately 6 percent of the companies surveyed use the caption "Cash," 83 percent use "Cash and cash equivalents," and 4 percent use a caption such as "Cash and marketable securities" or similar terminology.

ILLUSTRATION 6-2
Classification of Cash-Related Items

Classification of Cash, Cash Equivalents, and Noncash Items

Item	Classification	Comment
Cash	Cash	If unrestricted, report as cash. If restricted, identify and classify as current and noncurrent assets.
Petty cash and change funds	Cash	Report as cash.
Short-term paper	Cash equivalents	Investments with maturity of less than 3 months, often combined with cash.
Short-term paper	Temporary investments	Investments with maturity of 3 to 12 months.
Postdated checks and IOU's	Receivables	Assumed to be collectible.
Travel advances	Receivables	Assumed to be collected from employees or deducted from their salaries.
Postage on hand (as stamps or in postage meters)	Prepaid expenses	May also be classified as office supplies inventory.
Bank overdrafts	Current liability	If right of offset exists, reduce cash.
Compensating balances	Cash separately classified as a deposit maintained as compensating balance	Classify as current or noncurrent in the balance sheet. Disclose separately in notes details of the arrangement.

WHAT DO THE NUMBERS MEAN?

TOO MUCH OF A GOOD THING?

Can it ever be a bad thing to have too much cash on hand? Maybe so. As the data in the following table indicate, **General Motors** and some other major companies have been stockpiling cash at levels not recently seen.

Company	Total Cash (in billions)
General Motors	$54.8
Berkshire Hathaway	$36.0
Ford Motor Company	$33.6
Hewlett-Packard	$13.9
Intel	$13.5

Given the low returns on cash, investors may ask why companies maintain such large cash balances. Some companies with good growth prospects plan to use these resources to fuel growth. They intend to step up spending on property, plant, and equipment or on research and development. Or they may hold cash in order to acquire other companies that have growth prospects. However, without good use for stockpiled cash, stockholders would be better served by a payout in the form of a cash dividend.

SECTION 2 *RECEIVABLES*

Receivables are claims held against customers and others for money, goods, or services. For financial statement purposes, companies classify receivables as either **current** (short-term) or **noncurrent** (long-term). Companies expect to collect **current receivables** within a year or during the current operating cycle, whichever is longer. They classify all other receivables as **noncurrent**. Receivables are further classified in the balance sheet as either trade or nontrade receivables.

OBJECTIVE 3
Define receivables and identify the different types of receivables.

Customers often owe a company amounts for goods bought or services rendered. A company may subclassify these **trade receivables**, usually the most significant item it possesses, into accounts receivable and notes receivable. **Accounts receivable** are oral promises of the purchaser to pay for goods and services sold. They represent "open accounts" resulting from short-term extensions of credit. A company normally collects them within 30 to 60 days. **Notes receivable** are written promises to pay a certain sum of money on a specified future date. They may arise from sales, financing, or other transactions. Notes may be short-term or long-term.

Nontrade receivables arise from a variety of transactions. Some examples of nontrade receivables are:

1 Advances to officers and employees.
2 Advances to subsidiaries.
3 Deposits paid to cover potential damages or losses.
4 Deposits paid as a guarantee of performance or payment.
5 Dividends and interest receivable.
6 Claims against:
   (a) Insurance companies for casualties sustained.
   (b) Defendants under suit.
   (c) Governmental bodies for tax refunds.
   (d) Common carriers for damaged or lost goods.
   (e) Creditors for returned, damaged, or lost goods.
   (f) Customers for returnable items (crates, containers, etc.).

Because of the peculiar nature of nontrade receivables, companies generally report them as separate items in the balance sheet. Illustration 6-3 shows the reporting of trade and non-trade receivables in the balance sheets of **Adolph Coors Company** and **Seaboard Corporation**.

ILLUSTRATION 6-3
Receivables Balance Sheet Presentations

Adolph Coors Company
(in thousands)

Current assets	
Cash and cash equivalents	$160,038
Short-term investments	96,190
Accounts and notes receivable	
Trade, less allowance for doubtful accounts of $299	106,962
Subsidiaries	11,896
Other, less allowance for certain claims of $584	7,751
Inventories	102,660
Other supplies, less allowance for obsolete supplies of $3,968	27,729
Prepaid expenses and other assets	12,848
Deferred tax asset	22,917
Total current assets	$548,991

Seaboard Corporation
(in thousands)

Current assets		
Cash and cash equivalents		$ 19,760
Short-term investments		91,375
Receivables		
Trade	$194,966	
Due from foreign affiliates	36,662	
Other	41,816	
		273,444
Allowance for doubtful receivables		(29,801)
Net receivables		243,643
Inventories		218,030
Deferred income taxes		14,132
Prepaid expenses and deposits		23,760
Total current assets		$610,700

The basic issues in accounting for accounts and notes receivable are the same: **recognition, valuation**, and **disposition**. We discuss these basic issues for accounts and notes receivable next.

RECOGNITION OF ACCOUNTS RECEIVABLE

OBJECTIVE 4
Explain accounting issues related to recognition of accounts receivable.

In most receivables transactions, the amount to be recognized is the exchange price between the two parties. **The exchange price is the amount due from the debtor** (a customer or a borrower). Some type of business document, often an invoice, serves as evidence of the exchange price. Two factors may complicate the measurement of the exchange price: (1) the availability of discounts (trade and cash discounts), and (2) the length of time between the sale and the due date of payments (the interest element).

Trade Discounts

Prices may be subject to a trade or quantity discount. Companies use such **trade discounts** to avoid frequent changes in catalogs, to alter prices for different quantities purchased, or to hide the true invoice price from competitors.

Trade discounts are commonly quoted in percentages. For example, say your textbook has a list price of $90, and the publisher sells it to college bookstores for list less a 30 percent trade discount. The publisher then records the receivable at $63 per textbook. The publisher, per normal practice, simply deducts the trade discount from the list price and bills the customer net.

As another example, **Maxwell House** at one time sold a 10-ounce jar of its instant coffee listing at $5.85 to supermarkets for $5.05, a trade discount of approximately 14 percent. The supermarkets in turn sold the instant coffee for $5.20 per jar. Maxwell House records the receivable and related sales revenue at $5.05 per jar, not $5.85.

Cash Discounts (Sales Discounts)

Companies offer **cash discounts (sales discounts)** to induce prompt payment. Cash discounts generally read in terms such as 2/10, n/30 (2 percent if paid within 10 days, gross amount due in 30 days), or 2/10, E.O.M., net 30, E.O.M. (2 percent if paid any time before the tenth day of the following month, with full payment received by the thirtieth of the following month).

Companies usually take sales discounts unless their cash is severely limited. Why? A company that receives a 1 percent reduction in the sales price for payment within 10 days, total payment due within 30 days, effectively earns 18.25 percent (.01 ÷ [20/365]), or at least avoids that rate of interest cost.

Companies usually record sales and related sales discount transactions by entering the receivable and sale at the gross amount. Under this method, companies recognize sales discounts only when they receive payment within the discount period. The income statement shows sales discounts as a deduction from sales to arrive at net sales.

Some contend that sales discounts not taken reflect penalties added to an established price to encourage prompt payment. That is, the seller offers sales on account at a slightly higher price than if selling for cash. The cash discount offered offsets the increase. Thus, customers who pay within the discount period actually purchase at the cash price. Those who pay after expiration of the discount period pay a penalty for the delay—an amount in excess of the cash price. Per this reasoning, companies record sales and receivables net. They subsequently debit any discounts not taken to Accounts Receivable and credit to Sales Discounts Forfeited. The entries in Illustration 6-4 show the difference between the gross and net methods.

ILLUSTRATION 6-4
Entries under Gross and Net Methods of Recording Cash (Sales) Discounts

Gross Method			Net Method		
Sales of $10,000, terms 2/10, n/30					
Accounts Receivable	10,000		Accounts Receivable	9,800	
Sales		10,000	Sales		9,800
Payment of $4,000 received within discount period					
Cash	3,920		Cash	3,920	
Sales Discounts	80		Accounts Receivable		3,920
Accounts Receivable		4,000			
Payment of $6,000 received after discount period					
Cash	6,000		Accounts Receivable	120	
Accounts Receivable		6,000	Sales Discounts Forfeited		120
			Cash	6,000	
			Accounts Receivable		6,000

If using the gross method, a company reports sales discounts as a deduction from sales in the income statement. Proper matching dictates that the company also reasonably estimates the expected discounts to be taken and charge that amount against sales. If using the net method, a company considers Sales Discounts Forfeited as an "Other revenue" item.[7]

Theoretically, the recognition of Sales Discounts Forfeited is correct. The receivable is stated closer to its realizable value, and the net sales figure measures the revenue earned from the sale. As a practical matter, however, companies seldom use the net method because it requires additional analysis and bookkeeping. For example, the net method requires adjusting entries to record sales discounts forfeited on accounts receivable that have passed the discount period.

Nonrecognition of Interest Element

Ideally, a company should measure receivables in terms of their present value, that is, the discounted value of the cash to be received in the future. When expected cash receipts require a waiting period, the receivable face amount is not worth the amount that the company ultimately receives.

To illustrate, assume that **Best Buy** makes a sale on account for $1,000 with payment due in four months. The applicable annual rate of interest is 12 percent, and payment is made at the end of four months. The present value of that receivable is not $1,000 but $961.54 ($1,000 × .96154). In other words, the $1,000 Best Buy receives four months from now is not the same as the $1,000 received today.

Theoretically, any revenue after the period of sale is interest revenue. In practice, companies ignore interest revenue related to accounts receivable because the amount of the discount is not usually material in relation to the net income for the period. The profession specifically excludes from present value considerations "receivables arising from transactions with customers in the normal course of business which are due in customary trade terms not exceeding approximately one year."[8]

UNDERLYING CONCEPTS

Materiality means it must make a difference to a decision maker. The FASB believes that present value concepts can be ignored for short-term receivables.

VALUATION OF ACCOUNTS RECEIVABLE

Reporting of receivables involves (1) classification and (2) valuation on the balance sheet. Classification involves determining the length of time each receivable will be outstanding. Companies classify receivables intended to be collected within a year or the operating cycle, whichever is longer, as current. All other receivables are classified as long-term.

[7] To the extent that discounts not taken reflect a short-term financing, some argue that companies could use an interest revenue account to record these amounts.

[8] "Interest on Receivables and Payables," *Opinions of the Accounting Principles Board No. 21* (New York: AICPA, 1971), par. 3(a).

OBJECTIVE 5
Explain accounting issues related to valuation of accounts receivable.

Companies value and report short-term receivables at net realizable value—the net amount they expect to receive in cash. Determining net realizable value requires estimating both uncollectible receivables and any returns or allowances to be granted.

Uncollectible Accounts Receivable

As one revered accountant aptly noted, the credit manager's idea of heaven probably would be a place where everyone (eventually) paid his or her debts.[9] The recent experiences of **Circuit City**, **Sears** (now **Sears Holdings**), **Target**, and **Kohls**, as shown in Illustration 6-5, indicate the importance of credit sales for many companies. Note that for Sears, increased bad debt expense led to a lower stock price, which prompted Sears to sell its credit card portfolio to **Citigroup** in 2003.

ILLUSTRATION 6-5
Credit and Its Costs

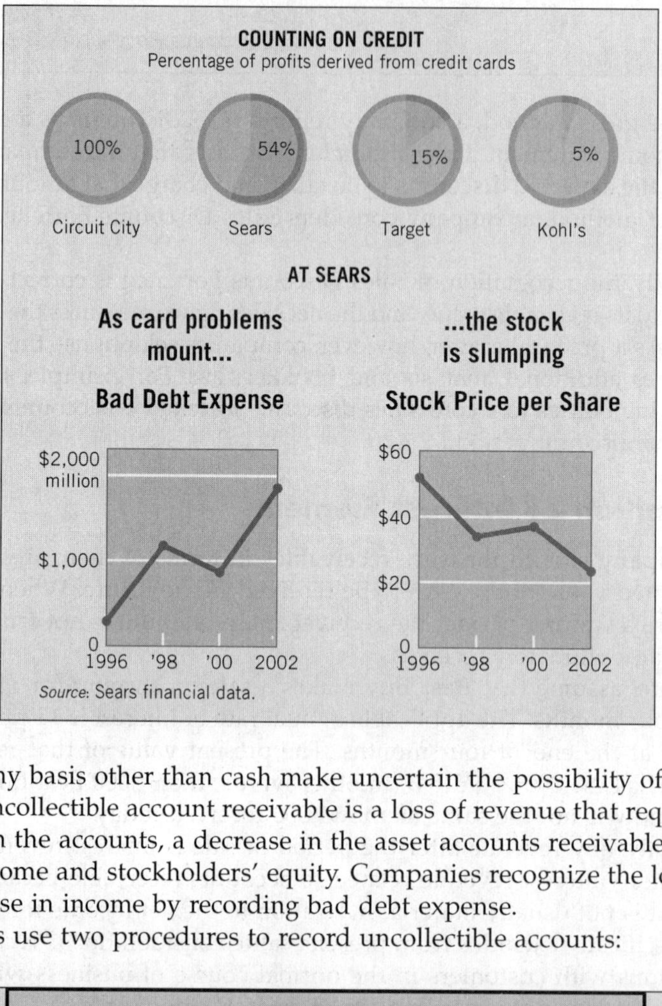

Sales on any basis other than cash make uncertain the possibility of collecting the account. An uncollectible account receivable is a loss of revenue that requires, through proper entry in the accounts, a decrease in the asset accounts receivable and a related decrease in income and stockholders' equity. Companies recognize the loss in revenue and the decrease in income by recording bad debt expense.

Companies use two procedures to record uncollectible accounts:

METHODS FOR RECORDING UNCOLLECTIBLES

1 *DIRECT WRITE-OFF METHOD.* No entry is made until a specific account has definitely been established as uncollectible. Then the loss is recorded by crediting Accounts Receivable and debiting Bad Debt Expense.

2 *ALLOWANCE METHOD.* An estimate is made of the expected uncollectible accounts from all sales made on account or from the total of outstanding receivables. This estimate is entered as an expense and an indirect reduction in accounts receivable (via an increase in the allowance account) in the period in which the sale is recorded.

[9]William J. Vatter, *Managerial Accounting* (Englewood Cliffs, N.J.: Prentice-Hall, 1950), p. 60.

The **direct write-off method** records the bad debt in the period in which a company determines that it cannot collect a specific receivable. In contrast, the **allowance method** enters the expense on an estimated basis in the accounting period in which the sales on account occur.

Supporters of the **direct write-off method** (which is used for tax purposes) contend that it records facts, not estimates. It assumes that a good account receivable resulted from each sale, and that later events revealed certain accounts to be uncollectible and worthless. From a practical standpoint this method is simple and convenient to apply. But the direct write-off method is theoretically deficient: It usually fails to match costs with revenues of the period. Nor does it result in receivables being stated at estimated realizable value on the balance sheet. **As a result, using the direct write-off method is not considered appropriate, except when the amount uncollectible is immaterial.**

Advocates of the **allowance method** believe that companies should record bad debt expense in the same period as the sale, to properly match expenses and revenues and to achieve a proper carrying value for accounts receivable. They contend that although estimates are involved, companies can predict the percentage of uncollectible receivables from past experiences, present market conditions, and an analysis of the outstanding balances. Many companies set their credit policies to provide for a certain percentage of uncollectible accounts. (In fact, many feel that failure to reach that percentage means that they are losing sales due to overly restrictive credit policies.)

The FASB considers the collectibility of receivables a loss contingency. Thus, the allowance method is appropriate in situations where it is probable that an asset has been impaired and that the amount of the loss can be reasonably estimated.[10]

A receivable is a prospective cash inflow. The probability of its collection must be considered in valuing cash flows. These estimates normally are based either on (1) percentage of sales or (2) outstanding receivables.

Percentage-of-Sales (Income Statement) Approach

UNDERLYING CONCEPTS

The percentage-of-sales method illustrates the matching principle, which relates expenses to revenues earned.

If there is a fairly stable relationship between previous years' credit sales and bad debts, then a company can convert that relationship into a percentage and use it to determine this year's bad debt expense.

The **percentage-of-sales approach** matches costs with revenues because it relates the charge to the period in which a company records the sale. To illustrate, assume that Chad Shumway Corp. estimates from past experience that about 2 percent of credit sales become uncollectible. If Chad Shumway has credit sales of $400,000 in 2007, it records bad debt expense using the percentage-of-sales method as follows.

Bad Debt Expense	8,000	
Allowance for Doubtful Accounts		8,000

The Allowance for Doubtful Accounts is a valuation account (i.e., a contra asset), subtracted from trade receivables on the balance sheet.[11] The amount of bad debt expense and the related credit to the allowance account are unaffected by any balance currently existing in the allowance account. Because the bad debt expense estimate is related to a nominal account (Sales), any balance in the allowance is ignored. Therefore, the percentage of sales method achieves a proper matching of cost and revenues. This method is frequently referred to as the **income statement approach**.

Percentage-of-Receivables (Balance Sheet) Approach

Using past experience, a company can estimate the percentage of its outstanding receivables that will become uncollectible, without identifying specific accounts. This procedure provides a reasonably accurate estimate of the receivables' realizable value. But,

---

[10]"Accounting for Contingencies," *Statement of Financial Accounting Standards No. 5* (Stamford, Conn.: FASB, 1975), par. 8.

[11]The account description employed for the allowance account is usually Allowance for Doubtful Accounts or simply Allowance. *Accounting Trends and Techniques—2004*, for example, indicates that approximately 86 percent of the companies surveyed used "allowance" in their description.

it does not fit the concept of matching cost and revenues. Rather, it simply reports receivables in the balance sheet at net realizable value. Hence it is referred to as the **percentage-of-receivables** (or **balance sheet) approach.**

Companies may apply this method using one **composite rate** that reflects an estimate of the uncollectible receivables. Or, companies may set up an **aging schedule** of accounts receivable, which applies a different percentage based on past experience to the various age categories. An aging schedule also identifies which accounts require special attention by indicating the extent to which certain accounts are past due. The following schedule of Wilson & Co. is an example.

ILLUSTRATION 6-6
Accounts Receivable Aging Schedule

WILSON & CO.
AGING SCHEDULE

Name of Customer	Balance Dec. 31	Under 60 days	61–90 days	91–120 days	Over 120 days
Western Stainless Steel Corp.	$ 98,000	$ 80,000	$18,000		
Brockway Steel Company	320,000	320,000			
Freeport Sheet & Tube Co.	55,000				$55,000
Allegheny Iron Works	74,000	60,000		$14,000	
	$547,000	$460,000	$18,000	$14,000	$55,000

Summary

Age	Amount	Percentage Estimated to be Uncollectible	Required Balance in Allowance
Under 60 days old	$460,000	4%	$18,400
61–90 days old	18,000	15%	2,700
91–120 days old	14,000	20%	2,800
Over 120 days	55,000	25%	13,750
Year-end balance of allowance for doubtful accounts			$37,650

Wilson reports bad debt expense of $37,650 for this year, assuming that no balance existed in the allowance account.

To change the illustration slightly, **assume that the allowance account had a credit balance of $800 before adjustment**. In this case, Wilson adds $36,850 ($37,650 – $800) to the allowance account, and makes the following entry.

Bad Debt Expense	36,850	
Allowance for Doubtful Accounts		36,850

Wilson therefore states the balance in the Allowance account at $37,650. **If the Allowance balance before adjustment had a debit balance of $200,** then Wilson records bad debt expense of $37,850 ($37,650 desired balance + $200 debit balance). In the percentage-of-receivables method, Wilson **cannot ignore** the balance in the allowance account, because the percentage is related to a real account (Accounts Receivable).

Companies usually do not prepare an aging schedule to determine bad debt expense. Rather, they prepare it as a control device to determine the composition of receivables and to identify delinquent accounts. Companies base the estimated loss percentage developed for each category on previous loss experience and the advice of credit department personnel.

wiley.com/college/kieso

Tutorial on Recording Uncollectible Accounts

Whether using a composite rate or an aging schedule, the primary objective of the percentage of outstanding receivables method for financial statement purposes is to report receivables in the balance sheet at net realizable value. However, it is deficient in that it may not match the bad debt expense to the period in which the sale takes place.

The allowance for doubtful accounts as a percentage of receivables will vary, depending on the industry and the economic climate. Companies such as **Eastman Kodak**, **General Electric**, and **Monsanto** have recorded allowances ranging from $3 to $6 per

$100 of accounts receivable. Other large companies, such as **CPC International** ($1.48), **Texaco** ($1.23), and **USX Corp.** ($0.78), have had bad debt allowances of less than $1.50 per $100. At the other extreme are hospitals that allow for $15 to $20 per $100 of accounts receivable.[12]

WHAT DO THE NUMBERS MEAN?

GOING FOR BROKE

The start of the new millennium has been a tough one for companies and their investors, creditors, and employees. **Enron**, **Kmart**, and **WorldCom** all declared bankruptcy—with WorldCom representing the largest bankruptcy ever. The trend seems to be continuing.

It is not surprising that banks and other creditors are raising their lending standards to guard against future loan defaults. Even so, some question whether creditors have set up reasonable bad debt allowances to ensure that financial performance is reported accurately. Indeed, one recent analysis for hospitals (mentioned in our opening story) indicates that additional bad debt expense needed to properly reflect future write-offs could result in an earnings hit of as much as 18 percent for some hospitals. That will be tough medicine for these companies to swallow.

Source: Adapted from: Julie Creswell, "First Going for Broke," *Fortune* (February 18, 2002), pp. 24–25; Bethany McLean, "Reality Check-up," *Fortune* (January 12, 2004), pp. 140.

In summary, the percentage-of-receivables method results in a more accurate valuation of receivables on the balance sheet. From a matching viewpoint, the percentage-of-sales approach provides the better results. Illustration 6-7 relates these methods to the basic theory.

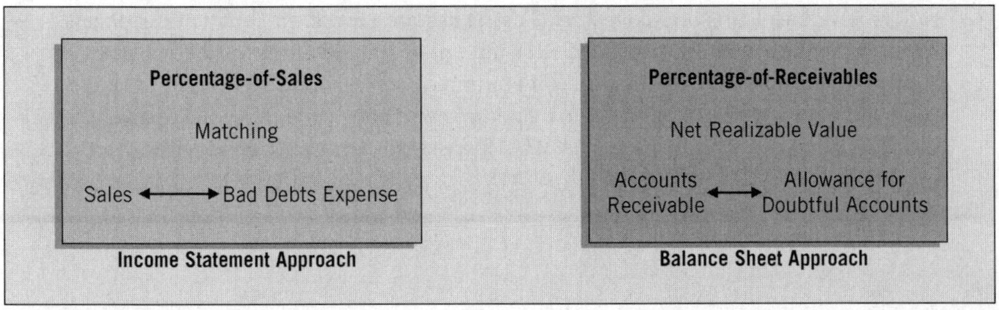

ILLUSTRATION 6-7
Comparison of Methods for Estimating Uncollectibles

The account title employed for the allowance account is usually Allowance for Doubtful Accounts or simply Allowance.

[12]A U.S. Department of Commerce study indicated, as a general rule, the following relationships between the age of accounts receivable and their uncollectibility.

30 days or less	4% uncollectible
31–60 days	10% uncollectible
61–90 days	17% uncollectible
91–120 days	26% uncollectible

After 120 days, an approximate 3–4 percent increase in uncollectibles for every 30 days outstanding occurs for the remainder of the first year.

INTERNATIONAL INSIGHT

The U.S. has criticized some countries' use of excess reserves to manage income. These same countries would argue that **Suntrust Banks'** accounting for loan losses is a similar practice.

Regardless of the method chosen, determining the expense associated with uncollectible accounts requires a large degree of judgment. Recent concern exists that, similar to **Nortel** in our opening story, some banks use this judgment to manage earnings. By overestimating the amounts of uncollectible loans in a good earnings year, the bank can "save for a rainy day" in a future period. In future (less-profitable) periods, banks can reduce the overly conservative allowance for loan loss account to increase earnings. In this regard, the SEC brought action against **Suntrust Banks,** requiring a reversal of $100 million of bad debt expense. This reversal increased aftertax profit by $61 million.[13]

Collection of Accounts Receivable Written Off

When a company determines a particular account receivable to be uncollectible, it removes the balance from the books by debiting Allowance for Doubtful Accounts and crediting Accounts Receivable. If it eventually collects on a receivable that it previously wrote off, it first reestablishes the receivable by debiting Accounts Receivable and crediting Allowance for Doubtful Accounts. The company then debits Cash and credits the customer's account for the amount received.

If using the direct write-off approach, the company debits the amount collected to Cash and credits a revenue account entitled Uncollectible Amounts Recovered, with proper notation in the customer's account.

WHAT DO THE NUMBERS MEAN?

COLLECTION IS A CLICK AWAY

What do lenders do with uncollectible receivables? After they record bad debts on their books, they next to try to collect what they can from the deadbeat customers. Some lenders auction their bad loans in the market for distressed debt, usually paying a fee of 5–15 percent to a distressed debt broker, who arranges the sale.

Recently, several Web sites have sprung up to provide a meeting place between lenders with bad loans and collectors. These sites are sort of an "eBay of deadbeats." For example, **Bank One Corp.** listed $211 million of unpaid credit card receivables on **DebtforSale.com.** While the lendors generally recover less than 10 percent of the face value of the receivables in an auction, by going online they can reduce the costs of their bad debts. Online services charge just 0.5–1 percent for their auction services.

Source: Adapted from P. Gogoi, "An eBay of Deadbeats," *Business Week* (September 18, 2000), p. 124.

RECOGNITION OF NOTES RECEIVABLE

A note receivable is supported by a formal **promissory note**, a written promise to pay a certain sum of money at a specific future date. Such a note is a negotiable instrument that a **maker** signs in favor of a designated **payee** who may legally and readily sell or otherwise transfer the note to others. Although notes contain an interest element because of the time value of money, companies classify them as interest-bearing or noninterest-bearing. **Interest-bearing notes** have a stated rate of interest. **Zero-interest-bearing notes** (noninterest-bearing) include interest as part of their face amount. Notes receivable are considered fairly liquid, even if long-term, because companies may easily convert them to cash (although they might pay a fee to do so).

[13]Recall from our earnings management discussion in Chapter 4 that increasing or decreasing income through management manipulation can reduce the quality of financial reports.

Companies frequently accept notes receivable from customers who need to extend the payment period of an outstanding receivable. Or they require notes from high-risk or new customers. In addition, companies often use notes in loans to employees and subsidiaries, and in the sales of property, plant, and equipment. In some industries (e.g., the pleasure and sport boat industry) notes support all credit sales. The majority of notes, however, originate from lending transactions. The basic issues in accounting for notes receivable are the same as those for accounts receivable: **recognition, valuation, and disposition.**

Companies generally record short-term notes at face value (less allowances) because the interest implicit in the maturity value is immaterial. A general rule is that notes treated as cash equivalents (maturities of three months or less and easily converted to cash) are not subject to premium or discount amortization.

However, companies should record and report long-term notes receivable at the **present value of the cash they expect to collect**. When the interest stated on an interest-bearing note equals the effective (market) rate of interest, the note sells at face value.[14] When the stated rate differs from the market rate, the cash exchanged (present value) differs from the face value of the note. Companies then record this difference, either a discount or a premium, and amortize it over the life of a note to approximate the effective (market) interest rate. This illustrates one of the many situations in which time value of money concepts are applied to accounting measurement.

OBJECTIVE 6
Explain accounting issues related to recognition of notes receivable.

Note Issued at Face Value

To illustrate the discounting of a note issued at face value, assume that Bigelow Corp. lends Scandinavian Imports $10,000 in exchange for a $10,000, three-year note bearing interest at 10 percent annually. The market rate of interest for a note of similar risk is also 10 percent. We show the time diagram depicting both cash flows in Illustration 6-8.

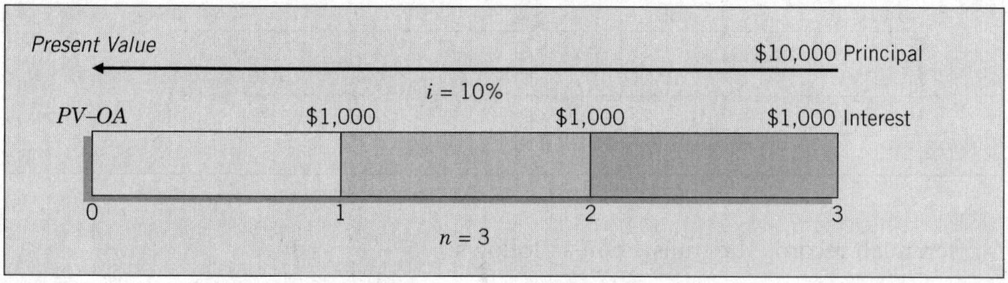

ILLUSTRATION 6-8
Time Diagram for Note Issued at Face Value

Bigelow computes the present value or exchange price of the note as follows.

Face value of the note		$10,000
Present value of the principal:		
$10,000 ($PVF_{3,10\%}$) = $10,000 × .75132	$7,513	
Present value of the interest:		
$1,000 ($PVF\text{-}OA_{3,10\%}$) = $1,000 × 2.48685	2,487	
Present value of the note		10,000
Difference		$ –0–

ILLUSTRATION 6-9
Present Value of Note—Stated and Market Rates the Same

[14]The **stated interest rate**, also referred to as the face rate or the coupon rate, is the rate contracted as part of the note. The **effective-interest rate**, also referred to as the *market rate* or the *effective yield*, is the rate used in the market to determine the value of the note —that is, the discount rate used to determine present value.

You can use a financial calculator to solve this problem.

Calculator Solution for Present Value of Note Receivable

	Inputs	Answer
N	3	
I	10	
PV	?	−10,000
PMT	1,000	
FV	10,000	

In this case, the present value of the note equals its face value, because the effective and stated rates of interest are also the same. Bigelow records the receipt of the note as follows.

Notes Receivable	10,000	
Cash		10,000

Bigelow recognizes the interest earned each year as follows.

Cash	1,000	
Interest Revenue		1,000

Note Not Issued at Face Value

Zero-Interest-Bearing Notes

If a company receives a zero-interest-bearing note, its present value is the cash paid to the issuer. Because the company knows both the future amount and the present value of the note, it can compute the interest rate. This rate is often referred to as the **implicit interest rate**. Companies record the difference between the future (face) amount and the present value (cash paid) as a discount and amortize it to interest revenue over the life of the note.

To illustrate, Jeremiah Company receives a three-year, $10,000 zero-interest-bearing note, the present value of which is $7,721.80. The implicit rate that equates the total cash to be received ($10,000 at maturity) to the present value of the future cash flows ($7,721.80) is 9 percent (the present value of 1 for three periods at 9 percent is .77218). We show the time diagram depicting the one cash flow in Illustration 6-10.

ILLUSTRATION 6-10
Time Diagram for Zero-Interest-Bearing Note

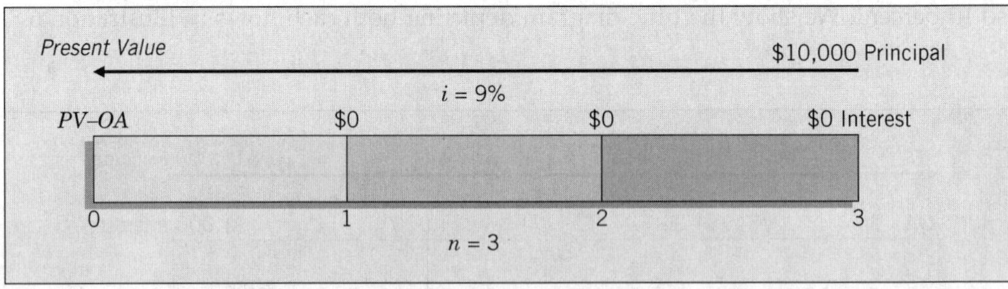

Calculator Solution for Effective-Interest Rate on Note

	Inputs	Answer
N	3	
I	?	9
PV	−7,721.80	
PMT	0	
FV	10,000	

Jeremiah records the transaction as follows:

Notes Receivable	10,000.00	
Discount on Notes Receivable ($10,000 − $7,721.80)		2,278.20
Cash		7,721.80

The Discount on Notes Receivable is a valuation account. Companies report it on the balance sheet as a contra-asset account to notes receivable. They then amortize the discount, and recognize interest revenue annually using the **effective-interest method**. Illustration 6-11 shows the three-year discount amortization and interest revenue schedule.

Jeremiah records interest revenue at the end of the first year using the effective-interest method as follows.

Discount on Notes Receivable	694.96	
Interest Revenue ($7,721.80 × 9%)		694.96

The amount of the discount, $2,278.20 in this case, represents the interest revenue Jeremiah will receive from the note over the three years.

Interest-Bearing Notes

Often the stated rate and the effective rate differ. The zero-interest-bearing note is one example.

ILLUSTRATION 6-11
Discount Amortization Schedule—Effective-Interest Method

SCHEDULE OF NOTE DISCOUNT AMORTIZATION
EFFECTIVE-INTEREST METHOD
0% NOTE DISCOUNTED AT 9%

	Cash Received	Interest Revenue	Discount Amortized	Carrying Amount of Note
Date of issue				$7,721.80
End of year 1	$ -0-	$ 694.96[a]	$ 694.96[b]	8,416.76[c]
End of year 2	-0-	757.51	757.51	9,174.27
End of year 3	-0-	825.73[d]	825.73	10,000.00
	$ -0-	$2,278.20	$2,278.20	

[a]$7,721.80 × .09 = $694.96
[b]$694.96 − 0 = $694.96
[c]$7,721.80 + $694.96 = $8,416.76
[d]5¢ adjustment to compensate for rounding

To illustrate a more common situation, assume that Morgan Corp. makes a loan to Marie Co. and receives in exchange a three-year, $10,000 note bearing interest at 10 percent annually. The market rate of interest for a note of similar risk is 12 percent. We show the time diagram depicting both cash flows in Illustration 6-12.

ILLUSTRATION 6-12
Time Diagram for Interest-Bearing Note

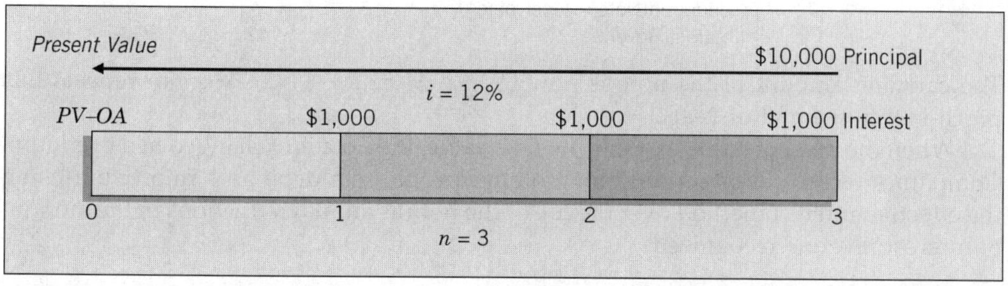

Morgan computes the present value of the two cash flows as follows.

ILLUSTRATION 6-13
Computation of Present Value—Effective Rate Different from Stated Rate

Face value of the note		$10,000
Present value of the principal:		
$10,000 ($PVF_{3,12\%}$) = $10,000 × .71178	$7,118	
Present value of the interest:		
$1,000 ($PVF\text{-}OA_{3,12\%}$) = $1,000 × 2.40183	2,402	
Present value of the note		9,520
Difference (Discount)		$ 480

In this case, because the effective rate of interest (12 percent) exceeds the stated rate (10 percent), the present value of the note is less than the face value. That is, Morgan exchanged the note at a **discount**. Morgan records the receipt of the note at a discount as follows.

Notes Receivable	10,000	
Discount on Notes Receivable		480
Cash		9,520

Morgan then amortizes the discount and recognizes interest revenue annually using the **effective-interest method**. Illustration 6-14 shows the three-year discount amortization and interest revenue schedule.

ILLUSTRATION 6-14
Discount Amortization Schedule—Effective-Interest Method

SCHEDULE OF NOTE DISCOUNT AMORTIZATION
EFFECTIVE-INTEREST METHOD
10% NOTE DISCOUNTED AT 12%

	Cash Received	Interest Revenue	Discount Amortized	Carrying Amount of Note
Date of issue				$ 9,520
End of year 1	$1,000[a]	$1,142[b]	$142[c]	9,662[d]
End of year 2	1,000	1,159	159	9,821
End of year 3	1,000	1,179	179	10,000
	$3,000	$3,480	$480	

[a]$10,000 × 10% = $1,000
[b]$9,520 × 12% = $1,142
[c]$1,142 − $1,000 = $142
[d]$9,520 + $142 = $9,662

On the date of issue, the note has a present value of $9,520. Its unamortized discount—additional interest revenue spread over the three-year life of the note—is $480.

At the end of year 1, Morgan receives $1,000 in cash. But its interest revenue is $1,142 ($9,520 × 12%). The difference between $1,000 and $1,142 is the amortized discount, $142. Morgan records receipt of the annual interest and amortization of the discount for the first year as follows (amounts per amortization schedule).

Cash	1,000	
Discount on Notes Receivable	142	
Interest Revenue		1,142

The carrying amount of the note is now $9,662 ($9,520 + $142). Morgan repeats this process until the end of year 3.

When the present value exceeds the face value, the note is exchanged at a premium. Companies record the premium on a note receivable as a debit and amortize it using the effective-interest method over the life of the note as annual reductions in the amount of interest revenue recognized.

Notes Received for Property, Goods, or Services

When a **note is received in exchange for property, goods, or services** in a bargained transaction entered into at arm's length, the stated interest rate is presumed to be fair unless:

1. No interest rate is stated, or
2. The stated interest rate is unreasonable, or
3. The face amount of the note is materially different from the current cash sales price for the same or similar items or from the current market value of the debt instrument.[15]

Calculator Solution for Effective-Interest Rate on Note

	Inputs	Answer
N	5	
I	?	12
PV	-20,000	
PMT	0	
FV	35,247	

In these circumstances, the company measures the present value of the note by the fair value of the property, goods, or services or by an amount that reasonably approximates the market value of the note.

To illustrate, Oasis Development Co. sold a corner lot to Rusty Pelican as a restaurant site. Oasis accepted in exchange a five-year note having a maturity value of $35,247 and no stated interest rate. The land originally cost Oasis $14,000. At the date of sale the land had a fair market value of $20,000. Given the criterion above, Oasis uses the fair market value of the land, $20,000, as the present value of the note. Oasis therefore records the sale as:

Notes Receivable	35,247	
Discount on Notes Receivable ($35,247 − $20,000)		15,247
Land		14,000
Gain on Sale of Land ($20,000 − $14,000)		6,000

[15]"Interest on Receivables and Payables," *Opinions of the Accounting Principles Board No. 21* (New York: AICPA, 1971), par. 12.

Oasis amortizes the discount to interest revenue over the five-year life of the note using the effective-interest method.

Choice of Interest Rate

In note transactions, other factors involved in the exchange, such as the fair market value of the property, goods, or services, determine the effective or real interest rate. But, if a company cannot determine that fair value, and if the note has no ready market, determining the present value of the note is more difficult. To estimate the present value of a note under such circumstances, the company must approximate an applicable interest rate that may differ from the stated interest rate. This process of interest-rate approximation is called **imputation**. The resulting interest rate is called an **imputed interest rate**.

The prevailing rates for similar instruments, from issuers with similar credit ratings, affect the choice of a rate. Restrictive covenants, collateral, payment schedule, and the existing prime interest rate also impact the choice. A company determines the imputed interest rate when it receives the note. It ignores any subsequent changes in prevailing interest rates.

VALUATION OF NOTES RECEIVABLE

OBJECTIVE 7
Explain accounting issues related to valuation of notes receivable.

Like accounts receivable, companies record and report short-term notes receivable at their net realizable value—that is, at their face amount less all necessary allowances. The primary notes receivable allowance account is Allowance for Doubtful Accounts. The computations and estimations involved in valuing short-term notes receivable and in recording bad debt expense and the related allowance **exactly parallel that for trade accounts receivable**. Companies estimate the amount of uncollectibles by using either a percentage of sales revenue or an analysis of the receivables.

Long-term notes receivable, however, pose additional estimation problems. For evidence, we need only look at the problems that financial institutions, most notably money-center banks, have had in collecting receivables from energy loans, real estate loans, and loans to less-developed countries.[16]

A company considers a note receivable **impaired** when collecting all amounts due (both principal and interest) will likely not occur.

WHAT DO THE NUMBERS MEAN?

PUTTING THE SQUEEZE ON

When the economy slows, lenders such as **J.P. Morgan** and **First Chicago** get stingier in granting new loans or renewing loans to existing customers. This tightening of loans is referred to as a "credit squeeze."

However, it is sometimes difficult for banks to cut back on lending when the economy goes from good times to bad. When times are good and banks are competing for lending business, lenders often grant business customers "lines of credit" as a sweetener to close a loan. In contrast to a term loan that is supported by a note, a line of credit allows borrowing on a day-to-day basis.

When times turn bad, the bank can cut back on loans via notes receivable, but it still must honor the lines of credit, even to weak customers. For example, **Xerox Inc.** got a $7 billion line of credit before it hit the skids. Although denied by the traditional loan markets, Xerox has been able to draw on its line of credit to make ends meet. Thus, what seemed like of good competitive tool in good times has put the squeeze on *lenders* when times have turned bad.

Source: Adapted from H. Timmons and D. Sparks, "Feeling a Credit Squeeze," *Business Week* (December 4, 2000), pp. 148–149.

[16] A wise person once said that a bank lending money to a Third World country is like lending money to one's children: You should never expect to get the interest, let alone the principal.

DISPOSITION OF ACCOUNTS AND NOTES RECEIVABLE

OBJECTIVE 8
Explain accounting issues related to disposition of accounts and notes receivable.

In the normal course of events, companies collect accounts and notes receivable when due and then remove them from the books. However, the growing size and significance of credit sales and receivables has led to changes in this "normal course of events." **In order to accelerate the receipt of cash from receivables, the owner may transfer accounts or notes receivables to another company for cash.**

There are various reasons for this early transfer. First, for competitive reasons, providing sales financing for customers is virtually mandatory in many industries. In the sale of durable goods, such as automobiles, trucks, industrial and farm equipment, computers, and appliances, most sales are on an installment contract basis. Many major companies in these industries have created wholly-owned subsidiaries specializing in receivables financing. For example, **General Motors Corp.** has **General Motors Acceptance Corp. (GMAC)**, and **John Deere** has **John Deere Credit**.

Second, the **holder** may sell receivables because money is tight and access to normal credit is unavailable or too expensive. Also, a firm may sell its receivables, instead of borrowing, to avoid violating existing lending agreements.

Finally, billing and collection of receivables are often time-consuming and costly. Credit card companies such as **MasterCard**, **VISA**, **American Express**, **Diners Club**, **Discover**, and others take over the collection process and provide merchants with immediate cash.

Conversely, some **purchasers** of receivables buy them to obtain the legal protection of ownership rights afforded a purchaser of assets versus the lesser rights afforded a secured creditor. In addition, banks and other lending institutions may need to purchase receivables because of legal lending limits. That is, they cannot make any additional loans but they can buy receivables and charge a fee for this service.

The transfer of receivables to a third party for cash happens in one of two ways:

1. Secured borrowing.
2. Sales of receivables.

Secured Borrowing

A company often uses receivables as collateral in a borrowing transaction. In fact, a creditor often requires that the debtor designate (assign) or pledge[17] receivables as security for the loan. If the loan is not paid when due, the creditor can convert the collateral to cash —that is, to collect the receivables.

To illustrate, on March 1, 2007, Howat Mills, Inc. provides (assigns) $700,000 of its accounts receivable to Citizens Bank as collateral for a $500,000 note. Howat Mills continues to collect the accounts receivable; the account debtors are not notified of the arrangement. Citizens Bank assesses a finance charge of 1 percent of the accounts receivable and interest on the note of 12 percent. Howat Mills makes monthly payments to the bank for all cash it collects on the receivables. Illustration 6-15 shows the entries for the secured borrowing for Howatt Mills and Citizens Bank.

In addition to recording the collection of receivables, Howat Mills must recognize all discounts, returns and allowances, and bad debts. Each month Howat Mills uses the proceeds from the collection of the accounts receivable to retire the note obligation. In addition, it pays interest on the note.[18]

[17]If a company transfers the receivables for custodial purposes, the custodial arrangement is often referred to as a **pledge**.

[18]What happens if Citizens Bank collected the transferred accounts receivable rather than Howat Mills? Citizens Bank would simply remit the cash proceeds to Howat Mills, and Howat Mills would make the same entries shown in Illustration 6-15. As a result, Howat Mills reports these "collaterized" receivables as an asset on the balance sheet.

Howat Mills, Inc.			Citizens Bank		
Transfer of accounts receivable and issuance of note on March 1, 2007					
Cash	493,000		Notes Receivable	500,000	
Finance Charge	7,000*		Finance Revenue		7,000*
Notes Payable		500,000	Cash		493,000
*(1% × $700,000)					
Collection in March of $440,000 of accounts less cash discounts of $6,000 plus receipt of $14,000 sales returns					
Cash	434,000				
Sales Discounts	6,000				
Sales Returns	14,000		(No entry)		
Accounts Receivable		454,000			
($440,000 + $14,000 = $454,000)					
Remitted March collections plus accrued interest to the bank on April 1					
Interest Expense	5,000*		Cash	439,000	
Notes Payable	434,000		Interest Revenue		5,000*
Cash		439,000	Notes Receivable		434,000
*($500,000 × .12 × 1/12)					
Collection in April of the balance of accounts less $2,000 written off as uncollectible					
Cash	244,000				
Allowance for Doubtful Accounts	2,000		(No entry)		
Accounts Receivable		246,000*			
*($700,000 − $454,000)					
Remitted the balance due of $66,000 ($500,000 − $434,000) on the note plus interest on May 1					
Interest Expense	660*		Cash	66,660	
Notes Payable	66,000		Interest Revenue		660*
Cash		66,660	Notes Receivable		66,000
*($66,000 × .12 × 1/12)					

ILLUSTRATION 6-15
Entries for Transfer of Receivables—Secured Borrowing

Sales of Receivables

Sales of receivables have increased substantially in recent years. A common type is a sale to a factor. **Factors** are finance companies or banks that buy receivables from businesses for a fee and then collect the remittances directly from the customers. **Factoring receivables** is traditionally associated with the textile, apparel, footwear, furniture, and home furnishing industries.[19] Illustration 6-16 shows a typical factoring arrangement.

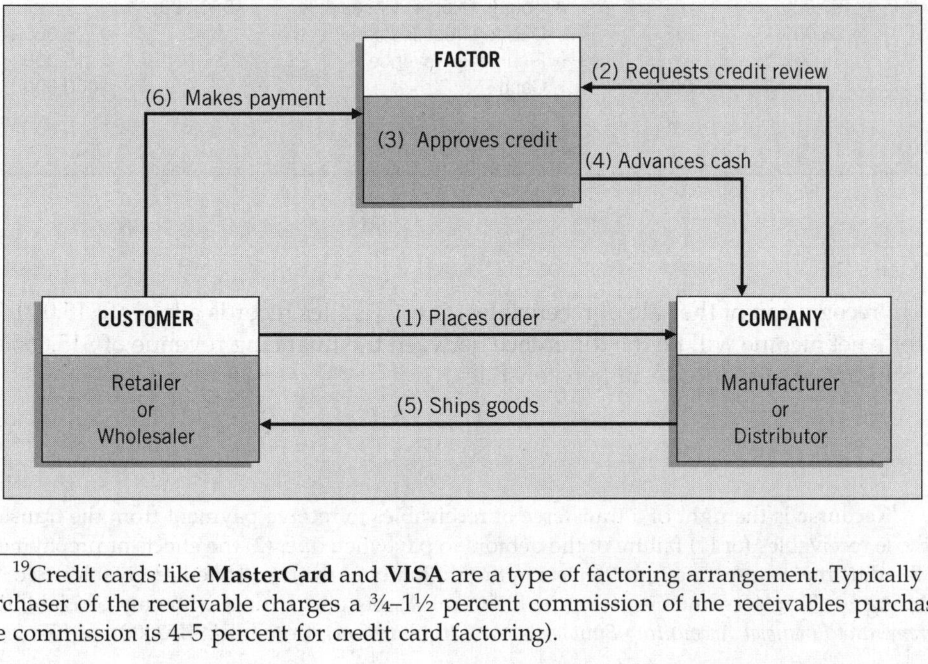

ILLUSTRATION 6-16
Basic Procedures in Factoring

[19]Credit cards like **MasterCard** and **VISA** are a type of factoring arrangement. Typically the purchaser of the receivable charges a ¾–1½ percent commission of the receivables purchased (the commission is 4–5 percent for credit card factoring).

A recent phenomenon in the sale (transfer) of receivables is securitization. **Securitization** takes a pool of assets such as credit card receivables, mortgage receivables, or car loan receivables, and sells shares in these pools of interest and principal payments. This, in effect, creates securities backed by these pools of assets. Virtually every asset with a payment stream and a long-term payment history is a candidate for securitization.

What are the differences between factoring and securitization? Factoring usually involves sale to only one company, fees are high, the quality of the receivables is low, and the seller afterward does not service the receivables. In a securitization, many investors are involved, margins are tight, the receivables are of higher quality, and the seller usually continues to service the receivables.

In either a factoring or a securitization transaction, a company sells receivables on either a **without recourse** or a **with recourse** basis.[20]

Sale without Recourse

When buying receivables **without recourse**, the purchaser assumes the risk of collectibility and absorbs any credit losses. The transfer of accounts receivable in a nonrecourse transaction is an outright sale of the receivables both in form (transfer of title) and substance (transfer of control). In nonrecourse transactions, as in any sale of assets, the seller debits Cash for the proceeds and credits Accounts Receivable for the face value of the receivables. The seller recognizes the difference, reduced by any provision for probable adjustments (discounts, returns, allowances, etc.), as a Loss on the Sale of Receivables. The seller uses a Due from Factor account (reported as a receivable) to account for the proceeds retained by the factor to cover probable sales discounts, sales returns, and sales allowances.

Comprehensive Illustration of Sale Without Recourse

To illustrate, Crest Textiles, Inc. factors $500,000 of accounts receivable with Commercial Factors, Inc., on a **without recourse** basis. Crest Textiles transfers the receivable records to Commercial Factors, which will receive the collections. Commercial Factors assesses a finance charge of 3 percent of the amount of accounts receivable and retains an amount equal to 5 percent of the accounts receivable (for probable adjustments). Crest Textiles and Commercial Factors make the following journal entries for the receivables transferred without recourse.

ILLUSTRATION 6-17
Entries for Sale of Receivables Without Recourse

Crest Textiles, Inc.			Commercial Factors, Inc.		
Cash	460,000		Accounts (Notes) Receivable	500,000	
Due from Factor	25,000*		Due to Crest Textiles		25,000
Loss on Sale of Receivables	15,000**		Financing Revenue		15,000
Accounts (Notes) Receivable		500,000	Cash		460,000
*(5% × $500,000)					
**(3% × $500,000)					

In recognition of the sale of receivables, Crest Textiles records a loss of $15,000. The factor's net income will be the difference between the financing revenue of $15,000 and the amount of any uncollectible receivables.

[20]**Recourse** is the right of a transferee of receivables to receive payment from the transferor of those receivables for (1) failure of the debtors to pay when due, (2) the effects of prepayments, or (3) adjustments resulting from defects in the eligibility of the transferred receivables. See "Accounting for Transfers and Servicing of Financial Assets and Extinguishments of Liabilities," *Statement of Financial Accounting Standards No. 140* (Stamford, Conn.: FASB, 2000), p. 155.

Sale with Recourse

For receivables sold **with recourse**, the seller guarantees payment to the purchaser in the event the debtor fails to pay. To record this type of transaction, the seller uses a **financial components approach**, because the seller has a continuing involvement with the receivable.[21] In this approach, each party to the sale only recognizes the assets and liabilities that it controls after the sale.

To illustrate, assume the same information as in Illustration 6-17 for Crest Textiles and for Commercial Factors, except that Crest Textiles sold the receivables on a with-recourse basis. Crest Textiles determines that this recourse obligation has a fair value of $6,000. To determine the loss on the sale of the receivables, Crest Textiles computes the net proceeds from the sale as follows.

ILLUSTRATION 6-18
Net Proceeds Computation

Cash received	$460,000	
Due from factor	25,000	$485,000
Less: Recourse obligation		6,000
Net proceeds		$479,000

Net proceeds are cash or other assets received in a sale less any liabilities incurred. Crest Textiles then computes the loss as follows.

ILLUSTRATION 6-19
Loss on Sale Computation

Carrying (book) value	$500,000
Net proceeds	479,000
Loss on sale of receivables	$ 21,000

Illustration 6-20 shows the journal entries for both Crest Textiles and Commercial Factors for the receivables sold with recourse.

ILLUSTRATION 6-20
Entries for Sale of Receivables with Recourse

Crest Textiles, Inc.			Commercial Factors, Inc.		
Cash	460,000		Accounts Receivable	500,000	
Due from Factor	25,000		Due to Crest Textiles		25,000
Loss on Sale of Receivables	21,000		Financing Revenue		15,000
Accounts (Notes) Receivable		500,000	Cash		460,000
Recourse Liability		6,000			

[21]Accounting standards before *SFAS No. 140* generally required that the transferor account for financial assets transferred as an inseparable unit that had been entirely sold or entirely retained. Those standards were difficult to apply and produced inconsistent and arbitrary results. Values are now assigned to such components as the recourse provision, servicing rights, and agreement to reacquire.

Tutorial on the Disposition of Receivables

In this case, Crest Textiles recognizes a loss of $21,000. In addition, it records a liability of $6,000 to indicate the probable payment to Commercial Factors for uncollectible receivables. If Commercial Factors collects all the receivables, Crest Textiles eliminates its recourse liability and increases income. Commercial Factors' net income is the financing revenue of $15,000. It will have no bad debts related to these receivables.

WHAT DO THE NUMBERS MEAN?

UGLY DUCKLINGS

Ugly Duckling is a used-car dealer that has carved out a niche by selling cars to customers with questionable credit histories. Ugly Duckling and other "sub-prime lenders" earn a profit by loaning money to riskier borrowers so they can purchase automobiles or homes. To compensate for the higher probability of default of these customers, sub-prime lenders charge higher rates of interest on these high-risk loans. In many instances these companies package their sub-prime loans and sell them as securities. However, recognition of gains on these transfers of receivables is appropriate only if Ugly Duckling can reasonably estimate the proportion of the loans that borrowers will not repay (the receivables are sold with recourse).

However, estimating loan defaults is difficult. If sub-prime lenders fail to set rates high enough to cover unexpected higher rates of default, a severe cash squeeze will result. In addition, if too many of the loans that it sells then default, Ugly Duckling will have to take them back, thereby eliminating any gain it recorded on the original sale. Indeed, in one year alone, **ContiFinancial** had to write off over $654 million in sub-prime loans. Similarly, bank regulators had to step in and take over **Superior Bank FSB**, which specialized in sub-prime loans, because it overestimated the value of its sub-prime loans.

Thus, the sub-prime lending business is a risky one. Depending on default and interest rate assumptions on these receivables, companies like Ugly Duckling may not survive to grow into lending swans.

Secured Borrowing versus Sale

INTERNATIONAL INSIGHT

The IASB has a similar conceptual approach to the sale of receivables, although it provides more flexibility in implementation.

The FASB concluded that a sale occurs only if the seller surrenders control of the receivables to the buyer. The following three conditions must be met before a company can record a sale:

1. The transferred asset has been isolated from the transferor (put beyond reach of the transferor and its creditors).
2. The transferees have obtained the right to pledge or exchange either the transferred assets or beneficial interests in the transferred assets.
3. The transferor does not maintain effective control over the transferred assets through an agreement to repurchase or redeem them before their maturity.

If the three conditions are met, a sale occurs. Otherwise, the transferor should record the transfer as a secured borrowing. If sale accounting is appropriate, a company must still consider assets obtained and liabilities incurred in the transaction. Illustration 6-21 shows the rules of accounting for transfers of receivables. As it shows, if there is continuing involvement in a sale transaction, a company must record the assets obtained and liabilities incurred.

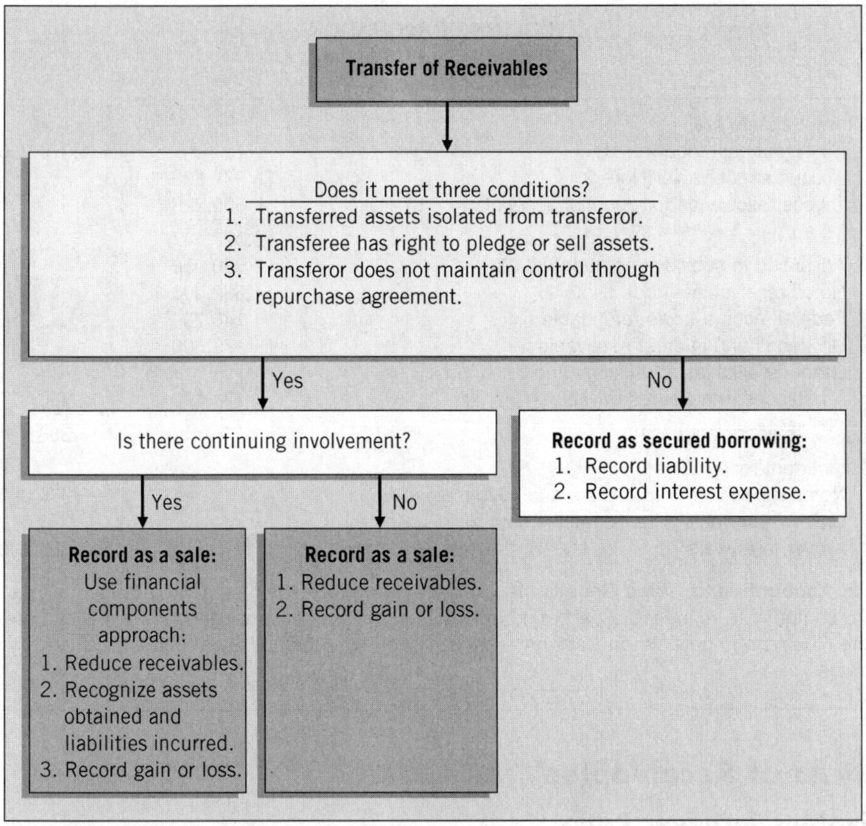

ILLUSTRATION 6-21
Accounting for Transfers of Receivables

PRESENTATION AND ANALYSIS

Presentation of Receivables

OBJECTIVE 9
Describe how to report and analyze receivables.

The general rules in classifying receivables are:

1 Segregate the different types of receivables that a company possesses, if material.
2 Appropriately offset the valuation accounts against the proper receivable accounts.
3 Determine that receivables classified in the current assets section will be converted into cash within the year or the operating cycle, whichever is longer.
4 Disclose any loss contingencies that exist on the receivables.
5 Disclose any receivables designated or pledged as collateral.
6 Disclose all significant concentrations of credit risk arising from receivables.[22]

The assets sections of Colton Corporation's balance sheet in Illustration 6-22 show many of the disclosures required for receivables.

[22]Concentrations of credit risk exist when receivables have common characteristics that may affect their collection. These common characteristics might be companies in the same industry or same region of the country. For example, **Quantum Corporation** reported that sales of its disk drives to its top five customers (including **Hewlett-Packard**) represented nearly 40 percent of its revenues in 2003. Financial statements users want to know if a substantial amount of receivables from such sales are to customers facing uncertain economic conditions. No numerical guidelines are provided as to what is meant by a "concentration of credit risk."

Three items should be disclosed with an identified concentration: (1) information on the characteristic that determines the concentration, (2) the amount of loss that could occur upon nonperformance, and (3) information on any collateral related to the receivable. "Disclosures about Fair Value of Financial Instruments," *Statement of Financial Accounting Standards No. 107* (Norwalk, Conn.: FASB, 1991), par. 15.

ILLUSTRATION 6-22
Disclosure of Receivables

Additional Disclosures of Receivables

COLTON CORPORATION
BALANCE SHEET (PARTIAL)
AS OF DECEMBER 31, 2007

Current assets		
Cash and cash equivalents		$ 1,870,250
Accounts receivable (Note 2)	$8,977,673	
Less: Allowance for doubtful accounts	500,226	
	8,477,447	
Advances to subsidiaries due 9/30/08	2,090,000	
Notes receivable—trade (Note 2)	1,532,000	
Federal income taxes refundable	146,704	
Dividends and interest receivable	75,500	
Other receivables and claims (including debit balances in accounts payable)	174,620	12,496,271
Total current assets		14,366,521
Noncurrent receivables		
Notes receivable from officers and key employees		376,090
Claims receivable (litigation settlement to be collected over four years)		585,000

Note 2: Accounts and Notes Receivable. In November 2007, the Company arranged with a finance company to refinance a part of its indebtedness. The loan is evidenced by a 12% note payable. The note is payable on demand and is secured by substantially all the accounts receivable.

INTERNATIONAL INSIGHT

Holding receivables that it will pay in a foreign currency represents risk that the exchange rate may move against the company. This results in a decrease in the amount collected in terms of U.S. dollars. Companies engaged in cross-border transactions often "hedge" these receivables by buying contracts to exchange currencies at specified amounts at future dates.

Analysis of Receivables

Receivables Turnover Ratio

Analysts frequently compute financial ratios to evaluate the liquidity of a company's accounts receivable. To assess the liquidity of the receivables, they use the **receivables turnover ratio**. This ratio measures the number of times, on average, a company collects receivables during the period. The ratio is computed by dividing net sales by average (net) receivables outstanding during the year. Theoretically, the numerator should include only net credit sales, but this information is frequently unavailable. However, if the relative amounts of credit and cash sales remain fairly constant, the trend indicated by the ratio will still be valid. Barring significant seasonal factors, average receivables outstanding can be computed from the beginning and ending balances of net trade receivables.

To illustrate, **Circuit City** reported 2004 net sales of $9,745 million, its beginning and ending accounts receivable balances were $380 million and $580 million, respectively. Illustration 6-23 shows the computation of its accounts receivables turnover ratio.

ILLUSTRATION 6-23
Computation of Accounts Receivable Turnover

$$\frac{\text{Net Sales}}{\text{Average Trade Receivables (net)}} = \text{Accounts Receivable Turnover}$$

$$\frac{\$9{,}745}{(\$580 + \$380)/2} = 20.3 \text{ times, or every 18 days } (365 \div 20.3)$$

UNDERLYING CONCEPTS

Providing information that will help users assess a company's current liquidity and prospective cash flows is a primary objective of accounting.

This information[23] shows how successful the company is in collecting its outstanding receivables. If possible, an aging schedule should also be prepared to help determine how long receivables have been outstanding. A satisfactory receivables turnover may have resulted because certain receivables were collected quickly though others have been outstanding for a relatively long period. An aging schedule would reveal such patterns.

[23]Often the receivables turnover is transformed to **days to collect accounts receivable** or **days outstanding**—an average collection period. In this case, 20.3 is divided into 365 days, resulting in 18 days. Several figures other than 365 could be used. A common alternative is 360 days because it is divisible by 30 (days) and 12 (months). *Use 365 days in any homework computations.*

QUESTIONS

1. What may be included under the heading of "cash"?

2. In what accounts should the following items be classified?

(a) Coins and currency.

(b) U.S. Treasury (government) bonds.

(c) Certificate of deposit.

(d) Cash in a bank that is in receivership.

(e) NSF check (returned with bank statement).

(f) Deposit in foreign bank (exchangeability limited).

(g) Postdated checks.

(h) Cash to be used for retirement of long-term bonds.

(i) Deposits in transit.

(j) 100 shares of **Dell** stock (intention is to sell in one year or less).

(k) Savings and checking accounts.

(l) Petty cash.

(m) Stamps.

(n) Travel advances.

3. Define a "compensating balance." How should a compensating balance be reported?

4. Michael Tilsen Thomas Inc. reported in a recent annual report "Restricted cash for debt redemption." What section of the balance sheet would report this item?

5. What are the reasons that a company gives trade discounts? Why are trade discounts not recorded in the accounts like cash discounts?

6. What are two methods of recording accounts receivable transactions when a cash discount situation is involved? Which is more theoretically correct? Which is used in practice more of the time? Why?

7. What are the basic problems that occur in the valuation of accounts receivable?

8. What is the theoretical justification of the allowance method as contrasted with the direct write-off method of accounting for bad debts?

9. Indicate how well the percentage-of-sales method and the aging method accomplish the objectives of the allowance method of accounting for bad debts.

10. Of what merit is the contention that the allowance method lacks the objectivity of the direct write-off method? Discuss in terms of accounting's measurement function.

11. Explain how the accounting for bad debts can be used for earnings management.

12. Because of calamitous earthquake losses, Kishwaukee Company, one of your client's oldest and largest customers, suddenly and unexpectedly became bankrupt. Approximately 30% of your client's total sales have been made to Kishwaukee Company during each of the past several years. The amount due from Kishwaukee Company—none of which is collectible—equals 22% of total accounts receivable, an amount that is considerably in excess of what was determined to be an adequate provision for doubtful accounts at the close of the preceding year. How would your client record the write-off of the Kishwaukee Company receivable if it is using the allowance method of accounting for bad debts? Justify your suggested treatment.

13. What is the normal procedure for handling the collection of accounts receivable previously written off using the direct write-off method? The allowance method?

14. On January 1, 2007, John Singer Co. sells property for which it had paid $690,000 to Sargent Company, receiving in return Sargent's zero-interest-bearing note for $1,000,000 payable in 5 years. What entry would John Singer make to record the sale, assuming that John Singer frequently sells similar items of property for a cash sales price of $620,000?

15. What is "imputed interest"? In what situations is it necessary to impute an interest rate for notes receivable? What are the considerations in imputing an appropriate interest rate?

16. Indicate three reasons why a company might sell its receivables to another company.

17. When is the financial components approach to recording the transfers of receivables used? When should a transfer of receivables be recorded as a sale?

18. Hale Hardware is planning to factor some of its receivables. The cash received will be used to pay for inventory purchases. The factor has indicated that it will require "recourse" on the sold receivables. Explain to the controller of Hale Hardware what "recourse" is and how the recourse will be reflected in Hale's financial statements after the sale of the receivables.

19. Outkast Outfitters Company includes in its trial balance for December 31 an item for Accounts Receivable $769,000. This balance consists of the following items:

Due from regular customers	$523,000
Refund receivable on prior year's income taxes (an established claim)	15,500
Travel advance to employees	22,000
Loan to wholly owned subsidiary	45,500
Advances to creditors for goods ordered	61,000
Accounts receivable assigned as security for loans payable	75,000
Notes receivable past due plus interest on these notes	27,000
Total	$769,000

Illustrate how these items should be shown in the balance sheet as of December 31.

20. What is the accounts receivable turnover ratio, and what type of information does it provide?

21. You are evaluating Hawthorn Downs Racetrack for a potential loan. An examination of the notes to the financial statements indicates restricted cash at year-end amounts to $100,000. Explain how you would use this information in evaluating Hawthorn's liquidity.

CHAPTER SEVEN

VALUATION OF INVENTORIES: A COST-BASIS APPROACH

Inventories in the Crystal Ball

A substantial increase in inventory may be a leading indicator of an upcoming decline in profit margins. Take the auto industry as an example. Detroit's inventories have been growing for several years because the domestic manufacturers like to run the factories at full capacity, even if they are not selling cars as fast as they can make them. The current arrangement is particularly tough for **General Motors**. It overproduces and then tries to push the sales with incentives and month-long "blow-out" sales. GM is hoping that the ever-growing market will cover the problem until customer demand grows to the point where the cars are purchased without so many incentives.

But recently, all that was growing was GM inventories. Not too long ago, the average sticker on a Cadillac DeVille was $54,193, but the net price after incentives was $42,211. This meant that the factory was giving up a substantial amount of profit through rebates, dealer cash, or lease or interest rate subsidies. A similar deal could be had at **Ford**, which was selling Explorers for $25,745 net, a 24 percent reduction for various factory incentives. But inventories at GM and Ford continued to grow, even with these significant incentives.[1]

These data concern investors. As one analyst remarked, "When inventory grows faster than sales, profits drop." That is, when companies face slowing sales and growing inventory, then markdowns in prices usually result. These markdowns, in turn, lead to lower sales revenue and income, thereby squeezing profit margins on sales.[2]

Research supporting these observations indicates that increases in retailers' inventory translate into lower prices and lower net income.[3] Interestingly, the same research found that for manufacturers, only increases in finished goods inventory lead to future profit declines. Increases in raw materials and work-in-process inventories signal that the company is building its inventory to meet increased demand. Therefore, future sales and income will be higher. These research results reinforce the usefulness of the GAAP requirement for manufacturers to disclose their inventory components on the balance sheet or in related notes.

---

[1]J. Flint, "Inventories: Too Much of a Good Thing," *Forbes.com* (September 21, 2004).

[2]S. Pulliam, "Heard on the Street," *Wall Street Journal* (May 21, 1997), p. C1.

[3]Victor Bernard and J. Noel, "Do Inventory Disclosures Predict Sales and Earnings?" *Journal of Accounting, Auditing, and Finance* (March 1991), pp. 145–182.

Learning Objectives

After studying this chapter, you should be able to:

1 Identify major classifications of inventory.
2 Distinguish between perpetual and periodic inventory systems.
3 Identify the effects of inventory errors on the financial statements.
4 Understand the items to include as inventory cost.
5 Describe and compare the cost flow assumptions used to account for inventories.
6 Explain the significance and use of a LIFO reserve.
7 Understand the effect of LIFO liquidations.
8 Explain the dollar-value LIFO method.
9 Identify the major advantages and disadvantages of LIFO.
10 Understand why companies select given inventory methods.

PREVIEW OF CHAPTER 7

As our opening story indicates, information on inventories and changes in inventory helps to predict financial performance. In this chapter we discuss the basic issues related to accounting and reporting for inventory. The content and organization of the chapter are as follows.

VALUATION OF INVENTORIES: A COST-BASIS APPROACH

- **INVENTORY CLASSIFICATION AND CONTROL**
  - Classification
  - Control
  - Basic inventory valuation issues
- **PHYSICAL GOODS INCLUDED IN INVENTORY**
  - Goods in transit
  - Consigned goods
  - Special sales agreements
  - Inventory errors
- **COSTS INCLUDED IN INVENTORY**
  - Product costs
  - Period costs
  - Purchase discounts
- **COST FLOW ASSUMPTIONS**
  - Specific identification
  - Average cost
  - FIFO
  - LIFO
- **LIFO: SPECIAL ISSUES**
  - LIFO reserve
  - LIFO liquidation
  - Dollar-value LIFO
  - Comparison of LIFO approaches
  - Advantages of LIFO
  - Disadvantages of LIFO
- **BASIS FOR SELECTION**
  - Summary of inventory valuation methods

INVENTORY CLASSIFICATION AND CONTROL

Classification

OBJECTIVE 1
Identify major classifications of inventory.

Inventories are asset items that a company holds for sale in the ordinary course of business, or goods that it will use or consume in the production of goods to be sold. The description and measurement of inventory require careful attention. The investment in inventories is frequently the largest current asset of merchandising (retail) and manufacturing businesses.

A **merchandising concern**, such as **Wal-Mart**, usually purchases its merchandise in a form ready for sale. It reports the cost assigned to unsold units left on hand as **merchandise inventory**. Only one inventory account, Merchandise Inventory, appears in the financial statements.

Manufacturing concerns, on the other hand, produce goods to sell to merchandising firms. Many of the largest U.S. businesses are manufacturers, such as **Boeing**, **IBM**, **ExxonMobil**, **Procter & Gamble**, **Ford**, and **Motorola**. Although the products they produce may differ, manufacturers normally have three inventory accounts—Raw Materials, Work in Process, and Finished Goods.

UNDERLYING CONCEPTS

Because inventory provides future economic benefits to the company (revenue from sales), it meets the definition of an asset. Inventory costs will be matched against revenue in the period that sales occur.

A company reports the cost assigned to goods and materials on hand but not yet placed into production as **raw materials inventory**. Raw materials include the wood to make a baseball bat or the steel to make a car. These materials can be traced directly to the end product.

At any point in a continuous production process some units are only partially processed. The cost of the raw material for these unfinished units, plus the direct labor

: applied specifically to this material and a ratable share of manufacturing overhead :s, constitute the **work in process inventory**.

Companies report the costs identified with the completed but unsold units on hand he end of the fiscal period as **finished goods inventory**. Illustration 7-1 contrasts financial statement presentation of inventories of **Wal-Mart** (a merchandising com- y) with those of **Caterpillar** (a manufacturing company.) The remainder of the bal- e sheet is essentially similar for the two types of companies.

ILLUSTRATION 7-1
Comparison of Presentation of Current Assets for Merchandising and Manufacturing Companies

Merchandising Company
Wal-Mart
Balance Sheet
January 31, 2004

Current assets (in millions)	
Cash and cash equivalents	$ 5,199
Receivables	1,254
Inventories	26,612
Prepaid expenses and other	1,356
Total current assets	$34,421

Manufacturing Company
Caterpillar
Balance Sheet
December 31, 2004

Current assets (in millions)		
Cash		$ 445
Accounts receivable		13,969
Inventories		
Raw materials	$1,592	
Work in process	664	
Finished goods	2,209	
Supplies	210	
Total inventories		4,675
Other current assets		1,767
Total current assets		$20,856

As indicated above, a manufacturing company, like **Caterpillar**, also might include lanufacturing or Factory **Supplies Inventory** account. In it, Caterpillar would in- le such items as machine oils, nails, cleaning material, and the like—supplies that used in production but are not the primary materials being processed.

Illustration 7-2 shows the differences in the flow of costs through a merchandising ıpany and a manufacturing company.

Additional Inventory Disclosures

ILLUSTRATION 7-2
Flow of Costs through Manufacturing and Merchandising Companies

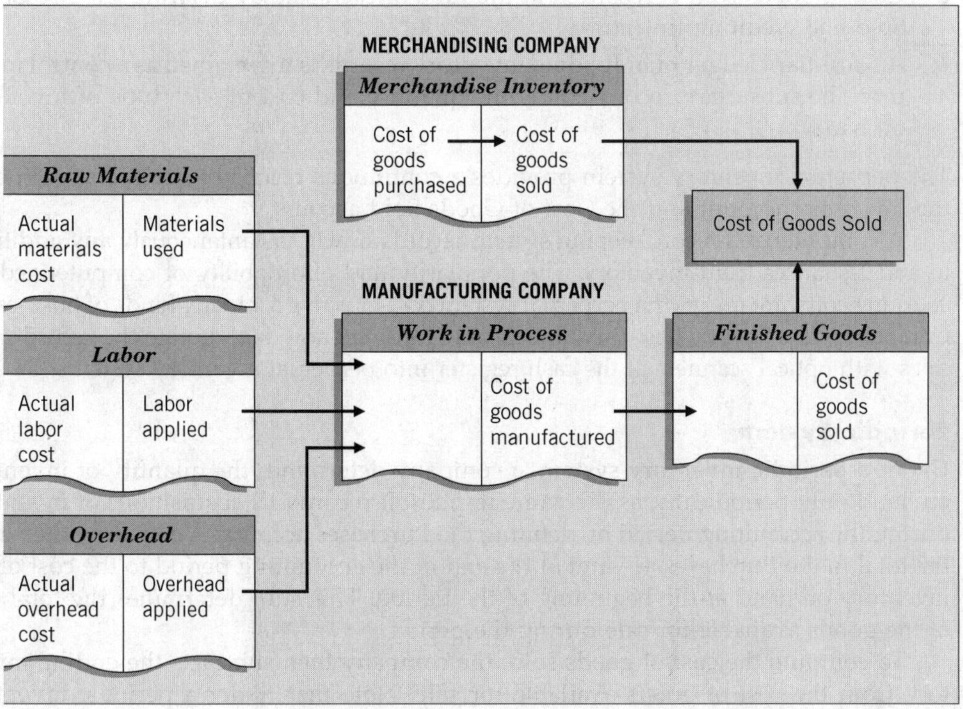

Control

For various reasons, management is vitally interested in inventory planning and control. Whether a company manufactures or merchandises goods, it needs an accurate accounting system with up-to-date records. It may lose sales and customers if it does not stock products in the desired style, quality, and quantity. Further, companies must monitor inventory levels carefully to limit the financing costs of carrying large amounts of inventory.

Companies use one of two types of systems for maintaining accurate inventory records—the perpetual system or the periodic system.

WHAT DO THE NUMBERS MEAN?

STAYING LEAN

With the introduction and use of "just-in-time" (JIT) inventory order systems and better supplier relationships, many companies have leaner inventory levels.

Wal-Mart provides a classic example of the use of tight inventory controls. Department managers use a scanner that when placed over the bar code corresponding to a particular item, will tell them how many of the items the store sold yesterday, last week, and over the same period last year. It will tell them how many of those items are in stock, how many are on the way, and how many the neighboring Wal-Marts are carrying (in case one store runs out). Such practices have helped Wal-Mart become one of the top-ranked companies on the Fortune 500 in terms of sales.

Perpetual System

OBJECTIVE 2
Distinguish between perpetual and periodic inventory systems.

A **perpetual inventory system** continuously tracks changes in the Inventory account. That is, a company records all purchases and sales (issues) of goods directly in the Inventory account **as they occur**. The accounting features of a perpetual inventory system are as follows.

1. Purchases of merchandise for resale or raw materials for production are debited to Inventory rather than to Purchases.
2. Freight-in, purchase returns and allowances, and purchase discounts are debited to Inventory rather than in separate accounts.
3. Cost of goods sold is recorded at the time of each sale by debiting Cost of Goods Sold and crediting Inventory.
4. A subsidiary ledger of individual inventory records is maintained as a control measure. The subsidiary records show the quantity and cost of each type of inventory on hand.

The perpetual inventory system provides a continuous record of the balances in both the Inventory account and the Cost of Goods Sold account.

A computerized recordkeeping system records nearly instantaneously any additions to and issuances from inventory. The popularity and affordability of computerized accounting software makes the perpetual system cost-effective for many kinds of businesses. Companies like **Target**, **Best Buy**, and **Sears Holdings** now incorporate the recording of sales with optical scanners at the cash register into perpetual inventory systems.

Periodic System

Under a **periodic inventory system**, a company determines the quantity of inventory on hand only periodically, as the name implies. It records all acquisitions of inventory during the accounting period by debiting the Purchases account. A company then adds the total in the Purchases account at the end of the accounting period to the cost of the inventory on hand at the beginning of the period. This sum determines the total cost of the goods available for sale during the period.

To compute the cost of goods sold, the company then subtracts the ending inventory from the cost of goods available for sale. Note that under a periodic inventory em, the cost of goods sold is a residual amount that depends on a physically counted ing inventory.

Once a year, companies take the **physical inventory count** required by a periodic em.[4] However, most companies need more current information regarding their in- tory levels to protect against stockouts or overpurchasing and to aid in preparation ıonthly or quarterly financial data. As a consequence, many companies use a **modi- l perpetual inventory system**. This system provides detailed inventory records of eases and decreases in quantities only—not dollar amounts. It is merely a memo- lum device outside the double-entry system, which helps in determining the level ıventory at any point in time.

Whether a company maintains a perpetual inventory in quantities and dollars or uantities only, or has no perpetual inventory record at all, it probably takes a phys- inventory once a year. No matter what type of inventory records companies use, all face the danger of loss and error. Waste, breakage, theft, improper entry, fail- to prepare or record requisitions, and other similar possibilities may cause the in- tory records to differ from the actual inventory on hand. Thus all companies need odic verification of the inventory records by actual count, weight, or measurement, ı the counts compared with the detailed inventory records. A company corrects the rds to agree with the quantities actually on hand.

Insofar as possible, companies should take the physical inventory near the end of r fiscal year, to properly report inventory quantities in their annual accounting re- s. Because this is not always possible, however, physical inventories taken within or three months of the year's end are satisfactory, if a company maintains detailed entory records with a fair degree of accuracy.

To illustrate the difference between a perpetual and a periodic system, assume that nire Company had the following transactions during the current year.

Beginning inventory	100 units at $ 6 = $ 600
Purchases	900 units at $ 6 = $5,400
Sales	600 units at $12 = $7,200
Ending inventory	400 units at $ 6 = $2,400

Fesmire records these transactions during the current year as shown in Illustration 7-3.

ILLUSTRATION 7-3
Comparative Entries—Perpetual vs. Periodic

Perpetual Inventory System			Periodic Inventory System		
Beginning inventory, 100 units at $6:					
e inventory account shows the inventory hand at $600.			The inventory account shows the inventory on hand at $600.		
Purchase 900 units at $6:					
entory	5,400		Purchases	5,400	
Accounts Payable		5,400	Accounts Payable		5,400
Sale of 600 units at $12:					
counts Receivable	7,200		Accounts Receivable	7,200	
Sales		7,200	Sales		7,200
st of Goods Sold (600 at $6)	3,600		(No entry)		
nventory		3,600			
End-of-period entries for inventory accounts, 400 units at $6:					
entry necessary.			Inventory (ending, by count)	2,400	
e account, Inventory, shows the ending			Cost of Goods Sold	3,600	
alance of $2,400			Purchases		5,400
00 + $5,400 − $3,600).			Inventory (beginning)		600

[4]In recent years, some companies have developed methods of determining inventories, in- ing statistical sampling, that are sufficiently reliable to make unnecessary an annual physi- ount of each item of inventory.

When a company uses a perpetual inventory system and a difference exists between the perpetual inventory balance and the physical inventory count, it needs a separate entry to adjust the perpetual inventory account. To illustrate, assume that at the end of the reporting period, the perpetual inventory account reported an inventory balance of $4,000. However, a physical count indicates $3,800 is actually on hand. The entry to record the necessary write-down is as follows.

Inventory Over and Short	200	
Inventory		200

Perpetual inventory overages and shortages generally represent a misstatement of cost of goods sold. The difference results from normal and expected shrinkage, breakage, shoplifting, incorrect recordkeeping, and the like. Inventory Over and Short therefore adjusts Cost of Goods Sold. In practice, companies sometimes report Inventory Over and Short in the "Other revenues and gains" or "Other expenses and losses" section of the income statement, depending on its balance. Note that a company using the periodic inventory system does not report the account Inventory Over and Short. The reason: The periodic method does not have accounting records against which to compare the physical count. Instead, a company buries inventory overages and shortages in cost of goods sold.

BASIC ISSUES IN INVENTORY VALUATION

Goods sold (or used) during an accounting period seldom correspond exactly to the goods bought (or produced) during that period. As a result, inventories either increase or decrease during the period. Companies must then allocate the cost of all the goods available for sale (or use) between the goods that were sold or used and those that are still on hand. The **cost of goods available for sale or use** is the *sum* of (1) the cost of the goods on hand at the beginning of the period, and (2) the cost of the goods acquired or produced during the period. The **cost of goods sold** is the *difference* between (1) the cost of goods available for sale during the period and (2) the cost of goods on hand at the end of the period. Illustration 7-4 shows these calculations.

ILLUSTRATION 7-4
Computation of Cost of Goods Sold

Beginning inventory, Jan. 1	$100,000
Cost of goods acquired or produced during the year	800,000
Total cost of goods available for sale	900,000
Ending inventory, Dec. 31	200,000
Cost of goods sold during the year	$700,000

Valuing inventories can be complex. It requires determining the following.

1 **The physical goods to include in inventory** (who owns the goods?—goods in transit, consigned goods, special sales agreements).

2 **The costs to include in inventory** (product vs. period costs).

3 **The cost flow assumption to adopt** (specific identification, average cost, FIFO, LIFO, retail, etc.).

We explore these basic issues in the next three sections.

PHYSICAL GOODS INCLUDED IN INVENTORY

Technically, a company should record purchases when it obtains legal title to the goods. In practice, however, a company records acquisitions when it receives the goods. Why? Because it is difficult to determine the exact time of legal passage of title for every purchase. In addition, no material error likely results from such a practice if consistently lied. Illustration 7-5 indicates the general guidelines companies use in evaluating ether the seller or buyer reports an item as inventory. Exceptions to the general delines can arise for goods in transit and consigned goods.

ILLUSTRATION 7-5
Guidelines for Determining Ownership

ods in Transit

netimes purchased merchandise remains in transit—not yet received—at the end of scal period. The accounting for these shipped goods depends on who owns them. example, a company like **Walgreens** determines ownership by applying the ssage of title" rule. If a supplier ships goods to Walgreens **f.o.b. shipping point**, passes to Walgreens when the supplier delivers the goods to the common carrier, acts as an agent for Walgreens. (The abbreviation f.o.b. stands for free on board.) ne supplier ships the goods **f.o.b. destination**, title passes to Walgreens only when ceives the goods from the common carrier. "Shipping point" and "destination" are n designated by a particular location, for example, f.o.b. Denver.

When Walgreens obtains legal title to goods, it must record them as purchases in that l period, assuming a periodic inventory system. Thus, goods shipped to Walgreens . shipping point, but in transit at the end of the period, belong to Walgreens. It should w the purchase in its records, because legal title to these goods passed to Walgreens n shipment of the goods. To disregard such purchases results in understating inven- es and accounts payable in the balance sheet, and understating purchases and ending entories in the income statement.

nsigned Goods

npanies market certain products through a **consignment** shipment. Under this ngement, a company like Williams' Art Gallery (the consignor) ships various art chandise to **Sotheby's Holdings** (the consignee), who acts as Williams' agent in ing the **consigned goods**. Sotheby's agrees to accept the goods without any liabil- except to exercise due care and reasonable protection from loss or damage, until it s the goods to a third party. When Sotheby's sells the goods, it remits the revenue, a selling commission and expenses incurred in accomplishing the sale, to Williams.

Goods out on consignment remain the property of the consignor (Williams in the mple above). Williams thus includes the goods in its inventory at purchase price or duction cost. Occasionally, and only for a significant amount, the consignor shows inventory out on consignment as a separate item. Sometimes a consignor reports inventory on consignment in the notes to the financial statements. For example, **le Clothes, Inc.** reported the following related to consigned goods: "Inventories sist of finished goods shipped on consignment to customers of the Company's sub- ary **April-Marcus, Inc.** "

The consignee makes no entry to the inventory account for goods received. Remember, these goods remain the property of the consignor until sold. In fact, the consignee should be extremely careful *not* to include any of the goods consigned as a part of inventory.

Special Sales Agreements

As we indicated earlier, transfer of legal title is the general guideline used to determine whether a company should include an item in inventory. Unfortunately, transfer of legal title and the underlying substance of the transaction often do not match. For example, legal title may have passed to the purchaser, but the seller of the goods retains the risks of ownership. Conversely, transfer of legal title may not occur, but the economic substance of the transaction is such that the seller no longer retains the risks of ownership.

Three special sales situations are illustrated here to indicate the types of problems companies encounter in practice. These are:

1. Sales with buyback agreement.
2. Sales with high rates of return.
3. Sales on installment.

Sales with Buyback Agreement

Sometimes an enterprise finances its inventory without reporting either the liability or the inventory on its balance sheet. This approach, often referred to as a **product financing arrangement**, usually involves a "sale" with either an implicit or explicit "buyback" agreement.

To illustrate, Hill Enterprises transfers ("sells") inventory to Chase, Inc. and simultaneously agrees to repurchase this merchandise at a specified price over a specified period of time. Chase then uses the inventory as collateral and borrows against it. Chase uses the loan proceeds to pay Hill, which repurchases the inventory in the future. Chase employs the proceeds from repayment to meet its loan obligation.

The essence of this transaction is that Hill Enterprises is financing its inventory—and retaining risk of ownership—even though it transferred to Chase technical legal title to the merchandise. By structuring a transaction in this manner, Hill avoids personal property taxes in certain states. Other advantages of this transaction for Hill are the removal of the current liability from its balance sheet and the ability to manipulate income. For Chase, the purchase of the goods may solve a LIFO liquidation problem (discussed later), or Chase may enter into a similar reciprocal agreement at a later date.

UNDERLYING CONCEPTS

Recognizing revenue at the time the inventory is "parked" violates the revenue recognition principle. This principle requires that the earning process be substantially completed. In this case, the economic benefits remain under the control of the seller.

These arrangements are often described in practice as "**parking transactions**." In this situation, Hill simply parks the inventory on Chase's balance sheet for a short period of time. When a repurchase agreement exists at a set price and this price covers all costs of the inventory plus related holding costs, Hill should report the inventory and related liability on its books.[5]

Sales with High Rates of Return

In industries such as publishing, music, toys, and sporting goods, formal or informal agreements often exist that permit purchasers to return inventory for a full or partial refund.

To illustrate, Quality Publishing Company sells textbooks to Campus Bookstores with an agreement that Campus may return for full credit any books not sold. Historically, Campus Bookstores returned approximately 25 percent of the textbooks from Quality Publishing. How should Quality Publishing report its sales transactions?

One alternative is to record the sale at the full amount and establish an estimated sales returns and allowances account. A second possibility is to not record any sale until circumstances indicate the amount of inventory the buyer will return. The key question

[5] "Accounting for Product Financing Arrangements," *Statement of Financial Accounting Standards No. 49* (Stamford, Conn.: FASB, 1981).

Jnder what circumstances should Quality Publishing consider the inventory sold? answer is that **when Quality Publishing can reasonably estimate the amount of ırns**, it should consider the goods sold. Conversely, if returns are unpredictable, ılity Publishing should not consider the goods sold and it should not remove the ds from its inventory.[6]

es on Installment

ods sold on installment" describes any type of sale in which the sale agreement re-es payment in periodic installments over an extended period of time. Because the of loss from uncollectibles is higher in installment-sale situations than in other sales sactions, the seller sometimes withholds legal title to the merchandise until the er has made all the payments.

The question is whether the seller should consider the inventory sold, even though le-title has not passed. The answer is that **the seller should exclude the goods from its ntory if it can reasonably estimate the percentage of bad debts.**

UNDERLYING CONCEPTS

For goods sold on installment, companies should recognize revenues because they have been substantially earned and are reasonably estimable. Collection is not the most critical event if bad debts can be reasonably estimated.

PARKING!

In one of the more elaborate accounting frauds, employees at **Kurzweil Applied Intelligence Inc.** booked millions of dollars in phony inventory sales during a two-year period that straddled two audits and an initial public stock offering. They dummied up phony shipping documents and logbooks to support bogus sales transactions. Then they shipped high-tech equipment, not to customers, but to a public warehouse for "temporary" storage, where some of it sat for 17 months. (Kurzweil still had ownership.)

To foil auditors' attempts to verify the existence of the inventory, Kurzweil employees moved the goods from warehouse to warehouse. To cover the fraudulently recorded sales transactions as auditors closed in, the employees brought back the still-hidden goods, under the pretense that the goods were returned by customers. When auditors uncovered the fraud, the bottom dropped out of Kurzweil's stock.

Source: Adapted from "Anatomy of a Fraud," *Business Week* (September 16, 1996), pp. 90–94.

WHAT DO THE NUMBERS MEAN?

ect of Inventory Errors

ıs incorrectly included or excluded in determining cost of goods sold through inven- misstatements will result in errors in the financial statements. Let's look at two cases, ıming a periodic inventory system.

OBJECTIVE 3
Identify the effects of inventory errors on the financial statements.

ling Inventory Misstated

at would happen if **IBM** correctly records its beginning inventory and purchases, fails to include some items in ending inventory? In this situation, we would have following effects on the financial statements at the end of the period.

Balance Sheet		Income Statement	
Inventory	Understated	Cost of goods sold	Overstated
Retained earnings	Understated		
Working capital (current assets less current liabilities)	Understated	Net income	Understated
Current ratio (current assets divided by current liabilities)	Understated		

ILLUSTRATION 7-6
Financial Statement Effects of Misstated Ending Inventory

[6]"Revenue Recognition When Right of Return Exists," *Statement of Financial Accounting Stan-s No. 48* (Stamford, Conn.: FASB, 1981).

UNDERLYING CONCEPTS

When inventory is misstated, its presentation lacks representational usefulness.

If ending inventory is understated, working capital and the current ratio are understated. If cost of goods sold is overstated, then net income is understated.

To illustrate the effect on net income over a two-year period (2006–2007), assume that Jay Weiseman Corp. understates its ending inventory by $10,000 in 2006; all other items are correctly stated. The effect of this error is to decrease net income in 2006 and to increase net income in 2007. The error is counterbalanced (offset) in 2007 because beginning inventory is understated and net income is overstated. As Illustration 7-7 shows, the income statement misstates the net income figures for both 2006 and 2007, although the *total* for the two years is correct.

ILLUSTRATION 7-7
Effect of Ending Inventory Error on Two Periods

JAY WEISEMAN CORP.
(All figures assumed)

	Incorrect Recording		Correct Recording	
	2006	2007	2006	2007
Revenues	$100,000	$100,000	$100,000	$100,000
Cost of goods sold				
Beginning inventory	25,000	20,000	25,000	30,000
Purchased or produced	45,000	60,000	45,000	60,000
Goods available for sale	70,000	80,000	70,000	90,000
Less: Ending inventory	20,000*	40,000	30,000	40,000
Cost of goods sold	50,000	40,000	40,000	50,000
Gross profit	50,000	60,000	60,000	50,000
Administrative and selling expenses	40,000	40,000	40,000	40,000
Net income	$ 10,000	$ 20,000	$ 20,000	$ 10,000
	Total income for two years = $30,000		Total income for two years = $30,000	

*Ending inventory understated by $10,000 in 2006.

If Weiseman *overstates* ending inventory in 2006, the reverse effect occurs: Inventory, working capital, current ratio, and net income are overstated and cost of goods sold is understated. The effect of the error on net income will be counterbalanced in 2007, but the income statement misstates both years' net income figures.

Purchases and Inventory Misstated

Suppose that Bishop Company does not record as a purchase certain goods that it owns and does not count them in ending inventory. The effect on the financial statements (assuming this is a purchase on account) is as follows.

ILLUSTRATION 7-8
Financial Statement Effects of Misstated Purchases and Inventory

Balance Sheet		Income Statement	
Inventory	Understated	Purchases	Understated
Retained earnings	No effect	Cost of goods sold	No effect
Accounts payable	Understated	Net income	No effect
Working capital	No effect	Inventory (ending)	Understated
Current ratio	Overstated		

Omission of goods from purchases and inventory results in an understatement of inventory and accounts payable in the balance sheet; it also results in an understatement of purchases and ending inventory in the income statement. However, the omission of such goods does not affect net income for the period. Why not? Because Bishop understates both purchases and ending inventory by the same amount—the error is eby offset in cost of goods sold. Total working capital is unchanged, but the current ɔ is overstated because of the omission of equal amounts from inventory and ac-nts payable.

To illustrate the effect on the current ratio, assume that Bishop *understated* accounts able and ending inventory by $40,000. Illustration 7-9 shows the understated and ect data.

ILLUSTRATION 7-9
Effects of Purchases and Ending Inventory Errors

Purchases and Ending Inventory Understated		Purchases and Ending Inventory Correct	
Current assets	$120,000	Current assets	$160,000
Current liabilities	$ 40,000	Current liabilities	$ 80,000
Current ratio	3 to 1	Current ratio	2 to 1

understated data indicate a current ratio of 3 to 1, whereas the correct ratio is 2 to 'hus, understatement of accounts payable and ending inventory can lead to a ndow dressing" of the current ratio. That is, Bishop can make the current ratio ap-r better than it is.

If Bishop *overstates* both purchases (on account) and ending inventory, then the ef-s on the balance sheet are exactly the reverse: The financial statements overstate in-tory and accounts payable, and understate the current ratio. The overstatement does affect cost of goods sold and net income because the errors offset one another. Sim-y, working capital is not affected.

We cannot overemphasize the importance of proper inventory measurement in senting accurate financial statements. For example, **Leslie Fay**, a women's arel maker, had accounting irregularities that wiped out one year's net income caused a restatement of the prior year's earnings. One reason: It inflated entory and deflated cost of goods sold. **Anixter Bros. Inc.** had to restate its income $1.7 million because an accountant in the antenna manufacturing division rstated the ending inventory, thereby reducing its cost of sales. Similarly, **AM rnational** allegedly recorded as sold products that were only being rented. As sult, inaccurate inventory and sales figures inappropriately added $7.9 million retax income.

STS INCLUDED IN INVENTORY

OBJECTIVE 4
Understand the items to include as inventory cost.

of the most important problems in dealing with inventories concerns the dollar ount at which to carry the inventory in the accounts. **Companies generally account the acquisition of inventories, like other assets, on a cost basis.**

oduct Costs

duct costs are those costs that "attach" to the inventory. As a result, a company rds product costs in the inventory account. These costs are directly connected with ging the goods to the buyer's place of business and converting such goods to a sal-condition. Such charges include freight charges on goods purchased, other direct s of acquisition, and labor and other production costs incurred in processing the ds up to the time of sale.

It seems proper also to allocate to inventories a share of any buying costs or ex-ses of a purchasing department, storage costs, and other costs incurred in storing andling the goods before their sale. However, because of the practical difficulties olved in allocating such costs and expenses, companies usually exclude these items aluing inventories.

A manufacturing company's costs include direct materials, direct labor, and man-turing overhead costs. Manufacturing overhead costs include indirect materials, indirect labor, and various costs, such as depreciation, taxes, insurance, and heat and electricity.

WHAT DO THE NUMBERS MEAN?

IT WAS THE WILD WEST

The practice of promotional payments, also known as vendor allowances, is widespread in the retail world. Eager to meet sales targets or promote their products through shelf placements and in store advertisements, vendors have been happy to grease the palms of retailers with rebates, allowances, and price breaks.

The question is, "How should retailers account for these payments?" Until recently some retailers recorded the payments as a reduction of selling expense. Unfortunately, in some of these cases the retailers had not actually sold the goods. Others accounted for them as a reduction of cost of goods sold.

Recently the SEC sued three executives of **Kmart Holding** and some Kmart vendors for their role in a $24 million accounting fraud that booked vendor allowances early. The scheme apparently allowed some Kmart managers to meet internal profit-margin targets. Similarly, **Royal Ahold** (a large Dutch supermarket operator) discovered that its U.S. Foodservice unit had improperly accounted for vendor payments, resulting in overstated earnings of at least $500 million. In addition, it found inflated profits at two of its other subsidiaries, also caused by improper accounting for vendor payments.

One analyst noted that it was like "the Wild West out there" because the lack of rules about when to recognize these payments and how to classify them allowed a certain amount of lawlessness. As a result, the FASB recently ruled that unless certain conditions are met, these payments must reduce cost of goods sold on the income statement. The accounting now appears right, but it took some frauds to close the accounting gap in this area.

Source: C. Schneider, "Retailers and Vendor Allowances," *CFO.com* (August 13, 2003).

Period Costs

Period costs are those costs that are indirectly related to the acquisition or production of goods. Period costs such as selling expenses and, under ordinary circumstances, general and administrative expenses are therefore not included as part as part of inventory cost.

UNDERLYING CONCEPTS

In capitalizing interest, companies apply both constraints—materiality and cost/benefit.

Yet, conceptually, these expenses are as much a cost of the product as the initial purchase price and related freight charges attached to the product. Why then do companies exclude these costs from inventoriable items? Because companies generally consider selling expenses as more directly related to the cost of goods sold than to the unsold inventory. In addition, period costs, especially administrative expenses, are so unrelated or indirectly related to the immediate production process that any allocation is purely arbitrary.[7]

Interest is another period cost. Companies usually expense **interest costs** associated with getting inventories ready for sale. Supporters of this approach argue that interest costs are really a **cost of financing**. Others contend that interest costs incurred to finance activities associated with readying inventories for sale are as much a **cost**

[7]Companies should not record abnormal freight, handling costs, and amounts of wasted materials (spoilage) as inventory costs. If the costs associated with the actual level of spoilage or product defects are greater than the costs associated with normal spoilage or defects, the company should charge the excess as an expense in the current period. "Inventory Costs: An Amendment of ARB No. 43, Chapter 4," *Statement of Financial Accounting Standards No. 151* (Norwalk, Conn.: FASB 2004.)

he asset as materials, labor, and overhead. Therefore, they reason, companies uld capitalize interest costs.

The FASB ruled that companies should capitalize interest costs related to as- constructed for internal use or assets produced as discrete projects (such as ɔs or real estate projects) for sale or lease.[8] The FASB emphasized that these dis- e projects should take considerable time, entail substantial expenditures, and be ly to involve significant amounts of interest cost. A company should not capi- ze interest costs for inventories that it routinely manufactures or otherwise pro- es in large quantities on a repetitive basis. In this case, the informational bene- loes not justify the cost.

atment of Purchase Discounts

use of a **Purchase Discounts** account in a periodic inventory system indicates that company is reporting its purchases and accounts payable at the gross amount. If a ıpany uses this **gross method**, it reports purchase discounts as a deduction from chases on the income statement.

Another approach is to record the purchases and accounts payable at an amount **of the cash discounts**. In this approach, the company records failure to take a chase discount within the discount period in a Purchase Discounts Lost account. company uses this **net method**, it considers purchase discounts lost as a finan- expense and reports it in the "Other expenses and losses" section of the income ement. This treatment is considered better for two reasons: (1) It provides a ect reporting of the cost of the asset and related liability. (2) It can measure ıagement inefficiency by holding management responsible for discounts not ɛn.

To illustrate the difference between the gross and net methods, assume the fol- ing transactions.

ILLUSTRATION 7-10
Entries under Gross and Net Methods

Gross Method			Net Method		
rchase cost $10,000, terms 2/10, net 30:					
rchases	10,000		Purchases	9,800	
Accounts Payable		10,000	Accounts Payable		9,800
oices of $4,000 are paid within discount period:					
counts Payable	4,000		Accounts Payable	3,920	
Purchase Discounts		80	Cash		3,920
Cash		3,920			
oices of $6,000 are paid after discount period:					
counts Payable	6,000		Accounts Payable	5,880	
Cash		6,000	Purchase Discounts Lost	120	
			Cash		6,000

UNDERLYING CONCEPTS

Not using the net method because of resultant difficulties is an example of the application of the cost/benefit constraint.

Many believe that the somewhat more complicated net method is not justified by resulting benefits. This could account for the widespread use of the less logical but pler gross method. In addition, some contend that management is reluctant to re- : in the financial statements the amount of purchase discounts lost.

[8]"Capitalization of Interest Cost," *Statement of Financial Accounting Standards No. 34* (Stam- , Conn.: FASB, 1979). The reporting rules related to interest cost capitalization have their test impact in accounting for long-term assets. We therefore discuss them in Chapter 9.

YOU MAY NEED A MAP

WHAT DO THE NUMBERS MEAN?

Does it really matter *where* a company reports certain costs in its income statement, as long as it includes them all as expenses in computing income?

For e-tailers, such as **Amazon.com** or **Drugstore.com**, *where* they report certain selling costs does appear to be important. Contrary to well-established retailer practices, these companies insist on reporting some selling costs—fulfillment costs related to inventory shipping and warehousing—as part of administrative expenses, instead of as cost of goods sold. This practice is allowable within GAAP, *if* applied consistently and adequately disclosed. Although the practice doesn't affect the bottom line, it does make the e-tailers' gross margins look better. For example, at one time Amazon.com reported $265 million of these costs in one quarter. Some experts thought Amazon.com should include those charges in costs of goods sold, which would substantially lower its gross profit, as shown below.

(in millions)

	E-tailer Reporting	Traditional Reporting
Sales	$2,795	$2,795
Cost of goods sold	2,132	2,397
Gross profit	$ 663	$ 398
Gross margin %	24%	14%

Similarly, if **Drugstore.com** and **eToys.com** made similar adjustments, their gross margins would go from positive to negative.

Thus, if you want to be able to compare the operating results of e-tailers to other traditional retailers, it might be a good idea to have a good accounting map in order to navigate their income statements and how they report certain selling costs.

Source: Adapted from P. Elstrom, "The End of Fuzzy Math?" *Business Week*, e.Biz—Net Worth (December 11, 2000). See also *EITF No. 00–10*, "Accounting for Shipping and Handling Fees and Costs." Under this standard, companies must disclose the accounting policy for classifying these selling costs in income.

WHICH COST FLOW ASSUMPTION TO ADOPT?

OBJECTIVE 5
Describe and compare the cost flow assumptions used to account for inventories.

During any given fiscal period, companies typically purchase merchandise at several different prices. If a company prices inventories at cost and it made numerous purchases at different unit costs, which cost price should it use? Conceptually, a specific identification of the given items sold and unsold seems optimal. But this measure often proves both expensive and impossible to achieve. Consequently, companies use one of several systematic inventory **cost flow assumptions.**

Indeed, the actual physical flow of goods and the cost flow assumption often greatly differ. **There is no requirement that the cost flow assumption adopted be consistent with the physical movement of goods.** A company's major objective in selecting a method should be to choose the one that, under the circumstances, most clearly reflects periodic income.[9]

To illustrate, assume that Call-Mart Inc. had the following transactions in its first month of operations.

Date	Purchases	Sold or Issued	Balance
March 2	2,000 @ $4.00		2,000 units
March 15	6,000 @ $4.40		8,000 units
March 19		4,000 units	4,000 units
March 30	2,000 @ $4.75		6,000 units

[9]"Restatement and Revision of Accounting Research Bulletins," *Accounting Research Bulletin No. 43* (New York: AICPA, 1953), Ch. 4, Statement 4.

From this information, Call-Mart computes the ending inventory of 6,000 units and cost of goods available for sale (beginning inventory + purchases) of $43,900 [(2,000 4.00) + (6,000 @ $4.40) + (2,000 @ $4.75)]. The question is, which price or prices ıld it assign to the 6,000 units of ending inventory? The answer depends on which flow assumption it uses.

ecific Identification

cific identification calls for identifying each item sold and each item in inventory. ɔmpany includes in cost of goods sold the costs of the specific items sold. It includes ıventory the costs of the specific items on hand. This method may be used only in ances where it is practical to separate physically the different purchases made. As sult, most companies only use this method when handling a relatively small num- of costly, easily distinguishable items. In the retail trade this includes some types :welry, fur coats, automobiles, and some furniture. In manufacturing it includes spe- orders and many products manufactured under a job cost system.

To illustrate, assume that Call-Mart Inc.'s 6,000 units of inventory consists of 1,000 :s from the March 2 purchase, 3,000 from the March 15 purchase, and 2,000 from March 30 purchase. Illustration 7-11 shows how Call-Mart computes the ending in- tory and cost of goods sold.

ILLUSTRATION 7-11
Specific Identification Method

Date	No. of Units	Unit Cost	Total Cost
March 2	1,000	$4.00	$ 4,000
March 15	3,000	4.40	13,200
March 30	2,000	4.75	9,500
Ending inventory	6,000		$26,700

Cost of goods available for sale (computed in previous section)	$43,900
Deduct: Ending inventory	26,700
Cost of goods sold	$17,200

This method appears ideal. Specific identification matches actual costs against ac- revenue. Thus, a company reports ending inventory at actual cost. In other words, **ler specific identification the cost flow matches the physical flow of the goods.** closer observation, however, this method has certain deficiencies.

Some argue that specific identification allows a company to manipulate net income. example, assume that a wholesaler purchases identical plywood early in the year ıree different prices. When it sells the plywood, the wholesaler can select either the est or the highest price to charge to expense. It simply selects the plywood from a :ific lot for delivery to the customer. A business manager, therefore, can manipulate income by delivering to the customer the higher- or lower-priced item, depending vhether the company seeks lower or higher reported earnings for the period.

Another problem relates to the arbitrary allocation of costs that sometimes occurs ı specific inventory items. For example, a company often faces difficulty in relating ɔping charges, storage costs, and discounts directly to a given inventory item. This ılts in allocating these costs somewhat arbitrarily, leading to a "breakdown" in the :ision of the specific identification method.[10]

[10]The motion picture industry provides a good illustration of the cost allocation problem. n actors receive a percentage of net income for a given movie or television program. Some rs, however, have alleged that their programs have been extremely profitable to the motion ıre studios but they have received little in the way of profit sharing. Actors contend that the ios allocate additional costs to successful projects to avoid sharing profits.

Average Cost

As the name implies, the **average cost method** prices items in the inventory on the basis of the average cost of all similar goods available during the period. To illustrate use of the periodic inventory method (amount of inventory computed at the end of the period), Call-Mart computes the ending inventory and cost of goods sold using a **weighted-average method** as follows.

ILLUSTRATION 7-12
Weighted-Average Method—Periodic Inventory

Date of Invoice	No. Units	Unit Cost	Total Cost
March 2	2,000	$4.00	$ 8,000
March 15	6,000	4.40	26,400
March 30	2,000	4.75	9,500
Total goods available	10,000		$43,900

Weighted-average cost per unit $\frac{\$43,900}{10,000} = \$4.39$

Inventory in units 6,000 units
Ending inventory 6,000 × \$4.39 = \$26,340

Cost of goods available for sale	$43,900
Deduct: Ending inventory	26,340
Cost of goods sold	$17,560

In computing the average cost per unit, Call-Mart includes the beginning inventory, if any, both in the total units available and in the total cost of goods available.

Companies use the **moving-average method** with perpetual inventory records. Illustration 7-13 shows the application of the average cost method for perpetual records.

ILLUSTRATION 7-13
Moving-Average Method—Perpetual Inventory

Date	Purchased		Sold or Issued	Balance	
March 2	(2,000 @ $4.00)	$ 8,000		(2,000 @ $4.00)	$ 8,000
March 15	(6,000 @ 4.40)	26,400		(8,000 @ 4.30)	34,400
March 19			(4,000 @ $4.30) $17,200	(4,000 @ 4.30)	17,200
March 30	(2,000 @ 4.75)	9,500		(6,000 @ 4.45)	26,700

In this method, Call-Mart computes a **new average unit cost** each time it makes a purchase. For example, on March 15, after purchasing 6,000 units for $26,400, Call-Mart has 8,000 units costing $34,400 ($8,000 plus $26,400) on hand. The average unit cost is $34,400 divided by 8,000, or $4.30. Call-Mart uses this unit cost in costing withdrawals until it makes another purchase. At that point, Call-Mart computes a new average unit cost. Accordingly, the company shows the cost of the 4,000 units withdrawn on March 19 at $4.30, for a total cost of goods sold of $17,200. On March 30, following the purchase of 2,000 units for $9,500, Call-Mart determines a new unit cost of $4.45, for an ending inventory of $26,700.

Companies often use average cost methods for practical rather than conceptual reasons. These methods are simple to apply and objective. They are not as subject to income manipulation as some of the other inventory pricing methods. In addition, proponents of the average cost methods reason that measuring a specific physical flow of inventory is often impossible. Therefore, it is better to cost items on an average-price basis. This argument is particularly persuasive when dealing with similar inventory items.

First-In, First-Out (FIFO)

The **FIFO (first-in, first-out) method** assumes that a company uses goods in the order in which it purchases them. In other words, the FIFO method assumes that **the first goods purchased are the first used** (in a manufacturing concern) **or the first sold** (in erchandising concern). The inventory remaining must therefore represent the most nt purchases.

To illustrate, assume that Call-Mart uses the periodic inventory system. It deter-es its cost of the ending inventory by taking the cost of the most recent purchase working back until it accounts for all units in the inventory. Call-Mart determines nding inventory and cost of goods sold as shown in Illustration 7-14.

ILLUSTRATION 7-14
FIFO Method—Periodic Inventory

Date	No. Units	Unit Cost	Total Cost
March 30	2,000	$4.75	$ 9,500
March 15	4,000	4.40	17,600
Ending inventory	6,000		$27,100

Cost of goods available for sale	$43,900
Deduct: Ending inventory	27,100
Cost of goods sold	$16,800

If Call-Mart instead uses a perpetual inventory system in quantities and dollars, it ches a cost figure to each withdrawal. Then the cost of the 4,000 units removed on ch 19 consists of the cost of the items purchased on March 2 and March 15. stration 7-15 shows the inventory on a FIFO basis perpetual system for Call-Mart.

ILLUSTRATION 7-15
FIFO Method—Perpetual Inventory

Date	Purchased		Sold or Issued	Balance	
rch 2	(2,000 @ $4.00)	$ 8,000		2,000 @ $4.00	$ 8,000
rch 15	(6,000 @ 4.40)	26,400		2,000 @ 4.00 6,000 @ 4.40	34,400
rch 19			2,000 @ $4.00 2,000 @ 4.40 ($16,800)	4,000 @ 4.40	17,600
rch 30	(2,000 @ 4.75)	9,500		4,000 @ 4.40 2,000 @ 4.75	27,100

Here, the ending inventory is $27,100, and the cost of goods sold is $16,800 [(2,000 00) + (2,000 @ $4.40)].

Notice that in these two FIFO examples, the cost of goods sold ($16,800) and end-inventory ($27,100) are the same. **In all cases where FIFO is used, the inventory cost of goods sold would be the same at the end of the month whether a per-ıal or periodic system is used.** Why? Because the same costs will always be first nd, therefore, first out. This is true whether a company computes cost of goods sold sells goods throughout the accounting period (the perpetual system) or as a resid-at the end of the accounting period (the periodic system).

One objective of FIFO is to approximate the physical flow of goods. When the phys-flow of goods is actually first-in, first-out, the FIFO method closely approximates ific identification. At the same time, it prevents manipulation of income. With FIFO, mpany cannot pick a certain cost item to charge to expense.

Another advantage of the FIFO method is that the ending inventory is close to cur-cost. Because the first goods in are the first goods out, the ending inventory amount sists of the most recent purchases. This is particularly true with rapid inventory ıover. This approach generally approximates replacement cost on the balance sheet en price changes have not occurred since the most recent purchases.

However, the FIFO method fails to match current costs against current revenues he income statement. A company charges the oldest costs against the more current enue, possibly distorting gross profit and net income.

Last-In, First-Out (LIFO)

INTERNATIONAL INSIGHT

International accounting standards do not permit LIFO.

The **LIFO (last-in, first-out) method** matches the cost of the last goods purchased against revenue. If Call-Mart Inc. uses a periodic inventory system, it assumes that **the cost of the total quantity sold or issued during the month comes from the most recent purchases.** Call Mart prices the ending inventory by using the total units as a basis of computation and disregards the exact dates of sales or issuances. For example, assume that the cost of the 4,000 units withdrawn absorbed the 2,000 units purchased on March 30 and 2,000 of the 6,000 units purchased on March 15. Illustration 7-16 shows how Call-Mart computes the inventory and related cost of goods sold, using the periodic inventory method.

ILLUSTRATION 7-16
LIFO Method—Periodic Inventory

Date of Invoice	No. Units	Unit Cost	Total Cost
March 2	2,000	$4.00	$ 8,000
March 15	4,000	4.40	17,600
Ending inventory	6,000		$25,600

Goods available for sale	$43,900
Deduct: Ending inventory	25,600
Cost of goods sold	$18,300

If Call-Mart keeps a perpetual inventory record in quantities and dollars, use of the LIFO method results in **different ending inventory and cost of goods sold amounts than the amounts calculated under the periodic method.** Illustration 7-17 shows these differences under the perpetual method.

ILLUSTRATION 7-17
LIFO Method—Perpetual Inventory

Date	Purchased		Sold or Issued	Balance	
March 2	(2,000 @ $4.00)	$ 8,000		2,000 @ $4.00	$ 8,000
March 15	(6,000 @ 4.40)	26,400		2,000 @ 4.00 6,000 @ 4.40	34,400
March 19			(4,000 @ $4.40) $17,600	2,000 @ 4.00 2,000 @ 4.40	16,800
March 30	(2,000 @ 4.75)	9,500		2,000 @ 4.00 2,000 @ 4.40 2,000 @ 4.75	26,300

wiley.com/college/kieso

Tutorial on Inventory Methods

The month-end periodic inventory computation presented in Illustration 7-16 (inventory $25,600 and cost of goods sold $18,300) shows a different amount from the perpetual inventory computation (inventory $26,300 and cost of goods sold $17,600). The periodic system matches the total withdrawals for the month with the total purchases for the month in applying the last-in, first-out method. In contrast, the perpetual system matches each withdrawal with the immediately preceding purchases. In effect, the periodic computation assumed that Call Mart included the cost of the goods that it purchased on March 30 in the sale or issue on March 19.

SPECIAL ISSUES RELATED TO LIFO

LIFO Reserve

OBJECTIVE 6
Explain the significance and use of a LIFO reserve.

Many companies use LIFO for tax and external reporting purposes. However, they maintain a FIFO, average cost, or standard cost system for internal reporting purposes. There are several reasons to do so: (1) Companies often base their pricing decisions on a FIFO, average, or standard cost assumption, rather than on a LIFO basis. (2) Record-keeping on some other basis is easier because the LIFO assumption usually does not approximate the physical flow of the product. (3) Profit-sharing and other bonus arrangements often depend on a non-LIFO inventory assumption. Finally, (4) the use of a pure LIFO system is troublesome for interim periods, which require estimates of year-end quantities and prices.

The difference between the inventory method used for internal reporting purposes and LIFO is the Allowance to Reduce Inventory to LIFO or the **LIFO reserve**. The change in the allowance balance from one period to the next is the **LIFO effect**. The LIFO effect is the adjustment that companies must make to the accounting records in a given year.

To illustrate, assume that Acme Boot Company uses the FIFO method for internal reporting purposes and LIFO for external reporting purposes. At January 1, 2007, the Allowance to Reduce Inventory to LIFO balance is $20,000. At December 31, 2007, the balance should be $50,000. As a result, Acme Boot realizes a LIFO effect of $30,000 and makes the following entry at year-end.

Cost of Goods Sold	30,000	
Allowance to Reduce Inventory to LIFO		30,000

Acme Boot deducts the Allowance to Reduce Inventory to LIFO from inventory to ensure that it states the inventory on a LIFO basis at year-end.

Companies should disclose either the LIFO reserve or the replacement cost of the inventory, as shown in Illustration 7-18.[11]

ILLUSTRATION 7-18
Note Disclosures of LIFO Reserve

American Maize-Products Company

Inventories (Note 3)	$80,320,000

Note 3: Inventories. At December 31, $31,516,000 of inventories were valued using the LIFO method. This amount is less than the corresponding replacement value by $3,765,000.

Brown Shoe Company, Inc.
(in thousands)

	Current Year	Previous Year
Inventories, (Note 1)	$365,989	$362,274

Note 1 (partial): Inventories. Inventories are valued at the lower of cost or market determined principally by the last-in, first-out (LIFO) method. If the first-in, first-out (FIFO) cost method had been used, inventories would have been $11,709 higher in the current year and $13,424 higher in the previous year.

Additional LIFO Reserve Disclosures

LIFO Liquidation

OBJECTIVE 7
Understand the effect of LIFO liquidations.

Up to this point, we have emphasized a **specific-goods approach** to costing LIFO inventories (also called **traditional LIFO** or **unit LIFO**). This approach is often unrealistic for two reasons:

1. When a company has many different inventory items, the accounting cost of tracking each inventory item is expensive.
2. Erosion of the LIFO inventory can easily occur. Referred to as **LIFO liquidation**, this often distorts net income and leads to substantial tax payments.

[11]The AICPA Task Force on LIFO Inventory Problems, *Issues Paper* (New York: AICPA, November 30, 1984), pars. 2–24. The SEC has endorsed this issues paper, and therefore the paper has authoritative status for GAAP purposes.

WHAT DO THE NUMBERS MEAN?

COMPARING APPLES TO APPLES

Investors commonly use the current ratio to evaluate a company's liquidity. They compute the current ratio as current assets divided by current liabilities. A higher current ratio indicates that a company is better able to meet its current obligations when they come due. However, it is not meaningful to compare the current ratio for a company using LIFO to one for a company using FIFO. It would be like comparing apples to oranges, since the two companies measure inventory (and cost of goods sold) differently.

To make the current ratio comparable on an apples-to-apples basis, analysts use the LIFO reserve. The following adjustments should do the trick:

Inventory Adjustment: LIFO inventory + LIFO reserve = FIFO inventory

(For cost of goods sold, add the *change* in the LIFO reserve to LIFO cost of goods sold to yield the comparable FIFO amount.)

For **Brown Shoe, Inc.** (see Illustration 7-18), with current assets of $487.8 million and current liabilities of $217.8 million, the current ratio using LIFO is: $487.8 ÷ $217.8 = 2.2. After adjusting for the LIFO effect, Brown's current ratio under FIFO would be: ($487.8 + $11.7) ÷ $217.8 = 2.3.

Thus, without the LIFO adjustment, the Brown Shoe current ratio is understated.

To understand the LIFO liquidation problem, assume that Basler Co. has 30,000 pounds of steel in its inventory on December 31, 2007, with cost determined on a specific-goods LIFO approach.

	Ending Inventory (2007)		
	Pounds	Unit Cost	LIFO Cost
2004	8,000	$ 4	$ 32,000
2005	10,000	6	60,000
2006	7,000	9	63,000
2007	5,000	10	50,000
	30,000		$205,000

As indicated, the ending 2007 inventory for Basler comprises costs from past periods. These costs are called **layers** (increases from period to period). The first layer is identified as the base layer. Illustration 7-19 shows the layers for Basler.

ILLUSTRATION 7-19
Layers of LIFO Inventory

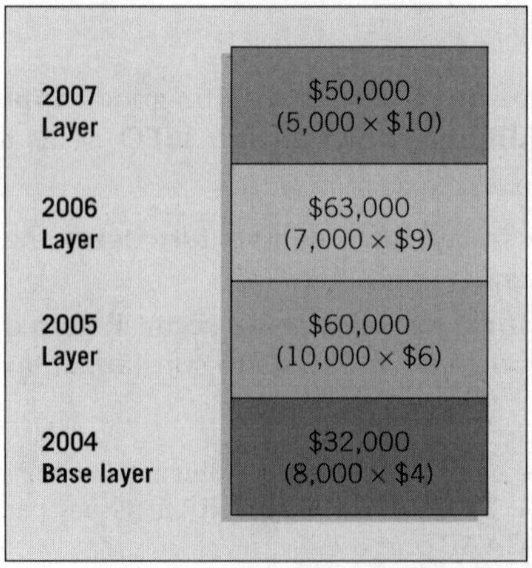

e the increased price of steel over the 4-year period. In 2008, due to metal short-, Basler had to liquidate much of its inventory (a LIFO liquidation). At the end of 3, only 6,000 pounds of steel remained in inventory. Because the company uses LIFO, er liquidates the most recent layer, 2007, first, followed by the 2006 layer, and so The result: Basler matches costs from preceding periods against sales revenues re-ed in current dollars. As Illustration 7-20 shows, this leads to a distortion in net in-e and increased taxable income in the current period. Unfortunately **LIFO liqui-ons can occur frequently when using a specific-goods LIFO approach.**

ILLUSTRATION 7-20
LIFO Liquidation

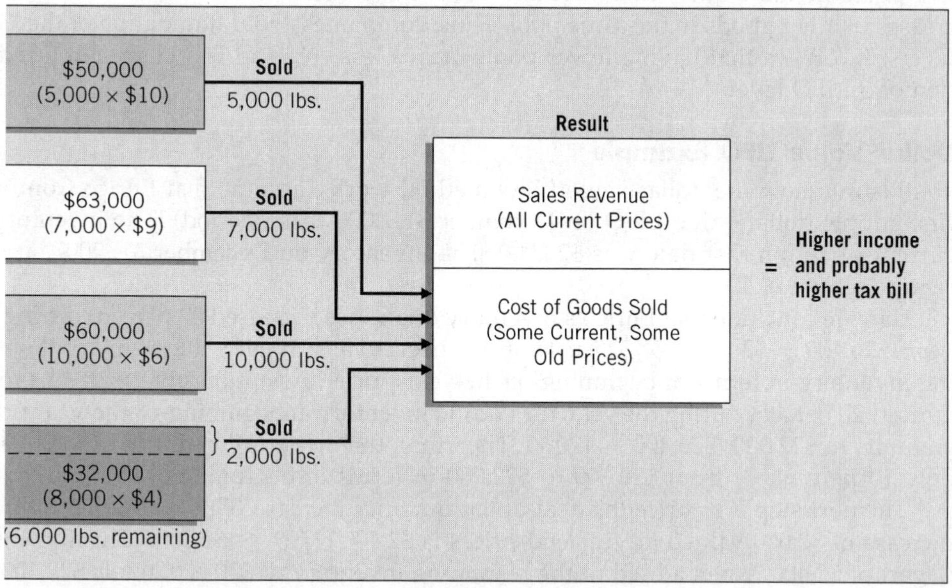

To alleviate the LIFO liquidation problems and to simplify the accounting, com-ies can combine goods into pools. A **pool** groups items of a similar nature. Thus, ead of only identical units, a company combines, and counts as a group, a number imilar units or products. This method, the **specific-goods pooled LIFO approach**, ally results in fewer LIFO liquidations. Why? Because the reduction of one quan-in the pool may be offset by an increase in another.

The specific-goods pooled LIFO approach eliminates some of the disadvantages of specific-goods (traditional) accounting for LIFO inventories. This pooled approach, g quantities as its measurement basis, however, creates other problems.

First, most companies continually change the mix of their products, materials, and luction methods. As a result, in employing a pooled approach using quantities, panies must continually redefine the pools. This can be time consuming and costly. ond, even when practical, the approach often results in an erosion ("LIFO liquida-") of the layers, thereby losing much of the LIFO costing benefit. An erosion of the rs results due to replacement of a specific good or material in the pool with an-r good or material. The new item may not be similar enough to be treated as part ie old pool. Therefore a company may need to recognize any inflationary profit de-ed on the old goods as it replaces them.

llar-Value LIFO

OBJECTIVE 8
Explain the dollar-value LIFO method.

dollar-value LIFO method overcomes the problems of redefining pools and erod-layers. **The dollar-value LIFO method determines and measures any increases decreases in a pool in terms of total dollar value, not the physical quantity of goods in the inventory pool.**

Such an approach has two important advantages over the specific-goods pooled roach. First, companies may include a broader range of goods in a dollar-value

LIFO pool. Second, a dollar-value LIFO pool permits replacement of goods that are similar items, similar in use, or interchangeable. (In contrast, a specific-goods LIFO pool only allows replacement of items that are substantially identical.)

Thus, dollar-value LIFO techniques help protect LIFO layers from erosion. Because of this advantage, companies frequently use the dollar-value LIFO method in practice.[12] Companies use the more traditional LIFO approaches only when dealing with few goods and expecting little change in product mix.

Tutorial on Dollar-Value LIFO

Under the dollar-value LIFO method, one pool may contain the entire inventory. However, companies generally use several pools.[13] In general, the more goods included in a pool, the more likely that increases in the quantities of some goods will offset decreases in other goods in the same pool. Thus, companies avoid liquidation of the LIFO layers. It follows that having fewer pools means less cost and less chance of a reduction of a LIFO layer.[14]

Dollar-Value LIFO Example

To illustrate how the dollar-value LIFO method works, assume that Enrico Company first adopts dollar-value LIFO on December 31, 2006 (base period). The inventory at current prices on that date was $20,000. The inventory on December 31, 2007, at current prices is $26,400.

Can we conclude that Enrico's inventory quantities increased 32 percent during the year ($26,400 ÷ $20,000 = 132%)? First, we need to ask: What is the value of the ending inventory in terms of beginning-of-the-year prices? Assuming that prices have increased 20 percent during the year, the ending inventory at beginning-of-the-year prices amounts to $22,000 ($26,400 ÷ 120%). Therefore, the inventory quantity has increased only 10 percent, or from $20,000 to $22,000 in terms of beginning-of-the-year prices.

The next step is to price this real-dollar quantity increase. This real-dollar quantity increase of $2,000 valued at year-end prices is $2,400 (120% × $2,000). This increment (layer) of $2,400, when added to the beginning inventory of $20,000, totals $22,400 for the December 31, 2007, inventory, as shown below.

First layer—(beginning inventory) in terms of 100	$20,000
Second layer—(2007 increase) in terms of 120	2,400
Dollar-value LIFO inventory, December 31, 2007	$22,400

Note that a layer forms only when the ending inventory at base-year prices exceeds the beginning inventory at base-year prices. And only when a new layer forms must Enrico compute a new index.

[12]A study by James M. Reeve and Keith G. Stanga disclosed that the vast majority of respondent companies applying LIFO use the dollar-value method or the dollar-value retail method to apply LIFO. Only a small minority of companies use the specific-goods (unit LIFO) approach or the specific-goods pooling approach. See J.M. Reeve and K.G. Stanga, "The LIFO Pooling Decision," *Accounting Horizons* (June 1987), p. 27.

[13]The Reeve and Stanga study (ibid.) reports that most companies have only a few pools—the median is six for retailers and three for nonretailers. But the distributions are highly skewed; some companies have 100 or more pools. Retailers that use LIFO have significantly more pools than nonretailers. About a third of the nonretailers (mostly manufacturers) use a single pool for their entire LIFO inventory.

[14]A later study shows that when quantities are increasing, multiple pools over a period of time may produce (under rather general conditions) significantly higher cost of goods sold deductions than a single-pool approach. When a stock-out occurs, a single-pool approach may lessen the layer liquidation for that year, but it may not erase the cumulative cost of goods sold advantage accruing to the use of multiple pools built up over the preceding years. See William R. Coon and Randall B. Hayes, "The Dollar Value LIFO Pooling Decision: The Conventional Wisdom Is Too General," *Accounting Horizons* (December 1989), pp. 57–70.

Comprehensive Dollar-Value LIFO Example

To illustrate the use of the dollar-value LIFO method in a more complex situation, assume that Bismark Company develops the following information.

December 31	Inventory at End-of-Year Prices	÷	Price Index (percentage)	=	End-of-Year Inventory at Base-Year Prices
(Base year) 2004	$200,000		100		$200,000
2005	299,000		115		260,000
2006	300,000		120		250,000
2007	351,000		130		270,000

At December 31, 2004, Bismark computes the ending inventory under dollar-value LIFO as $200,000, as Illustration 7-21 shows.

ILLUSTRATION 7-21
Computation of 2004 Inventory at LIFO Cost

Ending Inventory at Base-Year Prices	Layer at Base-Year Prices		Price Index (percentage)		Ending Inventory at LIFO Cost
$200,000	$200,000	×	100	=	$200,000

At December 31, 2005, a comparison of the ending inventory at base-year prices ($260,000) with the beginning inventory at base-year prices ($200,000) indicates that the quantity of goods (in base-year prices) increased $60,000 ($260,000 − $200,000). Bismark prices this increment (layer) at the 2005 index of 115 percent to arrive at a new layer of $69,000. Ending inventory for 2005 is $269,000, composed of the beginning inventory of $200,000 and the new layer of $69,000. Illustration 7-22 shows the computations.

ILLUSTRATION 7-22
Computation of 2005 Inventory at LIFO Cost

Ending Inventory at Base-Year Prices	Layers at Base-Year Prices		Price Index (percentage)		Ending Inventory at LIFO Cost
$260,000	→2004 $200,000	×	100	=	$200,000
	→2005 60,000	×	115	=	69,000
	$260,000				$269,000

At December 31, 2006, a comparison of the ending inventory at base-year prices ($250,000) with the beginning inventory at base-year prices ($260,000) indicates a decrease in the quantity of goods of $10,000 ($250,000 − $260,000). If the ending inventory at base-year prices is less than the beginning inventory at base-year prices, **a company must subtract the decrease from the most recently added layer. When a decrease occurs, the company "peels off" previous layers at the prices in existence when it added the layers.** In Bismark's situation, this means that it removes $10,000 in base-year prices from the 2005 layer of $60,000 at base-year prices. It values the balance of $50,000 ($60,000 − $10,000) at base-year prices at the 2005 price index of 115 percent. As a result, it now values this 2005 layer at $57,500 ($50,000 × 115%). Therefore, Bismark computes the ending inventory at $257,500, consisting of the beginning inventory of $200,000 and the second layer of $57,500. Illustration 7-23 shows the computations for 2006.

ILLUSTRATION 7-23
Computation of 2006 Inventory at LIFO Cost

Ending Inventory at Base-Year Prices	Layers at Base-Year Prices		Price Index (percentage)		Ending Inventory at LIFO Cost
$250,000	2004 $200,000	×	100	=	$200,000
	2005 50,000	×	115	=	57,500
	$250,000				$257,500

Note that if Bismark eliminates a layer or base (or portion thereof), it cannot rebuild it in future periods. That is, the layer is gone forever.

At December 31, 2007, a comparison of the ending inventory at base-year prices ($270,000) with the beginning inventory at base-year prices ($250,000) indicates an increase in the quantity of goods (in base-year prices) of $20,000 ($270,000 − $250,000). After converting the $20,000 increase to the 2007 price index, the ending inventory is $283,500, composed of the beginning layer of $200,000, a 2005 layer of $57,500, and a 2007 layer of $26,000 ($20,000 × 130%). Illustration 7-24 shows this computation.

ILLUSTRATION 7-24
Computation of 2007 Inventory at LIFO Cost

Ending Inventory at Base-Year Prices	Layers at Base-Year Prices		Price Index (percentage)		Ending Inventory at LIFO Cost
$270,000	2004 $200,000	×	100	=	$200,000
	2005 50,000	×	115	=	57,500
	2007 20,000	×	130	=	26,000
	$270,000				$283,500

The ending inventory at base-year prices must always equal the total of the layers at base-year prices. Checking that this situation exists will help to ensure correct dollar-value computations.

Selecting a Price Index

Obviously, price changes are critical in dollar-value LIFO. How do companies determine the price indexes? Many companies use the general price-level index that the federal government prepares and publishes each month. The most popular general external price-level index is the **Consumer Price Index for Urban Consumers** (CPI-U).[15] Companies also use more-specific external price indexes. For instance, various organizations compute and publish daily indexes for most commodities (gold, silver, other metals, corn, wheat, and other farm products). Many trade associations prepare indexes for specific product lines or industries. Any of these indexes may be used for dollar-value LIFO purposes.

When a relevant specific external price index is not readily available, a company may compute its own specific internal price index. The desired approach is to price ending inventory at the most current cost. Therefore, a company that chose to compute its own specific internal price index would ordinarily determine current cost by referring to the actual cost of the goods it most recently had purchased. The price index provides a measure of the change in price or cost levels between the base year and the current year. The company then computes the index for each year after the base year. The general formula for computing the index is as follows.

[15]Indexes may be **general** (composed of several commodities, goods, or services) or **specific** (for one commodity, good, or service). Additionally, they may be **external** (computed by an outside party, such as the government, commodity exchange, or trade association) or **internal** (computed by the enterprise for its own product or service).

ILLUSTRATION 7-25
Formula for Computing a Price Index

$$\frac{\text{Ending Inventory for the Period at Current Cost}}{\text{Ending Inventory for the Period at Base-Year Cost}} = \text{Price Index for Current Year}$$

This approach is generally referred to as the **double-extension method**. As its name implies, the value of the units in inventory is extended at *both* base-year prices and current-year prices.

To illustrate this computation, assume that Toledo Company's base-year inventory (January 1, 2007) consisted of the following.

Items	Quantity	Cost per Unit	Total Cost
A	1,000	$ 6	$ 6,000
B	2,000	20	40,000
January 1, 2007, inventory at base-year costs			$46,000

Examination of the ending inventory indicates that the company holds 3,000 units of Item A and 6,000 units of Item B on December 31, 2007. The most recent actual purchases related to these items were as follows.

Items	Purchase Date	Quantity Purchased	Cost per Unit
A	December 1, 2007	4,000	$ 7
B	December 15, 2007	5,000	25
B	November 16, 2007	1,000	22

Toledo double-extends the inventory as shown in Illustration 7-26.

ILLUSTRATION 7-26
Double-Extension Method of Determining a Price Index

	12/31/07 Inventory at Base-Year Costs			**12/31/07 Inventory at Current-Year Costs**		
Items	Units	Base-Year Cost per Unit	Total	Units	Current-Year Cost per Unit	Total
A	3,000	$ 6	$ 18,000	3,000	$ 7	$ 21,000
B	6,000	20	120,000	5,000	25	125,000
B				1,000	22	22,000
			$138,000			$168,000

After the inventories are double-extended, Toledo uses the formula in Illustration 7-25 to develop the index for the current year (2007), as follows.

ILLUSTRATION 7-27
Computation of 2007 Index

$$\frac{\text{Ending Inventory for the Period at Current Cost}}{\text{Ending Inventory for the Period at Base-Year Cost}} = \frac{\$168{,}000}{\$138{,}000} = 121.74\%$$

Toledo then applies this index (121.74%) to the layer added in 2007. Note in this illustration that Toledo used the most recent actual purchases to determine current cost; alternatively, it could have used other approaches such as FIFO and average cost. Whichever flow assumption is adopted, a company must use it consistently from one period to another.

Use of the double-extension method is time consuming and difficult where substantial technological change has occurred or where many items are involved. That is, as time passes, the company must determine a new base-year cost for new products, and must keep a base-year cost for each inventory item.[16]

Comparison of LIFO Approaches

We present three different approaches to computing LIFO inventories in this chapter—specific-goods LIFO, specific-goods pooled LIFO, and dollar-value LIFO. As we indicated earlier, the use of the specific-goods LIFO is unrealistic. Most companies have numerous goods in inventory at the end of a period. Costing (pricing) them on a unit basis is extremely expensive and time consuming.

The specific-goods pooled LIFO approach reduces recordkeeping and clerical costs. In addition, it is more difficult to erode the layers because the reduction of one quantity in the pool may be offset by an increase in another. Nonetheless, the pooled approach using quantities as its measurement basis can lead to untimely LIFO liquidations.

As a result, **most companies using a LIFO system employ dollar-value LIFO.** Although the approach appears complex, the logic and the computations are actually quite simple, after determining an appropriate index.

However, problems do exist with the dollar-value LIFO method. The selection of the items to be put in a pool can be subjective.[17] Such a determination, however, is extremely important because manipulation of the items in a pool without conceptual justification can affect reported net income. For example, the SEC noted that some companies have set up pools that are easy to liquidate. As a result, to increase income, a company simply decreases inventory, thereby matching low-cost inventory items to current revenues.

To curb this practice, the SEC has taken a much harder line on the number of pools that companies may establish. In a well-publicized case, **Stauffer Chemical Company** increased the number of LIFO pools from 8 to 280, boosting its net income by $16,515,000 or approximately 13 percent.[18] Stauffer justified the change in its Annual Report on the basis of "achieving a better matching of cost and revenue." The SEC required Stauffer to reduce the number of its inventory pools, contending that some pools were inappropriate and alleging income manipulation.

Major Advantages of LIFO

OBJECTIVE 9
Explain the major advantages and disadvantages of LIFO.

One obvious advantage of LIFO approaches is that the LIFO cost flow often approximates the physical flow of the goods in and out of inventory. For instance, in a coal pile, the last coal in is the first coal out because it is on the top of the pile. The coal remover is not going to take the coal from the bottom of the pile! The coal taken first is the coal placed on the pile last.

However, this is one of only a few situations where the actual physical flow corresponds to LIFO. Therefore most adherents of LIFO use other arguments for its widespread use, as follows.

[16]To simplify the analysis, companies may use another approach, initially sanctioned by the Internal Revenue Service for tax purposes. Under this method, a company obtains an index from an outside source or by double-extending only a sample portion of the inventory. For example, the IRS allows all companies to use as their inflation rate for a LIFO pool 80% of the inflation rate reported by the appropriate consumer or producer price indexes prepared by the Bureau of Labor Statistics (BLS). Once the company obtains the index, it divides the ending inventory at current cost by the index to find the base-year cost. Using generally available external indexes greatly simplifies LIFO computations, and frees companies from having to compute internal indexes.

[17]It is suggested that companies analyze how inventory purchases are affected by price changes, how goods are stocked, how goods are used, and if future liquidations are likely. See William R. Cron and Randall Hayes, ibid., p. 57.

[18]Commerce Clearing House, *SEC Accounting Rules* (Chicago: CCH, 1983), par. 4035.

Matching

LIFO matches the more recent costs against current revenues to provide a better measure of current earnings. During periods of inflation, many challenge the quality of non-LIFO earnings, noting that failing to match current costs against current revenues **creates transitory or "paper" profits ("inventory profits")**. Inventory profits occur when the inventory costs matched against sales are less than the inventory replacement cost. This results in understating the cost of goods sold and overstating profit. Using LIFO (rather than a method such as FIFO) matches current costs against revenues, thereby reducing inventory profits.

Tax Benefits/Improved Cash Flow

LIFO's popularity mainly stems from its tax benefits. As long as the price level increases and inventory quantities do not decrease, a deferral of income tax occurs. Why? Because a company matches the items it most recently purchased (at the higher price level) against revenues. For example, when **Fuqua Industries** switched to LIFO, it realized a tax savings of about $4 million. Even if the price level decreases later, the company still temporarily deferred its income taxes. Thus, use of LIFO in such situations improves a company's cash flow.[19]

The tax law requires that if a company uses LIFO for tax purposes, it must also use LIFO for financial accounting purposes[20] (although neither tax law nor GAAP requires a company to pool its inventories in the same manner for book and tax purposes). This requirement is often referred to as the **LIFO conformity rule**. Other inventory valuation methods do not have this requirement.

Future Earnings Hedge

With LIFO, future price declines will not substantially affect a company's future reported earnings. The reason: Since the company records the most recent inventory as sold first, there is not much ending inventory at high prices vulnerable to a price decline. Thus LIFO eliminates or substantially minimizes write-downs to market as a result of price decreases. In contrast, inventory costed under FIFO is more vulnerable to price declines, which can reduce net income substantially.

Major Disadvantages of LIFO

Despite its advantages, LIFO has the following drawbacks.

Reduced Earnings

Many corporate managers view the lower profits reported under the LIFO method in inflationary times as a distinct disadvantage. They would rather have higher reported profits than lower taxes. Some fear that investors may misunderstand an accounting change to LIFO, and that the lower profits may cause the price of the company's stock to fall.

Inventory Understated

LIFO may have a distorting effect on a company's balance sheet. The inventory valuation is normally outdated because the oldest costs remain in inventory. This understatement makes the working capital position of the company appear worse than it

[19]In periods of rising prices, the use of fewer pools will translate into greater income tax benefits through the use of LIFO. The use of fewer pools allows companies to offer inventory reductions on some items and inventory increases in others. In contrast, the use of more pools increases the likelihood of liquidating old, low-cost inventory layers and incurring negative tax consequences. See Reeve and Stanga, ibid., pp. 28–29.

[20]Management often selects an accounting procedure because a lower tax results from its use, instead of an accounting method that is conceptually more appealing. Throughout this textbook, we identify accounting procedures that provide income tax benefits to the user.

really is. A good example is **Caterpillar**, which uses LIFO costing for most of its inventory, valued at $4.7 billion at year-end 2004. Under FIFO costing, Caterpillar's inventories have a value of $6.8 billion—almost 50 percent higher than the LIFO amount.

The magnitude and direction of this variation between the carrying amount of inventory and its current price depend on the degree and direction of the price changes and the amount of inventory turnover. The combined effect of rising product prices and avoidance of inventory liquidations increases the difference between the inventory carrying value at LIFO and current prices of that inventory. This magnifies the balance sheet distortion attributed to the use of LIFO.

Physical Flow

LIFO does not approximate the physical flow of the items except in specific situations (such as the coal pile discussed earlier). Originally companies could use LIFO only in certain circumstances. This situation has changed over the years. Now, physical flow characteristics no longer determine whether a company may employ LIFO.

Involuntary Liquidation/Poor Buying Habits

If a company eliminates the base or layers of old costs, it may match old, irrelevant costs against current revenues. A distortion in reported income for a given period may result, as well as detrimental income tax consequences.[21]

Because of the liquidation problem, LIFO may cause poor buying habits. A company may simply purchase more goods and match these goods against revenue to avoid charging the old costs to expense. Furthermore, recall that with LIFO, a company may attempt to manipulate its net income at the end of the year simply by altering its pattern of purchases.[22]

One survey uncovered the following reasons why companies reject LIFO.[23]

ILLUSTRATION 7-28
Why Do Companies Reject LIFO? Summary of Responses

Reasons to Reject LIFO	Number	% of Total*
No expected tax benefits		
No required tax payment	34	16%
Declining prices	31	15
Rapid inventory turnover	30	14
Immaterial inventory	26	12
Miscellaneous tax related	38	17
	159	74%
Regulatory or other restrictions	26	12%
Excessive cost		
High administrative costs	29	14%
LIFO liquidation–related costs	12	6
	41	20%
Other adverse consequences		
Lower reported earnings	18	8%
Bad accounting	7	3
	25	11%

*Percentage totals more than 100% as some companies offered more than one explanation.

[21]The AICPA Task Force on LIFO Inventory Problems recommends that companies disclose the effects on income of LIFO inventory liquidations in the notes to the financial statements, but that they do not afford special treatment to the effects in the income statement. *Issues Paper* (New York: AICPA, 1984), pp. 36–37.

[22]For example, **General Tire and Rubber** accelerated raw material purchases at the end of the year to minimize the book profit from a liquidation of LIFO inventories and to minimize income taxes for the year.

[23]Michael H. Granof and Daniel Short, "Why Do Companies Reject LIFO?" *Journal of Accounting, Auditing, and Finance* (Summer 1984), pp. 323–333, Table 1, p. 327.

BASIS FOR SELECTION OF INVENTORY METHOD

OBJECTIVE 10
Understand why companies select given inventory methods.

How does a company choose among the various inventory methods? Although no absolute rules can be stated, preferability for LIFO usually occurs in either of the following circumstances: (1) if selling prices and revenues have been increasing faster than costs, thereby distorting income, and (2) in situations where LIFO has been traditional, such as department stores and industries where a fairly constant "base stock" is present (such as refining, chemicals, and glass).[24]

Conversely, LIFO is probably inappropriate in the following circumstances: (1) where prices tend to lag behind costs; (2) in situations where specific identification is traditional, such as in the sale of automobiles, farm equipment, art, and antique jewelry; or (3) where unit costs tend to decrease as production increases, thereby nullifying the tax benefit that LIFO might provide.[25]

Tax consequences are another consideration. Switching from FIFO to LIFO usually results in an immediate tax benefit. However, switching from LIFO to FIFO can result in a substantial tax burden. For example, when **Chrysler** (now **DaimlerChrysler**) changed from LIFO to FIFO, it became responsible for an additional $53 million in taxes that the company had deferred over 14 years of LIFO inventory valuation. Why, then, would Chrysler, and other companies, change to FIFO? The major reason was the profit crunch of that era. Although Chrysler showed a loss of $7.6 million after the switch, the loss would have been $20 million *more* if the company had not changed its inventory valuation from LIFO to FIFO.

It is questionable whether companies should switch from LIFO to FIFO for the sole purpose of increasing reported earnings. Intuitively one would assume that companies with higher reported earnings would have a higher share valuation (common stock price). However, some studies have indicated that the users of financial data exhibit a much higher sophistication than might be expected. Share prices are the same and, in some cases, even higher under LIFO in spite of lower reported earnings.[26]

The concern about reduced income resulting from adoption of LIFO has even less substance now because the IRS has relaxed the LIFO conformity rule which requires a company employing LIFO for tax purposes to use it for book purposes as well. The IRS has relaxed restrictions against providing non-LIFO income numbers as supplementary information. As a result, companies now provide supplemental non-LIFO disclosures. While not intended to override the basic LIFO method adopted for financial reporting, these disclosures may be useful in comparing operating income and working capital with companies not on LIFO.

For example, **JCPenney, Inc.** a LIFO user, presented the information in its annual report as shown in Illustration 7-29.

---

[24]*Accounting Trends and Techniques—2004* reports that of 833 inventory method disclosures, 251 used LIFO, 384 used FIFO, 167 used average cost, and 31 used other methods. Because of steady or falling raw materials costs and costs savings from electronic data interchange and just-in-time technologies in recent years, many businesses using LIFO no longer experience substantial tax benefits. Even some companies for which LIFO is creating a benefit are finding that the administrative costs associated with LIFO are higher than the LIFO benefit obtained. As a result, some companies are moving to FIFO or average cost.

[25]See Barry E. Cushing and Marc J. LeClere, "Evidence on the Determinants of Inventory Accounting Policy Choice," *The Accounting Review* (April 1992), pp. 355–366, Table 4, p. 363, for a list of factors hypothesized to affect FIFO–LIFO choices.

[26]See, for example, Shyam Sunder, "Relationship Between Accounting Changes and Stock Prices: Problems of Measurement and Some Empirical Evidence," *Empirical Research in Accounting: Selected Studies, 1973* (Chicago: University of Chicago), pp. 1–40. But see Robert Moren Brown, "Short-Range Market Reaction to Changes to LIFO Accounting Using Preliminary Earnings Announcement Dates," *The Journal of Accounting Research* (Spring 1980), which found that companies that do change to LIFO suffer a short-run decline in the price of their stock.

ILLUSTRATION 7-29
Supplemental Non-LIFO Disclosure

JCPenney, Inc.

Some companies in the retail industry use the FIFO method in valuing part or all of their inventories. Had JCPenney used the FIFO method and made no other assumptions with respect to changes in income resulting therefrom, income and income per share from continuing operations would have been:

Income from continuing operations (in millions)	$325
Income from continuing operations per share	$4.63

INTERNATIONAL INSIGHT

Many U.S. companies that have international operations use LIFO for U.S. purposes but use FIFO for their foreign subsidiaries.

Relaxation of the LIFO conformity rule has led some companies to select LIFO as their inventory valuation method because they will be able to disclose FIFO income numbers in the financial reports if they so desire.[27]

Companies often combine inventory methods. For example, **John Deere** uses LIFO for most of its inventories, and prices the remainder using FIFO. **Hershey Foods** follows the same practice. One reason for these practices is that certain product lines can be highly susceptible to deflation instead of inflation. In addition, if the level of inventory is unstable, unwanted involuntary liquidations may result in certain product lines if using LIFO. Finally, for high inventory turnover in certain product lines, a company cannot justify LIFO's additional recordkeeping and expense. In such cases, a company often uses average cost because it is easy to compute.[28]

Although a company may use a variety of inventory methods to assist in accurate computation of net income, once it selects a pricing method, it must apply it consistently thereafter. If conditions indicate that the inventory pricing method in use is unsuitable, the company must seriously consider all other possibilities before selecting another method. It should clearly explain any change and disclose its effect in the financial statements.

Inventory Valuation Methods—Summary Analysis

The preceding sections of this chapter described a number of inventory valuation methods. Here we present a brief summary of the three major inventory methods to show the effects these valuation methods have on the financial statements. This comparison assumes periodic inventory procedures and the following selected data.

Selected Data

Beginning cash balance		$ 7,000
Beginning retained earnings		$10,000
Beginning inventory:	4,000 units @ $3	$12,000
Purchases:	6,000 units @ $4	$24,000
Sales:	5,000 units @ $12	$60,000
Operating expenses		$10,000
Income tax rate		40%

[27]Note that a company can use one variation of LIFO for financial reporting purposes and another for tax without violating the LIFO conformity rule. Such a relaxation has caused many problems because the general approach to accounting for LIFO has been "whatever is good for tax is good for financial reporting."

[28]For an interesting discussion of the reasons for and against the use of FIFO and average cost, see Michael H. Granof and Daniel G. Short "For Some Companies, FIFO Accounting Makes Sense," *Wall Street Journal* (August 30, 1982), and the subsequent rebuttal by Gary C. Biddle "Taking Stock of Inventory Accounting Choices," *Wall Street Journal* (September 15, 1982).

Illustration 7-30 shows the comparative results on net income of the use of average cost, FIFO, and LIFO.

ILLUSTRATION 7-30
Comparative Results of Average Cost, FIFO, and LIFO Methods

	Average Cost	FIFO	LIFO
Sales	$60,000	$60,000	$60,000
Cost of goods sold	18,000[a]	16,000[b]	20,000[c]
Gross profit	42,000	44,000	40,000
Operating expenses	10,000	10,000	10,000
Income before taxes	32,000	34,000	30,000
Income taxes (40%)	12,800	13,600	12,000
Net income	$19,200	$20,400	$18,000

[a]4,000 @ $3 = $12,000
6,000 @ $4 = 24,000
$36,000

$36,000 ÷ 10,000 = $3.60
$3.60 × 5,000 = $18,000

[b]4,000 @ $3 = $12,000
1,000 @ $4 = 4,000
$16,000

[c]5,000 @ $4 = $20,000

Notice that gross profit and net income are lowest under LIFO, highest under FIFO, and somewhere in the middle under average cost.

Illustration 7-31 shows the final balances of selected items at the end of the period.

ILLUSTRATION 7-31
Balances of Selected Items Under Alternative Inventory Valuation Methods

	Inventory	Gross Profit	Taxes	Net Income	Retained Earnings	Cash
Average Cost	$18,000 (5,000 × $3.60)	$42,000	$12,800	$19,200	$29,200 ($10,000 + $19,200)	$20,200[a]
FIFO	$20,000 (5,000 × $4)	$44,000	$13,600	$20,400	$30,400 ($10,000 + $20,400)	$19,400[a]
LIFO	$16,000 (4,000 × $3) (1,000 × $4)	$40,000	$12,000	$18,000	$28,000 ($10,000 + $18,000)	$21,000[a]

[a]Cash at year-end	=	Beg. Balance	+	Sales	−	Purchases	−	Operating expenses	−	Taxes
Average cost—$20,200	=	$7,000	+	$60,000	−	$24,000	−	$10,000	−	$12,800
FIFO—$19,400	=	$7,000	+	$60,000	−	$24,000	−	$10,000	−	$13,600
LIFO—$21,000	=	$7,000	+	$60,000	−	$24,000	−	$10,000	−	$12,000

LIFO results in the highest cash balance at year-end (because taxes are lower). This example assumes that prices are rising. The opposite result occurs if prices are declining.

QUESTIONS

1. In what ways are the inventory accounts of a retailing company different from those of a manufacturing company?

2. Why should inventories be included in (a) a statement of financial position and (b) the computation of net income?

3. What is the difference between a perpetual inventory and a physical inventory? If a company maintains a perpetual inventory, should its physical inventory at any date be equal to the amount indicated by the perpetual inventory records? Why?

4. Mariah Carey, Inc. indicated in a recent annual report that approximately $19 million of merchandise was received on consignment. Should Mariah Carey, Inc. report this amount on its balance sheet? Explain.

5. What is a product financing arrangement? How should

product financing arrangements be reported in the financial statements?

6. Where, if at all, should the following items be classified on a balance sheet?

(a) Goods out on approval to customers.

(b) Goods in transit that were recently purchased f.o.b. destination.

(c) Land held by a realty firm for sale.

(d) Raw materials.

(e) Goods received on consignment.

(f) Manufacturing supplies.

7. At the balance sheet date Paula Abdul Company held title to goods in transit amounting to $214,000. This amount was omitted from the purchases figure for the year and also from the ending inventory. What is the effect of this omission on the net income for the year as calculated when the books are closed? What is the effect on the company's financial position as shown in its balance sheet? Is materiality a factor in determining whether an adjustment for this item should be made?

8. Define "cost" as applied to the valuation of inventories.

9. Distinguish between product costs and period costs as they relate to inventory.

10. **Ford Motor Co.** is considering alternate methods of accounting for the cash discounts it takes when paying suppliers promptly. One method suggested was to report these discounts as financial income when payments are made. Comment on the propriety of this approach.

11. Konerko Inc. purchases 300 units of an item at an invoice cost of $30,000. What is the cost per unit? If the goods are shipped f.o.b. shipping point and the freight bill was $1,500, what is the cost per unit if Konerko Inc. pays the freight charges? If these items were bought on 2/10, n/30 terms and the invoice and the freight bill were paid within the 10-day period, what would be the cost per unit?

12. Specific identification is sometimes said to be the ideal method of assigning cost to inventory and to cost of goods sold. Briefly indicate the arguments for and against this method of inventory valuation.

13. FIFO, weighted average, and LIFO methods are often used instead of specific identification for inventory valuation purposes. Compare these methods with the specific identification method, discussing the theoretical propriety of each method in the determination of income and asset valuation.

14. How might a company obtain a price index in order to apply dollar-value LIFO?

15. Describe the LIFO double-extension method. Using the following information, compute the index at December 31, 2007, applying the double-extension method to a LIFO pool consisting of 25,500 units of product A and 10,350 units of product B. The base-year cost of product A is $10.20 and of product B is $37.00. The price at December 31, 2007, for product A is $19.00 and for product B is $45.60.

16. As compared with the FIFO method of costing inventories, does the LIFO method result in a larger or smaller net income in a period of rising prices? What is the comparative effect on net income in a period of falling prices?

17. What is the dollar-value method of LIFO inventory valuation? What advantage does the dollar-value method have over the specific goods approach of LIFO inventory valuation? Why will the traditional LIFO inventory costing method and the dollar-value LIFO inventory costing method produce different inventory valuations if the composition of the inventory base changes?

18. Explain the following terms.

(a) LIFO layer. **(b)** LIFO reserve. **(c)** LIFO effect.

19. On December 31, 2006, the inventory of Mario Lemieux Company amounts to $800,000. During 2007, the company decides to use the dollar-value LIFO method of costing inventories. On December 31, 2007, the inventory is $1,026,000 at December 31, 2007, prices. Using the December 31, 2006, price level of 100 and the December 31, 2007, price level of 108, compute the inventory value at December 31, 2007, under the dollar-value LIFO method.

20. In an article that appeared in the *Wall Street Journal*, the phrases "phantom (paper) profits" and "high LIFO profits" through involuntary liquidation were used. Explain these phrases.

CHAPTER EIGHT

INVENTORIES: ADDITIONAL VALUATION ISSUES

What Do Inventory Changes Tell Us?

Department stores face an ongoing challenge: They need to keep enough inventory to meet customer demand, but not to accumulate too much inventory. If demand falls short of expectations, the department store may be forced to reduce prices on its existing inventory, thus losing sales revenue.

For example, the following table shows recent annual sales and inventory trends for major retailers, compared to the prior year.

Company	Sales	Inventory
Nordstrom	+10.59%	+ 1.73%
Federated Department Stores	+ 2.40%	− 2.95%
JCPenney	+ 3.59%	+ 0.41%
Wal-Mart	+11.63%	+ 9.06%
May Department Stores	+ 8.23%	+13.34%
Target	+11.62%	+18.83%
Best Buy	+17.21%	+25.52%
Circuit City	− 1.97%	+ 7.63%
Sears	−12.22%	+ 4.01%

Source: Company reports, fiscal years 2003 and 2004.

For over half of these retailers, inventories grew faster than sales from one year to the next—a trend that should raise warning flags for investors. Rising levels of inventories indicate that fewer shoppers are turning out to buy merchandise compared to activity in the prior period. As one analyst remarked, ". . . when inventory grows faster than sales, profits drop." That is, when retailers face slower sales and growing inventory, markdowns in prices are usually not far behind. These markdowns, in turn, lead to lower sales revenue and income.

Bankruptcies of retailers like **Ames Department Stores**, **Montgomery Ward**, and **Bradlees Stores** indicate the consequences of poor inventory management. And more recently, **Kmart**, which filed for bankruptcy in January 2002 and has since been acquired by **Sears Holdings**, was in an inventory "Catch-22." In order to work out of bankruptcy, Kmart needed to keep its shelves stocked so that customers would continue to shop in its remaining stores. However, vendors who were worried about Kmart's ability to manage its inventory were reluctant to ship goods without assurances that they would get paid. Thus, investors, creditors, and vendors keep an eye on information about inventories in the retail industry.

Learning Objectives

After studying this chapter, you should be able to:

1. Describe and apply the lower-of-cost-or-market rule.
2. Explain when companies value inventories at net realizable value.
3. Explain when companies use the relative sales value method to value inventories.
4. Discuss accounting issues related to purchase commitments.
5. Determine ending inventory by applying the gross profit method.
6. Determine ending inventory by applying the retail inventory method.
7. Explain how to report and analyze inventory.

PREVIEW OF CHAPTER 8

As our opening story indicates, information on inventories and changes in inventory helps to predict financial performance—in particular, profits. In this chapter we discuss some of the valuation and estimation concepts that companies use to develop relevant inventory information. The content and organization of the chapter are as follows.

INVENTORIES: ADDITIONAL VALUATION ISSUES

- **LOWER-OF-COST-OR-MARKET**
  - Ceiling and floor
  - How LCM works
  - Application of LCM
  - "Market"
  - Evaluation of rule
- **VALUATION BASES**
  - Net realizable value
  - Relative sales value
  - Purchase commitments
- **GROSS PROFIT METHOD**
  - Gross profit percentage
  - Evaluation of method
- **RETAIL INVENTORY METHOD**
  - Concepts
  - Conventional method
  - Special items
  - Evaluation of method
- **PRESENTATION AND ANALYSIS**
  - Presentation
  - Analysis

LOWER-OF-COST-OR-MARKET

OBJECTIVE 1
Describe and apply the lower-of-cost-or-market rule.

Inventories are recorded at their cost. However, if inventory declines in value below its original cost, a major departure from the historical cost principle occurs. Whatever the reason for a decline—obsolescence, price-level changes, or damaged goods—a company should write down the inventory to market to report this loss. **A company abandons the historical cost principle when the future utility (revenue-producing ability) of the asset drops below its original cost.** Companies therefore **report inventories at the lower-of-cost-or-market** at each reporting period.

Illustration 8-1 shows how **Eastman Kodak** and **Best Buy** reported this information.

ILLUSTRATION 8-1
Lower-of-Cost-or-Market Disclosures

EASTMAN KODAK

Notes to Financial Statements

The company reduces the carrying value to a lower-of-cost-or-market basis for those items that are excess, obsolete, or slow moving based on management's analysis of inventory levels and future sales forecasts.

BEST BUY

Notes to Financial Statements

Merchandise inventories are recorded at the lower of average cost or market.

Recall that **cost** is the acquisition price of inventory computed using one of the historical cost-based methods—specific identification, average cost, FIFO, or LIFO. The term **market** in the phrase "the lower-of-cost-or-market" (LCM) generally means the cost to replace the item by purchase or reproduction. For a retailer like **Nordstrom**, the term "market" refers to the market in which it purchases goods, not the market in which it sells them. For a manufacturer like **William Wrigley Jr.**, the term "market" refers to the cost to reproduce. Thus the rule really means that **companies value goods at cost or cost to replace, whichever is lower.**

For example, say **Target** purchased a **Timex** calculator wristwatch for $30 for resale. Target can sell the wristwatch for $48.95 and replace it for $25. It should therefore value the wristwatch at $25 for inventory purposes under the lower-of-cost-or-market rule. Target can use the lower-of-cost-or-market rule of valuation after applying any of the cost flow methods discussed above to determine the inventory cost.

UNDERLYING CONCEPTS

The use of the lower-of-cost-or-market rule is an excellent example of the conservatism constraint.

A departure from cost is justified because **a company should charge a loss of utility against revenues in the period in which the loss occurs,** not in the period of sale. Note also that the lower-of-cost-or-market method is **a conservative approach to inventory valuation.** That is, when doubt exists about the value of an asset, a company should use the lower value for the asset, which also reduces net income.

Lower-of-Cost-or-Market—Ceiling and Floor

Why use replacement cost to represent market value? Because a decline in the replacement cost of an item usually reflects or predicts a decline in selling price. Using replacement cost allows a company to maintain a consistent rate of gross profit on sales (normal profit margin). Sometimes, however, a reduction in the replacement cost of an item fails to indicate a corresponding reduction in its utility. This requires using two additional valuation limitations to value ending inventory—net realizable value and net realizable value less a normal profit margin.

Net realizable value (NRV) is the estimated selling price in the ordinary course of business, less reasonably predictable costs of completion and disposal (often referred to as net selling price). A normal profit margin is subtracted from that amount to arrive at **net realizable value less a normal profit margin.**

To illustrate, assume that Jerry Mander Corp. has unfinished inventory with a sales value of $1,000, estimated cost of completion of $300, and a normal profit margin of 10 percent of sales. Jerry Mander determines the following net realizable value.

ILLUSTRATION 8-2
Computation of Net Realizable Value

Inventory—sales value	$1,000
Less: Estimated cost of completion and disposal	300
Net realizable value	700
Less: Allowance for normal profit margin (10% of sales)	100
Net realizable value less a normal profit margin	$ 600

The general lower-of-cost-or-market rule is: A company values inventory at the lower-of-cost-or-market, with market limited to an amount that is not more than net realizable value or less than net realizable value less a normal profit margin.[1]

The **upper (ceiling)** is the net realizable value of inventory. The **lower (floor)** is the the net realizable value less a normal profit margin. What is the rationale for these two limitations? Establishing these limits for the value of the inventory prevents companies from over- or understating inventory.

[1]"Restatement and Revision of Accounting Research Bulletins," *Accounting Research Bulletin No. 43* (New York: AICPA, 1953), Ch. 4, par. 8.

The maximum limitation, **not to exceed the net realizable value (ceiling),** prevents overstatement of the value of obsolete, damaged, or shopworn inventories. That is, if the replacement cost of an item exceeds its net realizable value, a company should not report inventory at replacement cost. The company can receive only the selling price less cost of disposal. To report the inventory at replacement cost would result in an overstatement of inventory and understatement of the loss in the current period.

To illustrate, assume that **Staples** paid $1,000 for a color laser printer that it can now replace for $900. The printer's net realizable value is $700. At what amount should Staples report the laser printer in the financial statements? To report the replacement cost of $900 overstates the ending inventory and understates the loss for the period. Therefore, Staples should report the printer at $700.

The minimum limitation (floor) is **not to be less than net realizable value reduced by an allowance for an approximately normal profit margin.** The floor establishes a value below which a company should not price inventory, regardless of replacement cost. It makes no sense to price inventory below net realizable value less a normal margin. This minimum amount (floor) measures what the company can receive for the inventory and still earn a normal profit. Use of a floor deters understatement of inventory and overstatement of the loss in the current period.

UNDERLYING CONCEPTS

Setting a floor and a ceiling increases the relevancy of the inventory presentation. The inventory figure provides a better understanding of how much revenue the inventory will generate.

Illustration 8-3 graphically presents the guidelines for valuing inventory at the lower-of-cost-or-market.

ILLUSTRATION 8-3
Inventory Valuation—
Lower of Cost or Market

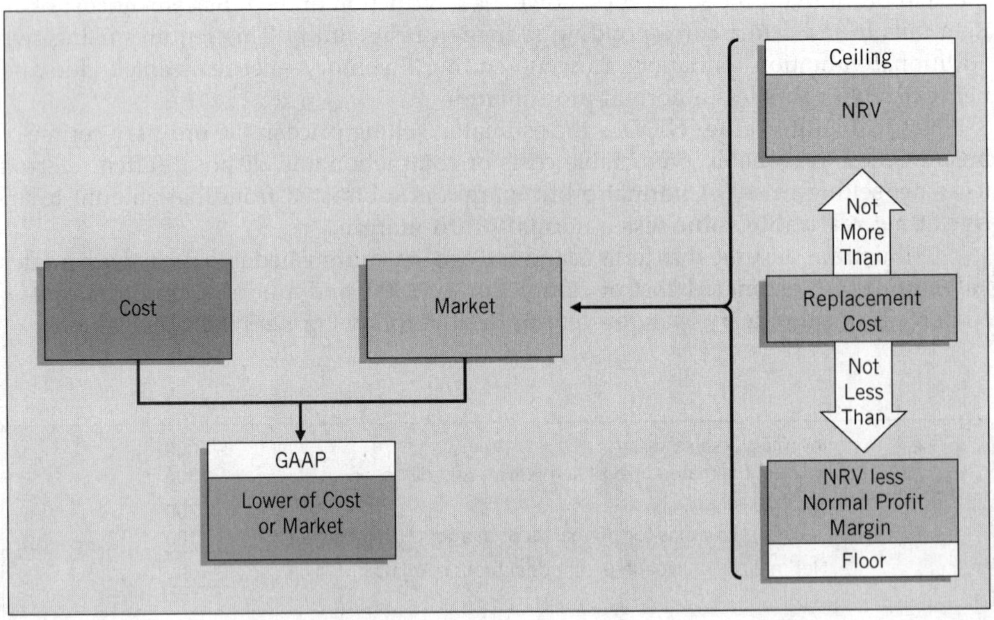

How Lower-of-Cost-or-Market Works

The **designated market value** is the amount that a company compares to cost. It is **always the middle value of three amounts**: replacement cost, net realizable value, and net realizable value less a normal profit margin. To illustrate how to compute designated market value, assume the information relative to the inventory of Regner Foods, Inc., as shown in Illustration 8-4.

Regner Foods then compares designated market value to cost to determine the lower-of-cost-or-market. It determines the final inventory value as shown in Illustration 8-5.

ILLUSTRATION 8-4
Computation of Designated Market Value

Food	Replacement Cost	Net Realizable Value (Ceiling)	Net Realizable Value Less a Normal Profit Margin (Floor)	Designated Market Value
Spinach	$ 88,000	$120,000	$104,000	$104,000
Carrots	90,000	100,000	70,000	90,000
Cut beans	45,000	40,000	27,500	40,000
Peas	36,000	72,000	48,000	48,000
Mixed vegetables	105,000	92,000	80,000	92,000

Designated Market Value Decision:

Spinach	Net realizable value less a normal profit margin is selected because it is the middle value.
Carrots	Replacement cost is selected because it is the middle value.
Cut beans	Net realizable value is selected because it is the middle value.
Peas	Net realizable value less a normal profit margin is selected because it is the middle value.
Mixed vegetables	Net realizable value is selected because it is the middle value.

ILLUSTRATION 8-5
Determining Final Inventory Value

Food	Cost	Replacement Cost	Net Realizable Value (Ceiling)	Net Realizable Value Less a Normal Profit Margin (Floor)	Designated Market Value	Final Inventory Value
Spinach	$ 80,000	$ 88,000	$120,000	$104,000	$104,000	$ 80,000
Carrots	100,000	90,000	100,000	70,000	90,000	90,000
Cut beans	50,000	45,000	40,000	27,500	40,000	40,000
Peas	90,000	36,000	72,000	48,000	48,000	48,000
Mixed vegetables	95,000	105,000	92,000	80,000	92,000	92,000
						$350,000

Final Inventory Value:

Spinach	Cost ($80,000) is selected because it is lower than designated market value (net realizable value less a normal profit margin).
Carrots	Designated market value (replacement cost, $90,000) is selected because it is lower than cost.
Cut beans	Designated market value (net realizable value, $40,000) is selected because it is lower than cost.
Peas	Designated market value (net realizable value less a normal profit margin, $48,000) is selected because it is lower than cost.
Mixed vegetables	Designated market value (net realizable value, $92,000) is selected because it is lower than cost.

The application of the lower-of-cost-or-market rule incorporates only losses in value that occur in the normal course of business from such causes as style changes, shift in demand, or regular shop wear. A company reduces damaged or deteriorated goods to net realizable value. When material, it may carry such goods in separate inventory accounts.

Methods of Applying Lower-of-Cost-or-Market

In the Regner Foods illustration, we assumed that the company applied the lower-of-cost-or-market rule to each individual type of food. However, companies may apply the lower-of-cost-or-market rule either directly to each item, to each category, or to the total of the inventory. If a company follows a major category or total inventory approach in applying the lower-of-cost-or-market rule, increases in market prices tend to offset decreases in market prices. To illustrate, assume that Regner Foods separates its food products into two major categories, frozen and canned, as shown in Illustration 8-6.

ILLUSTRATION 8-6
Alternative Applications of Lower-of-Cost-or-Market

			Lower-of-Cost-or-Market By:		
	Cost	Designated Market	**Individual Items**	**Major Categories**	**Total Inventory**
Frozen					
Spinach	$ 80,000	$104,000	$ 80,000		
Carrots	100,000	90,000	90,000		
Cut beans	50,000	40,000	40,000		
Total frozen	230,000	234,000		$230,000	
Canned					
Peas	90,000	48,000	48,000		
Mixed vegetables	95,000	92,000	92,000		
Total canned	185,000	140,000		140,000	
Total	$415,000	$374,000	$350,000	$370,000	$374,000

If Regner Foods applied the lower-of-cost-or-market rule to individual items, the amount of inventory is $350,000. If applying the rule to major categories, it jumps to $370,000. If applying LCM to the total inventory, it totals $374,000. Why this difference? When a company uses a major categories or total inventory approach, market values higher than cost offset market values lower than cost. For Regner Foods, using the major categories approach partially offsets the high market value for spinach. Using the total inventory approach totally offsets it.

Companies usually price inventory on an item-by-item basis. In fact, tax rules require that companies use an individual-item basis barring practical difficulties. In addition, the individual-item approach gives the most conservative valuation for balance sheet purposes.[2] Often, a company prices inventory on a total-inventory basis when it offers only one end product (comprised of many different raw materials). If it produces several end products, a company might use a category approach instead. The method selected should be the one that most clearly reflects income. **Whichever method a company selects, it should apply the method consistently from one period to another.**[3]

Recording "Market" Instead of Cost

One of two methods is used for recording inventory at market. One method, referred to as the **direct method**, substitutes the (lower) market value figure for cost when valuing the inventory. As a result, the company does not report a loss in the income statement because the cost of goods sold already includes the amount of the loss. The second method, referred to as the **indirect method** or **allowance method**, does not change the cost amount. Rather, it establishes a separate contra asset account and a loss account to record the write-off.

We use the following inventory data to illustrate entries under both methods.

Cost of goods sold (before adjustment to market)	$108,000
Ending inventory (cost)	82,000
Ending inventory (at market)	70,000

[2]If a company uses dollar-value LIFO, determining the LIFO cost of an individual item may be more difficult. The company might decide that it is more appropriate to apply the lower-of-cost-or-market rule to the total amount of each pool. The AICPA Task Force on LIFO Inventory Problems concluded that the most reasonable approach to applying the lower-of-cost-or-market provisions to LIFO inventories is to base the determination on reasonable groupings of items. A pool constitutes a reasonable grouping.

[3]Inventory accounting for financial statement purposes can be different from income tax purposes. For example, companies cannot use the lower-of-cost-or-market rule with LIFO for tax purposes. However, companies may use the lower-of-cost-or-market and LIFO for financial accounting purposes.

Illustration 8-7 shows the entries for both the direct and indirect methods, assuming the use of a **perpetual** inventory system.

ILLUSTRATION 8-7
Accounting for the Reduction of Inventory to Market—Perpetual Inventory System

Direct Method			Indirect or Allowance Method		
To reduce inventory from cost to market:					
Cost of Goods Sold	12,000		Loss Due to Market		
Inventory		12,000	Decline of Inventory	12,000	
			Allowance to Reduce		
			Inventory to Market		12,000

Identifying the loss due to market decline shows the loss separate from cost of goods sold in the income statement (but not as an extraordinary item). The advantage of this approach is that it does not distort the cost of goods sold.

Illustration 8-8 contrasts the differing amounts reported in the income statements under the two methods, using data from the preceding illustration.

ILLUSTRATION 8-8
Income Statement Presentation—Direct and Indirect Methods of Reducing Inventory to Market

Direct Method	
Revenue from sales	$200,000
Cost of goods sold (after adjustment to market*)	120,000
Gross profit on sales	$ 80,000
Indirect or Allowance Method	
Revenue from sales	$200,000
Cost of goods sold	108,000
Gross profit on sales	92,000
Loss due to market decline of inventory	12,000
	$ 80,000

*Cost of goods sold (before adjustment to market)	$ 108,000
Difference between inventory at cost and market ($82,000–$70,000)	12,000
Cost of goods sold (after adjustment to market)	$ 120,000

The direct-method presentation buries the loss in the cost of goods sold. The indirect-method presentation is preferable, because it clearly discloses the loss resulting from the market decline of inventory prices.

Using the indirect method, the company would report the Allowance to Reduce Inventory to Market on the balance sheet as a $12,000 deduction from the inventory. This deduction permits both the income statement and the balance sheet to show the ending inventory of $82,000, although the balance sheet shows a net amount of $70,000. It also keeps subsidiary inventory ledgers and records in correspondence with the control account without changing unit prices.

Use of an allowance account permits balance sheet disclosure of the inventory at cost and at the lower of cost or market. However, it raises the problem of how to dispose of the balance of the allowance account in the following period. If the company still has on hand the merchandise in question, it should retain the allowance account. If it does not keep that account, the company will overstate beginning inventory and cost of goods. However, **if the company has sold the goods**, then it should close the account. It then establishes a "new allowance account" for any decline in inventory value that takes place in the current year.[4]

UNDERLYING CONCEPTS

The income statement under the direct method presentation lacks *representational faithfulness.* The cost of goods sold does not represent what it purports to represent. However, allowing this presentation illustrates the concept of materiality. That is, the presentation does not affect net income and would not "change the judgment of a reasonable person."

[4]The AICPA Task Force on LIFO Inventory Problems concluded that for LIFO inventories, companies should close the allowance from the prior year and should base the allowance at the end of the year on a new lower-of-cost-or-market computation. *Issues Paper* (New York: AICPA, November 30, 1984), pp. 50–55.

Some accountants leave the allowance account on the books. They merely adjust the balance at the next year-end to agree with the discrepancy between cost and the lower-of-cost-or-market at that balance sheet date. Thus, if prices are falling, the company records a loss. If prices are rising, the company recovers a loss recorded in prior years, and it records a "gain," as shown in Illustration 8-9. Note that this "gain" is not really a gain, but a recovery of a previously recognized loss.

ILLUSTRATION 8-9
Effect on Net Income of Reducing Inventory to Market

Date	Inventory at Cost	Inventory at Market	Amount Required in Valuation Account	Adjustment of Valuation Account Balance	Effect on Net Income
Dec. 31, 2006	$188,000	$176,000	$12,000	$12,000 inc.	Loss
Dec. 31, 2007	194,000	187,000	7,000	5,000 dec.	Gain
Dec. 31, 2008	173,000	174,000	0	7,000 dec.	Gain
Dec. 31, 2009	182,000	180,000	2,000	2,000 inc.	Loss

UNDERLYING CONCEPTS

The inconsistency in the presentation of inventory is an example of the trade-off between *relevancy and reliability*. Market is more relevant than cost, and cost is more reliable than market. Apparently, relevance takes precedence in a down market, and reliability is more important in an up market.

We can think of this net "gain" under the indirect method as the excess of the credit effect of closing the beginning allowance balance over the debit effect of setting up the current year-end allowance account. Recognizing a gain or loss has the same effect on net income as closing the allowance balance to beginning inventory or to cost of goods sold.

WHAT DO THE NUMBERS MEAN?

"PUT IT IN REVERSE"

The lower-of-cost-or-market rule is designed to provide timely information about the decline in the value of inventory. When the value of inventory declines, income takes a hit in the period of the write-down.

What happens in the periods after the write-down? For some companies, gross margins and bottom lines get a boost when they sell inventory that had been written down in a previous period. For example, as the following table shows, **Vishay Technologies**, **Transwitch**, and **Cisco Systems** reported gains from selling inventory that had previously been written down. The table also evaluates how clearly these companies disclosed the effects of the reversal of inventory write-downs.

Company	Gain from reversal	Disclosure
Vishay Inter-Technology	Not available	Poor—The semi-conductor company did not mention the gain in its earnings announcement. Two weeks later in an SEC filing, Vishay disclosed the gain on the inventory that it had written down.
Transwitch	$600,000	Poor—The company did not mention the gain in its earnings announcement. Three weeks later in an SEC filing, the company disclosed the gain on the inventory that it had written down.
Cisco Systems	$525 million	Full—The networking giant detailed in its earnings release and in SEC filings the gains from selling inventory it had previously written off.

For Transwitch, the reversal of fortunes amounted to 23 percent of net income. The problem is that the $600,000 credit had little to do with the company's ongoing operations, and the company did not do a good job disclosing the effect of the reversal on current-year profitability.

Even when companies do disclose a reversal, it is sometimes hard to determine the impact on income. For example, **Intel** disclosed that is had sold inventory that had been written down in prior periods but did not specify how much reserved inventory was sold.

After the recent accounting scandals, transparency of financial reporting has become a top priority. With better disclosure of the reversals that boost profits in the current period, financial transparency would also get a boost.

Source: S. E. Ante, "The Secret Behind Those Profit Jumps," *Business Week Online* (December 8, 2003).

Evaluation of the Lower-of-Cost-or-Market Rule

The lower-of-cost-or-market rule suffers some conceptual deficiencies:

1 A company recognizes decreases in the value of the the asset and the charge to expense in the period in which the loss in utility occurs—not in the period of sale. On the other hand, it recognizes increases in the value of the asset only at the point of sale. This inconsistent treatment can distort income data.

2 Application of the rule results in inconsistency because a company may value the inventory at cost in one year and at market in the next year.

3 Lower-of-cost-or-market values the inventory in the balance sheet conservatively, but its effect on the income statement may or may not be conservative. Net income for the year in which a company takes the loss is definitely lower. Net income of the subsequent period may be higher than normal if the expected reductions in sales price do not materialize.

4 Application of the lower-of-cost-or-market rule uses a "normal profit" in determining inventory values. Since companies estimate "normal profit" based on past experience (which they may not attain in the future), this subjective measure presents an opportunity for income manipulation.

Many financial statement users appreciate the lower-of-cost-or-market rule because they at least know that it prevents overstatement of inventory. In addition, recognizing all losses but anticipating no gains generally results in lower income.

VALUATION BASES

Valuation at Net Realizable Value

OBJECTIVE 2
Explain when companies value inventories at net realizable value.

For the most part, companies record inventory at cost or at the lower-of-cost-or-market.[5] However, many believe that for purposes of applying the lower-of-cost-or-market rule, companies should define "market" as **net realizable value** (selling price less estimated costs to complete and sell), rather than as replacement cost. This argument is based on the fact that the amount that companies will collect from this inventory in the future is the net realizable value.[6]

Under limited circumstances, support exists for **recording inventory at net realizable value**, even if that amount is above cost. GAAP permits this exception to the normal recognition rule under the following conditions: (1) when there is a controlled market with a quoted price applicable to all quantities, and (2) when no significant costs of disposal

[5]Manufacturing companies frequently employ a **standardized cost system** that predetermines the unit costs for material, labor, and manufacturing overhead and that values raw materials, work in process, and finished goods inventories at their standard costs. For financial reporting purposes, it is acceptable to price inventories at standard costs if there is no significant difference between the actual costs and standard costs. If there is a significant difference, companies should adjust the inventory amounts to actual cost. In *Accounting Research and Terminology Bulletin, Final Edition,* the profession notes that "**standard costs are acceptable if adjusted at reasonable intervals to reflect current conditions.**" **Burlington Industries** and **Hewlett-Packard** use standard costs for valuing at least a portion of their inventories.

[6]"The Accounting Basis of Inventories," *Acconting Research Study No. 13* (New York: AICPA, 1973) recommends that companies adopt net realizable value. We also should note that companies frequently fail to apply the rules of lower-of-cost-or-market in practice. For example, companies rarely compute and apply the lower limit—net realizable value less a normal markup—because it is a fairly subjective computation. In addition, companies often do not reduce inventory to market unless its disposition is expected to result in a loss. Furthermore, if the net realizable value of finished goods exceeds cost, companies usually assume that both work in process and raw materials do also. In practice, therefore, *ARB No. 43* is considered a guide, and accountants often exercise professional judgment in lieu of following this pronouncement literally.

INTERNATIONAL INSIGHT

The U.S. is the only country that defines *market* as something other than net realizable value.

are involved. For example, mining companies ordinarily report inventories of certain minerals (rare metals, especially) at selling prices because there is often a controlled market without significant costs of disposal. Similar treatment is given agricultural products that are immediately marketable at quoted prices.

A third reason for allowing valuation at net realizable value is that sometimes it is too difficult to obtain the cost figures. Cost figures are not difficult to determine in, say, a manufacturing plant, where the company combines various raw materials and purchased parts to create a finished product. The manufacturer can use the cost basis to account for various items in inventory, because it knows the cost of each individual component part. The situation is different in a meat-packing plant, however. The "raw material" consists of, say, cattle, each unit of which the company purchases as a whole and then divides into parts that are the products. Instead of one product out of many raw materials or parts, the meat-packing company makes many products from one "unit" of raw material. To allocate the cost of the animal "on the hoof" into the cost of, say, ribs, chuck, and shoulders, is a practical impossibility. It is much easier and more useful for the company to determine the market price of the various products and value them in the inventory at selling price less the various costs necessary to get them to market (costs such as shipping and handling). Hence, because of a peculiarity of the industry, meat-packing companies sometimes carry **inventories at sales price less distribution costs.**

Valuation Using Relative Sales Value

OBJECTIVE 3
Explain when companies use the relative sales value method to value inventories.

A special problem arises when a company buys a group of varying units in a single **lump-sum purchase**, also called a **basket purchase.**

To illustrate, assume that Woodland Developers purchases land for $1 million that it will subdivide into 400 lots. These lots are of different sizes and shapes but can be roughly sorted into three groups graded A, B, and C. As woodland sells the lots, it apportions the purchase cost of $1 million among the lots sold and the lots remaining on hand.

You might wonder why Woodland would not simply divide the total cost of $1 million by 400 lots, to get a cost of $2,500 for each lot. This approach would not recognize that the lots vary in size, shape, and attractiveness. Therefore, to accurately value each unit, the common and most logical practice is to allocate the total among the various units on the basis of their **relative sales value.**

Illustration 8-10 shows the allocation of relative sales value for the Woodland Developers example.

ILLUSTRATION 8-10
Allocation of Costs, Using Relative Sales Value

Lots	Number of Lots	Sales Price Per Lot	Total Sales Price	Relative Sales Price	Total Cost	Cost Allocated to Lots	Cost Per Lot
A	100	$10,000	$1,000,000	100/250	$1,000,000	$ 400,000	$4,000
B	100	6,000	600,000	60/250	1,000,000	240,000	2,400
C	200	4,500	900,000	90/250	1,000,000	360,000	1,800
			$2,500,000			$1,000,000	

Using the amounts given in the "Cost Per Lot" column, Woodland can determine the cost of lots sold and the gross profit as follows.

ILLUSTRATION 8-11
Determination of Gross Profit, Using Relative Sales Value

Lots	Number of Lots Sold	Cost Per Lot	Cost of Lots Sold	Sales	Gross Profit
A	77	$4,000	$308,000	$ 770,000	$ 462,000
B	80	2,400	192,000	480,000	288,000
C	100	1,800	180,000	450,000	270,000
			$680,000	$1,700,000	$1,020,000

The ending inventory is therefore $320,000 ($1,000,000 − $680,000).

Woodland also can compute this inventory amount another way. The ratio of cost to selling price for all the lots is $1 million divided by $2,500,000, or 40 percent. Accordingly, if the total sales price of lots sold is, say $1,700,000, then the cost of the lots sold is 40 percent of $1,700,000, or $680,000. The inventory of lots on hand is then $1 million less $680,000, or $320,000.

The petroleum industry widely uses the relative sales value method to value (at cost) the many products and by-products obtained from a barrel of crude oil.

Purchase Commitments—A Special Problem

OBJECTIVE 4
Discuss accounting issues related to purchase commitments.

In many lines of business, a company's survival and continued profitability depends on its having a sufficient stock of merchandise to meet customer demand. Consequently, it is quite common for a company to make **purchase commitments**, which are agreements to buy inventory weeks, months, or even years in advance. Generally, the seller retains title to the merchandise or materials covered in the purchase commitments. Indeed, the goods may exist only as natural resources as unplanted seed (in the case of agricultural commodities), or as work in process (in the case of a product).[7]

Usually it is neither necessary nor proper for the buyer to make any entries to reflect commitments for purchases of goods that the seller has not shipped. Ordinary orders, for which the buyer and seller will determine prices at the time of shipment and **which are subject to cancellation**, do not represent either an asset or a liability to the buyer. Therefore the buyer need not record such purchase commitments or report them in the financial statements.

What happens, though, if a buyer enters into a formal, noncancelable purchase contract? Even then, the buyer recognizes no asset or liability at the date of inception, **because the contract is "executory" in nature**: Neither party has fulfilled its part of the contract. However, if material, the buyer should disclose such contract details in a note to its financial statements. Illustration 8-12 shows an example of a purchase commitment disclosure.

Note 1: Contracts for the purchase of raw materials in 2007 have been executed in the amount of $600,000. The market price of such raw materials on December 31, 2006, is $640,000.

ILLUSTRATION 8-12
Disclosure of Purchase Commitment

In the disclosure in Illustration 8-12, the contract price was less than the market price at the balance sheet date. **If the contract price is greater than the market price, and the buyer expects that losses will occur when the purchase is effected, the buyer should recognize losses in the period during which such declines in market prices take place.**[8]

As an example, in the early 1980s many Northwest forest-product companies such as **Boise Cascade**, **Georgia-Pacific**, and **Weyerhaeuser** signed long-term timber-cutting contracts with the **U.S. Forest Service**. These contracts required that the companies pay $310 per thousand board feet for timber-cutting rights. Unfortunately, the market price for timber-cutting rights in late 1984 dropped to $80 per thousand board feet. As a result, a number of these companies had long-term contracts that, if fulfilled, would result in substantial future losses.

---

[7] A recent study noted that about 30 percent of public companies have purchase commitments outstanding, with an estimated value of $725 billion ("SEC Staff Report on Off-Balance Sheet Arrangements, Special Purpose Entities, and Related Issues,") http://www.sec.gov/news/studies/soxoffbalancerpt.pdf, June 2005). Purchase commitments are popular because the buyer can secure a supply of inventory at a known price. The seller also benefits in these arrangements by knowing how much to produce.

[8] *Accounting Research Bulletin No. 43*, op. cit., par. 16.

UNDERLYING CONCEPTS

Reporting the loss is *conservative*. However, reporting the decline in market price is debatable because no asset is recorded. This area demonstrates the need for good definitions of assets and liabilities.

To illustrate the accounting problem, assume that St. Regis Paper Co. signed timber-cutting contracts to be executed in 2007 at a price of $10,000,000. Assume further that the market price of the timber cutting rights on December 31, 2008, dropped to $7,000,000. St. Regis would make the following entry on December 31, 2008.

Unrealized Holding Gain or Loss—Income (Purchase Commitments)	3,000,000	
Estimated Liability on Purchase Commitments		3,000,000

St. Regis would report this unrealized holding loss in the income statement under "Other expenses and losses." And because the contract is to be executed within the next fiscal year, St. Regis would report the Estimated Liability on Purchase Commitments in the current liabilities section on the balance sheet. When St. Regis cuts the timber at a cost of $10 million, it would make the following entry.

Purchases (Inventory)	7,000,000	
Estimated Liability on Purchase Commitments	3,000,000	
Cash		10,000,000

The result of the purchase commitment was that St. Regis paid $10 million for a contract worth only $7 million. It recorded the loss in the previous period—when the price actually declined.

If St. Regis can partially or fully recover the contract price before it cuts the timber, it reduces the Estimated Liability on Purchase Commitments. In that case, it then reports in the period of the price increase a resulting gain for the amount of the partial or full recovery. For example, Congress permitted some of the forest-products companies to buy out of their contracts at reduced prices in order to avoid potential bankruptcies. To illustrate, assume that Congress permitted St. Regis to reduce its contract price and therefore its commitment by $1,000,000. The entry to record this transaction is as follows.

Estimated Liability on Purchase Commitments	1,000,000	
Unrealized Holding Gain or Loss—Income (Purchase Commitments)		1,000,000

If the market price at the time St. Regis cuts the timber is more than $2,000,000 below the contract price, St. Regis will have to recognize an additional loss in the period of cutting and record the purchase at the lower-of-cost-or-market.

Are purchasers at the mercy of market price declines? Not totally. Purchasers can protect themselves against the possibility of market price declines of goods under contract by hedging. In **hedging**, the purchaser in the purchase commitment simultaneously enters into a contract in which it agrees to sell in the future the same quantity of the same (or similar) goods at a fixed price. Thus the company holds a *buy position* in a purchase commitment and a *sell position* in a futures contract in the same commodity. The purpose of the hedge is to offset the price risk of the buy and sell positions: The company will be better off under one contract by approximately (maybe exactly) the same amount by which it is worse off under the other contract.

For example, St. Regis Paper Co. could have hedged its purchase commitment contract with a futures contract for timber rights of the same amount. In that case, its loss of $3,000,000 on the purchase commitment could have been offset by a $3,000,000 gain on the futures contract.

As easy as this makes it sound, accounting for purchase commitments is still unsettled and controversial. Some argue that companies should report purchase commitments as assets and liabilities at the time they sign the contract.[9] Others believe that the present recognition at the delivery date is more appropriate. *FASB Concepts Statement No. 6* states, "a purchase commitment involves both an item that might be recorded as an asset and an item that might be recorded as a liability. That is, it involves both a right to receive assets and an obligation to pay. . . . If both the right to receive assets and the obligation to pay were recorded at the time of the purchase commitment, the nature of the loss and the valuation account that records it when the price falls would be clearly seen." Although the discussion in *Concepts Statement No. 6* does not exclude the possibility of recording assets and liabilities for purchase commitments, it contains no conclusions or implications about whether companies should record them.[10]

THE GROSS PROFIT METHOD OF ESTIMATING INVENTORY

OBJECTIVE 5
Determine ending inventory by applying the gross profit method.

Companies take a physical inventory to verify the accuracy of the perpetual inventory records or, if no records exist, to arrive at an inventory amount. Sometimes, however, taking a physical inventory is impractical. In such cases, companies use substitute measures to approximate inventory on hand.

One substitute method of verifying or determining the inventory amount is the **gross profit method** (also called the **gross margin method)**. Auditors widely use this method in situations where they need only an estimate of the company's inventory (e.g., interim reports). Companies also use this method when fire or other catastrophe destroys either inventory or inventory records. The gross profit method relies on three assumptions:

1 The beginning inventory plus purchases equal total goods to be accounted for.
2 Goods not sold must be on hand.
3 The sales, reduced to cost, deducted from the sum of the opening inventory plus purchases, equal ending inventory.

To illustrate, assume that Cetus Corp. has a beginning inventory of $60,000 and purchases of $200,000, both at cost. Sales at selling price amount to $280,000. The gross profit on selling price is 30 percent. Cetus applies the gross margin method as follows.

ILLUSTRATION 8-13
Application of Gross Profit Method

Beginning inventory (at cost)		$ 60,000
Purchases (at cost)		200,000
Goods available (at cost)		260,000
Sales (at selling price)	$280,000	
Less: Gross profit (30% of $280,000)	84,000	
Sales (at cost)		196,000
Approximate inventory (at cost)		$ 64,000

[9]See, for example, Yuji Ijiri, *Recognition of Contractual Rights and Obligations, Research Report* (Stamford, Conn.: FASB, 1980), who argues that companies should capitalize firm purchase commitments. "Firm" means that it is unlikely that companies can avoid performance under the contract without a severe penalty.

Also, see Mahendra R. Gujarathi and Stanley F. Biggs, "Accounting for Purchase Commitments: Some Issues and Recommendations," *Accounting Horizons* (September 1988), pp. 75–78. They conclude, "Recording an asset and liability on the date of inception for the noncancelable purchase commitments is suggested as the first significant step towards alleviating the accounting problems associated with the issue. At year-end, the potential gains and losses should be treated as contingencies under *FASB 5* which provides a coherent structure for the accounting and informative disclosure for such gains and losses."

[10]"Elements of Financial Statements," *Statement of Financial Accounting Concepts No. 6* (Stamford, Conn.: FASB, 1985), pars. 251–253.

The current period's records contain all the information Cetus needs to compute inventory at cost, except for the gross profit percentage. Cetus determines the gross profit percentage by reviewing company policies or prior period records. In some cases, companies must adjust this percentage if they consider prior periods unrepresentative of the current period.[11]

Computation of Gross Profit Percentage

In most situations, the **gross profit percentage** is stated as a percentage of selling price. The previous illustration, for example, used a 30 percent gross profit on sales. Gross profit on selling price is the common method for quoting the profit for several reasons: (1) Most companies state goods on a retail basis, not a cost basis. (2) A profit quoted on selling price is lower than one based on cost. This lower rate gives a favorable impression to the consumer. (3) The gross profit based on selling price can never exceed 100 percent.[12]

In Illustration 8-13, the gross profit was a given. But how did Cetus derive that figure? To see how to compute a gross profit percentage, assume that an article cost $15 and sells for $20, a gross profit of $5. As shown in the computations in Illustration 8-14, this markup is ¼ or 25 percent of retail, and ⅓ or, 33⅓ percent of cost.

ILLUSTRATION 8-14
Computation of Gross Profit Percentage

$$\frac{\text{Markup}}{\text{Retail}} = \frac{\$5}{\$20} = 25\% \text{ at retail} \qquad \frac{\text{Markup}}{\text{Cost}} = \frac{\$5}{\$15} = 33\tfrac{1}{3}\% \text{ on cost}$$

Although companies normally compute the gross profit on the basis of selling price, you should understand the basic relationship between markup on cost and markup on selling price. For example, assume that a company marks up a given item by 25 percent. What, then, is the **gross profit on selling price**? To find the answer, assume that the item sells for $1. In this case, the following formula applies.

$$\text{Cost} + \text{Gross profit} = \text{Selling price}$$
$$C + .25C = SP$$
$$(1 + .25)C = SP$$
$$1.25C = \$1.00$$
$$C = \$0.80$$

[11]An alternative method of estimating inventory using the gross profit percentage is considered by some to be less complicated than the traditional method. This alternative method uses the standard income statement format as follows. (Assume the same data as in the Cetus example above.)

Sales		$280,000		$280,000
Cost of sales				
Beginning inventory	$ 60,000		$ 60,000	
Purchases	200,000		200,000	
Goods available for sale	260,000		260,000	
Ending inventory	(3) ?		(3) 64,000 Est.	
Cost of goods sold		(2) ?		(2)196,000 Est.
Gross profit on sales (30%)		(1) ?		(1) 84,000 Est.

Compute the unknowns as follows: first the gross profit amount, then cost of goods sold, and finally the ending inventory, as shown below.

(1) $280,000 × 30% = $84,000 (gross profit on sales).
(2) $280,000 − $84,000 = $196,000 (cost of goods sold).
(3) $260,000 − $196,000 = $64,000 (ending inventory).

[12]The terms *gross margin percentage, rate of gross profit,* and *percentage markup* are synonymous, although companies more commonly use *markup* in reference to cost and *gross profit* in reference to sales.

The gross profit equals \$0.20 (\$1.00 − \$0.80). The rate of gross profit on selling price is therefore 20 percent (\$0.20/\$1.00).

Conversely, assume that the gross profit on selling price is 20 percent. What is the **markup on cost**? To find the answer, again assume that the item sells for \$1. Again, the same formula holds:

$$\text{Cost} + \text{Gross profit} = \text{Selling price}$$

$$C + .20SP = SP$$

$$C = (1 - .20)SP$$

$$C = .80SP$$

$$C = .80(\$1.00)$$

$$C = \$0.80$$

As in the previous example, the markup equals \$0.20 (\$1.00 − \$0.80). The markup on cost is 25 percent (\$0.20/\$0.80).

Retailers use the following formulas to express these relationships:

$$\textbf{1. } \text{Gross profit on selling price} = \frac{\text{Percentage markup on cost}}{100\% + \text{Percentage markup on cost}}$$

$$\textbf{2. } \text{Percentage markup on cost} = \frac{\text{Gross profit on selling price}}{100\% - \text{Gross profit on selling price}}$$

ILLUSTRATION 8-15
Formulas Relating to Gross Profit

To understand how to use these formulas, consider their application in the following calculations.

Gross Profit on Selling Price		Percentage Markup on Cost
Given: 20%	⟶	$\frac{.20}{1.00 - .20} = 25\%$
Given: 25%	⟶	$\frac{.25}{1.00 - .25} = 33\frac{1}{3}\%$
$\frac{.25}{1.00 + .25} = 20\%$	⟵	Given: 25%
$\frac{.50}{1.00 + .50} = 33\frac{1}{3}\%$	⟵	Given: 50%

ILLUSTRATION 8-16
Application of Gross Profit Formulas

Because selling price exceeds cost, and with the gross profit amount the same for both, **gross profit on selling price will always be less than the related percentage based on cost.** Note that companies do not multiply sales by a cost-based markup percentage. Instead, they must convert the gross profit percentage to a percentage based on selling price.

Evaluation of Gross Profit Method

What are the major disadvantages of the gross profit method? One disadvantage is that **it provides an estimate.** As a result, companies must take a physical inventory once a year to verify the inventory. Second, the gross profit method **uses past percentages** in determining the markup. Although the past often provides answers to the future, a current rate is more appropriate. Note that whenever significant fluctuations occur, companies should adjust the percentage as appropriate. Third, companies must be **careful in applying a blanket gross profit rate.** Frequently, a store or department handles merchandise with widely varying rates of gross profit. In these situations, the company may need to apply the gross profit method by subsections, lines of merchandise, or a similar basis that classifies merchandise according to their respective rates of gross profit. The gross profit method is normally unacceptable for financial reporting purposes because it provides only an estimate. GAAP requires a physical inventory as additional verification of the inventory indicated in the records. Nevertheless, GAAP permits the gross profit method to determine ending inventory for interim (generally quarterly) reporting purposes, provided a company discloses the use of this method. Note that the gross profit method will follow closely the inventory method used (FIFO, LIFO, average cost) because it relies on historical records.

WHAT DO THE NUMBERS MEAN?

THE SQUEEZE

Managers and analysts closely follow gross profits. A small change in the gross profit rate can significantly affect the bottom line. In 1993, **Apple Computer** suffered a textbook case of shrinking gross profits. In response to pricing wars in the personal computer market, Apple had to quickly reduce the price of its signature Macintosh computers—reducing prices more quickly than it could reduce its costs. As a result its gross profit rate fell from 44 percent in 1992 to 40 percent in 1993. Though the drop of 4 percent seems small, its impact on the bottom line caused Apple's stock price to drop from $57 per share on June 1, 1993, to $27.50 by mid-July 1993.

As another example, **Debenham**, the second largest department store in the United Kingdom, experienced a 14 percentage share price decline. The cause? Mark-downs on slow moving inventory reduced its gross margin.

Source: Alison Smith, "Debenham's Shares Hit by Warning," *Financial Times* (July 24, 2002), p. 21.

RETAIL INVENTORY METHOD

OBJECTIVE 6
Determine ending inventory by applying the retail inventory method.

Accounting for inventory in a retail operation presents several challenges. Retailers with certain types of inventory may use the specific identification method to value their inventories. Such an approach makes sense when a retailer holds significant individual inventory units, such as automobiles, pianos, or fur coats. However, imagine attempting to use such an approach at **Target**, **True-Value Hardware**, **Sears Holdings**, or **Bloomingdale's**—high-volume retailers that have many different types of merchandise. It would be extremely difficult to determine the cost of each sale, to enter cost codes on the tickets, to change the codes to reflect declines in value of the merchandise, to allocate costs such as transportation, and so on.

An alternative is to compile the inventories at retail prices. For most retailers, an observable pattern between cost and price exists. The retailer can then use a formula to convert retail prices to cost. This method is called the **retail inventory method. It requires that the retailer keep a record of (1) the total cost and retail value of goods purchased, (2) the total cost and retail value of the goods available for sale, and (3) the sales for the period.** Use of the retail inventory method is very common. For example, **Safeway** supermarkets uses the retail inventory method, as does **Target Corp.**, **Wal-Mart**, and **Best Buy**.

Here is how it works at a company like **Best Buy**: Beginning with the retail value of the goods available for sale, Best Buy deducts the sales for the period. This calculation determines an estimated inventory (goods on hand) at retail. It next computes the **cost-to-retail ratio** for all goods. The formula for this computation is to divide the cost of total goods available for sale at cost by the total goods available at retail price. Finally, to obtain ending inventory at cost, Best Buy applies the cost-to-retail ratio to the ending inventory valued at retail. Illustration 8-17 shows the retail inventory method calculations for Best Buy (assumed data).

ILLUSTRATION 8-17
Retail Inventory Method

BEST BUY
(current period)

	Cost	Retail
Beginning inventory	$14,000	$ 20,000
Purchases	63,000	90,000
Goods available for sale	$77,000	110,000
Deduct: Sales		85,000
Ending inventory, at retail		$ 25,000

Ratio of cost to retail ($77,000 ÷ $110,000) = 70%
Ending inventory at cost (70% of $25,000) = $ 17,500

There are different versions of the retail inventory method. These include the **conventional** method (based on lower-of-average-cost-or-market), the **cost** method, the **LIFO retail** method, and the **dollar-value LIFO** retail method. Regardless of which version a company uses, the IRS, various retail associations, and the accounting profession all sanction use of the retail inventory method. One of its advantages is that a company like **Target** can approximate the inventory balance **without a physical count**. However, to avoid a potential overstatement of the inventory, Target makes periodic inventory counts. Such counts are especially important in retail operations where loss due to shoplifting or breakage is common.

The retail inventory method is particularly useful for any type of interim report, because such reports usually need a fairly quick and reliable measure of the inventory. Also, insurance adjusters often use this method to estimate losses from fire, flood, or other type of casualty. This method also acts as a **control device** because a company will have to explain any deviations from a physical count at the end of the year. Finally, the retail method **expedites the physical inventory count** at the end of the year. The crew taking the physical inventory need record only the retail price of each item. The crew does not need to look up each item's invoice cost, thereby saving time and expense.

Retail-Method Concepts

The amounts shown in the "Retail" column of Illustration 8-17 represent the original retail prices, assuming no price changes. In practice, though, retailers frequently mark up or mark down the prices they charge buyers.

For retailers, the term **markup** means an additional markup of the original retail price. (In another context, such as the gross profit discussion, we often think of markup on the basis of cost.) **Markup cancellations** are decreases in prices of merchandise that the retailer had marked up above the original retail price.

In a competitive market, retailers often need to use **markdowns**, which are decreases in the original sales prices. Such cuts in sales prices may be necessary because of a decrease in the general level of prices, special sales, soiled or damaged goods, overstocking, and market competition. Markdowns are common in retailing these days. **Markdown cancellations** occur when the markdowns are later offset by increases in the prices of goods that the retailer had marked down—such as after a one-day sale, for example. Neither a markup cancellation nor a markdown cancellation can exceed the original markup or markdown.

To illustrate these concepts, assume that Designer Clothing Store recently purchased 100 dress shirts from Marroway, Inc. The cost for these shirts was $1,500, or $15 a shirt. Designer Clothing established the selling price on these shirts at $30 a shirt. The shirts were selling quickly in anticipation of Father's Day, so the manager added a markup of $5 per shirt. This markup made the price too high for customers, and sales slowed. The manager then reduced the price to $32. At this point we would say that the shirts at Designer Clothing have had a markup of $5 and a markup cancellation of $3.

Right after Father's Day, the manager marked down the remaining shirts to a sale price of $23. At this point, an additional markup cancellation of $2 has taken place, and a $7 markdown has occurred. If the manager later increases the price of the shirts to $24, a markdown cancellation of $1 would occur.

Retail Inventory Method with Markups and Markdowns—Conventional Method

Retailers use markup and markdown concepts in developing the proper inventory valuation at the end of the accounting period. To obtain the appropriate inventory figures, companies must give proper treatment to markups, markup cancellations, markdowns, and markdown cancellations.

To illustrate the different possibilities, consider the data for In-Fusion Inc., shown in Illustration 8-18. In-Fusion can calculate its ending inventory at cost under two assumptions, A and B. (We'll explain the reasons for the two later.)

Assumption A: Computes a cost ratio after markups (and markup cancellations) but before markdowns.

Assumption B: Computes a cost ratio after both markups and markdowns (and cancellations).

ILLUSTRATION 8-18
Retail Inventory Method with Markups and Markdowns

	Cost	Retail
Beginning inventory	$ 500	$ 1,000
Purchases (net)	20,000	35,000
Markups		3,000
Markup cancellations		1,000
Markdowns		2,500
Markdown cancellations		2,000
Sales (net)		25,000

IN-FUSION INC.

	Cost		Retail
Beginning inventory	$ 500		$ 1,000
Purchases (net)	20,000		35,000
Merchandise available for sale	20,500		36,000
Add: Markups		$3,000	
Less: Markup cancellations		(1,000)	
Net markups			2,000
	20,500		38,000
(A) Cost-to-retail ratio	$\frac{\$20,500}{\$38,000}$	= 53.9%	
Deduct:			
Markdowns		2,500	
Less: Markdown cancellations		(2,000)	
Net markdowns			500
	$20,500		37,500
(B) Cost-to-retail ratio	$\frac{\$20,500}{\$37,500}$	= 54.7%	
Deduct: Sales (net)			25,000
Ending inventory at retail			$12,500

The computations for In-Fusion are:

Ending inventory at retail × Cost ratio = Value of ending inventory
Assumption A: $12,500 × 53.9% = $6,737.50
Assumption B: $12,500 × 54.7% = $6,837.50

The question becomes: Which assumption and which percentage should In-Fusion use to compute the ending inventory valuation? The answer depends on which retail inventory method In-Fusion chooses.

One approach uses only assumption A (a cost ratio using markups but not markdowns). It approximates the lower-of-average-cost-or-market. We will refer to this approach as the **conventional retail inventory method** or the **lower-of-cost-or-market approach.**

To understand why this method considers only the markups, not the markdowns, in the cost percentage, you must understand how a retail business operates. A markup normally indicates an increase in the market value of the item. On the other hand, a markdown means a decline in the utility of that item. Therefore, to approximate the lower-of-cost-or-market, we would consider markdowns a current loss and so would not include them in calculating the cost-to-retail ratio. Omitting the markdowns would make the cost-to-retail ratio lower, which leads to an approximate lower-of-cost-or-market.

An example will make the distinction between the two methods clear: In-Fusion purchased two items for $5 apiece; the original sales price was $10 each. One item was subsequently written down to $2. Assuming no sales for the period, **if markdowns are considered** in the cost-to-retail ratio (assumption B—the **cost method**), we compute the ending inventory in the following way.

ILLUSTRATION 8-19
Retail Inventory Method Including Markdowns—Cost Method

Markdowns Included in Cost-to-Retail Ratio

	Cost	Retail
Purchases	$10	$20
Deduct: Markdowns		8
Ending inventory, at retail		$12

Cost-to-retail ratio $\frac{\$10}{\$12} = 83.3\%$

Ending inventory at cost ($12 × .833) = $10

This approach (the cost method) reflects an **average cost** of the two items of the commodity without considering the loss on the one item. It values ending inventory at $10.

If markdowns are not considered in the cost-to-retail ratio (assumption A—the **conventional retail method)**, we compute the ending inventory as follows.

ILLUSTRATION 8-20
Retail Inventory Method Excluding Markdowns—Conventional Method (LCM)

Markdowns Not Included in Cost-to-Retail Ratio

	Cost	Retail
Purchases	$10	$20

Cost-to-retail ratio $\frac{\$10}{\$20} = 50\%$

	Cost	Retail
Deduct: Markdowns		8
Ending inventory, at retail		$12

Ending inventory, at cost ($12 × .50) = $6

Under this approach (the conventional retail method, in which markdowns are **not considered)**, ending inventory would be $6. The inventory valuation of $6 reflects two inventory items, one inventoried at $5 and the other at $1. It reflects the fact that In-Fusion reduced the sales price from $10 to $2, and reduced the cost from $5 to $1.[13]

[13]This figure is not really market (replacement cost), but it is net realizable value less the normal margin that is allowed. In other words, the sale price of the goods written down is $2, but subtracting a normal margin of 50 percent ($5 cost, $10 price), the figure becomes $1.

To approximate the lower-of-cost-or-market, In-Fusion must establish the **cost-to-retail ratio**. It does this by dividing the cost of goods available for sale by the sum of the original retail price of these goods plus the net markups. This calculation excludes markdowns and markdown cancellations. Illustration 8-21 shows the basic format for the retail inventory method using the lower-of-cost-or-market approach along with the In-Fusion Inc. information.

ILLUSTRATION 8-21
Comprehensive Conventional Retail Inventory Method Format

IN-FUSION INC.

	Cost		Retail
Beginning inventory	$ 500.00		$ 1,000.00
Purchases (net)	20,000.00		35,000.00
Totals	20,500.00		36,000.00
Add: Net markups			
Markups		$3,000.00	
Markup cancellations		1,000.00	2,000.00
Totals	$20,500.00 ←		→ 38,000.00
Deduct: Net markdowns			
Markdowns		2,500.00	
Markdown cancellations		2,000.00	500.00
Sales price of goods available			37,500.00
Deduct: Sales (net)			25,000.00
Ending inventory, at retail			$12,500.00

$$\text{Cost-to-retail ratio} = \frac{\text{Cost of goods available}}{\text{Original retail price of goods available, plus net markups}}$$

$$= \frac{\$20,500}{\$38,000} = 53.9\%$$

Ending inventory at lower of cost or market (53.9% × $12,500.00) = $ 6,737.50

Because an averaging effect occurs, an exact lower-of-cost-or-market inventory valuation is ordinarily not obtained, but an adequate approximation can be achieved. In contrast, adding net markups **and** deducting net markdowns yields **approximate cost**.

Special Items Relating to Retail Method

The retail inventory method becomes more complicated when we consider such items as freight-in, purchase returns and allowances, and purchase discounts. In the retail method, we treat such items as follows.

- **Freight costs** are part of the purchase cost.
- **Purchase returns** are ordinarily considered as a reduction of the price at both cost and retail.
- **Purchase discounts and allowances** usually are considered as a reduction of the cost of purchases.

In short, the treatment for the items affecting the cost column of the retail inventory approach follows the computation for cost of goods available for sale.[14]

Note also that **sales returns and allowances** are considered as proper adjustments to gross sales. However, when sales are recorded gross, companies do not recognize **sales discounts**. To adjust for the sales discount account in such a situation would provide an ending inventory figure at retail that would be overvalued.

[14]When the purchase allowance is not reflected by a reduction in the selling price, no adjustment is made to the retail column.

In addition, a number of special items require careful analysis:

- **Transfers-in** from another department are reported in the same way as purchases from an outside enterprise.
- **Normal shortages** (breakage, damage, theft, shrinkage) should reduce the retail column because these goods are no longer available for sale. Such costs are reflected in the selling price because a certain amount of shortage is considered normal in a retail enterprise. As a result, companies do not consider this amount in computing the cost-to-retail percentage. Rather, to arrive at ending inventory at retail, they show normal shortages as a deduction similar to sales.
- **Abnormal shortages,** on the other hand, are deducted from both the cost and retail columns and reported as a special inventory amount or as a loss. To do otherwise distorts the cost-to-retail ratio and overstates ending inventory.
- **Employee discounts** (given to employees to encourage loyalty, better performance, and so on) are deducted from the retail column in the same way as sales. These discounts should not be considered in the cost-to-retail percentage because they do not reflect an overall change in the selling price.

Illustration 8-22 shows some of these concepts. The company, Extreme Sport Apparel, determines its inventory using the conventional retail inventory method.

ILLUSTRATION 8-22
Conventional Retail Inventory Method—Special Items Included

EXTREME SPORT APPAREL

	Cost		Retail
Beginning inventory	$ 1,000		$ 1,800
Purchases	30,000		60,000
Freight-in	600		—
Purchase returns	(1,500)		(3,000)
Totals	30,100		58,800
Net markups			9,000
Abnormal shortage	(1,200)		(2,000)
Totals	$28,900 ←	→	65,800
Deduct:			
Net markdowns			1,400
Sales		$36,000	
Sales returns		(900)	35,100
Employee discounts			800
Normal shortage			1,300
			$27,200

$$\text{Cost-to-retail ratio} = \frac{\$28,900}{\$65,800} = 43.9\%$$

Ending inventory at lower of cost or market (43.9% × $27,200) = $11,940.80

Evaluation of Retail Inventory Method

Companies like **Gap Inc., Circuit City**, or your local department store use the retail inventory method of computing inventory for the following reasons: (1) to permit the computation of net income without a physical count of inventory, (2) as a control measure in determining inventory shortages, (3) in regulating quantities of merchandise on hand, and (4) for insurance information.

One characteristic of the retail inventory method is that it **has an averaging effect on varying rates of gross profit.** This can be problematic when companies apply the method to an entire business, where rates of gross profit vary among departments. There is no allowance for possible distortion of results because of such differences.

Companies refine the retail method under such conditions by computing inventory separately by departments or by classes of merchandise with similar gross profits. In addition, the reliability of this method assumes that the distribution of items in inventory is similar to the "mix" in the total goods available for sale.

PRESENTATION AND ANALYSIS

Presentation of Inventories

OBJECTIVE 7
Explain how to report and analyze inventory.

Accounting standards require financial statement disclosure of the composition of the inventory, inventory financing arrangements, and the inventory costing methods employed. The standards also require the consistent application of costing methods from one period to another.

Manufacturers should report the inventory composition either in the balance sheet or in a separate schedule in the notes. The relative mix of raw materials, work in process, and finished goods helps in assessing liquidity and in computing the stage of inventory completion.

Significant or unusual financing arrangements relating to inventories may require note disclosure. Examples include transactions with related parties, product financing arrangements, firm purchase commitments, involuntary liquidation of LIFO inventories, and pledging of inventories as collateral. Companies should present inventories pledged as collateral for a loan in the current assets section rather than as an offset to the liability.

wiley.com/college/kieso
Additional Inventory Disclosures

A company should also report the basis on which it states inventory amounts (lower-of-cost-or-market) and the method used in determining cost (LIFO, FIFO, average cost, etc.). For example, the annual report of **Mumford of Wyoming** contains the following disclosures.

ILLUSTRATION 8-23
Disclosure of Inventory Methods

Mumford of Wyoming

Note A: Significant Accounting Policies

Live feeder cattle and feed—last-in, first-out (LIFO) cost, which is below approximate market	$854,800
Live range cattle—lower of principally identified cost or market	$1,240,500
Live sheep and supplies—lower of first-in, first-out (FIFO) cost or market	$674,000
Dressed meat and by-products—principally at market less allowances for distribution and selling expenses	$362,630

The preceding illustration shows that a company can use different pricing methods for different elements of its inventory. If Mumford changes the method of pricing any of its inventory elements, it must report a change in accounting principle. For example, if Mumford changes its method of accounting for live sheep from FIFO to average cost, it should separately report this change, along with the effect on income, in the current and prior periods. Changes in accounting principle require an explanatory paragraph in the auditor's report describing the change in method.

Fortune Brands, Inc. reported its inventories in its annual report as follows (note the "trade practice" followed in classifying inventories among the current assets).

ILLUSTRATION 8-24
Disclosure of Trade Practice in Valuing Inventories

Fortune Brands, Inc.

Current assets	
Inventories (Note 2)	
Leaf tobacco	$ 563,424,000
Bulk whiskey	232,759,000
Other raw materials, supplies and work in process	238,906,000
Finished products	658,326,000
	$1,693,415,000

Note 2: Inventories

Inventories are priced at the lower of cost (average; first-in, first-out; and minor amounts at last-in, first-out) or market. In accordance with generally recognized trade practice, the leaf tobacco and bulk whiskey inventories are classified as current assets, although part of such inventories due to the duration of the aging process, ordinarily will not be sold within one year.

The following inventory disclosures by **Newmont Gold Company** reveal the use of different bases of valuation, including market value, for different classifications of inventory.

ILLUSTRATION 8-25
Disclosure of Different Bases of Valuation

Newmont Gold Company

Current assets	
Inventories (Note 2)	$44,303,000
Noncurrent assets	
Inventories—ore in stockpiles (Note 2)	$5,250,000

Note 2: Inventories

Inventories included in current assets at December 31 were:

Ore and in-process inventory	$11,303,000
Gold bullion and gold precipitates	24,209,000
Materials and supplies	8,791,000
	$44,303,000

Ore and in-process inventory and materials and supplies are stated at the lower of average cost or net realizable value. Gold bullion and gold precipitates are stated at market value, less a provision for estimated refining and delivery charges. Expenditures capitalized as ore and in-process inventory include labor, material and other production costs.

Noncurrent inventories are stated at the lower of average cost or net realizable value and represent ore in stockpiles anticipated to be processed in future years.

Analysis of Inventories

As our opening story illustrates, the amount of inventory that a company carries can have significant economic consequences. As a result, companies must manage inventories. But, inventory management is a double-edged sword. It requires constant attention. On the one hand, management wants to stock a great variety and quantity of items. Doing so will provide customers with the greatest selection. However, such an inventory policy may incur excessive carrying costs (e.g., investment, storage, insurance, taxes, obsolescence, and damage). On the other hand, low inventory levels lead to stockouts, lost sales, and disgruntled customers.

Using financial ratios helps companies to chart a middle course between these two dangers. Common ratios used in the management and evaluation of inventory levels are inventory turnover and a related measure, average days to sell the inventory.

Inventory Turnover Ratio

The **inventory turnover ratio** measures the number of times on average a company sells the inventory during the period. It measures the liquidity of the inventory. To compute inventory turnover, divide the cost of goods sold by the average inventory on hand during the period.

Barring seasonal factors, analysts compute average inventory from beginning and ending inventory balances. For example, in its 2004 annual report **Kellogg Company** reported a beginning inventory of $649.8 million, an ending inventory of $681 million, and cost of goods sold of $5,299 million for the year. Illustration 8-26 shows the inventory turnover formula and Kellogg Company's 2004 ratio computation below.

ILLUSTRATION 8-26
Inventory Turnover Ratio

$$\text{Inventory Turnover} = \frac{\text{Cost of Goods Sold}}{\text{Average Inventory}}$$

$$= \frac{\$5{,}299}{(\$681 + \$649.8)/2} = 8 \text{ times}$$

Average Days to Sell Inventory

A variant of the inventory turnover ratio is the **average days to sell inventory**. This measure represents the average number of days' sales for which a company has inventory on hand. For example, the inventory turnover for Kellogg Company of 8 times divided into 365 is approximately 45.6 days.

There are typical levels of inventory in every industry. However, companies that keep their inventory at lower levels with higher turnovers than those of their competitors, and that still can satisfy customer needs, are the most successful.

QUESTIONS

1. Where there is evidence that the utility of inventory goods, as part of their disposal in the ordinary course of business, will be less than cost, what is the proper accounting treatment?

2. Explain the rationale for the ceiling and floor in the lower-of-cost-or-market method of valuing inventories.

3. Why are inventories valued at the lower-of-cost-or-market? What are the arguments against the use of the LCM method of valuing inventories?

4. What approaches may be employed in applying the lower-of-cost-or-market procedure? Which approach is normally used and why?

5. In some instances accounting principles require a departure from valuing inventories at cost alone. Determine the proper unit inventory price in the following cases.

	Cases 1	2	3	4	5
Cost	$15.90	$16.10	$15.90	$15.90	$15.90
Net realizable value	14.30	19.20	15.20	10.40	16.40
Net realizable value less normal profit	12.80	17.60	13.75	8.80	14.80
Market (replacement cost)	14.80	17.20	12.80	9.70	16.80

6. What method(s) might be used in the accounts to record a loss due to a price decline in the inventories? Discuss.

7. What factors might call for inventory valuation at sales prices (net realizable value or market price)?

8. Under what circumstances is relative sales value an appropriate basis for determining the price assigned to inventory?

9. At December 31, 2008, Kidman Co. has outstanding purchase commitments for purchase of 150,000 gallons, at $6.40 per gallon, of a raw material to be used in its manufacturing process. The company prices its raw material inventory at cost or market, whichever is lower. Assuming that the market price as of December 31, 2008, is $5.90, how would you treat this situation in the accounts?

10. What are the major uses of the gross profit method?

11. Distinguish between gross profit as a percentage of cost and gross profit as a percentage of sales price. Convert the following gross profit percentages based on cost to gross profit percentages based on sales price: 20% and 33⅓%. Convert the following gross profit percentages based on sales price to gross profit percentages based on cost: 33⅓% and 60%.

12. Carole Lombard Co. with annual net sales of $6 million maintains a markup of 25% based on cost. Lombard's expenses average 15% of net sales. What is Lombard's gross profit and net profit in dollars?

13. A fire destroys all of the merchandise of Rosanna Arquette Company on February 10, 2008. Presented below is information compiled up to the date of the fire.

Inventory, January 1, 2008	$ 400,000
Sales to February 10, 2008	1,750,000
Purchases to February 10, 2008	1,140,000
Freight-in to February 10, 2008	60,000
Rate of gross profit on selling price	40%

What is the approximate inventory on February 10, 2008?

14. What conditions must exist for the retail inventory method to provide valid results?

15. The conventional retail inventory method yields results that are essentially the same as those yielded by the lower-of-cost-or-market method. Explain. Prepare an illustration of how the retail inventory method reduces inventory to market.

16. **(a)** Determine the ending inventory under the conventional retail method for the furniture department of Gin Blossoms Department Stores from the following data.

	Cost	Retail
Inventory, Jan. 1	$ 149,000	$ 283,500
Purchases	1,400,000	2,160,000
Freight-in	70,000	
Markups, net		92,000
Markdowns, net		48,000
Sales		2,235,000

(b) If the results of a physical inventory indicated an inventory at retail of $240,000, what inferences would you draw?

17. **Deere and Company** reported inventory in its balance sheet as follows:

Inventories	$1,999,100,000

What additional disclosures might be necessary to present the inventory fairly?

18. Of what significance is inventory turnover to a retail store?

C H A P T E R N I N E

ACQUISITION AND DISPOSITION OF PROPERTY, PLANT, AND EQUIPMENT

Where Have All the Assets Gone?

Investments in long-lived assets, such as property, plant, and equipment, are important elements in many companies' balance sheets. As the chart below indicates, major companies, such as **Southwest Airlines** and **Wal-Mart**, recently reported property, plant, and equipment (PP&E) as a percent of total assets ranging from 54 percent up to nearly 77 percent.

However, for various strategic reasons, many companies are now shedding property, plant, and equipment. Instead, they are paying others to manufacture and assemble products—functions they previously performed in their own facilities. Companies are also reducing fixed assets by outsourcing warehousing and distribution. Such logistics outsourcing can cut companies' own costs for keeping and managing inventories, and spare them the need to invest in advanced tracking technologies increasingly required by retailers. In a recent year more than 80 percent of the country's 100 biggest companies used third-party logistics providers.[1] As a result, some companies such as **Nortel** and **Lucent** are decreasing their investment in long-lived assets, as the following chart shows.

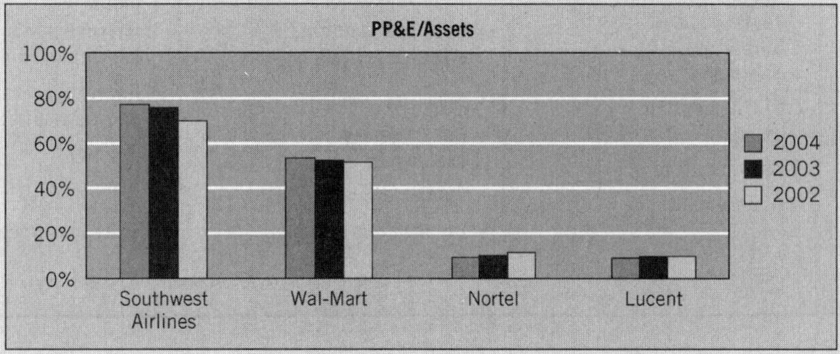

Nortel is a good example of these strategies. It has sold and outsourced certain facilities in order to reduce its direct manufacturing activities and costs. Nortel also sold its training and headset businesses. Further, it has aggressively outsourced other operations to reduce costs. Reductions in these areas will enable Nortel and other outsourcing companies to concentrate on their core operations and better manage investments in property, plant and equipment.

[1]Adapted from Chapter 1 in Grady Means and David Schneider, *MetaCapitalism: The e-Business Revolution and the Design of 21st-Century Companies and Markets* (New York: John Wiley and Sons, 2000); and Kris Maher, "Global Goods Jugglers," *Wall Street Journal Online* (July 5, 2005).

Learning Objectives

After studying this chapter, you should be able to:

1 Describe property, plant, and equipment.
2 Identify the costs to include in initial valuation of property, plant, and equipment.
3 Describe the accounting problems associated with self-constructed assets.
4 Describe the accounting problems associated with interest capitalization.
5 Understand accounting issues related to acquiring and valuing plant assets.
6 Describe the accounting treatment for costs subsequent to acquisition.
7 Describe the accounting treatment for the disposal of property, plant, and equipment.

PREVIEW OF CHAPTER 9

As we indicate in the opening story, a company like **Southwest Airlines** has a substantial investment in property, plant, and equipment. Conversely, other companies, such as **Nortel**, have a minor investment in these types of assets. In this chapter, we discuss the proper accounting for the acquisition, use, and disposition of property, plant, and equipment. The content and organization of the chapter are as follows.

ACQUISITION AND DISPOSITION OF PROPERTY, PLANT, AND EQUIPMENT

ACQUISITION
- Acquisition costs: Land, buildings, equipment
- Self-constructed assets
- Interest costs
- Observations

VALUATION
- Cash discounts
- Deferred contracts
- Lump-sum purchases
- Stock issuance
- Nonmonetary exchanges
- Contributions
- Other valuation methods

COSTS SUBSEQUENT TO ACQUISITION
- Additions
- Improvements and replacements
- Rearrangement and reinstallation
- Repairs
- Summary

DISPOSITIONS
- Sale
- Involuntary conversion
- Miscellaneous problems

OBJECTIVE 1
Describe property, plant, and equipment.

Companies like **Boeing**, **Target**, and **Starbucks** use assets of a durable nature. Such assets are called **property, plant, and equipment**. Other terms commonly used are **plant assets** and **fixed assets**. We use these terms interchangeably throughout this textbook.

Property, plant, and equipment include land, building structures (offices, factories, warehouses), and equipment (machinery, furniture, tools). The major characteristics of property, plant, and equipment are as follows.

1 **They are acquired for use in operations and not for resale.** Only assets used in normal business operations are classified as property, plant, and equipment. For example, an idle building is more appropriately classified separately as an investment. Land developers or subdividers classify land as inventory.

2 **They are long-term in nature and usually depreciated.** Property, plant, and equipment yield services over a number of years. Companies allocate the cost of the investment in these assets to future periods through periodic depreciation charges. The exception is land, which is depreciated only if a material decrease in value occurs, such as a loss in fertility of agricultural land because of poor crop rotation, drought, or soil erosion.

3 **They possess physical substance.** Property, plant, and equipment are tangible assets characterized by physical existence or substance. This differentiates them from intangible assets, such as patents or goodwill. Unlike raw material, however, property, plant, and equipment do not physically become part of a product held for resale.

UNDERLYING CONCEPTS

Market value is relevant to inventory but less so for property, plant, and equipment which, consistent with the going concern assumption, are held for use in the business, not for sale like inventory.

ACQUISITION AND VALUATION OF PROPERTY, PLANT, AND EQUIPMENT

OBJECTIVE 2
Identify the costs to include in initial valuation of property, plant, and equipment.

Most companies use historical cost as the basis for valuing property, plant, and equipment. **Historical cost measures the cash or cash equivalent price of obtaining the asset and bringing it to the location and condition necessary for its intended use.** For example, companies like **Kellogg Co.** consider the purchase price, freight costs, sales taxes, and installation costs of a productive asset as part of the asset's cost. It then allocates these costs to future periods through depreciation. Further, Kellogg **adds to the asset's cost** any related costs incurred **after the asset's acquisition**, such as additions, improvements, or replacements, **if they provide future service potential**. Otherwise, Kellogg expenses these costs immediately.

Disagreement does exist concerning differences between historical cost and other valuation methods (such as replacement cost or fair market value) **arising after acquisition**. *APB Opinion No. 6* states, "property, plant, and equipment should not be written up to reflect appraisal, market, or current values which are above cost." Although the opinion notes minor exceptions, current standards indicate that departures from historical cost are rare. The main reasons for this position are as follows:

INTERNATIONAL INSIGHT

In many nations, such as Great Britain and Brazil, companies may revalue their fixed assets at amounts above historical cost. These revaluations may be at appraisal values or at amounts linked to a specified index.

1 At the date of acquisition, cost reflects fair value.

2 Historical cost involves actual, not hypothetical, transactions and so is the most reliable.

3 Companies should not anticipate gains and losses but should recognize gains and losses only when the asset is sold.

Cost of Land

All expenditures made to acquire land and ready it for use are considered part of the land cost. Thus, when **Wal-Mart** or **Home Depot** purchases land on which to build a new store, its land costs typically include (1) the purchase price; (2) closing costs, such as title to the land, attorney's fees, and recording fees; (3) costs incurred in getting the land in condition for its intended use, such as grading, filling, draining, and clearing; (4) assumption of any liens, mortgages, or encumbrances on the property; and (5) any additional land improvements that have an indefinite life.

Expanded Discussion of Alternative Valuation Methods

For example, when Home Depot purchases land for the purpose of constructing a building, it considers all costs incurred up to the excavation for the new building as land costs. **Removal of old buildings—clearing, grading, and filling—is a land cost because this activity is necessary to get the land in condition for its intended purpose.** Home Depot treats any proceeds from getting the land ready for its intended use, such as salvage receipts on the demolition of an old building or the sale of cleared timber, as **reductions in the price of the land.**

In some cases, when Home Depot purchases land, it may assume certain obligations on the land such as back taxes or liens. In such situations, the cost of the land is the cash paid for it, plus the encumbrances. In other words, if the purchase price of the land is \$50,000 cash, but Home Depot assumes accrued property taxes of \$5,000 and liens of \$10,000, its land cost is \$65,000.

Home Depot also might incur **special assessments** for local improvements, such as pavements, street lights, sewers, and drainage systems. It should charge these costs to the Land account because they are relatively permanent in nature. That is, after installation, they are maintained by the local government. In addition, Home Depot should charge any permanent improvements it makes, such as landscaping, to the Land account. It records separately any **improvements with limited lives**, such as private driveways, walks, fences, and parking lots, as Land Improvements. These costs are depreciated over their estimated lives.

Generally, land is part of property, plant, and equipment. However, if the major purpose of acquiring and holding land is speculative, a company more appropriately classifies the land as an **investment**. If a real estate concern holds the land for resale, it should classify the land as **inventory**.

In cases where land is held as an investment, what accounting treatment should be given for taxes, insurance, and other direct costs incurred while holding the land? Many believe these costs should be capitalized. The reason: They are not generating revenue from the investment at this time. Companies generally use this approach except when the asset is currently producing revenue (such as rental property).

Cost of Buildings

INTERNATIONAL INSIGHT

Under international accounting standards, historical cost is the benchmark (preferred) treatment for property, plant, and equipment. However, companies may also use revalued amounts. If using revaluation, companies must revalue the class of assets regularly.

The cost of buildings should include all expenditures related directly to their acquisition or construction. These costs include (1) materials, labor, and overhead costs incurred during construction and (2) professional fees and building permits. Generally, companies contract others to construct their buildings. Companies consider all costs incurred, from excavation to completion, as part of the building costs.

But how should companies account for an old building that is on the site of a newly proposed building? Is the cost of removal of the old building a cost of the land or a cost of the new building? Recall that **if a company purchases land with an old building on it, then the cost of demolition less its salvage value is a cost of getting the land ready for its intended use and relates to the land rather than to the new building**. In other words, all costs of getting an asset ready for its intended use are costs of that asset.

Cost of Equipment

The term "equipment" in accounting includes delivery equipment, office equipment, machinery, furniture and fixtures, furnishings, factory equipment, and similar fixed assets. The cost of such assets includes the purchase price, freight and handling charges incurred, insurance on the equipment while in transit, cost of special foundations if required, assembling and installation costs, and costs of conducting trial runs. Costs thus include all expenditures incurred in acquiring the equipment and preparing it for use.

Self-Constructed Assets

OBJECTIVE 3
Describe the accounting problems associated with self-constructed assets.

Occasionally companies construct their own assets. Determining the cost of such machinery and other fixed assets can be a problem. Without a purchase price or contract price, the company must allocate costs and expenses to arrive at the cost of the **self-constructed asset**. Materials and direct labor used in construction pose no problem. A company can trace these costs directly to work and material orders related to the fixed assets constructed.

However, the assignment of indirect costs of manufacturing creates special problems. These indirect costs, called **overhead** or burden, include power, heat, light, insurance, property taxes on factory buildings and equipment, factory supervisory labor, depreciation of fixed assets, and supplies.

Companies can handle indirect costs in one of two ways:

1 *Assign no fixed overhead to the cost of the constructed asset.* The major argument for this treatment is that indirect overhead is generally fixed in nature; it does not increase as a result of constructing one's own plant or equipment. This approach assumes that the company will have the same costs regardless of whether it constructs the asset or not. Therefore, to charge a portion of the overhead costs to the equipment will normally reduce current expenses and consequently overstate income of the current period. However, the company would assign to the cost of the constructed asset variable overhead costs that increase as a result of the construction.

2 *Assign a portion of all overhead to the construction process.* This approach, called a **full-costing approach**, is appropriate if one believes that costs attach to all products and assets manufactured or constructed. Under this approach, a company assigns a portion of all overhead to the construction process, as it would to normal production. Advocates say that failure to allocate overhead costs understates the initial cost of the asset and results in an inaccurate future allocation.

Companies should assign to the asset **a pro rata portion** of the fixed overhead to determine its cost. Companies use this treatment extensively because many believe that it results in a better matching of costs with revenues.

If the allocated overhead results in recording construction costs in excess of the costs that an outside independent producer would charge, the company should record the excess overhead as a period loss rather than capitalize it. This avoids capitalizing the asset at more than its probable market value.[2]

Interest Costs During Construction

OBJECTIVE 4
Describe the accounting problems associated with interest capitalization.

The proper accounting for interest costs has been a long-standing controversy. Three approaches have been suggested to account for the interest incurred in financing the construction of property, plant, and equipment:

1 *Capitalize no interest charges during construction.* Under this approach, interest is considered a cost of financing and not a cost of construction. Some contend that if a company had used stock (equity) financing rather than debt, it would not incur this cost. The major argument against this approach is that the use of cash, whatever its source, has an associated implicit interest cost, which should not be ignored.

2 *Charge construction with all costs of funds employed, whether identifiable or not.* This method maintains that the cost of construction should include the cost of financing, whether by cash, debt, or stock. Its advocates say that all costs necessary to get an asset ready for its intended use, including interest, are part of the asset's cost. Interest, whether actual or imputed, is a cost, just as are labor and materials. A major criticism of this approach is that imputing the cost of equity capital (stock) is subjective and outside the framework of a historical cost system.

3 *Capitalize only the actual interest costs incurred during construction.* This approach agrees in part with the logic of the second approach—that interest is just as much a cost as are labor and materials. But this approach capitalizes only interest costs incurred through debt financing. (That is, it does not try to determine the cost of equity financing.) Under this approach, a company that uses debt financing will have an asset of higher cost than a company that uses stock financing. Some consider this approach unsatisfactory because they believe the cost of an asset should be the same whether it is financed with cash, debt, or equity.

Illustration 9-1 shows how a company might add interest costs (if any) to the cost of the asset under the three capitalization approaches.

---

[2] The Accounting Standards Executive Committee (AcSEC) of the AICPA has issued an exposure draft related to property, plant, and equipment. In this exposure draft, AcSEC argues against allocation of overhead. Instead, it basically supports capitalization of only direct costs (costs directly related to the specific activities involved in the construction process). AcSEC was concerned that the allocation of overhead costs may lead to overly aggressive allocations and therefore misstatements of income. In addition, not reporting these costs as period costs during the construction period may affect comparisons of period costs and resulting net income from one period to the next. See Accounting Standards Executive Committee, "Accounting for Certain Costs and Activities Related to Property, Plant, and Equipment," Exposure Draft (New York: AICPA, June 29, 2001).

ILLUSTRATION 9-1
Capitalization of Interest Costs

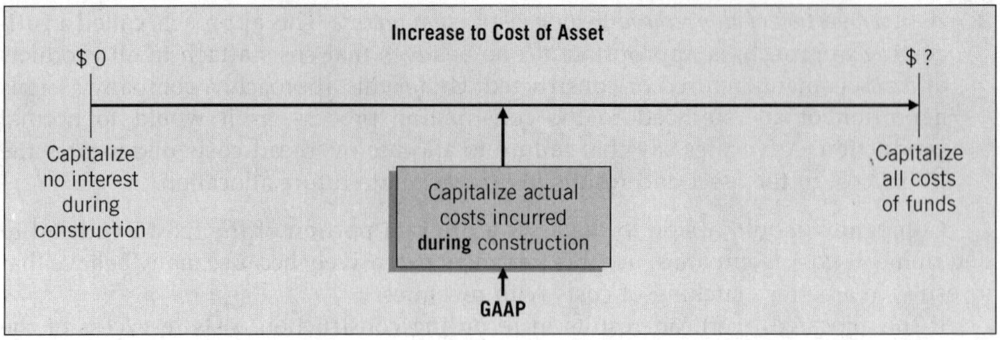

GAAP requires the third approach—capitalizing actual interest (with modification). This method follows the concept that the **historical cost of acquiring an asset includes all costs (including interest) incurred to bring the asset to the condition and location necessary for its intended use.** The rationale for this approach is that during construction, the asset is not generating revenues. Therefore, a company should defer (capitalize) interest costs.[3] Once construction is complete, the asset is ready for its intended use and a company can earn revenues. At this point the company should report interest as an expense and match it to these revenues. It follows that the company should expense any interest cost incurred in purchasing an asset that is ready for its intended use.

To implement this general approach, companies consider three items:

1. Qualifying assets.
2. Capitalization period.
3. Amount to capitalize.

Qualifying Assets

To qualify for interest capitalization, assets must require a period of time to get them ready for their intended use. A company capitalizes interest costs starting with the first expenditure related to the asset. Capitalization continues until the company substantially readies the asset for its intended use.

Assets that qualify for interest cost capitalization include assets under construction for a company's own use (including buildings, plants, and large machinery) and assets intended for sale or lease that are constructed or otherwise produced as discrete projects (e.g., ships or real estate developments).

Examples of assets that do not qualify for interest capitalization are (1) assets that are in use or ready for their intended use, and (2) assets that the company does not use in its earnings activities and that are not undergoing the activities necessary to get them ready for use. Examples of this second type include land remaining undeveloped and assets not used because of obsolescence, excess capacity, or need for repair.

INTERNATIONAL INSIGHT

Under international accounting standards, companies may capitalize interest, but it is not the preferred treatment. The benchmark treatment is to expense interest in the period incurred.

Capitalization Period

The **capitalization period** is the period of time during which a company must capitalize interest. It begins with the presence of three conditions:

1. Expenditures for the asset have been made.
2. Activities that are necessary to get the asset ready for its intended use are in progress.
3. Interest cost is being incurred.

Interest capitalization **continues as long as these three conditions are present**. The capitalization period ends when the asset is substantially complete and ready for its intended use.

[3]"Capitalization of Interest Cost," *Statement of Financial Accounting Standards No. 34* (Stamford, Conn.: FASB, 1979).

Amount to Capitalize

The amount of interest to capitalize is limited to the lower of actual interest cost incurred during the period or avoidable interest. **Avoidable interest** is the amount of interest cost during the period that a company could theoretically avoid if it had not made expenditures for the asset. If the actual interest cost for the period is $90,000 and the avoidable interest is $80,000, the company capitalizes only $80,000. Or, if the actual interest cost is $80,000 and the avoidable interest is $90,000, it still capitalizes only $80,000. In no situation should interest cost include a cost of capital charge for stockholders' equity. Furthermore, GAAP requires interest capitalization for a qualifying asset only if its effect, compared with the effect of expensing interest, is material.[4]

To apply the avoidable interest concept, a company determines the potential amount of interest that it may capitalize during an accounting period by multiplying the interest rate(s) by the **weighted-average accumulated expenditures** for qualifying assets during the period.

Weighted-Average Accumulated Expenditures. In computing the weighted-average accumulated expenditures, a company weights the construction expenditures by the amount of time (fraction of a year or accounting period) that it can incur interest cost on the expenditure.

To illustrate, assume a 17-month bridge construction project with current-year payments to the contractor of $240,000 on March 1, $480,000 on July 1, and $360,000 on November 1. The company computes the weighted-average accumulated expenditures for the year ended December 31 as follows.

ILLUSTRATION 9-2
Computation of Weighted-Average Accumulated Expenditures

Expenditures					
Date	Amount	×	Capitalization Period*	=	Weighted-Average Accumulated Expenditures
March 1	$ 240,000		10/12		$200,000
July 1	480,000		6/12		240,000
November 1	360,000		2/12		60,000
	$1,080,000				$500,000

*Months between date of expenditure and date interest capitalization stops or end of year, whichever comes first (in this case December 31).

To compute the weighted-average accumulated expenditures, a company weights the expenditures by the amount of time that it can incur interest cost on each one. For the March 1 expenditure, the company associates 10 months' interest cost with the expenditure. For the expenditure on July 1, it incurs only 6 months' interest costs. For the expenditure made on November 1, the company incurs only 2 months of interest cost.

Interest Rates. Companies follow these principles in selecting the appropriate interest rates to be applied to the weighted-average accumulated expenditures:

1 For the portion of weighted-average accumulated expenditures that is less than or equal to any amounts borrowed specifically to finance construction of the assets, **use the interest rate incurred on the specific borrowings.**

[4] Ibid., summary paragraph.

2 For the portion of weighted-average accumulated expenditures that is greater than any debt incurred specifically to finance construction of the assets, **use a weighted average of interest rates incurred on all other outstanding debt during the period.**[5]

Illustration 9-3 shows the computation of a weighted-average interest rate for debt greater than the amount incurred specifically to finance construction of the assets.

ILLUSTRATION 9-3
Computation of Weighted-Average Interest Rate

	Principal	Interest
12%, 2-year note	$ 600,000	$ 72,000
9%, 10-year bonds	2,000,000	180,000
7.5%, 20-year bonds	5,000,000	375,000
	$7,600,000	$627,000

$$\text{Weighted-average interest rate} = \frac{\text{Total interest}}{\text{Total principal}} = \frac{\$627{,}000}{\$7{,}600{,}000} = 8.25\%$$

Comprehensive Example of Interest Capitalization

To illustrate the issues related to interest capitalization, assume that on November 1, 2006, Shalla Company contracted Pfeifer Construction Co. to construct a building for $1,400,000 on land costing $100,000 (purchased from the contractor and included in the first payment). Shalla made the following payments to the construction company during 2007.

January 1	March 1	May 1	December 31	Total
$210,000	$300,000	$540,000	$450,000	$1,500,000

Pfeifer Construction completed the building, ready for occupancy, on December 31, 2007. Shalla had the following debt outstanding at December 31, 2007.

Specific Construction Debt	
1. 15%, 3-year note to finance purchase of land and construction of the building, dated December 31, 2006, with interest payable annually on December 31	$750,000
Other Debt	
2. 10%, 5-year note payable, dated December 31, 2003, with interest payable annually on December 31	$550,000
3. 12%, 10-year bonds issued December 31, 2002, with interest payable annually on December 31	$600,000

Shalla computed the weighted-average accumulated expenditures during 2003 as shown in Illustration 9-4.

ILLUSTRATION 9-4
Computation of Weighted-Average Accumulated Expenditures

Expenditures			Current Year		
Date	Amount	×	Capitalization Period	=	Weighted-Average Accumulated Expenditures
January 1	$ 210,000		12/12		$210,000
March 1	300,000		10/12		250,000
May 1	540,000		8/12		360,000
December 31	450,000		0		0
	$1,500,000				$820,000

[5]The interest rate to be used may rely exclusively on an average rate of all the borrowings, if desired. For our purposes, we use the specific borrowing rate followed by the average interest rate because we believe it to be more conceptually consistent. Either method can be used; *FASB Statement No. 34* does not provide explicit guidance on this measurement. For a discussion of this issue and others related to interest capitalization, see Kathryn M. Means and Paul M. Kazenski, "SFAS 34: Recipe for Diversity," *Accounting Horizons* (September 1988); and Wendy A. Duffy, "A Graphical Analysis of Interest Capitalization," *Journal of Accounting Education* (Fall 1990).

Note that the expenditure made on December 31, the last day of the year, does not have any interest cost.

Shalla computes the avoidable interest as shown in Illustration 9-5.

ILLUSTRATION 9-5
Computation of Avoidable Interest

Weighted-Average Accumulated Expenditures	×	Interest Rate	=	Avoidable Interest
$750,000		.15 (construction note)		$112,500
70,000[a]		.1104 (weighted average of other debt)[b]		7,728
$820,000				$120,228

[a]The amount by which the weighted-average accumulated expenditures exceeds the specific construction loan.

[b]Weighted-average interest rate computation:

	Principal	Interest
10%, 5-year note	$ 550,000	$ 55,000
12%, 10-year bonds	600,000	72,000
	$1,150,000	$127,000

$$\text{Weighted-average interest rate} = \frac{\text{Total interest}}{\text{Total principal}} = \frac{\$127,000}{\$1,150,000} = 11.04\%$$

The company determines the actual interest cost, which represents the maximum amount of interest that it may capitalize during 2007, as shown in Illustration 9-6.

ILLUSTRATION 9-6
Computation of Actual Interest Cost

Construction note	$750,000 × .15	=	$112,500
5-year note	$550,000 × .10	=	55,000
10-year bonds	$600,000 × .12	=	72,000
Actual interest			$239,500

The interest cost that Shalla capitalizes is the lesser of $120,228 (avoidable interest) and $239,500 (actual interest), or $120,228.

Shalla records the following journal entries during 2007:

January 1		
Land	100,000	
Building (or Construction in Process)	110,000	
Cash		210,000
March 1		
Building	300,000	
Cash		300,000
May 1		
Building	540,000	
Cash		540,000
December 31		
Building	450,000	
Cash		450,000
Building (Capitalized Interest)	120,228	
Interest Expense ($239,500 − $120,228)	119,272	
Cash ($112,500 + $55,000 + $72,000)		239,500

wiley.com/college/kieso

Tutorial on Interest Capitalization

Shalla should write off capitalized interest cost as part of depreciation over the useful life of the assets involved and not over the term of the debt. It should disclose the total interest cost incurred during the period, with the portion charged to expense and the portion capitalized indicated.

At December 31, 2007, Shalla discloses the amount of interest capitalized either as part of the nonoperating section of the income statement or in the notes accompanying the financial statements. We illustrate both forms of disclosure, in Illustrations 9-7 and 9-8.

ILLUSTRATION 9-7
Capitalized Interest Reported in the Income Statement

Income from operations		XXXX
Other expenses and losses:		
Interest expense	$239,500	
Less: Capitalized interest	120,228	119,272
Income before taxes on income		XXXX
Income taxes		XXX
Net income		XXXX

ILLUSTRATION 9-8
Capitalized Interest Disclosed in a Note

Note 1: Accounting Policies. *Capitalized Interest.* During 2007 total interest cost was $239,500, of which $120,228 was capitalized and $119,272 was charged to expense.

Special Issues Related to Interest Capitalization

Two issues related to interest capitalization merit special attention:

1. Expenditures for land.
2. Interest revenue.

Expenditures for Land. When a company purchases land with the intention of developing it for a particular use, interest costs associated with those expenditures qualify for interest capitalization. If it purchases land as a site for a structure (such as a plant site), **interest costs capitalized during the period of construction are part of the cost of the plant, not the land**. Conversely, if the company develops land for lot sales, it includes any capitalized interest cost as part of the acquisition cost of the developed land. However, it should **not** capitalize interest costs involved in purchasing land held **for speculation** because the asset is ready for its intended use.

INTERNATIONAL INSIGHT

Under international accounting standards *(IAS No. 23)*, companies may capitalize interest, but it is not the preferred treatment. Thus, the financial statements of U.S. and IAS companies may not be comparable if capitalized interest costs are significant and the IAS company uses the preferred treatment. However, an analyst can convert the U.S. GAAP numbers to be comparable to the IAS company.

Interest Revenue. Companies frequently borrow money to finance construction of assets. They temporarily invest the excess borrowed funds in interest-bearing securities until they need the funds to pay for construction. During the early stages of construction, interest revenue earned may exceed the interest cost incurred on the borrowed funds.

Should companies offset interest revenue against interest cost when determining the amount of interest to capitalize as part of the construction cost of assets? In general, **companies should not net or offset interest revenue against interest cost**. Temporary or short-term investment decisions are not related to the interest incurred as part of the acquisition cost of assets. Therefore, companies should capitalize the interest incurred on qualifying assets whether or not they temporarily invest excess funds in short-term securities. Some criticize this approach because a company can defer the interest cost but report the interest revenue in the current period.

Observations

The interest capitalization requirement, while now universally adopted, is still debated. From a conceptual viewpoint, many believe that, for the reasons mentioned earlier, companies should either capitalize **no interest cost** or **all interest costs**, actual or imputed.

WHAT'S IN YOUR INTEREST?

WHAT DO THE NUMBERS MEAN?

The requirement to capitalize interest can significantly impact financial statements. For example, when earnings of building manufacturer **Jim Walter's Corporation** dropped from $1.51 to $1.17 per share, the company offset 11 cents per share of the decline by capitalizing the interest on coal mining projects and several plants under construction.

How do statement users determine the impact of interest capitalization on a company's bottom line? They examine the notes to the financial statements. Companies with material interest capitalization must disclose the amounts of capitalized interest relative to total interest costs. For example, **Anadarko Petroleum Corporation** capitalized nearly 30 percent of its total interest costs in a recent year and provided the following footnote related to capitalized interest.

Financial Footnotes

Total interest costs incurred during the year were $82,415,000. Of this amount, the Company capitalized $24,716,000. Capitalized interest is included as part of the cost of oil and gas properties. The capitalization rates are based on the Company's weighted-average cost of borrowings used to finance the expenditures.

VALUATION

Like other assets, **companies should record property, plant, and equipment at the fair market value of what they give up or at the fair value of the asset received, whichever is more clearly evident**. However, the process of asset acquisition sometimes obscures fair market value. For example, if a company buys land and buildings together for one price, how does it determine separate values for the land and buildings? We examine these types of accounting problems in the following sections.

Cash Discounts

OBJECTIVE 5
Understand accounting issues related to acquiring and valuing plant assets.

When a company purchases plant assets subject to cash discounts for prompt payment, how should it report the discount? If it takes the discount, the company should consider the discount as a reduction in the purchase price of the asset. But should the company reduce the asset cost even if it does not take the discount?

Two points of view exist on this question. One approach considers the discount—whether taken or not—as a reduction in the cost of the asset. The rationale for this approach is that the real cost of the asset is the cash or cash equivalent price of the asset. In addition, some argue that the terms of cash discounts are so attractive that failure to take them indicates management error or inefficiency.

Proponents of the other approach argue that failure to take the discount should not always be considered a loss. The terms may be unfavorable, or it might not be prudent for the company to take the discount. At present, companies use both methods, though most prefer the former method.

Deferred-Payment Contracts

Companies frequently purchase plant assets on long-term credit contracts, using notes, mortgages, bonds, or equipment obligations. **To properly reflect cost, companies account for assets purchased on long-term credit contracts at the present value of the consideration exchanged between the contracting parties at the date of the transaction.**

For example, Greathouse Company purchases an asset today in exchange for a $10,000 zero-interest-bearing note payable four years from now. The company would not record the asset at $10,000. Instead, the present value of the $10,000 note establishes the exchange price of the transaction (the purchase price of the asset). Assuming an appropriate interest rate of 9 percent at which to discount this single payment of $10,000 due four years from now, Greathouse records this asset at $7,084.30 ($10,000 × .70843). [See Table 6-2 for the present value of a single sum, $PV = \$10,000\ (PVF_{4,9\%})$.]

When no interest rate is stated, or if the specified rate is unreasonable, the company imputes an appropriate interest rate. The objective is to approximate the interest rate that the buyer and seller would negotiate at arm's length in a similar borrowing transaction. In imputing an interest rate, companies consider such factors as the borrower's credit rating, the amount and maturity date of the note, and prevailing interest rates. **The company uses the cash exchange price of the asset acquired (if determinable) as the basis for recording the asset and measuring the interest element.**

To illustrate, Sutter Company purchases a specially built robot spray painter for its production line. The company issues a $100,000, five-year, zero-interest-bearing note to Wrigley Robotics, Inc. for the new equipment. The prevailing market rate of interest for obligations of this nature is 10 percent. Sutter is to pay off the note in five $20,000 installments, made at the end of each year. Sutter cannot readily determine the fair market value of this specially built robot. Therefore Sutter approximates the robot's value by establishing the market value (present value) of the note. Entries for the date of purchase and dates of payments, plus computation of the present value of the note, are as follows.

Date of Purchase

Equipment	75,816*	
Discount on Notes Payable	24,184	
Notes Payable		100,000

*Present value of note = $20,000 (*PVF-OA*$_{5,10\%}$)
= $20,000 (3.79079); Table 6-4
= $75,816

End of First Year

Interest Expense	7,582	
Notes Payable	20,000	
Cash		20,000
Discount on Notes Payable		7,582

Interest expense in the first year under the effective-interest approach is $7,582 [($100,000 − $24,184) × 10%]. The entry at the end of the second year to record interest and principal payment is as follows.

End of Second Year

Interest Expense	6,340	
Notes Payable	20,000	
Cash		20,000
Discount on Notes Payable		6,340

Interest expense in the second year under the effective-interest approach is $6,340 [($100,000 − $24,184) − ($20,000 − $7,582)] × 10%.

If Sutter did not impute an interest rate for deferred-payment contracts, it would record the asset at an amount greater than its fair value. In addition, Sutter would understate interest expense in the income statement for all periods involved.

Lump-Sum Purchases

A special problem of pricing fixed assets arises when a company purchases a group of plant assets at a single **lump-sum price**. When this common situation occurs, the company allocates the total cost among the various assets on the basis of their relative fair market values. The assumption is that costs will vary in direct proportion to fair value. This is the same principle that companies apply to allocate a lump-sum cost among different inventory items.

To determine fair market value, a company should use valuation techniques that are appropriate in the circumstances. In some cases, a single valuation technique will be appropriate. In other cases, multiple valuation approaches might have to be used.

To illustrate, Norduct Homes, Inc. decides to purchase several assets of a small heating concern, Comfort Heating, for $80,000. Comfort Heating is in the process of liquidation. Its assets sold are:

	Book Value	Fair Market Value
Inventory	$30,000	$ 25,000
Land	20,000	25,000
Building	35,000	50,000
	$85,000	$100,000

Norduct Homes allocates the $80,000 purchase price on the basis of the relative fair market values (assuming specific identification of costs is impracticable) in the following manner.

ILLUSTRATION 9-9
Allocation of Purchase Price—Relative Fair Market Value Basis

Inventory	$\frac{\$25,000}{\$100,000} \times \$80,000 = \$20,000$
Land	$\frac{\$25,000}{\$100,000} \times \$80,000 = \$20,000$
Building	$\frac{\$50,000}{\$100,000} \times \$80,000 = \$40,000$

Issuance of Stock

When companies acquire property by issuing securities, such as common stock, the par or stated value of such stock fails to properly measure the property cost. If trading of the stock is active, **the market value of the stock issued is a fair indication of the cost of the property acquired. The stock is a good measure of the current cash equivalent price.**

For example, Upgrade Living Co. decides to purchase some adjacent land for expansion of its carpeting and cabinet operation. In lieu of paying cash for the land, the company issues to Deedland Company 5,000 shares of common stock (par value $10) that have a fair market value of $12 per share. Upgrade Living Co. records the following entry.

Land (5,000 × $12)	60,000	
Common Stock		50,000
Additional Paid-In Capital		10,000

If the company cannot determine the market value of the common stock exchanged, it establishes the market value of the property. It then uses the value of the property as the basis for recording the asset and issuance of the common stock.[6]

[6]The valuation approaches that should be used are the market, income, or cost approach, or a combination of these approaches. The *market approach* uses observable prices and other relevant information generated by market transactions involving comparable assets. The *income approach* uses valuation techniques to convert future amounts (for example, cash flows or earnings) to a single present value amount (discounted). The *cost approach* is based on the amount that currently would be required to replace the service capacity of an asset (often referred to as current replacement cost). In determining the fair value, the company should assume the highest and best use of the asset ("Fair Value Measurement," Proposed *Statement of Financial Accounting Standard* (Norwalk, Conn.: FASB, October 21, 2005).

Exchanges of Nonmonetary Assets

The proper accounting for exchanges of nonmonetary assets, such as property, plant, and equipment, is controversial.[7] Some argue that companies should account for these types of exchanges based on the fair value of the asset given up or the fair value of the asset received, with a gain or loss recognized. Others believe that they should account for exchanges based on the recorded amount (book value) of the asset given up, with no gain or loss recognized. Still others favor an approach that recognizes losses in all cases, but defers gains in special situations.

Ordinarily companies account for the exchange of **nonmonetary assets** on the basis of **the fair value of the asset given up or the fair value of the asset received, whichever is clearly more evident.**[8] Thus, companies **should recognize immediately** any gains or losses on the exchange. The rationale for immediate recognition is that most transactions have **commercial substance**, and therefore gains and losses should be recognized.

Meaning of Commercial Substance

As indicated above, fair value is the basis for measuring an asset acquired in a nonmonetary exchange if the transaction has commercial substance. An exchange has **commercial substance** if the future cash flows change as a result of the transaction. That is, if the two parties' economic positions change, the transaction has commercial substance.

For example, Andrew Co. exchanges some if its equipment for land held by Roddick Inc. It is likely that the timing and amount of the cash flows arising for the land will differ significantly from the cash flows arising from the equipment. As a result, both Andrew Co. and Roddick Inc. are in different economic positions. Therefore, the exchange has commercial substance, and the companies recognize a gain or loss on the exchange.

What if companies exchange similar assets, such as one truck for another truck?[9] Even in an exchange of similar assets, a change in the economic position of the company can result. For example, let's say the useful life of the truck received is significantly longer than that of the truck given up. The cash flows for the trucks can differ significantly. As a result, the transaction has commercial substance, and the company should use fair value as a basis for measuring the asset received in the exchange.

However, it is possible to exchange similar assets but not have a significant difference in cash flows. That is, the company is in the same economic position as before the exchange. In that case, the company recognizes a loss but generally defers a gain.

As we will see in the examples below, use of fair value generally results in recognizing a gain or loss at the time of the exchange. Consequently companies must

---

[7] Nonmonetary assets are items whose price in terms of the monetary unit may change over time. Monetary assets—cash and short- or long-term accounts and notes receivable—are fixed in terms of units of currency by contract or otherwise.

[8] "Accounting for Nonmonetary Transactions," *Opinions of the Accounting Principles Board No. 29* (New York: AICPA, 1973), par 18, and "Exchanges of Nonmonetary Assets, an Amendment of *APB Opinion No. 29*," *Statement of Financial Accounting Standards No. 153* (Norwalk, Conn: FASB, 2004).

[9] In previous accounting standards, the primary factor in determining whether to recognize gains on exchanges was whether the assets were "similar" in nature. This approach was problematic due to the subjectivity of determining similarity in the assets being exchanged. The new commercial-substance condition addresses this concern and contributes to international accounting convergence. The FASB and the IASB have agreed to resolve differences between the U.S. GAAP and International Financial Reporting Standards (IFRS). With the commercial-substance approach, U.S. GAAP and IFRS are now in agreement.

determine if the transaction has commercial substance. To make this determination, they must carefully evaluate the cash flow characteristics of the assets exchanged.[10]

Illustration 9-10 summarizes asset exchange situations and the related accounting.

ILLUSTRATION 9-10
Accounting for Exchanges

Type of Exchange	Accounting Guidance
Exchange has commercial substance.	Recognize gains and losses immediately.
Exchange lacks commercial substance—no cash received.	Defer gains; recognize losses immediately.
Exchange lacks commercial substance—cash received.	Recognize partial gain; recognize losses immediately.*

*If cash is 25% or more of the fair value of the exchange, recognize entire gain because earnings process is complete.

As Illustration 9-10 indicates, companies immediately recognize losses they incur on all exchanges. The accounting for gains depends on whether the exchange has commercial substance. If the exchange has commercial substance, the company recognizes the gain immediately. However, the profession modifies the rule for immediate recognition of a gain when an exchange lacks commercial substance: If the company receives no cash in such an exchange, it defers recognition of a gain. If the company receives cash in such an exchange, it recognizes part of the gain immediately.

To illustrate the accounting for these different types of transactions, we examine various loss and gain exchange situations.

Exchanges—Loss Situation

When a company exchanges nonmonetary assets and a loss results, the company recognizes the loss immediately. The rationale: Companies should not value assets at more than their cash equivalent price; if the loss were deferred, assets would be overstated. Therefore, companies recognize a loss immediately whether the exchange has commercial substance or not.

For example, Information Processing, Inc. trades its used machine for a new model at Jerrod Business Solutions Inc. The exchange has commercial substance. The used machine has a book value of $8,000 (original cost $12,000 less $4,000 accumulated depreciation) and a fair value of $6,000. The new model lists for $16,000. Jerrod gives Information Processing a trade-in allowance of $9,000 for the used machine. Information Processing computes the cost of the new asset as follows.

ILLUSTRATION 9-11
Computation of Cost of New Machine

List price of new machine	$16,000
Less: Trade-in allowance for used machine	9,000
Cash payment due	7,000
Fair value of used machine	6,000
Cost of new machine	$13,000

[10]The determination of the commercial substance of a transaction requires significant judgment. In determining whether future cash flows change, it is necessary to do one of two things: (1) Determine whether the risk, timing, and amount of cash flows arising for the asset received differ from the cash flows associated with the outbound asset. Or, (2) evaluate whether cash flows are affected with the exchange versus without the exchange. Also note that if companies cannot determine fair values of the assets exchanged, then they should use recorded book values in accounting for the exchange.

Information Processing records this transaction as follows:

Equipment	13,000	
Accumulated Depreciation—Equipment	4,000	
Loss on Disposal of Equipment	2,000	
Equipment		12,000
Cash		7,000

We verify the loss on the disposal of the used machine as follows:

ILLUSTRATION 9-12
Computation of Loss on Disposal of Used Machine

Fair value of used machine	$6,000
Book value of used machine	8,000
Loss on disposal of used machine	$2,000

Why did Information Processing not use the trade-in allowance or the book value of the old asset as a basis for the new equipment? The company did not use the trade-in allowance because it included a price concession (similar to a price discount). Few individuals pay list price for a new car. Dealers such as Jerrod often inflate trade-in allowances on the used car so that actual selling prices fall below list prices. To record the car at list price would state it at an amount in excess of its cash equivalent price because of the new car's inflated list price. Similarly, use of book value in this situation would overstate the value of the new machine by $2,000.[11]

Exchanges—Gain Situation

Has Commercial Substance. Now let's consider the situation in which a nonmonetary exchange has commercial substance and a gain is realized. In such a case, a company usually records the cost of a nonmonetary asset acquired in exchange for another nonmonetary asset at the **fair value of the asset given up**, and immediately recognizes a gain. The company should use the **fair value of the asset received** only if it is more clearly evident than the fair value of the asset given up.

To illustrate, Interstate Transportation Company exchanged a number of used trucks plus cash for a semi-truck. The used trucks have a combined book value of $42,000 (cost $64,000 less $22,000 accumulated depreciation). Interstate's purchasing agent, experienced in the second-hand market, indicates that the used trucks have a fair market value of $49,000. In addition to the trucks, Interstate must pay $17,000 cash for the semi-truck. Interstate computes the cost of the semi-truck as follows.

ILLUSTRATION 9-13
Computation of Semi-Truck Cost

Fair value of trucks exchanged	$49,000
Cash paid	17,000
Cost of semi-truck	$66,000

Interstate records the exchange transaction as follows:

Semi-truck	66,000	
Accumulated Depreciation—Trucks	22,000	
Trucks		64,000
Gain on Disposal of Used Trucks		7,000
Cash		17,000

The gain is the difference between the fair value of the used trucks and their book value. We verify the computation as follows.

[11] Recognize that for Jerrod (the dealer), the asset given up in the exchange is considered inventory. As a result, Jerrod records a sale and related cost of goods sold. The used machine received by Jerrod is recorded at fair value.

ILLUSTRATION 9-14
Computation of Gain on Disposal of Used Trucks

Fair value of used trucks		$49,000
Cost of used trucks	$64,000	
Less: Accumulated depreciation	22,000	
Book value of used trucks		42,000
Gain on disposal of used trucks		$ 7,000

In this case, Interstate is in a different economic position, and therefore the transaction has commercial substance. Thus, it **recognizes a gain.**

Lacks Commercial Substance—No Cash Received. We now assume that the Interstate Transportation Company exchange lacks commercial substance. That is, the economic position of Interstate did not change significantly as a result of this exchange. In this case, Interstate defers the gain of $7,000 and reduces the basis of the semi-truck. Illustration 9-15 shows two different but acceptable computations to illustrate this reduction.

ILLUSTRATION 9-15
Basis of Semi-Truck—Fair Value vs. Book Value

Fair value of semi-truck	$66,000		Book value of used trucks	$42,000
Less: Gain deferred	7,000	OR	Plus: Cash paid	17,000
Basis of semi-truck	$59,000		Basis of semi-truck	$59,000

Interstate records this transaction as follows:

Semi-truck	59,000	
Accumulated Depreciation—Trucks	22,000	
Trucks		64,000
Cash		17,000

If the exchange lacks commercial substance, the company recognizes the gain (reflected in the basis of the semi-truck) when it later sells the semi-truck, not at the time of the exchange.

Lacks Commercial Substance—Some Cash Received. When a company receives cash (sometimes referred to as "boot") in an exchange that lacks commercial substance, it may immediately recognize a portion of the gain.[12] Illustration 9-16 shows the general formula for gain recognition when an exchange includes some cash.

ILLUSTRATION 9-16
Formula for Gain Recognition, Some Cash Received

$$\frac{\text{Cash Received (Boot)}}{\text{Cash Received (Boot)} + \text{Fair Value of Other Assets Received}} \times \text{Total Gain} = \text{Recognized Gain}$$

To illustrate, assume that Queenan Corporation traded in used machinery with a book value of $60,000 (cost $110,000 less accumulated depreciation $50,000) and a fair value of $100,000. It receives in exchange a machine with a fair value of $90,000 plus cash of $10,000. Illustration 9-17 shows calculation of the total gain on the exchange.

ILLUSTRATION 9-17
Computation of Total Gain

Fair value of machine exchanged	$100,000
Book value of machine exchanged	60,000
Total gain	$ 40,000

[12]When the monetary consideration is significant, i.e., **25 percent or more** of the fair value of the exchange, both parties consider the transaction a **monetary exchange**. Such "monetary" exchanges rely on the fair values to measure the gains or losses that are recognized in their entirety. *EITF Issue No. 86-29*, "Nonmonetary Transactions: Magnitude of Boot and the Exception to the Use of Fair Value," *Emerging Issues Task Force Abstracts* (October 1, 1987).

Generally, when a transaction lacks commercial substance, a company defers any gain. But because Queenan received $10,000 in cash, it recognizes a partial gain. The portion of the gain a company recognizes is the ratio of monetary assets (cash in this case) to the total consideration received. Queenan computes the partial gain as follows:

ILLUSTRATION 9-18
Computation of Gain Based on Ratio of Cash Received

$$\frac{\$10,000}{\$10,000 + \$90,000} \times \$40,000 = \$4,000$$

Because Queenan recognizes only a gain of $4,000 on this transaction, it defers the remaining $36,000 ($40,000 − $4,000) and reduces the basis (recorded cost) of the new machine. Illustration 9-19 shows the computation of the basis.

ILLUSTRATION 9-19
Computation of Gain Based on Ratio of Cost Received

Fair value of new machine	$90,000		Book value of old machine	$60,000
Less: Gain deferred	36,000	OR	Portion of book value presumed sold	6,000*
Basis of new machine	$54,000		Basis of new machine	$54,000

$$^{*}\ \frac{\$10,000}{\$100,000} \times \$60,000 = \$6,000$$

Queenan records the transaction with the following entry.

Cash	10,000	
Machine	54,000	
Accumulated Depreciation—Machine	50,000	
Machine		110,000
Gain on Disposal of Machine		4,000

The rationale for the treatment of a partial gain is as follows: Before a nonmonetary exchange that includes some cash, a company has an unrecognized gain, which is the difference between the book value and the fair value of the old asset. When the exchange occurs, a portion of the fair value is converted to a more liquid asset. The ratio of this liquid asset to the total consideration received is the portion of the total gain that the company realizes. Thus, the company recognizes and records that amount.

Illustration 9-20 presents in summary form the accounting requirements for recognizing gains and losses on exchanges of nonmonetary assets.[13]

ILLUSTRATION 9-20
Summary of Gain and Loss Recognition on Exchanges of Nonmonetary Assets

1. Compute the total gain or loss on the transaction. This amount is equal to the difference between the fair value of the asset given up and the book value of the asset given up.
2. If a loss is computed in step 1, always recognize the entire loss.
3. If a gain is computed in step 1,
   (a) and the exchange has commercial substance, recognize the entire gain.
   (b) and the exchange lacks commercial substance,
      (1) and no cash is involved, no gain is recognized.
      (2) and some cash is given, no gain is recognized.
      (3) and some cash is received, the following portion of the gain is recognized:

$$\frac{\text{Cash Received (Boot)}}{\text{Cash Received (Boot)} + \text{Fair Value of Other Assets Received}} \times \text{Total Gain}^{*}$$

*If the amount of cash exchanged is 25% or more, recognize entire gain.

[13]Adapted from an article by Robert Capettini and Thomas E. King, "Exchanges of Nonmonetary Assets: Some Changes," *The Accounting Review* (January 1976).

Companies disclose in their financial statements nonmonetary exchanges during a period. Such disclosure indicates the nature of the transaction(s), the method of accounting for the assets exchanged, and gains or losses recognized on the exchanges.[14]

ABOUT THOSE SWAPS

WHAT DO THE NUMBERS MEAN?

In a press release, Roy Olofson, former vice president of finance for **Global Crossing**, accused company executives of improperly describing the company's revenue to the public. He said the company had improperly recorded long-term sales immediately rather than over the term of the contract, had improperly booked as cash transactions swaps of capacity with other carriers, and had fired him when he blew the whistle.

The accounting for the swaps involves exchanges of similar network capacity. Companies have said they engage in such deals because swapping is quicker and less costly than building segments of their own networks, or because such pacts provide redundancies to make their own networks more reliable. In one expert's view, an exchange of similar network capacity is the equivalent of trading a blue truck for a red truck—it shouldn't boost a company's revenue.

But Global Crossing and **Qwest**, among others, counted as revenue the money received from the other company in the swap. (In general, in transactions involving leased capacity, the companies booked the revenue over the life of the contract.) Some of these companies then treated their own purchases as capital expenditures, which were not run through the income statement. Instead, the spending led to the addition of assets on the balance sheet (and an inflated bottom line.)

The SEC questioned some of these capacity exchanges, because it appeared they were a device to pad revenue. This reaction was not surprising, since revenue growth was a key factor in the valuation of companies such as Global Crossing and Qwest during the craze for tech stocks in the late 1990s and 2000.

Source: Adapted from Henny Sender, "Telecoms Draw Focus for Moves in Accounting," *Wall Street Journal* (March 26, 2002), p. C7.

Accounting for Contributions

Companies sometimes receive or make contributions (donations or gifts). Such contributions, **nonreciprocal transfers**, transfer assets in one direction. A contribution is often some type of asset (such as cash, securities, land, buildings, or use of facilities), but it also could be the forgiveness of a debt.

When companies acquire assets as donations, a strict cost concept dictates that the valuation of the asset should be zero. However, a departure from the cost principle seems justified; the only costs incurred (legal fees and other relatively minor expenditures) are not a reasonable basis of accounting for the assets acquired. To record nothing is to ignore the economic realities of an increase in wealth and assets. Therefore, companies use the **fair value of the asset** to establish its value on the books.

What then is the proper accounting for the credit in this transaction? Some believe the credit should be made to Donated Capital (an additional paid-in capital account). This approach views the increase in assets from a donation as contributed capital, rather than as earned revenue.

Others argue that companies should report donations as revenues from contributions. Their reasoning is that only the owners of a business contribute capital. At issue in this approach is whether the company should report revenue immediately or over the period that the asset is employed. For example, to attract new industry a city may

[14] "Accounting for Nonmonetary Transactions," op. cit., par. 28.

offer land, but the receiving enterprise may incur additional costs in the future (e.g., transportation or higher state income taxes) because the location is not the most desirable. As a consequence, some argue that company should defer the revenue and recognize it as the costs are incurred.

The FASB's position is that **in general, companies should recognize contributions received as revenues in the period received.**[15] Companies measure contributions at the fair value of the assets received.[16] To illustrate, Max Wayer Meat Packing, Inc. has recently accepted a donation of land with a fair value of $150,000 from the Memphis Industrial Development Corp. In return Max Wayer Meat Packing promises to build a packing plant in Memphis. Max Wayer's entry is:

Land	150,000	
Contribution Revenue		150,000

When a company contributes a nonmonetary asset, it should record the amount of the donation as an expense at the fair value of the donated asset. If a difference exists between the fair value of the asset and its book value, the company should recognize a gain or loss. To illustrate, Kline Industries donates land to the city of Los Angeles for a city park. The land cost $80,000 and has a fair market value of $110,000. Kline Industries records this donation as follows:

Contribution Expense	110,000	
Land		80,000
Gain on Disposal of Land		30,000

In some cases, companies promise to give (pledge) some type of asset in the future. Should companies record this promise immediately or when they give the assets? If the promise is **unconditional** (depends only on the passage of time or on demand by the recipient for performance), the company should report the contribution expense and related payable immediately. If the promise is **conditional**, the company recognizes expense in the period benefited by the contribution, generally when it transfers the asset.

Other Asset Valuation Methods

The exception to the historical cost principle for assets acquired through donation is based on fair value. Another exception is the **prudent cost** concept. This concept states that if for some reason a company ignorantly paid too much for an asset originally, it is theoretically preferable to charge a loss immediately.

For example, assume that a company constructs an asset at a cost much greater than its present economic usefulness. It would be appropriate to charge these excess costs as a loss to the current period, rather than capitalize them as part of the cost of the asset. In practice, the need to use the prudent cost approach seldom develops. Companies typically either use good reasoning in paying a given price or fail to recognize that they have overpaid.

What happens, on the other hand, if a company makes a bargain purchase or internally constructs a piece of equipment at a cost savings? Such savings should not result in immediate recognition of a gain under any circumstances.

---

[15]"Accounting for Contributions Received and Contributions Made," *Statement of Financial Accounting Standards No. 116* (Norwalk, Conn.: FASB, 1993). The scope of this standard excludes transfers of assets from governmental units to business enterprises. However, we believe that the basic requirements should hold also for these types of contributions. Therefore, companies should record all assets at fair value and all credits as revenue.

[16]"Accounting for Nonmonetary Transactions," op. cit., par. 18. Also, *FASB No. 116* indicates that companies should record expenses on contributions made at the fair value of the assets given up.

COSTS SUBSEQUENT TO ACQUISITION

OBJECTIVE 6
Describe the accounting treatment for costs subsequent to acquisition.

After installing plant assets and readying them for use, a company incurs additional costs that range from ordinary repairs to significant additions. The major problem is allocating these costs to the proper time periods. **In general, costs incurred to achieve greater future benefits should be capitalized, whereas expenditures that simply maintain a given level of services should be expensed.** In order to capitalize costs, one of three conditions must be present:

1 The useful life of the asset must be increased.
2 The quantity of units produced from the asset must be increased.
3 The quality of the units produced must be enhanced.

For example, a company like **Boeing** should expense expenditures that do not increase an asset's future benefits. That is, it expenses immediately ordinary repairs that maintain the existing condition of the asset or restore it to normal operating efficiency.

UNDERLYING CONCEPTS

Expensing long-lived ashtrays and waste baskets is an application of the materiality constraint.

Companies expense most expenditures below an established arbitrary minimum amount, say, $100 or $500. Although conceptually this treatment may be incorrect, expediency demands it. Otherwise, companies would set up depreciation schedules for such items as wastepaper baskets and ashtrays.

DISCONNECTED

WHAT DO THE NUMBERS MEAN?

It all started with a check of the books by an internal auditor for WorldCom Inc. The telecom giant's newly installed chief executive had asked for a financial review, and the auditor was spot-checking records of capital expenditures. She found the company was using an unorthodox technique to account for one of its biggest expenses: charges paid to local telephone networks to complete long-distance calls.

Instead of recording these charges as operating expenses, WorldCom recorded a significant portion as capital expenditures. The maneuver was worth hundreds of millions of dollars to WorldCom's bottom line. It effectively turned a loss for all of 2001 and the first quarter of 2002 into a profit. The graph below compares WorldCom's accounting to that under GAAP. Soon after this discovery, WorldCom filed for bankruptcy.

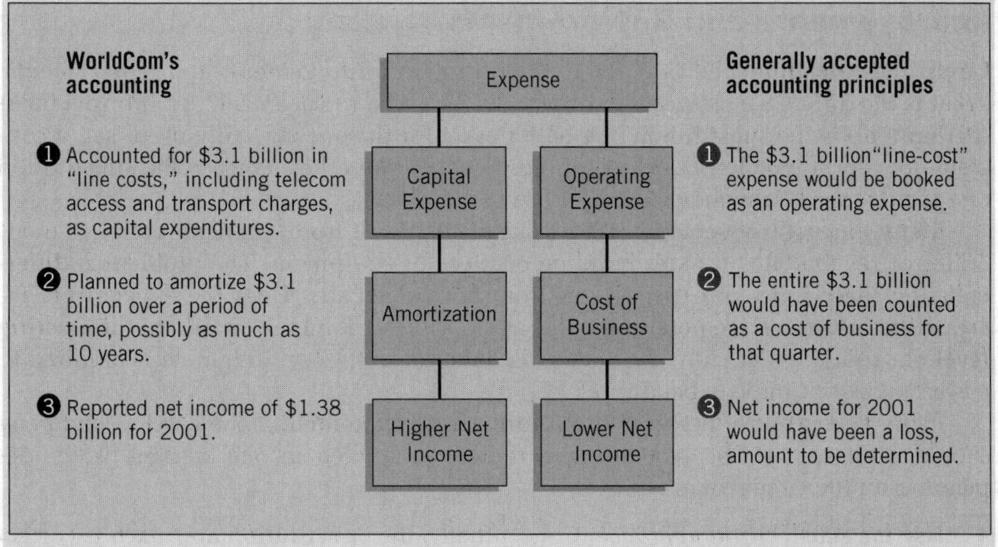

Source: Adapted from Jared Sandberg, Deborah Solomon, and Rebecca Blumenstein, "Inside WorldCom's Unearthing of a Vast Accounting Scandal," *Wall Street Journal* (June 27, 2002,), p. A1.

The distinction between a **capital (asset) expenditure** and a **revenue (expense) expenditure** is not always clear-cut. Yet, in most cases, **consistent application of a capital/expense policy** is more important than attempting to provide general theoretical guidelines for each transaction. Generally, companies incur four major types of expenditures relative to existing assets.

MAJOR TYPES OF EXPENDITURES

ADDITIONS. Increase or extension of existing assets.

IMPROVEMENTS AND REPLACEMENTS. Substitution of an improved asset for an existing one.

REARRANGEMENT AND REINSTALLATION. Movement of assets from one location to another.

REPAIRS. Expenditures that maintain assets in condition for operation.

Additions

Additions should present no major accounting problems. By definition, **companies capitalize any addition to plant assets because a new asset is created**. For example, the addition of a wing to a hospital, or of an air conditioning system to an office, increases the service potential of that facility. Companies should capitalize such expenditures and match them against the revenues that will result in future periods.

One problem that arises in this area is the accounting for any changes related to the existing structure as a result of the addition. Is the cost incurred to tear down an old wall to make room for the addition, a cost of the addition or an expense or loss of the period? The answer is that it depends on the original intent. If the company had anticipated building an addition later, then this cost of removal is a proper cost of the addition. But if the company had not anticipated this development, it should properly report the removal as a loss in the current period on the basis of inefficient planning. Normally, the company retains the carrying amount of the old wall in the accounts, although theoretically the company should remove it.

Improvements and Replacements

Companies substitute one asset for another through **improvements** and **replacements**. What is the difference between an improvement and a replacement? An **improvement** (**betterment**) is the substitution of a **better asset** for the one currently used (say, a concrete floor for a wooden floor). A **replacement**, on the other hand, is the substitution of a **similar asset** (a wooden floor for a wooden floor).

Many times improvements and replacements result from a general policy to modernize or rehabilitate an older building or piece of equipment. The problem is differentiating these types of expenditures from normal repairs. Does the expenditure increase the **future service potential** of the asset? Or does it merely **maintain the existing level** of service? Frequently, the answer is not clear-cut. Good judgment is required to correctly classify these expenditures.

If the expenditure increases the future service potential of the asset, a company should capitalize it. The accounting is therefore handled in one of three ways, depending on the circumstances:

1 *Use the substitution approach.* Conceptually, the **substitution approach** is correct if the carrying amount of the old asset is available. It is then a simple matter to remove the cost of the old asset and replace it with the cost of the new asset.

To illustrate, Instinct Enterprises decides to replace the pipes in its plumbing system. A plumber suggests that the company use plastic tubing in place of the cast iron pipes and copper tubing. The old pipe and tubing have a book value of $15,000 (cost of $150,000 less accumulated depreciation of $135,000), and a scrap value of $1,000. The plastic tubing system costs $125,000. If Instinct pays $124,000 for the new tubing after exchanging the old tubing, it makes the following entry:

Plumbing System	125,000	
Accumulated Depreciation	135,000	
Loss on Disposal of Plant Assets	14,000	
Plumbing System		150,000
Cash ($125,000 − $1,000)		124,000

The problem is determining the book value of the old asset. Generally, the components of a given asset depreciate at different rates. However, generally no separate accounting is made. For example, the tires, motor, and body of a truck depreciate at different rates, but most companies use one rate for the entire truck. Companies can set separate depreciation rates, but it is often impractical. If a company cannot determine the carrying amount of the old asset, it adopts one of two other approaches.

2 *Capitalize the new cost.* Another approach capitalizes the improvement and keeps the carrying amount of the old asset on the books. The justification for this approach is that the item is sufficiently depreciated to reduce its carrying amount almost to zero. Although this assumption may not always be true, the differences are often insignificant. Companies usually handle improvements in this manner.

3 *Charge to accumulated depreciation.* In cases when a company does not improve the quantity or quality of the asset itself, but instead extends its useful life, the company debits the expenditure to Accumulated Depreciation rather than to an asset account. The theory behind this approach is that the replacement extends the useful life of the asset and thereby recaptures some or all of the past depreciation. The net carrying amount of the asset is the same whether debiting the asset or accumulated depreciation.

Rearrangement and Reinstallation

Companies incur **rearrangement and reinstallation costs** to benefit future periods. An example is the rearrangement and reinstallation of machines to facilitate future production.

If a company like **Eastman Kodak** can determine or estimate the original installation cost and the accumulated depreciation to date, it handles the rearrangement and reinstallation cost as a replacement. If not, which is generally the case, Eastman Kodak should capitalize the new costs (if material in amount) as an asset to be amortized over future periods expected to benefit. If these costs are immaterial, if they cannot be separated from other operating expenses, or if their future benefit is questionable, the company should immediately expense them.

Repairs

A company makes **ordinary repairs** to maintain plant assets in operating condition. It charges ordinary repairs to an expense account in the period incurred, on the basis that **it is the primary period benefited**. Maintenance charges that occur regularly include replacing minor parts, lubricating and adjusting equipment, repainting, and cleaning. A company treats these as ordinary operating expenses.

It is often difficult to distinguish a repair from an improvement or replacement. The major consideration is whether the expenditure benefits more than one year or one operating cycle, whichever is longer. If a **major repair** (such as an overhaul) occurs, several periods will benefit. A company should handle the cost as an addition, improvement, or replacement.[17]

If companies prepare income statements for short periods of time, say, monthly or quarterly, the same principles apply. Ordinary repairs and other regular maintenance charges for an annual period may benefit several quarters, and companies may need to allocate the cost among those periods. A company will often find it advantageous to concentrate its repair program at a certain time of the year, perhaps during the period of least activity or when the plant is shut down for vacation. Short-term comparative statements might be misleading if the company shows such expenditures as expenses of the quarter in which they were incurred. To give comparability to monthly or quarterly income statements, a company might use an account such as Allowance for Repairs so that it can better assign repair costs to the periods benefited.

To illustrate, Cricket Tractor Company estimated that its total repair expense for the year would be $720,000. It decided to charge each quarter for a portion of the repair cost even though the total cost for the year would occur in only two quarters.

End of First Quarter (zero repair costs incurred)		
Repair Expense	180,000	
Allowance for Repairs (¼ × $720,000)		180,000
End of Second Quarter ($344,000 repair costs incurred)		
Allowance for Repairs	344,000	
Cash, Wages Payable, Inventory, etc.		344,000
Repair Expense	180,000	
Allowance for Repairs (¼ × $720,000)		180,000
End of Third Quarter (zero repair costs incurred)		
Repair Expense	180,000	
Allowance for Repairs (¼ × $720,000)		180,000
End of Fourth Quarter ($380,800 repair costs incurred)		
Allowance for Repairs	380,800	
Cash, Wages Payable, Inventory, etc.		380,800
Repair Expense	184,800	
Allowance for Repairs ($344,000 + $380,800 − $180,000 − $180,000 − $180,000)		184,800

Companies should not carry over a balance in the Allowance for Repairs account to the following year. The fourth quarter would normally absorb the variation from estimates. If a company prepares balance sheets during the year, it will add or subtract the Allowance account from the property, plant, and equipment section to determine a proper valuation.[18]

Summary of Costs Subsequent to Acquisition

Illustration 9-21 summarizes the accounting treatment for various costs incurred subsequent to the acquisition of capitalized assets.

[17] AcSEC has proposed (see footnote 2) that companies expense as incurred costs involved for planned major expenditures unless they represent an *additional* component or the *replacement* of an existing component. The "expense as incurred" approach is justified on the basis that these costs are relatively consistent from period to period, that they are not separately identifiable assets or property units in and of themselves, and that they serve only to restore assets to their original operating condition.

[18] Some might argue that the Allowance for Repairs account should be reported as a liability, because it has a credit balance. However, reporting a liability is inappropriate: To whom do you owe the amount? Placement in the stockholders' equity section is also illogical because no addition to the stockholders' investment has taken place.

ILLUSTRATION 9-21
Summary of Costs Subsequent to Acquisition of Property, Plant, and Equipment

Type of Expenditure	Normal Accounting Treatment
Additions	Capitalize cost of addition to asset account.
Improvements and replacements	(a) **Carrying value known:** Remove cost of and accumulated depreciation on old asset, recognizing any gain or loss. Capitalize cost of improvement/replacement. (b) **Carrying value unknown:** 1. If the asset's useful life is extended, debit accumulated depreciation for cost of improvement/replacement. 2. If the quantity or quality of the asset's productivity is increased, capitalize cost of improvement/replacement to asset account.
Rearrangement and reinstallation	(a) If original installation cost is **known**, account for cost of rearrangement/reinstallation as a replacement (carrying value known). (b) If original installation cost is **unknown** and rearrangement/reinstallation cost is **material** in amount and benefits future periods, capitalize as an asset. (c) If original installation cost is **unknown** and rearrangement/reinstallation cost is **not material or future benefit is questionable**, expense the cost when incurred.
Repairs	(a) **Ordinary:** Expense cost of repairs when incurred. (b) **Major:** As appropriate, treat as an addition, improvement, or replacement.

DISPOSITIONS OF PLANT ASSETS

OBJECTIVE 7
Describe the accounting treatment for the disposal of property, plant, and equipment.

A company, like **Intel**, may retire plant assets voluntarily or dispose of them by sale, exchange, involuntary conversion, or abandonment. Regardless of the type of disposal, depreciation must be taken up to the date of disposition. Then, Intel should remove all accounts related to the retired asset. Generally, the book value of the specific plant asset does not equal its disposal value. As a result, a gain or loss develops. The reason: Depreciation is an estimate of cost allocation and not a process of valuation. **The gain or loss is really a correction of net income** for the years during which Intel used the fixed asset.

Intel should show gains or losses on the disposal of plant assets in the income statement along with other items from customary business activities. However, if it sold, abandoned, spun off, or otherwise disposed of the "operations of a component of a business," then it should report the results separately in the discontinued operations section of the income statement. That is, Intel should report any gain or loss from disposal of a business component with the related results of discontinued operations.

Sale of Plant Assets

Companies record depreciation for the period of time between the date of the last depreciation entry and the date of sale. To illustrate, assume that Barret Company recorded depreciation on a machine costing $18,000 for 9 years at the rate of $1,200 per year. If it sells the machine in the middle of the tenth year for $7,000, Barret records depreciation to the date of sale as:

Depreciation Expense	600	
Accumulated Depreciation—Machinery		600

The entry for the sale of the asset then is:

Cash	7,000	
Accumulated Depreciation—Machinery [($1,200 × 9) + $600]	11,400	
Machinery		18,000
Gain on Disposal of Machinery		400

The book value of the machinery at the time of the sale is $6,600 ($18,000 – $11,400). Because the machinery sold for $7,000, the amount of the gain on the sale is $400.

Involuntary Conversion

Sometimes an asset's service is terminated through some type of **involuntary conversion** such as fire, flood, theft, or condemnation. Companies report the difference between the amount recovered (e.g., from a condemnation award or insurance recovery), if any, and the asset's book value as a gain or loss. They treat these gains or losses like any other type of disposition. In some cases, these gains or losses may be reported as extraordinary items in the income statement, **if the conditions of the disposition are unusual and infrequent in nature.**

To illustrate, Camel Transport Corp. had to sell a plant located on company property that stood directly in the path of an interstate highway. For a number of years the state had sought to purchase the land on which the plant stood, but the company resisted. The state ultimately exercised its right of eminent domain, which the courts upheld. In settlement, Camel received $500,000, which substantially exceeded the $200,000 book value of the plant and land (cost of $400,000 less accumulated depreciation of $200,000). Camel made the following entry.

Cash	500,000	
Accumulated Depreciation—Plant Assets	200,000	
Plant Assets		400,000
Gain on Disposal of Plant Assets		300,000

If the conditions surrounding the condemnation are judged to be unusual and infrequent, Camel's gain of $300,000 is reported as an extraordinary item.

Some object to the recognition of a gain or loss in certain *involuntary* conversions. For example, the federal government often condemns forests for national parks. The paper companies that owned these forests must report a gain or loss on the condemnation. However, companies such as **Georgia-Pacific** contend that no gain or loss should be reported because they must replace the condemned forest land immediately and so are in the same economic position as they were before. The issue is whether condemnation and subsequent purchase should be viewed as one or two transactions. *FASB Interpretation No. 30* rules against the companies by requiring "that gain or loss be recognized when a nonmonetary asset is involuntarily converted to monetary assets even though an enterprise reinvests or is obligated to reinvest the monetary assets in replacement nonmonetary assets."[19]

Miscellaneous Problems

If a company scraps or abandons an asset without any cash recovery, it recognizes a loss equal to the asset's book value. If scrap value exists, the gain or loss that occurs is the difference between the asset's scrap value and its book value. If an asset still can be used even though it is fully depreciated, it may be kept on the books at historical cost less depreciation.

Companies must disclose in notes to the financial statements the amount of fully depreciated assets in service. For example, **Petroleum Equipment Tools Inc.** in its annual report disclosed, "The amount of fully depreciated assets included in property, plant, and equipment at December 31 amounted to approximately $98,900,000."

[19] "Accounting for Involuntary Conversions of Nonmonetary Assets to Monetary Assets," *FASB Interpretation No. 30* (Stamford, Conn.: FASB, 1979), summary paragraph.

QUESTIONS

1. What are the major characteristics of plant assets?
2. Esplanade Inc. owns land that it purchased on January 1, 2000, for $420,000. At December 31, 2007, its current value is $770,000 as determined by appraisal. At what amount should Esplanade report this asset on its December 31, 2007, balance sheet? Explain.
3. Name the items, in addition to the amount paid to the former owner or contractor, that may properly be included as part of the acquisition cost of the following plant assets.
   (a) Land.
   (b) Machinery and equipment.
   (c) Buildings.
4. Indicate where the following items would be shown on a balance sheet.
   (a) A lien that was attached to the land when purchased.
   (b) Landscaping costs.
   (c) Attorney's fees and recording fees related to purchasing land.
   (d) Variable overhead related to construction of machinery.
   (e) A parking lot servicing employees in the building.
   (f) Cost of temporary building for workers during construction of building.
   (g) Interest expense on bonds payable incurred during construction of a building.
   (h) Assessments for sidewalks that are maintained by the city.
   (i) The cost of demolishing an old building that was on the land when purchased.
5. Two positions have normally been taken with respect to the recording of fixed manufacturing overhead as an element of the cost of plant assets constructed by a company for its own use:
   (a) It should be excluded completely.
   (b) It should be included at the same rate as is charged to normal operations.

   What are the circumstances or rationale that support or deny the application of these methods?
6. The Buildings account of Diego Rivera Inc. includes the following items that were used in determining the basis for depreciating the cost of a building.
   (a) Organization and promotion expenses.
   (b) Architect's fees.
   (c) Interest and taxes during construction.
   (d) Interest revenue on investments held to fund construction of a building.

   Do you agree with these charges? If not, how would you deal with each of the items above in the corporation's books and in its annual financial statements?
7. Jones Company has purchased two tracts of land. One tract will be the site of its new manufacturing plant, while the other is being purchased with the hope that it will be sold in the next year at a profit. How should these two tracts of land be reported in the balance sheet?
8. One financial accounting issue encountered when a company constructs its own plant is whether the interest cost on funds borrowed to finance construction should be capitalized and then amortized over the life of the assets constructed. What is the justification for capitalizing such interest?
9. Provide examples of assets that do not qualify for interest capitalization.
10. What interest rates should be used in determining the amount of interest to be capitalized? How should the amount of interest to be capitalized be determined?
11. How should the amount of interest capitalized be disclosed in the notes to the financial statements? How should interest revenue from temporarily invested excess funds borrowed to finance the construction of assets be accounted for?
12. Discuss the basic accounting problem that arises in handling each of the following situations.
    (a) Assets purchased by issuance of capital stock.
    (b) Acquisition of plant assets by gift or donation.
    (c) Purchase of a plant asset subject to a cash discount.
    (d) Assets purchased on a long-term credit basis.
    (e) A group of assets acquired for a lump sum.
    (f) An asset traded in or exchanged for another asset.
13. Yukio Mishima Industries acquired equipment this year to be used in its operations. The equipment was delivered by the suppliers, installed by Mishima, and placed into operation. Some of it was purchased for cash with discounts available for prompt payment. Some of it was purchased under long-term payment plans for which the interest charges approximated prevailing rates. What costs should Mishima capitalize for the new equipment purchased this year? Explain.
14. Adam Mickiewicz Co. purchased for $2,200,000 property that included both land and a building to be used in operations. The seller's book value was $300,000 for the land and $900,000 for the building. By appraisal, the fair market value was estimated to be $500,000 for the land and $2,000,000 for the building. At what amount should Mickiewicz report the land and the building at the end of the year?
15. Richardson Co. acquires machinery by paying $10,000 cash and signing a $5,000, 2-year, zero-interest-bearing note payable. The note has a present value of $4,058, and Richardson purchased a similar machine last month for $13,500. At what cost should the new equipment be

recorded?

16. Sean May is evaluating two recent transactions involving exchanges of equipment. In one case, the exchange has commercial substance. In the second situation, the exchange lacks commercial substance. Explain to Sean the differences in accounting for these two situations.

17. Saadi Company purchased a heavy-duty truck on July 1, 2004, for $30,000. It was estimated that it would have a useful life of 10 years and then would have a trade-in value of $6,000. It was traded on August 1, 2008, for a similar truck costing $39,000; $13,000 was allowed as trade-in value (also fair value) on the old truck and $26,000 was paid in cash. A comparison of expected cash flows for the trucks indicates the exchange lacks commercial substance. What is the entry to record the trade-in? The company uses the straight-line method.

18. Once equipment has been installed and placed in operation, subsequent expenditures relating to this equipment are frequently thought of as repairs or general maintenance and, hence, chargeable to operations in the period in which the expenditure is made. Actually, determination of whether such an expenditure should be charged to operations or capitalized involves a much more careful analysis of the character of the expenditure. What are the factors that should be considered in making such a decision? Discuss fully.

19. What accounting treatment is normally given to the following items in accounting for plant assets?

(a) Additions.

(b) Major repairs.

(c) Improvements and replacements.

20. New machinery, which replaced a number of employees, was installed and put in operation in the last month of the fiscal year. The employees had been dismissed after payment of an extra month's wages, and this amount was added to the cost of the machinery. Discuss the propriety of the charge. If it was improper, describe the proper treatment.

21. To what extent do you consider the following items to be proper costs of the fixed asset? Give reasons for your opinions.

(a) Overhead of a business that builds its own equipment.

(b) Cash discounts on purchases of equipment.

(c) Interest paid during construction of a building.

(d) Cost of a safety device installed on a machine.

(e) Freight on equipment returned before installation, for replacement by other equipment of greater capacity.

(f) Cost of moving machinery to a new location.

(g) Cost of plywood partitions erected as part of the remodeling of the office.

(h) Replastering of a section of the building.

(i) Cost of a new motor for one of the trucks.

22. Recently, Michelangelo Manufacturing Co. presented the account "Allowance for Repairs" in the long-term liabilities section. Evaluate this procedure.

23. Dimitri Enterprises has a number of fully depreciated assets that are still being used in the main operations of the business. Because the assets are fully depreciated, the president of the company decides not to show them on the balance sheet or disclose this information in the notes. Evaluate this procedure.

24. What are the general rules for how gains or losses on retirement of plant assets should be reported in income?

CHAPTER TEN

DEPRECIATION AND IMPAIRMENTS

Do They Matter?

The axiom on Wall Street has been that huge one-time charges don't really count. These highly unusual events don't truly reflect how a company is faring, so Wall Street ignores them. In the last few years write-offs have approached all-time highs. For example, over one-third of the companies surveyed by *Accounting Trends and Techniques* in 2004 reported asset impairments.

However, some companies have taken write-offs so regularly that they really are a reflection of ongoing business. When you adjust for the write-offs, earnings turn out to be far worse—and the companies' shares of stock turn out to be far more expensive. Presented below are data from three companies that recently had charges every year for five consecutive years.

Company	Net Income Before Write-Offs ($ mil)	Net Income After Write-Offs ($ mil)	Percentage Difference	EPS	EPS Adjusted	P/E	P/E Adjusted
International Paper	$591	$ 95	84%	$2.82	$0.46	15	90
Waste Management	755	130	83	1.43	0.25	18	102
Fortune Brands	322	61	81	3.30	0.63	13	67

For example, the data show that International Paper's adjusted earnings come in closer to $0.46 per share than $2.82. This means that its price-to-earnings ratio is closer to 90 than to 15. In short, these companies may be overpriced and are likely set for stock price declines.

One reason for more write-offs may be the tougher U.S. guidelines to determine when companies should consider property, plant, and equipment as impaired. These impairment rules are catching on internationally. Twenty-six Japanese companies adopted impairment standards similar to the U.S. standards, resulting in a combined loss of ¥814.1 billion (yen) in fiscal 2004. Adoption of the impairment standard both signals that the recent economic downturn was behind these companies and introduces more transparent accounting. Thus, while impairments are on the rise in the United States and elsewhere, investors are now receiving better information about fixed-asset values in financial statements.[1]

[1] Adapted from "Were Profits Inflated?" *Business Week* (March 4, 2002), p. 14, and from Michael K. Ozanian, "The Secret Charges, *Forbes* (March 4, 2002), p. 102. See also "Losses Pile Up under Stricter Accounting," *International Herald Tribune* (June 2, 2004).

Learning Objectives

After studying this chapter, you should be able to:

1. Explain the concept of depreciation.
2. Identify the factors involved in the depreciation process.
3. Compare activity, straight-line, and decreasing-charge methods of depreciation.
4. Explain special depreciation methods.
5. Explain the accounting issues related to asset impairment.
6. Explain how to report and analyze property, plant, equipment, and natural resources.

PREVIEW OF CHAPTER 10

As noted in the opening story, both U.S. and foreign companies are affected by impairment rules. These rules recognize that when economic conditions deteriorate, companies may need to write off an asset's cost to indicate the decline in its usefulness. The purpose of this chapter is to examine the depreciation process and the methods of writing off the cost of tangible assets and natural resources. The content and organization of the chapter are as follows.

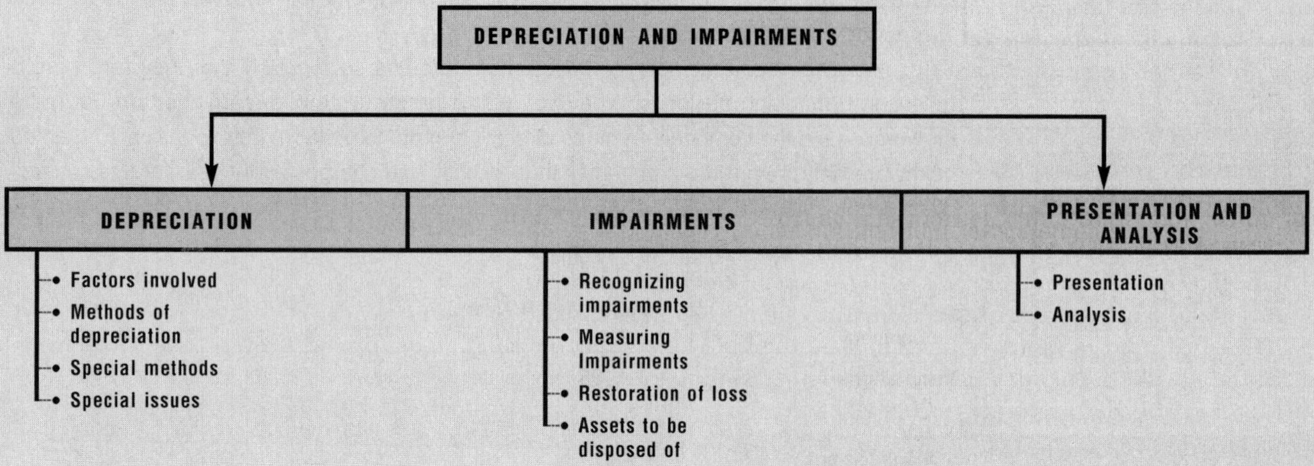

DEPRECIATION—A METHOD OF COST ALLOCATION

OBJECTIVE 1
Explain the concept of depreciation.

Most individuals at one time or another purchase and trade in an automobile. The automobile dealer and the buyer typically discuss what the trade-in value of the old car is. Also, they may talk about what the trade-in value of the new car will be in several years. In both cases a decline in value is considered to be an example of depreciation.

To accountants, however, depreciation is not a matter of valuation. Rather, **depreciation is a means of cost allocation. Depreciation is the accounting process of allocating the cost of tangible assets to expense in a systematic and rational manner to those periods expected to benefit from the use of the asset.** For example, a company like **Goodyear** (one of the world's largest tire manufacturers) does not depreciate assets on the basis of a decline in their fair market value. Instead, it depreciates through systematic charges to expense.

This approach is employed because the value of the asset may fluctuate between the time the asset is purchased and the time it is sold or junked. Attempts to measure these interim value changes have not been well received because values are difficult to measure objectively. Therefore, Goodyear charges the asset's cost to depreciation expense over its estimated life. It makes no attempt to value the asset at fair market value between acquisition and disposition. Companies use the cost allocation approach because it matches costs with revenues and because fluctuations in market value are uncertain and difficult to measure.

When companies write off the cost of long-lived assets over a number of periods, they typically use the term **depreciation**. They use the term **depletion** to describe the reduction in the cost of natural resources (such as timber, gravel, oil, and coal) over a period of time. The expiration of intangible assets, such as patents or copyrights, is called **amortization**.

Factors Involved in the Depreciation Process

OBJECTIVE 2
Identify the factors involved in the depreciation process.

Before establishing a pattern of charges to revenue, a company must answer three basic questions:

1. What depreciable base is to be used for the asset?
2. What is the asset's useful life?
3. What method of cost apportionment is best for this asset?

The answers to these questions involve combining several estimates into one single figure. Note the calculations assume perfect knowledge of the future, which is never attainable.

Depreciable Base for the Asset

Tutorial on Depreciation Methods

The base established for depreciation is a function of two factors: the original cost, and salvage or disposal value. We discussed historical cost in Chapter 9. **Salvage value** is the estimated amount that a company will receive when it sells the asset or removes it from service. It is the amount to which a company writes down or depreciates the asset during its useful life. If an asset has a cost of $10,000 and a salvage value of $1,000, its **depreciation base** is $9,000.

ILLUSTRATION 10-1
Computation of Depreciation Base

Original cost	$10,000
Less: Salvage value	1,000
Depreciation base	$ 9,000

From a practical standpoint, companies often assign a zero salvage value. Some long-lived assets, however, have substantial salvage values.

Estimation of Service Lives

The service life of an asset often differs from its physical life. A piece of machinery may be physically capable of producing a given product for many years beyond its service life. But a company may not use the equipment for all that time because the cost of producing the product in later years may be too high. For example, the old Slater cotton mill in Pawtucket, Rhode Island, is preserved in remarkable physical condition as an historic landmark in U.S. industrial development, although its service life was terminated many years ago.[2]

Companies retire assets for two reasons: **physical factors** (such as casualty or expiration of physical life) and **economic factors** (obsolescence). Physical factors are the wear and tear, decay, and casualties that make it difficult for the asset to perform indefinitely. These physical factors set the outside limit for the service life of an asset.

We can classify the economic or functional factors into three categories:

1. **Inadequacy** results when an asset ceases to be useful to a company because the demands of the firm have changed. An example would be the need for a larger building to handle increased production. Although the old building may still be sound, it may have become inadequate for the company's purpose.
2. **Supersession** is the replacement of one asset with another more efficient and economical asset. Examples would be the replacement of the mainframe computer with a PC network, or the replacement of the Boeing 767 with the Boeing 787.
3. **Obsolescence** is the catchall for situations not involving inadequacy and supersession.

[2]Taken from J. D. Coughlan and W. K. Strand, *Depreciation Accounting, Taxes and Business Decisions* (New York: The Ronald Press, 1969), pp. 10–12.

Because the distinction between these categories appears artificial, it is probably best to consider economic factors collectively instead of trying to make distinctions that are not clear-cut.

To illustrate the concepts of physical and economic factors, consider a new nuclear power plant. Which is more important in determining the useful life of a nuclear power plant—physical factors or economic factors? The limiting factors seem to be (1) ecological considerations, (2) competition from other power sources, and (3) safety concerns. Physical life does not appear to be the primary factor affecting useful life. Although the plant's physical life may be far from over, the plant may become obsolete in 10 years.

For a house, physical factors undoubtedly are more important than the economic or functional factors relative to useful life. Whenever the physical nature of the asset primarily determines useful life, maintenance plays an extremely vital role. The better the maintenance, the longer the life of the asset.[3]

In most cases, a company estimates the useful life of an asset based on its past experience with the same or similar assets. Others use sophisticated statistical methods to establish a useful life for accounting purposes. And in some cases, companies select arbitrary service lives. In a highly industrial economy such as that of the United States, where research and innovation are so prominent, technological factors have as much effect, if not more, on service lives of tangible plant assets as physical factors do.

WHAT DO THE NUMBERS MEAN?

ALPHABET DUPE

Some companies try to imply that depreciation is not a cost. For example, in their press releases they will often make a bigger deal over earnings before interest, taxes, depreciation, and amortization (often referred to as EBITDA) than net income under GAAP. They like it because it "dresses up" their earnings numbers. Some on Wall Street buy this hype because they don't like the allocations that are required to determine net income. Some banks, without batting an eyelash, even let companies base their loan covenants on EBITDA.

For example, look at **Premier Parks**, which operates the Six Flags chain of amusement parks. Premier touts its EBITDA performance. But that number masks a big part of how the company operates—and how it spends its money. Premier argues that analysts should ignore depreciation for big-ticket items like roller coasters because the rides have a long life. Critics, however, say that the amusement industry has to spend as much as 50 percent of its EBITDA just to keep its rides and attractions current. Those expenses are not optional—let the rides get a little rusty, and ticket sales start to tail off. That means analysts really should view depreciation associated with the costs of maintaining the rides (or buying new ones) as an everyday expense. It also means investors in those companies should have strong stomachs.

What's the risk of trusting a fad accounting measure? Just look at a recent year's bankruptcy numbers. Of the 147 companies tracked by Moody's that defaulted on their debt, most borrowed money based on EBITDA performance. The bankers in those deals probably wish they had looked at a few other factors. Maybe it's time more investors did so too.

Source: Adapted from Herb Greenberg, Alphabet Dupe: Why EBITDA Falls Short," *Fortune* (July 10, 2000), p. 240.

[3]The airline industry also illustrates the type of problem involved in estimation. In the past, aircraft were assumed not to wear out—they just became obsolete. However, some jets have been in service as long as 20 years, and maintenance of these aircraft has become increasingly expensive. In addition, some recent air disasters have heightened the public's concern about worn-out aircraft. As a result, some airlines now replace aircraft not because of obsolescence but because of physical deterioration.

Methods of Depreciation

The third factor involved in the depreciation process is the **method** of cost apportionment. The profession requires that the depreciation method employed be "systematic and rational." Companies may use a number of depreciation methods, as follows.

1. Activity method (units of use or production).
2. Straight-line method.
3. Decreasing charge methods (accelerated):
   (a) Sum-of-the-years'-digits.
   (b) Declining-balance method.
4. Special depreciation methods:
   (a) Group and composite methods.
   (b) Hybrid or combination methods.[4]

UNDERLYING CONCEPTS

Depreciation attempts to match the cost of an asset to the periods that benefit from the use of that asset.

To illustrate these depreciation methods, assume that Stanley Coal Mines recently purchased an additional crane for digging purposes. Illustration 10-2 contains the pertinent data concerning this purchase.

Cost of crane	$500,000
Estimated useful life	5 years
Estimated salvage value	$ 50,000
Productive life in hours	30,000 hours

ILLUSTRATION 10-2
Data Used to Illustrate Depreciation Methods

Activity Method

OBJECTIVE 3
Compare activity, straight-line, and decreasing-charge methods of depreciation.

The **activity method** (also called the **variable-charge** or **units-of-production approach**) assumes that depreciation is **a function of use or productivity, instead of the passage of time**. A company considers the life of the asset in terms of either the **output** it provides (units it produces), or an **input** measure such as the number of hours it works. Conceptually, the proper cost association relies on output instead of hours used, but often the output is not easily measurable. In such cases, an input measure such as machine hours is a more appropriate method of measuring the dollar amount of depreciation charges for a given accounting period.

The crane poses no particular depreciation problem. Stanley can measure the usage (hours) relatively easily. If Stanley uses the crane for 4,000 hours the first year, the depreciation charge is:

$$\frac{\text{(Cost less salvage)} \times \text{Hours this year}}{\text{Total estimated hours}} = \text{Depreciation charge}$$

$$\frac{(\$500{,}000 - \$50{,}000) \times 4{,}000}{30{,}000} = \$60{,}000$$

ILLUSTRATION 10-3
Depreciation Calculation, Activity Method—Crane Example

The major limitation of this method is that it is inappropriate in situations in which depreciation is a function of time instead of activity. For example, a building steadily deteriorates due to the elements (time) regardless of its use. In addition, where economic or functional factors affect an asset, independent of its use, the activity method loses much of its significance. For example, if a company is expanding rapidly, a particular building may soon become obsolete for its intended purposes. In both cases, activity is irrelevant. Another problem in using an activity method is the difficulty of estimating units of output or service hours received.

[4]*Accounting Trends and Techniques—2004* reports that of its 600 surveyed companies, for reporting purposes, 580 used straight-line, 22 used declining-balance, 5 used sum-of-the-years'-digits, 41 used an accelerated method (not specified), and 30 used units of production.

In cases where loss of services results from activity or productivity, the activity method matches costs and revenues the best. Companies that desire low depreciation during periods of low productivity, and high depreciation during high productivity, either adopt or switch to an activity method. In this way, a plant running at 40 percent of capacity generates 60 percent lower depreciation charges. **Inland Steel**, for example, switched to units-of-production depreciation at one time and reduced its losses by $43 million, or $1.20 per share.[5]

Straight-Line Method

UNDERLYING CONCEPTS

If benefits flow on a "straight-line" basis, then justification exists for matching the cost of the asset on a straight-line basis with these benefits.

The **straight-line method** considers depreciation a **function of time rather than a function of usage.** Companies widely use this method because of its simplicity. The straight-line procedure is often the most conceptually appropriate, too. When creeping obsolescence is the primary reason for a limited service life, the decline in usefulness may be constant from period to period. Stanley computes the depreciation charge for the crane as follows.

ILLUSTRATION 10-4
Depreciation Calculation, Straight-Line Method—Crane Example

$$\frac{\text{Cost less salvage}}{\text{Estimated service life}} = \text{Depreciation charge}$$

$$\frac{\$500{,}000 - \$50{,}000}{5} = \$90{,}000$$

The major objection to the straight-line method is that it rests on two tenuous assumptions: (1) The asset's economic usefulness is the same each year, and (2) the repair and maintenance expense is essentially the same each period.

One additional problem that occurs in using straight-line—as well as some others—is that distortions in the rate of return analysis (income/assets) develop. Illustration 10-5 indicates how the rate of return increases, given constant revenue flows, because the asset's book value decreases.

ILLUSTRATION 10-5
Depreciation and Rate of Return Analysis—Crane Example

Year	Depreciation Expense	Undepreciated Asset Balance (book value)	Income (after depreciation expense)	Rate of Return (Income ÷ Assets)
0		$500,000		
1	$90,000	410,000	$100,000	24.4%
2	90,000	320,000	100,000	31.2%
3	90,000	230,000	100,000	43.5%
4	90,000	140,000	100,000	71.4%
5	90,000	50,000	100,000	200.0%

Decreasing-Charge Methods

UNDERLYING CONCEPTS

The matching concept does not justify a constant charge to income. If the benefits from the asset decline as the asset ages, then a decreasing charge to income better matches cost to benefits.

The **decreasing-charge methods** provide for a higher depreciation cost in the earlier years and lower charges in later periods. Because these methods allow for higher early-year charges than in the straight-line method, they are often called **accelerated depreciation methods.**

What is the main justification for this approach? The rationale is that companies should charge more depreciation in earlier years because the asset is most productive in its earlier years. Furthermore, the accelerated methods provide a constant cost because the depreciation charge is lower in the later periods, at the time when the repair and maintenance costs are often higher. Generally, companies use one of two decreasing-charge methods: the sum-of-the-years'-digits method, or the declining-balance method.

[5]"Double Standard," *Forbes* (November 22, 1982), p. 178.

Sum-of-the-Years'-Digits. The **sum-of-the-years'-digits method** results in a decreasing depreciation charge based on a decreasing fraction of depreciable cost (original cost less salvage value). Each fraction uses the sum of the years as a denominator (5 + 4 + 3 + 2 + 1 = 15). The numerator is the number of years of estimated life remaining as of the beginning of the year. In this method, the numerator decreases year by year, and the denominator remains constant (5/15, 4/15, 3/15, 2/15, and 1/15). At the end of the asset's useful life, the balance remaining should equal the salvage value. Illustration 10-6 shows this method of computation.[6]

ILLUSTRATION 10-6
Sum-of-the-Years'-Digits Depreciation Schedule—Crane Example

Year	Depreciation Base	Remaining Life in Years	Depreciation Fraction	Depreciation Expense	Book Value, End of Year
1	$450,000	5	5/15	$150,000	$350,000
2	450,000	4	4/15	120,000	230,000
3	450,000	3	3/15	90,000	140,000
4	450,000	2	2/15	60,000	80,000
5	450,000	1	1/15	30,000	50,000[a]
		15	15/15	$450,000	

[a]Salvage value.

Declining-Balance Method. The **declining-balance method** utilizes a depreciation rate (expressed as a percentage) that is some multiple of the straight-line method. For example, the double-declining rate for a 10-year asset is 20 percent (double the straight-line rate, which is 1/10 or 10 percent). Companies apply the constant rate to the declining book value each year.

Unlike other methods, the declining-balance method **does not deduct the salvage value** in computing the depreciation base. The declining-balance rate is multiplied by the book value of the asset at the beginning of each period. Since the depreciation charge reduces the book value of the asset each period, applying the constant-declining-balance rate to a successively lower book value results in lower depreciation charges each year. This process continues until the book value of the asset equals its estimated salvage value. At that time the company discontinues depreciation.

Companies use various multiples in practice. For example, the **double-declining-balance method** depreciates assets at twice (200 percent) the straight-line rate. Illustration 10-7 shows Stanley's depreciation charges if using the double-declining approach.

ILLUSTRATION 10-7
Double-Declining Depreciation Schedule—Crane Example

Year	Book Value of Asset First of Year	Rate on Declining Balance[a]	Depreciation Expense	Balance Accumulated Depreciation	Book Value, End of Year
1	$500,000	40%	$200,000	$200,000	$300,000
2	300,000	40%	120,000	320,000	180,000
3	180,000	40%	72,000	392,000	108,000
4	108,000	40%	43,200	435,200	64,800
5	64,800	40%	14,800[b]	450,000	50,000

[a]Based on twice the straight-line rate of 20% ($90,000/$450,000 = 20%; 20% × 2 = 40%).
[b]Limited to $14,800 because book value should not be less than salvage value.

---

[6]What happens if the estimated service life of the asset is, let us say, 51 years? How would we calculate the sum-of-the-years'-digits? Fortunately mathematicians have developed the following formula that permits easy computation:

$$\frac{n(n+1)}{2} = \frac{51(51+1)}{2} = 1{,}326$$

Companies often switch from the declining-balance method to the straight-line method near the end of the asset's useful life to ensure that they depreciate the asset only to its salvage value.[7]

Special Depreciation Methods

OBJECTIVE 4
Explain special depreciation methods.

Sometimes companies adopt special depreciation methods. Reasons for doing so might be that a company's assets have unique characteristics, or the nature of the industry. Two of these special methods are:

1 Group and composite methods.
2 Hybrid or combination methods.

Group and Composite Methods

Companies often depreciate multiple-asset accounts using one rate. For example, **AT&T** might depreciate telephone poles, microwave systems, or switchboards by groups.

Two methods of depreciating multiple-asset accounts exist: the group method and the composite method. The choice of method depends on the nature of the assets involved. Companies frequently use the **group method** when the assets are similar in nature and have approximately the same useful lives. They use the **composite approach** when the assets are dissimilar and have different lives. The group method more closely approximates a single-unit cost procedure because the dispersion from the average is not as great. The computation for group or composite methods is essentially the same: find an average and depreciate on that basis.

Companies determine the **composite depreciation rate** by dividing the depreciation per year by the total cost of the assets. To illustrate, Mooney Motors establishes the composite depreciation rate for its fleet of cars, trucks, and campers as shown in Illustration 10-8.

ILLUSTRATION 10-8
Depreciation Calculation, Composite Basis

Asset	Original Cost	Residual Value	Depreciable Cost	Estimated Life (yrs.)	Depreciation per Year (straight-line)
Cars	$145,000	$25,000	$120,000	3	$40,000
Trucks	44,000	4,000	40,000	4	10,000
Campers	35,000	5,000	30,000	5	6,000
	$224,000	$34,000	$190,000		$56,000

$$\text{Composite depreciation rate} = \frac{\$56{,}000}{\$224{,}000} = 25\%$$

Composite life = 3.39 years ($190,000 ÷ $56,000)

If there are no changes in the asset account, Mooney will depreciate the group of assets to the residual or salvage value at the rate of $56,000 ($224,000 × 25%) a

[7]A pure form of the declining-balance method (sometimes appropriately called the "fixed percentage of book value method") has also been suggested as a possibility. This approach finds a rate that depreciates the asset exactly to salvage value at the end of its expected useful life. The formula for determination of this rate is as follows:

$$\text{Depreciation rate} = 1 - \sqrt[n]{\frac{\text{Salvage value}}{\text{Acquisition cost}}}$$

The life in years is n. After computing the depreciation rate, a company applies it on the declining book value of the asset from period to period, which means that depreciation expense will be successively lower. This method is not used extensively in practice due to cumbersome computations. Further, it is not permitted for tax purposes.

year. As a result, it will take Mooney 3.39 years to depreciate these assets. The length of time it takes a company to depreciate it assets on a composite basis is called the **composite life**.

We can highlight the differences between the group or composite method and the single-unit depreciation method by looking at asset retirements. If Mooney retires an asset before, or after, the average service life of the group is reached, it buries the resulting gain or loss in the Accumulated Depreciation account. This practice is justified because Mooney will retire some assets before the average service life and others after the average life. For this reason, the debit to Accumulated Depreciation is the difference between original cost and cash received. Mooney does not record a gain or loss on disposition.

To illustrate, suppose that Mooney Motors sold one of the campers with a cost of $5,000 for $2,600 at the end of the third year. The entry is:

Accumulated Depreciation	2,400	
Cash	2,600	
Cars, Trucks, and Campers		5,000

If Mooney purchases a new type of asset (mopeds, for example), it must compute a new depreciation rate and apply this rate in subsequent periods.

Illustration 10-9 presents a typical financial statement disclosure of the group depreciation method for **Ampco-Pittsburgh Corporation**.

ILLUSTRATION 10-9
Disclosure of Group Depreciation Method

Ampco-Pittsburgh Corporation

Depreciation rates are based on estimated useful lives of the asset groups. Gains or losses on normal retirements or replacements of depreciable assets, subject to composite depreciation methods, are not recognized; the difference between the cost of the assets retired or replaced and the related salvage value is charged or credited to the accumulated depreciation.

The group or composite method simplifies the bookkeeping process and tends to average out errors caused by over- or under-depreciation. As a result, gains or losses on disposals of assets do not distort periodic income.

On the other hand, the unit method has several advantages over the group or composite methods: (1) It simplifies the computation mathematically. (2) It identifies gains and losses on disposal. (3) It isolates depreciation on idle equipment. (4) It represents the best estimate of the depreciation of each asset, not the result of averaging the cost over a longer period of time. As a consequence, companies generally use the unit method. Unless stated otherwise, you should use the unit method in homework problems.[8]

Hybrid or Combination Methods

In addition to the depreciation methods already discussed, companies are free to develop their own special or tailor-made depreciation methods. GAAP requires only that the method result in the allocation of an asset's cost over the asset's life in a **systematic and rational manner**.

[8] AcSEC has indicated in an exposure draft that companies should use the unit approach whenever feasible. In fact, it indicates that an even better way to depreciate property, plant, and equipment is to use *component depreciation*. Under component depreciation, a company should depreciate over its expected useful life any part or portion of property, plant, and equipment that can be separately identified as an asset. For example, a company could separate the various components of a building (e.g., roof, heating and cooling system, elevator, leasehold improvements) and depreciate each component over its useful life.

For example, the steel industry widely uses a hybrid depreciation method, called the **production variable method** that is a combination straight-line/activity approach. The following note from **WHX Corporation**'s annual report explains one variation of this method.

ILLUSTRATION 10-10
Disclosure of Hybrid Depreciation Method

WHX Corporation

The Company utilizes the modified units of production method of depreciation which recognizes that the depreciation of steelmaking machinery is related to the physical wear of the equipment as well as a time factor. The modified units of production method provides for straight-line depreciation charges modified (adjusted) by the level of raw steel production. In the prior year, depreciation under the modified units of production method was $21.6 million or 40% less than straight-line depreciation, and in the current year it was $1.1 million or 2% more than straight-line depreciation.

wiley.com/college/kieso

Expanded Discussion—Special Depreciation Methods

DECELERATING DEPRECIATION

WHAT DO THE NUMBERS MEAN?

Which depreciation method should management select? Many believe that the method that best matches revenues with expenses should be used. For example, if revenues generated by the asset are constant over its useful life, select straight-line depreciation. On the other hand, if revenues are higher (or lower) at the beginning of the asset's life, then use a decreasing (or increasing) method. Thus, if a company can reliably estimate revenues from the asset, selecting a depreciation method that best matches costs with those revenues would seem to provide the most useful information to investors and creditors for assessing the future cash flows from the asset.

Managers in the real estate industry face a different challenge when considering depreciation choices. Real estate managers object to traditional depreciation methods because in their view, real estate often does not decline in value. In addition, because real estate is highly debt-financed, most real estate concerns report losses in earlier years of operations when the sum of depreciation and interest exceeds the revenue from the real estate project. As a result, real estate companies, like **Kimco Realty**, argue for some form of **increasing-charge** method of depreciation (lower depreciation at the beginning and higher depreciation at the end). With such a method, companies would report higher total assets and net income in the earlier years of the project.[9]

Special Depreciation Issues

We still need to discuss several special issues related to depreciation:

1. How should companies compute depreciation for partial periods?
2. Does depreciation provide for the replacement of assets?
3. How should companies handle revisions in depreciation rates?

[9]In this regard, real estate investment trusts (REITs) often report (in addition to net income) an earnings measure, funds from operations (FFO), that adjusts income for depreciation expense and other noncash expenses. This method is not GAAP. There is mixed empirical evidence about whether FFO or GAAP income is more useful to real estate investment trust investors. See, for example, Richard Gore and David Stott, "Toward a More Informative Measure of Operating Performance in the REIT Industry: Net Income vs. FFO," *Accounting Horizons* (December 1998); and Linda Vincent, "The Information Content of FFO for REITs," *Journal of Accounting and Economics* (January 1999).

Depreciation and Partial Periods

Companies seldom purchase plant assets on the first day of a fiscal period or dispose of them on the last day of a fiscal period. A practical question is: How much depreciation should a company charge for the partial periods involved?

In computing depreciation expense for partial periods, companies must determine the depreciation expense for the full year and then prorate this depreciation expense between the two periods involved. This process should continue throughout the useful life of the asset.

Assume, for example, that Steeltex Company purchases an automated drill machine with a 5-year life for $45,000 (no salvage value) on June 10, 2006. The company's fiscal year ends December 31. Steeltex therefore charges depreciation for only 6⅔ months during that year. The total depreciation for a full year (assuming straight-line depreciation) is $9,000 ($45,000/5). The depreciation for the first, partial year is therefore:

$$\frac{6\frac{2}{3}}{12} \times \$9{,}000 = \$5{,}000$$

The partial-period calculation is relatively simple when Steeltex uses straight-line depreciation. But how is partial-period depreciation handled when it uses an accelerated method such as sum-of-the-years'-digits or double-declining balance? As an illustration, assume that Steeltex purchased another machine for $10,000 on July 1, 2006, with an estimated useful life of five years and no salvage value. Illustration 10-11 shows the depreciation figures for 2006, 2007, and 2008.

ILLUSTRATION 10-11
Calculation of Partial-Period Depreciation, Two Methods

	Sum-of-the-Years'-Digits	Double-Declining Balance
1st full year	(5/15 × $10,000) = $3,333.33	(40% × $10,000) = $4,000
2nd full year	(4/15 × 10,000) = 2,666.67	(40% × 6,000) = 2,400
3rd full year	(3/15 × 10,000) = 2,000.00	(40% × 3,600) = 1,440
Depreciation from July 1, 2006, to December 31, 2006		
	6/12 × $3,333.33 = $1,666.67	6/12 × $4,000 = $2,000
Depreciation for 2007		
	6/12 × $3,333.33 = $1,666.67	6/12 × $4,000 = $2,000
	6/12 × 2,666.67 = 1,333.33	6/12 × 2,400 = 1,200
	$3,000.00	$3,200
		or ($10,000 − $2,000) × 40% = $3,200
Depreciation for 2008		
	6/12 × $2,666.67 = $1,333.33	6/12 × $2,400 = $1,200
	6/12 × 2,000.00 = 1,000.00	6/12 × 1,440 = 720
	$2,333.33	$1,920
		or ($10,000 − $5,200) × 40% = $1,920

Sometimes a company like Steeltex modifies the process of allocating costs to a partial period to handle acquisitions and disposals of plant assets more simply. It may compute depreciation for the full period on the opening balance in the asset account and not charge depreciation on acquisitions during the year. It then charges a full year of depreciation in the year of disposal. Other variations charge one-half year's depreciation both in the year of acquisition and in the year of disposal (referred to as the **half-year convention**), or charge a full year in the year of acquisition and none in the year of disposal.

In fact, Steeltex may adopt any one of these several fractional-year policies in allocating cost to the first and last years of an asset's life so long as it applies the method consistently. However, **unless otherwise stipulated, companies normally compute depreciation on the basis of the nearest full month.**

Illustration 10-12 shows depreciation allocated under five different fractional-year policies using the straight-line method on the $45,000 automated drill machine purchased by Steeltex Company on June 10, 2006, discussed earlier.

ILLUSTRATION 10-12
Fractional-Year Depreciation Policies

Machine Cost = $45,000	Depreciation Allocated per Period Over 5-Year Life*					
Fractional-Year Policy	2006	2007	2008	2009	2010	2011
1. Nearest fraction of a year.	$5,000[a]	$9,000	$9,000	$9,000	$9,000	$4,000[b]
2. Nearest full month.	5,250[c]	9,000	9,000	9,000	9,000	3,750[d]
3. Half year in period of acquisition and disposal.	4,500	9,000	9,000	9,000	9,000	4,500
4. Full year in period of acquisition, none in period of disposal.	9,000	9,000	9,000	9,000	9,000	–0–
5. None in period of acquisition, full year in period of disposal.	–0–	9,000	9,000	9,000	9,000	9,000

[a]6.667/12 ($9,000) [b]5.333/12 ($9,000) [c]7/12 ($9,000) [d]5/12 ($9,000)
*Rounded to nearest dollar.

Depreciation and Replacement of Fixed Assets

A common misconception about depreciation is that it provides funds for the replacement of fixed assets. Depreciation is like other expenses in that it reduces net income. It differs, though, in that **it does not involve a current cash outflow.**

To illustrate why depreciation does not provide funds for replacement of plant assets, assume that a business starts operating with plant assets of $500,000 that have a useful life of five years. The company's balance sheet at the beginning of the period is:

Plant assets	$500,000	Owners' equity	$500,000

If we assume that the company earns no revenue over the five years, the income statements are:

	Year 1	Year 2	Year 3	Year 4	Year 5
Revenue	$ –0–	$ –0–	$ –0–	$ –0–	$ –0–
Depreciation	(100,000)	(100,000)	(100,000)	(100,000)	(100,000)
Loss	$(100,000)	$(100,000)	$(100,000)	$(100,000)	$(100,000)

Total depreciation of the plant assets over the five years is $500,000. The balance sheet at the end of the five years therefore is:

Plant assets	–0–	Owners' equity	–0–

This extreme example illustrates that depreciation **in no way** provides funds for the replacement of assets. **The funds for the replacement of the assets come from the revenues** (generated through use of the asset). Without the revenues, no income materializes and no cash inflow results.

Revision of Depreciation Rates

When purchasing a plant asset, companies carefully determine depreciation rates based on past experience with similar assets and other pertinent information. The provisions for depreciation are only estimates, however. They may need to revise them during the life of the asset. Unexpected physical deterioration or unforeseen obsolescence may decrease the estimated useful life of the asset. Improved maintenance procedures, revision of operating procedures, or similar developments may prolong the life of the asset beyond the expected period.[10]

For example, assume that **International Paper Co.** purchased machinery with an original cost of $90,000. It estimates a 20-year life with no salvage value. However, during year 11, International Paper estimates that it will use the machine for an additional 20 years. Its total life, therefore, will be 30 years instead of 20. Depreciation has been recorded at the rate of 1/20 of $90,000, or $4,500 per year by the straight-line method. On the basis of a 30-year life, International Paper should have recorded depreciation as 1/30 of $90,000, or $3,000 per year. It has therefore overstated depreciation, and understated net income, by $1,500 for each of the past 10 years, or a total amount of $15,000. Illustration 10-13 shows this computation.

ILLUSTRATION 10-13
Computation of Accumulated Difference Due to Revisions

	Per Year	For 10 Years
Depreciation charged per books (1/20 × $90,000)	$4,500	$45,000
Depreciation based on a 30-year life (1/30 × $90,000)	3,000	30,000
Excess depreciation charged	$1,500	$15,000

International Paper should report this change in estimate in the current and prospective periods. It should not make any changes in previously reported results. And it does not adjust opening balances nor attempt to "catch up" for prior periods. The reason? Changes in estimates are a continual and inherent part of any estimation process. Continual restatement of prior periods would occur for revisions of estimates unless handled prospectively. Therefore, no entry is made at the time the change in estimate occurs. Charges for depreciation in subsequent periods (assuming use of the straight-line method) are determined by **dividing the remaining book value less any salvage value by the remaining estimated life.**

ILLUSTRATION 10-14
Computing Depreciation after Revision of Estimated Life

Machinery	$90,000
Less: Accumulated depreciation	45,000
Book value of machinery at end of 10th year	$45,000

Depreciation (future periods) = $45,000 book value ÷ 20 years remaining life = $2,250

The entry to record depreciation for each of the remaining 20 years is:

Depreciation Expense	2,250	
Accumulated Depreciation—Machinery		2,250

[10]As an example of a change in operating procedures, **General Motors** (GM) used to write off its tools—such as dies and equipment used to manufacture car bodies—over the life of the body type. Through this procedure, it expensed tools twice as fast as **Ford** and three times as fast as **DaimlerChrysler**. However, it slowed the depreciation process on these tools and lengthened the lives on its plant and equipment. These revisions reduced depreciation and amortization charges by approximately $1.23 billion, or $2.55 per share, in the year of the change. In Chapter 18, we provide a more complete discussion of changes in estimates.

DEPRECIATION CHOICES

WHAT DO THE NUMBERS MEAN?

The amount of depreciation expense recorded depends on both the depreciation method used and estimates of service lives and salvage values of the assets. Differences in these choices and estimates can significantly impact a company's reported results and can make it difficult to compare the depreciation numbers of different companies.

For example, when **Willamette Industries** extended the estimated service lives of its machinery and equipment by five years, it increased income by nearly $54 million.

An analyst determines the impact of these management choices and judgments on the amount of depreciation expense by examining the notes to financial statements. For example, Willamette Industries provided the following note to its financial statements.

Note 4: Property, Plant, and Equipment (partial)

	Range of Useful Lives
Land	—
Buildings	15–35
Machinery & equipment	5–25
Furniture & fixtures	3–15

During the year, the estimated service lives for most machinery and equipment were extended five years. The change was based upon a study performed by the company's engineering department, comparisons to typical industry practices, and the effect of the company's extensive capital investments which have resulted in a mix of assets with longer productive lives due to technological advances. As a result of the change, net income was increased by $54,000,000.

IMPAIRMENTS

OBJECTIVE 5
Explain the accounting issues related to asset impairment.

The general accounting standard of **lower-of-cost-or-market for inventories does not apply to property, plant, and equipment**. Even when property, plant, and equipment has suffered partial obsolescence, accountants have been reluctant to reduce the asset's carrying amount. Why? Because, unlike inventories, it is difficult to arrive at a fair value for property, plant, and equipment that is not subjective and arbitrary.

For example, **Falconbridge Ltd. Nickel Mines** had to decide whether to write off all or a part of its property, plant, and equipment in a nickel-mining operation in the Dominican Republic. The project had been incurring losses because nickel prices were low and operating costs were high. Only if nickel prices increased by approximately 33 percent would the project be reasonably profitable. Whether a write-off was appropriate depended on the future price of nickel. Even if the company decided to write off the asset, how much should be written off?

UNDERLYING CONCEPTS

The *going concern concept* assumes that the company can recover the investment in its assets. Under GAAP companies do not report the fair value of long-lived assets because a going concern does not plan to sell such assets. However, if the assumption of being able to recover the cost of the investment is not valid, then a company should report a reduction in value.

Recognizing Impairments

As discussed in the opening story, the FASB and international accounting standard-setters have developed rules for recognizing impairments on long-lived assets.[11] According to these standards, when the carrying amount of an asset is not recoverable, a company records a write-off. This write-off is referred to as an **impairment**.

[11] "Accounting for the Impairment or Disposal of Long-lived Assets," *Statement of Financial Accounting Standards No. 144* (Norwalk, Conn.: 2001).

Various events and changes in circumstances might lead to an impairment. Examples are:

a. A significant decrease in the market value of an asset.

b. A significant change in the extent or manner in which an asset is used.

c. A significant adverse change in legal factors or in the business climate that affects the value of an asset.

d. An accumulation of costs significantly in excess of the amount originally expected to acquire or construct an asset.

e. A projection or forecast that demonstrates continuing losses associated with an asset.

These events or changes in circumstances indicate that the company may not be able to recover the carrying amount of the asset. In that case, a **recoverability test** is used to determine whether an impairment has occurred.

To apply the first step of the recoverability test, a company like **UPS** estimates the future net cash flows expected from the **use of that asset and its eventual disposition.** If the sum of the expected future net cash flows (undiscounted) is **less than the carrying amount** of the asset, UPS considers the asset impaired. Conversely, if the sum of the expected future net cash flows (undiscounted) is **equal to or greater than the carrying amount** of the asset, no impairment has occurred.

The recoverability test therefore screens for asset impairment. For example, if the expected future net cash flows from an asset are $400,000 and its carrying amount is $350,000, no impairment has occurred. However, if the expected future net cash flows are $300,000, an impairment has occurred. The rationale for the recoverability test relies on a basic presumption: A balance sheet should report long-lived assets at no more than the carrying amounts that are recoverable.

Measuring Impairments

If the recoverability test indicates an impairment, UPS computes a loss. The **impairment loss** is the amount by which the carrying amount of the asset **exceeds its fair value.** How does UPS determine the fair value of an asset? It is measured based on the market value if an active market for the asset exists. If no active market exists, UPS uses the **present value of expected future net cash flows to determine fair value.**

To summarize, the process of determining an impairment loss is as follows.

1 Review events or changes in circumstances for possible impairment.

2 If the review indicates impairment, apply the recoverability test. If the sum of the expected future net cash flows from the long-lived asset is less than the carrying amount of the asset, an impairment has occurred.

3 Assuming an impairment, the impairment loss is the amount by which the carrying amount of the asset exceeds the fair value of the asset. The fair value is the market value or the present value of expected future net cash flows.

Impairment—Example 1

M. Alou Inc. has an asset that, due to changes in its use, it reviews for possible impairment. The asset's carrying amount is $600,000 ($800,000 cost less $200,000 accumulated depreciation). Alou determines the expected future net cash flows (undiscounted) from the use of the asset and its eventual disposal to be $650,000.

The recoverability test indicates that the $650,000 of expected future net cash flows from the asset's use exceed the carrying amount of $600,000. As a result, no impairment occurred. (Recall that the undiscounted future net cash flows must be less than the carrying amount for Alou to deem an asset to be impaired and to measure the impairment loss.) Therefore, M. Alou Inc. does not recognize an impairment loss in this case.

Impairment—Example 2

Assume the same facts as in Example 1, except that the expected future net cash flows from Alou's asset are $580,000 (instead of $650,000). The recoverability test indicates that the expected future net cash flows of $580,000 from the use of the asset are less than its carrying amount of $600,000. Therefore an impairment has occurred.

The difference between the carrying amount of Alou's asset and its fair value is the impairment loss. Assuming this asset has a market value of $525,000, Illustration 10-15 shows the loss computation.

ILLUSTRATION 10-15
Computation of Impairment Loss

Carrying amount of the equipment	$600,000
Fair value of equipment (market value)	525,000
Loss on impairment	$ 75,000

M. Alou records the impairment loss as follows.

Loss on Impairment	75,000	
Accumulated Depreciation		75,000

M. Alou Inc. reports the impairment loss as part of income from continuing operations, in the "Other expenses and losses" section. Generally, Alou **should not report this loss as an extraordinary item.** Costs associated with an impairment loss are the same costs that would flow through operations and that it would report as part of continuing operations. Alou will continue to use these assets in operations. Therefore, it should not report the loss below "Income from continuing operations."

A company that recognizes an impairment loss should disclose the asset(s) impaired, the events leading to the impairment, the amount of the loss, and how it determined fair value (disclosing the interest rate used, if appropriate).

Restoration of Impairment Loss

After recording an impairment loss, the reduced carrying amount of an asset held for use becomes its new cost basis. A company does not change the new cost basis except for depreciation or amortization in future periods or for additional impairments.

To illustrate, assume that Damon Company at December 31, 2006, has equipment with a carrying amount of $500,000. Damon determines this asset is impaired and writes it down to its fair value of $400,000. At the end of 2007, Damon determines that the fair value of the asset is $480,000. The carrying amount of the equipment should not change in 2007 except for the depreciation taken in 2007. Damon **may not restore an impairment loss for an asset held for use.** The rationale for not writing the asset up in value is that the new cost basis puts the impaired asset on an equal basis with other assets that are unimpaired.

INTERNATIONAL INSIGHT

International accounting standards permit write-ups for subsequent recoveries of impairment. U.S. GAAP prohibits those write-ups, except for assets to be disposed of.

Impairment of Assets to Be Disposed of

What happens if a company intends to dispose of the impaired asset, instead of holding it for use? Recently **Kroger** recorded an impairment loss of $54 million on property, plant, and equipment it no longer needs due to store closures. In this case, Kroger reports the impaired asset at the lower of cost or net realizable value (fair value less cost to sell). Because Kroger intends to dispose of the assets in a short period of time, it uses net realizable value in order to provide a better measure of the net cash flows that it will receive from these assets.

Kroger does not depreciate or amortize assets held for disposal during the period it holds them. The rationale is that depreciation is inconsistent with the notion of assets to be disposed of and with the use of the lower of cost or net realizable value. In other words, **assets held for disposal are like inventory; companies should report them at the lower of cost or net realizable value.**

Because Kroger will recover assets held for disposal through sale rather than through operations, it continually revalues them. Each period, the assets are reported at the lower of cost or net realizable value. Thus **Kroger can write up or down an asset held for disposal in future periods, as long as the carrying value after the write-up never exceeds the carrying amount of the asset before the impairment.** Companies should report losses or gains related to these impaired assets as part of **income from continuing operations.**

Illustration 10-16 summarizes the key concepts in accounting for impairments.

ILLUSTRATION 10-16
Graphic of Accounting for Impairments

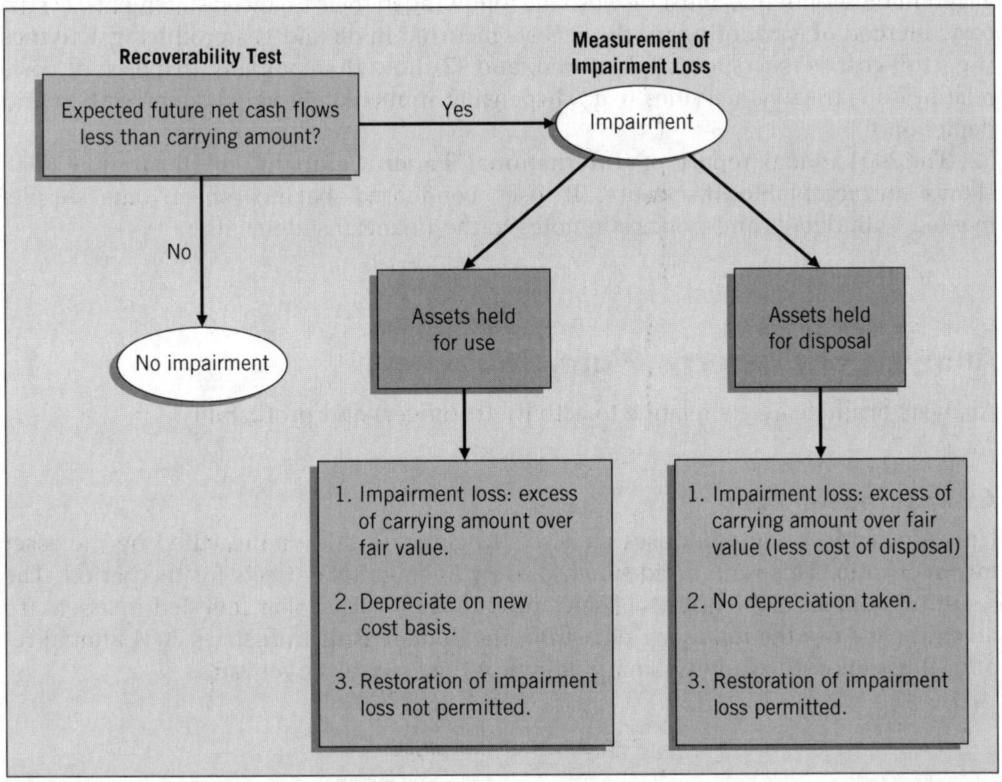

PRESENTATION AND ANALYSIS

Presentation of Property, Plant, Equipment, and Natural Resources

OBJECTIVE 6
Explain how to report and analyze property, plant, equipment, and natural resources.

A company should disclose the basis of valuation—usually historical cost—for property, plant, equipment, and natural resources along with pledges, liens, and other commitments related to these assets. It should not offset any liability secured by property, plant, equipment, and natural resources against these assets. Instead, this obligation should be reported in the liabilities section. The company should segregate property, plant, and equipment not currently employed as producing assets in the business (such as idle facilities or land held as an investment) from assets used in operations.

When depreciating assets, a company credits a valuation account normally called Accumulated Depreciation. Using an Accumulated Depreciation account permits the user of the financial statements to see the original cost of the asset and the amount of depreciation that the company charged to expense in past years.

When depleting natural resources, some companies use an Accumulated Depletion account. Many, however, simply credit the natural resource account directly. The rationale for this approach is that the natural resources are physically consumed, making direct reduction of the cost of the natural resources appropriate.

Because of the significant impact on the financial statements of the depreciation method(s) used, companies should disclose the following.

a. Depreciation expense for the period.
b. Balances of major classes of depreciable assets, by nature and function.
c. Accumulated depreciation, either by major classes of depreciable assets or in total.
d. A general description of the method or methods used in computing depreciation with respect to major classes of depreciable assets.[12]

Special disclosure requirements relate to the oil and gas industry. Companies engaged in these activities must disclose the following in their financial statements: (1) the basic method of accounting for those costs incurred in oil and gas producing activities (e.g., full-cost versus successful-efforts), and (2) how the company disposes of costs relating to extractive activities (e.g., dispensing immediately versus depreciation and depletion.)[13]

The 2004 annual report of **International Paper Company** in Illustration 10-18 shows an acceptable disclosure. It uses condensed balance sheet data supplemented with details and policies in notes to the financial statements.

Analysis of Property, Plant, Equipment

Analysts evaluate assets relative to activity (turnover) and profitability.

Additional Property, Plant, and Equipment Disclosures

Asset Turnover Ratio

How efficiently a company uses its assets to generate sales is measured by the **asset turnover ratio**. This ratio divides net sales by average total assets for the period. The resulting number is the dollars of sales produced by each dollar invested in assets. To illustrate, we use the following data from the **Tootsie Roll Industries** 2004 annual report. Illustration 10-17 shows computation of the asset turnover ratio.

Tootsie Roll Industries

	(in millions)
Net sales	$420.1
Total assets, 12/31/04	811.8
Total assets, 12/31/03	665.3
Net income	64.2

ILLUSTRATION 10-17
Asset Turnover Ratio

$$\text{Asset turnover} = \frac{\text{Net sales}}{\text{Average total assets}}$$

$$= \frac{\$420.1}{(\$811.8 + \$665.3)/2}$$

$$= .569$$

[12]"Omnibus Opinion—1967," *Opinions of the Accounting Principles Board No. 12* (New York: AICPA, 1967), par. 5. Some believe that companies should disclose the average useful life of the assets or the range of years of asset life to help users understand the age and life of property, plant, and equipment.

[13]Public companies, in addition to these two required disclosures, must include as supplementary information numerous schedules reporting reserve quantities; capitalized costs; acquisition, exploration, and development activities; and a standardized measure of discounted future net cash flows related to proved oil and gas reserve quantities. See "Disclosures about Oil and Gas Producing Activities," *Statement of Financial Accounting Standards Board No. 69* (Stamford, Conn.: FASB, 1982).

ILLUSTRATION 10-18
Disclosures for Property, Plant, Equipment, and Natural Resources

International Paper Company

Consolidated Balance Sheet (partial)

In millions at December 31	2004	2003
Assets		
Total current assets	$ 9,319	$11,096
Plants, properties and equipment, net	13,432	13,260
Forestlands	3,936	3,979
Investments	679	678
Goodwill	4,994	4,793
Deferred charges and other assets	1,857	1,719
Total assets	$34,217	$35,525

Note 1 (partial)

Plants, Properties and Equipment Plants, properties and equipment are stated at cost, less accumulated depreciation. Expenditures for betterments are capitalized whereas normal repairs and maintenance are expensed as incurred. The units-of-production method of depreciation is used for major pulp and paper mills and certain wood products facilities and the straight-line method for other plants and equipment. Annual straight-line depreciation rates are, for buildings, 2 1/2% to 8 1/2%, and, for machinery and equipment, 5% to 33%.

Forestlands At December 31, 2004, International Paper and its subsidiaries owned or controlled about 6.8 million acres of forestlands in the United States, 1.2 million acres in Brazil, 785,000 acres in New Zealand, and had, through licenses and forest management agreements, harvesting rights on government owned forestlands in Russia. Forestlands include owned property as well as certain timber harvesting rights with terms of one or more years, and are stated at cost, less cost of timber harvested (COTH). Costs attributable to timber are charged against income as trees are cut. The rate charged is determined annually based on the relationship of incurred costs to estimated current merchantable volume.

Effective January 1, 2002, International Paper prospectively changed its method of accounting for mid-rotation fertilization expenditures to include such expenditures in the capitalized cost of forestlands. Accordingly, these costs are included as part of the COTH as trees are sold.

Note 11 (partial)

Plants, properties and equipment by major classification were:

In millions at December 31	2004	2003
Pulp, paper and packaging facilities		
Mills	$22,165	$21,234
Packaging plants	5,874	5,826
Wood products facilities	1,411	1,232
Other plants, properties and equipment	1,925	2,091
Gross cost	31,375	30,383
Less: Accumulated depreciation	17,943	17,123
Plants, properties and equipment, net	$13,432	$13,260

The asset turnover ratio shows that Tootsie Roll generated sales of $0.57 per dollar of assets in the year ended December 31, 2004.

Asset turnover ratios vary considerably among industries. For example, a large utility like **Ameren** has a ratio of 0.32 times. A large grocery chain like **Kroger** has a ratio of 2.73 times. Thus, in comparing performance among companies based on the asset turnover ratio, you need to consider the ratio within the context of the industry in which a company operates.

Profit Margin on Sales Ratio

Another measure for analyzing the use of property, plant, and equipment is the **profit margin on sales ratio** (rate of return on sales). Calculated as net income divided by net sales, this profitability ratio does not, by itself, answer the question of how profitably a company uses its assets. But by relating the profit margin on sales to the asset turnover during a period of time, we can ascertain how profitably the company used assets during that period of time in a measure of the rate of return on assets. Using the Tootsie Roll Industries data shown above, we compute the profit margin on sales ratio and the rate of return on assets as follows.

ILLUSTRATION 10-19
Profit Margin on Sales

$$\text{Profit margin on sales} = \frac{\text{Net income}}{\text{Net sales}} = \frac{\$64.2}{\$420.1} = 15.28\%$$

$$\text{Rate of return on assets} = \text{Profit margin on sales} \times \text{Asset turnover} = 15.28\% \times .569 = 8.7\%$$

Rate of Return on Assets

The rate of return a company achieves through use of its assets is the **rate of return on assets (ROA)**. Rather than using the profit margin on sales, we can compute it directly by dividing net income by average total assets. Using Tootsie Roll's data, we compute the ratio as follows.

ILLUSTRATION 10-20
Rate of Return on Assets

$$\text{Rate of return on assets} = \frac{\text{Net income}}{\text{Average total assets}} = \frac{\$64.2}{(\$811.8 + \$665.3)/2} = 8.7\%$$

The 8.7 percent rate of return computed in this manner equals (with rounding) the 8.7 percent rate computed by multiplying the profit margin on sales by the asset turnover. The rate of return on assets measures profitability well because it combines the effects of profit margin and asset turnover.

QUESTIONS

1. Distinguish between depreciation, depletion, and amortization.
2. Identify the factors that are relevant in determining the annual depreciation charge, and explain whether these factors are determined objectively or whether they are based on judgment.
3. Some believe that accounting depreciation measures the decline in the value of fixed assets. Do you agree? Explain.
4. Explain how estimation of service lives can result in unrealistically high valuations of fixed assets.
5. The plant manager of a manufacturing firm suggested in a conference of the company's executives that accountants should speed up depreciation on the machinery in the finishing department because improvements were rapidly making those machines obsolete and a depreciation fund big enough to cover their replacement is needed. Discuss

the accounting concept of depreciation and the effect on a business concern of the depreciation recorded for plant assets, paying particular attention to the issues raised by the plant manager.

6. For what reasons are plant assets retired? Define inadequacy, supersession, and obsolescence.

7. What basic questions must be answered before the amount of the depreciation charge can be computed?

8. Elizabeth Ashley Company purchased a machine on January 2, 2006, for $600,000. The machine has an estimated useful life of 5 years and a salvage value of $100,000. Depreciation was computed by the 150% declining-balance method. What is the amount of accumulated depreciation at the end of December 31, 2007?

9. Linda Blair Company purchased machinery for $120,000 on January 1, 2007. It is estimated that the machinery will have a useful life of 20 years, salvage value of $15,000, production of 84,000 units, and working hours of 42,000. During 2007 the company uses the machinery for 14,300 hours, and the machinery produces 20,000 units. Compute depreciation under the straight-line, units-of-output, working hours, sum-of-the-years'-digits, and declining-balance (use 10% as the annual rate) methods.

10. What are the major factors considered in determining what depreciation method to use?

11. Under what conditions is it appropriate for a business to use the composite method of depreciation for its plant assets? What are the advantages and disadvantages of this method?

12. If Brad Pitt, Inc. uses the composite method and its composite rate is 7.5% per year, what entry should it make when plant assets that originally cost $50,000 and have been used for 10 years are sold for $16,000?

13. A building that was purchased December 31, 1982, for $2,400,000 was originally estimated to have a life of 50 years with no salvage value at the end of that time. Depreciation has been recorded through 2006. During 2007 an examination of the building by an engineering firm discloses that its estimated useful life is 15 years after 2006. What should be the amount of depreciation for 2007?

14. Armand Assante, president of Flatbush Company, has recently noted that depreciation increases cash provided by operations and therefore depreciation is a good source of funds. Do you agree? Discuss.

15. Melanie Mayron purchased a computer for $6,000 on July 1, 2007. She intends to depreciate it over 4 years using the double-declining balance method. Salvage value is $1,000. Compute depreciation for 2008.

16. Astaire Inc. is considering the write-down of its long-term plant because of a lack of profitability. Explain to the management of Astaire how to determine whether a write-off is permitted.

17. Last year Wilde Company recorded an impairment on an asset held for use. Recent appraisals indicate that the asset has increased in value. Should Wilde record this recovery in value?

18. Kuga Co. has equipment with a carrying amount of $700,000. The expected future net cash flows from the equipment are $705,000, and its fair value is $590,000. The equipment is expected to be used in operations in the future. What amount (if any) should Kuga report as an impairment to its equipment?

19. Explain how gains or losses on impaired assets should be reported in income.

20. It has been suggested that plant and equipment could be replaced more quickly if depreciation rates for income tax and accounting purposes were substantially increased. As a result, business operations would receive the benefit of more modern and more efficient plant facilities. Discuss the merits of this proposition.

21. Neither depreciation on replacement cost nor depreciation adjusted for changes in the purchasing power of the dollar has been recognized as generally accepted accounting principles for inclusion in the primary financial statements. Briefly present the accounting treatment that might be used to assist in the maintenance of the ability of a company to replace its productive capacity.

22. **Target Corporation** in 2004 reported net income of $3.2 billion, net sales of $45.7 billion, and average total assets of $29.8 billion. What is Target's asset turnover ratio? What is Target's rate of return on assets?

CHAPTER ELEVEN

INTANGIBLE ASSETS

Untouchable

As shown in the graph below, tangible assets as a percent of all assets have declined dramatically in the last 50 years. Consequently, companies today increasingly derive value from intangible assets—intellectual property, technology, or reputation. Many well-known companies make most of their money from intangible assets: **Microsoft Corp.**'s software, **Pfizer Inc.**'s drug patents, and **Walt Disney Co.**'s film and television productions.

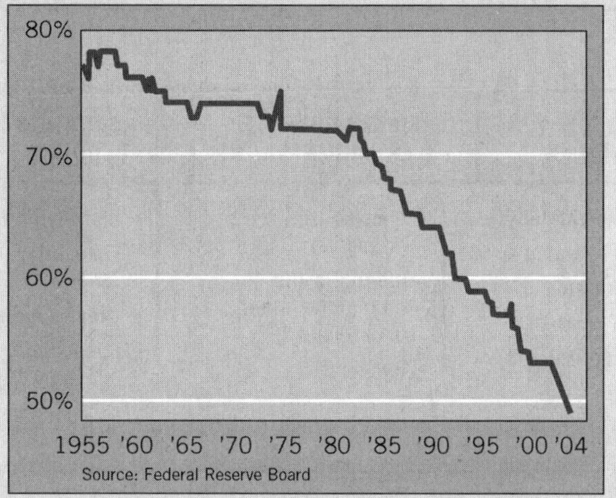

Tangible assets as a percentage of all assets of nonfinancial businesses

However, the experience at **Winstar Communications** illustrates how quickly the value of intangible assets can erode. Just before Winstar filed for bankruptcy, it listed $5 billion in assets, a large share comprised of questionable intangible assets related to its customer base. Within just a few months, its assets fetched just $42 *million.* Winstar's investors and creditors learned the shocking speed at which the value of such assets can decline.

Perhaps Federal Reserve Chairman Alan Greenspan's remarks are relevant in these turbulent times: ". . . a firm is inherently fragile if its value-added emanates more from conceptual as distinct from physical assets. Trust and reputation can vanish overnight. A factory cannot."[1]

[1]Adapted from Greg Ip, "The Rise and Fall of Intangible Assets Leads to Shorter Company Life Spans, *Wall Street Journal Online* (April 4, 2002).

Learning Objectives

After studying this chapter, you should be able to:

1 Describe the characteristics of intangible assets.
2 Identify the costs to include in the initial valuation of intangible assets.
3 Explain the procedure for amortizing intangible assets.
4 Describe the types of intangible assets.
5 Explain the conceptual issues related to goodwill.
6 Describe the accounting procedures for recording goodwill.
7 Explain the accounting issues related to intangible-asset impairments.
8 Identify the conceptual issues related to research and development costs.
9 Describe the accounting for research and development and similar costs.
10 Indicate the presentation of intangible assets and related items.

PREVIEW OF CHAPTER 11

As our opening story indicates, the accounting and reporting of intangibles is taking on increasing importance in this information age, especially for companies like **Microsoft Corp.**, **Pfizer Inc.**, and **Walt Disney Co.** In this chapter we explain the basic conceptual and reporting issues related to intangible assets. The content and organization of the chapter are as follows.

INTANGIBLE ASSETS

- **INTANGIBLE ASSET ISSUES**
  - Characteristics
  - Valuation
  - Amortization
- **TYPES OF INTANGIBLES**
  - Marketing-related
  - Customer-related
  - Artistic-related
  - Contract-related
  - Technology-related
  - Goodwill
- **IMPAIRMENT OF INTANGIBLES**
  - Limited-life intangibles
  - Indefinite-life intangibles other than goodwill
  - Goodwill
- **RESEARCH AND DEVELOPMENT COSTS**
  - Identifying R&D
  - Accounting for R&D
  - Other similar costs
  - Conceptual questions
- **PRESENTATION OF INTANGIBLES AND RELATED ITEMS**
  - Intangible assets
  - R&D costs

INTANGIBLE ASSET ISSUES

Characteristics

OBJECTIVE 1
Describe the characteristics of intangible assets.

Gap Inc.'s most important asset is its brand image, not its store fixtures. **Coca-Cola**'s success comes from its secret formula for making Coke, not its plant facilities. **America Online**'s subscriber base provides its most important asset, not its Internet connection equipment. As these examples show, we have an economy dominated today by information and service providers. For these companies, their major assets are often intangible in nature. Accounting for these intangibles is difficult.

What exactly are intangible assets? **Intangible assets** have two main characteristics.[2]

1. **They lack physical existence.** Unlike tangible assets such as property, plant, and equipment, intangible assets derive their value from the rights and privileges granted to the company using them.
2. **They are not financial instruments.** Assets such as bank deposits, accounts receivable, and long-term investments in bonds and stocks also lack physical substance. However, they are not classified as intangibles, because these assets are financial instruments. They derive their value from the right (claim) to receive cash or cash equivalents in the future.

In most cases, intangible assets provide benefits over a period of years. Therefore, companies normally classify them as long-term assets. We discuss the most common types

[2] "Goodwill and Other Intangible Assets," *Statement of Financial Accounting Standards No. 142* (Norwalk, Conn.: FASB, 2001).

of intangibles (patents, copyrights, franchises or licenses, trademarks or trade names, and goodwill) later in the chapter.

Valuation

Purchased Intangibles

Intangibles purchased from another party are **recorded at cost**. Cost includes all costs of acquisition and expenditures necessary to make the intangible asset ready for its intended use. Typical costs include purchase price, legal fees, and other incidental expenses.

OBJECTIVE 2
Identify the costs to include in the initial valuation of intangible assets.

If a company acquires intangibles for stock or in exchange for other assets, **the cost of the intangible is the fair value of the consideration given or the fair value of the intangible received, whichever is more clearly evident**. When a company buys several intangibles, or a combination of intangibles and tangibles, in a "basket purchase," it should allocate the cost on the basis of fair values. Essentially the accounting treatment for purchased intangibles closely parallels that for purchased tangible assets.

UNDERLYING CONCEPTS

The basic attributes of intangibles, their uncertainty as to future benefits, and their uniqueness have discouraged valuation in excess of cost.

Internally Created Intangibles

Costs incurred internally to create intangibles are generally expensed. Thus, even though a company may incur substantial research and development costs to create an intangible, it expenses these costs.

How do companies justify this approach? Some argue that the costs incurred internally to create intangibles bear no relationship to their real value. Therefore, expensing these costs is appropriate. Others note that it is difficult to associate internal costs with a specific intangible. And others contend that due to the underlying subjectivity related to intangibles, companies should follow a conservative approach—that is, expense as incurred. As a result, **companies only capitalize direct costs** incurred in developing the intangible, such as legal costs.

Amortization of Intangibles

Intangibles have either a **limited (finite) useful life** or an **indefinite useful life**. For example, a company like **Walt Disney** has both types of intangibles. Walt Disney **amortizes** its **limited life** intangible assets. It **does not amortize** intangible assets with an **indefinite life**.

OBJECTIVE 3
Explain the procedure for amortizing intangible assets.

Limited-Life Intangibles

The allocation of the cost of intangible assets in a systematic way is called **amortization**. Walt Disney amortizes its limited-life intangibles by systematic charges to expense over their useful life. The useful life should reflect the periods over which these assets will contribute to cash flows. Walt Disney considers these factors in determining useful life:

1. The expected use of the asset by the company.
2. The expected useful life of another asset or a group of assets to which the useful life of the intangible asset may relate (such as lease rights to a studio lot).
3. Any legal, regulatory, or contractual provisions that may limit the useful life.
4. Any legal, regulatory, or contractual provisions that enable renewal or extension of the asset's legal or contractual life without substantial cost. This factor assumes that there is evidence to support renewal or extension. Disney also must be able to accomplish renewal or extension without material modifications of the existing terms and conditions.

5 The effects of obsolescence, demand, competition, and other economic factors. Examples include the stability of the industry, known technological advances, legislative action that results in an uncertain or changing regulatory environment, and expected changes in distribution channels.

6 The level of maintenance expenditure required to obtain the expected future cash flows from the asset. For example, a material level of required maintenance in relation to the carrying amount of the asset may suggest a very limited useful life.[3]

The amount of amortization expense for a limited-life intangible asset should reflect the pattern in which the company consumes or uses up the asset, if the company can reliably determine that pattern. For example, assume that Second Wave, Inc. purchases a license to provide a limited quantity of a gene product, called Mega. Second Wave should amortize the cost of the license following the pattern of use of Mega. If it cannot determine the pattern of production or consumption, Second Wave should use the straight-line method of amortization. (*For homework problems, assume the use of the straight-line method unless stated otherwise.*)

When Second Wave amortizes these licenses, it should show the charges as expenses. It should credit either the appropriate asset accounts or separate accumulated amortization accounts.

The amount of an intangible asset to be amortized should be its cost less residual value. The residual value is assumed to be zero unless at the end of its useful life the intangible asset has value to another company. For example, if Hardy Co. commits to purchasing an intangible asset from U2D Co. at the end of the asset's useful life, U2D Co. should reduce the cost of its intangible asset by the residual value. Similarly, U2D Co. should consider market values, if reliably determined, for residual values.

What happens if the life of a limited-life intangible asset changes? In that case the remaining carrying amount should be amortized over the revised remaining useful life. Companies should, on a regular basis, evaluate the limited-life intangibles for impairment. Similar to property, plant, and equipment, an impairment loss should be recognized if the carrying amount of the intangible is not recoverable and its carrying amount exceeds its fair value.

Indefinite-Life Intangibles

If no legal, regulatory, contractual, competitive, or other factors limit the useful life of an intangible asset, a company considers its useful life indefinite. **Indefinite** means that there is no foreseeable limit on the period of time over which the intangible asset is expected to provide cash flows. A company does not amortize an intangible asset with an indefinite life.

To illustrate, assume that Double Clik, Inc. acquired a trademark that it uses to distinguish a leading consumer product. It renews the trademark every 10 years at minimal cost. All evidence indicates that this trademark product will generate cash flows for an indefinite period of time. In this case, the trademark has an indefinite life; Double Clik does not record any amortization.

Companies should test indefinite-life intangibles for impairment at least annually. The **impairment test** for indefinite-life intangibles differs from the one for limited-life intangibles in that only the fair value test is performed. There is no recoverability test related to indefinite-life intangibles. The reason: Indefinite-life intangible assets might never fail the undiscounted cash flows recoverability test because cash flows could extend indefinitely into the future.

Illustration 11-1 summarizes the accounting treatment for intangible assets.

[3] Ibid, par. 11.

ILLUSTRATION 11-1
Accounting Treatment for Intangibles

Type of Intangible	Manner Acquired: Purchased	Manner Acquired: Internally Created	Amortization	Impairment Test
Limited-life intangibles	Capitalize	Expense*	Over useful life	Recoverability test and then fair value test
Indefinite-life intangibles	Capitalize	Expense*	Do not amortize	Fair value test

*Except for direct costs, such as legal costs.

TYPES OF INTANGIBLE ASSETS

OBJECTIVE 4
Describe the types of intangible assets.

As indicated, the accounting for intangible assets depends on whether the intangible has a limited or an indefinite life. There are many different types of intangibles, often classified into the following six major categories.[4]

1 Marketing-related intangible assets.
2 Customer-related intangible assets.
3 Artistic-related intangible assets.
4 Contract-related intangible assets.
5 Technology-related intangible assets.
6 Goodwill.

Marketing-Related Intangible Assets

Companies primarily use **marketing-related intangible assets** in the marketing or promotion of products or services. Examples are trademarks or trade names, newspaper mastheads, Internet domain names, and noncompetition agreements.

A common form of a marketing-related intangible asset is a trademark or trade name. A **trademark** or **trade name** is a word, phrase, or symbol that distinguishes or identifies a particular company or product. Under common law, the right to use a trademark or trade name, whether registered or not, rests exclusively with the original user as long as the original user continues to use it. Registration with the U.S. Patent and Trademark Office provides legal protection for an **indefinite number of renewals for periods of 10 years each**. Therefore a company that uses an established trademark or trade name may properly consider it to have an indefinite life. Trade names like Kleenex, Pepsi-Cola, Buick, Excedrin, Wheaties, and Sunkist create immediate product identification in our minds, thereby enhancing marketability.

If a company acquires a trademark or trade name, it capitalizes the cost at the purchase price. If a company develops a trademark or trade name, it capitalizes costs related to securing it, such as attorney fees, registration fees, design costs, consulting fees, and successful legal defense costs. However, it excludes research and development costs. When the total cost of a trademark or trade name is insignificant, a company may simply expense it. In most cases, the life of a trademark or trade name is indefinite. Therefore companies do not amortize its cost.

The value of a marketing-related intangible can be substantial. Consider Internet domain names. The name **Drugs.com** recently sold for $800,000. The bidding for the name **Loans.com** approached $500,000.

[4]This classification framework is based on "Business Combinations," *Statement of Financial Accounting Standards No. 141* (Norwalk, Conn.: FASB, 2001).

Company names themselves identify qualities and characteristics that companies work hard and spend much to develop. In a recent year an estimated 1,230 companies took on new names in an attempt to forge new identities, and paid over $250 million to corporate-identity consultants. Among these were **Primerica** (formerly American Can), **Navistar** (formerly International Harvester), and **Nissan** (formerly Datsun).[5]

Customer-Related Intangible Assets

Customer-related intangible assets result from interactions with outside parties. Examples include customer lists, order or production backlogs, and both contractual and noncontractual customer relationships.

To illustrate, assume that We-Market Inc. acquires the customer list of a large newspaper for $6,000,000 on January 1, 2007. This customer database includes name, contact information, order history, and demographic information. We-Market expects to benefit evenly from the information over a three-year period. In this case, the customer list is a limited-life intangible that We-Market should amortize on a straight-line basis over the three-year period.

We-Market records the purchase of the customer list and the amortization of the customer list at the end of each year as follows.

January 1, 2007		
Customer List	6,000,000	
Cash		6,000,000
(To record purchase of customer list)		
December 31, 2007, 2008, 2009		
Customer List Amortization Expense	2,000,000	
Customer List (or Accumulated Customer List Amortization)		2,000,000
(To record amortization expense)		

The preceding example assumed no residual value for the customer list. But what if We-Market determines that it can sell the list for $60,000 to another company at the end of three years? In that case We-Market should subtract this residual value from the cost in order to determine the proper amortization expense for each year. Amortization expense would therefore be $1,980,000, as shown in Illustration 11-2.

ILLUSTRATION 11-2
Calculation of Amortization Expense with Residual Value

Cost	$6,000,000
Residual value	60,000
Amortization base	$5,940,000
Amortization expense per period: $1,980,000 ($5,940,000 ÷ 3)	

Companies should assume a zero residual value unless the asset's useful life is less than the economic life and reliable evidence is available concerning the residual value.[6]

[5]To illustrate how various intangibles arise from a given product, consider how the creators of the highly successful game Trivial Pursuit protected their creation. First, they copyrighted the 6,000 questions that are at the heart of the game. Then they shielded the Trivial Pursuit name by applying for a registered trademark. As a third mode of protection, they obtained a design patent on the playing board's design as a unique graphic creation.

[6]"Goodwill and Other Intangible Assets," *Statement of Financial Accounting Standards No. 142* (Norwalk, Conn.: FASB, 2001), par. B55.

Artistic-Related Intangible Assets

Artistic-related intangible assets involve ownership rights to plays, literary works, musical works, pictures, photographs, and video and audiovisual material. Copyrights protect these ownership rights.

A **copyright** is a federally granted right that all authors, painters, musicians, sculptors, and other artists have in their creations and expressions. A copyright is granted for the **life of the creator plus 70 years**. It gives the owner, or heirs, the exclusive right to reproduce and sell an artistic or published work. Copyrights are not renewable. Companies may capitalize the costs of acquiring and defending a copyright. However, they must expense the research and development costs involved as incurred.

Copyrights can be valuable. For example, the **Walt Disney Company** faced the loss of its copyright on Mickey Mouse, which could have affected sales of billions of dollars of Mickey-related goods and services (including theme parks). This copyright was so valuable that Disney and many other big entertainment companies fought all the way to the Supreme Court (and won) an extension of copyright lives from 50 to 70 years. Another example of the value of these intangibles is **Really Useful Group**, which owns copyrights on the musicals of Andrew Lloyd Webber—*Cats, Phantom of the Opera, Jesus Christ-Superstar,* and others. It has little hard assets, yet analysts value it at over $300 million.

Generally, the useful life of the copyright is less than its legal life (life of the creator plus 70 years). Thus, Really Useful Group should allocate the costs of its copyrights to the years in which it expects to receive the benefits. The difficulty of determining the number of years over which it will receive benefits normally encourages a company like Really Useful Group to write off these costs over a fairly short period of time.

Contract-Related Intangible Assets

Contract-related intangible assets represent the value of rights that arise from contractual arrangements. Examples are franchise and licensing agreements, construction permits, broadcast rights, and service or supply contracts. A common form of contract-based intangible asset is a franchise.

A **franchise** is a contractual arrangement under which the franchisor grants the franchisee the right to sell certain products or services, to use certain trademarks or trade names, or to perform certain functions, usually within a designated geographical area. We deal with franchises everyday, from driving in an automobile purchased from a **Toyota** dealer, to eating lunch at **McDonald's**, to living in a home purchased through a **Century 21** real estate broker, or to vacationing at a **Marriott** resort.

The franchisor, having developed a unique concept or product, protects its concept or product through a patent, copyright, or trademark or trade name. The franchisee acquires the right to exploit the franchisor's idea or product by signing a franchise agreement.

A municipality (or other governmental body) and a company that uses public property often enter into another type of franchise arrangement. In such cases, a municipality allows a privately owned company to use public property in performing its services. Examples are the use of public waterways for a ferry service, the use of public land for telephone or electric lines, the use of phone lines for cable TV, the use of city streets for a bus line, or the use of the airwaves for radio or TV broadcasting. Such operating rights, obtained through agreements with governmental units or agencies, are frequently referred to as **licenses** or **permits**.

Franchises and licenses may be for a definite period of time, for an indefinite period of time, or perpetual. The company securing the franchise or license carries an intangible asset account entitled Franchise or License on its books, only when it can identify costs (such as a lump-sum payment in advance or legal fees and other expenditures) with the acquisition of the operating right. **A company should amortize the cost of a franchise (or license) with a limited life as operating expense over the life of the franchise.** It should not amortize a franchise with an indefinite life, or a perpetual franchise, but instead should carry it at cost.

Annual payments made under a franchise agreement should be entered as operating expenses in the period in which they are incurred. The payments do not represent an asset since they do not relate to future rights to use public property.

SWEET TO SOUR

WHAT DO THE NUMBERS MEAN?

Krispy Kreme, the doughnut maker once dubbed the "hottest brand in the land," has taken a series of beatings. The latest: a formal inquiry by the Securities and Exchange Commission in October 2004 into its accounting. The problem seems to be with franchises Krispy Kreme reacquired a few years ago from owners who wanted to exit the business. Krispy Kreme decided to book most of the purchase price as an intangible asset called "reacquired franchise rights," which it does not amortize, or write-down, over time.

Management justified the accounting based on its belief that reacquired franchise rights have "indefinite lives." But critics charge that this artificially inflates profits and doesn't reflect the cost of the stores on its balance sheet. To compound its woes, some of the reacquired franchises were purchased from related parties, at prices some allege were too generous.

Accounting experts say it's unclear whether Krispy Kreme's method violates GAAP. One research firm found that all of the companies it follows with reacquired franchise rights amortize the costs over time. Krispy Kreme's methods are "definitely not conservative," according to one analyst.

The SEC probe couldn't have come at a worse time. Krispy Kreme's profits have plunged, and the stock lost about 75 percent of its value in the last year. Given the company's tumbling profits and hyper-aggressive accounting, investors should expect restatements and a big write-down when its auditor performs its annual impairment test. In other words, Krispy Kreme's outlook has gone from sweet to sour.

Source: Adapted from David Stires, "Accounting," *Fortune* (November 1, 2004), p. 42.

Technology-Related Intangible Assets

Technology-related intangible assets relate to innovations or technological advances. Examples are patented technology and trade secrets granted by the U.S. Patent and Trademark Office. A **patent** gives the holder exclusive right to use, manufacture, and sell a product or process **for a period of 20 years** without interference or infringement by others. With this exclusive right, fortunes can be made. For example, companies such as **Merck**, **Polaroid**, and **Xerox** were founded on patents.[7] The two principal kinds of patents are **product patents**, which cover actual physical products, and **process patents**, which govern the process of making products.

If a company like **Qualcomm** purchases a patent from an inventor (or other owner), the purchase price represents its cost. Qualcomm can capitalize other costs incurred in connection with securing a patent, as well as attorneys' fees and other unrecovered costs of a successful legal suit to protect the patent, as part of the patent cost. However, it **must expense as incurred** any research and development costs related to the **development** of the product, process, or idea that it subsequently patents. We will discuss accounting for research and development costs in the next part.

[7]Consider the opposite result: Sir Alexander Fleming, who discovered penicillin, decided not to use a patent to protect his discovery. He hoped that companies would produce it more quickly to help save sufferers. Companies, however, refused to develop it because they did not have the patent shield and, therefore, were afraid to make the investment.

Qualcomm should amortize the cost of a patent over its legal life or its useful life (the period benefits are received), whichever is **shorter**. If it owns a patent from the date it is granted, and Qualcomm expects the patent to be useful during its entire legal life, the company should amortize it over 20 years. If it appears that the patent will be useful for a shorter period of time, say, for five years, it should amortize its cost over five years.

Changing demand, new inventions superseding old ones, inadequacy, and other factors often limit the useful life of a patent to less than the legal life. For example, the useful life of patents in the pharmaceutical and drug industry is frequently less than the legal life because of the testing and approval period that follows their issuance. A typical drug patent has 5 to 11 years knocked off its 20-year legal life. Why? Because a drug-maker spends one to four years on animal tests, four to six years on human tests, and two to three years for the Food and Drug Administration to review the tests. All this time occurs after issuing the patent but before the product goes on a pharmacist's shelves.

PATENT BATTLES

WHAT DO THE NUMBERS MEAN?

From bioengineering to software design to the Internet, global competition is bringing battles over patents to the boiling point. For example, **Priceline.com** filed suit against **Microsoft** for launching Hotel Price Matcher, a service that operates much like the name-your-own-price-system Priceline pioneered.

Do you ever wonder who thought of the technology that saves your shipping and credit card information when you shop online? It was **Amazon.com**, which patented "one-click" shopping. To protect its technology, Amazon.com filed a complaint against **Barnesandnoble.com**, its rival in the Web-retailing wars, alleging infringement on its patent for one-click shopping. Even though Amazon.com and Barnesandnoble.com settled their dispute, patent battles continue between online retailers and independent software developers, claiming that companies like Amazon.com are unfairly undercutting its competition through these "business-method" patents.

Source: Adapted from "Battle over Patents Threatens to Damp Web's Innovative Spirit," *Wall Street Journal* (November 8, 1999); and L. Rohde, "Amazon, Barnes and Noble Settle Patent Dispute, *CNN.com* (March 8, 2002).

A company charges all legal fees and other costs incurred in successfully defending a patent suit to Patents, an asset account, because such a suit establishes the legal rights of the holder of the patent. Such costs should be amortized along with acquisition cost, over the remaining useful life of the patent.

Amortization expense should reflect the pattern, if reliably determined, in which a company uses up the patent.[8] A company may credit amortization of patents directly to the Patents account or to an Accumulated Patent Amortization account. To illustrate, assume that Harcott Co. incurs $180,000 in legal costs on January 1, 2007 to successfully defend a patent. The patent's useful life is 20 years, amortized on a straight-line basis. Harcott records the legal fees and the amortization at the end of 2007 as follows.

January 1, 2007		
Patents	180,000	
Cash		180,000
(To record legal fees related to patent)		
December 31, 2007		
Patent Amortization Expense	9,000	
Patents (or Accumulated Patent Amortization)		9,000
(To record amortization of patent)		

[8]Companies may compute amortization on a units-of-production basis in a manner similar to that described for depreciation on property, plant, and equipment. See Chapter 10.

We've said that a patent's useful life should not extend beyond its legal life of 20 years. However, companies often make small modifications or additions that lead to a new patent. For example, **Astra Zeneca Plc** filed for additional patents on minor modifications to its heartburn drug, Prilosec. The effect may be to extend the life of the old patent. In that case Astra Zeneca can apply the unamortized costs of the old patent to the new patent if the new patent provides essentially the same benefits.[9] Alternatively, if a patent becomes impaired because demand drops for the product, the asset should be written down or written off immediately to expense.

WHAT DO THE NUMBERS MEAN?

THE VALUE OF A SECRET FORMULA

The nuclear secrets contained within the Los Alamos nuclear lab seem easier to check out than a library book. But **The Coca-Cola Company** has managed to keep the recipe for the world's best-selling soft drink under wraps for more than 100 years. How has it done so?

Coca-Cola offers almost no information about its lifeblood. The only written copy of the formula resides in a bank vault in Atlanta. This handwritten sheet is available to no one except by vote of Coca-Cola's board of directors.

Can't science offer some clues? Coke purportedly contains 17 to 18 ingredients. That includes the usual caramel color and corn syrup, as well as a blend of oils known as 7X (rumored to be a mix of orange, lemon, cinnamon, and others). Distilling natural products like these is complicated, since they're made of thousands of compounds. One ingredient you will not find is cocaine. Although the original formula did contain trace amounts, today's Coke doesn't. When was it removed? That too is a secret.

Some experts indicate that the power of the Coca-Cola formula and related brand image account for almost 95 percent of Coke's $150 billion stock value.

Source: Adapted from Reed Tucker, "How Has Coke's Formula Stayed a Secret?" *Fortune* (July 24, 2000), p. 42.

Goodwill

OBJECTIVE 5
Explain the conceptual issues related to goodwill.

Although companies may capitalize certain costs to develop specifically identifiable assets such as patents and copyrights, the amounts capitalized are generally insignificant. But companies do record material amounts of intangible assets when purchasing intangible assets, particularly in situations involving the purchase of another business (often referred to as a business combination).

In a business combination, a company assigns the cost (purchase price), where possible, to the identifiable tangible and intangible net assets. It records the remainder in an intangible asset account called **Goodwill**. Goodwill is often referred to as the most intangible of intangible assets, because it is only identified with the business as a whole. The only way to sell it is to sell the business.

The problem of determining the proper cost to allocate to intangible assets in a business combination is complex. Many different types of intangibles may be considered, such as those we discussed earlier. It is extremely difficult not only to identify certain types of intangibles but also to assign a value to them in a business combination.

[9] Another example is **Eli Lilly**'s drug Prozac (prescribed to treat depression). In 1998 this product accounted for 43 percent of Eli Lilly's sales. The patent on Prozac expired in 2001, and the company was unable to extend its protection with a second-use patent for the use of Prozac to treat appetite disorders. Sales of the product slipped substantially as generic equivalents entered the market.

As a result, companies only record identifiable intangible assets that they can reliably measure. They record all other intangible assets, too difficult to identify or measure, as goodwill.[10]

Recording Goodwill

OBJECTIVE 6
Describe the accounting procedures for recording goodwill.

Internally Created Goodwill. **Goodwill generated internally should not be capitalized in the accounts.** The reason? Measuring the components of goodwill is simply too complex, and associating any costs with future benefits is too difficult. The future benefits of goodwill may have no relationship to the costs incurred in the development of that goodwill. To add to the mystery, goodwill may even exist in the absence of specific costs to develop it. Finally, because no objective transaction with outside parties takes place, a great deal of subjectivity—even misrepresentation—may occur.

UNDERLYING CONCEPTS

Capitalizing goodwill only when it is purchased in an arm's-length transaction, and not capitalizing any goodwill generated internally, is another example of reliability winning out over relevance.

Purchased Goodwill. Goodwill is recorded only when an entire business is purchased. Because goodwill is a "going concern" valuation, it cannot be separated from the business as a whole. To record goodwill, a company compares the fair market value of the net tangible and identifiable intangible assets with the purchase price of the acquired business. The difference is considered goodwill. This is why goodwill is sometimes referred to as a "plug," or "gap filler," or "**master valuation**" account. **Goodwill is the residual—the excess of cost over fair value of the identifiable net assets acquired.**

To illustrate, Multi-Diversified, Inc. decides that it needs a parts division to supplement its existing tractor distributorship. The president of Multi-Diversified is interested in buying a small concern in Chicago (Tractorling Company). Illustration 11-3 presents the balance sheet of Tractorling Company.

ILLUSTRATION 11-3
Tractorling Balance Sheet

TRACTORLING CO.
BALANCE SHEET
AS OF DECEMBER 31, 2007

Assets		Equities	
Cash	$ 25,000	Current liabilities	$ 55,000
Receivables	35,000	Capital stock	100,000
Inventories	42,000	Retained earnings	100,000
Property, plant, and equipment, net	153,000		
Total assets	$255,000	Total equities	$255,000

After considerable negotiation, Tractorling Company decides to accept Multi-Diversified's offer of $400,000. What, then, is the value of the goodwill, if any?

Expanded Discussion—Valuing Goodwill

The answer is not obvious. Tractorling's historical cost-based balance sheet does not disclose the fair market values of its identifiable assets. Suppose, though, that as the negotiations progress, Multi-Diversified investigates Tractorling's underlying assets to determine their fair market values. Such an investigation may be accomplished

[10]*SFAS No. 141* provides detailed guidance regarding the recognition of identifiable intangible assets in a business combination. Using this guidance, it was expected that companies would recognize more identifiable intangible assets, and less goodwill, in the financial statements as a result of business combinations. According to *Accounting Trends and Techniques* (AICPA 2004), companies surveyed reported nearly twice as many identifiable intangible assets compared to the survey in 2001. There was little change in the number of survey companies reporting goodwill.

either through a purchase audit undertaken by Multi-Diversified's auditors or by an independent appraisal from some other source. The investigation determines the valuations shown in Illustration 11-4.

ILLUSTRATION 11-4
Fair Market Value of Tractorling's Net Assets

Fair Market Values	
Cash	$ 25,000
Receivables	35,000
Inventories	122,000
Property, plant, and equipment, net	205,000
Patents	18,000
Liabilities	(55,000)
Fair market value of net assets	$350,000

Normally, differences between current fair market value and book value are more common among long-term assets than in the current assets category. Cash obviously poses no problems as to value. And receivables normally are fairly close to current valuation, although they may at times need certain adjustments due to inadequate bad debt provisions. Liabilities usually are stated at book value. However, if interest rates have changed since the company incurred the liabilities, a different valuation (such as present value based on expected cash flows) might be appropriate. Careful analysis must be made to determine that no unrecorded liabilities are present.

The $80,000 difference in Tractorling's inventories ($122,000 − $42,000) could result from a number of factors, the most likely being that the company uses LIFO. Recall that during periods of inflation, LIFO better matches expenses against revenues. However, it also creates a balance sheet distortion. Ending inventory consists of older layers costed at lower valuations.

In many cases, the values of long-term assets such as property, plant, and equipment, and intangibles may have increased substantially over the years. This difference could be due to inaccurate estimates of useful lives, continual expensing of small expenditures (say, less than $300), inaccurate estimates of salvage values, and the discovery of some unrecorded assets (as in Tractorling's case, where analysis determines Patents have a fair value of $18,000). Or, fair values may have substantially increased.

Since the investigation now determines the fair market value of net assets to be $350,000, why would Multi-Diversified pay $400,000? Undoubtedly, Tractorling points to its established reputation, good credit rating, top management team, well-trained employees, and so on. These factors make the value of the business greater than $350,000. At the same time, Multi-Diversified places a premium on the future earning power of these attributes as well as the basic asset structure of the company today. At this point in the negotiations, price can be a function of many factors. The most important is probably sheer skill at the bargaining table.

Multi-Diversified labels the difference between the purchase price of $400,000 and the fair market value of $350,000 as goodwill. Goodwill is viewed as one or a group of unidentifiable values (intangible assets), the cost of which "is measured by the difference between the cost of the group of assets or enterprise acquired and the sum of the assigned costs of individual tangible and identifiable intangible assets acquired less liabilities assumed."[11] This procedure for valuation, a **master valuation**

[11]The FASB expressed concern about measuring goodwill as a residual, but noted that there is no real measurement alternative since goodwill is not separable from the company as a whole. "Business Combinations," *Statement of Financial Accounting Standards No. 141* (Norwalk, Conn.: FASB, 2001), par. B145.

approach, assumes goodwill covers all the values that cannot be specifically identified with any identifiable tangible or intangible asset. Illustration 11-5 shows this approach.

ILLUSTRATION 11-5
Determination of Goodwill—Master Valuation Approach

Assigned to purchase price of $400,000	Cash	$ 25,000
	Receivables	35,000
	Inventories	122,000
	Property, plant, and equipment, net	205,000
	Patents	18,000
	Liabilities	(55,000)
	Fair maket value of net identifiable assets	$350,000
	Purchase price	400,000
	Value assigned to goodwill	$ 50,000

Multi-Diversified records this transaction as follows.

Cash	25,000	
Receivables	35,000	
Inventories	122,000	
Property, Plant, and Equipment	205,000	
Patents	18,000	
Goodwill	50,000	
Liabilities		55,000
Cash		400,000

Companies often identify goodwill on the balance sheet as the **excess of cost over the fair value** of the net assets acquired.

Goodwill Write-off

Companies that recognize goodwill in a business combination **consider it to have an indefinite life and therefore should not amortize it**. The reason: Investors find the amortization charge of little use in evaluating financial performance. In addition, although goodwill may decrease over time, predicting the actual life of goodwill and an appropriate pattern of amortization is extremely difficult.

Furthermore, goodwill often is the largest intangible asset on a company's balance sheet and the investment community wants to know the amount invested in goodwill. Therefore, **companies only adjust its carrying value when goodwill is impaired**. This approach significantly impacts the income statements of some companies. For example, **AOL Time Warner** (now **Time Warner**), **AT&T**, and other companies wrote off $750 billion of goodwill in a recent year. (See "What Do the Numbers Mean?" discussion on the next page.)

Some believe that goodwill's value eventually disappears. Therefore, they argue companies should charge goodwill to expense over the periods affected. Amortizing goodwill better matches expense with revenues. Others note that the accounting treatment for purchased goodwill and goodwill created internally should be consistent. They point out that companies immediately expense goodwill created internally and thus it does not appear as an asset. Companies should follow the same treatment, they argue, for purchased goodwill. Even though these arguments may have some merit, nonamortization of goodwill combined with an adequate impairment test should provide the most useful financial information to the investment community.

Negative Goodwill—Badwill

Negative goodwill (often referred to as a **bargain purchase** or **badwill)** arises when the fair value of the assets acquired exceeds the purchase price of the assets. This situation results from a market imperfection. In this case, the seller would have been better off to sell the assets individually than in total. However, situations do occur (e.g., a forced liquidation or distressed sale due to the death of a company founder), in which the purchase price is less than the value of the net identifiable assets. This results in a credit, which is referred to as **negative goodwill** or, alternatively, as **excess of fair value over the cost acquired**, **badwill**, or **bargain purchase**.

The FASB requires that companies recognize this remaining excess as an extraordinary gain. The Board noted that extraordinary gain treatment is appropriate in order to highlight the excess, and to reflect the unusual nature and infrequent occurrence of the item. Some disagree with the approach, as it results in a gain at the time of the purchase. However, we believe that the Board took a practical approach, given that this transaction rarely occurs.[12]

WHAT DO THE NUMBERS MEAN?

REAL NEWS OR JUST BOOKKEEPING?

Companies used 2002 to take massive write-offs. As Chief Investment Strategist Abby Joseph Cohen of **Goldman Sachs** noted, "Simply stated, many companies are writing off not only the kitchen sink but the bathtub as well." For instance, **AOL Time Warner Inc.** (now **Time Warner**) had a goodwill write-down in the first quarter of that year that—by itself—reduced S&P 500 earnings by $2 to $4 on an after-tax basis, Ms. Cohen said.

In her investment letter, Ms. Cohen attributed companies' massive write-downs to "the air"—that is, a confluence of the impacts from the September 11, 2001, terrorist attacks, the official announcement that the country is in a recession, and new rules for the write-down of goodwill.

Though earnings hits can be tough to swallow in the quarter in which they are taken, they often are not of lasting impact psychologically or operationally. "The quarter in which the write-offs are recorded typically bears the statistical brunt, but may not be reflective of performance in future quarters," according to Ms. Cohen.

Goodwill impairment issues continue to grab their share of business headlines. For example, **Hewlett-Packard** has received a fair amount of criticism for it failure to take goodwill impairment charges on goodwill arising from its merger with **Compaq**. HP's chief financial officer acknowledges the issue, but plays down its significance: "There's no question that if profitability doesn't improve, there will be an impairment charge." He makes the case that it wouldn't matter much, given that it would be just a bookkeeping entry. What do you think? Is an impairment charge just an entry or can it provide some new information about the merits of the merger with Compaq?

Source: Carol J. Loomis, "Why Carly's Big Bet Is Failing," *Fortune* (February 7, 2005), p. 50.

IMPAIRMENT OF INTANGIBLE ASSETS

OBJECTIVE 7
Explain the accounting issues related to intangible-asset impairments.

In some cases, the carrying amount of a long-lived asset (property, plant, and equipment or intangible assets) is not recoverable. Therefore, a company needs a write-off. As discussed in Chapter 10, this write-off is referred to as an **impairment**.

Impairment of Limited-Life Intangibles

The rules that apply to **impairments of property, plant, and equipment also apply to limited-life intangibles**. As discussed in Chapter 10, a company should review property, plant, and equipment for impairment at certain points—whenever events or

[12] "Business Combinations," *Statement of Financial Accounting Standards No. 141* (Norwalk, Conn.: FASB, 2001), pars. B187–B192.

changes in circumstances indicate that the carrying amount of the assets may not be recoverable.

In performing this **recoverability test**, the company estimates the future cash flows expected from use of the assets and its eventual disposal. If the sum of the expected future net cash flows (undiscounted) is less than the carrying amount of the asset, the company would measure and recognize an impairment loss.[13] The company then uses the **fair value test**. This test measures the impairment loss by comparing the asset's fair value with its carrying amount. The impairment loss is the carrying amount of the asset less the fair value of the impaired asset. As with other impairments, the loss on the limited-life intangible is reported as part of income from continuing operations. The entry generally appears in the "Other expenses and losses" section.

To illustrate, assume that Lerch, Inc. has a patent on how to extract oil from shale rock. Unfortunately, reduced oil prices adversely affected the shale oil technology. Thus, the patent has provided little income to date. As a result, Lerch performs a **recoverability test**. It finds that the expected net future cash flows from this patent are $35 million, and Lerch's patent has a carrying amount of $60 million. Because the expected future net cash flows of $35 million are less than the carrying amount of $60 million, Lerch must determine an impairment loss.

Discounting the expected net future cash flows at its market rate of interest, Lerch determines the fair value of its patent to be $20 million. Illustration 11-6 shows the impairment loss computation (based on fair value).

ILLUSTRATION 11-6
Computation of Loss on Impairment of Patent

Carrying amount of patent	$60,000,000
Fair value (based on present value computation)	20,000,000
Loss on impairment	$40,000,000

Lerch records this loss as follows:

Loss on Impairment	40,000,000	
Patents		40,000,000

After recognizing the impairment, the reduced carrying amount of the patents is its new cost basis. Lerch should amortize the patent's new cost over its remaining useful life or legal life, whichever is shorter. Even if oil prices increase in subsequent periods, and the value of the patent increases, Lerch **may not recognize restoration of the previously recognized impairment loss.**

Impairment of Indefinite-Life Intangibles Other Than Goodwill

Indefinite-life intangibles (other than goodwill) should be tested for impairment at least annually. The impairment test for an indefinite-life asset other than goodwill is a **fair value test**. This test compares the fair value of the intangible asset with the asset's carrying amount. If the fair value of the intangible asset is less than the carrying amount, an impairment is recognized. Companies use this one-step test because many indefinite-life assets easily meet the recoverability test (because cash flows may extend many years into the future). **As a result, the recoverability test is not used.**

To illustrate, assume that Arcon Radio purchased a broadcast license for $2,000,000. The license is renewable every 10 years if the company provides appropriate service and does not violate Federal Communications Commission (FCC) rules and procedures. Arcon Radio has renewed the license with the FCC twice, at a minimal cost. Because

[13] "Accounting for the Impairment or Disposal of Long-lived Assets," *Statement of Financial Accounting Standards No. 144* (Norwalk, Conn.: 2001).

it expects cash flows to last indefinitely, Arcon Radio reports the license as an indefinite-life intangible asset. Recently the FCC decided to no longer renew broadcast licenses, but to auction these licenses to the highest bidder. Arcon Radio expects cash flows for the remaining two years of its existing license. Arcon Radio performs an impairment test and determines that the fair value of the intangible asset is $1,500,000. It therefore reports an impairment loss of $500,000, computed as follows.

ILLUSTRATION 11-7
Computation of Loss on Impairment of Broadcast License

Carrying amount of broadcast license	$2,000,000
Fair value of broadcast license	1,500,000
Loss on impairment	$ 500,000

Arcon Radio now reports the license at $1,500,000, its fair value. Even if the value of the license increases in the remaining two years, Arcon Radio may not restore the previously recognized impairment loss.

Impairment of Goodwill

The impairment rule for goodwill is a two-step process. First, a company should compare the fair value of the reporting unit to its carrying amount, including goodwill. If the fair value of the reporting unit exceeds the carrying amount, it does not consider goodwill impaired. The company does not have to do anything else.

To illustrate, assume that Kohlbuy Corporation has three divisions in its company. It purchased one division, Pritt Products, four years ago for $2 million. Unfortunately, Pritt experienced operating losses over the last three quarters. Kohlbuy management is now reviewing the division for purposes of recognizing an impairment. Illustration 11-8 lists the Pritt Division's net assets, including the associated goodwill of $900,000 from the purchase.

ILLUSTRATION 11-8
Net Assets of Pritt Division, Including Goodwill

Cash	$ 200,000
Receivables	300,000
Inventory	700,000
Property, plant, and equipment (net)	800,000
Goodwill	900,000
Less: Accounts and notes payable	(500,000)
Net assets	$2,400,000

Kohlbuy determines that the fair value of Pritt Division is $2,800,000. **As a result, it does not recognize any impairment, because the fair value of the division exceeds the carrying amount of the net assets.**

However, if the fair value of Pritt Division is less than the carrying amount of the net assets, then Kohlbuy performs a second step to determine possible impairment. In the second step, Kohlbuy determines the fair value of the goodwill (implied value of goodwill) and compares it to its carrying amount. To illustrate, assume that the fair value of the Pritt Division is $1,900,000 instead of $2,800,000. Illustration 11-9 computes the implied value of the goodwill in this case.[14]

[14] Illustration 11-9 assumes that the carrying amount equals the fair value of net identifiable assets (excluding goodwill). If different, companies use the fair value of the net identifiable assets (excluding goodwill) to determine the implied goodwill.

ILLUSTRATION 11-9
Determination of Implied Value of Goodwill

Fair value of Pritt Division	$1,900,000
Net identifiable assets (excluding goodwill) ($2,400,000 − $900,000)	1,500,000
Implied value of goodwill	$ 400,000

Kohlbuy then compares the implied value of the goodwill to the recorded goodwill to determine impairment, as shown in Illustration 11-10.

ILLUSTRATION 11-10
Measurement of Goodwill Impairment

Carrying amount of goodwill	$900,000
Implied value of goodwill	400,000
Loss on impairment	$500,000

Illustration 11-11 summarizes the impairment tests for various intangible assets.

ILLUSTRATION 11-11
Summary of Intangible Asset Impairment Tests

Type of Intangible Asset	Impairment Test
Limited life	Recoverability test, then fair value test
Indefinite life other than goodwill	Fair value test
Goodwill	Fair value test on reporting unit, then fair value test on implied goodwill

RESEARCH AND DEVELOPMENT COSTS

OBJECTIVE 8
Identify the conceptual issues related to research and development costs.

Research and development (R&D) costs are not in themselves intangible assets. We present the accounting for R&D costs here, however, because research and development activities frequently result in the development of something that a company patents or copyrights (such as a new product, process, idea, formula, composition, or literary work).

Many companies spend considerable sums of money on research and development to create new products or processes, to improve present products, and to discover new knowledge that may be valuable at some future date. Illustration 11-12 shows the outlays for R&D made by selected U.S. companies.

ILLUSTRATION 11-12
R&D Outlays, as a Percentage of Sales and Profits

Company	R&D ($ million)	R&D/Sales	R&D/Net Income
Caterpillar	$ 928.0	3.07%	45.60%
Deere & Co.	611.6	3.06%	43.50%
Dell	463.0	0.94%	15.22%
General Mills	158.0	1.43%	14.98%
Hewlett-Packard	3,506.0	4.39%	100.26%
Johnson & Johnson	5,203.0	10.99%	61.15%
Kellogg	148.9	1.55%	16.72%
Merck	4,010.2	17.48%	68.98%

INTERNATIONAL INSIGHT

International accounting standards require the capitalization of appropriate development expenditures. This conflicts with U.S. GAAP.

Two difficulties arise in accounting for these research and development (R&D) expenditures: (1) identifying the costs associated with particular activities, projects, or achievements, and (2) determining the magnitude of the future benefits and length of time over which such benefits may be realized. Because of these latter uncertainties, the accounting practice in this area has been simplified. **Companies must expense all research and development costs when incurred.**[15]

Identifying R&D Activities

Illustration 11-13 shows the definitions for **research activities** and **development activities**. These definitions differentiate research and development costs from similar costs.[16]

ILLUSTRATION 11-13
R&D Activities

Research Activities	Development Activities
 Planned search or critical investigation aimed at discovery of new knowledge.	 Translation of research findings or other knowledge into a plan or design for a new product or process or for a significant improvement to an existing product or process whether intended for sale or use.
Examples Laboratory research aimed at discovery of new knowledge; searching for applications of new research findings.	**Examples** Conceptual formulation and design of possible product or process alternatives; construction of prototypes and operation of pilot plants.

Note that R&D activities do not include routine or periodic alterations to existing products, production lines, manufacturing processes, and other ongoing operations, even though these alterations may represent improvements. For example, routine ongoing efforts to refine, enrich, or improve the qualities of an existing product are not considered R&D activities.

Accounting for R&D Activities

OBJECTIVE 9
Describe the accounting for research and development and similar costs.

The costs associated with R&D activities and the accounting treatments accorded them are as follows.

1. *Materials, Equipment, and Facilities.* Expense the entire costs, **unless the items have alternative future uses** (in other R&D projects or otherwise), in which case carry as inventory and allocate as consumed; or capitalize and depreciate as used.
2. *Personnel.* Expense salaries, wages, and other related costs of personnel engaged in R&D as incurred.
3. *Purchased Intangibles.* Expense the entire cost, **unless the items have alternative future uses** (in other R&D projects or otherwise), in which case capitalize and amortize.
4. *Contract Services.* Expense the costs of services performed by others in connection with the R&D as incurred.
5. *Indirect Costs.* Include a reasonable allocation of indirect costs in R&D costs, except for general and administrative cost, which must be clearly related in order to be included in R&D.[17]

[15] "Accounting for Research and Development Costs," *Statement of Financial Accounting Standards No. 2* (Stamford, Conn.: FASB, 1974), par. 12.

[16] Ibid., par. 8.

[17] Ibid., par. 11.

Consistent with item 1 above, if a company owns a research facility consisting of buildings, laboratories, and equipment that conducts R&D activities and that has alternative future uses (in other R&D projects or otherwise), it should capitalize the facility as an operational asset. The company accounts for depreciation and other costs related to such research facilities as R&D expenses.[18]

To illustrate, assume that Next Century Incorporated develops, produces, and markets laser machines for medical, industrial, and defense uses.[19] Illustration 11-14 lists the types of expenditures related to its laser machine activities, along with the recommended accounting treatment.

ILLUSTRATION 11-14
Sample R&D Expenditures and Their Accounting Treatment

Next Century Incorporated

Type of Expenditure	Accounting Treatment
1. Construction of long-range research facility for use in current and future projects (three-story, 400,000-square-foot building).	Capitalize and depreciate as R&D expense.
2. Acquisition of R&D equipment for use on current project only.	Expense immediately as R&D.
3. Acquisition of machinery to be used on current and future R&D projects.	Capitalize and depreciate as R&D expense.
4. Purchase of materials to be used on current and future R&D projects.	Inventory and allocate to R&D projects; expense as consumed.
5. Salaries of research staff designing new laser bone scanner.	Expense immediately as R&D.
6. Research costs incurred under contract with New Horizon, Inc., and billable monthly.	Record as a receivable (reimbursable expenses).
7. Material, labor, and overhead costs of prototype laser scanner.	Expense immediately as R&D.
8. Costs of testing prototype and design modifications.	Expense immediately as R&D.
9. Legal fees to obtain patent on new laser scanner.	Capitalize as patent and amortize to overhead as part of cost of goods manufactured.
10. Executive salaries.	Expense as operating expense (general and administrative).
11. Cost of marketing research to promote new laser scanner.	Expense as operating expense (selling).
12. Engineering costs incurred to advance the laser scanner to full production stage.	Expense immediately as R&D.
13. Costs of successfully defending patent on laser scanner.	Capitalize as patent and amortize to overhead as part of cost of goods manufactured.
14. Commissions to sales staff marketing new laser scanner.	Expense as operating expense (selling).

[18]Companies in **the extractive industries** can use the following accounting treatment for the unique costs of research, exploration, and development activities and for those costs that are similar to but not classified as R&D costs: (1) expense as incurred, (2) capitalize and either depreciate or amortize over an appropriate period of time, or (3) accumulate as part of inventoriable costs. Choice of the appropriate accounting treatment for such costs is based on the degree of certainty of future benefits and the principle of matching revenues and expenses.

[19]Sometimes companies conduct R&D activities for other companies under a contractual arrangement. In this case, the contract usually specifies that the company performing the R&D work be reimbursed for all direct costs and certain specific indirect costs, plus a profit element. Because reimbursement is expected, the company doing the R&D work records the R&D costs as a receivable. The company for whom the work has been performed reports these costs as R&D and expenses them as incurred.

For a more complete discussion of how an enterprise should account for funding of its R&D by others, see "Research and Development Arrangements," *Statement of Financial Accounting Standards No. 68* (Stamford, Conn.: FASB, 1982).

Other Costs Similar to R&D Costs

Many costs have characteristics similar to research and development costs. Examples are:

1 Start-up costs for a new operation.
2 Initial operating losses.
3 Advertising costs.
4 Computer software costs.

For the most part, these costs are expensed as incurred, similar to the accounting for R&D costs. We briefly explain these costs in the following sections.

Start-Up Costs

Start-up costs are incurred for one-time activities to start a new operation. Examples include opening a new plant, introducing a new product or service, or conducting business in a new territory or with a new class of customers. Start-up costs include **organizational costs**, such as legal and state fees incurred to organize a new business entity.

The accounting for start-up costs is straightforward: **Expense start-up costs as incurred.** The profession recognizes that companies incur start-up costs with the expectation of future revenues or increased efficiencies. However, to determine the amount and timing of future benefits is so difficult that a conservative approach—expensing these costs as incurred—is required.[20]

To illustrate the type of costs that companies expense as start-up costs, assume that U.S.-based Hilo Beverage Company decides to construct a new plant in Brazil. This represents Hilo's first entry into the Brazilian market. As part of its overall strategy, Hilo plans to introduce the company's major U.S. brands into Brazil, on a locally produced basis. The following costs might be involved:

1 Travel-related costs; costs related to employee salaries; and costs related to feasibility studies, accounting, tax, and government affairs.
2 Training of local employees related to product, maintenance, computer systems, finance, and operations.
3 Recruiting, organizing, and training related to establishing a distribution network.

Hilo Beverage should expense all these start-up costs as incurred.

Start-up activities commonly occur at the same time as activities such as the acquisition of assets. For example, as it is incurring start-up costs for the new plant, Hilo also probably is buying or building property, plant, equipment, and inventory. Hilo should not immediately expense the costs of these assets. Instead, it should charge them to operations and report them on the balance sheet using appropriate GAAP reporting guidelines.

Initial Operating Losses

Some contend that companies should be allowed to capitalize initial operating losses incurred in the start-up of a business. They argue that such operating losses are a cost of starting a business and are unavoidable.

For example, assume that Hilo lost money in its first year of operations and wishes to capitalize this loss. Hilo's CEO argues that as the company becomes profitable, it will offset these losses in future periods. What do *you* think? We believe that this approach is unsound, since losses have no future service potential and therefore cannot be considered an asset.

---

[20] "Reporting on the Costs of Start-up Activities," *Statement of Position 98-5* (New York: AICPA, 1998).

GAAP requires that operating losses during the early years should not be capitalized. In short, **the accounting and reporting standards should be no different for an enterprise trying to establish a new business than they are for other enterprises.**[21]

Advertising Costs

Over the years, **PepsiCo** has hired various pop stars, such as Britney Spears and Beyoncé, to advertise its products. How should it report such advertising costs related to its star spokespeople? Pepsi could expense the costs in various ways:

1. When they have completed their singing assignments.
2. The first time the advertising runs.
3. Over the estimated useful life of the advertising.
4. In an appropriate fashion to each of the three periods identified above.
5. Over the period revenues are expected to result.

For the most part, Pepsi must expense advertising costs as incurred or the first time the advertising takes place. These two alternatives are permitted because whichever approach is followed, the results are essentially the same. On the other hand, companies record as assets any tangible assets used in advertising, such as billboards or blimps. The rationale is that such assets do have alternative future uses. Again the

BRANDED

WHAT DO THE NUMBERS MEAN?

For many companies, developing a strong brand image is as important as developing the products they sell. Now more than ever, companies see the power of a strong brand, enhanced by significant and effective advertising investments.

As the following chart indicates, the value of brand investments is substantial. **Coca-Cola** heads the list with an estimated brand value of nearly $70 billion.

The World's 10 Most Valuable Brands
(in billions)

1 **Coca-Cola**	$67.3	6 **Disney**	$27.1
2 **Microsoft**	61.3	7 **McDonald's**	25.0
3 **IBM**	53.8	8 **Nokia**	24.0
4 **GE**	44.1	9 **Toyota**	22.7
5 **Intel**	33.5	10 **Marlboro**	22.1

Source: 2004 data, from Interbrand Corp. and J. P. Morgan Chase.

Occasionally you may find the value of a brand included in a company's financial statements under goodwill. But generally you won't find the estimated values of brands recorded in companies' balance sheets. The reason? The subjectivity that goes into estimating a brand's value. In some cases, analysts base an estimate of brand value on opinion polls or on some multiple of ad spending. In estimating the brand values shown above, **Interbrand Corp.** estimates the percentage of the overall future revenues the brand will generate and then discounts the net cash flows, to arrive at a present value. Some analysts believe that information on brand values is relevant. Others voice valid concerns about the reliability of brand value estimates due to subjectivity in the estimates for revenues, costs, and the risk component of the discount rate.

Source: Adapted from Gerry Khermouch, "The Best Global Brands," *Businessweek* (August 5, 2002), pp. 93–95; and D. Brady, R. D. Hof, and A. Reinhardt, "Cult Brands," *Businessweek Online* (August 2, 2004).

[21]"Accounting and Reporting by Development Stage Enterprises," *Statement of Financial Accounting Standards No. 7* (Stamford, Conn.: FASB, 1975), par. 10. A company is considered to be in the developing stages when it is directing its efforts toward establishing a new business and either the company has not started the principal operations or it has earned no significant revenue.

profession has taken a conservative approach to recording advertising costs because defining and measuring the future benefits can be so difficult.[22]

Computer Software Costs

UNDERLYING CONCEPTS

The requirement that companies expense all R&D costs as incurred is an example of the conflict between relevance and reliability. Here, this requirement leans strongly in support of reliability, as well as conservatism, consistency, and comparability. No attempt is made to match costs and revenues.

A special problem arises in distinguishing R&D costs from selling and administrative activities. The FASB's intent was that companies exclude from the definition of R&D activities the acquisition, development, or improvement of a product or process **for use in their selling or administrative activities.** For example, the costs of software incurred by an airline in improving its computerized reservation system, or the costs incurred in developing a management information system **are not** research and development costs.

Accounting for computer software costs is a specialized and complicated accounting topic.

Conceptual Questions

The requirement that companies expense immediately all R&D costs (as well as start-up costs) incurred internally is a conservative, practical solution. It ensures consistency in practice and uniformity among companies. But the practice of immediately writing off expenditures made in the expectation of benefiting future periods is conceptually incorrect.

Proponents of immediate expensing contend that from an income statement standpoint, long-run application of this standard frequently makes little difference. They argue that because of the ongoing nature of most companies' R&D activities, the amount of R&D cost charged to expense each accounting period is about the same, whether there is immediate expensing or capitalization and subsequent amortization. Others criticize this practice. They believe that the balance sheet should report an intangible asset related to expenditures that have future benefit. To preclude capitalization of all R&D expenditures removes from the balance sheet what may be a company's most valuable asset. This standard represents one of the many trade-offs made among relevance, reliability, and cost-benefit considerations.[23]

PRESENTATION OF INTANGIBLES AND RELATED ITEMS

Presentation of Intangible Assets

OBJECTIVE 10
Indicate the presentation of intangible assets and related items.

The reporting of intangible assets differs from the reporting of property, plant, and equipment in that contra accounts are not normally shown for intangibles. (See Illustration 11-15.) On the balance sheet, companies should report all intangible assets other than goodwill as a separate item. If goodwill is present, companies should report it separately. The FASB concluded that since goodwill and other intangible assets differ significantly from other types of assets, this disclosure benefits users of the balance sheet.

[22]"Reporting on Advertising Costs," *Statement of Position 93-7* (New York: AICPA, 1993). Note that there are some exceptions for immediate expensing of advertising costs when they relate to direct-response advertising, but this subject is beyond the scope of this book.

[23]Research findings indicate that capitalizing R&D costs may be helpful to investors. For example, one study showed a significant relationship between R&D outlays and subsequent benefits in the form of increased productivity, earnings, and shareholder value for R&D–intensive companies. Baruch Lev and Theodore Sougiannis, "The Capitalization, Amortization, and Value-Relevance of R&D," *Journal of Accounting and Economics* (February 1996).

Another study found that there was a significant decline in earnings usefulness for companies that were forced to switch from capitalizing to expensing R&D costs, and that the decline appears to persist over time. Martha L. Loudder and Bruce K. Behn, "Alternative Income Determination Rules and Earnings Usefulness: The Case of R&D Costs," *Contemporary Accounting Research* (Fall 1995).

On the income statement, companies should present amortization expense and impairment losses for intangible assets other than goodwill as part of continuing operations. Goodwill impairment losses should also be presented as a separate line item in the continuing operations section, unless the goodwill impairment is associated with a discontinued operation.

ILLUSTRATION 11-15
Intangible Asset Disclosures

HARBAUGH COMPANY

Balance Sheet (partial)
(in thousands)

Intangible Assets (Note C)	$3,840
Goodwill (Note D)	2,575

Income Statement (partial)
(in thousands)

as part of Continuing operations

Amortization expense	$380
Impairment losses (goodwill)	46

Note C: Acquired Intangible Assets

	As of December 31, 2007	
	Gross Carrying Amount	Accumulated Amortization
Amortized intangible assets		
Trademark	$2,000	$(100)
Customer list	500	(310)
Other	60	(10)
Total	$2,560	$(420)
Unamortized intangible assets		
Licenses	$1,300	
Trademark	400	
Total	$1,700	

Aggregate Amortization Expense

For year ended 12/31/07	$380

Estimated Amortization Expense

For year ended 12/31/08	$200
For year ended 12/31/09	90
For year ended 12/31/10	70
For year ended 12/31/11	60
For year ended 12/31/12	50

Note D: Goodwill

The changes in the carrying amount of goodwill for the year ended December 31, 2007, are as follows:

($000s)	Technology Segment	Communications Segment	Total
Balance as of January 1, 2007	$1,413	$904	$2,317
Goodwill acquired during year	189	115	304
Impairment losses	—	(46)	(46)
Balance as of December 31, 2007	$1,602	$973	$2,575

The Communications segment is tested for impairment in the third quarter, after the annual forecasting process. Due to an increase in competition in the Texas and Louisiana cable industry, operating profits and cash flows were lower than expected in the fourth quarter of 2006 and the first and second quarters of 2007. Based on that trend, the earnings forecast for the next 5 years was revised. In September 2007, a goodwill impairment loss of $46 was recognized in the Communications reporting unit. The fair value of that reporting unit was estimated using the expected present value of future cash flows.

The notes to the financial statements should include information about acquired intangible assets, including the aggregate amortization expense for each of the succeeding 5 years. The notes should include information about changes in the carrying amount of goodwill during the period. As noted earlier, Illustration 11-15 shows the type of disclosure made related to intangible assets in the financial statements and related notes for Harbaugh Company.

Presentation of Research and Development Costs

wiley.com/college/kieso

Additional Disclosures of Intangibles and R&D Costs

Acceptable accounting practice requires that companies disclose in the financial statements (generally in the notes) the total R&D costs charged to expense each period for which they present an income statement. **Merck & Co., Inc.**, a global research pharmaceutical company, reported both internal and acquired research and development in its recent income statement, as shown in Illustration 11-16.

ILLUSTRATION 11-16
Income Statement Disclosure of R&D Costs

Merck & Co., Inc.

(in millions)	Years Ended December 31		
	2004	2003	2002
Sales	$22,938.6	$22,485.9	$21,445.8
Costs, expenses, and other			
Materials and production	4,959.8	4,436.9	4,004.9
Marketing and administrative	7,346.3	6,394.9	5,652.2
Research and development	4,010.2	3,279.9	2,677.2
Equity income from affiliates	(1,008.2)	(474.2)	(644.7)
Other (income) expense, net	(344.0)	(203.2)	104.5
	$14,964.1	$13,434.3	$11,794.1

In addition, Merck provides a discussion about R&D expenditures in its annual report, as shown in Illustration 11-17.

ILLUSTRATION 11-17
Merck's R&D Disclosure

Merck & Co., Inc.

Research and development in the pharmaceutical industry is inherently a long-term process. The following data show an unbroken trend of year-to-year increases in the Company's research and development spending. For the period 1995 to 2004, the compounded annual growth rate in research and development was 13%.

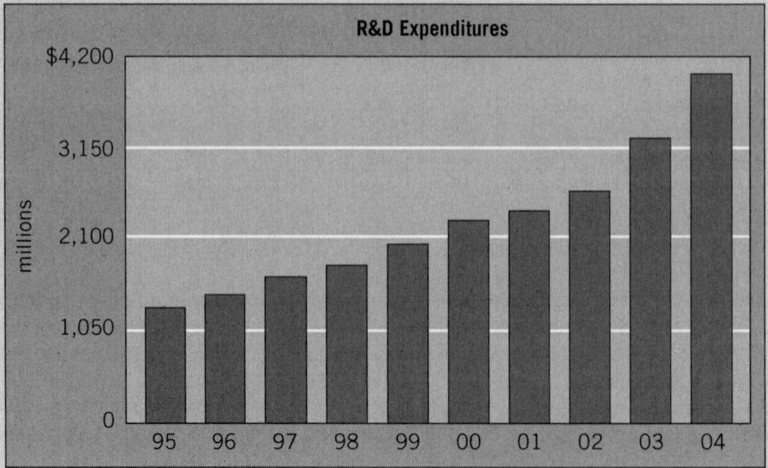

QUESTIONS

1. What are the two main characteristics of intangible assets?
2. If intangibles are acquired for stock, how is the cost of the intangible determined?
3. Intangibles have either a limited useful life or an indefinite useful life. How should these two different types of intangibles be amortized?
4. Why does the accounting profession make a distinction between internally created intangibles and purchased intangibles?
5. In 2006 Sheila Wright Corp. spent $420,000 for "goodwill" visits by sales personnel to key customers. The purpose of these visits was to build a solid, friendly relationship for the future and to gain insight into the problems and needs of the companies served. How should this expenditure be reported?
6. What are factors to be considered in estimating the useful life of an intangible asset?
7. What should be the pattern of amortization for a limited-life intangible?
8. **Columbia Sportswear Company** acquired a trademark that is helpful in distinguishing one of its new products. The trademark is renewable every 10 years at minimal cost. All evidence indicates that this trademark product will generate cash flows for an indefinite period of time. How should this trademark be amortized?
9. Michael Redd Company spent $190,000 developing a new process, $45,000 in legal fees to obtain a patent, and $91,000 to market the process that was patented, all in the year 2006. How should these costs be accounted for in 2006?
10. Yellow 3 purchased a patent for $450,000 which has an estimated useful life of 10 years. Its pattern of use or consumption cannot be reliably determined. Prepare the entry to record the amortization of the patent in its first year of use.
11. Explain the difference between artistic-related intangible assets and contract-related intangible assets.
12. What is goodwill? What is negative goodwill?
13. Under what circumstances is it appropriate to record goodwill in the accounts? How should goodwill, properly recorded on the books, be written off in order to conform with generally accepted accounting principles?
14. In examining financial statements, financial analysts often write off goodwill immediately. Evaluate this procedure.
15. Astaire Inc. is considering the write-off of a limited life intangible because of its lack of profitability. Explain to the management of Astaire how to determine whether a write-off is permitted.
16. Last year Blair Company recorded an impairment on an intangible asset held for use. Recent appraisals indicate that the asset has increased in value. Should Blair record this recovery in value?
17. Explain how losses on impaired intangible assets should be reported in income.
18. Mills Company determines that its goodwill is impaired. It finds that its implied goodwill is $380,000 and its recorded goodwill is $400,000. The fair value of its identifiable assets is $1,450,000. What is the amount of goodwill impaired?
19. What is the nature of research and development costs?
20. Research and development activities may include (a) personnel costs, (b) materials and equipment costs, and (c) indirect costs. What is the recommended accounting treatment for these three types of R&D costs?
21. Which of the following activities should be expensed currently as R&D costs?
    (a) Testing in search for or evaluation of product or process alternatives.
    (b) Engineering follow-through in an early phase of commercial production.
    (c) Legal work in connection with patent applications or litigation, and the sale or licensing of patents.
22. Indicate the proper accounting for the following items.
    (a) Organization costs.
    (b) Advertising costs.
    (c) Operating losses.
23. In 2005, Cassie Logan Corporation developed a new product that will be marketed in 2006. In connection with the development of this product, the following costs were incurred in 2005: research and development costs $420,000; materials and supplies consumed $60,000; and compensation paid to research consultants $125,000. It is anticipated that these costs will be recovered in 2008. What is the amount of research and development costs that Cassie Logan should record in 2005 as a charge to expense?
24. Recently, a group of university students decided to incorporate for the purposes of selling a process to recycle the waste product from manufacturing cheese. Some of the initial costs involved were legal fees and office expenses incurred in starting the business, state incorporation fees, and stamp taxes. One student wishes to charge these costs against revenue in the current period. Another wishes to defer these costs and amortize them in the future. Which student is correct?
25. An intangible asset with an estimated useful life of 30 years was acquired on January 1, 1996, for $450,000. On January 1, 2006, a review was made of intangible assets and their expected service lives, and it was determined that this asset had an estimated useful life of 30 more years from the date of the review. What is the amount of amortization for this intangible in 2006?

C H A P T E R T W E L V E

CURRENT LIABILITIES AND CONTINGENCIES

Now You See It, Now You Don't

A look at the liabilities side of the balance sheet of the German company **Beru AG Corporation**, dated March 31, 2003, shows how international standards are changing the reporting of financial information. Here is how one liability was shown on this date:

Anticipated losses arising from pending transactions	3,285,000 euros

Do you believe a liability should be reported for such transactions? *Anticipated losses* means the losses have not yet occurred; *pending transactions* mean that the condition that might cause the loss has also not occurred. So where is the liability? To whom does the company owe something? Where is the obligation?

U.S. GAAP provides guidance on this subject. A company can accrue a liability for a contingency only if an obligation has arisen from a past event, if payment is probable, and if the company can reasonably estimate the obligation. In short, under U.S. GAAP, companies cannot accrue anticipated future losses today.

German accounting rules are more permissive. They permit companies to report liabilities for possible future events. In essence, the establishment of this general-purpose "liability" provides a buffer for Beru if losses do materialize. If you take a more skeptical view, you might say the accounting rules let Beru smooth its income by charging expenses in good years and reducing expenses in bad years.

The story has a happy ending, from a U.S. accounting point of view. As we indicated earlier in the text, European companies switched to International Financial Reporting Standards (IFRS) in 2005. Because IFRS are similar to U.S. GAAP, liabilities like "Anticipated losses from pending transactions" disappear. So when we look at Beru's 2005 financial statements, we find a note stating that the company has reported as liabilities only obligations arising from past transactions that can be reasonably estimated.

Learning Objectives

After studying this chapter, you should be able to:

1. Describe the nature, type, and valuation of current liabilities.
2. Explain the classification issues of short-term debt expected to be refinanced.
3. Identify types of employee-related liabilities.
4. Identify the criteria used to account for and disclose gain and loss contingencies.
5. Explain the accounting for different types of loss contingencies.
6. Indicate how to present and analyze liabilities and contingencies.

PREVIEW OF CHAPTER 12

As our opening story indicates, the convergence of U.S. GAAP with IFRS should lead to improved reporting of liabilities. In this chapter we explain the basic issues related to accounting and reporting for current and contingent liabilities. The content and organization of the chapter are as follows.

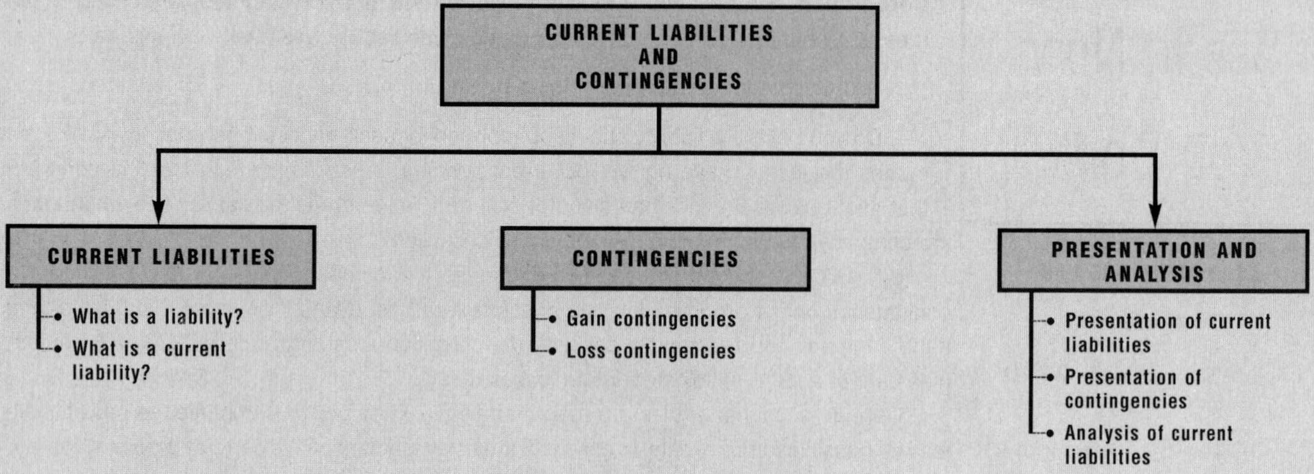

SECTION 1 | *CURRENT LIABILITIES*

WHAT IS A LIABILITY?

UNDERLYING CONCEPTS

To determine the appropriate classification of specific financial instruments, companies need proper definitions of assets, liabilities, and equities. They often use the conceptual framework definitions as the basis for resolving controversial classification issues.

The question, "What is a liability?" is not easy to answer. For example, is preferred stock a liability or an ownership claim? The first reaction is to say that preferred stock is in fact an ownership claim, and companies should report it as part of stockholders' equity. In fact, preferred stock has many elements of debt as well.[1] The issuer (and in some cases the holder) often has the right to call the stock within a specific period of time—making it similar to a repayment of principal. The dividend on the preferred stock is in many cases almost guaranteed (the cumulative provision)—making it look like interest. As a result, preferred stock is but one of many financial instruments that are difficult to classify.[2]

To help resolve some of these controversies, the FASB, as part of its conceptual framework study, defined **liabilities** as **"probable future sacrifices of economic benefits arising from present obligations of a particular entity to transfer assets**

[1]This illustration is not just a theoretical exercise. In practice, a number of preferred stock issues have all the characteristics of a debt instrument, except that they are called and legally classified as preferred stock. In some cases, the IRS has even permitted companies to treat the dividend payments as interest expense for tax purposes.

[2]The FASB has issued a new standard for addressing this issue: "Accounting for Certain Financial Instruments with Characteristics of Both Liabilities and Equity," *Statement of Financial Accounting Standards No. 150* (Norwalk, Conn.: FASB, 2003).

or provide services to other entities in the future as a result of past transactions or events."[3] In other words, a liability has three essential characteristics:

1. It is a present obligation that entails settlement by probable future transfer or use of cash, goods, or services.
2. It is an unavoidable obligation.
3. The transaction or other event creating the obligation has already occurred.

Because liabilities involve future disbursements of assets or services, one of their most important features is the date on which they are payable. A company must satisfy currently maturing obligations in the ordinary course of business to continue operating. Liabilities with a more distant due date do not, as a rule, represent a claim on the company's current resources. They are therefore in a slightly different category. This feature gives rise to the basic division of liabilities into (1) current liabilities and (2) long-term debt.

WHAT IS A CURRENT LIABILITY?

OBJECTIVE 1
Describe the nature, type, and valuation of current liabilities.

Recall that current assets are cash or other assets that companies reasonably expect to convert into cash, sell, or consume in operations within a single operating cycle or within a year (if completing more than one cycle each year). **Current liabilities** are **"obligations whose liquidation is reasonably expected to require use of existing resources properly classified as current assets, or the creation of other current liabilities."[4]** This definition has gained wide acceptance because it recognizes operating cycles of varying lengths in different industries. This definition also considers the important relationship between current assets and current liabilities.[5]

The **operating cycle** is the period of time elapsing between the acquisition of goods and services involved in the manufacturing process and the final cash realization resulting from sales and subsequent collections. Industries that manufacture products requiring an aging process, and certain capital-intensive industries, have an operating cycle of considerably more than one year. On the other hand, most retail and service establishments have several operating cycles within a year.

Here are some typical current liabilities:

1. Accounts payable.
2. Notes payable.
3. Current maturities of long-term debt.
4. Short-term obligations expected to be refinanced.
5. Dividends payable.
6. Customer advances and deposits.
7. Unearned revenues.
8. Sales taxes payable.
9. Income taxes payable.
10. Employee-related liabilities.

Accounts Payable

Accounts payable, or **trade accounts payable**, are balances owed to others for goods, supplies, or services purchased on open account. Accounts payable arise because of the time lag between the receipt of services or acquisition of title to assets and the payment

[3]"Elements of Financial Statements of Business Enterprises," *Statement of Financial Accounting Concepts No. 6* (Stamford, Conn.: FASB, 1980).

[4]Committee on Accounting Procedure, American Institute of Certified Public Accountants, "Accounting Research and Terminology Bulletins," Final Edition (New York: AICPA, 1961), p. 21.

[5]The FASB affirmed this concept of "maturity within one year or the operating cycle whichever is longer" in its definition of short-term obligations in *Statement No. 6*. "Classification of Short-term Obligations Expected to Be Refinanced," *Statement of Financial Accounting Standards No. 6* (Stamford, Conn.: FASB, 1975), par. 2.

for them. The terms of the sale (e.g., 2/10, n/30 or 1/10, E.O.M.) usually state this period of extended credit, commonly 30 to 60 days.

Most companies record liabilities for purchases of goods upon receipt of the goods. If title has passed to the purchaser before receipt of the goods, the company should record the transaction at the time of title passage. A company must pay special attention to transactions occurring near the end of one accounting period and at the beginning of the next. It needs to ascertain that the record of goods received (the inventory) agrees with the liability (accounts payable), and that it records both in the proper period.

Measuring the amount of an account payable poses no particular difficulty. The invoice received from the creditor specifies the due date and the exact outlay in money that is necessary to settle the account. The only calculation that may be necessary concerns the amount of cash discount. See Chapter 7 for illustrations of entries related to accounts payable and purchase discounts.

Notes Payable

Notes payable are written promises to pay a certain sum of money on a specified future date. They may arise from purchases, financing, or other transactions. Some industries require notes (often referred to as **trade notes payable**) as part of the sales/purchases transaction in lieu of the normal extension of open account credit. Notes payable to banks or loan companies generally arise from cash loans. Companies classify notes as short-term or long-term, depending on the payment due date. Notes may also be interest-bearing or zero-interest-bearing.

Interest-Bearing Note Issued

Assume that Castle National Bank agrees to lend $100,000 on March 1, 2007, to Landscape Co. if Landscape signs a $100,000, 6 percent, four-month note. Landscape records the cash received on March 1 as follows:

March 1		
Cash	100,000	
Notes Payable		100,000
(To record issuance of 6%, 4-month note to Castle National Bank)		

If Landscape prepares financial statements semiannually, it makes the following adjusting entry to recognize interest expense and interest payable of $2,000 ($100,000 × 6% × 4/12) at June 30:

June 30		
Interest Expense	2,000	
Interest Payable		2,000
(To accrue interest for 4 months on Castle National Bank note)		

If Landscape prepares financial statements monthly, its adjusting entry at the end of each month is $500 ($100,000 × 6% × 1/12).

At maturity (July 1), Landscape must pay the face value of the note ($100,000) plus $2,000 interest ($100,000 × 6% × 4/12). Landscape records payment of the note and accrued interest as follows.

July 1		
Notes Payable	100,000	
Interest Payable	2,000	
Cash		102,000
(To record payment of Castle National Bank interest-bearing note and accrued interest at maturity)		

Zero-Interest-Bearing Note Issued

A company may issue a zero-interest-bearing note instead of an interest-bearing note. A zero-interest-bearing note does not explicitly state an interest rate on the face of the note. **Interest is still charged**, however. At maturity the borrower must pay back an amount greater than the cash received at the issuance date. In other words, the borrower receives in cash the present value of the note. The present value equals the face value of the note at maturity minus the interest or discount charged by the lender for the term of the note. In essence, the bank takes its fee "up front" rather than on the date the note matures.

To illustrate, assume that Landscape issues a $102,000, four-month, zero-interest-bearing note to Castle National Bank. The present value of the note is $100,000.[6] Landscape records this transaction as follows.

March 1		
Cash	100,000	
Discount on Notes Payable	2,000	
Notes Payable		102,000
(To record issuance of 4-month, zero-interest-bearing note to Castle National Bank)		

Landscape credits the Notes Payable account for the face value of the note, which is $2,000 more than the actual cash received. It debits the difference between the cash received and the face value of the note to Discount on Notes Payable. **Discount on Notes Payable is a contra account to Notes Payable, and therefore is subtracted from Notes Payable on the balance sheet.** Illustration 12-1 shows the balance sheet presentation on March 1.

ILLUSTRATION 12-1
Balance Sheet Presentation of Discount

Current liabilities		
Notes payable	102,000	
Less: Discount on notes payable	2,000	100,000

The amount of the discount, $2,000 in this case, represents the cost of borrowing $100,000 for 4 months. Accordingly, Landscape charges the discount to interest expense over the life of the note. That is, the Discount on Notes Payable balance **represents interest expense chargeable to future periods**. Thus, Landscape should not debit Interest Expense for $2,000 at the time of obtaining the loan. We discuss additional accounting issues related to notes payable in Chapter 13.

Current Maturities of Long-Term Debt

PepsiCo reports as part of its current liabilities the portion of bonds, mortgage notes, and other long-term indebtedness that matures within the next fiscal year. It categorizes this amount as **current maturities of long-term debt**. Companies, like PepsiCo, exclude long-term debts maturing currently as current liabilities if they are to be:

1. retired by assets accumulated for this purpose that properly have not been shown as current assets,
2. refinanced, or retired from the proceeds of a new debt issue, or
3. converted into capital stock.

In these situations, the use of current assets or the creation of other current liabilities does not occur. Therefore, classification as a current liability is inappropriate. A company should disclose the plan for liquidation of such a debt either parenthetically or by a note to the financial statements. When only a part of a long-term debt is to be

[6]The bank discount rate used in this example to find the present value is 5.96 percent.

paid within the next 12 months, as in the case of serial bonds that it retires through a series of annual installments, **the company reports the maturing portion of long-term debt as a current liability,** and the remaining portion as a long-term debt.

However, a company should classify as current any liability that is **due on demand** (callable by the creditor) or will be due on demand within a year (or operating cycle, if longer). Liabilities often become callable by the creditor when there is a violation of the debt agreement. For example, most debt agreements specify a given level of equity to debt be maintained, or specify that working capital be of a minimum amount. If the company violates an agreement, it must classify the debt as current because it is a reasonable expectation that existing working capital will be used to satisfy the debt. Only if a company can show that it is **probable** that it will cure (satisfy) the violation within the grace period specified in the agreements can it classify the debt as noncurrent.[7]

Short-Term Obligations Expected to Be Refinanced

OBJECTIVE 2
Explain the classification issues of short-term debt expected to be refinanced.

Short-term obligations are debts scheduled to mature within one year after the date of a company's balance sheet or within its operating cycle, whichever is longer. Some **short-term obligations** are **expected to be refinanced** on a long-term basis. These short-term obligations will not require the use of working capital during the next year (or operating cycle).[8]

At one time, the accounting profession generally supported the exclusion of short-term obligations from current liabilities if they were "expected to be refinanced." But the profession provided no specific guidelines, so companies determined whether a short-term obligation was "expected to be refinanced" based solely on management's **intent** to refinance on a long-term basis. Classification was not clear-cut. For example, a company might obtain a five-year bank loan but handle the actual financing with 90-day notes, which it must keep turning over (renewing). In this case, is the loan a long-term debt or a current liability? Another example was the **Penn Central Railroad** before it went bankrupt. The railroad was deep into short-term debt but classified it as long-term debt. Why? Because the railroad believed it had commitments from lenders to keep refinancing the short-term debt. When those commitments suddenly disappeared, it was "good-bye Pennsy." As the Greek philosopher Epictetus once said, "Some things in this world are not and yet appear to be."

Refinancing Criteria

To resolve these classification problems, the accounting profession has developed authoritative criteria for determining the circumstances under which short-term obligations may be properly excluded from current liabilities. A company is required to exclude a short-term obligation from current liabilities if **both** of the following conditions are met:

1 It must **intend to refinance** the obligation on a long-term basis.
2 It must **demonstrate an ability** to consummate the refinancing.[9]

Intention to refinance on a long-term basis means that the company intends to refinance the short-term obligation so that it will not require the use of working capital during the ensuing fiscal year (or operating cycle, if longer).

---

[7]"Classification of Obligations That Are Callable by the Creditor," *Statement of Financial Accounting Standards No. 78* (Stamford, Conn.: FASB, 1983).

[8]*Refinancing a short-term obligation on a long-term basis* means either replacing it with a long-term obligation or equity securities, or renewing, extending, or replacing it with short-term obligations for an uninterrupted period extending beyond one year (or the operating cycle, if longer) from the date of the enterprise's balance sheet.

[9]"Classification of Short-term Obligations Expected to Be Refinanced," *Statement of Financial Accounting Standards No. 6* (Stamford, Conn.: FASB, 1975), pars. 10 and 11.

The company demonstrates the **ability** to consummate the refinancing by:

(a) **Actually refinancing** the short-term obligation by issuing a long-term obligation or equity securities after the date of the balance sheet but before it is issued; or

(b) Entering into a **financing agreement** that clearly permits the company to refinance the debt on a long-term basis on terms that are readily determinable.

If an actual refinancing occurs, the portion of the short-term obligation to be excluded from current liabilities may not exceed the proceeds from the new obligation or equity securities used to retire the short-term obligation. For example, **Montavon Winery** had \$3,000,000 of short-term debt. Subsequent to the balance sheet date, but before issuing the balance sheet, the company issued 100,000 shares of common stock, intending to use the proceeds to liquidate the short-term debt at its maturity. If Montavon's net proceeds from the sale of the 100,000 shares total \$2,000,000, it can exclude from current liabilities only \$2,000,000 of the short-term debt.

An additional question is whether a company should exclude from current liabilities a short-term obligation if it is paid off after the balance sheet date and replaced by long-term debt before the balance sheet is issued. To illustrate, Marquardt Company pays off short-term debt of \$40,000 on January 17, 2008, and issues long-term debt of \$100,000 on February 3, 2008. Marquardt's financial statements, dated December 31, 2007, are to be issued March 1, 2008. Should Marquardt exclude the \$40,000 short-term debt from current liabilities? No—here's why: Repayment of the short-term obligation required the use of **existing** current assets **before** the company obtained funds through long-term financing. Therefore, Marquardt must include the short-term obligations in current liabilities at the balance sheet date (see graphical presentation below).

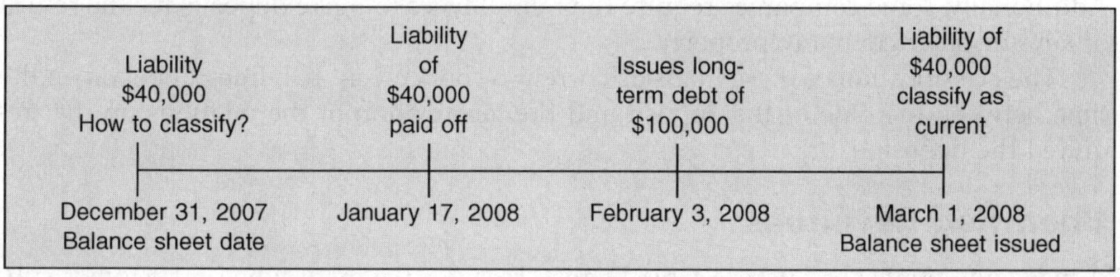

ILLUSTRATION 12-2
Short-Term Debt Paid Off after Balance Sheet Date and Later Replaced by Long-Term Debt

WHAT ABOUT THAT SHORT-TERM DEBT?

WHAT DO THE NUMBERS MEAN?

The evaluation of credit quality involves more than simply assessing a company's ability to repay loans. Credit analysts also evaluate debt management strategies. Analysts and investors will reward what they view as prudent management decisions with lower debt service costs and a higher stock price. The wrong decisions can bring higher debt costs and lower stock prices.

General Electric Capital Corp., a subsidiary of **General Electric**, recently experienced the negative effects of market scrutiny of its debt management policies. Analysts complained that GE had been slow to refinance its mountains of short-term debt. GE had issued these current obligations, with maturities of 270 days or less, when interest rates were low. However, in light of expectations that the Fed would raise interest rates, analysts began to worry about the higher interest costs GE would pay when it refinanced these loans. Some analysts recommended that it was time to reduce dependence on short-term credit. The reasoning goes that a shift to more dependable long-term debt, thereby locking in slightly higher rates for the long-term, is the better way to go.

Thus, scrutiny of GE debt strategies led to analysts' concerns about GE's earnings prospects. Investors took the analysis to heart, and GE experienced a 2-day 6 percent drop in its stock price.

Source: Adapted from Steven Vames, "Credit Quality, Stock Investing Seem to Go Hand in Hand," *Wall Street Journal* (April 1, 2002), p. R4.

Dividends Payable

UNDERLYING CONCEPTS

Preferred dividends in arrears do represent a probable future economic sacrifice, but the expected sacrifice does not result from a past transaction or past event. The sacrifice will result from a future event (declaration by the board of directors). Note disclosure improves the predictive value of the financial statements.

A **cash dividend payable** is an amount owed by a corporation to its stockholders as a result of board of directors' authorization. At the date of declaration the corporation assumes a liability that places the stockholders in the position of creditors in the amount of dividends declared. Because companies always pay cash dividends within one year of declaration (generally within three months), they classify them as current liabilities.

On the other hand, companies do not recognize accumulated but undeclared dividends on cumulative preferred stock as a liability. Why? Because **preferred dividends in arrears** are not an obligation until the board of directors authorizes the payment Nevertheless, companies should disclose the amount of cumulative dividends unpaid in a note, or show it parenthetically in the capital stock section.

Dividends payable in the form of additional shares of stock are not recognized as a liability. Such **stock dividends** (as we discuss in Chapter 14) do not require future outlays of assets or services. Companies generally report such undistributed stock dividends in the stockholders' equity section because they represent retained earnings in the process of transfer to paid-in capital.

Customer Advances and Deposits

Current liabilities may include **returnable cash deposits** received from customers and employees. Companies may receive deposits from customers to guarantee performance of a contract or service or as guarantees to cover payment of expected future obligations. For example, a company like **Alltel Corp.** often requires a deposit on equipment that customers use to connect to the Internet or to access its other services. Alltel also may receive deposits from customers as guarantees for possible damage to property. Additionally, some companies require their employees to make deposits for the return of keys or other company property.

The classification of these items as current or noncurrent liabilities depends on the time between the date of the deposit and the termination of the relationship that required the deposit.

Unearned Revenues

A magazine publisher, such as **Golf Digest**, receives payment when a customer subscribes to its magazines. An airline company, such as **American Airlines**, sells tickets for future flights. And software companies, like **Microsoft**, issue coupons that allow customers to upgrade to the next version of their software. How do these companies account for **unearned revenues** that they receive before delivering goods or rendering services?

1 Upon receipt of the advance, debit Cash, and credit a current liability account identifying the source of the unearned revenue.

2 Upon earning the revenue, debit the unearned revenue account, and credit an earned revenue account.

To illustrate, assume that Allstate University sells 10,000 season football tickets at $50 each for its five-game home schedule. Allstate University records the sales of season tickets as follows:

August 6		
Cash	500,000	
Unearned Football Ticket Revenue		500,000
(To record sale of 10,000 season tickets)		

After each game, Allstate University makes the following entry.

September 7		
Unearned Football Ticket Revenue	100,000	
Football Ticket Revenue		100,000
(To record football ticket revenues earned)		

Unearned Football Ticket Revenue is, therefore, unearned revenue. Allstate University reports it as a current liability in the balance sheet. As revenue is earned, a transfer from unearned revenue to earned revenue occurs. Unearned revenue is material for some companies: In the airline industry, tickets sold for future flights represent almost 50 percent of total current liabilities.

Illustration 12-3 shows specific unearned and earned revenue accounts used in selected types of businesses.

ILLUSTRATION 12-3
Unearned and Earned Revenue Accounts

Type of Business	Account Title: Unearned Revenue	Account Title: Earned Revenue
Airline	Unearned Passenger Ticket Revenue	Passenger Revenue
Magazine publisher	Unearned Subscription Revenue	Subscription Revenue
Hotel	Unearned Rental Revenue	Rental Revenue
Auto dealer	Unearned Warranty Revenue	Warranty Revenue
Retailers	Unearned Gift Card Revenue	Sales Revenue

The balance sheet should report obligations for any commitments that are redeemable in goods and services. The income statement should report revenues earned during the period.

MICROSOFT'S LIABILITIES—GOOD OR BAD?

WHAT DO THE NUMBERS MEAN?

Users of financial statements generally examine current liabilities to assess a company's liquidity and overall financial flexibility. Companies must pay many current liabilities, such as accounts payable, wages payable, and taxes payable, sooner rather than later. A substantial increase in these liabilities should raise a red flag about a company's financial position.

This is not the case for all current liabilities. For example, **Microsoft** has a current liability entitled "Unearned revenue" that has increased substantially year after year. Unearned revenue is a liability that arises from sales of Microsoft products such as *Windows* and *Office*. At the time of a sale, customers pay not only for the current version of the software but also for future upgrades. Microsoft recognizes sales revenue from the current version of the software and records as a liability (unearned revenue) the value of future upgrades to the software that it "owes" to customers.

Market analysts read such an increase in unearned revenue as a positive signal about Microsoft's sales and profitability. When Microsoft's sales are growing, its unearned revenue account increases. Thus, an *increase* in a liability is good news about Microsoft sales. At the same time, a decline in unearned revenue is bad news. As one analyst noted, a slowdown or reversal of the growth in Microsoft's unearned revenues indicates slowing sales, which is bad news for investors. Thus, increases in current liabilities can sometimes be viewed as good signs instead of bad.

Source: Adapted from David Bank, "Some Fans Cool to Microsoft, Citing Drop in Old Indicator," *Wall Street Journal* (October 28, 1999).

Sales Taxes Payable

Retailers like **Wal-Mart**, **Circuit City**, and **Gap** must collect sales taxes from customers on transfers of tangible personal property and on certain services and then must remit these taxes to the proper governmental authority. GAP, for example, sets up a liability to provide for taxes collected from customers but not yet remitted to the tax authority. The Sales Taxes Payable account should reflect the liability for sales taxes due various governments.

The entry below illustrates use of the Sales Taxes Payable account on a sale of $3,000 when a 4 percent sales tax is in effect.

Cash or Accounts Receivable	3,120	
Sales		3,000
Sales Taxes Payable		120

Sometimes the sales tax collections credited to the liability account are not equal to the liability as computed by the governmental formula. In such a case, GAP makes an adjustment of the liability account by recognizing a gain or a loss on sales tax collections.

Many companies do not segregate the sales tax and the amount of the sale at the time of sale. Instead, the company credits both amounts in total in the Sales account. Then, to reflect correctly the actual amount of sales and the liability for sales taxes, the company would debit the Sales account for the amount of the sales taxes due the government on these sales, and would credit the Sales Taxes Payable account for the same amount.

To illustrate, assume that the Sales account balance of $150,000 includes sales taxes of 4 percent. Thus, the amount recorded in the Sales account is comprised of the sales amount plus sales tax of 4 percent of the sales amount. Sales therefore are $144,230.77 ($150,000 ÷ 1.04) and the sales tax liability is $5,769.23 ($144,230.77 × 0.04; or $150,000 − $144,230.77). The following entry would record the amount due the taxing unit.

Sales	5,769.23	
Sales Taxes Payable		5,769.23

Income Taxes Payable

Expanded Discussion of Property Taxes Payable

Any federal or state income tax varies in proportion to the amount of annual income. Using the best information and advice available, a business must prepare an income tax return and compute the income tax payable resulting from the operations of the current period. Corporations should classify as a current liability the taxes payable on net income, as computed per the tax return.[10] Unlike a corporation, proprietorships and partnerships are not taxable entities. Because the individual proprietor and the members of a partnership are subject to personal income taxes on their share of the business's taxable income, income tax liabilities do not appear on the financial statements of proprietorships and partnerships.

Most corporations must make periodic tax payments throughout the year in an authorized bank depository or a Federal Reserve Bank. These payments are based upon estimates of the total annual tax liability. As the estimated total tax liability changes, the periodic contributions also change. If in a later year the taxing authority assesses an additional tax on the income of an earlier year, the company should credit Income Taxes Payable and charge the related debit to current operations.

Differences between taxable income under the tax laws and accounting income under generally accepted accounting principles sometimes occur. Because of these differences, the amount of income tax payable to the government in any given year may differ substantially from income tax expense as reported on the financial statements. Chapter 17 is devoted solely to income tax matters and presents an extensive discussion of this complex topic.

Employee-Related Liabilities

OBJECTIVE 3
Identify types of employee-related liabilities.

Companies also report as a current liability amounts owed to employees for salaries or wages at the end of an accounting period. In addition, they often also report as current liabilities the following items related to employee compensation.

[10] Corporate taxes are based on a progressive tax rate structure. Companies with taxable income of $50,000 or less are taxed at a 15 percent rate; higher levels of income are taxed at rates ranging up to 39 percent.

1 Payroll deductions.
2 Compensated absences.
3 Bonuses.

Payroll Deductions

The most common types of payroll deductions are taxes, insurance premiums, employee savings, and union dues. **To the extent that a company has not remitted the amounts deducted to the proper authority at the end of the accounting period, it should recognize them as current liabilities.**

Social Security Taxes. Since January 1, 1937, Social Security legislation has provided federal old age, survivor, and disability insurance (O.A.S.D.I.) benefits for certain individuals and their families. Funds for these payments come from taxes levied on both the employer and the employee. Employers collect the employee's share of this tax by deducting it from the employee's gross pay, and remit it to the government along with their share. The government taxes both the employer and the employee at the same rate, currently 6.2 percent based on the employee's gross pay up to a $90,000 annual limit. The O.A.S.D.I. tax is usually referred to as F.I.C.A. (the Federal Insurance Contribution Act).

In 1965 Congress passed the first federal health insurance program for the aged—popularly known as **Medicare**. This two-part program alleviates the high cost of medical care for those over age 65. A separate Hospital Insurance tax, paid by both the employee and the employer at the rate of 1.45 percent on the employee's total compensation, finances the Basic Plan, which provides hospital and other institutional services. The Voluntary Plan covers the major part of doctors' bills and other medical and health services. Monthly payments from all who enroll, plus matching funds from the federal government, finance this plan.

The combination of the O.A.S.D.I. tax (F.I.C.A.) and the federal Hospital Insurance Tax is commonly referred to as the **Social Security tax**. The combined rate for these taxes, 7.65 percent on an employee's wages to $90,000 and 1.45 percent in excess of $90,000, changes intermittently by acts of Congress. **Companies should report the amount of unremitted employee and employer Social Security tax on gross wages paid as a current liability.**

Unemployment Taxes. Another payroll tax levied by the federal government in cooperation with state governments provides a system of unemployment insurance. All employers who meet the following criteria are subject to the Federal Unemployment Tax Act (F.U.T.A.): (1) those who paid wages of $1,500 or more during any calendar quarter in the year or preceding year, or (2) those who employed at least one individual on at least one day in each of 20 weeks during the current or preceding calendar year.

Only employers pay the unemployment tax. The rate of this tax is 6.2 percent on the first $7,000 of compensation paid to each employee during the calendar year. The employer receives a tax credit not to exceed 5.4 percent for contributions paid to a state plan for unemployment compensation. Thus, if an employer is subject to a state unemployment tax of 5.4 percent or more, it pays only 0.8 percent tax to the federal government.

State unemployment compensation laws differ both from the federal law and among various states. Therefore, employers must refer to the unemployment tax laws in each state in which they pay wages and salaries. The normal state tax may range from 3 percent to 7 percent or higher. However, all states provide for some form of **merit rating**, which reduces the state contribution rate. Employers who display by their benefit and contribution experience that they provide steady employment may receive this reduction—if the size of the state fund is adequate. In order not to penalize an employer who has earned a reduction in the state contribution rate, federal law allows a credit of 5.4 percent, even when the effective state contribution rate is less than 5.4 percent.

To illustrate, Appliance Repair Co. has a taxable payroll of $100,000. It is subject to a federal rate of 6.2 percent and a state contribution rate of 5.7 percent. However, its stable employment experience reduces the company's state rate to 1 percent. Appliance Repair computes its federal and state unemployment taxes as shown in Illustration 12-4.

ILLUSTRATION 12-4
Computation of Unemployment Taxes

State unemployment tax payment (1% × $100,000)	$1,000
Federal unemployment tax [(6.2% − 5.4%) × $100,000]	800
Total federal and state unemployment tax	$1,800

Companies pay federal unemployment tax quarterly, and file a tax form annually. Companies also generally pay state contributions quarterly as well. Because both the federal and the state unemployment taxes accrue on earned compensation, companies should record the amount of accrued but unpaid employer contributions **as an operating expense and as a current liability when preparing financial statements at year-end.**

Income Tax Withholding. Federal and some state income tax laws require employers to withhold from each employee's pay the applicable income tax due on those wages. The employer computes the amount of income tax to withhold according to a government-prescribed formula or withholding tax table. That amount depends on the length of the pay period and each employee's taxable wages, marital status, and claimed dependents. If the income tax withheld plus the employee and the employer Social Security taxes exceeds specified amounts per month, the employer must make remittances to the government during the month. Illustration 12-5 summarizes payroll deductions and liabilities.

ILLUSTRATION 12-5
Summary of Payroll Liabilities

Item	Who Pays	
Income tax withholding FICA taxes—employee share Union dues	Employee	Employer reports these amounts as liabilities until remitted.
FICA taxes—employer share Federal unemployment State unemployment	Employer	

Payroll Deductions Example. Assume a weekly payroll of $10,000 entirely subject to F.I.C.A. and Medicare (7.65%), federal (0.8%) and state (4%) unemployment taxes, with income tax withholding of $1,320 and union dues of $88 deducted. The company records the wages and salaries paid and the **employee payroll deductions** as follows:

Wages and Salaries Expense	10,000	
Withholding Taxes Payable		1,320
F.I.C.A. Taxes Payable		765
Union Dues Payable to Local No. 257		88
Cash		7,827

It records the **employer payroll taxes** as follows:

Payroll Tax Expense	1,245	
F.I.C.A. Taxes Payable		765
Federal Unemployment Tax Payable		80
State Unemployment Tax Payable		400

The employer must remit to the government its share of F.I.C.A. tax along with the amount of F.I.C.A. tax deducted from each employee's gross compensation. It should record all unremitted employer F.I.C.A. taxes as payroll tax expense and payroll tax payable.[11]

Compensated Absences

Compensated absences are paid absences from employment—such as vacation, illness, and holidays. Companies should accrue a liability for the cost of compensation for future absences if **all of the following conditions** exist.[12]

(a) The employer's obligation relating to employees' rights to receive compensation for future absences is attributable to employees' services **already rendered.**

(b) The obligation relates to the rights that **vest or accumulate.**

(c) Payment of the compensation is **probable.**

(d) The amount can be **reasonably estimated.**[13]

UNDERLYING CONCEPTS

When these four conditions exist, all elements in the definition of a liability exist. In addition, the matching concept requires that the company report the expense for the services in the same period as the revenue was generated.

Illustration 12-6 shows an example of an accrual for compensated absences, in an excerpt from the balance sheet of **Clarcor Inc.**

ILLUSTRATION 12-6
Balance Sheet Presentation of Accrual for Compensated Absences

Clarcor Inc.

Current liabilities	
Accounts payable	$ 6,308
Accrued salaries, wages and commissions	2,278
Compensated absences	2,271
Accrued pension liabilities	1,023
Other accrued liabilities	4,572
	$16,452

If an employer meets conditions (a), (b), and (c) but does not accrue a liability because of a failure to meet condition (d), it should disclose that fact. Illustration 12-7 shows an example of such a disclosure, in a note from the financial statements of **Gotham Utility Company.**

[11] A manufacturing company allocates all of the payroll costs (wages, payroll taxes, and fringe benefits) to appropriate cost accounts such as Direct Labor, Indirect Labor, Sales Salaries, Administrative Salaries, and the like. This abbreviated and somewhat simplified discussion of payroll costs and deductions is not indicative of the volume of records and clerical work that may be involved in maintaining a sound and accurate payroll system.

[12] "Accounting for Compensated Absences," *Statement of Financial Accounting Standards No. 43* (Stamford, Conn.: FASB, 1980), par. 6.

[13] *FASB Statement No. 112*, "Employers' Accounting for Postemployment Benefits," requires that companies apply these same four conditions to **postemployment benefits**. "Employers' Accounting for Postemployment Benefits," *Statement of Financial Accounting Standards No. 112* (Norwalk, Conn.: FASB, November 1992), par. 18. Companies provide **postemployment benefits** to past or inactive employees **after employment but prior to retirement**. Examples include salary continuation, supplemental unemployment benefits, severance pay, job training, and continuation of health and life insurance coverage.

ILLUSTRATION 12-7
Disclosure of Policy for Compensated Absences

Gotham Utility Company

Employees of the Company are entitled to paid vacation, personal, and sick days off, depending on job status, length of service, and other factors. Due to numerous differing union contracts and other agreements with nonunion employees, it is impractical to estimate the amount of compensation for future absences, and, accordingly, no liability has been reported in the accompanying financial statements. The Company's policy is to recognize the cost of compensated absences when actually paid to employees; compensated absence payments to employees totaled $2,786,000.

The following considerations are relevant to the accounting for compensated absences. **Vested rights** exist when an employer has an obligation to make payment to an employee even after terminating his or her employment. Thus, vested rights are not contingent on an employee's future service. **Accumulated rights** are those that employees can carry forward to future periods if not used in the period in which earned. For example, assume that you earn four days of vacation pay as of December 31, the end of your employer's fiscal year. Company policy is that you will be paid for this vacation time even if you terminate employment. In this situation, your four days of vacation pay are vested, and your employer must accrue the amount.

Now assume that your vacation days are not vested, but that you can carry the four days over into later periods. Although the rights are not vested, they are accumulated rights for which the employer must make an accrual. However, the amount of the accrual is adjusted to allow for estimated forfeitures due to turnover.

A modification of the general rules relates to the issue of **sick pay**. If sick pay benefits vest, a company must accrue them. If sick pay benefits accumulate but do not vest, a company may choose whether to accrue them. Why this distinction? Companies may administer compensation designated as sick pay in one of two ways. In some companies, employees receive sick pay only if illness causes their absence. Therefore, these companies may or may not accrue a liability because its payment depends on future employee illness. Other companies allow employees to accumulate unused sick pay and take compensated time off from work even when not ill. For this type of sick pay, a company must accrue a liability because the company will pay it, regardless of whether employees become ill.

Companies should recognize the expense and related liability for compensated absences in the year earned by employees. For example, if new employees receive rights to two weeks' paid vacation at the beginning of their second year of employment, a company considers the vacation pay to be earned during the first year of employment.

What rate should a company use to accrue the compensated absence cost—the current rate or an estimated future rate? *FASB Statement No. 43* is silent on this subject. Therefore, companies will likely use the current rather than future rate. The future rate is less certain and raises time value of money issues. To illustrate, assume that Amutron Inc. began operations on January 1, 2006. The company employs 10 individuals and pays each $480 per week. Employees earned 20 unused vacation weeks in 2006. In 2007, the employees used the vacation weeks, but now they each earn $540 per week. Amutron accrues the accumulated vacation pay on December 31, 2006, as follows.

Wages Expense	9,600	
Vacation Wages Payable ($480 × 20)		9,600

At December 31, 2006, the company reports on its balance sheet a liability of $9,600. In 2007, it records the payment of vacation pay as follows.

Vacation Wages Payable	9,600	
Wages Expense	1,200	
Cash ($540 × 20)		10,800

In 2007 the use of the vacation weeks extinguishes the liability. Note that Amutron records the difference between the amount of cash paid and the reduction in the liability account as an adjustment to Wages Expense in the period when paid. This difference arises because it accrues the liability account at the rates of pay in effect during the period when employees *earned* the compensated time. The cash paid, however, depends on the rates in effect during the period when employees *used* the compensated time. If Amutron used the future rates of pay to compute the accrual in 2006, then the cash paid in 2007 would equal the liability.[14]

Bonus Agreements

Many companies give a **bonus** to certain or all employees in addition to their regular salaries or wages. Frequently the bonus amount depends on the company's yearly profit. For example, employees at **Ford Motor Company** share in the success of the company's operations on the basis of a complicated formula using net income as its primary basis for computation. A company may consider **bonus payments to employees** as additional wages and should include them as a deduction in determining the net income for the year.

To illustrate the entries for an employee bonus, assume that Palmer Inc. shows income for the year 2007 of $100,000. It will pay out bonuses of $10,700 in January 2008. Palmer makes an adjusting entry dated December 31, 2007, to record the bonuses as follows.

Employees' Bonus Expense	10,700	
Profit-Sharing Bonus Payable		10,700

In January 2008, when Palmer pays the bonus, it makes this journal entry:

Profit-Sharing Bonus Payable	10,700	
Cash		10,700

Palmer should show the expense account in the income statement as an operating expense. **The liability, Profit-Sharing Bonus Payable, is usually payable within a short period of time. Companies should include it as a current liability in the balance sheet.** Similar to bonus agreements are contractual agreements for **conditional expenses.** Examples would be agreements covering rents or royalty payments conditional on the amount of revenues earned or the quantity of product produced or extracted. Conditional expenses based on revenues or units produced are usually less difficult to compute than bonus arrangements.

For example, assume that a lease calls for a fixed rent payment of $500 per month and 1 percent of all sales over $300,000 per year. The company's annual rent obligation would amount to $6,000 plus $0.01 of each dollar of revenue over $300,000. Or, a royalty agreement may give to a patent owner $1 for every ton of product resulting from the patented process, or give to a mineral rights owner $0.50 on every barrel of oil extracted. As the company produces or extracts each additional unit of product, it creates an additional obligation, usually a current liability.

INTERNATIONAL INSIGHT

In Japan, companies do not treat bonuses to members of the board of directors and to the Commercial Code auditors as expenses. Instead, they consider such bonuses to be a distribution of profits and charge them against retained earnings.

CONTINGENCIES

SECTION 2

Companies often are involved in situations where uncertainty exists about whether an obligation to transfer cash or other assets has arisen and/or the amount that will be required to settle the obligation. For example:

- **Merck** may be a defendant in a lawsuit, and any payment is contingent upon the outcome of a settlement or an administrative or court proceeding.

[14]Some companies have obligations for benefits paid to employees after they retire. The accounting and reporting standards for postretirement benefit payments are complex. These standards relate to two different types of **postretirement benefits**: (1) pensions, and (2) postretirement health care and life insurance benefits.

- **Ford Motor Co.** provides a warranty for a car it sells, and any payments are contingent on the number of cars that qualify for benefits under the warranty.
- **Briggs & Stratton** acts as a guarantor on a loan for another entity, and any payment is contingent on whether the other entity defaults.

Broadly, these situations are called contingencies. A **contingency** is "an existing condition, situation, or set of circumstances involving uncertainty as to possible gain **(gain contingency)** or loss **(loss contingency)** to an enterprise that will ultimately be resolved when one or more future events occur or fail to occur."[15]

GAIN CONTINGENCIES

OBJECTIVE 4
Identify the criteria used to account for and disclose gain and loss contingencies.

Gain contingencies are claims or rights to receive assets (or have a liability reduced) whose existence is uncertain but which may become valid eventually. The typical gain contingencies are:

1. Possible receipts of monies from gifts, donations, bonuses, and so on.
2. Possible refunds from the government in tax disputes.
3. Pending court cases with a probable favorable outcome.
4. Tax loss carryforwards (discussed in Chapter 17).

Companies follow a conservative policy in this area. Except for tax loss carryforwards, they do not record gain contingencies. A company discloses gain contingencies in the notes only when a high probability exists for realizing them. As a result, it is unusual to find information about contingent gains in the financial statements and the accompanying notes. Illustration 12-8 presents an example of a disclosure gain contingency.

ILLUSTRATION 12-8
Disclosure of Gain Contingency

BMC Industries, Inc.

Note 13: Legal Matters. In the first quarter, a U.S. District Court in Miami, Florida, awarded the Company a $5.1 million judgment against **Barth Industries** (Barth) of Cleveland, Ohio and its parent, **Nesco Holdings, Inc.** (Nesco). The judgment relates to an agreement under which Barth and Nesco were to help automate the plastic lens production plant in Fort Lauderdale, Florida. The Company has not recorded any income relating to this judgment because Barth and Nesco have filed an appeal.

LOSS CONTINGENCIES

Loss contingencies involve possible losses. A liability incurred as a result of a loss contingency is by definition a contingent liability. **Contingent liabilities** depend on the occurrence of one or more future events to confirm either the amount payable, the payee, the date payable, or its existence. That is, these factors depend on a contingency.

When a loss contingency exists, the likelihood that the future event or events will confirm the incurrence of a liability can range from probable to remote. The FASB uses the terms **probable, reasonably possible**, and **remote** to identify three areas within that range and assigns the following meanings.

Probable. The future event or events are likely to occur.

Reasonably possible. The chance of the future event or events occurring is more than remote but less than likely.

Remote. The chance of the future event or events occurring is slight.

[15]"Accounting for Contingencies," *Statement of Financial Accounting Standards No. 5* (Stamford, Conn.: FASB, 1975), par. 1. According to *Accounting Trends and Techniques—2004*, the most common gain contingencies are related to operating loss carryforwards and other tax credits. The most common loss contingencies are related to litigation, environmental, and insurance losses.

Companies should accrue an estimated loss from a loss contingency by a charge to expense and a liability recorded only if **both** of the following conditions are met.[16]

1 Information available prior to the issuance of the financial statements indicates that it is **probable that a liability has been incurred** at the date of the financial statements.

2 The amount of the loss can be **reasonably estimated**.

To record a liability, a company does not need to know the exact payee nor the exact date payable. **What a company must know is whether it is probable that it incurred a liability.**

To meet the second criterion, a company needs to be able to reasonably determine an amount for the liability. To determine a reasonable estimate of the liability, a company may use its own experience, experience of other companies in the industry, engineering or research studies, legal advice, or educated guesses by qualified personnel. Illustration 12-9 shows an accrual recorded for a loss contingency, from the annual report of **Quaker State Oil Refining Company**.

ILLUSTRATION 12-9
Disclosure of Accrual for Loss Contingency

Quaker State Oil Refining Company

Note 5: Contingencies. During the period from November 13 to December 23, a change in an additive component purchased from one of its suppliers caused certain oil refined and shipped to fail to meet the Company's low-temperature performance requirements. The Company has recalled this product and has arranged for reimbursement to its customers and the ultimate consumers of all costs associated with the product. Estimated cost of the recall program, net of estimated third party reimbursement, in the amount of $3,500,000 has been charged to current operations.

Use of the terms probable, reasonably possible, and remote to classify contingencies involves judgment and subjectivity. Illustration 12-10 lists examples of loss contingencies and the general accounting treatment accorded them.

ILLUSTRATION 12-10
Accounting Treatment of Loss Contingencies

Usually Accrued

Loss Related to:

1. Collectibility of receivables
2. Obligations related to product warranties and product defects
3. Premiums offered to customers

Not Accrued

Loss Related to:

4. Risk of loss or damage of enterprise property by fire, explosion, or other hazards
5. General or unspecified business risks
6. Risk of loss from catastrophes assumed by property and casualty insurance companies, including reinsurance companies

May Be Accrued*

Loss Related to:

7. Threat of expropriation of assets
8. Pending or threatened litigation
9. Actual or possible claims and assessments**
10. Guarantees of indebtedness of others
11. Obligations of commercial banks under "standby letters of credit"
12. Agreements to repurchase receivables (or the related property) that have been sold

*Should be accrued when both criteria—probable and reasonably estimable—are met.
**Estimated amounts of losses incurred prior to the balance sheet date but settled subsequently should be accrued as of the balance sheet date.

[16]We discuss loss contingencies that result in the incurrence of a liability in this chapter. We discuss loss contingencies that result in the impairment of an asset (e.g., collectibility of receivables or threat of expropriation of assets) in other sections of this textbook.

Practicing accountants express concern over the diversity that now exists in the interpretation of "probable," "reasonably possible," and "remote." Current practice relies heavily on the exact language used in responses received from lawyers (such language is necessarily biased and protective rather than predictive). As a result, accruals and disclosures of contingencies vary considerably in practice. Some of the more common loss contingencies are:[17]

1. Litigation, claims, and assessments.
2. Guarantee and warranty costs.
3. Premiums and coupons.
4. Environmental liabilities.

As discussed in the opening story, companies do not record or report in the notes to the financial statements general risk contingencies inherent in business operations (e.g., the possibility of war, strike, uninsurable catastrophes, or a business recession).

Litigation, Claims, and Assessments

OBJECTIVE 5
Explain the accounting for different types of loss contingencies.

Companies must consider the following factors, among others, in determining whether to record a liability with respect to **pending or threatened litigation** and actual or possible **claims** and **assessments.**

1. The **time period** in which the underlying cause of action occurred.
2. The **probability** of an unfavorable outcome.
3. The ability to make a **reasonable estimate** of the amount of loss.

To report a loss and a liability in the financial statements, **the cause for litigation must have occurred on or before the date of the financial statements.** It does not matter that the company became aware of the existence or possibility of the lawsuit or claims after the date of the financial statements but before issuing them. To evaluate the probability of an unfavorable outcome, a company considers the following: the nature of the litigation; the progress of the case; the opinion of legal counsel; its own and others' experience in similar cases; and any management response to the lawsuit.

Companies can seldom predict the outcome of pending litigation, however, with any assurance. And, even if evidence available at the balance sheet date does not favor the company, it is hardly reasonable to expect the company to publish in its financial statements a dollar estimate of the probable negative outcome. Such specific disclosures might weaken the company's position in the dispute and encourage the plaintiff to intensify its efforts. A typical example of the wording of such a disclosure is the note to the financial statements of **Apple Computer, Inc.**, relating to its litigation concerning repetitive stress injuries, as shown in Illustration 12-11.

ILLUSTRATION 12-11
Disclosure of Litigation

Apple Computer, Inc.

"Repetitive Stress Injury" Litigation. The Company is named in numerous lawsuits (fewer than 100) alleging that the plaintiff incurred so-called "repetitive stress injury" to the upper extremities as a result of using keyboards and/or mouse input devices sold by the Company. On October 4, in a trial of one of these cases (*Dorsey v. Apple*) in the United States District Court for the Eastern District of New York, the jury rendered a verdict in favor of the Company, and final judgment in favor of the Company has been entered. The other cases are in various stages of pretrial activity. These suits are similar to those filed against other major suppliers of personal computers. Ultimate resolution of the litigation against the Company may depend on progress in resolving this type of litigation in the industry overall.

[17] *Accounting Trends and Techniques—2004* reports that of the 600 companies surveyed, companies report loss contingencies for the following: litigation, 506; environmental, 245; insurance, 122; governmental investigation, 94; possible tax assessments, 76; and others, 47.

With respect to **unfiled suits** and **unasserted claims and assessments**, a company must determine (1) the degree of **probability** that a suit may be filed or a claim or assessment may be asserted, and (2) the **probability** of an unfavorable outcome. For example, assume that the Federal Trade Commission investigates the Nawtee Company for restraint of trade, and institutes enforcement proceedings. Private claims of triple damages for redress often follow such proceedings. In this case, Nawtee must determine the probability of the claims being asserted **and** the probability of triple damages being awarded. If both are probable, if the loss is reasonably estimable, and if the cause for action is dated on or before the date of the financial statements, then Nawtee should accrue the liability.[18]

Guarantee and Warranty Costs

A **warranty (product guarantee)** is a promise made by a seller to a buyer to make good on a deficiency of quantity, quality, or performance in a product. Manufacturers commonly use it as a sales promotion technique. Automakers, for instance, "hyped" their sales by extending their new-car warranty to seven years or 100,000 miles. For a specified period of time following the date of sale to the consumer, the manufacturer may promise to bear all or part of the cost of replacing defective parts, to perform any necessary repairs or servicing without charge, to refund the purchase price, or even to "double your money back."

Warranties and guarantees entail future costs. These additional costs, sometimes called "after costs" or "post-sale costs," frequently are significant. Although the future cost is indefinite as to amount, due date, and even customer, a liability is probable in most cases. Companies should recognize this liability in the accounts if they can reasonably estimate it. The estimated amount of the liability includes all the costs that the company will incur after sale and delivery and that are incident to the correction of defects or deficiencies required under the warranty provisions. Warranty costs are a classic example of a loss contingency.

Companies use two basic methods of accounting for warranty costs: (1) the cash-basis method and (2) the accrual method.

Cash Basis

Under the **cash-basis method**, companies expense warranty costs as incurred. In other words, a **seller or manufacturer charges warranty costs to the period in which it complies with the warranty**. The company does not record a liability for future costs arising from warranties, nor does it charge the period of sale. Companies frequently justify use of this method, the only one recognized for income tax purposes, on the basis of expediency when warranty costs are immaterial or when the warranty period is relatively short. A company must use the cash-basis method when it does not accrue a warranty liability in the year of sale either because:

1. it is not probable that a liability has been incurred, or
2. it cannot reasonably estimate the amount of the liability.

Accrual Basis

If it is probable that customers will make warranty claims and a company can reasonably estimate the costs involved, the company must use the accrual method. Under the **accrual method**, companies charge warranty costs to operating expense **in the year of sale**. The accrual method is the generally accepted method. Companies should use it whenever the warranty is an integral and inseparable part of the sale and is viewed as a loss contingency. We refer to this approach as the **expense warranty approach**.

---

[18] Companies need not disclose contingencies involving an unasserted claim or assessment when no claimant has come forward unless (1) it is considered probable that a claim will be asserted, and (2) there is a reasonable possibility that the outcome will be unfavorable.

Example of Expense Warranty Approach. To illustrate the expense warranty method, assume that Denson Machinery Company begins production on a new machine in July 2006, and sells 100 units at $5,000 each by its year-end, December 31, 2006. Each machine is under warranty for one year. Denson estimates, based on past experience with a similar machine, that the warranty cost will average $200 per unit. Further, as a result of parts replacements and services rendered in compliance with machinery warranties, it incurs $4,000 in warranty costs in 2006 and $16,000 in 2007.

1 Sale of 100 machines at $5,000 each, July through December 2006:

Cash or Accounts Receivable	500,000	
Sales		500,000

2 Recognition of warranty expense, July through December 2006:

Warranty Expense	4,000	
Cash, Inventory, Accrued Payroll		4,000
(Warranty costs incurred)		
Warranty Expense	16,000	
Estimated Liability under Warranties		16,000
(To accrue estimated warranty costs)		

The December 31, 2006, balance sheet reports "Estimated liability under warranties" as a current liability of $16,000, and the income statement for 2006 reports "Warranty expense" of $20,000.

3 Recognition of warranty costs incurred in 2007 (on 2006 machinery sales):

Estimated Liability under Warranties	16,000	
Cash, Inventory, or Accrued Payroll		16,000
(Warranty costs incurred)		

If Denson Machinery applies the cash-basis method, it reports $4,000 as warranty expense in 2006 and $16,000 as warranty expense in 2007. It records all of the sale price as revenue in 2006. In many instances, application of the cash-basis method fails to match the warranty costs relating to the products sold during a given period with the revenues derived from such products. As such, **it violates the matching principle**. Where ongoing warranty policies exist year after year, the differences between the cash and the expense warranty bases probably would not be so great.

Sales-Warranty Approach. A warranty is sometimes **sold separately from the product**. For example, when you purchase a television set or DVD player, you are entitled to the manufacturer's warranty. You also will undoubtedly be offered an extended warranty on the product at an additional cost.[19]

In this case, the seller should recognize separately the sale of the television or DVD player, with the manufacturer's warranty and the sale of the extended warranty.[20] This approach is referred to as the **sales-warranty approach. Companies defer revenue on the sale of the extended warranty** and generally recognize it on a straight-line basis over the life of the contract. The seller of the warranty defers revenue because it has an obligation to perform services over the life of the contract. The seller should only defer and amortize costs that vary with and are directly related to the sale of the contracts (mainly commissions). It expenses those costs, such as employees' salaries, advertising, and general and administrative expenses that it would have incurred even if it did not sell a contract.

[19]A company separately prices a contract **if the customer has the option to purchase** the services provided under the contract for an expressly stated amount separate from the price of the product. An extended warranty or product maintenance contract usually meets these conditions.

[20]"Accounting for Separately Extended Warranty and Product Maintenance Contracts," *FASB Technical Bulletin No. 90–1* (Stamford, Conn.: FASB, 1990).

To illustrate, assume you purchase a new automobile from Hanlin Auto for \$20,000. In addition to the regular warranty on the auto (the manufacturer will pay for all repairs for the first 36,000 miles or three years, whichever comes first), you purchase at a cost of \$600 an extended warranty that protects you for an additional three years or 36,000 miles. Hanlin Auto records the sale of the automobile (with the regular warranty) and the sale of the extended warranty on January 2, 2006, as follows:

Cash	20,600	
Sales		20,000
Unearned Warranty Revenue		600

It recognizes revenue at the end of the fourth year (using straight-line amortization) as follows.

Unearned Warranty Revenue	200	
Warranty Revenue		200

Because the extended warranty contract only starts after the regular warranty expires, Hanlin Auto defers revenue recognition until the fourth year. If it incurs the costs of performing services under the extended warranty contract on other than a straight-line basis (as historical evidence might indicate), Hanlin Auto should recognize revenue over the contract period in proportion to the costs it expected to incur in performing services under the contract.[21]

Premiums and Coupons

Numerous companies offer premiums (either on a limited or continuing basis) to customers in return for boxtops, certificates, coupons, labels, or wrappers. The **premium** may be silverware, dishes, a small appliance, a toy, or free transportation. Also, **printed coupons** that can be redeemed for a cash discount on items purchased are extremely popular.[22] A more recent marketing innovation is the **cash rebate**, which the buyer can obtain by returning the store receipt, a rebate coupon, and Universal Product Code (UPC label) or "bar code" to the manufacturer.

Companies offer premiums, coupon offers, and rebates to stimulate sales. Thus companies should charge the **costs of premiums and coupons to expense in the period of the sale** that benefits from the plan. The period that benefits is not necessarily the period in which the company offered the premium. At the end of the accounting period many premium offers may be outstanding and must be redeemed when presented in subsequent periods. In order to reflect the existing current liability and to match costs with revenues, the company estimates the number of outstanding premium offers that customers will present for redemption. The company then charges the cost of premium offers to Premium Expense. It credits the outstanding obligations to an account titled Estimated Liability for Premiums.

UNDERLYING CONCEPTS

Warranties and coupons are loss contingencies that satisfy the conditions necessary for a liability. Regarding the income statement, the *matching principle* requires that companies report the related expense in the period in which the sale occurs.

The following example illustrates the accounting treatment for a premium offer. Fluffy Cakemix Company offered its customers a large nonbreakable mixing bowl in exchange for 25 cents and 10 boxtops. The mixing bowl costs Fluffy Cakemix Company 75 cents, and the company estimates that customers will redeem 60 percent of

[21]Ibid, par. 3. The FASB recently issued additional disclosure requirements for warranties. A company must disclose its accounting policy and the method used to determine its warranty liability, and must present a tabular reconciliation of the changes in the product warranty liability. *FASB Interpretation No. 45,* "Guarantor's Accounting and Disclosure Requirements for Guarantees, Including Indirect Guarantees of Indebtedness of Others" (Norwalk, Conn.: FASB, 2002).

[22]Approximately 4 percent of coupons are redeemed. Redeemed coupons eventually make their way to the corporate headquarters of the stores that accept them. From there they are shipped to clearinghouses operated by **A. C. Nielsen Company** (of TV-rating fame) that count them and report back to the manufacturers who, in turn, reimburse the stores.

the boxtops. The premium offer began in June 2007 and resulted in the transactions journalized below. Fluffy Cakemix Company records purchase of 20,000 mixing bowls at 75 cents as follows.

Inventory of Premium Mixing Bowls	15,000	
Cash		15,000

The entry to record sales of 300,000 boxes of cake mix at 80 cents would be:

Cash	240,000	
Sales		240,000

Fluffy records the actual redemption of 60,000 boxtops, the receipt of 25 cents per 10 boxtops, and the delivery of the mixing bowls as follows.

Cash [(60,000 ÷ 10) × $0.25]	1,500	
Premium Expense	3,000	
Inventory of Premium Mixing Bowls		4,500
Computation: (60,000 ÷ 10) × $0.75 = $4,500		

Finally, Fluffy makes an end-of-period adjusting entry for estimated liability for outstanding premium offers (boxtops) as follows.

Premium Expense	6,000	
Estimated Liability for Premiums		6,000

Computation:	
Total boxtops sold in 2007	300,000
Total estimated redemptions (60%)	180,000
Boxtops redeemed in 2007	60,000
Estimated future redemptions	120,000
Cost of estimated claims outstanding (120,000 ÷ 10) × ($0.75 − $0.25) = $6,000	

The December 31, 2007, balance sheet of Fluffy Cakemix Company reports an "Inventory of premium mixing bowls" of $10,500 as a current asset and "Estimated liability for premiums" of $6,000 as a current liability. The 2007 income statement reports a $9,000 "Premium expense" among the selling expenses.

WHAT DO THE NUMBERS MEAN?

FREQUENT FLYERS

Numerous companies offer premiums to customers in the form of a promise of future goods or services as an incentive for purchases today. Premium plans that have widespread adoption are the frequent-flyer programs used by all major airlines. On the basis of mileage accumulated, frequent-flyer members receive discounted or free airline tickets. Airline customers can earn miles toward free travel by making long-distance phone calls, staying in hotels, and charging gasoline and groceries on a credit card. Those free tickets represent an enormous potential liability because people using them may displace paying passengers.

When airlines first started offering frequent-flyer bonuses, everyone assumed that they could accommodate the free-ticket holders with otherwise-empty seats. That made the additional cost of the program so minimal that airlines didn't accrue it or report the small liability. But, as more and more paying passengers have been crowded off flights by frequent-flyer awardees, the loss of revenues has grown enormously. For example, **United Airlines** at one time reported a liability of $1.4 billion for advance ticket sales, some of which pertains to free frequent-flyer tickets.

Although the profession has studied the accounting for this transaction, no authoritative guidelines have been issued.

Environmental Liabilities

Estimates to clean up existing toxic waste sites total upward of $752 billion over a 30-year period. In addition, cost estimates of cleaning up our air and preventing future deterioration of the environment run even higher. The average environmental cost per company for various industries at one time was: high-tech companies, $2 million (6.1% of revenues); utilities, $340 million (6.1% of revenues); steel and metals, $50 million (2.9% of revenues), and oil companies, $430 million (1.9% of revenues).

These costs will only grow when considering "Superfund legislation." This federal legislation provides the Environmental Protection Agency (EPA) with the power to clean up waste sites and charge the clean-up costs to parties the EPA deems responsible for contaminating the site. These potentially responsible parties can have a significant liability.

In many industries, the construction and operation of long-lived assets involves obligations for the retirement of those assets. When a mining company opens up a strip mine, it may also commit to restore the land once it completes mining. Similarly, when an oil company erects an offshore drilling platform, it may be legally obligated to dismantle and remove the platform at the end of its useful life.

Accounting Recognition of Asset Retirement Obligations

A company must recognize an **asset retirement obligation (ARO)** when it has an existing legal obligation associated with the retirement of a long-lived asset and when it can reasonably estimate the amount of the liability. Companies should record the ARO at fair value.[23]

Obligating Events. Examples of existing legal obligations, which require recognition of a liability include, but are not limited to:

- decommissioning nuclear facilities,
- dismantling, restoring, and reclamation of oil and gas properties,
- certain closure, reclamation, and removal costs of mining facilities,
- closure and post-closure costs of landfills.

In order to capture the benefits of these long-lived assets, **the company is generally legally obligated for the costs associated with retirement of the asset, whether the company hires another party to perform the retirement activities or performs the activities with its own workforce and equipment**. AROs give rise to various recognition patterns. For example, the obligation may arise at the outset of the asset's use (e.g., erection of an oil-rig), or it may build over time (e.g., a landfill that expands over time).

Measurement. A company initially measures an ARO at fair value, which is defined as the amount that the company would pay in an active market to settle the ARO. While active markets do not exist for many AROs, companies should estimate fair value based on the best information available. Such information could include market prices of similar liabilities, if available. Alternatively, companies may use present value techniques to estimate fair value.

Recognition and Allocation. To record an ARO in the financial statements, a company includes the cost associated with the ARO in the carrying amount of the related long-lived asset, and records a liability for the same amount. It records an asset retirement cost as part of the related asset because these costs are tied to operating the asset and are necessary to prepare the asset for its intended use. Therefore, the specific asset (e.g., mine, drilling platform, nuclear power plant) should be increased because the future economic benefit comes from the use of this productive asset. **Companies should not**

[23]"Accounting for Asset Retirement Obligations," *Statement of Financial Accounting Standards No. 143* (Norwalk, Conn.: FASB, 2001).

record the capitalized asset retirement costs in a separate account because there is no future economic benefit that can be associated with these costs alone.

In subsequent periods, companies allocate the cost of the ARO to expense over the period of the related asset's useful life. Companies may use the straight-line method for this allocation, as well as other systematic and rational allocations.

Example of ARO Accounting Provisions. To illustrate the accounting for AROs, assume that on January 1, 2006, Wildcat Oil Company erected an oil platform in the Gulf of Mexico. Wildcat is legally required to dismantle and remove the platform at the end of its useful life, estimated to be five years. Wildcat estimates that dismantling and removal will cost $1,000,000. Based on a 10 percent discount rate, the present value of the asset retirement obligation is $620,920 ($1,000,000 × .62092). Wildcat records this ARO as follows.

January 1, 2006

Drilling Platform	620,920	
Asset Retirement Obligation		620,920

During the life of the asset, Wildcat allocates the asset retirement cost to expense. Using the straight-line method, Wildcat makes the following entries to record this expense.

December 31, 2006, 2007, 2008, 2009, 2010

Depreciation Expense ($620,920 ÷ 5)	124,184	
Accumulated Depreciation		124,184

In addition, Wildcat must accrue interest expense each period. Wildcat records interest expense and the related increase in the asset retirement obligation on December 31, 2006, as follows.

December 31, 2006

Interest Expense ($620,920 × 10%)	62,092	
Asset Retirement Obligation		62,092

On January 10, 2011, Wildcat contracts with Rig Reclaimers, Inc. to dismantle the platform at a contract price of $995,000. Wildcat makes the following journal entry to record settlement of the ARO.

January 10, 2011

Asset Retirement Obligation	1,000,000	
Gain on Settlement of ARO		5,000
Cash		995,000

Companies need to provide more extensive disclosure regarding environmental liabilities. In addition, companies should record more of these liabilities. The SEC believes that companies should not delay recognition of a liability due to significant uncertainty. The SEC argues that if the liability is within a range, and no amount within the range is the best estimate, then management should recognize the minimum amount of the range. That treatment is in accordance with *FASB Interpretation No. 14*, "Reasonable Estimation of the Amount of a Loss." The SEC also believes that companies should report environmental liabilities in the balance sheet independent of recoveries from third parties. Thus, companies may not net possible insurance recoveries against liabilities but must show them separately. Because there is much litigation regarding recovery of insurance proceeds, these "assets" appear to be gain contingencies. Therefore, companies should not be report these on the balance sheet.[24]

---

[24]As we indicated earlier, the FASB requires that, when some amount within the range appears at the time to be a better estimate than any other amount within the range, a company accrues that amount. When no amount within the range is a better estimate than any other amount, the company **accrues** the dollar amount at the low end of the range and **discloses** the dollar amount at the high end of the range. Unfortunately, in many cases, zero may arguably be the low point of the range, resulting in no liability being recognized. See *FASB Interpretation No. 14*, "Reasonable Estimation of the Amount of a Loss" (Stamford, Conn.: FASB, 1976), par. 3, and *FASB Statement No. 5*, "Accounting for Contingencies" (Stamford, Conn.: FASB, 1975).

MORE DISCLOSURE PLEASE

WHAT DO THE NUMBERS MEAN?

On November 19, 2001, Enron filed its third-quarter financial statements and reported on its balance sheet debt of approximately $13 billion. Yet on the same day, at a meeting to discuss its liquidity crisis, Enron informed its bankers that its debt was approximately $38 billion. Company officers described the difference of $25 billion as being either off-balance-sheet or on the balance sheet other than debt.

As a result of the Enron bankruptcy and other financial reporting scandals, Congress passed the Sarbanes-Oxley Act of 2002. One of its provisions mandates that the Securities and Exchange Commission conduct a study to determine the extent of off-balance-sheet transactions occurring in U.S. businesses.

Table 1 below indicates the extent of disclosure and recognition of contingent liabilities. The study classified contingent liabilities into three categories (1) litigation contingent liabilities, (2) environmental liabilities, and (3) guarantees. The statistics provided relate to reports filed by 10,100 companies listed on the U.S. stock exchanges in 2005.

Table 1

Type of Contingency	Companies Disclosing	Companies Recording
Litigation contingent liabilities	46.3%	5.1%
Environmental contingent liabilities	10.2%	5.1%
Guarantees	35.4%	10.2%

As Table 1 indicates, approximately 46 percent of companies disclosed litigation contingent liabilities, but only 5.1 percent recorded any liability related to these contingencies. On the other hand, 35 percent of the companies disclosed guarantees but a third of these companies (10.2 percent) recorded a liability for these contingencies.

Table 2 below shows the dollar amounts of the contingent liabilities companies disclosed and recorded.

Table 2

Type of Contingency	Companies Disclosing ($ millions)	Companies Recording ($ millions)
Litigation contingent liabilities	$52,354	$11,814
Environmental contingent liabilities	$23,414	$18,723
Guarantees	$46,535,399	$123,949

Table 2 indicates that companies disclosed litigation contingent liabilities of approximately $52 billion, but recorded only $11.8 billion as liabilities. Incredibly, companies disclosed more than *$46 trillion* of guarantees, a small fraction of which (just $124 billion) they recorded as liabilities.

The results of this study suggest that the FASB must continue to address the issue of contingencies to ensure that companies provide relevant and reliable information for these types of financial events.

Source: "Report and Recommendations Pursuant to Section 401(c) of the Sarbanes-Oxley Act of 2002 on Arrangements with Off-Balance Sheet Implications, Special Purpose Entities, and Transparency of Filings by Issuers," United States Securities and Exchange Commission, Office of Chief Accountant, Office of Economic Analyses, Division of Corporation Finance (June 2005).

Self-Insurance

As discussed earlier, contingencies are not recorded for general risks (e.g., losses that might arise due to poor expected economic conditions.) Similarly, companies do not record contingencies for more specific future risks such as allowances for repairs. The reason: These items do meet the definition of a liability because they do not arise from a past transaction but instead relate to future events.

UNDERLYING CONCEPTS

Even if companies can estimate the amount of losses with a high degree of certainty, the losses are not liabilities because they result from a future event and not from a past event.

Some companies take out insurance policies against the potential losses from fire, flood, storm, and accident. Other companies do not. The reasons: Some risks are not insurable, the insurance rates are prohibitive (e.g., earthquakes and riots), or they make a business decision to self-insure. Self-insurance is another item that is not recognized as a contingency.

Despite its name, **self-insurance** is **not insurance, but risk assumption**. Any company that assumes its own risks puts itself in the position of incurring expenses or losses as they occur. There is little theoretical justification for the establishment of a liability based on a hypothetical charge to insurance expense. This is "as if" accounting. The conditions for accrual stated in *FASB Statement No. 5* are not satisfied prior to the occurrence of the event. Until that time there is no diminution in the value of the property. And unlike an insurance company, which has contractual obligations to reimburse policyholders for losses, a company can have no such obligation to itself and, hence, no liability either before or after the occurrence of damage.[25]

The note shown in Illustration 12-12 from the annual report of **Adolph Coors Company** is typical of the self-insurance disclosure.

ILLUSTRATION 12-12
Disclosure of Self-Insurance

Adolph Coors Company

Notes to Financial Statements

Note 4: Commitments and Contingencies. It is generally the policy of the Company to act as a self-insurer for certain insurable risks consisting primarily of physical loss to corporate property, business interruption resulting from such loss, employee health insurance programs, and workers' compensation. Losses and claims are accrued as incurred.

Exposure to **risks of loss resulting from uninsured past injury to others**, however, is an existing condition involving uncertainty about the amount and timing of losses that may develop. In such a case, a contingency exists. A company with a fleet of vehicles for example, would have to accrue uninsured losses resulting from injury to others or damage to the property of others that took place prior to the date of the financial statements (if the experience of the company or other information enables it to make a reasonable estimate of the liability). However, it should not establish a liability for **expected future injury** to others or damage to the property of others, even if it can reasonably estimate the amount of losses.

SECTION 3 — *PRESENTATION AND ANALYSIS*

Presentation of Current Liabilities

OBJECTIVE 6
Indicate how to present and analyze liabilities and contingencies.

In practice, current liabilities are usually recorded and reported in financial statements at their full maturity value. Because of the short time periods involved, frequently less than one year, the difference between the present value of a current liability and the maturity value is usually not large. The profession accepts as immaterial any slight overstatement of liabilities that results from carrying current liabilities at maturity value.[26]

[25] "Accounting for Contingencies," *FASB Statement No. 5,* op. cit., par. 28. A commentary in *Forbes* (June 15, 1974), p. 42, stated its position on this matter quite succinctly: "The simple and unquestionable fact of life is this: Business is cyclical and full of unexpected surprises. Is it the role of accounting to disguise this unpleasant fact and create a fairyland of smoothly rising earnings? Or, should accounting reflect reality, warts and all—floods, expropriations and all manner of rude shocks?"

[26] "Interest on Receivables and Payables," *Opinions of the Accounting Principles Board No. 21* (New York: AICPA, 1971), par. 3. *APB Opinion No. 21* specifically exempts from present value measurements those payables arising from transactions with suppliers in the normal course of business that do not exceed approximately one year.

The current liabilities accounts are commonly presented as the first classification in the liabilities and stockholders' equity section of the balance sheet. Within the current liabilities section, companies may list the accounts in order of maturity, in descending order of amount, or in order of liquidation preference. Illustration 12-13 presents an excerpt of **Best Buy Company**'s financial statements that is representative of the reports of large corporations.

ILLUSTRATION 12-13
Balance Sheet Presentation of Current Liabilities

Best Buy Co.
(dollars in thousands)

	Feb. 26, 2005	Feb. 28, 2004
Current assets		
Cash and cash equivalents	$ 470	$ 245
Short-term investments	2,878	2,355
Receivables	375	343
Merchandise inventories	2,851	2,607
Other current assets	329	174
Total current assets	$6,903	$5,724
Current liabilities		
Accounts payable	$2,824	$2,460
Unredeemed gift card liabilities	410	300
Accrued compensation and related expenses	234	269
Accrued liabilities	844	724
Accrued income taxes	575	380
Current portion of long-term debt	72	368
Total current liabilities	$4,959	$4,501

wiley.com/college/kieso

Additional Disclosures of Current Liabilities

Detail and supplemental information concerning current liabilities should be sufficient to meet the requirement of full disclosure. Companies should clearly identify secured liabilities, as well as indicate the related assets pledged as collateral. If the due date of any liability can be extended, a company should disclose the details. Companies should not offset current liabilities against assets that it will apply to their liquidation. Finally, current maturities of long-term debt are classified as current liabilities.

A major exception exists when a company will pay a currently maturing obligation from assets classified as long-term. For example, if a company will retire a bond payable using a bond sinking fund that is classified as a long-term asset, it should report the bonds payable in the long-term liabilities section. Presentation of this debt in the current liabilities section would distort the working capital position of the enterprise.

If a company excludes a short-term obligation from current liabilities because of refinancing, it should include the following in the note to the financial statements:

1. A general description of the financing agreement.
2. The terms of any new obligation incurred or to be incurred.
3. The terms of any equity security issued or to be issued.

When a company expects to refinance on a long-term basis by issuing equity securities, it is not appropriate to include the short-term obligation in stockholders' equity. At the date of the balance sheet, the obligation is a liability and not stockholders' equity. Illustration 12-14 shows the disclosure requirements for an actual refinancing situation.

ILLUSTRATION 12-14
Actual Refinancing of Short-Term Debt

	December 31, 2006
Current liabilities	
Accounts payable	$ 3,600,000
Accrued payables	2,500,000
Income taxes payable	1,100,000
Current portion of long-term debt	1,000,000
Total current liabilities	$ 8,200,000
Long-term debt	
Notes payable refinanced in January 2007 (Note 1)	$ 2,000,000
11% bonds due serially through 2017	15,000,000
Total long-term debt	$17,000,000

Note 1: On January 19, 2007, the Company issued 50,000 shares of common stock and received proceeds totaling $2,385,000, of which $2,000,000 was used to liquidate notes payable that matured on February 1, 2007. Accordingly, such notes payable have been classified as long-term debt at December 31, 2006.

Presentation of Contingencies

Additional Disclosures of Contingencies

A company records a loss contingency and a liability if the loss is both probable and estimable. But, if the loss is **either probable or estimable but not both**, and if there is at least a **reasonable possibility** that a company may have incurred a liability, it must disclose the following in the notes.

1. The nature of the contingency.
2. An estimate of the possible loss or range of loss or a statement that an estimate cannot be made.

Illustration 12-15 presents an extensive litigation disclosure note from the financial statements of **Raymark Corporation**. The note indicates that Raymark charged actual losses to operations and that a further liability may exist, but that the company cannot currently estimate this liability.

ILLUSTRATION 12-15
Disclosure of Loss Contingency through Litigation

Raymark Corporation

Note I: Litigation. Raymark is a defendant or co-defendant in a substantial number of lawsuits alleging wrongful injury and/or death from exposure to asbestos fibers in the air. The following table summarizes the activity in these lawsuits:

Claims	
Pending at beginning of year	8,719
Received during year	4,494
Settled or otherwise disposed of	(1,445)
Pending at end of year	11,768
Average indemnification cost	$3,364
Average cost per case, including defense costs	$6,499
Trial activity	
Verdicts for the Company	23
Total trials	36

The following table presents the cost of defending asbestos litigation, together with related insurance and workers' compensation expenses.

Included in operating profit	$ 1,872,000
Nonoperating expense	9,077,000
Total	$10,949,000

The Company is seeking to reasonably determine its liability. However, it is not possible to predict which theory of insurance will apply, the number of lawsuits still to be filed, the cost of settling and defending the existing and unfiled cases, or the ultimate impact of these lawsuits on the Company's consolidated financial statements.

Companies should disclose certain other contingent liabilities, even though the possibility of loss may be remote, as follows.

1. Guarantees of indebtedness of others.
2. Obligations of commercial banks under "stand-by letters of credit."
3. Guarantees to repurchase receivables (or any related property) that have been sold or assigned.

Disclosure should include the nature and amount of the guarantee and, if estimable, the amount that the company can recover from outside parties.[27] **Cities Service Company** disclosed its guarantees of others' indebtedness in the following note.

INTERNATIONAL INSIGHT

U.S. GAAP provides more guidance on the content of disclosures about contingencies than do IFRS.

ILLUSTRATION 12-16
Disclosure of Guarantees of Indebtedness

Cities Service Company

Note 10: Contingent Liabilities. The Company and certain subsidiaries have guaranteed debt obligations of approximately $62 million of companies in which substantial stock investments are held. Also, under long-term agreements with certain pipeline companies in which stock interests are held, the Company and its subsidiaries have agreed to provide minimum revenue for product shipments. The Company has guaranteed mortgage debt ($80 million) incurred by a 50 percent owned tanker affiliate for construction of tankers which are under long-term charter contracts to the Company and others. It is not anticipated that any loss will result from any of the above described agreements.

Analysis of Current Liabilities

The distinction between current liabilities and long-term debt is important. It provides information about the liquidity of the company. Liquidity regarding a liability is the expected time to elapse before its payment. In other words, a liability soon to be paid is a current liability. A liquid company is better able to withstand a financial downturn. Also, it has a better chance of taking advantage of investment opportunities that develop.

Analysts use certain basic ratios such as net cash flow provided by operating activities to current liabilities, and the turnover ratios for receivables and inventory, to assess liquidity. Two other ratios used to examine liquidity are the current ratio and the acid-test ratio.

Current Ratio

The **current ratio** is the ratio of total current assets to total current liabilities. Illustration 12-17 shows its formula.

ILLUSTRATION 12-17
Formula for Current Ratio

$$\text{Current ratio} = \frac{\text{Current assets}}{\text{Current liabilities}}$$

The ratio is frequently expressed as a coverage of so many times. Sometimes it is called the **working capital ratio** because working capital is the excess of current assets over current liabilities.

[27] As discussed earlier (footnote 21), the FASB recently issued additional disclosure and recognition requirements for guarantees. The interpretation responds to confusion about the application of *SFAS No. 5* to guarantees used in certain transactions. The new rules expand existing disclosure requirements for most guarantees, including loan guarantees such as standby letters of credit. It also will result in companies recognizing more liabilities at fair value for the obligations assumed under a guarantee (*FASB Interpretation No. 45*, op. cit.).

A satisfactory current ratio does not disclose that a portion of the current assets may be tied up in slow-moving inventories. With inventories, especially raw materials and work in process, there is a question of how long it will take to transform them into the finished product and what ultimately will be realized in the sale of the merchandise. Eliminating the inventories, along with any prepaid expenses, from the amount of current assets might provide better information for short-term creditors. Therefore, some analysts use the acid-test ratio in place of the current ratio.

Acid-Test Ratio

Many analysts favor an **acid-test** or **quick ratio** that relates total current liabilities to cash, marketable securities, and receivables. Illustration 12-18 shows the formula for this ratio. As you can see, the acid-test ratio does not include inventories.

ILLUSTRATION 12-18
Formula for Acid-Test Ratio

$$\text{Acid-test ratio} = \frac{\text{Cash} + \text{Short-term investments} + \text{Net receivables}}{\text{Current liabilities}}$$

To illustrate the computation of these two ratios, we use the information for **Best Buy Co.** in Illustration 12-13. Illustration 12-19 shows the computation of the current and acid-test ratios for Best Buy.

ILLUSTRATION 12-19
Computation of Current and Acid-Test Ratios for Best Buy Co.

$$\text{Current ratio} = \frac{\text{Current assets}}{\text{Current liabilities}} = \frac{\$6{,}903}{\$4{,}959} = 1.39 \text{ times}$$

$$\text{Acid-test ratio} = \frac{\text{Cash} + \text{Short-term investments} + \text{Net receivables}}{\text{Current liabilities}} = \frac{\$3{,}723}{\$4{,}959} = 0.75 \text{ times}$$

From this information, it appears that Best Buy's current position is adequate. However, the acid-test ratio is well below 1. A comparison to another retailer, **Circuit City**, whose current ratio is 2.13 and whose acid-test ratio is 0.75, indicates that Best Buy is carrying less inventory than its industry counterparts.

QUESTIONS

1. Distinguish between a current liability and a long-term debt.
2. Assume that your friend Greg Jonas, who is a music major, asks you to define and discuss the nature of a liability. Assist him by preparing a definition of a liability and by explaining to him what you believe are the elements or factors inherent in the concept of a liability.
3. Why is the liabilities section of the balance sheet of primary significance to bankers?
4. How are current liabilities related by definition to current assets? How are current liabilities related to a company's operating cycle?
5. Jon Bryant, a newly hired loan analyst, is examining the current liabilities of a corporate loan applicant. He observes that unearned revenues have declined in the current year compared to the prior year. Is this a positive indicator about the client's liquidity? Explain.
6. How is present value related to the concept of a liability?
7. What is the nature of a "discount" on notes payable?
8. How should a debt callable by the creditor be reported in the debtor's financial statements?
9. Under what conditions should a short-term obligation be excluded from current liabilities?
10. What evidence is necessary to demonstrate the ability to consummate the refinancing of short-term debt?
11. Discuss the accounting treatment or disclosure that should be accorded a declared but unpaid cash dividend; an accumulated but undeclared dividend on cumulative preferred stock; a stock dividend distributable.
12. How does unearned revenue arise? Why can it be classified properly as a current liability? Give several examples of business activities that result in unearned revenues.

13. What are compensated absences?

14. Under what conditions must an employer accrue a liability for the cost of compensated absences?

15. Under what conditions is an employer required to accrue a liability for sick pay? Under what conditions is an employer permitted but not required to accrue a liability for sick pay?

16. Caitlin Carter operates a health food store, and she has been the only employee. Her business is growing, and she is considering hiring some additional staff to help her in the store. Explain to her the various payroll deductions that she will have to account for, including their potential impact on her financial statements, if she hires additional staff.

17. Define (a) a contingency and (b) a contingent liability.

18. Under what conditions should a contingent liability be recorded?

19. Distinguish between a current liability and a contingent liability. Give two examples of each type.

20. How are the terms "probable," "reasonably possible," and "remote" related to contingent liabilities?

21. Contrast the cash basis method and the accrual method of accounting for warranty costs.

22. Kren Company has had a record-breaking year in terms of growth in sales and profitability. However, market research indicates that it will experience operating losses in two of its major businesses next year. The controller has proposed that the company record a provision for these future losses this year, since it can afford to take the charge and still show good results. Advise the controller on the appropriateness of this charge.

23. How does the expense warranty approach differ from the sales warranty approach?

24. Zucker-Abrahams Airlines Inc. awards members of its Flightline program a second ticket at half price, valid for 2 years anywhere on its flight system, when a full-price ticket is purchased. How would you account for the full-fare and half-fare tickets?

25. Northeast Airlines Co. awards members of its Frequent Fliers Club one free round-trip ticket, anywhere on its flight system, for every 50,000 miles flown on its planes. How would you account for the free ticket award?

26. When must a company recognize an asset retirement obligation?

27. Should a liability be recorded for risk of loss due to lack of insurance coverage? Discuss.

28. What factors must be considered in determining whether or not to record a liability for pending litigation? For threatened litigation?

29. Within the current liabilities section, how do you believe the accounts should be listed? Defend your position.

30. How does the acid-test ratio differ from the current ratio? How are they similar?

31. When should liabilities for each of the following items be recorded on the books of an ordinary business corporation?

(a) Acquisition of goods by purchase on credit.

(b) Officers' salaries.

(c) Special bonus to employees.

(d) Dividends.

(e) Purchase commitments.

CHAPTER THIRTEEN

LONG-TERM LIABILITIES

Your Debt Is Killing My Stock

Traditionally, investors in the stock and bond markets operate in their own separate worlds. However, in recent volatile markets, even quiet murmurs in the bond market have been amplified into movements (usually negative) in stock prices. At one extreme, these gyrations heralded the demise of a company well before the investors could sniff out the problem.

The swift decline of **Enron** in late 2001 provided the ultimate lesson: A company with no credit is no company at all. As one analyst remarked, "You can no longer have an opinion on a company's stock without having an appreciation for its credit rating." Other energy companies, such as **Calpine**, **NRG Energy**, and **AES Corp.**, also felt the effect of Enron's troubles as lenders tightened or closed down the credit supply and raised interest rates on already-high levels of debt. The result? Stock prices took a hit.

Other industries are not immune from the negative stock price effects of credit problems. For example, analysts at **TheStreet.com** compiled a list of companies with high debt levels and low ability to cover interest costs. Among them is **Goodyear Tire and Rubber**, which reported debt six times greater than its equity. Goodyear is a classic example of how swift and crippling a heavy debt-load can be. Not too long ago, Goodyear had a high debt rating and was paying a good dividend. But with mounting operating losses, Goodyear's debt became a huge burden, its debt rating fell to junk-status, the company cut its dividend, and its stock price dropped 80%. This was yet another example of stock prices taking a hit due to concerns about credit quality. Thus, even if your investment tastes are in stocks, keep an eye on the liabilities.[1]

[1]Adapted from Steven Vames, "Credit Quality, Stock Investing Seem to Go Hand in Hand," *Wall Street Journal* (April 1, 2002), p. R4 and Herb Greenberg, "The Hidden Dangers of Debt," *Fortune* (July 21, 2003), p. 153.

Learning Objectives

After studying this chapter, you should be able to:

1. Describe the formal procedures associated with issuing long-term debt.
2. Identify various types of bond issues.
3. Describe the accounting valuation for bonds at date of issuance.
4. Apply the methods of bond discount and premium amortization.
5. Describe the accounting for the extinguishment of debt.
6. Explain the accounting for long-term notes payable.
7. Explain the reporting of off-balance-sheet financing arrangements.
8. Indicate how to present and analyze long-term debt.

PREVIEW OF CHAPTER 13

As our opening story indicates, investors pay considerable attention to a company's liabilities. The stock market severely punishes companies with high debt levels and the related impact of higher interest costs on income performance. In this chapter we explain the accounting issues related to long-term debt. The content and organization of the chapter are as follows.

LONG-TERM LIABILITIES

- **BONDS PAYABLE**
  - Issuing bonds
  - Types and ratings
  - Valuation
  - Effective-interest method
  - Costs of issuing
  - Treasury bonds
  - Extinguishment
- **LONG-TERM NOTES PAYABLE**
  - Notes issued at face value
  - Notes not issued at face value
  - Special situations
  - Mortgage notes payable
- **REPORTING AND ANALYSIS OF LONG-TERM DEBT**
  - Off-balance-sheet financing
  - Presentation and analysis

SECTION 1 *BONDS PAYABLE*

Long-term debt consists of probable future sacrifices of economic benefits arising from present obligations that are not payable within a year or the operating cycle of the company, whichever is longer. Bonds payable, long-term notes payable, mortgages payable, pension liabilities, and lease liabilities are examples of long-term liabilities.

A corporation, per its bylaws, usually requires approval by the board of directors and the stockholders before bonds or notes can be issued. The same holds true for other types of long-term debt arrangements.

OBJECTIVE 1
Describe the formal procedures associated with issuing long-term debt.

Generally, long-term debt has various **covenants** or **restrictions** that protect both lenders and borrowers. The indenture or agreement often includes the amounts authorized to be issued, interest rate, due date(s), call provisions, property pledged as security, sinking fund requirements, working capital and dividend restrictions, and limitations concerning the assumption of additional debt. Companies should describe these features in the body of the financial statements or the notes if important for a complete understanding of the financial position and the results of operations.

Although it would seem that these covenants provide adequate protection to the long-term debtholder, many bondholders suffer considerable losses when companies add more debt to the capital structure. Consider what can happen to bondholders in leveraged buyouts (LBOs), which are usually led by management. In an LBO of **RJR Nabisco**, for example, solidly rated 9⅜ percent bonds due in 2016 plunged 20 percent in value when management announced the leveraged buyout. Such a loss in value occurs because the additional debt added to the capital structure increases the likelihood of default. Although covenants protect bondholders, they can still suffer losses when debt levels get too high.

ISSUING BONDS

A bond arises from a contract known as a **bond indenture**. A bond represents a promise to pay: (1) a sum of money at a designated maturity date, plus (2) periodic interest at a specified rate on the maturity amount (face value). Individual bonds are evidenced by a paper certificate and typically have a $1,000 face value. Companies usually make bond interest payments semiannually, although the interest rate is generally expressed as an annual rate. The main purpose of bonds is to borrow for the long term when the amount of capital needed is too large for one lender to supply. By issuing bonds in $100, $1,000, or $10,000 denominations, a company can divide a large amount of long-term indebtedness into many small investing units, thus enabling more than one lender to participate in the loan.

A company may sell an entire bond issue to an investment bank which acts as a selling agent in the process of marketing the bonds. In such arrangements, investment banks may either underwrite the entire issue by guaranteeing a certain sum to the company, thus taking the risk of selling the bonds for whatever price they can get (firm underwriting). Or they may sell the bond issue for a commission on the proceeds of the sale (best-efforts underwriting). Alternatively, the issuing company may sell the bonds directly to a large institution, financial or otherwise, without the aid of an underwriter (private placement).

TYPES AND RATINGS OF BONDS

Below, we define some of the more common types of bonds found in practice.

OBJECTIVE 2
Identify various types of bond issues.

TYPES OF BONDS

SECURED AND UNSECURED BONDS. Secured bonds are backed by a pledge of some sort of collateral. Mortgage bonds are secured by a claim on real estate. Collateral trust bonds are secured by stocks and bonds of other corporations. Bonds not backed by collateral are **unsecured**. A **debenture bond** is unsecured. A "junk bond" is unsecured and also very risky, and therefore pays a high interest rate. Companies often use these bonds to finance leveraged buyouts.

TERM, SERIAL BONDS, AND CALLABLE BONDS. Bond issues that mature on a single date are called **term bonds**; issues that mature in installments are called **serial bonds**. Serially maturing bonds are frequently used by school or sanitary districts, municipalities, or other local taxing bodies that receive money through a special levy. **Callable bonds** give the issuer the right to call and retire the bonds prior to maturity.

CONVERTIBLE, COMMODITY-BACKED, AND DEEP-DISCOUNT BONDS. If bonds are convertible into other securities of the corporation for a specified time after issuance, they are **convertible bonds**.

Two types of bonds have been developed in an attempt to attract capital in a tight money market—commodity-backed bonds and deep-discount bonds. **Commodity-backed bonds** (also called **asset-linked bonds**) are redeemable in measures of a commodity, such as barrels of oil, tons of coal, or ounces of rare metal. To illustrate, **Sunshine Mining**, a silver-mining company, sold two issues of bonds redeemable with either $1,000 in cash or 50 ounces of silver, whichever is greater at maturity, and that have a stated interest rate of 8½ percent. The accounting problem is one of projecting the maturity value, especially since silver has fluctuated between $4 and $40 an ounce since issuance.

JCPenney Company sold the first publicly marketed long-term debt securities in the United States that do not bear interest. These **deep-discount bonds**, also referred to as **zero-interest debenture bonds**, are sold at a discount that provides the buyer's total interest payoff at maturity.

REGISTERED AND BEARER (COUPON) BONDS. Bonds issued in the name of the owner are **registered bonds** and require surrender of the certificate and issuance of a new certificate to complete a sale. A **bearer** or **coupon bond**, however, is not recorded in the name of the owner and may be transferred from one owner to another by mere delivery.

INCOME AND REVENUE BONDS. Income bonds pay no interest unless the issuing company is profitable. **Revenue bonds**, so called because the interest on them is paid from specified revenue sources, are most frequently issued by airports, school districts, counties, toll-road authorities, and governmental bodies.

WHAT DO THE NUMBERS MEAN?

ALL ABOUT BONDS

How do investors monitor their bond investments? Typically, they review the bond listings found in the newspaper or online. Corporate bond listings in the financial press show the coupon or interest rate, maturity date, and last price. However, because corporate bonds are more actively traded by large institutional investors, the listings also indicate the current yield and include the volume traded. Corporate bond listings would look like those below.

Bonds	Cur. Yld.	Vol	Close	Net Chg.
BosCelts 6s38	9.2	22	65 3/8	+1/4
PacBell 6 5/8 34	6.7	5	99 1/8	−1/8

The companies issuing the bonds are listed in the first column—in this case, the professional basketball team the **Boston Celtics**, and the telecommunications company **Pacific Bell**. Immediately after the names, comes the interest rate paid by the bond as a percentage of its par value. The Celtics' bond pays 6 percent; PacBell's pays 6 5/8 percent. (The small "s" in the Celtics' listing simply separates the interest rate from the year the bond matures, 2038.) The PacBell bond matures in 2034.

Reading on, the basketball team's bond has a current yield of 9.2 percent based on its closing price of $653.75 per $1,000. The volume traded on the exchange the day before amounted to $22,000, and the price rose $2.50. Similarly, PacBell had a volume of $5,000 and closed nearer its par value, $991.25, down $1.25 for the day.

Also, as indicated in the chapter, interest rates and the bond's term to maturity have a real effect on bond prices. For example, an increase in interest rates will lead to a decline in bond values; a decrease in interest rates will lead to a rise in bond values. These effects are shown in the data reported below, based on three different bond funds.

Bond Price Changes in Response to Interest Rate Changes	1% Interest Rate Increase	1% Interest Rate Decrease
Short-term fund (2–5 years)	−2.5%	+2.5%
Intermediate-term fund (5 years)	−5%	+5%
Long-term fund (10 years)	−10%	+10%

Source: Data from The Vanguard Group.

Another factor that affects bond prices is the call feature, which decreases the value of the bond. Investors must be rewarded for the risk that the issuer will call the bond if interest rates decline, which forces the investor to reinvest at lower rates.

Source: The Bond Market Association (*www.investinginbonds.com*).

OBJECTIVE 3
Describe the accounting valuation for bonds at date of issuance.

VALUATION OF BONDS PAYABLE—DISCOUNT AND PREMIUM

The issuance and marketing of bonds to the public does not happen overnight. It usually takes weeks or even months. First, the issuing company must arrange for underwriters that will help market and sell the bonds. Then it must obtain the Securities and Exchange

Commission's approval of the bond issue, undergo audits, and issue a prospectus (a document which describes the features of the bond and related financial information). Finally, the company must generally have the bond certificates printed. Frequently the issuing company establishes the terms of a bond indenture well in advance of the sale of the bonds. Between the time the company sets these terms and the time it issues the bonds, the market conditions and the financial position of the issuing corporation may change significantly. Such changes affect the marketability of the bonds and thus their selling price.

The selling price of a bond issue is set by the supply and demand of buyers and sellers, relative risk, market conditions, and the state of the economy. The investment community values a bond at the **present value of its expected future cash flows**, which consist of (1) interest and (2) principal. The rate used to compute the present value of these cash flows is the interest rate that provides an acceptable return on an investment commensurate with the issuer's risk characteristics.

INTERNATIONAL INSIGHT

IFRS for long-term debt permit valuation of long-term debt and other liabilities at fair value with gains and losses on changes in fair value recorded in income (referred to as the "fair value option").

The interest rate written in the terms of the bond indenture (and often printed on the bond certificate) is known as the **stated**, **coupon**, or **nominal rate**. The issuer of the bonds sets this rate. The stated rate is expressed as a percentage of the **face value** of the bonds (also called the **par value, principal amount**, or **maturity value**).

If the rate employed by the investment community (buyers) differs from the stated rate, the present value of the bonds computed by the buyers (and the current purchase price) will differ from the face value of the bonds. The difference between the face value and the present value of the bonds determines the actual price that buyers pay for the bonds. This difference is either a discount or premium.[2] If the bonds sell for less than face value, they sell at a **discount**. If the bonds sell for more than face value, they sell at a **premium**.

The rate of interest actually earned by the bondholders is called the **effective yield** or **market rate**. If bonds sell at a discount, the effective yield exceeds the stated rate. Conversely, if bonds sell at a premium, the effective yield is lower than the stated rate. Several variables affect the bond's price while it is outstanding, most notably the market rate of interest. There is an inverse relationship between the market interest rate and the price of the bond.

Here we consider an example to illustrate the computation of the **present value of a bond issue**. Assume that ServiceMaster issues $100,000 in bonds, due in five years with 9 percent interest payable annually at year-end. At the time of issue, the market rate for such bonds is 11 percent. The time diagram in Illustration 13-1 depicts both the interest and the principal cash flows.

ILLUSTRATION 13-1
Time Diagram for Bond Cash Flows

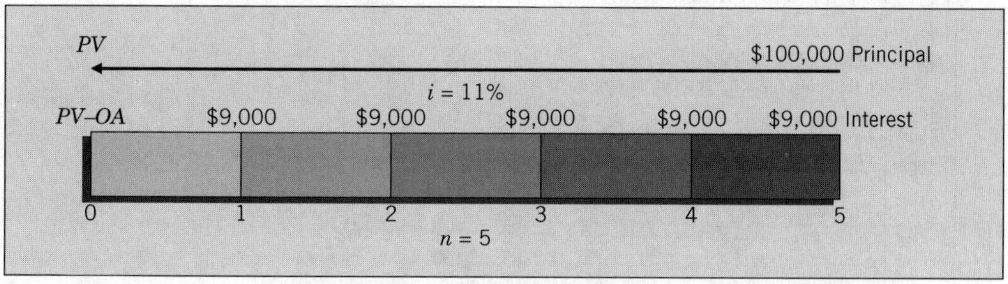

[2]Until the 1950s, corporations commonly issued bonds with low, even-percentage coupons (such as 4 percent) to demonstrate their financial solidity. Frequently, large discounts resulted. More recently, it has become acceptable to set the stated rate of interest on bonds in rather precise fractions (such as $10\frac{7}{8}$ percent). Companies usually attempt to align the stated rate as closely as possible with the market or effective rate at the time of issue.

Although discounts and premiums continue to occur, their absolute magnitude tends to be much smaller; many times it is immaterial. A study conducted in the mid-80's documented that of 685 new debt offerings, none were issued at a premium. Approximately 95 percent were issued either with no discount or at a price above 98. Now, however, zero-interest (deep discount) bonds are more popular, and they cause substantial discounts.

The actual principal and interest cash flows are discounted at an 11 percent rate for five periods as shown in Illustration 13-2.

ILLUSTRATION 13-2
Present Value Computation of Bond Selling at a Discount

Present value of the principal:	
$100,000 × .59345 (Table 6-2)	$59,345.00
Present value of the interest payments:	
$9,000 × 3.69590 (Table 6-4)	33,263.10
Present value (selling price) of the bonds	$92,608.10

By paying $92,608.10 at the date of issue, investors realize an effective rate or yield of 11 percent over the five-year term of the bonds. These bonds would sell at a discount of $7,391.90 ($100,000 − $92,608.10). The price at which the bonds sell is typically stated as a percentage of the face or par value of the bonds. For example, the ServiceMaster bonds sold for 92.6 (92.6% of par). If ServiceMaster had received $102,000, then the bonds sold for 102 (102% of par).

WHAT DO THE NUMBERS MEAN?

HOW'S MY RATING?

Two major publication companies, **Moody's Investors Service** and **Standard & Poor's Corporation**, issue quality ratings on every public debt issue. The following table summarizes the ratings issued by Standard & Poor's, along with historical default rates on bonds with different ratings. As expected, bonds receiving the highest quality rating of AAA have the lowest historical default rates. Bonds rated below BBB, which are considered below investment grade ("junk bonds"), experience default rates ranging from 20 to 50 percent.

Original Rating	AAA	AA	A	BBB	BB	B	CCC
Default Rate*	0.52%	1.31	2.32	6.64	19.52	35.76	54.38

*Percentage of defaults by issuers recently rated by Standard & Poor's, based on rating they were initially assigned. *Source*: Data from Standard & Poor's Corp.

Debt ratings reflect credit quality. The market closely monitors these ratings when determining the required yield and pricing of bonds at issuance and in periods after issuance, especially if a bond's rating is upgraded or downgraded. Data on recent upgrades and downgrades suggest there are a lot more fallen angels (downgraded debt) than rising stars (upgraded debt).

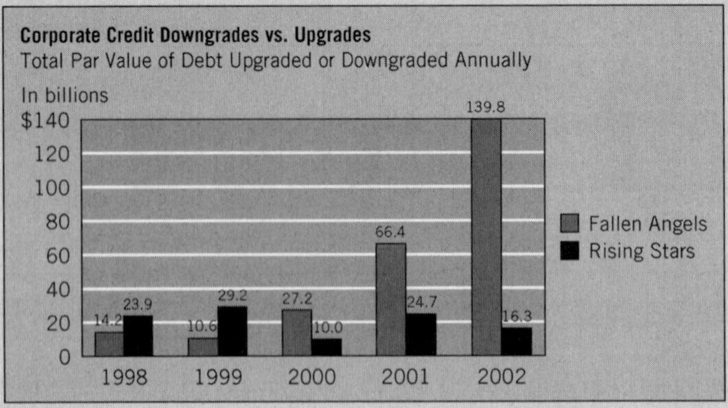

Source: J.P. Morgan Chase & Co.

Whereas the dollar amount of upgrades exceeded downgrades in 1999, the dollar amount of downgrades was more than seven times the rising-star amounts in 2002. It is not surprising, then, that bond investors and companies who issue bonds keep a close watch on debt ratings—both when bonds are issued and while the bonds are outstanding.

Source: A. Borrus, M. McNamee, and H. Timmons, "The Credit Raters: How They Work and How They Might Work Better," *Business Week* (April 8, 2002), pp. 38–40; and the T. Rowe Price Report (Winter 2003).

When bonds sell below face value, it means that investors demand a rate of interest **higher** than the stated rate. Usually this occurs because the investors can earn a greater rate on alternative investments of equal risk. They cannot change the stated rate, so they refuse to pay face value for the bonds. Thus, by changing the amount invested, they alter the effective rate of return. The investors receive interest at the stated rate computed on the face value, but they actually earn at **an effective rate that exceeds the stated rate because they paid less than face value for the bonds.** (Later in the chapter, in Illustrations 13-6 and 13-7, we show an illustration for a bond that sells at a premium.)

Bonds Issued at Par on Interest Date

When a company issues bonds on an interest payment date at par (face value), it accrues no interest. No premium or discount exists. The company simply records the cash proceeds and the face value of the bonds. To illustrate, if Buchanan Company issues at par 10-year term bonds with a par value of $800,000, dated January 1, 2007, and bearing interest at an annual rate of 10 percent payable semiannually on January 1 and July 1, it records the following entry:

Cash	800,000	
Bonds Payable		800,000

Buchanan records the first semiannual interest payment of $40,000 ($800,000 × .10 × 1/2) on July 1, 2007, as follows.

Bond Interest Expense	40,000	
Cash		40,000

It records accrued interest expense at December 31, 2007 (year-end) as follows.

Bond Interest Expense	40,000	
Bond Interest Payable		40,000

Bonds Issued at Discount or Premium on Interest Date

OBJECTIVE 4
Apply the methods of bond discount and premium amortization.

If Buchanan Company issues the $800,000 of bonds on January 1, 2007, at 97 (meaning 97 percent of par), it records the issuance as follows.

Cash ($800,000 × .97)	776,000	
Discount on Bonds Payable	24,000	
Bonds Payable		800,000

Recall from our earlier discussion that because of its relation to interest, **companies amortize the discount and charge it to interest expense over the period of time that the bonds are outstanding.**

The **straight-line method**[3] amortizes a constant amount each year. For example, using the bond discount of $24,000, Buchanan amortizes $2,400 to interest expense each year for 10 years ($24,000 ÷ 10 years). It records amortization annually as follows.

Bond Interest Expense	2,400	
Discount on Bonds Payable		2,400

At the end of the first year, 2007, following the amortization entry above, the unamortized balance in Discount on Bonds Payable is $21,600 ($24,000 − $2,400).

If Buchanan dates and sells the bonds on October 1, 2007, and if the fiscal year of the corporation ends on December 31, the discount amortized during 2007 would be only 3/12 of 1/10 of $24,000, or $600. Buchanan must also record three months of accrued interest on December 31.

[3]Although the effective-interest method is preferred for amortization of discount or premium, to keep these initial illustrations simple, we have chosen to use the straight-line method (which is acceptable if the results obtained are not materially different from those produced by the effective-interest method).

Premium on Bonds Payable is accounted for in a manner similar to that for Discount on Bonds Payable. If Buchanan dates and sells 10-year bonds with a par value of $800,000 on January 1, 2007, at 103, it records the issuance as follows.

Cash ($800,000 × 1.03)	824,000	
Premium on Bonds Payable		24,000
Bonds Payable		800,000

At the end of 2007 and for each year the bonds are outstanding, Buchanan amortizes the premium on a straight-line basis with the following entry.

Premium on Bonds Payable	2,400	
Bond Interest Expense		2,400

Amortization of a discount increases bond interest expense. Amortization of a premium decreases bond interest expense. Later in the chapter we discuss amortization of a discount or premium under the effective-interest method.

The issuer may call some bonds at a stated price after a certain date. This call feature gives the issuing corporation the opportunity to reduce its bonded indebtedness or take advantage of lower interest rates. **Whether callable or not, a company must amortize any premium or discount over the bond's life to maturity because early redemption (call of the bond) is not a certainty.**

Bonds Issued between Interest Dates

Companies usually make bond interest payments semiannually, on dates specified in the bond indenture. When companies issue bonds on other than the interest payment dates, **buyers of the bonds will pay the seller the interest accrued from the last interest payment date to the date of issue**. The purchasers of the bonds, in effect, pay the bond issuer in advance for that portion of the full six-months' interest payment to which they are not entitled because they have not held the bonds for that period. **Then, on the next semiannual interest payment date, purchasers will receive the full six-months' interest payment.**

To illustrate, assume that on March 1, 2007, Taft Corporation issues 10-year bonds, dated January 1, 2007, with a par value of $800,000. These bonds have an annual interest rate of 6 percent, payable semiannually on January 1 and July 1. Because Taft issues the bonds between interest dates, it records the bond issuance at **par plus accrued interest** as follows.

Cash	808,000	
Bonds Payable		800,000
Bond Interest Expense ($800,000 × .06 × 2/12)		8,000
(Interest Payable might be credited instead)		

The purchaser advances two months' interest. On July 1, 2007, four months after the date of purchase, Taft pays the purchaser six months' interest. Taft makes the following entry on July 1, 2007.

Bond Interest Expense	24,000	
Cash		24,000

The Bond Interest Expense account now contains a debit balance of $16,000, which represents the proper amount of interest expense—four months at 6 percent on $800,000.

The illustration above was simplified by having the January 1, 2007, bonds issued on March 1, 2007, **at par.** If, however, Taft issued the 6 percent bonds at 102, its March 1 entry would be:

Cash [($800,000 × 1.02) + ($800,000 × .06 × 2/12)]	824,000	
Bonds Payable		800,000
Premium on Bonds Payable ($800,000 × .02)		16,000
Bond Interest Expense		8,000

Taft would amortize the premium **from the date of sale** (March 1, 2007), not from the date of the bonds (January 1, 2007).

EFFECTIVE-INTEREST METHOD

The preferred procedure for amortization of a discount or premium is the **effective-interest method** (also called **present value amortization**). Under the effective-interest method, companies:

1. Compute bond interest expense first by multiplying the **carrying value** (book value) of the bonds at the beginning of the period by the effective interest rate.[4]
2. Determine the bond discount or premium amortization next by comparing the bond interest expense with the interest (cash) to be paid.

Illustration 13-3 depicts graphically the computation of the amortization.

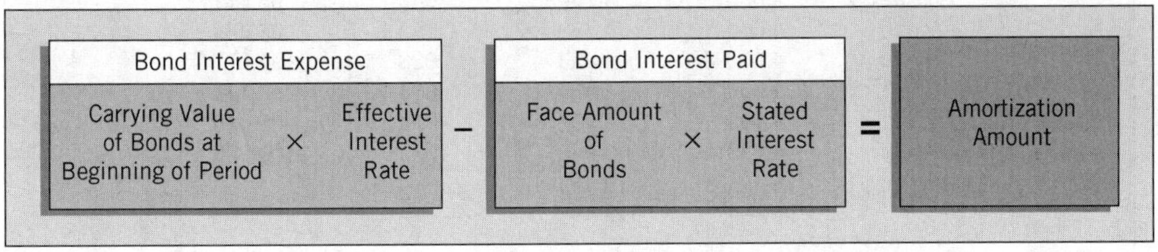

ILLUSTRATION 13-3
Bond Discount and Premium Amortization Computation

The effective-interest method produces a periodic interest expense equal to **a constant percentage of the carrying value of the bonds.** Since the percentage is the effective rate of interest incurred by the borrower at the time of issuance, the effective-interest method matches expenses with revenues better than the straight-line method.

Both the effective-interest and straight-line methods result in the **same total amount of interest expense over the term of the bonds.** However, when the annual amounts are materially different, generally accepted accounting principles require use of the effective-interest method.[5]

Bonds Issued at a Discount

To illustrate amortization of a discount under the effective-interest method, Evermaster Corporation issued $100,000 of 8 percent term bonds on January 1, 2007, due on January 1, 2012, with interest payable each July 1 and January 1. Because the investors required an effective-interest rate of 10 percent, they paid $92,278 for the $100,000 of bonds, creating a $7,722 discount. Evermaster computes the $7,722 discount as follows.[6]

ILLUSTRATION 13-4
Computation of Discount on Bonds Payable

Maturity value of bonds payable		$100,000
Present value of $100,000 due in 5 years at 10%, interest payable semiannually (Table 6-2); $FV(PVF_{10,5\%})$; ($100,000 × .61391)	$61,391	
Present value of $4,000 interest payable semiannually for 5 years at 10% annually (Table 6-4); $R(PVF\text{-}OA_{10,5\%})$; ($4,000 × 7.72173)	30,887	
Proceeds from sale of bonds		92,278
Discount on bonds payable		$ 7,722

[4]The **carrying value** is the face amount minus any unamortized discount or plus any unamortized premium. The term *carrying value* is synonymous with *book value.*

[5]"Interest on Receivables and Payables," *Opinions of the Accounting Principles Board No. 21* (New York: AICPA, 1971), par. 16.

[6]Because companies pay interest semiannually, the interest rate used is 5% $(10\% \times \frac{6}{12})$. The number of periods is 10 (5 years × 2).

The five-year amortization schedule appears in Illustration 13-5.

ILLUSTRATION 13-5
Bond Discount Amortization Schedule

Calculator Solution for Present Value of Bonds:

	Inputs	Answer
N	10	
I/YR	5	
PV	?	92,278
PMT	−4,000	
FV	−100,000	

SCHEDULE OF BOND DISCOUNT AMORTIZATION
EFFECTIVE-INTEREST METHOD—SEMIANNUAL INTEREST PAYMENTS
5-YEAR, 8% BONDS SOLD TO YIELD 10%

Date	Cash Paid	Interest Expense	Discount Amortized	Carrying Amount of Bonds
1/1/07				$ 92,278
7/1/07	$ 4,000[a]	$ 4,614[b]	$ 614[c]	92,892[d]
1/1/08	4,000	4,645	645	93,537
7/1/08	4,000	4,677	677	94,214
1/1/09	4,000	4,711	711	94,925
7/1/09	4,000	4,746	746	95,671
1/1/10	4,000	4,783	783	96,454
7/1/10	4,000	4,823	823	97,277
1/1/11	4,000	4,864	864	98,141
7/1/11	4,000	4,907	907	99,048
1/1/12	4,000	4,952	952	100,000
	$40,000	$47,722	$7,722	

[a]$4,000 = $100,000 × .08 × 6/12
[b]$4,614 = $92,278 × .10 × 6/12
[c]$614 = $4,614 − $4,000
[d]$92,892 = $92,278 + $614

Evermaster records the issuance of its bonds at a discount on January 1, 2007, as follows:

Cash	92,278	
Discount on Bonds Payable	7,722	
Bonds Payable		100,000

It records the first interest payment on July 1, 2007, and amortization of the discount as follows:

Bond Interest Expense	4,614	
Discount on Bonds Payable		614
Cash		4,000

Evermaster records the interest expense accrued at December 31, 2007 (year-end) and amortization of the discount as follows:

Bond Interest Expense	4,645	
Bond Interest Payable		4,000
Discount on Bonds Payable		645

Bonds Issued at a Premium

Now assume that for the bond issue described above, investors are willing to accept an effective interest rate of 6 percent. In that case, they would pay $108,530 or a premium of $8,530, computed as follows.

ILLUSTRATION 13-6
Computation of Premium on Bonds Payable

Maturity value of bonds payable		$100,000
Present value of $100,000 due in 5 years at 6%, interest payable semiannually (Table 6-2); $FV(PVF_{10,3\%})$; ($100,000 × .74409)	$74,409	
Present value of $4,000 interest payable semiannually for 5 years at 6% annually (Table 6-4); $R(PVF\text{-}OA_{10,3\%})$; ($4,000 × 8.53020)	34,121	
Proceeds from sale of bonds		108,530
Premium on bonds payable		$ 8,530

The five-year amortization schedule appears in Illustration 13-7.

ILLUSTRATION 13-7
Bond Premium Amortization Schedule

SCHEDULE OF BOND PREMIUM AMORTIZATION
EFFECTIVE-INTEREST METHOD—SEMIANNUAL INTEREST PAYMENTS
5-YEAR, 8% BONDS SOLD TO YIELD 6%

Date	Cash Paid	Interest Expense	Premium Amortized	Carrying Amount of Bonds
1/1/07				$108,530
7/1/07	$ 4,000[a]	$ 3,256[b]	$ 744[c]	107,786[d]
1/1/08	4,000	3,234	766	107,020
7/1/08	4,000	3,211	789	106,231
1/1/09	4,000	3,187	813	105,418
7/1/09	4,000	3,162	838	104,580
1/1/10	4,000	3,137	863	103,717
7/1/10	4,000	3,112	888	102,829
1/1/11	4,000	3,085	915	101,914
7/1/11	4,000	3,057	943	100,971
1/1/12	4,000	3,029	971	100,000
	$40,000	$31,470	$8,530	

[a]$4,000 = $100,000 × .08 × 6/12
[b]$3,256 = $108,530 × .06 × 6/12
[c]$744 = $4,000 − $3,256
[d]$107,786 = $108,530 − $744

Calculator Solution for Present Value of Bonds:

	Inputs	Answer
N	10	
I/YR	3	
PV	?	108,530
PMT	-4,000	
FV	-100,000	

Evermaster records the issuance of its bonds at a premium on January 1, 2007, as follows:

Cash	108,530	
Premium on Bonds Payable		8,530
Bonds Payable		100,000

Evermaster records the first interest payment on July 1, 2007, and amortization of the premium as follows:

Bond Interest Expense	3,256	
Premium on Bonds Payable	744	
Cash		4,000

Evermaster should amortize the discount or premium as an adjustment to interest expense over the life of the bond in such a way as to result in a **constant rate of interest** when applied to the carrying amount of debt outstanding at the beginning of any given period.

Accruing Interest

In our previous examples, the interest payment dates and the date the financial statements were issued were the same. For example, when Evermaster sold bonds at a premium, the two interest payment dates coincided with the financial reporting dates. However, what happens if Evermaster wishes to report financial statements at the end of February 2007? In this case, the company **prorates** the premium by the appropriate number of months, to arrive at the proper interest expense, as follows.

ILLUSTRATION 13-8
Computation of Interest Expense

Interest accrual ($4,000 × 2/6)	$1,333.33
Premium amortized ($744 × 2/6)	(248.00)
Interest expense (Jan.–Feb.)	$1,085.33

Evermaster records this accrual as follows.

Bond Interest Expense	1,085.33	
Premium on Bonds Payable	248.00	
Bond Interest Payable		1,333.33

If the company prepares financial statements six months later, it follows the same procedure. That is, the premium amortized would be as follows.

ILLUSTRATION 13-9
Computation of Premium Amortization

Premium amortized (March–June) ($744 × 4/6)	$496.00
Premium amortized (July–August) ($766 × 2/6)	255.33
Premium amortized (March–August 2004)	$751.33

The interest-accrual computation is much simpler if the company uses the straight-line method. For example, the total premium is $8,530, which Evermaster allocates evenly over the five-year period. Thus, premium amortization per month is $142.17 ($8,530 ÷ 60 months).

Classification of Discount and Premium

Discount on bonds payable is **not an asset**. It does not provide any future economic benefit. In return for the use of borrowed funds, a company must pay interest. A bond discount means that the company borrowed less than the face or maturity value of the bond. It therefore faces an actual (effective) interest rate higher than the stated (nominal) rate. Conceptually, discount on bonds payable is a liability valuation account. That is, it reduces the face or maturity amount of the related liability.[7] This account is referred to as a **contra account**.

Similarly, premium on bonds payable has no existence apart from the related debt. The lower interest cost results because the proceeds of borrowing exceed the face or maturity amount of the debt. Conceptually, premium on bonds payable is a *liability* valuation account. It adds to the face or maturity amount of the related liability.[8] This account is referred to as an **adjunct account**. As a result, **companies report bond discounts and bond premiums as a direct deduction from or addition to the face amount of the bond**.

COSTS OF ISSUING BONDS

The issuance of bonds involves engraving and printing costs, legal and accounting fees, commissions, promotion costs, and other similar charges. Companies are required to charge these costs to an asset account, often referred to as Unamortized Bond Issue Costs. Companies then allocate these Unamortized Bond Issue Costs over the life of the debt, in a manner similar to that used for discount on bonds.[9]

We disagree with this approach. Unamortized bond issue cost in our view is an expense (or a reduction of the related liability.)

Apparently the FASB also disagrees with the current GAAP treatment and notes in *Concepts Statement No. 6* that debt issue cost is not considered an asset because it provides no future economic benefit. The cost of issuing bonds, in effect, reduces the proceeds of the bonds issued and increases the effective interest rate. Companies may thus account for it the same as the unamortized discount.

[7] "Elements of Financial Statements of Business Enterprises," *Statement of Financial Accounting Concepts No. 6* (Stamford, Conn.: FASB, 1980).

[8] Ibid., par. 238.

[9] "Interest on Receivables and Payables," op. cit., par. 15.

There is an obvious difference between GAAP and *Concepts Statement No. 6*'s view of debt issue costs. However, until an issued standard supersedes existing GAAP, **unamortized bond issue costs are treated as a deferred charge and amortized over the life of the debt.**

To illustrate the accounting for costs of issuing bonds, assume that Microchip Corporation sold $20,000,000 of 10-year debenture bonds for $20,795,000 on January 1, 2007 (also the date of the bonds). Costs of issuing the bonds were $245,000. Microchip records the issuance of the bonds and amortization of the bond issue costs as follows.

January 1, 2007		
Cash	20,550,000	
Unamortized Bond Issue Costs	245,000	
Premium on Bonds Payable		795,000
Bonds Payable		20,000,000
(To record issuance of bonds)		
December 31, 2007		
Bond Issue Expense	24,500	
Unamortized Bond Issue Costs		24,500
(To amortize one year of bond issue costs—straight-line methods)		

Microchip continues to amortize the bond issue costs in the same way over the life of the bonds. Although the effective-interest method is preferred, in practice companies may use the straight-line method to amortize bond issue costs because it is easier and the results are not materially different.

TREASURY BONDS

Bonds payable that have been reacquired by the issuing corporation or its agent or trustee and have not been canceled are known as **treasury bonds**. Similar to treasury stock (discussed in Chapter 14), these bonds are reported on the balance sheet as a deduction from "Bonds payable." When the treasury bonds are later sold or canceled, the company credits the Treasury Bonds account.

EXTINGUISHMENT OF DEBT

OBJECTIVE 5
Describe the accounting for the extinguishment of debt.

How do companies record the payment of debt—often referred to as **extinguishment of debt**? If a company holds the bonds (or any other form of debt security) to maturity, the answer is straightforward: The company does not compute any gains or losses. It will have fully amortized any premium or discount and any issue costs at the date the bonds mature. As a result, the carrying amount will equal the maturity (face) value of the bond. As the maturity or face value will also equal the bond's market value at that time, no gain or loss exists.

In some cases, a company extinguishes debt before its maturity date.[10] The amount paid on extinguishment or redemption before maturity, including any call

[10]Some companies have attempted to extinguish debt through an in-substance defeasance. **In-substance defeasance** is an arrangement whereby a company provides for the future repayment of a long-term debt issue by placing purchased securities in an irrevocable trust. The company pledges the principal and interest of the securities in the trust to pay off the principal and interest of its own debt securities as they mature. However, it is not legally released from its primary obligation for the debt that is still outstanding. In some case, debt holders are not even aware of the transaction and continue to look to the company for repayment. This practice is not considered an extinguishment of debt, and therefore the company does not record a gain or loss.

premium and expense of reacquisition, is called the **reacquisition price**. On any specified date, the **net carrying amount** of the bonds is the amount payable at maturity, adjusted for unamortized premium or discount, and cost of issuance. Any excess of the net carrying amount over the reacquisition price is a **gain from extinguishment**. The excess of the reacquisition price over the net carrying amount is a **loss from extinguishment**. At the time of reacquisition, **the unamortized premium or discount, and any costs of issue applicable to the bonds, must be amortized up to the reacquisition date.**

To illustrate, assume that on January 1, 2000, General Bell Corp. issued at 97 bonds with a par value of $800,000, due in 20 years. It incurred bond issue costs totaling $16,000. Eight years after the issue date, General Bell calls the entire issue at 101 and cancels it.[11] At that time, the unamortized discount balance is $14,400, and the unamortized issue cost balance is $9,600. Illustration 13-10 indicates how General Bell computes the loss on redemption (extinguishment).

ILLUSTRATION 13-10
Computation of Loss on Redemption of Bonds

Reacquisition price ($800,000 × 1.01)		$808,000
Net carrying amount of bonds redeemed:		
Face value	$800,000	
Unamortized discount ($24,000* × 12/20)	(14,400)	
Unamortized issue costs ($16,000 × 12/20)		
(both amortized using straight-line basis)	(9,600)	776,000
Loss on redemption		$ 32,000

*[$800,000 × (1 − .97)]

General Bell records the reacquisition and cancellation of the bonds as follows:

Bonds Payable	800,000	
Loss on Redemption of Bonds	32,000	
Discount on Bonds Payable		14,400
Unamortized Bond Issue Costs		9,600
Cash		808,000

Note that it is often advantageous for the issuer to acquire the **entire** outstanding bond issue and replace it with a new bond issue bearing a lower rate of interest. The replacement of an existing issuance with a new one is called **refunding**. Whether the early redemption or other extinguishment of outstanding bonds is a nonrefunding or a refunding situation, a company should recognize the difference (gain or loss) between the reacquisition price and the net carrying amount of the redeemed bonds in income of the period of redemption.[12]

[11]The issuer of callable bonds must generally exercise the call on an interest date. Therefore, the amortization of any discount or premium will be up to date, and there will be no accrued interest. However, early extinguishments through purchases of bonds in the open market are more likely to be on other than an interest date. If the purchase is not made on an interest date, the discount or premium must be amortized, and the interest payable must be accrued from the last interest date to the date of purchase.

[12]Until recently, companies reported gains and losses on extinguishment of debt as extraordinary items. In response to concerns that such gains or losses are neither unusual nor infrequent, the FASB eliminated extraordinary item treatment for extinguishment of debt. "Recission of *FASB Statements No. 4, 44,* and *64* and Technical Corrections," *Statement of Accounting Standards No. 145* (Norwalk, Conn.: FASB, 2002).

DEAD-WEIGHT DEBT

WHAT DO THE NUMBERS MEAN?

As the opening story in the chapter indicated, high debt levels translate into high interest costs, which are a drag on profitability. The chart below shows that the ratio of interest payments to earnings has been on an upward trend. This is bad news for companies that have a lot of debt on their balance sheet.

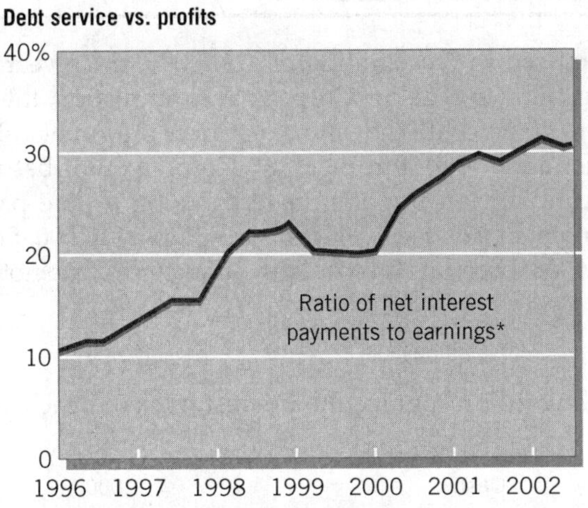

*Earnings before tax and interest
Data: HSBC Securities Inc., Commerce Dept.

However in a low interest rate environment, as experienced recently, companies with debt-laden balance sheets benefit when interest rates fall. **Exelon Corp.**, a Chicago-based energy company, is a good example. Exelon has been refinancing its long-term debt by retiring bonds with 6.5 percent rates in exchange for newly issued bonds with rates ranging from 3.7 percent to 5.9 percent. This refinancing saved Exelon approximately $30 million dollars in annual interest costs. Exelon was able to get out of its higher cost debt when the getting was good. Other debt-laden companies might not fare so well if interest rates rise before they can refinance.

Source: Adapted from Gregory Zuckerman, "Climb of Corporate Debt Trips Analysts' Alarm," *Wall Street Journal* (December 31, 2001), p. C1; and James Mehring, "The Dead Weight of Debt," *Business Week* (February 24, 2003), p. 60.

LONG-TERM NOTES PAYABLE

SECTION 2

OBJECTIVE 6
Explain the accounting for long-term notes payable.

The difference between current notes payable and **long-term notes payable** is the maturity date. As discussed in Chapter 12, short-term notes payable are those that companies expect to pay within a year or the operating cycle—whichever is longer. Long-term notes are similar in substance to bonds in that both have fixed maturity dates and carry either a stated or implicit interest rate. However, notes do not trade as readily as bonds in the organized public securities markets. Noncorporate and small corporate enterprises issue notes as their long-term instruments. Larger corporations issue both long-term notes and bonds.

Accounting for notes and bonds is quite similar. **Like a bond, a note is valued at the present value of its future interest and principal cash flows. The company amortizes any discount or premium over the life of the note,** just as it would the discount or premium on a bond.[13] Companies compute the present value of an **interest-bearing note**, record its issuance, and amortize any discount or premium and accrual of interest in the same way that they do for bonds.

As you might expect, accounting for long-term notes payable parallels accounting for long-term notes receivable as was presented in Chapter 6.

NOTES ISSUED AT FACE VALUE

In Chapter 6, we discussed the recognition of a $10,000, three-year note Scandinavian Imports issued at face value to Bigelow Corp. In this transaction, the stated rate and the effective rate were both 10 percent. The time diagram and present value computation in Chapter 6 (see Illustration 6-9) for Bigelow Corp. would be the same for the issuer of the note, Scandinavian Imports, in recognizing a note payable. Because the present value of the note and its face value are the same, $10,000, Scandinavian would recognize no premium or discount. It records the issuance of the note as follows.

Cash	10,000	
Notes Payable		10,000

Scandinavian Imports would recognize the interest incurred each year as follows.

Interest Expense	1,000	
Cash		1,000

NOTES NOT ISSUED AT FACE VALUE

Zero-Interest-Bearing Notes

Calculator Solution for Effective Interest on Note:

	Inputs	Answer
N	8	
I/YR	?	15
PV	-327	
PMT	0	
FV	1,000	

If a company issues a zero-interest-bearing (non-interest-bearing) note[14] solely for cash, it measures the note's present value by the cash received. The implicit interest rate is the **rate that equates the cash received with the amounts to be paid in the future**. The issuing company records the difference between the face amount and the present value (cash received) as **a discount and amortizes that amount to interest expense over the life of the note.**

An example of such a transaction is Beneficial Corporation's offering of $150 million of zero-coupon notes (deep-discount bonds) having an eight-year life. With a face value of $1,000 each, these notes sold for $327—a deep discount of $673 each. The present value of each note is the cash proceeds of $327. We can calculate the interest rate by determining the rate that equates the amount the investor currently pays with the amount to be received in the future. Thus, Beneficial amortizes the discount over the eight-year life of the notes using an effective interest rate of 15 percent.[15]

---

[13] According to *APB Opinion No. 21*, all payables that represent commitments to pay money at a determinable future date are subject to present value measurement techniques, except for the following specifically excluded types:

1. Normal accounts payable due within one year.
2. Security deposits, retainages, advances, or progress payments.
3. Transactions between parent and subsidiary.
4. Obligations payable at some indeterminable future date.

[14] Although we use the term "note" throughout this discussion, the basic principles and methodology apply equally to other long-term debt instruments.

[15] $\$327 = \$1{,}000(PVF_{8,i})$

$$PVF_{8,i} = \frac{\$327}{\$1{,}000} = .327$$

$.327 = 15\%$ (in Table 6-2 locate .32690).

To illustrate the entries and the amortization schedule, assume that Turtle Cove Company issued the three-year, $10,000, zero-interest-bearing note to Jeremiah Company illustrated in Chapter 6 (notes receivable). The implicit rate that equated the total cash to be paid ($10,000 at maturity) to the present value of the future cash flows ($7,721.80 cash proceeds at date of issuance) was 9 percent. (The present value of $1 for 3 periods at 9 percent is $0.77218.) Illustration 13-11 shows the time diagram for the single cash flow.

ILLUSTRATION 13-11
Time Diagram for Zero-Interest Note

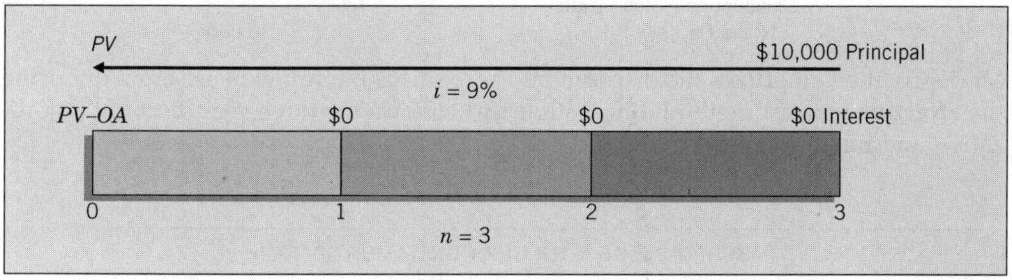

Turtle Cove records issuance of the note as follows.

Cash	7,721.80	
Discount on Notes Payable	2,278.20	
Notes Payable		10,000.00

Turtle Cove amortizes the discount and recognizes interest expense annually using the **effective-interest method**. Illustration 13-12 shows the three-year discount amortization and interest expense schedule. (This schedule is similar to the note receivable schedule of Jeremiah Company in Illustration 6-11.)

ILLUSTRATION 13-12
Schedule of Note Discount Amortization

SCHEDULE OF NOTE DISCOUNT AMORTIZATION
EFFECTIVE-INTEREST METHOD
0% NOTE DISCOUNTED AT 9%

	Cash Paid	Interest Expense	Discount Amortized	Carrying Amount of Note
Date of issue				$ 7,721.80
End of year 1	$-0-	$ 694.96[a]	$ 694.96[b]	8,416.76[c]
End of year 2	-0-	757.51	757.51	9,174.27
End of year 3	-0-	825.73[d]	825.73	10,000.00
	$-0-	$2,278.20	$2,278.20	

[a]$7,721.80 × .09 = $694.96
[b]$694.96 − 0 = $694.96
[c]$7,721.80 + $694.96 = $8,416.76
[d]5¢ adjustment to compensate for rounding

Turtle Cove records interest expense at the end of the first year using the effective-interest method as follows.

Interest Expense ($7,721.80 × 9%)	694.96	
Discount on Notes Payable		694.96

The total amount of the discount, $2,278.20 in this case, represents the expense that Turtle Cove Company will incur on the note over the three years.

Interest-Bearing Notes

The zero-interest-bearing note above is an example of the extreme difference between the stated rate and the effective rate. In many cases, the difference between these rates is not so great.

Consider the example from Chapter 6 where Marie Co. issued for cash a $10,000, three-year note bearing interest at 10 percent to Morgan Corp. The market rate of interest for a note of similar risk is 12 percent. Illustration 6-12 shows the time diagram depicting the cash flows and the computation of the present value of this note. In this case, because the effective rate of interest (12%) is greater than the stated rate (10%), the present value of the note is less than the face value. That is, the note is exchanged at a **discount**. Marie Co. records the issuance of the note as follows.

Cash	9,520	
Discount on Notes Payable	480	
Notes Payable		10,000

Marie Co. then amortizes the discount and recognizes interest expense annually using the **effective-interest method**. Illustration 13-13 shows the three-year discount amortization and interest expense schedule.

ILLUSTRATION 13-13
Schedule of Note Discount Amortization

SCHEDULE OF NOTE DISCOUNT AMORTIZATION
EFFECTIVE-INTEREST METHOD
10% NOTE DISCOUNTED AT 12%

	Cash Paid	Interest Expense	Discount Amortized	Carrying Amount of Note
Date of issue				$ 9,520
End of year 1	$1,000[a]	$1,142[b]	$142[c]	9,662[d]
End of year 2	1,000	1,159	159	9,821
End of year 3	1,000	1,179	179	10,000
	$3,000	$3,480	$480	

[a]$10,000 × 10% = $1,000
[b]$9,520 × 12% = $1,142
[c]$1,142 − $1,000 = $142
[d]$9,520 + $142 = $9,662

Marie Co. records payment of the annual interest and amortization of the discount for the first year as follows (amounts per amortization schedule).

Interest Expense	1,142	
Discount on Bonds Payable		142
Cash		1,000

When the present value exceeds the face value, Marie Co. exchanges the note at a premium. It does so by recording the premium as a credit and amortizing it using the effective-interest method over the life of the note as annual reductions in the amount of interest expense recognized.

SPECIAL NOTES PAYABLE SITUATIONS

Notes Issued for Property, Goods, and Services

Sometimes, companies may receive property, goods, or services in exchange for a note payable. When exchanging the debt instrument for property, goods, or services in a bargained transaction entered into at arm's length, the stated interest rate is presumed to be fair unless:

1. No interest rate is stated, or
2. The stated interest rate is unreasonable, or
3. The stated face amount of the debt instrument is materially different from the current cash sales price for the same or similar items or from the current market value of the debt instrument.

In these circumstances the company measures the present value of the debt instrument by the fair value of the property, goods, or services or by an amount that reasonably approximates the market value of the note.[16] If there is **no stated rate of interest, the amount of interest is the difference between the face amount of the note and the fair value of the property.**

For example, assume that Scenic Development Company sells land having a cash sale price of $200,000 to Health Spa, Inc. In exchange for the land, Health Spa gives a five-year, $293,866, zero-interest-bearing note. The $200,000 cash sale price represents the present value of the $293,866 note discounted at 8 percent for five years. Should both parties record the transaction on the sale date at the face amount of the note, which is $293,866? No—if they did, Health Spa's Land account and Scenic's sales would be overstated by $93,866 (the interest for five years at an effective rate of 8 percent). Similarly, interest revenue to Scenic and interest expense to Health Spa for the five-year period would be understated by $93,866.

Because the difference between the cash sale price of $200,000 and the $293,866 face amount of the note represents interest at an effective rate of 8 percent, the companies' transaction is recorded at the exchange date as follows.

ILLUSTRATION 13-14
Entries for Noncash Note Transactions

Health Spa, Inc. (Buyer)			Scenic Development Company (Seller)		
Land	200,000		Notes Receivable	293,866	
Discount on Notes Payable	93,866		Discount on Notes Rec.		93,866
Notes Payable		293,866	Sales		200,000

During the five-year life of the note, Health Spa amortizes annually a portion of the discount of $93,866 as a charge to interest expense. Scenic Development records interest revenue totaling $93,866 over the five-year period by also amortizing the discount. The effective-interest method is required, unless the results obtained from using another method are not materially different from those that result from the effective-interest method.

Choice of Interest Rate

In note transactions, the effective or market interest rate is either evident or determinable by other factors involved in the exchange, such as the fair market value of what is given or received. But, if a company cannot determine the fair value of the property, goods, services, or other rights, and if the note has no ready market, the problem of determining the present value of the note is more difficult. To estimate the present value of a note under such circumstances, a company must approximate an applicable interest rate that may differ from the stated interest rate. This process of interest-rate approximation is called **imputation**, and the resulting interest rate is called an **imputed interest rate**.

The prevailing rates for similar instruments of issuers with similar credit ratings affect the choice of a rate. Other factors such as restrictive covenants, collateral, payment schedule, and the existing prime interest rate also play a part. Companies determine the imputed interest rate when they issue a note; any subsequent changes in prevailing interest rates are ignored.

To illustrate, assume that on December 31, 2007, Wunderlich Company issued a promissory note to Brown Interiors Company for architectural services. The note has a face value of $550,000, a due date of December 31, 2012, and bears a stated interest rate of 2 percent, payable at the end of each year. Wunderlich cannot readily determine the fair value of the architectural services, nor is the note readily marketable. On the basis of Wunderlich's credit rating, the absence of collateral, the prime interest rate at that date, and the prevailing interest on Wunderlich's other outstanding debt, the

[16]"Interest on Receivables and Payables," op. cit., par. 12.

company imputes an 8 percent interest rate as appropriate in this circumstance. Illustration 13-15 shows the time diagram depicting both cash flows.

ILLUSTRATION 13-15
Time Diagram for Interest-Bearing Note

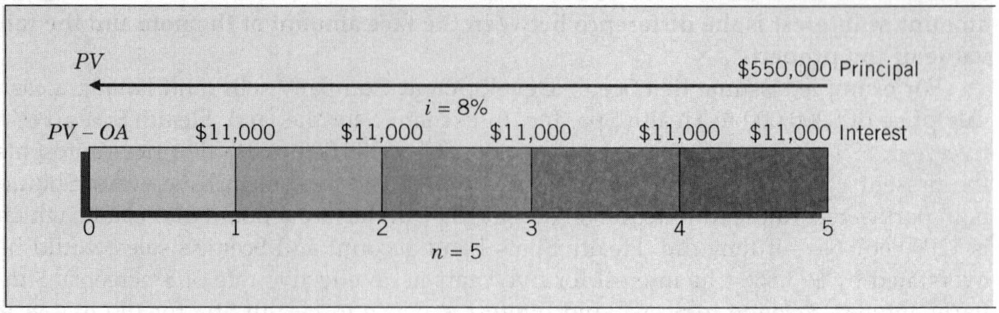

The present value of the note and the imputed fair value of the architectural services are determined as follows.

ILLUSTRATION 13-16
Computation of Imputed Fair Value and Note Discount

Face value of the note		$550,000
Present value of $550,000 due in 5 years at 8% interest payable annually (Table 6-2); $FV(PVF_{5,8\%})$; ($550,000 × .68058)	$374,319	
Present value of $11,000 interest payable annually for 5 years at 8%; $R(PVF\text{-}OA_{5,8\%})$; ($11,000 × 3.99271)	43,920	
Present value of the note		418,239
Discount on notes payable		$131,761

Wunderlich records issuance of the note in payment for the architectural services as follows.

December 31, 2007

Building (or Construction in Process)	418,239	
Discount on Notes Payable	131,761	
Notes Payable		550,000

The five-year amortization schedule appears below.

ILLUSTRATION 13-17
Schedule of Discount Amortization Using Imputed Interest Rate

SCHEDULE OF NOTE DISCOUNT AMORTIZATION
EFFECTIVE-INTEREST METHOD
2% NOTE DISCOUNTED AT 8% (IMPUTED)

Date	Cash Paid (2%)	Interest Expense (8%)	Discount Amortized	Carrying Amount of Note
12/31/07				$418,239
12/31/08	$11,000[a]	$ 33,459[b]	$ 22,459[c]	440,698[d]
12/31/09	11,000	35,256	24,256	464,954
12/31/10	11,000	37,196	26,196	491,150
12/31/11	11,000	39,292	28,292	519,442
12/31/12	11,000	41,558[e]	30,558	550,000
	$55,000	$186,761	$131,761	

[a]$550,000 × 2% = $11,000
[b]$418,239 × 8% = $33,459
[c]$33,459 − $11,000 = $22,459
[d]$418,239 + $22,459 = $440,698
[e]$3 adjustment to compensate for rounding.

Calculator Solution for the Fair Value of Services:

	Inputs	Answer
N	5	
I/YR	8	
PV	?	418,241*
PMT	−11,000	
FV	−550,000	

*Difference due to rounding.

Wunderlich records payment of the first year's interest and amortization of the discount as follows.

December 31, 2008

Interest Expense	33,459	
Discount on Notes Payable		22,459
Cash		11,000

MORTGAGE NOTES PAYABLE

The most common form of long-term notes payable is a mortgage note payable. A **mortgage note payable** is a promissory note secured by a document called a mortgage that pledges title to property as security for the loan. Individuals, proprietorships, and partnerships use mortgage notes payable more frequently than do corporations. (Corporations usually find that bond issues offer advantages in obtaining large loans.)

The borrower usually receives cash for the face amount of the mortgage note. In that case, the face amount of the note is the true liability, and no discount or premium is involved. When the lender assesses "points," however, the total amount received by the borrower is less than the face amount of the note.[17] Points raise the effective interest rate above the rate specified in the note. A **point** is 1 percent of the face of the note.

For example, assume that Harrick Co. borrows $1,000,000, signing a 20-year mortgage note with a stated interest rate of 10.75 percent as part of the financing for a new plant. If Associated Savings demands 4 points to close the financing, Harrick will receive 4 percent less than $1,000,000—or $960,000—but it will be obligated to repay the entire $1,000,000 at the rate of $10,150 per month. Because Harrick received only $960,000, and must repay $1,000,000, its effective interest rate is increased to approximately 11.3 percent on the money actually borrowed.

On the balance sheet, Harrick should report the mortgage note payable as a liability using a title such as "Mortgage Notes Payable" or "Notes Payable—Secured," with a brief disclosure of the property pledged in notes to the financial statements.

Mortgages may be payable in full at maturity or in installments over the life of the loan. If payable at maturity, Harrick classifies its mortgage payable as a long-term liability on the balance sheet until such time as the approaching maturity date warrants showing it as a current liability. If it is payable in installments, Harrick shows the current installments due as current liabilities, with the remainder as a long-term liability.

Lenders have partially replaced the traditional **fixed-rate mortgage** with alternative mortgage arrangements. Most lenders offer **variable-rate mortgages** (also called *floating-rate* or *adjustable-rate* mortgages) featuring interest rates tied to changes in the fluctuating market rate. Generally the variable-rate lenders adjust the interest rate at either one- or three-year intervals, pegging the adjustments to changes in the prime rate or the U.S. Treasury bond rate.

REPORTING AND ANALYSIS OF LONG-TERM DEBT

SECTION 3

Reporting of long-term debt is one of the most controversial areas in financial reporting. Because long-term debt has a significant impact on the cash flows of the company, reporting requirements must be substantive and informative. One problem is that the definition of a liability established in *Concepts Statement No. 6* and the recognition criteria established in *Concepts Statement No. 5* are sufficiently imprecise that some continue to argue that certain obligations need not be reported as debt.

OFF-BALANCE-SHEET FINANCING

OBJECTIVE 7
Explain the reporting of off-balance-sheet financing arrangements.

What do **Krispy Kreme**, **Cisco**, **Enron**, and **Adelphia Communications** have in common? They all have been accused of using off-balance-sheet financing to minimize the reporting of debt on their balance sheets. **Off-balance-sheet financing** is an attempt to

[17]Points, in mortgage financing, are analogous to the original issue discount of bonds.

borrow monies in such a way to prevent recording the obligations. It has become an issue of extreme importance. Many allege that Enron, in one of the largest corporate failures on record, hid a considerable amount of its debt off the balance sheet. As a result, any company that uses off-balance-sheet financing today risks investors dumping their stock. Consequently (as discussed in the opening story), their share price will suffer. Nevertheless, a considerable amount of off-balance-sheet financing continues to exist. As one writer noted, "The basic drives of humans are few: to get enough food, to find shelter, and to keep debt off the balance sheet."

Different Forms

Off-balance-sheet financing can take many different forms:

1 **Non-Consolidated Subsidiary:** Under GAAP, a parent company does not have to consolidate a subsidiary company that is less than 50 percent owned. In such cases, the parent therefore does not report the assets and liabilities of the subsidiary. All the parent reports on its balance sheet is the investment in the subsidiary. As a result, users of the financial statements may not understand that the subsidiary has considerable debt for which the parent may ultimately be liable if the subsidiary runs into financial difficulty.

2 **Special Purpose Entity (SPE):** A company creates a **special purpose entity** to perform a special project. To illustrate, assume that Clarke Company decides to build a new factory. However, management does not want to report the plant or the borrowing used to fund the construction on its balance sheet. It therefore creates an SPE, the purpose of which is to build the plant. (This arrangement is called a **project financing arrangement**.) The SPE finances and builds the plant. In return, Clarke guarantees that it or some outside party will purchase all the products produced by the plant. (Some refer to this as a **take-or-pay contract**). As a result, Clarke might not report the asset or liability on its books. The accounting rules in this area are complex.

3 **Operating Leases:** Another way that companies keep debt off the balance sheet is by leasing. Instead of owning the assets, companies lease them. Again, by meeting certain conditions, the company has to report only rent expense each period and to provide note disclosure of the transaction. Note that SPEs often use leases to accomplish off-balance-sheet treatment.

Rationale

Why do companies engage in off-balance-sheet financing? A major reason is that many believe that **removing debt enhances the quality of the balance sheet** and permits credit to be obtained more readily and at less cost.

Second, loan covenants often limit the amount of debt a company may have. As a result, the company uses off-balance-sheet financing, because **these types of commitments might not be considered in computing the debt limitation.**

Third, some argue that the asset side of the balance sheet is severely understated. For example, companies that use LIFO costing for inventories and depreciate assets on an accelerated basis will often have carrying amounts for inventories and property, plant, and equipment that are much lower than their current values. As an offset to these lower values, some believe that part of the debt does not have to be reported. In other words, **if companies report assets at current values**, less pressure would undoubtedly exist for off-balance-sheet financing arrangements.

Whether the arguments above have merit is debatable. The general idea of "out of sight, out of mind" may not be true in accounting. Many users of financial statements indicate that they factor these off-balance-sheet financing arrangements into their computations when assessing debt to equity relationships. Similarly, many loan covenants also attempt to account for these complex arrangements. Nevertheless, many companies still believe that benefits will accrue if they omit certain obligations from the balance sheet.

As a response to off-balance-sheet financing arrangements, the FASB has increased disclosure (note) requirements. This response is consistent with an "efficient markets" philosophy: the important question is not whether the presentation is off-balance-sheet or not, but whether the items are disclosed at all. In addition, the SEC, in response to the Sarbanes-Oxley Act of 2002, now requires companies to provide related information in their management discussion and analysis sections. Specifically, companies must disclose (1) all contractual obligations in a tabular format and (2) contingent liabilities and commitments in either a textual or tabular format.[18]

We believe that recording more obligations on the balance sheet will enhance financial reporting. Given the problems with companies such as **Enron**, **Dynergy**, **Williams Company**, **Adelphia Communications**, and **Calpine**, and the new Sarbanes-Oxley requirements, we expect that less off-balance-sheet financing will occur in the future.

OBLIGATED

WHAT DO THE NUMBERS MEAN?

The off-balance-sheet world is slowly but surely becoming more on-balance-sheet. New interpretations on guarantees (discussed in Chapter 12) and variable interest entities are doing their part to increase the amount of debt reported on corporate balance sheets.

In addition, the SEC recently issued a rule that requires companies to disclose off-balance-sheet arrangements and contractual obligations that currently have, or are reasonably likely to have, a material future effect on the companies' financial condition. Companies now must include a tabular disclosure (following a prescribed format) in the management discussion and analysis section of the annual report. Presented below is **Best Buy**'s tabular disclosure of its contractual obligations.

Best Buy Co.
Contractual Obligations

The following table presents information regarding our contractual obligations by fiscal year ($ in millions):

		Payments due by period			
Contractual Obligations	**Total**	**Less than 1 year**	**1–3 years**	**3–5 years**	**More than 5 years**
Long-term debt obligations	$ 425	$ 2	$ 408	$ 12	$ 3
Capital lease obligations	13	5	4	3	1
Master lease obligations	55	55	—	—	—
Financing lease obligations	107	10	17	19	61
Interest payments	218	23	37	32	126
Operating lease obligations	5,850	541	1,065	997	3,247
Purchase obligations	1,514	689	404	259	162
Total	$8,182	$1,325	$1,935	$1,322	$3,600

Note: For more information refer to Note 4, Debt; Note 7, Leases; and Note 11, Contingencies and Commitments, respectively, in the Notes to Consolidated Financial Statements.

Enron's abuse of off-balance-sheet financing to hide debt was shocking and inappropriate. One silver lining in the Enron debacle however is that the standard-setting bodies in the accounting profession are now providing increased guidance on companies' reporting of contractual obligations. We believe the new SEC rule which requires companies to report their obligations over a period of time will be extremely useful to the investment community.

INTERNATIONAL INSIGHT

There is no comparable institution to the SEC in international securities markets. As a result, many international companies (those not registered with the SEC) are not required to provide disclosures such as those related to contractual obligations.

[18]It is unlikely that the FASB will be able to stop all types of off-balance-sheet transactions. Financial engineering is the Holy Grail of Wall Street. Developing new financial instruments and arrangements to sell and market to customers is not only profitable, but also adds to the prestige of the investment firms that create them. Thus, new financial products will continue to appear that will test the ability of the FASB to develop appropriate accounting standards for them.

PRESENTATION AND ANALYSIS OF LONG-TERM DEBT

OBJECTIVE 8
Indicate how to present and analyze long-term debt.

Presentation of Long-Term Debt

Companies that have large amounts and numerous issues of long-term debt frequently report only one amount in the balance sheet, supported with comments and schedules in the accompanying notes. Long-term debt that **matures within one year** should be reported as a current liability, unless using noncurrent assets to accomplish retirement.

ILLUSTRATION 13-18
Long-Term Debt Disclosure

Best Buy Co.
(dollars in millions)

	February 26, 2005	February 28, 2004
Total current assets	$6,903	$5,724
Current liabilities		
Accounts payable	$2,824	$2,460
Unredeemed gift card liabiliities	410	300
Accrued compensation and related expenses	234	269
Accrued liabilities	844	724
Accrued income taxes	575	380
Current portion of long-term debt	72	368
Total current liabilities	4,959	4,501
Long-term liabilities	358	247
Long-term debt	528	482

4. Debt (in part)	February 26, 2005	February 28, 2004
Convertible subordinated debentures, unsecured, due 2022, interest rate 2.25%	$402	$402
Convertible debentures, unsecured, due 2021, interest rate 2.75%	—	353
Master lease obligations, due 2006, interest rate 5.9%	55	58
Capital lease obligations, due 2005, interest rate ranging from 5.9% to 8.0%	13	16
Financing lease obligations, due 2008 to 2022, interest rates ranging from 5.6% to 6.0%	107	—
Mortgage and other debt, interest rates ranging from 1.8% to 8.9%	23	21
Total debt	600	850
Less: Current portion	(72)	(368)
Total long-term debt	$528	$482

The mortgage and other debt are secured by certain property and equipment with a net book value of $98 and $97 at February 26, 2005, and February 28, 2004, respectively.

The future maturities of long-term debt, including master and capitalized leases, consist of the following:

Fiscal Year	
2006	$ 72
2007	415
2008	14
2009	14
2010	20
Thereafter	65
	$600

The fair value of long-term debt approximated $603 and $902 as of February 26, 2005, and February 28, 2004, respectively, based on the ask prices quoted from external sources, compared with carrying values of $600 and $850, respectively.

If the company plans to refinance debt, convert it into stock, or retire it from a bond retirement fund, it should continue to report the debt as noncurrent. However, the company should disclose the method it will use in its liquidation.[19]

Note disclosures generally indicate the nature of the liabilities, maturity dates, interest rates, call provisions, conversion privileges, restrictions imposed by the creditors, and assets designated or pledged as security. Companies should show any assets pledged as security for the debt in the assets section of the balance sheet. The fair value of the long-term debt should also be disclosed if it is practical to estimate fair value. Finally, companies must disclose future payments for sinking fund requirements and maturity amounts of long-term debt during each of the next five years.[20] These disclosures aid financial statement users in evaluating the amounts and timing of future cash flows. Illustration 13-18 shows an example of the type of information provided for **Best Buy Co.** Note that if the company has any off-balance-sheet financing, it must provide extensive note disclosure.[21]

Analysis of Long-Term Debt

Long-term creditors and stockholders are interested in a company's long-run solvency, particularly its ability to pay interest as it comes due and to repay the face value of the debt at maturity. Debt to total assets and times interest earned are two ratios that provide information about debt-paying ability and long-run solvency.

Debt to Total Assets Ratio

The **debt to total assets ratio** measures the percentage of the total assets provided by creditors. To compute it, divide total debt (both current and long-term liabilities) by total assets, as Illustration 13-19 shows.

$$\text{Debt to total assets} = \frac{\text{Total debt}}{\text{Total assets}}$$

ILLUSTRATION 13-19
Computation of Debt to Total Assets Ratio

The higher the percentage of debt to total assets, the greater the risk that the company may be unable to meet its maturing obligations.

Times Interest Earned Ratio

The **times interest earned ratio** indicates the company's ability to meet interest payments as they come due. As shown in Illustration 13-20, it is computed by dividing income before interest expense and income taxes by interest expense.

$$\text{Times interest earned} = \frac{\text{Income before income taxes and interest expense}}{\text{Interest expense}}$$

ILLUSTRATION 13-20
Computation of Times Interest Earned Ratio

To illustrate these ratios, we use data from **Best Buy**'s 2005 annual report. Best Buy has total liabilities of $5,845 million, total assets of $10,294 million, interest expense of $44 million, income taxes of $509 million, and net income of $984 million. We

[19] "Balance Sheet Classification of Short-Term Obligations Expected to Be Refinanced," *FASB Statement of Financial Accounting Standards No. 6* (Stamford, Conn.: FASB, 1975), par. 15. Also see "Disclosure of Information about Capital Structure," *FASB Statement of Financial Accounting Standards No. 129* (Norwalk, Conn.: 1997), par. 4.

[20] "Disclosure of Long-Term Obligations," *FASB Statement of Financial Accounting Standards No. 47* (Stamford, Conn.: 1981), par. 10.

[21] Ibid.

compute Best Buy's debt to total assets and times interest earned ratios as shown in Illustration 13-21.

ILLUSTRATION 13-21
Computation of Long-Term Debt Ratios for Best Buy

$$\text{Debt to total assets} = \frac{\$5{,}845}{\$10{,}294} = 56.8\%$$

$$\text{Times interest earned} = \frac{(\$984 + \$44 + \$509)}{\$44} = 35 \text{ times}$$

Even though Best Buy has a relatively high debt to total assets percentage of 56.8 percent, its interest coverage of 35 times indicates it can easily meet its interest payments as they come due.

QUESTIONS

1. (a) From what sources might a corporation obtain funds through long-term debt? (b) What is a bond indenture? What does it contain? (c) What is a mortgage?

2. **Potlatch Corporation** has issued various types of bonds such as term bonds, income bonds, and debentures. Differentiate between term bonds, mortgage bonds, collateral trust bonds, debenture bonds, income bonds, callable bonds, registered bonds, bearer or coupon bonds, convertible bonds, commodity-backed bonds, and deep discount bonds.

3. Distinguish between the following interest rates for bonds payable:

(a) yield rate
(b) nominal rate
(c) stated rate
(d) market rate
(e) effective rate

4. Distinguish between the following values relative to bonds payable:

(a) maturity value
(b) face value
(c) market value
(d) par value

5. Under what conditions of bond issuance does a discount on bonds payable arise? Under what conditions of bond issuance does a premium on bonds payable arise?

6. How should discount on bonds payable be reported on the financial statements? Premium on bonds payable?

7. What are the two methods of amortizing discount and premium on bonds payable? Explain each.

8. Zeno Company sells its bonds at a premium and applies the effective interest method in amortizing the premium. Will the annual interest expense increase or decrease over the life of the bonds? Explain.

9. **Briggs and Stratton** recently reported unamortized debt issue costs of $5.1 million. How should the costs of issuing these bonds be accounted for and classified in the financial statements?

10. Where should treasury bonds be shown on the balance sheet?

11. What is the "call" feature of a bond issue? How does the call feature affect the amortization of bond premium or discount?

12. Why would a company wish to reduce its bond indebtedness before its bonds reach maturity? Indicate how this can be done and the correct accounting treatment for such a transaction.

13. How are gains and losses from extinguishment of a debt classified in the income statement? What disclosures are required of such transactions?

14. What is done to record properly a transaction involving the issuance of a non-interest-bearing long-term note in exchange for property?

15. How is the present value of a non-interest-bearing note computed?

16. When is the stated interest rate of a debt instrument presumed to be fair?

17. What are the considerations in imputing an appropriate interest rate?

18. Differentiate between a fixed-rate mortgage and a variable-rate mortgage.

19. What disclosures are required relative to long-term debt and sinking fund requirements?

20. What is off-balance-sheet financing? Why might a company be interested in using off-balance-sheet financing?

21. What are some forms of off-balance-sheet financing?

22. What are take-or-pay contracts and through-put contracts?

CHAPTER FOURTEEN

STOCKHOLDERS' EQUITY

Everything Else Equal?

Not all dividend payers are created equal. Some stocks provide a good dividend yield but also promise strong earnings growth. These stocks could provide a healthy one-two punch for investors. A good example is Seattle's **Plum Creek Timber**. It pays a dividend of close to 4.2 percent, and it also expects earnings to expand about 6 percent in the next year.

General Motors has a seemingly healthy dividend of 5.8 percent. But the big automaker had a loss of $1.1 billion in a recent quarter, and it is having trouble reducing its onerous health-care benefits. There is concern that GM may be forced to trim its dividend at some point to conserve cash. The following chart shows that dividends are an important part of total stock returns.

While the Dow Jones Industrial Average price (pink shading) has grown 260% over the past 15 years–leaving investors with $3^1/_2$ times as much money–the rise including dividends (blue shading) was 408%.

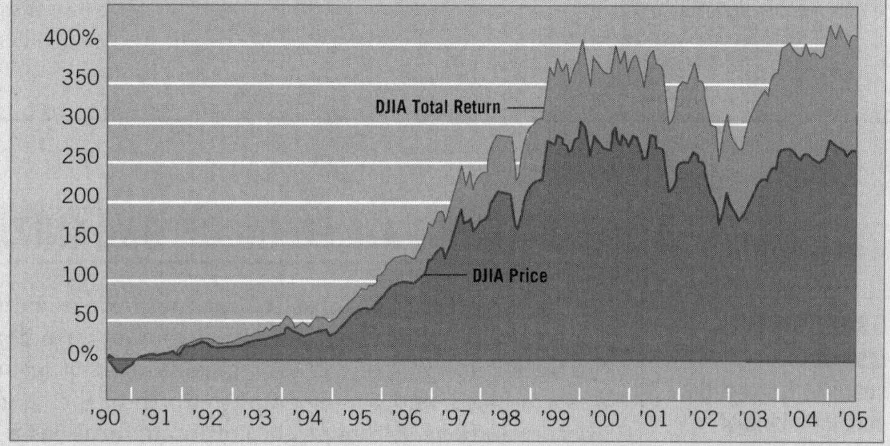

Source: WSJ Marketing Data Group

As one analyst noted, "Investors have consistently underappreciated the value of compounding dividends in a portfolio. And dividends usually provide a strong degree of downside protection for a portfolio." But be wary when focusing on high-dividend stocks. Those with problems may find it difficult to keep their dividend payments going in the future.

Source: Adapted from Gary Zuckerman, "When Dividends Are Sweet, Be Choosy," *Wall Street Journal Online* (July 3, 2005).

Learning Objectives

After studying this chapter, you should be able to:

1. Discuss the characteristics of the corporate form of organization.
2. Identify the key components of stockholders' equity.
3. Explain the accounting procedures for issuing shares of stock.
4. Describe the accounting for treasury stock.
5. Explain the accounting for and reporting of preferred stock.
6. Describe the policies used in distributing dividends.
7. Identify the various forms of dividend distributions.
8. Explain the accounting for small and large stock dividends, and for stock splits.
9. Indicate how to present and analyze stockholders' equity.

PREVIEW OF CHAPTER 14

As our opening story indicates, dividends combined with other information about a company can provide useful information to investors. In this chapter we explain the accounting issues for dividend transactions, as well as other transactions related to the stockholders' equity of a corporation. The content and organization of the chapter are as follows.

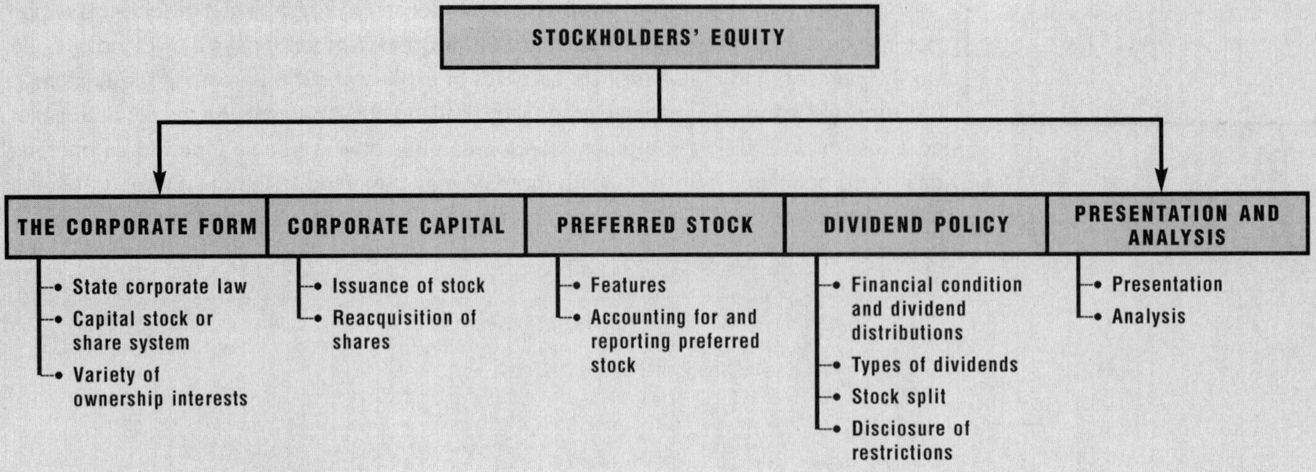

THE CORPORATE FORM OF ORGANIZATION

OBJECTIVE 1
Discuss the characteristics of the corporate form of organization.

Of the three **primary forms of business organization**—the proprietorship, the partnership, and the corporation—the corporate form dominates. The corporation is by far the leader in terms of the aggregate amount of resources controlled, goods and services produced, and people employed. All of the "Fortune 500" largest industrial firms are corporations. Although the corporate form has a number of advantages (as well as disadvantages) over the other two forms, its principal advantage is its facility for attracting and accumulating large amounts of capital.

The special characteristics of the corporate form that affect accounting include:

1 Influence of state corporate law.
2 Use of the capital stock or share system.
3 Development of a variety of ownership interests.

State Corporate Law

Anyone who wishes to establish a corporation must submit **articles of incorporation** to the state in which incorporation is desired. After fulfilling requirements, the state issues a corporation charter, thereby recognizing the company as a legal entity subject to state law. Regardless of the number of states in which a corporation has operating divisions, it is incorporated in only one state.

It is to the company's advantage to incorporate in a state whose laws favor the corporate form of business organization. **General Motors**, for example, is incorporated in Delaware; **U.S. Steel** is a New Jersey corporation. Some corporations have increasingly been incorporating in states with laws favorable to existing management. For example, to thwart possible unfriendly takeovers, at one time, **Gulf Oil** changed its state of incorporation to Delaware. There, the board of directors alone, without a vote of the shareholders, may approve certain tactics against takeovers.

Each state has its own business incorporation act. The accounting for stockholders' equity follows the provisions of these acts. In many cases states have adopted the principles contained in the Model Business Corporate Act prepared by the American Bar Association. State laws are complex and vary both in their provisions and in their definitions of certain terms. Some laws fail to define technical terms. As a result, terms often mean one thing in one state and another thing in a different state. These problems may be further compounded because legal authorities often interpret the effects and restrictions of the laws differently.

Capital Stock or Share System

Stockholders' equity in a corporation generally consists of a large number of units or shares. Within a given class of stock each share exactly equals every other share. The number of shares possessed determines each owner's interest. If a company has one class of stock divided into 1,000 shares, a person who owns 500 shares controls one-half of the ownership interest. One holding 10 shares has a one-hundredth interest.

INTERNATIONAL INSIGHT

In the United States, stockholders are treated equally as far as access to financial information. That is not always the case in other countries. For example, in Mexico, foreign investors as well as minority investors often have difficulty obtaining financial data. These restrictions are rooted in the habits of companies that, for many years, were tightly controlled by a few stockholders and managers.

Each share of stock has certain rights and privileges. Only by special contract can a company restrict these rights and privileges at the time it issues the shares. Owners must examine the articles of incorporation, stock certificates, and the provisions of the state law to ascertain such restrictions on or variations from the standard rights and privileges. In the absence of restrictive provisions, each share carries the following rights:

1. To share proportionately in profits and losses.
2. To share proportionately in management (the right to vote for directors).
3. To share proportionately in corporate assets upon liquidation.
4. To share proportionately in any new issues of stock of the same class—called the **preemptive right.**[1]

The first three rights are self-explanatory. The last right is used to protect each stockholder's proportional interest in the company. **The preemptive right protects an existing stockholder from involuntary dilution of ownership interest.** Without this right, stockholders might find their interest reduced by the issuance of additional stock without their knowledge, and at prices unfavorable to them. However, many corporations have eliminated the preemptive right. Why? Because this right makes it inconvenient for corporations to issue large amounts of additional stock, as they frequently do in acquiring other companies.

The share system easily allows one individual to transfer an interest in a company to another investor. For example, individuals owning shares in **Circuit City may sell them to others at any time and at any price without obtaining the consent of the company or other stockholders**. Each share is personal property of the owner, who may dispose of it at will. Circuit City simply maintains a list or subsidiary ledger of stockholders as a guide to dividend payments, issuance of stock rights, voting proxies, and the like. Because owners freely and frequently transfer shares, Circuit City must revise the subsidiary ledger of stockholders periodically, generally in advance of every dividend payment or stockholders' meeting.

In addition, the major stock exchanges require ownership controls that the typical corporation finds uneconomic to provide. Thus, corporations often use **registrars and transfer agents** who specialize in providing services for recording and transferring stock. The Uniform Stock Transfer Act and the Uniform Commercial Code govern the negotiability of stock certificates.

Variety of Ownership Interests

In every corporation one class of stock must represent the basic ownership interest. That class is called common stock. **Common stock** is the residual corporate interest that bears the ultimate risks of loss and receives the benefits of success. It is guaranteed

[1]This privilege is referred to as a **stock right** or **warrant**. The warrants issued in these situations are of short duration, unlike the warrants issued with other securities.

neither dividends nor assets upon dissolution. But common stockholders generally control the management of the corporation and tend to profit most if the company is successful. In the event that a corporation has only one authorized issue of capital stock, that issue is by definition common stock, whether so designated in the charter or not.

INTERNATIONAL INSIGHT

The U.S. and British systems of corporate governance and finance depend to a large extent on equity financing and the widely dispersed ownership of shares traded in highly liquid markets. The German and Japanese systems have relied more on debt financing, interlocking stock ownership, banker/directors, and worker/shareholder rights.

In an effort to broaden investor appeal, corporations may offer two or more classes of stock, each with different rights or privileges. In the preceding section we pointed out that each share of stock of a given issue has the same four inherent rights as other shares of the same issue. By special stock contracts between the corporation and its stockholders, however, the stockholder may sacrifice certain of these rights in return for other special rights or privileges. Thus special classes of stock, usually called **preferred stock**, are created. In return for any special preference, the preferred stockholder always sacrifices some of the inherent rights of common stock ownership.

A common type of preference is to give the preferred stockholders a prior claim on earnings. The corporation thus assures them a dividend, usually at a stated rate, before it distributes any amount to the common stockholders. In return for this preference the preferred stockholders may sacrifice their right to a voice in management or their right to share in profits beyond the stated rate.

WHAT DO THE NUMBERS MEAN?

CLASSY STOCK

Some companies grant preferences to different shareholders by issuing different classes of common stock. Blue-chip newspaper companies, such as **The New York Times, Dow Jones**, and **The Washington Post**, have two classes of stock. Also, **Ford** and **Comcast** are two-class companies.

Sometimes these different classes of shares trade at dramatically different prices. For example, **Molex** has issued both common shares and Class A common stock, with the common shares trading at up to a 14 percent premium over the Class A shares. Why the difference in price? The most common explanation is voting rights. In the Molex case, the common shareholders get one vote per share; Class A shares don't get to vote.

For most retail investors, voting rights are not that important. But for family-controlled companies, issuing newer classes of lower or non-voting stock effectively creates currency for acquisitions, increases liquidity, or puts a public value on the company without diluting the family's voting control. Thus, investors must carefully compare the apparent bargain prices for some classes of stock—they may end up as second-class citizens with no voting rights.

Source: Adapted from Lauren Rublin, "Separate but Equal," *Barons Online* (August 16, 1999); and Andy Serwer, "Dual-Listed Companies Aren't Fair or Balanced," *Fortune* (September 20, 2004), p. 83.

CORPORATE CAPITAL

OBJECTIVE 2
Identify the key components of stockholders' equity.

Owner's equity in a corporation is defined as stockholders' equity, shareholders' equity, or corporate capital. The following three categories normally appear as part of stockholders' equity:

1 Capital stock.
2 Additional paid-in capital.
3 Retained earnings.

The first two categories, capital stock and additional paid-in capital, constitute contributed (paid-in) capital. **Retained earnings** represents the earned capital of the company. **Contributed capital (paid-in capital)** is the total amount paid in on capital stock—the amount provided by stockholders to the corporation for use in the business. Contributed capital includes items such as the par value of all outstanding stock and premiums less discounts on issuance. **Earned capital** is the capital that develops from profitable operations. It consists of all undistributed income that remains invested in the company.

Stockholders' equity is the difference between the assets and the liabilities of the company. That is, the owners' or stockholders' interest in a company like **Walt Disney Co.** is a **residual interest**.[2] **Stockholders' (owners') equity** represents the cumulative net contributions by stockholders plus retained earnings. As a residual interest, stockholders' equity has no existence apart from the assets and liabilities of Disney—stockholders' equity equals net assets. Stockholders' equity is not a claim to specific assets but a claim against a portion of the total assets. Its amount is not specified or fixed; it depends on Disney's profitability. Stockholders' equity grows if it is profitable. It shrinks, or may disappear entirely, if Disney loses money.

Issuance of Stock

OBJECTIVE 3
Explain the accounting procedures for issuing shares of stock.

In issuing stock, companies follow these procedures: First, the state must authorize the stock, generally in a certificate of incorporation or charter. Next, the corporation offers shares for sale, entering into contracts to sell stock. Then, after receiving amounts for the stock, the corporation issues shares. The corporation generally makes no entry in the general ledger accounts when it receives its stock authorization from the state of incorporation.

We discuss the accounting problems involved in the issuance of stock under the following topics.

1. Accounting for par value stock.
2. Accounting for no-par stock.
3. Accounting for stock issued in combination with other securities (lump-sum sales).
4. Accounting for stock issued in noncash transactions.
5. Accounting for costs of issuing stock.

Par Value Stock

The par value of a stock has no relationship to its fair market value. At present, the par value associated with most capital stock issuances is very low. For example, **PepsiCo**'s par value is $0.01, **Kellogg**'s is $0.25, and **Hershey**'s is $1. Such values contrast dramatically with the situation in the early 1900s, when practically all stock issued had a par value of $100. Low par values help companies avoid the contingent liability associated with stock sold below par.[3]

To show the required information for issuance of par value stock, corporations maintain accounts for each class of stock as follows.

1. ***Preferred Stock or Common Stock.*** Together, these two stock accounts reflect the par value of the corporation's issued shares. The company credits these accounts

---

[2]"Elements of Financial Statements," *Statement of Financial Accounting Concepts No. 6* (Stamford, Conn.: FASB, 1985), par. 60.

[3]Companies rarely, if ever, issue stock at a value below par value. If issuing stock below par, the company records the discount as a debit to Additional Paid-in Capital. In addition, the corporation may call on the original purchaser or the current holder of the shares issued below par to pay in the amount of the discount to prevent creditors from sustaining a loss upon liquidation of the corporation.

when it originally issues the shares. It makes no additional entries in these accounts unless it issues additional shares or retires them.

2 *Additional Paid-in Capital (also called Paid-in Capital in Excess of Par).* The **Additional Paid-in Capital** account indicates any excess over par value paid in by stockholders in return for the shares issued to them. Once paid in, the excess over par becomes a part of the corporation's additional paid-in capital. The individual stockholder has no greater claim on the excess paid in than all other holders of the same class of shares.

No-Par Stock

Many states permit the issuance of capital stock without par value, called **no-par stock**. The reasons for issuance of no-par stock are twofold: First, issuance of no-par stock **avoids the contingent liability** (see footnote 3) that might occur if the corporation issued par value stock at a discount. Second, some confusion exists over the relationship (or rather the absence of a relationship) between the par value and fair market value. If shares have no par value, **the questionable treatment of using par value as a basis for fair value never arises.** This is particularly advantageous whenever issuing stock for property items such as tangible or intangible fixed assets.

A major disadvantage of no-par stock is that some states levy a high tax on these issues. In addition, in some states the total issue price for no-par stock may be considered legal capital, which could reduce the flexibility in paying dividends.

Corporations sell no-par shares, like par value shares, for whatever price they will bring. However, unlike par value shares, corporations issue them without a premium or a discount. The exact amount received represents the credit to common or preferred stock. For example, Video Electronics Corporation is organized with authorized common stock of 10,000 shares without par value. Video Electronics makes only a memorandum entry for the authorization, inasmuch as no amount is involved. If Video Electronics then issues 500 shares for cash at $10 per share, it makes the following entry:

Cash	5,000	
Common Stock—No-Par Value		5,000

If it issues another 500 shares for $11 per share, Video Electronics makes this entry:

Cash	5,500	
Common Stock—No-Par Value		5,500

True no-par stock should be carried in the accounts at issue price without any additional paid-in capital or discount reported. But some states require that no-par stock have a **stated value**. The stated value is a minimum value below which a company cannot issue it. Thus, instead of being no-par stock, such stated-value stock becomes, in effect, stock with a very low par value. It thus is open to all the criticism and abuses that first encouraged the development of no-par stock.[4]

If no-par stock has a stated value of $5 per share but sells for $11, all such amounts in excess of $5 are recorded as additional paid-in capital, which in many states is fully or partially available for dividends. Thus, no-par value stock, with a low stated value, permits a new corporation to commence its operations with additional paid-in capital that may exceed its stated capital. For example, if a company issued 1,000 of the shares with a $5 stated value at $15 per share for cash, it makes the following entry.

Cash	15,000	
Common Stock		5,000
Paid-in Capital in Excess of Stated Value		10,000

[4] *Accounting Trends and Techniques—2004* indicates that its 600 surveyed companies reported 655 issues of outstanding common stock, 570 par value issues, and 54 no-par issues; 6 of the no-par issues were shown at their stated (assigned) values.

Most corporations account for no-par stock with a stated value as if it were par value stock with par equal to the stated value.

Stock Issued with Other Securities (Lump-Sum Sales)

Generally, corporations sell classes of stock separately from one another. The reason to do so is to track the proceeds relative to each class, as well as relative to each lot. Occasionally, a corporation issues two or more classes of securities for a single payment or lump sum, in the acquisition of another company. The accounting problem in such **lump-sum sales** is how to allocate the proceeds among the several classes of securities. Companies use one of two methods of allocation: (1) the proportional method and (2) the incremental method.

Proportional Method. If the fair market value or other sound basis for determining relative value is available for each class of security, **the company allocates the lump sum received among the classes of securities on a proportional basis.** For instance, assume a company issues 1,000 shares of $10 stated value common stock having a market value of $20 a share, and 1,000 shares of $10 par value preferred stock having a market value of $12 a share, for a lump sum of $30,000. Illustration 14-1 shows how the company allocates the $30,000 to the two classes of stock.

ILLUSTRATION 14-1
Allocation in Lump-Sum Securities Issuance—Proportional Method

Fair market value of common (1,000 × $20) =	$20,000
Fair market value of preferred (1,000 × $12) =	12,000
Aggregate fair market value	$32,000
Allocated to common: $\frac{\$20,000}{\$32,000} \times \$30,000$ =	$18,750
Allocated to preferred: $\frac{\$12,000}{\$32,000} \times \$30,000$ =	11,250
Total allocation	$30,000

Incremental Method. In instances where a company cannot determine the fair market value of all classes of securities, it may use the incremental method. It uses the market value of the securities as a basis for those classes that it knows, and allocates the remainder of the lump sum to the class for which it does not know the market value. For instance, if a company issues 1,000 shares of $10 stated value common stock having a market value of $20, and 1,000 shares of $10 par value preferred stock having no established market value, for a lump sum of $30,000, it allocates the $30,000 to the two classes as shown in Illustration 14-2.

ILLUSTRATION 14-2
Allocation in Lump-Sum Securities Issuance—Incremental Method

Lump-sum receipt	$30,000
Allocated to common (1,000 × $20)	20,000
Balance allocated to preferred	$10,000

If a company cannot determine fair value for any of the classes of stock involved in a lump-sum exchange, it may need to use other approaches. It may rely on an expert's appraisal. Or, if the company knows that one or more of the classes of securities issued will have a determinable market value in the near future, it may use a best estimate basis with the intent to adjust later, upon establishment of the future market value.

Stock Issued in Noncash Transactions

Accounting for the issuance of shares of stock for property or services involves an issue of valuation. **The general rule is: Companies should record stock issued for services or property other than cash at either the fair value of the stock issued or the fair value of the noncash consideration received, whichever is more clearly determinable.**

If a company can readily determine both, and the transaction results from an arm's-length exchange, there will probably be little difference in their fair values. In such cases the basis for valuing the exchange should not matter.

If a company cannot readily determine either the fair value of the stock it issues or the property or services it receives, it should employ an appropriate valuation technique. Depending on available data, the valuation may be based on market transactions involving comparable assets or the use of discounted expected future cash flows. Companies should avoid the use of the book, par, or stated values as a basis of valuation for these transactions.

A company may exchange unissued stock or treasury stock (issued shares that it has reacquired but not retired) for property or services. If it uses treasury shares, the cost of the treasury shares should not be considered the decisive factor in establishing the fair value of the property or services. Instead, it should use the fair value of the treasury stock, if known, to value the property or services. Otherwise, if it does not know the fair value of the treasury stock, it should use the fair value of the property or services received, if determinable.

The following series of transactions illustrates the procedure for recording the issuance of 10,000 shares of $10 par value common stock for a patent for Marlowe Company, in various circumstances.

1 Marlowe cannot readily determine the fair value of the patent, but it knows the fair value of the stock is $140,000.

Patent	140,000	
Common Stock (10,000 shares × $10 per share)		100,000
Paid-in Capital in Excess of Par		40,000

2 Marlowe cannot readily determine the fair value of the stock, but it determines the fair value of the patent is $150,000.

Patent	150,000	
Common Stock (10,000 shares × $10 per share)		100,000
Paid-in Capital in Excess of Par		50,000

3 Marlowe cannot readily determine the fair value of the stock nor the fair value of the patent. An independent consultant values the patent at $125,000 based on discounted expected cash flows.

Patent	125,000	
Common Stock (10,000 shares × $10 share)		100,000
Paid-in Capital in Excess of Par		25,000

In corporate law, the board of directors has the power to set the value of noncash transactions. However, boards sometimes abuse this power. The issuance of stock for property or services has resulted in cases of overstated corporate capital through intentional overvaluation of the property or services received. The overvaluation of the stockholders' equity resulting from inflated asset values creates **watered stock**. The corporation should eliminate the "water" by simply writing down the overvalued assets.

If, as a result of the issuance of stock for property or services, a corporation undervalues the recorded assets, it creates **secret reserves**. An understated corporate structure (secret reserve) may also result from other methods: excessive depreciation or amortization charges, expensing capital expenditures, excessive write-downs of inventories or receivables, or any other understatement of assets or overstatement of liabilities. An example of a liability overstatement is an excessive provision for estimated product warranties that ultimately results in an understatement of owners' equity, thereby creating a secret reserve.

Costs of Issuing Stock

When a company like **Walgreens** issues stock, it should report direct costs incurred to sell stock, such as underwriting costs, accounting and legal fees, printing costs, and taxes, as a reduction of the amounts paid in. Walgreens therefore debits issue costs to Additional Paid-in Capital because they are unrelated to corporate operations. In effect, **issue costs are a cost of financing**. As such, issue costs should reduce the proceeds received from the sale of the stock.

Walgreens should expense management salaries and other indirect costs related to the stock issue because it is difficult to establish a relationship between these costs and the sale proceeds. In addition, Walgreens expenses recurring costs, primarily registrar and transfer agents' fees, as incurred.

THE CASE OF THE DISAPPEARING RECEIVABLE

WHAT DO THE NUMBERS MEAN?

Sometimes companies issue stock but may not receive cash in return. As a result, a company records a receivable.

Controversy existed regarding the presentation of this receivable on the balance sheet. Some argued that the company should report the receivable as an asset similar to other receivables. Others argued that the company should report the receivable as a deduction from stockholders' equity (similar to the treatment of treasury stock). The SEC settled this issue: It requires companies to use the contra-equity approach because the risk of collection in this type of transaction is often very high.

This accounting issue surfaced in **Enron**'s accounting. Starting in early 2000, Enron issued shares of its common stock to four "special-purpose entities," in exchange for which it received a note receivable. Enron then increased its assets (by recording a receivable) and stockholders' equity, a move the company now calls an accounting error. As a result of this accounting treatment, Enron overstated assets and stockholders' equity by $172 million in its 2000 audited financial statements and by $828 million in its unaudited 2001 statements. This $1 billion overstatement was 8.5 percent of Enron's previously reported stockholders' equity at that time.

As Lynn Turner, former chief accountant of the SEC, noted, "It is a basic accounting principle that you don't record equity until you get cash, and a note doesn't count as cash." Situations like this led investors, creditors, and suppliers to lose faith in the credibility of Enron, which eventually caused its bankruptcy.

Source: Adapted from Jonathan Weil, "Basic Accounting Tripped Up Enron—Financial Statements Didn't Add Up—Auditors Overlook a Simple Rule," *Wall Street Journal* (November 11, 2001), p. C1.

Reacquisition of Shares

OBJECTIVE 4
Describe the accounting for treasury stock.

Companies often buy back their own shares. In fact, share buybacks now exceed dividends as a form of distribution to stockholders.[5] For example, **Dell**, **Yahoo**, and **The Home Depot** had buybacks recently of $10 billion, $3 billion, and $2 billion, respectively. Illustration 14-3 indicates that buybacks are increasing dramatically.

[5] At the beginning of the 1990s the situation was just the opposite. That is, share buybacks were less than half the level of dividends. Companies are extremely reluctant to reduce or eliminate their dividends, because they believe that the market negatively views this action.

ILLUSTRATION 14-3
Stock Buybacks on the Rise

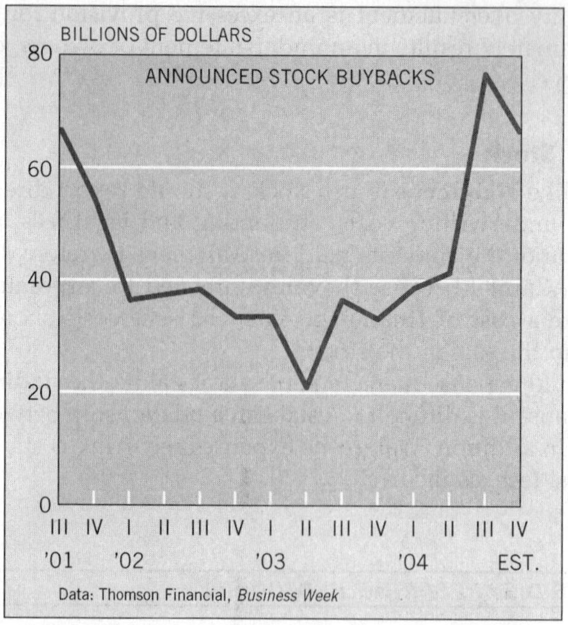

Source: *Business Week* (November 29, 2004), p.116.

Corporations purchase their outstanding stock for several reasons:

1. ***To provide tax-efficient distributions of excess cash to shareholders.*** Capital gain rates on sales of stock to the company by the stockholders have been approximately half the ordinary tax rate for many investors. This advantage has been somewhat diminished by recent changes in the tax law related to dividends.
2. ***To increase earnings per share and return on equity.*** Reducing both shares outstanding and stockholders' equity often enhances certain performance ratios. However, strategies to hype performance measures might increase performance in the short-run, but these tactics add no real long-term value.
3. ***To provide stock for employee stock compensation contracts or to meet potential merger needs.*** **Honeywell Inc.** reported that it would use part of its purchase of one million common shares for employee stock option contracts. Other companies acquire shares to have them available for business acquisitions.
4. ***To thwart takeover attempts or to reduce the number of stockholders.*** By reducing the number of shares held by the public, existing owners and managements bar "outsiders" from gaining control or significant influence. When Ted Turner attempted to acquire **CBS**, CBS started a substantial buyback of its stock. Companies may also use stock purchases to eliminate dissident stockholders.
5. ***To make a market in the stock.*** As one company executive noted, "Our company is trying to establish a floor for the stock." Purchasing stock in the marketplace creates a demand. This may stabilize the stock price or, in fact, increase it.

Some publicly held corporations have chosen to "go private," that is, to eliminate public (outside) ownership entirely by purchasing all of their outstanding stock. Companies often accomplish such a procedure through a **leveraged buyout (LBO)**, in which the company borrows money to finance the stock repurchases.

After reacquiring shares, a company may either retire them or hold them in the treasury for reissue. If not retired, such shares are referred to as **treasury stock (treasury shares)**. Technically, treasury stock is a corporation's own stock, reacquired after having been issued and fully paid.

Underlying Concepts

As we indicated in Chapter 2, an asset should have probable future economic benefits. Treasury stock simply reduces common stock outstanding.

Treasury stock is not an asset. When a company purchases treasury stock, a reduction occurs in both assets and stockholders' equity. It is inappropriate to imply that a corporation can own a part of itself. A corporation may sell treasury stock to obtain funds, but that does not make treasury stock a balance sheet asset. When a corporation buys back some of its own outstanding stock, it has not acquired an asset; it reduces net assets.

The possession of treasury stock does not give the corporation the right to vote, to exercise preemptive rights as a stockholder, to receive cash dividends, or to receive assets upon corporate liquidation. **Treasury stock is essentially the same as unissued capital stock.** No one advocates classifying unissued capital stock as an asset in the balance sheet.[6]

SIGNALS TO BUY?

WHAT DO THE NUMBERS MEAN?

Market analysts sometimes look to stock buybacks as a buy signal for a stock. That strategy is not that surprising if you look at the performance of companies that did buybacks. For example, in one study, buyback companies outperformed similar companies without buybacks by an average of 23 percent. In a recent three-year period, companies followed by **Buybackletter.com** were up 16.4 percent, while the S&P 500 Stock Index was up just 7.1 percent in that period. Why the premium? Well, the conventional wisdom is that companies who buy back shares believe their shares are undervalued. Thus, analysts view the buyback announcement as an important piece of inside information about future company prospects.

On the other hand, buy-backs can actually hurt businesses and their shareholders over the long-run. Whether the buy-back is a good thing appears to depend a lot on why the company did the buy-back and what the repurchased shares were used for. One study found that companies often increased their buybacks when earnings growth slowed. This allowed the companies to prop up earnings per share (based on fewer shares outstanding). Furthermore, many buybacks do not actually result in a net reduction in shares outstanding. For example, companies, such as **Microsoft**, bought back shares to meet share demands for stock option exercises, resulting in higher net shares outstanding when it re-issued the repurchased shares to the option holders upon exercise. In this case the buyback actually indicated a further dilution in the share ownership in the buyback company.

This does not mean you should never trust a buy-back signal. But if the buy-back is intended to manage the company's earnings or if the buy-back results in dilution, take a closer look.

Source: Adapted from Ann Tergesen, "When Buybacks Are Signals to Buy," *Business Week Online* (October 1, 2001); and Rachel Beck, "Stock BuyBacks Not Always Good for the Company, Shareholders," *Naples [FL] Daily News* (March 7, 2004). p. I1.

Purchase of Treasury Stock

Companies use two general methods of handling treasury stock in the accounts: the cost method and the par value method. Both methods are generally acceptable. The cost method enjoys more widespread use.[7]

Discussion of Using Par or Stated Value for Treasury Stock Transactions

- The **cost method** results in debiting the Treasury Stock account for the reacquisition cost and in reporting this account as a deduction from the total paid-in capital **and** retained earnings on the balance sheet.
- The **par** or **stated value method** records all transactions in treasury shares at their par value and reports the treasury stock as a deduction from capital stock only.

[6]The possible justification for classifying these shares as assets is that the company will use them to liquidate a specific liability that appears on the balance sheet. *Accounting Trends and Techniques—2004* reported that out of 600 companies surveyed, 398 disclosed treasury stock, but none classified it as an asset.

[7]*Accounting Trends and Techniques—2004* indicates that of its selected list of 600 companies, 384 carried common stock in treasury at cost and only 2 at par or stated value; 2 companies carried preferred stock in treasury at cost and none at par or stated value.

No matter which method a company uses, most states consider the cost of the treasury shares acquired as a restriction on retained earnings.

Companies generally use the cost method to account for treasury stock. This method derives its name from the fact that a company maintains the Treasury Stock account at the cost of the shares purchased.[8] Under the cost method, the company debits the Treasury Stock account for the cost of the shares acquired. Upon reissuance of the shares, it credits the account for this same cost. The original price received for the stock does not affect the entries to record the acquisition and reissuance of the treasury stock.

To illustrate, assume that Pacific Company issued 100,000 shares of $1 par value common stock at a price of $10 per share. In addition, it has retained earnings of $300,000. Illustration 14-4 shows the stockholders' equity section on December 31, 2006, before purchase of treasury stock.

ILLUSTRATION 14-4
Stockholders' Equity with No Treasury Stock

Stockholders' equity	
Paid-in capital	
Common stock, $1 par value, 100,000 shares issued and outstanding	$ 100,000
Additional paid-in capital	900,000
Total paid-in capital	1,000,000
Retained earnings	300,000
Total stockholders' equity	$1,300,000

On January 20, 2007, Pacific acquires 10,000 shares of its stock at $11 per share. Pacific records the reacquisition as follows:

January 20, 2007		
Treasury Stock	110,000	
Cash		110,000

Note that Pacific debited Treasury Stock for the cost of the shares purchased. The original paid-in capital account, Common Stock, is not affected because the number of issued shares does not change. The same is true for the Additional Paid-in Capital account. Pacific deducts treasury stock from total paid-in capital and retained earnings in the stockholders' equity section.

Illustration 14-5 shows the stockholders' equity section for Pacific after purchase of the treasury stock.

ILLUSTRATION 14-5
Stockholders' Equity with Treasury Stock

Stockholders' equity	
Paid-in capital	
Common stock, $1 par value, 100,000 shares issued and 90,000 outstanding	$ 100,000
Additional paid-in capital	900,000
Total paid-in capital	1,000,000
Retained earnings	300,000
Total paid-in capital and retained earnings	1,300,000
Less: Cost of treasury stock (10,000 shares)	110,000
Total stockholders' equity	$1,190,000

[8]If making numerous acquisitions of blocks of treasury shares at different prices, a company may use inventory costing methods—such as specific identification, average, or FIFO—to identify the cost at date of reissuance.

Pacific subtracts the cost of the treasury stock from the total of common stock, additional paid-in capital, and retained earnings. It therefore reduces stockholders' equity. Many states require a corporation to restrict retained earnings for the cost of treasury stock purchased. The restriction keeps intact the corporation's legal capital that it temporarily holds as treasury stock. When the corporation sells the treasury stock, it lifts the restriction.

Pacific discloses both the number of shares issued (100,000) and the number in the treasury (10,000). The difference is the number of shares of stock outstanding (90,000). The term **outstanding stock** means the number of shares of issued stock that stockholders own.

Sale of Treasury Stock

Companies usually reissue or retire treasury stock. When selling treasury shares, the accounting for the sale depends on the price. If the selling price of the treasury stock equals its cost, the company records the sale of the shares by debiting Cash and crediting Treasury Stock. In cases where the selling price of the treasury stock is not equal to cost, then accounting for treasury stock sold **above cost** differs from the accounting for treasury stock sold **below cost**. However, the sale of treasury stock either above or below cost increases both total assets and stockholders' equity.

Sale of Treasury Stock above Cost. When the selling price of shares of treasury stock exceeds its cost, a company credits the difference to Paid-in Capital from Treasury Stock. To illustrate, assume that Pacific acquired 10,000 shares of its treasury stock at $11 per share. It now sells 1,000 shares at $15 per share on March 10. Pacific records the entry as follows.

March 10, 2007

Cash	15,000	
Treasury Stock		11,000
Paid-in Capital from Treasury Stock		4,000

There are two reasons why Pacific does not credit $4,000 to Gain on Sale of Treasury Stock: (1) Gains on sales occur when selling **assets**; treasury stock is not an asset. (2) A gain or loss should not be recognized from stock transactions with its own stockholders. Thus, Pacific should not include paid-in capital arising from the sale of treasury stock in the measurement of net income. Instead, it lists paid-in capital from treasury stock separately on the balance sheet, as a part of paid-in capital.

Sale of Treasury Stock below Cost. When a corporation sells treasury stock below its cost, it usually debits the excess of the cost over selling price to Paid-in Capital from Treasury Stock. Thus, if Pacific sells an additional 1,000 shares of treasury stock on March 21 at $8 per share, it records the sale as follows.

March 21, 2007

Cash	8,000	
Paid-in Capital from Treasury Stock	3,000	
Treasury Stock		11,000

We can make several observations based on the two sale entries (sale above cost and sale below cost): (1) Pacific credits Treasury Stock at cost in each entry. (2) Pacific uses Paid-in Capital from Treasury Stock for the difference between the cost and the resale price of the shares. (3) Neither entry affects the original paid-in capital account, Common Stock.

After eliminating the credit balance in Paid-in Capital from Treasury Stock, the corporation debits any additional excess of cost over selling price to Retained Earnings. To illustrate, assume that Pacific sells an additional 1,000 shares at $8 per share on April 10. Illustration 14-6 shows the balance in the Paid-in Capital from Treasury Stock account (before the April 10 purchase).

ILLUSTRATION 14-6
Treasury Stock Transactions in Paid-in Capital Account

Paid-in Capital from Treasury Stock			
Mar. 21	3,000	Mar. 10	4,000
		Balance	1,000

In this case, Pacific debits $1,000 of the excess to Paid-in Capital from Treasury Stock. It debits the remainder to Retained Earnings. The entry is:

April 10, 2007		
Cash	8,000	
Paid-in Capital from Treasury Stock	1,000	
Retained Earnings	2,000	
Treasury Stock		11,000

Retiring Treasury Stock

The board of directors may approve the retirement of treasury shares. This decision results in cancellation of the treasury stock and a reduction in the number of shares of issued stock. Retired treasury shares have the status of authorized and unissued shares. The accounting effects are similar to the sale of treasury stock except that corporations debit the **paid-in capital accounts applicable to the retired shares** instead of cash. For example, if a corporation originally sells the shares at par, it debits Common Stock for the par value per share. If it originally sells the shares at $3 above par value, it also debits Paid-in Capital in Excess of Par Value for $3 per share at retirement.

PREFERRED STOCK

OBJECTIVE 5
Explain the accounting for and reporting of preferred stock.

As noted earlier, **preferred stock** is a special class of shares that possesses certain preferences or features not possessed by the common stock.[9] The following features are those most often associated with preferred stock issues.

1. Preference as to dividends.
2. Preference as to assets in the event of liquidation.
3. Convertible into common stock.
4. Callable at the option of the corporation.
5. Nonvoting.

The features that distinguish preferred from common stock may be of a more restrictive and negative nature than preferences. For example, the preferred stock may be nonvoting, noncumulative, and nonparticipating.

Companies usually issue preferred stock with a par value, expressing the dividend preference as a **percentage of the par value**. Thus, holders of 8 percent preferred stock with a $100 par value are entitled to an annual dividend of $8 per share. This stock is commonly referred to as 8 percent preferred stock. In the case of no-par preferred stock, a corporation expresses a dividend preference as a **specific dollar amount** per share, for example, $7 per share. This stock is commonly referred to as $7 preferred stock.

A preference as to dividends does not assure the payment of dividends. It merely assures that the corporation must pay the stated dividend rate or amount applicable to the preferred stock before paying any dividends on the common stock.

[9] *Accounting Trends and Techniques—2004* reports that of its 600 surveyed companies, 84 had preferred stock outstanding; 73 had one class of preferred, and 9 had two classes.

A company often issues preferred stock (instead of debt) because of a high debt-to-equity ratio. In other instances, it issues preferred stock through private placements with other corporations at a lower-than-market dividend rate because the acquiring corporation receives largely tax-free dividends (owing to the IRS's 70 percent or 80 percent dividends received deduction).

Features of Preferred Stock

A corporation may attach whatever preferences or restrictions, in whatever combination it desires, to a preferred stock issue, as long as it does not specifically violate its state incorporation law. Also, it may issue more than one class of preferred stock. We discuss the most common features attributed to preferred stock below.

Cumulative Preferred Stock

Cumulative preferred stock requires that if a corporation fails to pay a dividend in any year, it must make it up in a later year before paying any dividends to common stockholders. If the directors fail to declare a dividend at the normal date for dividend action, the dividend is said to have been "passed." Any passed dividend on cumulative preferred stock constitutes a **dividend in arrears**. Because no liability exists until the board of directors declares a dividend, a corporation does not record a dividend in arrears as a liability but discloses it in a note to the financial statements. A corporation seldom issues noncumulative preferred stock because a passed dividend is lost forever to the preferred stockholder. As a result, this stock issue would be less marketable.

Participating Preferred Stock

Holders of **participating preferred stock** share ratably with the common stockholders in any profit distributions beyond the prescribed rate. That is, 5 percent preferred stock, if fully participating, will receive not only its 5 percent return, but also dividends at the same rates as those paid to common stockholders if paying amounts in excess of 5 percent of par or stated value to common stockholders. Note that participating preferred stock may be only partially participating. Although seldom used, examples of companies that have issued participating preferreds are **LTV Corporation, Southern California Edison,** and **Allied Products Corporation.**

Convertible Preferred Stock

Convertible preferred stock allows stockholders, at their option, to exchange preferred shares for common stock at a predetermined ratio. The convertible preferred stockholder not only enjoys a preferred claim on dividends but also has the option of converting into a common stockholder with unlimited participation in earnings.

Callable Preferred Stock

Callable preferred stock permits the corporation at its option to call or redeem the outstanding preferred shares at specified future dates and at stipulated prices. Many preferred issues are callable. The corporation usually sets the call or redemption price slightly above the original issuance price and commonly states it in terms related to the par value. The callable feature permits the corporation to use the capital obtained through the issuance of such stock until the need has passed or it is no longer advantageous.

The existence of a call price or prices tends to set a ceiling on the market value of the preferred shares unless they are convertible into common stock. When a corporation redeems preferred stock, it must pay any dividends in arrears.

Redeemable Preferred Stock

Recently, more and more issuances of preferred stock have features that make the security more like debt (legal obligation to pay) than an equity instrument. For example, **redeemable preferred stock** has a mandatory redemption period or a redemption feature that the issuer cannot control.

Previously, public companies were not permitted to report these debt-like preferreds in equity, but they were not required to report them as a liability either. There were concerns about classification of these debt-like securities, which may have been reported as equity or in the "mezzanine" section of balance sheets between debt and equity. There also was diversity in practice as to how dividends on these securities were reported. The FASB recently issued a standard that affects the accounting for certain hybrid instruments and requires debt-like securities, like redeemable preferred stock to be classified as liabilities and be measured and accounted for similar to liabilities.[10]

Accounting for and Reporting Preferred Stock

The accounting for preferred stock at issuance is similar to that for common stock. A corporation allocates proceeds between the par value of the preferred stock and additional paid-in capital. To illustrate, assume that Bishop Co. issues 10,000 shares of $10 par value preferred stock for $12 cash per share. Bishop records the issuance as follows:

Cash	120,000	
Preferred Stock		100,000
Paid-in Capital in Excess of Par		20,000

Thus, Bishop maintains separate accounts for these different classes of shares.

In contrast to convertible bonds (recorded as a liability on the date of issue) corporations consider convertible preferred stock as a part of stockholders' equity. In addition, when exercising convertible preferred stocks, there is no theoretical justification for recognition of a gain or loss. A company recognizes no gain or loss when dealing with stockholders in their capacity as business owners. Instead, the company **employs the book value method**: debit Preferred Stock, along with any related Additional Paid-in Capital; credit Common Stock and Additional Paid-in Capital (if an excess exists).

Preferred stock generally has no maturity date. Therefore, no legal obligation exists to pay the preferred stockholder. As a result, companies classify preferred stock as part of stockholders' equity. Companies generally report preferred stock at par value as the first item in the stockholders' equity section. They report any excess over par value as part of additional paid-in capital. They also consider dividends on preferred stock as a distribution of income and not an expense. Companies must disclose the pertinent rights of the preferred stock outstanding.[11]

DIVIDEND POLICY

OBJECTIVE 6
Describe the policies used in distributing dividends.

As indicated in the opening story, dividend payouts can be important signals to the market. The practice of paying dividends declined sharply in the 1980s and 1990s as companies focused on growth and plowed profits back into the business. A resurgence in dividend payouts is due in large part to the dividend tax cut of 2003, which reduced the rate of tax on dividends to 14 percent (quite a bit lower than the ordinary income rate charged in the past). In addition, investors who were burned by accounting scandals in recent years began demanding higher payouts in the form of dividends. Why?

[10] "Accounting for Certain Financial Instruments with Characteristics of Both Liabilities and Equity," *Statement of Financial Accounting Standards No. 150* (Norwalk Conn.: FASB, 2003). *SFAS No. 150* represents completion of the first phase in a broader project on liabilities and equity. In phase two, the FASB will deal with the accounting for compound financial instruments (e.g., convertible debt) that have characteristics of liabilities and equity, the definition of an ownership relationship, and the definition of liabilities (an amendment to *FASB Concepts Statement No. 6*, "Elements of Financial Statements.")

[11] "Disclosure of Information about Capital Structure," *Statement of Financial Accounting Standards No. 129* (Norwalk, Conn.: FASB, 1997).

A dividend check provides proof that at least some portion of a company's profits is genuine.[12]

Determining the proper amount of dividends to pay is a difficult financial management decision. Companies that are paying dividends are extremely reluctant to reduce or eliminate their dividend. They fear that the securities market might negatively view this action. As a consequence, companies that have been paying cash dividends will make every effort to continue to do so. In addition, the type of shareholder the company has (taxable or nontaxable, retail investor or institutional investor) plays a large role in determining dividend policy.

Very few companies pay dividends in amounts equal to their legally available retained earnings. The major reasons are as follows.

1. To maintain agreements (bond covenants) with specific creditors, to retain all or a portion of the earnings, in the form of assets, to build up additional protection against possible loss.
2. To meet state corporation requirements, that earnings equivalent to the cost of treasury shares purchased be restricted against dividend declarations.
3. To retain assets that would otherwise be paid out as dividends, to finance growth or expansion. This is sometimes called internal financing, reinvesting earnings, or "plowing" the profits back into the business.
4. To smooth out dividend payments from year to year by accumulating earnings in good years and using such accumulated earnings as a basis for dividends in bad years.
5. To build up a cushion or buffer against possible losses or errors in the calculation of profits.

The reasons above are self-explanatory except for the second. The laws of some states require that the corporation restrict its legal capital from distribution to stockholders, to protect against loss for creditors.[13] The applicable state law determines the legality of a dividend.

Financial Condition and Dividend Distributions

Effective management of a company requires attention to more than the legality of dividend distributions. Management must also consider economic conditions, most importantly, liquidity. Assume an extreme situation as shown in Illustration 14-7.

ILLUSTRATION 14-7
Balance Sheet, Showing a Lack of Liquidity

BALANCE SHEET

Plant assets	$500,000	Capital stock	$400,000
	$500,000	Retained earnings	100,000
			$500,000

The depicted company has a retained earnings credit balance. Unless restricted, it can declare a dividend of $100,000. But because all its assets are plant assets used in operations, payment of a cash dividend of $100,000 would require the sale of plant assets or borrowing.

[12]Jeff Opdyke, "Tax Cut, Shareholder Pressure Stoke Surge in Dividends," *Wall Street Journal Online* (January 18, 2005).

[13]If the corporation buys its own outstanding stock, it reduces its legal capital and distributes assets to stockholders. If permitted, the corporation could, by purchasing treasury stock at any price desired, return to the stockholders their investments and leave creditors with little or no protection against loss.

Even if a balance sheet shows current assets, as in Illustration 14-8, the question remains as to whether the company needs those cash assets for other purposes.

ILLUSTRATION 14-8
Balance Sheet, Showing Cash but Minimal Working Capital

BALANCE SHEET

Cash	$100,000	Current liabilities		$ 60,000
Plant assets	460,000	Capital stock	$400,000	
	$560,000	Retained earnings	100,000	500,000
				$560,000

The existence of current liabilities strongly implies that the company needs some of the cash to meet current debts as they mature. In addition, day-by-day cash requirements for payrolls and other expenditures not included in current liabilities also require cash.

Thus, before declaring a dividend, management must consider **availability of funds to pay the dividend**. A company should not pay a dividend unless both the present and future financial position warrant the distribution.

The SEC encourages companies to disclose their dividend policy in their annual report, especially those that (1) have earnings but fail to pay dividends, or (2) do not expect to pay dividends in the foreseeable future. In addition, the SEC encourages companies that consistently pay dividends to indicate whether they intend to continue this practice in the future.

Types of Dividends

OBJECTIVE 7
Identify the various forms of dividend distributions.

Companies generally base dividend distributions either on accumulated profits (that is, retained earnings) or on some other capital item such as additional paid-in capital. Dividends are of the following types.

1. Cash dividends.
2. Property dividends.
3. Liquidating dividends.
4. Stock dividends.

Although commonly paid in cash, companies occasionally pay dividends in stock or some other asset.[14] **All dividends, except for stock dividends, reduce the total stockholders' equity in the corporation.** When declaring a stock dividend, the corporation does not pay out assets or incur a liability. It issues additional shares of stock to each stockholder and nothing more.

The natural expectation of any stockholder who receives a dividend is that the corporation has operated successfully. As a result, he or she is receiving a share of its profits. A company should disclose a **liquidating dividend**—that is, a dividend not based on retained earnings—to the stockholders so that they will not misunderstand its source.

Cash Dividends

The board of directors votes on the declaration of **cash dividends**. Upon approval of the resolution, the board declares a dividend. Before paying it, however, the company must prepare a current list of stockholders. For this reason there is usually a time lag between declaration and payment. For example, the board of directors might approve

[14] *Accounting Trends and Techniques—2004* reported that of its 600 surveyed companies, 370 paid a cash dividend on common stock, 54 paid a cash dividend on preferred stock, 4 issued stock dividends, and 7 issued or paid dividends in kind. Some companies declare more than one type of dividend in a given year.

a resolution at the January 10 (**date of declaration**) meeting, and declare it payable February 5 (**date of payment**) to all stockholders of record January 25 (**date of record**).[15] In this example, the period from January 10 to January 25 gives time for the company to complete and register any transfers in process. The time from January 25 to February 5 provides an opportunity for the transfer agent or accounting department, depending on who does this work, to prepare a list of stockholders as of January 25 and to prepare and mail dividend checks.

A declared cash dividend is a liability. Because payment is generally required very soon, it is usually a current liability. Companies use the following entries to record the declaration and payment of an ordinary dividend payable in cash. For example, Roadway Freight Corp. on June 10 declared a cash dividend of 50 cents a share on 1.8 million shares payable July 16 to all stockholders of record June 24.

At date of declaration (June 10)		
Retained Earnings (Cash Dividends Declared)	900,000	
Dividends Payable		900,000
At date of record (June 24)		
No entry		
At date of payment (July 16)		
Dividends Payable	900,000	
Cash		900,000

To set up a ledger account that shows the amount of dividends declared during the year, Roadway Freight might debit Cash Dividends Declared instead of Retained Earnings at the time of declaration. It then closes this account to Retained Earnings at year-end.

A company may declare dividends either as a certain percent of par, such as a 6 percent dividend on preferred stock, or as an amount per share, such as 60 cents per share on no-par common stock. In the first case, the rate multiplied by the par value of outstanding shares equals the total dividend. In the second, the dividend equals the amount per share multiplied by the number of shares outstanding. **Companies do not declare or pay cash dividends on treasury stock.**

Dividend policies vary among corporations. Some companies, such as **Bank of America, Clorox Co.**, and **Tootsie Roll Industries**, take pride in a long, unbroken string of quarterly dividend payments. They would lower or pass the dividend only if forced to do so by a sustained decline in earnings or a critical shortage of cash.

"Growth" companies, on the other hand, pay little or no cash dividends because their policy is to expand as rapidly as internal and external financing permit. For example, **Questcor Pharmaceuticals Inc.** has never paid cash dividends to its common stockholders. These investors hope that the price of their shares will appreciate in value. The investors will then realize a profit when they sell their shares. Many companies focus more on increasing share price, stock repurchase programs, and corporate earnings than on dividend payout.

INTERNATIONAL INSIGHT

As a less preferred but still allowable treatment, international accounting standards permit companies to reduce equity by the amount of proposed dividends prior to their legal declaration.

Property Dividends

Dividends payable in assets of the corporation other than cash are called **property dividends** or **dividends in kind**. Property dividends may be merchandise, real estate, or investments, or whatever form the board of directors designates. **Ranchers Exploration and Development Corp.** reported one year that it would pay a fourth-quarter dividend in gold bars instead of cash. Because of the obvious difficulties of divisibility of

[15]Theoretically, the ex-dividend date is the day after the date of record. However, to allow time for transfer of the shares, the stock exchanges generally advance the ex-dividend date two to four days. Therefore, the party who owns the stock on the day prior to the expressed ex-dividend date receives the dividends. The party who buys the stock on and after the ex-dividend date does not receive the dividend. Between the declaration date and the ex-dividend date, the market price of the stock includes the dividend.

units and delivery to stockholders, the usual property dividend is in the form of securities of other companies that the distributing corporation holds as an investment.

For example, after ruling that **DuPont**'s 23 percent stock interest in **General Motors** violated antitrust laws, the Supreme Court ordered DuPont to divest itself of the GM stock within 10 years. The stock represented 63 million shares of GM's 281 million shares then outstanding. DuPont could not sell the shares in one block of 63 million. Further, it could not sell 6 million shares annually for the next 10 years without severely depressing the value of the GM stock. DuPont solved its problem by declaring a property dividend and distributing the GM shares as a dividend to its own stockholders.

When declaring a property dividend, the corporation should **restate at fair value the property it will distribute, recognizing any gain or loss** as the difference between the property's fair value and carrying value at date of declaration. The corporation may then record the declared dividend as a debit to Retained Earnings (or Property Dividends Declared) and a credit to Property Dividends Payable, at an amount equal to the fair value of the distributed property. Upon distribution of the dividend, the corporation debits Property Dividends Payable and credits the account containing the distributed asset (restated at fair value).

For example, Trendler, Inc. transferred to stockholders some of its investments in marketable securities costing $1,250,000 by declaring a property dividend on December 28, 2006, to be distributed on January 30, 2007, to stockholders of record on January 15, 2007. At the date of declaration the securities have a market value of $2,000,000. Trendler makes the following entries.

At date of declaration (December 28, 2006)		
Investments in Securities	750,000	
Gain on Appreciation of Securities		750,000
Retained Earnings (Property Dividends Declared)	2,000,000	
Property Dividends Payable		2,000,000
At date of distribution (January 30, 2007)		
Property Dividends Payable	2,000,000	
Investments in Securities		2,000,000

Liquidating Dividends

Some corporations use paid-in capital as a basis for dividends. Without proper disclosure of this fact, stockholders may erroneously believe the corporation has been operating at a profit. To avoid this type of deception, intentional or unintentional, a clear statement of the source of every dividend should accompany the dividend check.

Dividends based on other than retained earnings are sometimes described as **liquidating dividends.** This term implies that such dividends are a return of the stockholder's investment rather than of profits. In other words, **any dividend not based on earnings reduces corporate paid-in capital and to that extent, it is a liquidating dividend**. Companies in the extractive industries may pay dividends equal to the total of accumulated income and depletion. The portion of these dividends in excess of accumulated income represents a return of part of the stockholder's investment.

For example, McChesney Mines Inc. issued a "dividend" to its common stockholders of $1,200,000. The cash dividend announcement noted that stockholders should consider $900,000 as income and the remainder a return of capital. McChesney Mines records the dividend as follows:

At date of declaration		
Retained Earnings	900,000	
Additional Paid-in Capital	300,000	
Dividends Payable		1,200,000
At date of payment		
Dividends Payable	1,200,000	
Cash		1,200,000

In some cases, management simply decides to cease business and declares a liquidating dividend. In these cases, liquidation may take place over a number of years to ensure an orderly and fair sale of assets. For example, when **Overseas National Airways** dissolved, it agreed to pay a liquidating dividend to its stockholders over a period of years equivalent to $8.60 per share. Each liquidating dividend payment in such cases reduces paid-in capital.

Stock Dividends

If management wishes to "capitalize" part of the earnings (i.e., reclassify amounts from earned to contributed capital), and thus retain earnings in the business on a permanent basis, it may issue a stock dividend. In this case, **the company distributes no assets.** Each stockholder maintains exactly the same proportionate interest in the corporation and the same total book value after the company issues the stock dividend. Of course, the book value per share is lower because each stockholder holds more shares.

A **stock dividend** therefore is the issuance by a corporation of its own stock to its stockholders on a pro rata basis, without receiving any consideration. In recording a stock dividend, some believe that the company should transfer the **par value of the stock issued** as a dividend from retained earnings to capital stock. Others believe that it should transfer the **fair value of the stock issued**—its market value at the declaration date—from retained earnings to capital stock and additional paid-in capital.

UNDERLYING CONCEPTS

By requiring fair value, the intent was to punish companies that used stock dividends. This approach violates the neutrality concept (that is, that standards-setting should be even-handed).

The fair value position was adopted, at least in part, in order to influence the stock dividend policies of corporations. Evidently in 1941 both the New York Stock Exchange and many in the accounting profession regarded periodic stock dividends as objectionable. They believed that the term dividend when used with a distribution of additional stock was misleading because investors' net assets did not increase as a result of this "dividend." As a result, these groups decided to make it more difficult for corporations to sustain a series of such stock dividends out of their accumulated earnings, by requiring the use of fair market value when it substantially exceeded book value.[16]

OBJECTIVE 8
Explain the accounting for small and large stock dividends, and for stock splits.

When the stock dividend is less than 20–25 percent of the common shares outstanding at the time of the dividend declaration, the company is therefore required to transfer the **fair market value** of the stock issued from retained earnings. Stock dividends of less than 20–25 percent are often referred to as **small (ordinary) stock dividends**. This method of handling stock dividends is justified on the grounds that "many recipients of stock dividends look upon them as distributions of corporate earnings and usually in an amount equivalent to the fair value of the additional shares received."[17] We consider this argument unconvincing. It is generally agreed that stock dividends are not income to the recipients. Therefore, sound accounting should not recommend procedures simply because some recipients think they are income.

To illustrate a small stock dividend, assume that Vine Corporation has outstanding 1,000 shares of $100 par value capital stock and retained earnings of $50,000. If Vine declares a 10 percent stock dividend, it issues 100 additional shares to current stockholders. If the fair value of the stock at the time of the stock dividend is $130 per share, the entry is:

At date of declaration

Retained Earnings (Stock Dividend Declared)	13,000	
Common Stock Dividend Distributable		10,000
Paid-in Capital in Excess of Par		3,000

[16]This was perhaps the earliest instance of "economic consequences" affecting an accounting pronouncement. The Committee on Accounting Procedure described its action as required by "proper accounting and corporate policy." See Stephen A. Zeff, "The Rise of 'Economic Consequences,'" *The Journal of Accountancy* (December 1978), pp. 53–66.

[17]American Institute of Certified Public Accountants, *Accounting Research and Terminology Bulletins*, No. 43 (New York: AICPA, 1961), Ch. 7, par. 10. One study concluded that *small* stock dividends do not always produce significant amounts of extra value on the date after issuance (ex date) and that *large* stock dividends almost always fail to generate extra value on the ex-dividend date. Taylor W. Foster III and Don Vickrey, "The Information Content of Stock Dividend Announcements," *The Accounting Review*, Vol. LIII, No. 2 (April 1978), pp. 360–370.

Note that the stock dividend does not affect any asset or liability. The entry merely reflects a reclassification of stockholders' equity. If Vine prepares a balance sheet between the dates of declaration and distribution, it should show the common stock dividend distributable in the stockholders' equity section as an addition to capital stock (whereas it shows cash or property dividends payable as current liabilities).

When issuing the stock, the entry is:

At date of distribution		
Common Stock Dividend Distributable	10,000	
Common Stock		10,000

No matter what the fair value is at the time of the stock dividend, each stockholder retains the same proportionate interest in the corporation.

Some state statutes specifically prohibit the issuance of stock dividends on treasury stock. In those states that permit treasury shares to participate in the distribution accompanying a stock dividend or stock split, the planned use of the treasury shares influences corporate practice. For example, if a corporation issues treasury shares in connection with employee stock options, the treasury shares may participate in the distribution because the corporation usually adjusts the number of shares under option for any stock dividends or splits. But no useful purpose is served by issuing additional shares to the treasury stock without a specific purpose, since they are essentially equivalent to authorized but unissued shares.

To continue with our example of the effect of the small stock dividend, note in Illustration 14-9 that the stock dividend does not change the total stockholders' equity. Also note that it does not change the proportion of the total shares outstanding held by each stockholder.

ILLUSTRATION 14-9
Effects of a Small (10%) Stock Dividend

Before dividend	
Capital stock, 1,000 shares of $100 par	$100,000
Retained earnings	50,000
Total stockholders' equity	$150,000
Stockholders' interests:	
A. 400 shares, 40% interest, book value	$ 60,000
B. 500 shares, 50% interest, book value	75,000
C. 100 shares, 10% interest, book value	15,000
	$150,000
After declaration but before distribution of 10% stock dividend	
If fair value ($130) is used as basis for entry:	
Capital stock, 1,000 shares at $100 par	$100,000
Common stock distributable, 100 shares at $100 par	10,000
Paid-in capital in excess of par	3,000
Retained earnings ($50,000 − $13,000)	37,000
Total stockholders' equity	$150,000
After declaration and distribution of 10% stock dividend	
If fair value ($130) is used as basis for entry:	
Capital stock, 1,100 shares at $100 par	$110,000
Paid-in capital in excess of par	3,000
Retained earnings ($50,000 − $13,000)	37,000
Total stockholders' equity	$150,000
Stockholders' interest:	
A. 440 shares, 40% interest, book value	$ 60,000
B. 550 shares, 50% interest, book value	75,000
C. 110 shares, 10% interest, book value	15,000
	$150,000

Stock Split

If a company has undistributed earnings over several years, and accumulates a sizable balance in retained earnings, the market value of its outstanding shares likely increases. Stock issued at prices less than $50 a share can easily attain a market value in excess of $200 a share. The higher the market price of a stock, however, the less readily some investors can purchase it.

The managements of many corporations believe that better public relations depend on wider ownership of the corporation stock. They therefore target a market price sufficiently low to be within range of the majority of potential investors. To reduce the market value of shares, they use the common device of a **stock split**. For example, after its stock price increased by 25-fold, **Qualcomm Inc.** split its stock 4-for-1. Qualcomm's stock had risen above $500 per share, raising concerns that Qualcomm could not meet an analyst target of $1,000 per share. The split reduced the analysts' target to $250, which it could better meet with wider distribution of shares at lower trading prices.

From an accounting standpoint, Qualcomm **records no entry for a stock split**. However, it enters a memorandum note to indicate the changed par value of the shares and the increased number of shares. Illustration 14-10 shows the lack of change in stockholders' equity for a 2-for-1 stock split on 1,000 shares of $100 par value stock with the par being halved upon issuance of the additional shares.

ILLUSTRATION 14-10
Effects of a Stock Split

Stockholders' Equity before 2-for-1 Split		Stockholders' Equity after 2-for-1 Split	
Common stock, 1,000 shares at $100 par	$100,000	Common stock, 2,000 shares at $50 par	$100,000
Retained earnings	50,000	Retained earnings	50,000
	$150,000		$150,000

WHAT DO THE NUMBERS MEAN?

SPLITSVILLE

Stock splits were all the rage in the booming stock market of the 1990s. Of major companies on the **New York Stock Exchange**, fewer than 80 companies split shares in 1990. By 1998, with stock prices soaring, over 200 companies split shares. Although the split does not increase a stockholder's proportionate ownership of the company, studies show that split shares usually outperform those that don't split, as well as the market as a whole, for several years after the split. In addition, the splits help the company keep the shares in more attractive price ranges.

What about when the market "turns south"? A number of companies who split their shares in the boom markets of the 1990s have since seen their share prices decline to a point considered too low. For example, since **Ameritrade**'s 12-for-1 split in 1999, its stock price declined over 74 percent, so that it was trading around $6 per share in March 2002. And **Lucent** traded at less than $5 a share following a 4-for-1 split. For some investors, these low-priced stocks are unattractive because some brokerage commissions rely on the number of shares traded, not the dollar amount. Others are concerned that low-priced shares are easier for would-be scamsters to manipulate.

Some companies are considering reverse stock splits in which, say, 5 shares are consolidated into one. Thus, a stock previously trading at $5 per share would be part of an unsplit share trading at $25. Unsplitting might thus avoid some of the negative consequences of a low trading price. The downside to this strategy is that analysts might view reverse splits as additional bad news about the direction of the stock price. For example, **Webvan**, a failed Internet grocer, did a 1-for-25 reverse split just before it entered bankruptcy.

Source: Adapted from David Henry, "Stocks: The Case for Unsplitting," *BusinessWeek Online* (April 1, 2002).

Stock Split and Stock Dividend Differentiated

From a legal standpoint, a stock split differs from a stock dividend. How? A stock split increases the number of shares outstanding and decreases the par or stated value per share. **A stock dividend, although it increases the number of shares outstanding, does not decrease the par value; thus it increases the total par value of outstanding shares.**

The reasons for issuing a stock dividend are numerous and varied. Stock dividends can be primarily a publicity gesture, **because many consider stock dividends as dividends**. Another reason is that the corporation may simply wish to retain profits in the business by capitalizing a part of retained earnings. In such a situation, it makes a transfer on declaration of a stock dividend from earned capital to contributed capital.

A corporation may also use a stock dividend, like a stock split, to increase the marketability of the stock, although marketability is often a secondary consideration. If the stock dividend is large, it has the same effect on market price as a stock split. **Whenever corporations issue additional shares for the purpose of reducing the unit market price, then the distribution more closely resembles a stock split than a stock dividend. This effect usually results only if the number of shares issued is more than 20–25 percent of the number of shares previously outstanding.**[18] A stock dividend of more than 20–25 percent of the number of shares previously outstanding is called a **large stock dividend.**[19] Such a distribution should not be called a stock dividend but instead "a split-up effected in the form of a dividend" or "stock split."

Also, since a split-up effected in the form of a dividend does not alter the par value per share, companies generally are required to transfer the par value amount from retained earnings. In other words, companies transfer from retained earnings to capital stock **the par value of the stock issued**, as opposed to a transfer of the market value of the shares issued as in the case of a small stock dividend.[20] For example, **Brown Group, Inc.** at one time authorized a 2-for-1 split, effected in the form of a stock dividend. As a result of this authorization, it distributed approximately 10.5 million shares, and transferred more than $39 million representing the par value of the shares issued from Retained Earnings to the Common Stock account.

To illustrate a large stock dividend (stock split-up effected in the form of a dividend), Rockland Steel, Inc. declared a 30 percent stock dividend on November 20, payable December 29 to stockholders of record December 12. At the date of declaration, 1,000,000 shares, par value $10, are outstanding and with a fair market value of $200 per share. The entries are:

At date of declaration (November 20)

Retained Earnings	3,000,000	
Common Stock Dividend Distributable		3,000,000

Computation:	1,000,000 shares	300,000 Additional shares
	× 30%	× $10 Par value
	300,000	$3,000,000

At date of distribution (December 29)

Common Stock Dividend Distributable	3,000,000	
Common Stock		3,000,000

---

[18]*Accounting Research and Terminology Bulletin No. 43*, par. 13.

[19]The SEC has added more precision to the 20–25 percent rule. Specifically, the SEC indicates that companies should consider distributions of 25 percent or more as a "split-up effected in the form of a dividend." Companies should account for distributions of less than 25 percent as a stock dividend. The SEC more precisely defined GAAP here. As a result, public companies follow the SEC rule.

[20]Often, a company records a split-up effected in the form of a dividend as a debit to Paid-in Capital instead of Retained Earnings to indicate that this transaction should affect only paid-in capital accounts. No reduction of retained earnings is required except as indicated by legal requirements. For homework purposes, assume that the debit is to Retained Earnings. See, for example, Taylor W. Foster III and Edmund Scribner, "Accounting for Stock Dividends and Stock Splits: Corrections to Textbook Coverage," *Issues in Accounting Education* (February 1998).

Illustration 14-11 summarizes and compares the effects in the balance sheet and related items of various types of dividends and stock splits.

ILLUSTRATION 14-11
Effects of Dividends and Stock Splits on Financial Statement Elements

Effect on:	Declaration of Cash Dividend	Payment of Cash Dividend	Declaration and Distribution of Small Stock Dividend	Declaration and Distribution of Large Stock Dividend	Declaration and Distribution of Stock Split
Retained earnings	Decrease	–0–	Decrease[a]	Decrease[b]	–0–
Capital stock	–0–	–0–	Increase[b]	Increase[b]	–0–
Additional paid-in capital	–0–	–0–	Increase[c]	–0–	–0–
Total stockholders' equity	Decrease	–0–	–0–	–0–	–0–
Working capital	Decrease	–0–	–0–	–0–	–0–
Total assets	–0–	Decrease	–0–	–0–	–0–
Number of shares outstanding	–0–	–0–	Increase	Increase	Increase

[a]Market value of shares. [b]Par or stated value of shares. [c]Excess of market value over par.

INTERNATIONAL INSIGHT

Switzerland allows companies to create income reserves. That is, companies reduce income in years with good profits by allocating it to reserves on the balance sheet. In less profitable years, companies then reallocate from the reserves to improve income. This "smoothes" income across years.

Disclosure of Restrictions on Retained Earnings

Many corporations restrict retained earnings or dividends, without any formal journal entries. Such restrictions are **best disclosed by note**. Parenthetical notations are sometimes used, but restrictions imposed by bond indentures and loan agreements commonly require an extended explanation. Notes provide a medium for more complete explanations and free the financial statements from abbreviated notations. The note disclosure should reveal the source of the restriction, pertinent provisions, and the amount of retained earnings subject to restriction, or the amount not restricted.

Restrictions may be based on the retention of a certain retained earnings balance, the ability to maintain certain working capital requirements, additional borrowing, and other considerations. The example from the annual report of **Alberto-Culver Company** in Illustration 14-12 shows a note disclosing potential restrictions on retained earnings and dividends.

ILLUSTRATION 14-12
Disclosure of Restrictions on Retained Earnings and Dividends

Alberto-Culver Company

Note 3 (in part): The $200 million revolving credit facility, the term note due September 2000, and the receivables agreement impose restrictions on such items as total debt, working capital, dividend payments, treasury stock purchases, and interest expense. At year-end, the company was in compliance with these arrangements, and $220 million of consolidated retained earnings was not restricted as to the payment of dividends.

PRESENTATION AND ANALYSIS OF STOCKHOLDERS' EQUITY

Presentation

Balance Sheet

OBJECTIVE 9
Indicate how to present and analyze stockholders' equity.

Illustration 14-13 shows a comprehensive stockholders' equity section from the balance sheet of Frost Company that includes most of the equity items we discussed in this chapter.

ILLUSTRATION 14-13
Comprehensive Stockholders' Equity Presentation

FROST CORPORATION STOCKHOLDERS' EQUITY DECEMBER 31, 2007		
Capital stock		
Preferred stock, $100 par value, 7% cumulative, 100,000 shares authorized, 30,000 shares issued and outstanding		$ 3,000,000
Common stock, no par, stated value $10 per share, 500,000 shares authorized, 400,000 shares issued		4,000,000
Common stock dividend distributable, 20,000 shares		200,000
Total capital stock		7,200,000
Additional paid-in capital[21]		
Excess over par—preferred	$150,000	
Excess over stated value—common	840,000	990,000
Total paid-in capital		8,190,000
Retained earnings		4,360,000
Total paid-in capital and retained earnings		12,550,000
Less: Cost of treasury stock (2,000 shares, common)		(190,000)
Accumulated other comprehensive loss[22]		(360,000)
Total stockholders' equity		$12,000,000

Frost should disclose the pertinent rights and privileges of the various securities outstanding. For example, companies must disclose all of the following dividend and liquidation preferences, participation rights, call prices and dates, conversion or exercise prices and pertinent dates, sinking fund requirements, unusual voting rights, and significant terms of contracts to issue additional shares. Liquidation preferences should be disclosed in the equity section of the balance sheet, rather than in the notes to the financial statements, to emphasize the possible effect of this restriction on future cash flows.[23]

Statement of Stockholders' Equity

Reporting of Stockholders' Equity in Eastman-Kodak's Annual Report

The **statement of stockholders' equity** is frequently presented in the following basic format.

1. Balance at the beginning of the period.
2. Additions.
3. Deductions.
4. Balance at the end of the period.

---

[21] *Accounting Trends and Techniques—2004* reports that of its 600 surveyed companies, 535 had additional paid-in capital; 313 used the caption "Additional paid-in capital"; 111 used "Capital in excess of par or stated value" as the caption; 82 used "Paid-in capital" or "Additional capital"; and 29 used other captions.

[22] Companies may include a number of items in the "Accumulated other comprehensive loss." Among these items are "Foreign currency translation adjustments" (covered in advanced accounting), "Unrealized holding gains and losses for available-for-sale securities" (covered in Chapter 15), "Excess of additional pension liability over unrecognized prior service cost", "Guarantees of employee stock option plan (ESOP) debt," "Unearned or deferred compensation related to employee stock award plans," and others.

Accounting Trends and Techniques—2004 reports that of its 600 surveyed companies reporting other items in the equity section, 477 reported cumulative translation adjustments, 389 reported minimum pension liability adjustments, 268 reported unrealized losses/gains on certain investments, and 311 reported changes in the fair value of derivatives. A number of companies had more than one item.

[23] "Disclosure of Information about Capital Structure," *Statement of Financial Accounting Standards No. 129* (Norwalk, Conn.: FASB, February 1997), par. 4.

Companies must disclose changes in the separate accounts comprising stockholders' equity, to make the financial statements sufficiently informative.[24] Such changes may be disclosed in separate statements or in the basic financial statements or notes thereto.[25]

A **columnar format** for the presentation of changes in stockholders' equity items in published annual reports is gaining in popularity. An example is **Hewlett-Packard Company**'s statement of stockholders' equity, shown in Illustration 14-14.

ILLUSTRATION 14-14
Columnar Format for Statement of Stockholders' Equity

Hewlett-Packard Company and Subsidiaries
Consolidated Statement of Stockholders' Equity

(in millions, except number of shares in thousands)	Common Stock Number of Shares	Common Stock Par Value	Additional Paid-in Capital	Retained Earnings	Accumulated Other Comprehensive Income (Loss)	Total
Balance October 31, 2003	3,042,761	$30	$24,587	$13,332	$ (203)	$37,746
Net earnings				3,497		3,497
Net unrealized loss on available-for-sale securities					(20)	(20)
Net unrealized loss on cash flow hedges					(28)	(28)
Minimum pension liability, net of taxes					(13)	(13)
Cumulative translation adjustment					21	21
Comprehensive income						3,457
Assumption of stock options in connection with business acquisitions			15			15
Issuance of common stock in connection with employee stock plans and other	40,467		592			592
Repurchases of common stock	(172,468)	(1)	(3,100)	(208)		(3,309)
Tax benefit from employee stock plans			35			35
Dividends				(972)		(972)
Balance October 31, 2004	2,910,760	$29	$22,129	$15,649	$(243)	$37,564

Analysis

Analysts use stockholders' equity ratios to evaluate a company's profitability and long-term solvency. We discuss and illustrate the following three ratios below.

1 Rate of return on common stock equity.
2 Payout ratio.
3 Book value per share.

[24]If a company has other comprehensive income, and computes total comprehensive income only in the statement of stockholders' equity, it must display the statement of stockholders' equity with the same prominence as other financial statements. "Reporting Comprehensive Income," *Statement of Financial Accounting Standards No. 130* (Norwalk, Conn.: FASB, June 1997).

[25]*Accounting Trends and Techniques—2004* reports that of the 600 companies surveyed, 586 presented statements of stockholders' equity, 7 presented separate statements of retained earnings only, 2 presented combined statements of income and retained earnings, and 5 presented changes in equity items in the notes only.

Rate of Return on Common Stock Equity

wiley.com/college/kieso

Financial Analysis Primer

The **rate of return on common stock equity** measures profitability from the common stockholders' viewpoint. This ratio shows how many dollars of net income the company earned for each dollar invested by the owners. Return on equity (ROE) also helps investors judge the worthiness of a stock when the overall market is not doing well. For example, **Best Buy** shares dropped nearly 40 percent, along with the broader market in 2001–2002. But a review of its return on equity during this period and since shows a steady return of 20 to 22 percent while the overall market ROE declined from 16 percent to 8 percent. More importantly, Best Buy and other stocks, such as **3M** and **Procter & Gamble**, recovered their lost market value, while other stocks with less robust ROEs stayed in the doldrums.

Return on equity equals net income less preferred dividends, divided by average common stockholders' equity. For example, assume that Gerber's Inc. had net income of $360,000, declared and paid preferred dividends of $54,000, and average common stockholders' equity of $2,550,000. Illustration 14-15 shows how to compute Gerber's ratio.

ILLUSTRATION 14-15
Computation of Rate of Return on Common Stock Equity

$$\text{Rate of Return on Common Stock Equity} = \frac{\text{Net income} - \text{Preferred dividends}}{\text{Average common stockholders' equity}}$$

$$= \frac{\$360{,}000 - \$54{,}000}{\$2{,}550{,}000}$$

$$= 12\%$$

As shown in Illustration 14-15, when preferred stock is present, income available to common stockholders equals net income less preferred dividends. Similarly, the amount of common stock equity used in this ratio equals total stockholders' equity less the par value of preferred stock.

A company can improve its return on common stock equity through the prudent use of debt or preferred stock financing. **Trading on the equity** describes the practice of using borrowed money or issuing preferred stock in hopes of obtaining a higher rate of return on the money used. Shareholders win if return on the assets is higher than the cost of financing these assets. When this happens, the rate of return on common stock equity will exceed the rate of return on total assets. In short, the company is "trading on the equity at a gain." In this situation, the money obtained from bondholders or preferred stockholders earns enough to pay the interest or preferred dividends and leaves a profit for the common stockholders. On the other hand, if the cost of the financing is higher that the rate earned on the assets, the company is trading on equity at a loss and stockholders lose.

Payout Ratio

Another ratio of interest to investors, the **payout ratio**, is the ratio of cash dividends to net income. If preferred stock is outstanding, this ratio equals cash dividends paid to common stockholders, divided by net income available to common stockholders. For example, assume that Troy Co. has cash dividends of $100,000 and net income of $500,000, and no preferred stock outstanding. Illustration 14-16 shows the payout ratio computation.

ILLUSTRATION 14-16
Computation of Payout Ratio

$$\text{Payout Ratio} = \frac{\text{Cash dividends}}{\text{Net income} - \text{Preferred dividends}}$$

$$= \frac{\$100{,}000}{\$500{,}000}$$

$$= 20\%$$

As discussed in the opening story, it is important to some investors that the payout be sufficiently high to provide a good yield on the stock.[26]

Book Value per Share

A much-used basis for evaluating net worth is found in the book value or equity value per share of stock. **Book value per share** of stock is the amount each share would receive if the company were liquidated **on the basis of amounts reported on the balance sheet**. However, the figure loses much of its relevance if the valuations on the balance sheet fail to approximate fair market value of the assets. Book value per share equals common stockholders' equity divided by outstanding common shares. Assume that Chen Corporation's common stockholders' equity is $1,000,000 and it has 100,000 shares of common stock outstanding. Illustration 14-17 shows its book value per share computation.

$$\text{Book Value Per Share} = \frac{\text{Common stockholders' equity}}{\text{Outstanding shares}} = \frac{\$1{,}000{,}000}{100{,}000} = \$10 \text{ per share}$$

ILLUSTRATION 14-17
Computation of Book Value Per Share

QUESTIONS

1. In the absence of restrictive provisions, what are the basic rights of stockholders of a corporation?
2. Why is a preemptive right important?
3. Distinguish between common and preferred stock.
4. Why is the distinction between paid-in capital and retained earnings important?
5. Explain each of the following terms: authorized capital stock, unissued capital stock, issued capital stock, outstanding capital stock, and treasury stock.
6. What is meant by par value, and what is its significance to stockholders?
7. Describe the accounting for the issuance for cash of no-par value common stock at a price in excess of the stated value of the common stock.
8. Explain the difference between the proportional method and the incremental method of allocating the proceeds of lump sum sales of capital stock.
9. What are the different bases for stock valuation when assets other than cash are received for issued shares of stock?
10. Explain how underwriting costs and accounting and legal fees associated with the issuance of stock should be recorded.
11. For what reasons might a corporation purchase its own stock?
12. Discuss the propriety of showing:
    (a) Treasury stock as an asset.
    (b) "Gain" or "loss" on sale of treasury stock as additions to or deductions from income.
    (c) Dividends received on treasury stock as income.
13. What features or rights may alter the character of preferred stock?
14. Little Texas Inc. recently noted that its 4% preferred stock and 4% participating second preferred stock, which are both cumulative, have priority as to dividends up to 4% of their par value. Its participating preferred stock participates equally with the common stock in any dividends in excess of 4%. What is meant by the term participating? Cumulative?
15. Where in the financial statements is preferred stock normally reported?
16. List possible sources of additional paid-in capital.
17. Pleasant Dolls Inc. purchases 10,000 shares of its own previously issued $10 par common stock for $290,000. Assuming the shares are held in the treasury with intent to reissue, what effect does this transaction have on (a) net income, (b) total assets, (c) total paid-in capital, and (d) total stockholders' equity?
18. Indicate how each of the following accounts should be classified in the stockholders' equity section.
    (a) Common Stock
    (b) Retained Earnings
    (c) Paid-in Capital in Excess of Par Value
    (d) Treasury Stock
    (e) Paid-in Capital from Treasury Stock
    (f) Paid-in Capital in Excess of Stated Value
    (g) Preferred Stock
19. What factors influence the dividend policy of a company?

20. What are the principal considerations of a board of directors in making decisions involving dividend declarations? Discuss briefly.

21. Dividends are sometimes said to have been paid "out of retained earnings." What is the error, if any, in that statement?

22. Distinguish among: cash dividends, property dividends, liquidating dividends, and stock dividends.

23. Describe the accounting entry for a stock dividend, if any. Describe the accounting entry for a stock split, if any.

24. Stock splits and stock dividends may be used by a corporation to change the number of shares of its stock outstanding.
- **(a)** What is meant by a stock split effected in the form of a dividend?
- **(b)** From an accounting viewpoint, explain how the stock split effected in the form of a dividend differs from an ordinary stock dividend.
- **(c)** How should a stock dividend that has been declared but not yet issued be classified in a statement of financial position? Why?

25. The following comment appeared in the notes of Alvarado Corporation's annual report: "Such distributions, representing proceeds from the sale of James Buchanan, Inc. were paid in the form of partial liquidating dividends and were in lieu of a portion of the Company's ordinary cash dividends." How would a partial liquidating dividend be accounted for in the financial records?

26. This comment appeared in the annual report of Rodriguez Lopez Inc.: "The Company could pay cash or property dividends on the Class A common stock without paying cash or property dividends on the Class B common stock. But if the Company pays any cash or property dividends on the Class B common stock, it would be required to pay at least the same dividend on the Class A common stock." How is a property dividend accounted for in the financial records?

27. For what reasons might a company restrict a portion of its retained earnings?

28. How are restrictions of retained earnings reported?

CHAPTER FIFTEEN

INVESTMENTS

Who's in Control Here?

The Coca-Cola Company (Coke) owns 36 percent of the shares of **Coca-Cola Enterprises** (a U.S. bottling business); **PepsiCo Inc.** owns 46 percent of **The Pepsi Bottling Group (PBG)** and 41 percent of **PepsiAmericas**. These bottling businesses are very important to Coca-Cola and PepsiCo, because they are the primary distributors of Coke and Pepsi products. In return, these companies depend on Coca-Cola and PepsiCo to provide significant marketing and distribution development support. Indeed, it can be said that Coca-Cola and PepsiCo control the bottling companies, who would not exist without their support.

However, because The Coca-Cola Company and PepsiCo own less than 50 percent of the shares in these companies, they do not prepare consolidated financial statements. Instead, Coca-Cola and PepsiCo account for these investments using the *equity method.* Under the equity method, for example, Coca-Cola reports a single income item for its profits from the bottlers, and only the net amount of its investment in the balance sheet.

Equity-method accounting gives Coca-Cola and PepsiCo pristine balance sheets and income statements, by separating the assets and liabilities and the profit margins of these bottlers from its beverage-making business. What's more, the International Accounting Standards Board (IASB) has issued *IAS No. 28* which requires that companies use the equity method. Previously, many international companies were permitted to use either the equity method or proportional consolidation for investments similar to Coke's and Pepsi's. It is good news that both U.S. and international companies are following the same rules. (On negative side, however, some of these companies should be consolidated but are not.)

A final point: In response to a recent FASB interpretation, companies are now starting to consolidate more 20 to 50 percent–owned investments. Consolidation of entities, such as the Coke and Pepsi bottlers, may be required if the risks and rewards of those investments accrue primarily to Coke and Pepsi.[1] In fact, Coke has consolidated some of its bottling companies, which should result in the reporting of more complete information on these affiliated companies.

---

[1] *Financial Accounting Standards Interpretation No. 46(R),* "Consolidation of Variable Interest Entities (revised) —An Interpretation of *ARB No. 51*" (Norwalk, Conn.: FASB, December 2003.)

Learning Objectives

After studying this chapter, you should be able to:

1. Identify the three categories of debt securities and describe the accounting and reporting treatment for each category.
2. Understand the procedures for discount and premium amortization on bond investments.
3. Identify the categories of equity securities and describe the accounting and reporting treatment for each category.
4. Explain the equity method of accounting and compare it to the fair value method for equity securities.
5. Describe the disclosure requirements for investments in debt and equity securities.
6. Discuss the accounting for impairments of debt and equity investments.
7. Describe the accounting for transfer of investment securities between categories.

PREVIEW OF CHAPTER 15

As our opening story indicates, U.S. and international standard-setters are studying the measurement, recognition, and disclosure for certain investments. In this chapter we address the accounting for debt and equity investments. The content and organization of this chapter are as follows.

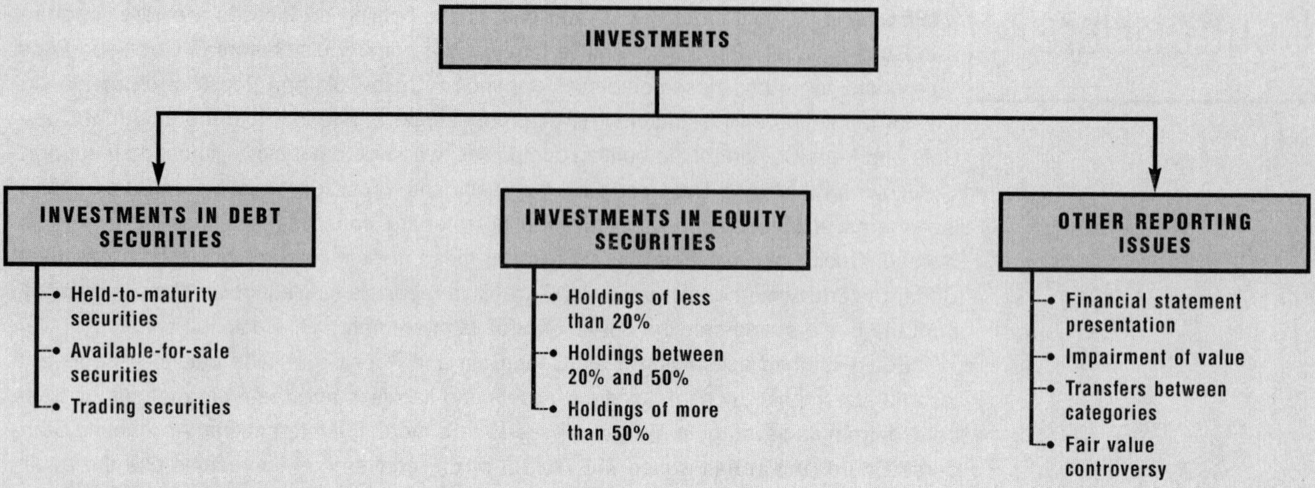

Companies have different motivations for investing in securities issued by other companies.[2] **One motivation is to earn a high rate of return.** For example, companies like **Coca-Cola** and **PepsiCo** can receive interest revenue from a debt investment or dividend revenue from an equity investment. In addition, they can realize capital gains on both types of securities. **Another motivation for investing (in equity securities) is to secure certain operating or financing arrangements with another company.** As in the opening story, **Coca-Cola** and **PepsiCo** are able to exercise some control over bottler companies based on its significant (but not controlling) equity investments.

To provide useful information, companies account for investments based on the type of security (debt or equity) and their intent with respect to the investment. As indicated in Illustration 15-1, we organize our study of investments by type of security. Within each section, we explain how the accounting for investments in debt and equity securities varies according to management intent.

[2]A **security** is a share, participation, or other interest in property or in an enterprise of the issuer or an obligation of the issuer that has the following three characteristics: (a) It either is represented by an instrument issued in bearer or registered form or, if not represented by an instrument, is registered in books maintained to record transfers by or on behalf of the issuer. (b) It is of a type commonly traded on securities exchanges or markets or, when represented by an instrument, is commonly recognized in any area in which it is issued or dealt in as a medium for investment. (c) It either is one of a class or series or by its terms is divisible into a class or series of shares, participations, interests, or obligations. From "Accounting for Certain Investments in Debt and Equity Securities," *Statement of Financial Accounting Standards No. 115* (Norwalk, Conn.: FASB, 1993), p. 48, par. 137.

Types of Security	Management Intent	Valuation Approach
Debt (Section 1)	No plans to sell	Amortized cost
	Plan to sell	Fair value
Equity (Section 2)	Plan to sell	Fair value
	Exercise some control	Equity method

ILLUSTRATION 15-1
Summary of Investment Accounting Approaches

INVESTMENTS IN DEBT SECURITIES — SECTION 1

Debt securities represent a creditor relationship with another entity. Debt securities include U.S. government securities, municipal securities, corporate bonds, convertible debt, and commercial paper. Trade accounts receivable and loans receivable are not debt securities because they do not meet the definition of a security.

Companies group investments in debt securities into three separate categories for accounting and reporting purposes:

OBJECTIVE 1
Identify the three categories of debt securities and describe the accounting and reporting treatment for each category.

- **Held-to-maturity**: Debt securities that the company has the positive intent and ability to hold to maturity.
- **Trading**: Debt securities bought and held primarily for sale in the near term to generate income on short-term price differences.
- **Available-for-sale**: Debt securities not classified as held-to-maturity or trading securities.

Illustration 15-2 identifies these categories, along with the accounting and reporting treatments required for each.

Category	Valuation	Unrealized Holding Gains or Losses	Other Income Effects
Held-to-maturity	Amortized cost	Not recognized	Interest when earned; gains and losses from sale.
Trading securities	Fair value	Recognized in net income	Interest when earned; gains and losses from sale.
Available-for-sale	Fair value	Recognized as other comprehensive income and as separate component of stockholders' equity	Interest when earned; gains and losses from sale.

ILLUSTRATION 15-2
Accounting for Debt Securities by Category

UNDERLYING CONCEPTS
Companies report debt securities at fair value not only because the information is relevant but also because it is reliable.

Amortized cost is the acquisition cost adjusted for the amortization of discount or premium, if appropriate. **Fair value** is the amount at which a company can exchange a financial instrument in a current transaction between willing parties, other than in a forced or liquidation sale.[3]

[3]Ibid., pp. 47–48. The fair value is **readily determinable** if SEC-registered exchanges provide its sale price or other quotations, or, for over-the-counter securities, recognized national publication systems publish the amounts.

HELD-TO-MATURITY SECURITIES

OBJECTIVE 2
Understand the procedures for discount and premium amortization on bond investments.

Only debt securities can be classified as held-to-maturity. By definition, equity securities have no maturity date. A company like **Starbucks** should classify a debt security as **held-to-maturity** only if it has **both (1) the positive intent** and **(2) the ability to hold those securities to maturity**. It should not classify a debt security as held-to-maturity if it intends to hold the security for an indefinite period of time. Likewise, if Starbucks anticipates that a sale may be necessary due to changes in interest rates, foreign currency risk, liquidity needs, or other asset-liability management reasons, it should not classify the security as held-to-maturity.[4]

Companies account for held-to-maturity securities **at amortized cost**, not fair value. If management intends to hold certain investment securities to maturity and has no plans to sell them, fair values (selling prices) are not relevant for measuring and evaluating the cash flows associated with these securities. Finally, because companies do not adjust held-to-maturity securities to fair value, these securities do not increase the volatility of either reported earnings or reported capital as do trading securities and available-for-sale securities.

Calculator Solution for Bond Price

	Inputs	Answer
N	10	
I	5	
PV	?	–92,278
PMT	4,000	
FV	100,000	

To illustrate the accounting for held-to-maturity debt securities, assume that Robinson Company purchased $100,000 of 8 percent bonds of Evermaster Corporation on January 1, 2006, at a discount, paying $92,278. The bonds mature January 1, 2011; interest is payable each July 1 and January 1. Robinson records the investment as follows:

January 1, 2006

Held-to-Maturity Securities	92,278	
Cash		92,278

Robinson uses a Held-to-Maturity Securities account to indicate the type of debt security purchased.

As indicated in Chapter 13, companies must amortize premium or discount using the **effective-interest method** unless some other method—such as the straight-line method—yields a similar result. They apply the effective-interest method to bond investments in a way similar to that for bonds payable. To compute interest revenue, companies compute the effective-interest rate or yield at the time of investment and apply that rate to the beginning carrying amount (book value) for each interest period. The investment carrying amount is increased by the amortized discount or decreased by the amortized premium in each period.

Illustration 15-3 shows the effect of the discount amortization on the interest revenue that Robinson records each period for its investment in Evermaster bonds. Robinson records the receipt of the first semiannual interest payment on July 1, 2006 (using the data in Illustration 15-3) as follows:

UNDERLYING CONCEPTS

The use of some simpler method that yields results similar to the effective-interest method is an application of the materiality concept.

July 1, 2006

Cash	4,000	
Held-to-Maturity Securities	614	
Interest Revenue		4,614

Because Robinson is on a calendar-year basis, it accrues interest and amortizes the discount at December 31, 2006, as follows.

December 31, 2006

Interest Receivable	4,000	
Held-to-Maturity Securities	645	
Interest Revenue		4,645

Again, Illustration 15-3 shows the interest and amortization amounts.

[4]The FASB defines situations where, even though a company sells a security before maturity, it has constructively held the security to maturity, and thus does not violate the held-to-maturity requirement. These include selling a security close enough to maturity (such as three months) so that interest rate risk is no longer an important pricing factor.

ILLUSTRATION 15-3
Schedule of Interest Revenue and Bond Discount Amortization—Effective-Interest Method

8% BONDS PURCHASED TO YIELD 10%

Date	Cash Received	Interest Revenue	Bond Discount Amortization	Carrying Amount of Bonds
1/1/06				$ 92,278
7/1/06	$ 4,000[a]	$ 4,614[b]	$ 614[c]	92,892[d]
1/1/07	4,000	4,645	645	93,537
7/1/07	4,000	4,677	677	94,214
1/1/08	4,000	4,711	711	94,925
7/1/08	4,000	4,746	746	95,671
1/1/09	4,000	4,783	783	96,454
7/1/09	4,000	4,823	823	97,277
1/1/10	4,000	4,864	864	98,141
7/1/10	4,000	4,907	907	99,048
1/1/11	4,000	4,952	952	100,000
	$40,000	$47,722	$7,722	

[a]$4,000 = $100,000 × .08 × 6/12
[b]$4,614 = $92,278 × .10 × 6/12
[c]$614 = $4,614 − $4,000
[d]$92,892 = $92,278 + $614

Robinson reports its investment in Evermaster bonds in its December 31, 2006, financial statements, as follows.

ILLUSTRATION 15-4
Reporting of Held-to-Maturity Securities

Balance Sheet

Current assets	
Interest receivable	$ 4,000
Long-term investments	
Held-to-maturity securities, at amortized cost	$93,537

Income Statement

Other revenues and gains	
Interest revenue	$ 9,259

Sometimes a company sells a held-to-maturity debt security so close to its maturity date that a change in the market interest rate would not significantly affect the security's fair value. Such a sale may be considered a sale at maturity and would not call into question the company's original intent to hold the investment to maturity. Let's assume, as an example, that Robinson Company sells its investment in Evermaster bonds on November 1, 2010, at 99¾ plus accrued interest. The discount amortization from July 1, 2010, to November 1, 2010, is $635 (4/6 × $952). Robinson records this discount amortization as follows.

November 1, 2010

Held-to-Maturity Securities	635	
Interest Revenue		635

Illustration 15-5 shows the computation of the realized gain on the sale.

ILLUSTRATION 15-5
Computation of Gain on Sale of Bonds

Selling price of bonds (exclusive of accrued interest)		$99,750
Less: Book value of bonds on November 1, 2010:		
Amortized cost, July 1, 2010	$99,048	
Add: Discount amortized for the period July 1, 2010, to November 1, 2010	635	
		99,683
Gain on sale of bonds		$ 67

Robinson records the sale of the bonds as:

November 1, 2010		
Cash	102,417	
Interest Revenue (4/6 × $4,000)		2,667
Held-to-Maturity Securities		99,683
Gain on Sale of Securities		67

The credit to Interest Revenue represents accrued interest for four months, for which the purchaser pays cash. The debit to Cash represents the selling price of the bonds plus accrued interest ($99,750 + $2,667). The credit to Held-to-Maturity Securities represents the book value of the bonds on the date of sale. The credit to Gain on Sale of Securities represents the excess of the selling price over the book value of the bonds.

AVAILABLE-FOR-SALE SECURITIES

UNDERLYING CONCEPTS

Recognizing unrealized gains and losses is an application of the concept of comprehensive income.

Companies, like **Amazon.com**, report **available-for-sale** securities at fair value. It records the unrealized gains and losses related to changes in the fair value of available-for-sale debt securities in an unrealized holding gain or loss account. Amazon adds (subtracts) this amount to other comprehensive income for the period. Other comprehensive income is then added to (subtracted from) accumulated other comprehensive income, which is shown as a separate component of stockholders' equity until realized. Thus, **companies report available-for-sale securities at fair value on the balance sheet, but do not report changes in fair value as part of net income until after selling the security**. This approach reduces the volatility of net income.

Example: Single Security

To illustrate the accounting for available-for-sale securities, assume that Graff Corporation purchases $100,000, 10 percent, five-year bonds on January 1, 2006, with interest payable on July 1 and January 1. The bonds sell for $108,111, which results in a bond premium of $8,111 and an effective interest rate of 8 percent.

Calculator Solution for Bond Price

	Inputs	Answer
N	10	
I	4	
PV	?	−108,111
PMT	5,000	
FV	100,000	

Graff records the purchase of the bonds as follows.[5]

January 1, 2006		
Available-for-Sale Securities	108,111	
Cash		108,111

Illustration 15-6 discloses the effect of the premium amortization on the interest revenue Graff records each period using the effective-interest method.

The entry to record interest revenue on July 1, 2006, is as follows.

July 1, 2006		
Cash	5,000	
Available-for-Sale Securities		676
Interest Revenue		4,324

At December 31, 2006, Graff makes the following entry to recognize interest revenue.

December 31, 2006		
Interest Receivable	5,000	
Available-for-Sale Securities		703
Interest Revenue		4,297

As a result, Graff reports revenue for 2006 of $8,621 ($4,324 + $4,297).

[5]Companies generally record investments acquired at par, at a discount, or at a premium in the accounts at cost, including brokerage and other fees but excluding the accrued interest. They generally do not record investments at maturity value. The use of a separate discount or premium account as a valuation account is acceptable procedure for investments, but in practice companies do not widely use it.

ILLUSTRATION 15-6
Schedule of Interest Revenue and Bond Premium Amortization—Effective-Interest Method

10% BONDS PURCHASED TO YIELD 8%

Date	Cash Received	Interest Revenue	Bond Premium Amortization	Carrying Amount of Bonds
1/1/06				$108,111
7/1/06	$ 5,000[a]	$ 4,324[b]	$ 676[c]	107,435[d]
1/1/07	5,000	4,297	703	106,732
7/1/07	5,000	4,269	731	106,001
1/1/08	5,000	4,240	760	105,241
7/1/08	5,000	4,210	790	104,451
1/1/09	5,000	4,178	822	103,629
7/1/09	5,000	4,145	855	102,774
1/1/10	5,000	4,111	889	101,885
7/1/10	5,000	4,075	925	100,960
1/1/11	5,000	4,040	960	100,000
	$50,000	$41,889	$8,111	

[a]$5,000 = $100,000 × .10 × 6/12
[b]$4,324 = $108,111 × .08 × 6/12
[c]$676 = $5,000 − $4,324
[d]$107,435 = $108,111 − $676

To apply the fair value method to these debt securities, assume that at year-end the fair value of the bonds is $105,000 and that the carrying amount of the investments is $106,732. Comparing this fair value with the carrying amount (amortized cost) of the bonds at December 31, 2006, Graff recognizes an unrealized holding loss of $1,732 ($106,732 − $105,000). It reports this loss as other comprehensive income. Graff makes the following entry.

December 31, 2006		
Unrealized Holding Gain or Loss—Equity	1,732	
Securities Fair Value Adjustment (Available-for-Sale)		1,732

Graff uses a valuation account instead of crediting the Available-for-Sale Securities account. The use of the **Securities Fair Value Adjustment (Available-for-Sale) account** enables the company to maintain a record of its amortized cost. Because the adjustment account has a credit balance in this case, Graff subtracts it from the balance of the Available-for-Sale Securities account to determine fair value. Graff reports this fair value amount on the balance sheet. At each reporting date, Graff reports the bonds at fair value with an adjustment to the Unrealized Holding Gain or Loss—Equity account.

Example: Portfolio of Securities

To illustrate the accounting for a portfolio of securities, assume that Webb Corporation has two debt securities classified as available-for-sale. Illustration 15-7 identifies the amortized cost, fair value, and the amount of the unrealized gain or loss.

ILLUSTRATION 15-7
Computation of Securities Fair Value Adjustment—Available-for-Sale Securities (2007)

AVAILABLE-FOR-SALE DEBT SECURITY PORTFOLIO
DECEMBER 31, 2007

Investments	Amortized Cost	Fair Value	Unrealized Gain (Loss)
Watson Corporation 8% bonds	$ 93,537	$103,600	$ 10,063
Anacomp Corporation 10% bonds	200,000	180,400	(19,600)
Total of portfolio	$293,537	$284,000	(9,537)
Previous securities fair value adjustment balance			–0–
Securities fair value adjustment—Cr.			$ (9,537)

The fair value of Webb's available-for-sale portfolio totals $284,000. The gross unrealized gains are $10,063, and the gross unrealized losses are $19,600, resulting in a net unrealized loss of $9,537. That is, the fair value of available-for-sale securities is $9,537 lower than its amortized cost. Webb makes an adjusting entry to a valuation allowance to record the decrease in value and to record the loss as follows.

December 31, 2007		
Unrealized Holding Gain or Loss—Equity	9,537	
Securities Fair Value Adjustment (Available-for-Sale)		9,537

Webb reports the unrealized holding loss of $9,537 as other comprehensive income and a reduction of stockholders' equity. Recall that companies exclude from net income any unrealized holding gains and losses related to available-for-sale securities.

Sale of Available-for-Sale Securities

If a company sells bonds carried as investments in available-for-sale securities before the maturity date, it must make entries to remove from the Available-for-Sale Securities account the amortized cost of bonds sold. To illustrate, assume that Webb Corporation sold the Watson bonds (from Illustration 15-7) on July 1, 2008, for $90,000, at which time it had an amortized cost of $94,214. Illustration 15-8 shows the computation of the realized loss.

ILLUSTRATION 15-8
Computation of Loss on Sale of Bonds

Amortized cost (Watson bonds)	$94,214
Less: Selling price of bonds	90,000
Loss on sale of bonds	$ 4,214

Webb records the sale of the Watson bonds as follows.

July 1, 2008		
Cash	90,000	
Loss on Sale of Securities	4,214	
Available-for-Sale Securities		94,214

Webb reports this realized loss in the "Other expenses and losses" section of the income statement. Assuming no other purchases and sales of bonds in 2008, Webb on December 31, 2008, prepares the information shown in Illustration 15-9.

ILLUSTRATION 15-9
Computation of Securities Fair Value Adjustment—Available-for-Sale (2008)

AVAILABLE-FOR-SALE DEBT SECURITY PORTFOLIO
DECEMBER 31, 2008

Investments	Amortized Cost	Fair Value	Unrealized Gain (Loss)
Anacomp Corporation 10% bonds (total portfolio)	$200,000	$195,000	$(5,000)
Previous securities fair value adjustment balance—Cr.			(9,537)
Securities fair value adjustment—Dr.			$ 4,537

Webb has an unrealized holding loss of $5,000. However, the Securities Fair Value Adjustment account already has a credit balance of $9,537. To reduce the adjustment account balance to $5,000, Webb debits it for $4,537, as follows.

December 31, 2008		
Securities Fair Value Adjustment (Available-for-Sale)	4,537	
Unrealized Holding Gain or Loss—Equity		4,537

WHAT IS FAIR VALUE?

WHAT DO THE NUMBERS MEAN?

In the fall of 2000, Wall Street brokerage firm **Morgan Stanley** told investors that rumor of big losses in its bond portfolio were "greatly exaggerated." As it turns out, Morgan Stanley also was exaggerating.

Recently, the SEC accused Morgan Stanley of violating securities laws by overstating the value of certain bonds by $75 million. The overvaluations stemmed more from wishful thinking than reality, in violation of generally accepted accounting principles, the SEC said. "In effect, Morgan Stanley valued its positions at the price at which it thought a willing buyer and seller should enter into an exchange, rather than at a price at which a willing buyer and a willing seller would enter into a current exchange," the SEC wrote.

Especially egregious, stated one accounting expert, were the SEC's findings that Morgan Stanley in some instances used its own more optimistic assumptions as a substitute for external pricing sources. "What that is saying is: 'Fair value is what you want the value to be. Pick a number...' That's especially troublesome."

As indicated in the text, the FASB has been working on a new standard for assessing what is fair and what isn't when it comes to assigning valuations. Concerns over the issue caught fire after the collapses of **Enron Corp.** and other energy traders that abused the wide discretion given them under fair-value accounting. Investors have expressed similar worries about some financial companies, which use internal—and subjectively designed—mathematical models to come up with valuations when market quotes aren't available.

Source: Adapted from Susanne Craig and Jonathan Weil, "SEC Targets Morgan Stanley Values," *Wall Street Journal* (November 8, 2004), p. C3.

Financial Statement Presentation

Webb's December 31, 2008, balance sheet and the 2008 income statement include the following items and amounts (the Anacomp bonds are long-term investments but are not intended to be held to maturity).

ILLUSTRATION 15-10
Reporting of Available-for-Sale Securities

Balance Sheet	
Current assets	
Interest receivable	$ xxx
Investments	
Available-for-sale securities, at fair value	$195,000
Stockholders' equity	
Accumulated other comprehensive loss	$ 5,000
Income Statement	
Other revenues and gains	
Interest revenue	$ xxx
Other expenses and losses	
Loss on sale of securities	$ 4,214

Some favor including the unrealized holding gain or loss in net income rather than showing it as other comprehensive income.[6] However, some companies, particularly financial institutions, note that recognizing gains and losses on assets, but not liabilities, introduces substantial volatility in net income. They argue that hedges often exist between assets and liabilities so that gains in assets are offset by losses in liabilities, and vice versa. In short, to recognize gains and losses only on the asset side is unfair and not representative of the economic activities of the company.

This argument convinced the FASB. As a result, companies **do not include in net income** these unrealized gains and losses. However, even this approach solves only

[6]In Chapter 4, we discussed the reporting of other comprehensive income and the concept of comprehensive income. "Reporting Comprehensive Income," *Statement of Financial Accounting Standards No. 130* (Norwalk, Conn.: FASB, 1997).

some of the problems, because **volatility of capital** still results. This is of concern to financial institutions because regulators restrict financial institutions' operations based on their level of capital. In addition, companies can still manage their net income by engaging in **gains trading** (i.e., selling the winners and holding the losers).

TRADING SECURITIES

Companies hold **trading securities** with the intention of selling them in a short period of time. "Trading" in this context means frequent buying and selling. Companies thus use trading securities to generate profits from short-term differences in price. Companies generally hold these securities for less than three months, some for merely days or hours.

Companies report trading securities at fair value, with unrealized holding gains and losses reported as part of net income. Similar to held-to-maturity or available-for-sale investments, they are required to amortize any discount or premium. A **holding gain or loss** is the net change in the fair value of a security from one period to another, exclusive of dividend or interest revenue recognized but not received. In short, the FASB says to adjust the trading securities to fair value, at each reporting date. In addition, companies report the change in value as part of net income, not other comprehensive income.

To illustrate, assume that on December 31, 2007, Western Publishing Corporation determined its trading securities portfolio to be as shown in Illustration 15-11. (Assume that 2007 is the first year that Western Publishing held trading securities.) At the date of acquisition, Western Publishing recorded these trading securities at cost, including brokerage commissions and taxes, in the account entitled Trading Securities. This is the first valuation of this recently purchased portfolio.

ILLUSTRATION 15-11
Computation of Securities Fair Value Adjustment—Trading Securities Portfolio (2007)

TRADING DEBT SECURITY PORTFOLIO
DECEMBER 31, 2007

Investments	Cost	Fair Value	Unrealized Gain (Loss)
Burlington Northern 10% bonds	$ 43,860	$ 51,500	$ 7,640
GM Corporation 11% bonds	184,230	175,200	(9,030)
Time Warner 8% bonds	86,360	91,500	5,140
Total of portfolio	$314,450	$318,200	3,750
Previous securities fair value adjustment balance			–0–
Securities fair value adjustment—Dr.			$ 3,750

INTERNATIONAL INSIGHT

IFRS provides for classification as trading, available for sale, or held-to-maturity for all types of financial assets. U.S. GAAP applies these classifications only to securities.

The total cost of Western Publishing's trading portfolio is $314,450. The gross unrealized gains are $12,780 ($7,640 + $5,140), and the gross unrealized losses are $9,030, resulting in a net unrealized gain of $3,750. The fair value of trading securities is $3,750 greater than its cost.

At December 31, Western Publishing makes an adjusting entry to a valuation allowance, referred to as Securities Fair Value Adjustment (Trading), to record the increase in value and to record the unrealized holding gain.

December 31, 2007		
Securities Fair Value Adjustment (Trading)	3,750	
Unrealized Holding Gain or Loss—Income		3,750

Because the Securities Fair Value Adjustment account balance is a debit, Western Publishing adds it to the cost of the Trading Securities account to arrive at a fair value for the trading securities. Western Publishing reports this fair value amount on the balance sheet.

When securities are actively traded, the FASB believes that the investments should be reported at fair value on the balance sheet. In addition, changes in fair value (unrealized gains and losses) should be reported in income. Such reporting on trading securities provides more relevant information to existing and prospective stockholders.

INVESTMENTS IN EQUITY SECURITIES | SECTION 2

OBJECTIVE 3
Identify the categories of equity securities and describe the accounting and reporting treatment for each category.

Equity securities represent ownership interests such as common, preferred, or other capital stock. They also include rights to acquire or dispose of ownership interests at an agreed-upon or determinable price, such as in warrants, rights, and call or put options. Companies do not treat convertible debt securities as equity securities. Nor do they treat as equity securities redeemable preferred stock (which must be redeemed for common stock). The cost of equity securities includes the purchase price of the security plus broker's commissions and other fees incidental to the purchase.

The degree to which one corporation **(investor)** acquires an interest in the common stock of another corporation **(investee)** generally determines the accounting treatment for the investment subsequent to acquisition. The classification of such investments depends on the percentage of the investee voting stock that is held by the investor:

1. Holdings of less than 20 percent (**fair value method**)—investor has passive interest.
2. Holdings between 20 percent and 50 percent (**equity method**)—investor has significant influence.
3. Holdings of more than 50 percent (**consolidated statements**)—investor has controlling interest.

Illustration 15-12 lists these levels of interest or influence and the corresponding valuation and reporting method that companies must apply to the investment.

ILLUSTRATION 15-12
Levels of Influence Determine Accounting Methods

Percentage of Ownership	0% ⟷	20% ⟷	50% ⟷	100%
Level of Influence	Little or None	Significant	Control	
Valuation Method	Fair Value Method	Equity Method	Consolidation	

The accounting and reporting for equity securities therefore depends upon the level of influence and the type of security involved, as shown in Illustration 15-13.

ILLUSTRATION 15-13
Accounting and Reporting for Equity Securities by Category

Category	Valuation	Unrealized Holding Gains or Losses	Other Income Effects
Holdings less than 20%			
1. Available-for-sale	Fair value	Recognized in "Other comprehensive income" and as separate component of stockholders' equity	Dividends declared; gains and losses from sale.
2. Trading	Fair value	Recognized in net income	Dividends declared; gains and losses from sale.
Holdings between 20% and 50%	Equity	Not recognized	Proportionate share of investee's net income.
Holdings more than 50%	Consolidation	Not recognized	Not applicable.

HOLDINGS OF LESS THAN 20%

When an investor has an interest of less than 20 percent, it is presumed that the investor has little or no influence over the investee. In such cases, if market prices are available subsequent to acquisition, the company values and reports the investment using the **fair value method**.[7] The fair value method requires that companies classify equity securities at acquisition as **available-for-sale securities** or **trading securities**. Because equity securities have no maturity date, companies cannot classify them as held-to-maturity.

Available-for-Sale Securities

Upon acquisition, companies record available-for-sale securities at cost.[8] To illustrate, assume that on November 3, 2007 Republic Corporation purchased common stock of three companies, each investment representing less than a 20 percent interest.

	Cost
Northwest Industries, Inc.	$259,700
Campbell Soup Co.	317,500
St. Regis Pulp Co.	141,350
Total cost	$718,550

Republic records these investments as follows.

November 3, 2007		
Available-for-Sale Securities	718,550	
Cash		718,550

On December 6, 2007, Republic receives a cash dividend of $4,200 on its investment in the common stock of Campbell Soup Co. It records the cash dividend as follows.

December 6, 2007		
Cash	4,200	
Dividend Revenue		4,200

All three of the investee companies reported net income for the year, but only Campbell Soup declared and paid a dividend to Republic. But, recall that when an investor owns less than 20 percent of the common stock of another corporation, it is presumed that the investor has relatively little influence on the investee. As a result, **net income earned by the investee is not a proper basis for recognizing income from the investment by the investor**. Why? Because the increased net assets resulting from profitable operations may be permanently retained for use in the investee's

[7]When market prices are unavailable, a company values the investment and reports it at cost in periods subsequent to acquisition. This approach is often referred to as the **cost method**. Companies recognize dividends when received. They value the portfolio and report it at acquisition cost. Companies only recognize gains or losses after selling the securities.

[8]Companies should record equity securities acquired in **exchange for noncash consideration** (property or services) at (1) the fair value of the consideration given, or (2) the fair value of the security received, whichever is more clearly determinable. Accounting for numerous purchases of securities requires the preservation of information regarding the cost of individual purchases, as well as the dates of purchases and sales. If **specific identification** is not possible, companies may use an **average cost** for multiple purchases of the same class of security. The **first-in, first-out method** (FIFO) of assigning costs to investments at the time of sale is also acceptable and normally employed.

business. Therefore, **the investor earns net income only when the investee declares cash dividends.**

At December 31, 2007, Republic's available-for-sale equity security portfolio has the cost and fair value shown in Illustration 15-14.

ILLUSTRATION 15-14
Computation of Securities Fair Value Adjustment—Available-for-Sale Equity Security Portfolio (2007)

AVAILABLE-FOR-SALE EQUITY SECURITY PORTFOLIO
DECEMBER 31, 2007

Investments	Cost	Fair Value	Unrealized Gain (Loss)
Northwest Industries, Inc.	$259,700	$275,000	$ 15,300
Campbell Soup Co.	317,500	304,000	(13,500)
St. Regis Pulp Co.	141,350	104,000	(37,350)
Total of portfolio	$718,550	$683,000	(35,550)
Previous securities fair value adjustment balance			–0–
Securities fair value adjustment—Cr.			$(35,550)

For Republic's available-for-sale equity securities portfolio, the gross unrealized gains are $15,300, and the gross unrealized losses are $50,850 ($13,500 + $37,350), resulting in a net unrealized loss of $35,550. The fair value of the available-for-sale securities portfolio is below cost by $35,550.

As with available-for-sale **debt** securities, Republic records the net unrealized gains and losses related to changes in the fair value of available-for-sale **equity** securities in an Unrealized Holding Gain or Loss—Equity account. Republic reports this amount as a **part of other comprehensive income and as a component of other accumulated comprehensive income (reported in stockholders' equity) until realized.** In this case, Republic prepares an adjusting entry debiting the Unrealized Holding Gain or Loss—Equity account and crediting the Securities Fair Value Adjustment account to record the decrease in fair value and to record the loss as follows.

December 31, 2007

Unrealized Holding Gain or Loss—Equity	35,550	
Securities Fair Value Adjustment (Available-for-Sale)		35,550

On January 23, 2008, Republic sold all of its Northwest Industries, Inc. common stock receiving net proceeds of $287,220. Illustration 15-15 shows the computation of the realized gain on the sale.

ILLUSTRATION 15-15
Computation of Gain on Sale of Stock

Net proceeds from sale	$287,220
Cost of Northwest shares	259,700
Gain on sale of stock	$ 27,520

Republic records the sale as follows.

January 23, 2008

Cash	287,220	
Available-for-Sale Securities		259,700
Gain on Sale of Stock		27,520

In addition, assume that on February 10, 2008, Republic purchased 20,000 shares of Continental Trucking at a market price of $12.75 per share plus brokerage commissions of $1,850 (total cost, $256,850).

Illustration 15-16 lists Republic's portfolio of available-for-sale securities, as of December 31, 2008.

ILLUSTRATION 15-16
Computation of Securities Fair Value Adjustment—Available-for-Sale Equity Security Portfolio (2008)

AVAILABLE-FOR-SALE EQUITY SECURITY PORTFOLIO
DECEMBER 31, 2008

Investments	Cost	Fair Value	Unrealized Gain (Loss)
Continental Trucking	$256,850	$278,350	$ 21,500
Campbell Soup Co.	317,500	362,550	45,050
St. Regis Pulp Co.	141,350	139,050	(2,300)
Total of portfolio	$715,700	$779,950	64,250
Previous securities fair value adjustment balance—Cr.			(35,550)
Securities fair value adjustment—Dr.			$ 99,800

At December 31, 2008, the fair value of Republic's available-for-sale equity securities portfolio exceeds cost by $64,250 (unrealized gain). The Securities Fair Value Adjustment account had a credit balance of $35,550 at December 31, 2008. To adjust its December 31, 2008, available-for-sale portfolio to fair value, the company debits the Securities Fair Value Adjustment account for $99,800 ($35,550 + $64,250). Republic records this adjustment as follows.

December 31, 2008		
Securities Fair Value Adjustment (Available-for-Sale)	99,800	
Unrealized Holding Gain or Loss—Equity		99,800

Trading Securities

The accounting entries to record trading equity securities are the same as for available-for-sale equity securities, except for recording the unrealized holding gain or loss. For trading equity securities, companies **report the unrealized holding gain or loss as part of net income**. Thus, the account titled Unrealized Holding Gain or Loss—Income is used.

HOLDINGS BETWEEN 20% AND 50%

An investor corporation may hold an interest of less than 50 percent in an investee corporation and thus not possess legal control. However, as shown in our opening story about **Coca-Cola**, an investment in voting stock of less than 50 percent can still give Coke (the investor) the ability to exercise significant influence over the operating and financial policies of its bottlers.[9] **Significant influence** may be indicated in several ways. Examples include representation on the board of directors, participation in policy-making processes, material intercompany transactions, interchange of managerial personnel, or technological dependency.

Another important consideration is the extent of ownership by an investor in relation to the concentration of other shareholdings. To achieve a reasonable degree of uniformity in application of the "significant influence" criterion, the profession concluded that an investment (direct or indirect) of 20 percent or more of the voting stock

[9] "The Equity Method of Accounting for Investments in Common Stock," *Opinions of the Accounting Principles Board No. 18* (New York: AICPA, 1971), par. 17.

of an investee should lead to a presumption that in the absence of evidence to the contrary, an investor has the ability to exercise significant influence over an investee.[10]

In instances of "significant influence" (generally an investment of 20 percent or more), the investor must account for the investment using the **equity method**.

Equity Method

OBJECTIVE 4
Explain the equity method of accounting and compare it to the fair value method for equity securities.

Under the **equity method** the investor and the investee acknowledge a substantive economic relationship. The company originally records the investment at the cost of the shares acquired but subsequently adjusts the amount each period for changes in the investee's net assets. That is, the **the investor's proportionate share of the earnings (losses) of the investee periodically increases (decreases) the investment's carrying amount. All dividends received by the investor from the investee also decrease the investment's carrying amount.** The equity method recognizes that investee's earnings increase investee's net assets, and that investee's losses and dividends decrease these net assets.

To illustrate the equity method and compare it with the fair value method, assume that Maxi Company purchases a 20 percent interest in Mini Company. To apply the fair value method in this example, assume that Maxi does not have the ability to exercise significant influence, and classifies the securities as available-for-sale. Where this example applies the equity method, assume that the 20 percent interest permits Maxi to exercise significant influence. Illustration 15-17 shows the entries.

ILLUSTRATION 15-17
Comparison of Fair Value Method and Equity Method

ENTRIES BY MAXI COMPANY					
Fair Value Method			Equity Method		
On January 2, 2007, Maxi Company acquired 48,000 shares (20% of Mini Company common stock) at a cost of $10 a share.					
Available-for-Sale-Securities	480,000		Investment in Mini Stock	480,000	
Cash		480,000	Cash		480,000
For the year 2007, Mini Company reported net income of $200,000; Maxi Company's share is 20%, or $40,000.					
No entry			Investment in Mini Stock	40,000	
			Revenue from Investment		40,000
At December 31, 2007, the 48,000 shares of Mini Company have a fair value (market price) of $12 a share, or $576,000.					
Securities Fair Value Adjustment (Available-for-Sale)	96,000		No entry		
Unrealized Holding Gain or Loss—Equity		96,000			
On January 28, 2008, Mini Company announced and paid a cash dividend of $100,000; Maxi Company received 20%, or $20,000.					
Cash	20,000		Cash	20,000	
Dividend Revenue		20,000	Investment in Mini Stock		20,000
For the year 2008, Mini reported a net loss of $50,000; Maxi Company's share is 20%, or $10,000.					
No entry			Loss on Investment	10,000	
			Investment in Mini Stock		10,000
At December 31, 2008, the Mini Company 48,000 shares have a fair value (market price) of $11 a share, or $528,000.					
Unrealized Holding Gain or Loss—Equity	48,000		No entry		
Securities Fair Value Adjustment (Available-for-Sale)		48,000			

[10]Cases in which an investment of 20 percent or more might not enable an investor to exercise significant influence include:

(1) The investee opposes the investor's acquisition of its stock.
(2) The investor and investee sign an agreement under which the investor surrenders significant shareholder rights.
(3) The investor's ownership share does not result in "significant influence" because majority ownership of the investee is concentrated among a small group of shareholders who operate the investee without regard to the views of the investor.
(4) The investor tries and fails to obtain representation on the investee's board of directors.

"Criteria for Applying the Equity Method of Accounting for Investments in Common Stock," *Interpretations of the Financial Accounting Standards Board No. 35* (Stamford, Conn.: FASB, 1981).

Note that under the fair value method, Maxi reports as revenue only the cash dividends received from Mini. **The earning of net income by Mini (the investee) is not considered a proper basis for recognition of income from the investment by Maxi (the investor).** Why? Mini may permanently retain in the business any increased net assets resulting from its profitable operation. Therefore, Maxi only earns revenue when it receives dividends from Mini.

Under the equity method, Maxi reports as revenue its share of the net income reported by Mini. Maxi records the cash dividends received from Mini as a decrease in the investment carrying value. As a result, Maxi records its share of the net income of Mini in the year when it is earned. With significant influence, Maxi can ensure that Mini will pay dividends, if desired, on any net asset increases resulting from net income. To wait until receiving a dividend ignores the fact that Maxi is better off if the investee has earned income.

INTERNATIONAL INSIGHT

IFRS permits companies to measure significant-influence investments using the equity, cost, or fair value methods.

Using dividends as a basis for recognizing income poses an additional problem. For example, assume that the investee reports a net loss. However, the investor exerts influence to force a dividend payment from the investee. In this case, the investor reports income, even though the investee is experiencing a loss. **In other words, using dividends as a basis for recognizing income fails to report properly the economics of the situation.**

For some companies, equity accounting can be a real pain to the bottom line. For example, **Amazon.com**, the pioneer of Internet retailing, at one time struggled to turn a profit. Furthermore, some of Amazon's equity investments had resulted in Amazon's earnings performance going from bad to worse. In a recent year, Amazon.com disclosed equity stakes in such companies as **Altera International**, **Basis Technology**, **Drugstore.com**, and **Eziba.com**. These equity investees reported losses that made Amazon's already bad bottom line even worse, accounting for up to 22 percent of its reported loss in one year alone.

Investee Losses Exceed Carrying Amount

UNDERLYING CONCEPTS

Revenue to be recognized should be earned and realized or realizable. A low level of ownership indicates that a company should defer the income from an investee until cash is received.

If an investor's share of the investee's losses exceeds the carrying amount of the investment, should the investor recognize additional losses? Ordinarily the investor should discontinue applying the equity method and not recognize additional losses.

If the investor's potential loss is not limited to the amount of its original investment (by guarantee of the investee's obligations or other commitment to provide further financial support), or if imminent return to profitable operations by the investee appears to be assured, the investor should recognize additional losses.[11]

HOLDINGS OF MORE THAN 50%

When one corporation acquires a voting interest of more than 50 percent in another corporation, it is said to have a **controlling interest**. In such a relationship, the investor corporation is referred to as the **parent** and the investee corporation as the **subsidiary**. Companies present the investment in the common stock of the subsidiary as a long-term investment on the separate financial statements of the parent.

INTERNATIONAL INSIGHT

In contrast to U.S. firms, financial statements of non-U.S. companies often include both consolidated (group) statements and parent company financial statements.

When the parent treats the subsidiary as an investment, the parent generally prepares **consolidated financial statements**. Consolidated financial statements treat the parent and subsidiary corporations as a single economic entity. (Advanced accounting courses extensively discuss the subject of when and how to prepare consolidated financial statements.) Whether or not consolidated financial statements are prepared, the parent company generally accounts for the investment in the subsidiary **using the equity method** as explained in this chapter.

[11] "The Equity Method of Accounting for Investments in Common Stock," op. cit., par. 19(i).

CONSOLIDATE THIS!

WHAT DO THE NUMBERS MEAN?

Presently the rules for consolidation seem very straightforward: If a company owns more than 50 percent of another company, it generally should be consolidated. If it owns less than 50 percent, it is generally not consolidated. However the FASB recognizes the artificiality of the present test. Determination of who really has control often relies on factors other than stock ownership.

In fact, specific guidelines force consolidation even though stock ownership is not above 50 percent in certain limited situations. For example, **Enron**'s failure to consolidate three special-purpose entities (SPEs) that it effectively controlled led to an overstatement of income of $569 million and overstatement of equity of $1.2 billion. In each of Enron's three SPEs, the GAAP guidelines would have led to consolidation. That is, the following factors indicate that consolidation should have occurred: the majority owner of the special-purpose entity (SPE) made only a modest investment; the activities of the SPE primarily benefited Enron; and the substantive risks and rewards related to the assets or debt of the SPE rested directly or indirectly with Enron.

The FASB has issued new guidelines related to SPEs, given all the reporting problems that have surfaced related to SPEs at Enron and other companies.

OTHER REPORTING ISSUES — SECTION 3

We have identified the basic issues involved in accounting for investments in debt and equity securities. In addition, the following issues relate to both of these types of securities.

1 Financial statement presentation.
2 Impairment of value.
3 Transfers between categories.
4 Fair value controversy.

FINANCIAL STATEMENT PRESENTATION OF INVESTMENTS

OBJECTIVE 5
Describe the disclosure requirements for investments in debt and equity securities.

Companies must present individual amounts for the three categories of investments either on the balance sheet or in the related notes. Illustration 15-18 summarizes the valuation and balance sheet classification of investments.

ILLUSTRATION 15-18
Investment Valuation and Classification

Investment Category	Valuation	Classification
Trading securities (debt and equity)	Fair value	Current asset.
Held-to-maturity (debt)	Amortized cost	Current or noncurrent based on maturity date of individual security.
Available-for-sale debt	Fair value	Depends on the circumstances. Current or noncurrent based on maturities and expectations as to sales and redemptions in the following year.
Available-for-sale equity	Fair value	Depends on the circumstances. Current or noncurrent based on expectations as to sales in the following year.

Actual Company Disclosures Related to Investments and Comprehensive Income

For securities classified as available-for-sale and separately for securities classified as held-to-maturity, a company should describe:

1. Aggregate fair value, gross unrealized holding gains, gross unrealized losses, and amortized cost basis by major security type (debt and equity).
2. Information about the contractual maturities of debt securities. The company may group maturity information, for example (a) within one year, (b) after one year through five years, (c) after five years through ten years, and (d) after ten years.

In classifying investments, evidence should support management's expressed intent, such as the history of the company's investment activities, events subsequent to the balance sheet date, and the nature and purpose of the investment.

Companies must be extremely careful with debt securities held to maturity. If a company prematurely sells a debt security in this category, the sale may "taint" the entire held-to-maturity portfolio. That is, a management's statement regarding "intent" is no longer credible. Therefore the company may have to reclassify the securities. This could lead to unfortunate consequences. An interesting by-product of this situation is that companies that wish to retire their debt securities early are finding it difficult to do so. The holder will not sell because the securities are classified as held-to-maturity.

Disclosures Related to Equity Investments

Disclosures Required under the Equity Method

The significance of an investment to the investor's financial position and operating results should determine the extent of disclosures. The following disclosures in the investor's financial statements generally apply to the equity method.

What do the numbers mean?

MORE DISCLOSURE PLEASE

As indicated in the last two sections, the level of disclosure for investment securities is extensive. How to account for investment securities is a particularly sensitive area, given the large amounts of equity investments involved. And presently companies report investments in equity securities at cost, equity, fair value, and full consolidation, depending on the circumstances. As a recent SEC study noted, "there are so many different accounting treatments for investments that it raises the question of whether they are all needed."

Presented below is an estimate of the percentage of companies on the major exchanges that have investments in the equity of other entities.

Investments in the Equity of Other Companies

Categorized by Accounting Treatment	Percent of Companies
Presenting consolidated financial statements	91.1%
Reporting equity method investments	23.5
Reporting cost method investments*	17.4
Reporting available-for-sale investments	37.4
Reporting trading investments	6.2

*If the equity investments are not publicly traded, the company often accounts for the investment under the cost method. Changes in value are therefore not recognized unless there is impairment.

As the table indicates, many companies have equity investments of some type. These investments can be substantial. For example, based on the table above, the total amount of equity-method investments appearing on company balance sheets is approximately $403 billion and the amount shown in the income statements in any one year for all companies is approximately $38 billion.

Source: "Report and Recommendations Pursuant to Section 401(c) of the Sarbanes-Oxley Act of 2002 on Arrangements with Off-Balance Sheet Implications, Special Purpose Entities, and Transparency of Filings by Issuers," United States Securities and Exchange Commission—Office of Chief Accountant, Office of Economic Analyses, Division of Corporation Finance (June 2005), pp. 36–39.

1 The name of each investee and the percentage of ownership of common stock.
2 The accounting policies of the investor with respect to investments in common stock.
3 The difference, if any, between the amount in the investment account and the amount of underlying equity in the net assets of the investee.
4 The aggregate value of each identified investment based on quoted market price (if available).
5 When equity-method investments are, in the aggregate, material in relation to the financial position and operating results of an investor, the company may need to present summarized information concerning assets, liabilities, and results of operations of the investees, either individually or in groups, as appropriate.

UNDERLYING CONCEPTS

The consolidation of financial results of different companies follows the economic entity assumption and disregards legal entities. The key objective is to provide useful information to financial statement users.

In addition, the investor should disclose the reasons for not using the equity method in cases of 20 percent or more ownership interest, and for using the equity method in cases of less than 20 percent ownership interest.

Reclassification Adjustments

As we indicated in Chapter 4, companies report changes in unrealized holding gains and losses related to available-for-sale securities as part of other comprehensive income. Companies may display the components of other comprehensive income in one of three ways: (1) in a combined statement of income and comprehensive income, (2) in a separate statement of comprehensive income that begins with net income, or (3) in a statement of stockholders' equity.

The reporting of changes in unrealized gains or losses in comprehensive income is straightforward unless a company sells securities during the year. In that case, double counting results when the company reports realized gains or losses as part of net income but also shows the amounts as part of other comprehensive income in the current period or in previous periods.

To ensure that gains and losses are not counted twice when a sale occurs, a **reclassification adjustment** is necessary. To illustrate, assume that Open Company has the following two available-for-sale securities in its portfolio at the end of 2006 (its first year of operations).

ILLUSTRATION 15-19
Available-for-Sale Security Portfolio (2006)

Investments	Cost	Fair Value	Unrealized Holding Gain (Loss)
Lehman Inc. common stocks	$ 80,000	$105,000	$25,000
Woods Co. common stocks	120,000	135,000	15,000
Total of portfolio	$200,000	$240,000	40,000
Previous securities fair value adjustment balance			–0–
Securities fair value adjustment—Dr.			$40,000

If Open Company reports net income in 2006 of $350,000, it presents a statement of comprehensive income as follows.

ILLUSTRATION 15-20
Statement of Comprehensive Income (2006)

OPEN COMPANY STATEMENT OF COMPREHENSIVE INCOME FOR THE YEAR ENDED DECEMBER 31, 2006	
Net income	$350,000
Other comprehensive income	
Holding gains arising during period	40,000
Comprehensive income	$390,000

During 2007, Open Company sold the Lehman Inc. common stock for $105,000 and realized a gain on the sale of $25,000 ($105,000 – $80,000). At the end of 2007, the fair value of the Woods Co. common stock increased an additional $20,000, to $155,000. Illustration 15-21 shows the computation of the change in the securities fair value adjustment account.

ILLUSTRATION 15-21
Available-for-Sale Security Portfolio (2007)

Investments	Cost	Fair Value	Unrealized Holding Gain (Loss)
Woods Co. common stocks	$120,000	$155,000	$35,000
Previous securities fair value adjustment balance—Dr.			(40,000)
Securities fair value adjustment—Cr.			$ (5,000)

Illustration 15-21 indicates that Open should report an unrealized holding loss of $5,000 in comprehensive income in 2007. In addition, Open realized a gain of $25,000 on the sale of the Lehman common stock. **Comprehensive income includes both realized and unrealized components.** Therefore Open recognizes a total holding gain (loss) in 2007 of $20,000, computed as follows.

ILLUSTRATION 15-22
Computation of Total Holding Gain (Loss)

Unrealized holding gain (loss)	$ (5,000)
Realized holding gain	25,000
Total holding gain recognized	$20,000

Open reports net income of $720,000 in 2007, which includes the realized gain on sale of the Lehman securities. Illustration 15-23 shows a statement of comprehensive income for 2007, indicating how Open reported the components of holding gains (losses).

ILLUSTRATION 15-23
Statement of Comprehensive Income (2007)

OPEN COMPANY
STATEMENT OF COMPREHENSIVE INCOME
FOR THE YEAR ENDED DECEMBER 31, 2007

Net income (includes $25,000 realized gain on Lehman shares)		$720,000
Other comprehensive income		
Total holding gains arising during period [$(5,000) + $25,000]	$20,000	
Less: Reclassification adjustment for gains included in net income	(25,000)	(5,000)
Comprehensive income		$715,000

In 2006, Open included the unrealized gain on the Lehman Co. common stock in comprehensive income. In 2007, Open sold the stock. It reported the realized gain in net income, which increased comprehensive income again. To avoid double counting this gain, Open makes a reclassification adjustment to eliminate the realized gain from the computation of comprehensive income in 2007.

A company may display reclassification adjustments on the face of the financial statement in which it reports comprehensive income. Or it may disclose these reclassification adjustments in the notes to the financial statements.

Comprehensive Example

To illustrate the reporting of investment securities and related gain or loss on available-for-sale securities, assume that on January 1, 2006, Hinges Co. had cash and common stock of $50,000.[12] At that date the company had no other asset, liability, or equity balance. On January 2, Hinges purchased for cash $50,000 of equity securities classified as available-for-sale. On June 30, Hinges sold part of the available-for-sale security portfolio, realizing a gain as shown in Illustration 15-24.

ILLUSTRATION 15-24
Computation of Realized Gain

Fair value of securities sold	$22,000
Less: Cost of securities sold	20,000
Realized gain	$ 2,000

Hinges did not purchase or sell any other securities during 2006. It received $3,000 in dividends during the year. At December 31, 2006, the remaining portfolio is as shown in Illustration 15-25.

ILLUSTRATION 15-25
Computation of Unrealized Gain

Fair value of portfolio	$34,000
Less: Cost of portfolio	30,000
Unrealized gain	$ 4,000

Illustration 15-26 shows the company's income statement for 2006.

ILLUSTRATION 15-26
Income Statement

HINGES CO.
INCOME STATEMENT
FOR THE YEAR ENDED DECEMBER 31, 2006

Dividend revenue	$3,000
Realized gains on investment in securities	2,000
Net income	$5,000

The company reports its change in the unrealized holding gain in a statement of comprehensive income as follows.

ILLUSTRATION 15-27
Statement of Comprehensive Income

HINGES CO.
STATEMENT OF COMPREHENSIVE INCOME
FOR THE YEAR ENDED DECEMBER 31, 2006

Net income		$5,000
Other comprehensive income:		
Holding gains arising during the period	$6,000	
Less: Reclassification adjustment for gains included in net income	2,000	4,000
Comprehensive income		$9,000

[12]We adapted this example from Dennis R. Beresford, L. Todd Johnson, and Cheri L. Reither, "Is a Second Income Statement Needed?" *Journal of Accountancy* (April 1996), p. 71.

Its statement of stockholders' equity appears in Illustration 15-28.

ILLUSTRATION 15-28
Statement of Stockholders' Equity

HINGES CO.
STATEMENT OF STOCKHOLDERS' EQUITY
FOR THE YEAR ENDED DECEMBER 31, 2006

	Common Stock	Retained Earnings	Accumulated Other Comprehensive Income	Total
Beginning balance	$50,000	$–0–	$–0–	$50,000
Add: Net income		5,000		5,000
Other comprehensive Income			4,000	4,000
Ending balance	$50,000	$5,000	$4,000	$59,000

The comparative balance sheet is shown in Illustration 15-29.

ILLUSTRATION 15-29
Comparative Balance Sheet

HINGES CO.
COMPARATIVE BALANCE SHEET

	1/1/06	12/31/06
Assets		
Cash	$50,000	$25,000
Available-for-sale securities		34,000
Total assets	$50,000	$59,000
Stockholders' equity		
Common stock	$50,000	$50,000
Retained earnings		5,000
Accumulated other comprehensive income		4,000
Total stockholders' equity	$50,000	$59,000

This example indicates how an unrealized gain or loss on available-for-sale securities affects all the financial statements. Note that a company must disclose the components that comprise accumulated other comprehensive income.

IMPAIRMENT OF VALUE

OBJECTIVE 6
Discuss the accounting for impairments of debt and equity investments.

A company should evaluate every investment, at each reporting date, to determine if it has suffered **impairment**—a loss in value that is other than temporary. For example, if an investee experiences a bankruptcy or a significant liquidity crisis, the investor may suffer a permanent loss. **If the decline is judged to be other than temporary, a company writes down the cost basis of the individual security to a new cost basis.** The company accounts for the write-down as a realized loss. Therefore, it includes the amount in net income.

For debt securities, a company uses the impairment test to determine whether "it is probable that the investor will be unable to collect all amounts due according to the contractual terms."

For equity securities, the guideline is less precise. Any time realizable value is lower than the carrying amount of the investment, a company must consider an impairment. Factors involved include the length of time and the extent to which the fair value has been less than cost; the financial condition and near-term prospects of the issuer; and the intent and ability of the investor company to retain its investment to allow for any anticipated recovery in fair value.

To illustrate an impairment, assume that Strickler Company holds available-for-sale bond securities with a par value and amortized cost of $1 million. The fair value of these securities is $800,000. Strickler has previously reported an unrealized loss on these securities of $200,000 as part of other comprehensive income. In evaluating the securities, Strickler now determines that it probably will not collect all amounts due. In this case, it reports the unrealized loss of $200,000 as a loss on impairment of $200,000. Strickler includes this amount in income, with the bonds stated at their new cost basis. It records this impairment as follows.

Loss on Impairment	200,000	
Securities Fair Value Adjustment (Available-for-Sale)	200,000	
Unrealized Holding Gain or Loss—Equity		200,000
Available-for-Sale Securities		200,000

The new cost basis of the investment in debt securities is $800,000. Strickler includes subsequent increases and decreases in the fair value of impaired available-for-sale securities as other comprehensive income.[13]

Companies base impairment for debt and equity securities on a fair value test. This test differs slightly from the impairment test for loans. The FASB rejected the discounted cash flow alternative for securities because of the availability of market price information.

THE IRONY OF IT ALL

WHAT DO THE NUMBERS MEAN?

The **Federal National Mortgage Association** (FNMA)—known as "Fannie Mae"—is a government-sponsored company that owns or guarantees about 25 percent of all the mortgages in the United States. Recently numerous articles have detailed accounting abuses by Fannie Mae. For example, Fannie Mae has acknowledged that some of its accounting polices do not comply with GAAP. It is now preparing to restate its financial statements back to 2001 and possibly to recognize at least $9 billion in losses related to derivatives.

Interestingly, Fannie Mae has caused much hardship for many of its brethren in the financial community (such as **DNB Financial, Independent Bank Corporation,** and **Wilmington Trust**). The reason: Many are holding security investments in Fannie Mae. And now the institutions are taking permanent write-downs on these securities because the losses appear to be other than temporary. (In other words, the Fannie Mae securities are impaired.) The irony is that a number of the companies that are taking impairment losses are the very ones that recently fought hard to make sure the FASB did not tighten up impairment accounting rules. Even more ironic is the fact the one of their fellow lobbyers (FNMA) is the source of their impairments!

TRANSFERS BETWEEN CATEGORIES

OBJECTIVE 7
Describe the accounting for transfer of investment securities between categories.

Companies account for transfers between any of the categories at fair value. Thus, if a company transfers available-for-sale securities to held-to-maturity investments, it records the new investment (held-to-maturity) at the date of transfer at **fair value** in the new category. Similarly, if it transfers held-to-maturity investments to available-for-sale investments, it records the new investments (available-for-sale) at **fair value**. This **fair value** rule assures that a company cannot omit recognition of fair value simply by transferring securities to the held-to-maturity category. Illustration 15-30 summarizes the accounting treatment for transfers.

[13]Companies may not amortize any discount related to the debt securities after recording the impairment. The new cost basis of impaired held-to-maturity securities does not change unless additional impairment occurs.

ILLUSTRATION 15-30
Accounting for Transfers

Examples of the Entries for Recording Transfers Between Categories

Type of Transfer	Measurement Basis	Impact of Transfer on Stockholders' Equity*	Impact of Transfer on Net Income*
Transfer from trading to available-for-sale	Security transferred at fair value at the date of transfer, which is the new cost basis of the security.	The unrealized gain or loss at the date of transfer increases or decreases stockholders' equity.	The unrealized gain or loss at the date of transfer is recognized in income.
Transfer from available-for-sale to trading	Security transferred at fair value at the date of transfer, which is the new cost basis of the security.	The unrealized gain or loss at the date of transfer increases or decreases stockholders' equity.	The unrealized gain or loss at the date of transfer is recognized in income.
Transfer from held-to-maturity to available-for-sale**	Security transferred at fair value at the date of transfer.	The separate component of stockholders' equity is increased or decreased by the unrealized gain or loss at the date of transfer.	None
Transfer from available-for-sale to held-to-maturity	Security transferred at fair value at the date of transfer.	The unrealized gain or loss at the date of transfer carried as a separate component of stockholders' equity is amortized over the remaining life of the security.	None

*Assumes that adjusting entries to report changes in fair value for the current period are not yet recorded.
***Statement No. 115* states that these types of transfers should be rare.

FAIR VALUE CONTROVERSY

The reporting of investment securities is controversial. Some believe that all securities should be reported at fair value; others believe they all should be stated at amortized cost. Others favor the present approach. In this section we look at some of the major unresolved issues.

Measurement Based on Intent

Companies classify debt securities as held-to-maturity, available-for-sale, or trading. As a result, companies can report three identical debt securities in three different ways in the financial statements. Some argue such treatment is confusing. Furthermore, the held-to-maturity category relies solely on intent, a subjective evaluation. What is not subjective is the market price of the debt instrument. In other words, the three classifications are subjective, resulting in arbitrary classifications.

Gains Trading

Companies can classify certain debt securities as held-to-maturity and therefore report them at amortized cost. Companies can classify other debt and equity securities as available-for-sale and report them at fair value with the unrealized gain or loss reported as other comprehensive income. In either case, a company can become involved in "gains trading" (also referred to as "cherry picking," "snacking," or "sell the best and keep the rest"). In **gains trading**, companies sell their "winners," reporting the gains in income, and hold on to the losers.

Liabilities Not Fairly Valued

Many argue that if companies report investment securities at fair value, they also should report liabilities at fair value. Why? By recognizing changes in value on only one side of the balance sheet (the asset side), a high degree of volatility can occur in the income and stockholders' equity amounts. Further, financial institutions are involved in asset and liability management (not just asset management). Viewing only one side may lead managers to make uneconomic decisions as a result of the accounting.

Although the Board sympathized with this view, it noted that companies still reported certain debt securities at amortized cost (held-to-maturity securities) and that this standard excluded other types of securities. In addition, serious valuation issues arose in relation to some types of liabilities. As a result, liabilities were excluded from consideration.[14]

Subjectivity of Fair Values

Some question the relevance of fair value measures for investments in securities, arguing in favor of reporting based on amortized cost. They believe that amortized cost provides relevant information: it focuses on the decision to acquire the asset, the earning effects of that decision that will be realized over time, and the ultimate recoverable value of the asset. They argue that fair value ignores those concepts. Instead, fair value focuses on the effects of transactions and events that do not involve the company, reflecting opportunity gains and losses whose recognition in the financial statements is, in their view, not appropriate until realized.

SUMMARY OF REPORTING TREATMENT OF SECURITIES

Illustration 15-31 summarizes the major debt and equity securities and their reporting treatment.

ILLUSTRATION 15-31
Summary of Treatment of Major Debt and Equity Securities

Category	Balance Sheet	Income Statement
Trading (debt and equity securities)	Investments shown at fair value. Current assets.	Interest and dividends are recognized as revenue. Unrealized holding gains and losses are included in net income.
Available-for-sale (debt and equity securities)	Investments shown at fair value. Current or long-term assets. Unrealized holding gains and losses are a separate component of stockholders' equity.	Interest and dividends are recognized as revenue. Unrealized holding gains and losses are **not** included in net income but in other comprehensive income.
Held-to-maturity (debt securities)	Investments shown at amortized cost. Current or long-term assets.	Interest is recognized as revenue.
Equity method and/or consolidation (equity securities)	Investments originally are carried at cost, are periodically adjusted by the investor's share of the investee's earnings or losses, and are decreased by all dividends received from the investee. Classified as long-term.	Revenue is recognized to the extent of the investee's earnings or losses reported subsequent to the date of investment.

wiley.com/college/kieso

Discussion of Special Issues Related to Investments

[14]In a recent exposure draft concerning valuation of financial instruments, the FASB indicated its support for valuing liabilities at fair value. "Fair Value Measurements," Proposed Statement of Financial Accounting Standards (Norwalk, Conn.: FASB, June 23, 2004).

QUESTIONS

1. Distinguish between a debt security and an equity security.
2. What purpose does the variety in bond features (types and characteristics) serve?
3. What is the cost of a long-term investment in bonds?
4. Identify and explain the three types of classifications for investments in debt securities.
5. When should a debt security be classified as held-to-maturity?
6. Explain how trading securities are accounted for and reported.
7. At what amount should trading, available-for-sale, and held-to-maturity securities be reported on the balance sheet?
8. On July 1, 2007, Ingalls Company purchased $2,000,000 of Wilder Company's 8% bonds, due on July 1, 2014. The bonds, which pay interest semiannually on January 1 and July 1, were purchased for $1,750,000 to yield 10%. Determine the amount of interest revenue Ingalls should report on its income statement for year ended December 31, 2007.
9. If the bonds in question 8 are classified as available-for-sale and they have a fair value at December 31, 2007, of $1,802,000, prepare the journal entry (if any) at December 31, 2007, to record this transaction.
10. Indicate how unrealized holding gains and losses should be reported for investment securities classified as trading, available-for-sale, and held-to-maturity.
11. (a) Assuming no Securities Fair Value Adjustment (Available-for-Sale) account balance at the beginning of the year, prepare the adjusting entry at the end of the year if Laura Company's available-for-sale securities have a market value $70,000 below cost. (b) Assume the same information as part (a), except that Laura Company has a debit balance in its Securities Fair Value Adjustment (Available-for-Sale) account of $10,000 at the beginning of the year. Prepare the adjusting entry at year-end.
12. Identify and explain the different types of classifications for investment in equity securities.
13. Why are held-to-maturity investments applicable only to debt securities?
14. Harry Company sold 10,000 shares of Potter Co. common stock for $27.50 per share, incurring $1,770 in brokerage commissions. These securities were classified as trading and originally cost $250,000. Prepare the entry to record the sale of these securities.
15. Distinguish between the accounting treatment for available-for-sale equity securities and trading equity securities.
16. What constitutes "significant influence" when an investor's financial interest is below the 50% level?
17. Explain how the investment account is affected by investee activities under the equity method.
18. When the equity method is applied, what disclosures should be made in the investor's financial statements?
19. Hatch Co. uses the equity method to account for investments in common stock. What accounting should be made for dividends received in excess of Hatch's share of investee's earnings subsequent to the date of investment?
20. Elizabeth Corp. has an investment with a carrying value (equity method) on its books of $170,000 representing a 40% interest in Dole Company, which suffered a $620,000 loss this year. How should Elizabeth Corp. handle its proportionate share of Dole's loss?
21. Where on the asset side of the balance sheet are trading securities, available-for-sale securities, and held-to-maturity securities reported? Explain.
22. Explain why reclassification adjustments are necessary.
23. Briefly discuss how a transfer of securities from the available-for-sale category to the trading category affects stockholders' equity and income.
24. When is a debt security considered impaired? Explain how to account for the impairment of an available-for-sale debt security.

CHAPTER SIXTEEN

REVENUE RECOGNITION

It's Back

Several years after passage, the accounting world continues to be preoccupied with the Sarbanes-Oxley Act of 2002 (SOX). Unfortunately, SOX did not solve one of the classic accounting issues—how to properly account for revenue. In fact, revenue recognition practices are the most prevalent reasons why accounting restatements increased dramatically in 2004. A number of the revenue recognition issues relate to possible fraudulent behavior by company executives and employees. Consider some of the recent SEC actions:

- The SEC charged the former co-chairman and CEO of **Qwest Communications International Inc.** and eight other former Qwest officers and employees with fraud and other violations of the federal securities laws. Three of these people fraudulently characterized nonrecurring revenue from one-time sales as revenue from recurring data and Internet services. The SEC release notes that internal correspondence likened Qwest's dependence on these transactions to fill the gap between actual and projected revenue to an addiction.
- The SEC filed a complaint against three former senior officers of **iGo Corp.**, alleging that the defendants collectively caused iGo to improperly recognize revenue on consignment sales and products that were not shipped or that were shipped after the end of a fiscal quarter.
- The SEC filed a complaint against the former CEO and chairman of **Homestore Inc.** and its former executive vice president of business development, alleging that they engaged in a fraudulent scheme to overstate advertising and subscription revenues. The scheme involved a complex structure of "round-trip" transactions using various third-party companies that, in essence, allowed Homestore to recognize its own cash as revenue.

Though the cases cited involved fraud and irregularity, not all revenue recognition errors are intentional. For example, in April 2005 **American Home Mortgage Investment Corp.** announced that it would reverse revenue recognized from its fourth-quarter 2004 loan securitization, and would recognize it in the first quarter of 2005 instead. As a result, American Home restated its financial results for 2004.[1]

So, how does a company ensure that revenue transactions are recorded properly? Some answers will become apparent after you study this chapter.

---

[1]Cheryl de Mesa Graziano, "Revenue Recognition: A Perennial Problem," *Financial Executive* (July 14, 2005), *www.fei.org/mag/articles/7-2005_revenue.cfm.*

Learning Objectives

After studying this chapter, you should be able to:

1 Apply the revenue recognition principle.
2 Describe accounting issues for revenue recognition at point of sale.
3 Apply the percentage-of-completion method for long-term contracts.
4 Apply the completed-contract method for long-term contracts.
5 Identify the proper accounting for losses on long-term contracts.
6 Describe the installment-sales method of accounting.
7 Explain the cost-recovery method of accounting.

PREVIEW OF CHAPTER 16

As indicated in the opening story, the issue of when revenue should be recognized is complex. The many methods of marketing products and services make it difficult to develop guidelines that will apply to all situations. This chapter provides you with general guidelines used in most business transactions. The content and organization of the chapter are as follows.

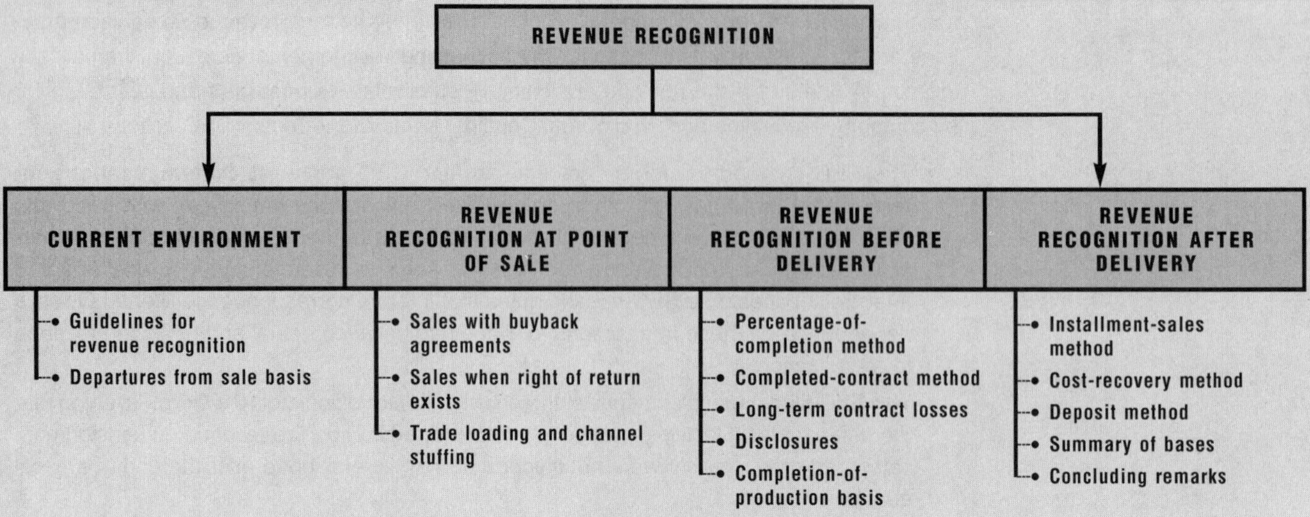

THE CURRENT ENVIRONMENT

According to one study, revenue recognition has been the largest single source of public-company restatements over the past decade. The study noted the following:

1. Restatements for improper revenue recognition result in larger drops in market capitalization than any other type of restatement.
2. Revenue problems caused eight of the top ten market value losses in a recent year.
3. Of the ten companies, the leading three lost $20 billion in market value in just three days following disclosure of revenue recognition problems.[2]

As a result of such revenue recognition problems, the SEC has increased its enforcement actions in this area (as evidenced in the opening story.) In some of these cases, companies made significant adjustments to previously issued financial statements. As Lynn Turner, former chief accountant of the SEC, indicated, "When people cross over the boundaries of legitimate reporting, the Commission will take appropriate action to ensure the fairness and integrity that investors need and depend on every day."[3]

Inappropriate recognition of revenue can occur in any industry. Products that are sold to distributors for resale pose different risks than products or services that are sold directly to customers. Sales in high-technology industries, where rapid product

[2]PricewaterhouseCoopers, "Current Developments for Audit Committees 2002" (Florham Park, N.J.: PricewaterhouseCoopers, 2002), p. 65.

[3]The Sarbanes-Oxley Act of 2002 also makes it clear that Congress will not tolerate abuses of the financial reporting process and that those who fail to adhere to "certain standards" will be prosecuted.

obsolescence is a significant issue, pose different risks than sale of inventory with a longer life, such as farm or construction equipment, automobiles, trucks, and appliances.[4]

As indicated in Chapter 9, telecom companies such as **Global Crossing** and **Qwest Communications** swapped fiber-optic capacity to increase revenue. The SEC has expressed concern that dot-coms also are increasing their revenue by including product sales in their revenue even though they are acting only as the distributor (intermediary) on behalf of other companies. Instead, dot-coms should be reporting only a distribution (brokerage) fee for selling another company's products.[5]

GROSSED OUT

WHAT DO THE NUMBERS MEAN?

Consider **Priceline.com**, the company made famous by William Shatner's ads about "naming your own price" for airline tickets and hotel rooms. In one of its quarterly SEC filings, Priceline reported that it earned $152 million in revenues. But that included the full amount customers paid for tickets, hotel rooms, and rental cars. Traditional travel agencies call that amount "gross bookings," not revenues. And much like regular travel agencies, Priceline keeps only a small portion of gross bookings—namely, the spread between the customers' accepted bids and the price it paid for the merchandise. The rest, which Priceline calls "product costs," it pays to the airlines and hotels that supply the tickets and rooms.

However, Priceline's product costs came to $134 million, leaving Priceline just $18 million of what it calls "gross profit" and what most other companies would call revenues. And that's before all of Priceline's other costs—like advertising and salaries—which netted out to a loss of $102 million. The difference isn't academic: Priceline stock traded at about 23 times its reported revenues but at a mind-boggling 214 times its "gross profit." This and other aggressive recognition practices led the SEC to issue stricter revenue recogniton guidance indicating that if a company performs as an agent or broker without assuming the risks and rewards of ownership of the goods, the company should report sales on a net (fee) basis.

Source: "Revenue Recognition in Financial Statements," *SEC Staff Accounting Bulletin No. 101* December 3, 1999) and "Revenue Recognition," *SEC Staff Accounting Bulletin No. 104* (December 17, 2003). See also Jeremy Kahn, "Presto Chango! Sales Are Huge," *Fortune* (March 20, 2000), p. 44.

Guidelines for Revenue Recognition

OBJECTIVE 1
Apply the revenue recognition principle.

In general, the guidelines for revenue recognition are quite broad. On top of the broad guidelines, certain industries have specific additional guidelines that provide further insight into when revenue should be recognized. The **revenue recognition principle** provides that companies should recognize revenue[6] (1) when it is realized

[4]Adapted from American Institute of Certified Public Accountants, Inc., *Audit Issues in Revenue Recognition* (New York: AICPA, 1999).

[5]"Revenue Recognition in Financial Statements," *SEC Staff Accounting Bulletin No. 101*, December 3, 1999).

[6]Recognition is "the process of formally recording or incorporating an item in the accounts and financial statements of an entity" (*SFAC No. 3*, par. 83). "Recognition includes depiction of an item in both words and numbers, with the amount included in the totals of the financial statements" (*SFAC No. 5*, par. 6). For an asset or liability, recognition involves recording not only acquisition or incurrence of the item but also later changes in it, including removal from the financial statements previously recognized.

Recognition is not the same as realization, although the two are sometimes used interchangeably in accounting literature and practice. *Realization* is "the process of converting noncash resources and rights into money and is most precisely used in accounting and financial reporting to refer to sales of assets for cash or claims to cash" (*SFAC No. 3*, par. 83).

or realizable and (2) when it is earned.[7] Therefore, proper revenue recognition revolves around three terms:

> Revenues are **realized** when a company exchanges goods and services for cash or claims to cash (receivables).
>
> Revenues are **realizable** when assets a company receives in exchange are readily convertible to known amounts of cash or claims to cash.
>
> Revenues are **earned** when a company has substantially accomplished what it must do to be entitled to the benefits represented by the revenues—that is, when the earnings process is complete or virtually complete.[8]

UNDERLYING CONCEPTS

Revenues are inflows of assets and/or settlements of liabilities from delivering or producing goods, providing services, or other earning activities that constitute a company's ongoing major or central operations during a period.

Four revenue transactions are recognized in accordance with this principle:

1. Companies recognize revenue from selling products at the date of sale. This date is usually interpreted to mean the date of delivery to customers.
2. Companies recognize revenue from services provided, when services have been performed and are billable.
3. Companies recognize revenue from permitting others to use enterprise assets, such as interest, rent, and royalties, as time passes or as the assets are used.
4. Companies recognize revenue from disposing of assets other than products at the date of sale.

These revenue transactions are diagrammed in Illustration 16-1.

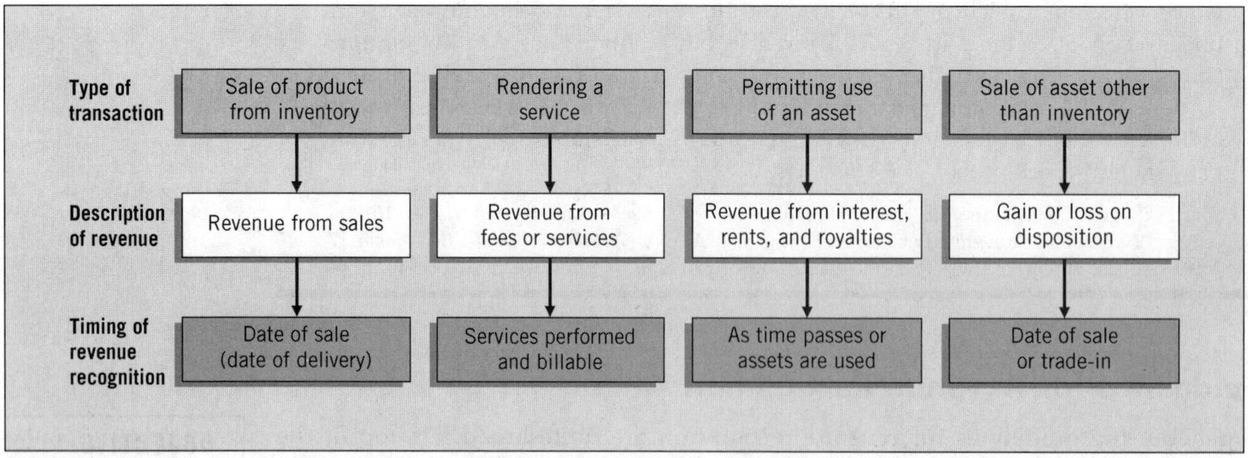

ILLUSTRATION 16-1
Revenue Recognition Classified by Nature of Transaction

The preceding statements are the basis of accounting for revenue transactions. Yet, in practice there are departures from the revenue recognition principle. Companies sometimes recognize revenue at other points in the earning process, owing in great measure to the considerable variety of revenue transactions.[9]

---

[7] "Recognition and Measurement in Financial Statements of Business Enterprises," *Statement of Financial Accounting Concepts No. 5* (Stamford, Conn.: FASB, 1984), par. 83.

[8] Gains (as contrasted to revenues) commonly result from transactions and other events that do not involve an "earning process." For gain recognition, being earned is generally less significant than being realized or realizable. Companies commonly recognize gains at the time of an asset's sale, disposition of a liability, or when prices of certain assets change.

[9] The FASB and IASB are now involved in a joint project on revenue recognition. The purpose of this project is to develop comprehensive conceptual guidance on when to recognize revenue. Presently, the boards are considering an approach that focuses on changes in assets and liabilities (rather than on earned and realized) as the basis for revenue recognition. It is hoped that this approach will lead to more consistent accounting in this area. (See *www.fasb.org/project/revenue_recognition.shtml*.)

Departures from the Sale Basis

An FASB study found some common **reasons for departures from the sale basis.**[10] One reason is a desire to **recognize earlier** than the time of sale the effect of earning activities. Earlier recognition is appropriate if there is a high degree of certainty about the amount of revenue earned. A second reason is a desire to **delay recognition** of revenue beyond the time of sale. Delayed recognition is appropriate if the degree of uncertainty concerning the amount of either revenue or costs is sufficiently high or if the sale does not represent substantial completion of the earnings process.

This chapter focuses on two of the four general types of revenue transactions described earlier: (1) selling products and (2) providing services. Both of these are **sales transactions.** (In several other sections of the textbook, we discuss the other two types of revenue transactions—revenue from permitting others to use enterprise assets, and revenue from disposing of assets other than products.) Our discussion of product sales transactions in this chapter is organized around the following topics:

Examples of Revenue Recognition Policies

1. Revenue recognition at point of sale (delivery).
2. Revenue recognition before delivery.
3. Revenue recognition after delivery.
4. Revenue recognition for special sales transactions—franchises and consignments.

Illustration 16-2 depicts this organization of revenue recognition topics.

ILLUSTRATION 16-2
Revenue Recognition Alternatives

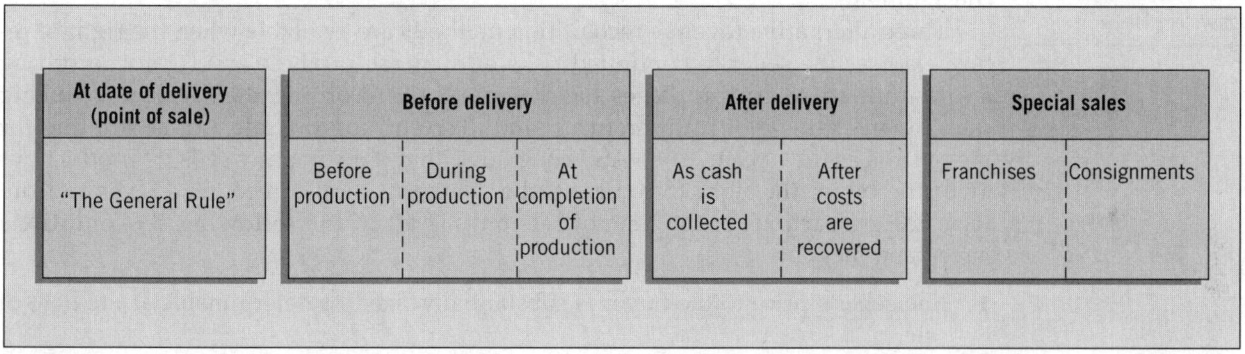

REVENUE RECOGNITION AT POINT OF SALE (DELIVERY)

OBJECTIVE 2
Describe accounting issues for revenue recognition at point of sale.

According to the FASB's *Concepts Statement No. 5*, companies usually meet the two conditions for recognizing revenue (being realized or realizable and being earned) by the time they deliver products or render services to customers.[11] Therefore, companies commonly recognize revenues from manufacturing and selling activities at **point of sale** (usually meaning delivery).[12] Implementation problems, however, can arise. We discuss three such problematic situations on the following pages.

[10]Henry R. Jaenicke, Survey of Present Practices in Recognizing Revenues, Expenses, Gains, and Losses, A Research Report (Stamford, Conn.: FASB, 1981), p. 11.

[11]The SEC believes that revenue is realized or realizable and earned when **all** of the following criteria are met: (1) Persuasive evidence of an arrangement exists; (2) delivery has occurred or services have been provided; (3) the seller's price to the buyer is fixed or determinable; and (4) collectibility is reasonably assured. See "Revenue Recognition in Financial Statements," *SEC Staff Accounting Bulletin No. 101* (December 3, 1999). The SEC provided more specific guidance because the general criteria were difficult to interpret.

[12]*Statement of Financial Accounting Concepts No. 5*, op. cit., par. 84.

Sales with Buyback Agreements

If a company sells a product in one period and agrees to buy it back in the next accounting period, has the company sold the product? As indicated in Chapter 7, legal title has transferred in this situation. However, the economic substance of the transaction is that the seller retains the risks of ownership. The FASB has curtailed recognition of revenue using this practice. When a repurchase agreement exists at a set price and this price covers all cost of the inventory plus related holding costs, the inventory and related liability remain on the seller's books.[13] In other words, no sale.

Sales When Right of Return Exists

Whether cash or credit sales are involved, a special problem arises with claims for returns and allowances. In Chapter 6, we presented the accounting treatment for normal returns and allowances. However, certain companies experience such a **high rate of returns**—a high ratio of returned merchandise to sales—that they find it necessary to postpone reporting sales until the return privilege has substantially expired.

UNDERLYING CONCEPTS

This is an example of *realized but unearned revenue.* When high rates of return exist and cannot be reasonably estimated, a question arises as to whether the earnings process has been substantially completed.

For example, in the publishing industry, the rate of return approaches 25 percent for hardcover books and 65 percent for some magazines. Other types of companies that experience high return rates are perishable food dealers, distributors who sell to retail outlets, recording-industry companies, and some toy and sporting goods manufacturers. Returns in these industries are frequently made either through a right of contract or as a matter of practice involving "guaranteed sales" agreements or consignments.

Three alternative revenue recognition methods are available when the right of return exposes the seller to continued risks of ownership. These are: (1) not recording a sale until all return privileges have expired; (2) recording the sale, but reducing sales by an estimate of future returns; and (3) recording the sale and accounting for the returns as they occur. The FASB concluded that if a company sells its product but gives the buyer the right to return it, the company should recognize revenue from the sales transactions at the time of sale **only if all of the following six conditions** have been met.[14]

1 The seller's price to the buyer is substantially fixed or determinable at the date of sale.

2 The buyer has paid the seller, or the buyer is obligated to pay the seller, and the obligation is not contingent on resale of the product.

3 The buyer's obligation to the seller would not be changed in the event of theft or physical destruction or damage of the product.

4 The buyer acquiring the product for resale has economic substance apart from that provided by the seller.

5 The seller does not have significant obligations for future performance to directly bring about resale of the product by the buyer.

6 The seller can reasonably estimate the amount of future returns.

What if the six conditions are not met? In that case, the company must recognize sales revenue and cost of sales either when the return privilege has substantially expired or when those six conditions subsequently are met, **whichever occurs first**. In the income statement, the company must reduce sales revenue and cost of sales by the amount of the estimated returns.

[13]"Accounting for Product Financing Arrangements," *Statement of Financial Accounting Standards No. 49* (Stamford, Conn.: FASB, 1981).

[14]"Revenue Recognition When Right of Return Exists," *Statement of Financial Accounting Standards No. 48* (Stamford, Conn.: FASB, 1981), par. 6.

Trade Loading and Channel Stuffing

Some companies record revenues at date of delivery with neither buyback nor unlimited return provisions. Although they appear to be following acceptable point-of-sale revenue recognition practices, they are recognizing revenues and earnings prematurely.

For example, the domestic cigarette industry at one time engaged in a distribution practice known as **trade loading**. As one commentator described this practice, "Trade loading is a crazy, uneconomic, insidious practice through which manufacturers—trying to show sales, profits, and market share they don't actually have—induce their wholesale customers, known as the trade, to buy more product than they can promptly resell."[15] In total, the cigarette industry appears to have exaggerated a couple years' operating profits by as much as $600 million by taking the profits from future years.

In the computer software industry, a similar practice is referred to as **channel stuffing**. When a software maker needed to make its financial results look good, it offered deep discounts to its distributors to overbuy, and then recorded revenue when the software left the loading dock.[16] Of course, the distributors' inventories become bloated and the marketing channel gets too filled with product, but the software maker's current-period financials are improved. However, financial results in future periods will suffer, unless the company repeats the process.

Trade loading and channel stuffing distort operating results and "window dress" financial statements. If used without an appropriate allowance for sales returns, channel stuffing is a classic example of booking tomorrow's revenue today. Business managers need to be aware of the ethical dangers of misleading the financial community by engaging in such practices to improve their financial statements.

INTERNATIONAL INSIGHT

General revenue recognition principles are provided by IFRS that are consistent with U.S. GAAP but contain limited detailed or industry-specific guidance.

NO TAKE-BACKS, REVISITED

WHAT DO THE NUMBERS MEAN?

You may recall from an earlier discussion (in Chapter 2) that investors in **Lucent Technologies** were negatively affected when Lucent violated one of the fundamental criteria for revenue recognition—the "no take-back" rule. This rule holds that revenue should not be booked on inventory that is shipped if the customer can return it at some point in the future. In this particular case, Lucent agreed to take back shipped inventory from its distributors, if the distributors were unable to sell the items to their customers.

In essence, Lucent was "stuffing the channel." By booking sales when goods were shipped, even though they most likely would get them back, Lucent was able to report continued sales growth. However, Lucent investors got a nasty surprise when distributors returned those goods and Lucent had to restate its financial results. The restatement erased $679 million in revenues, turning an operating profit into a loss. In response to this bad news, Lucent's stock price declined $1.31 per share, or 8.5 percent. Lucent is not alone in this practice. **Sunbeam** got caught stuffing the sales channel with barbeque grills and other outdoor items, which contributed to its troubles when it was forced to restate its earnings.

Investors can be tipped off to potential channel stuffing by carefully reviewing a company's revenue recognition policy for generous return policies and by watching inventory and receivable levels. When sales increase along with receivables, that's one sign that customers are not paying for goods shipped on credit. And growing inventory levels are an indicator that customers have all the goods they need. Both scenarios suggest a higher likelihood of goods being returned and revenues and income being restated. So remember, no take-backs!

Source: Adapted from S. Young, "Lucent Slashes First Quarter Outlook, Erases Revenue from Latest Quarter," *Wall Street Journal Online* (December 22, 2000); and Tracey Byrnes, "Too Many Thin Mints: Spotting the Practice of Channel Stuffing," *Wall Street Journal Online* (February 7, 2002).

---

[15] "The $600 Million Cigarette Scam," *Fortune* (December 4, 1989), p. 89.

[16] "Software's Dirty Little Secret," *Forbes* (May 15, 1989), p. 128.

REVENUE RECOGNITION BEFORE DELIVERY

wiley.com/college/kieso

Additional Disclosures of Revenue Recognition Policies

For the most part, companies recognize revenue at the point of sale (delivery) because at point of sale most of the uncertainties in the earning process are removed and the exchange price is known. Under certain circumstances, however, companies recognize revenue prior to completion and delivery. The most notable example is long-term construction contract accounting, which uses the percentage-of-completion method.

Long-term contracts frequently provide that the seller (builder) may bill the purchaser at intervals, as it reaches various points in the project. Examples of long-term contracts are construction-type contracts, development of military and commercial aircraft, weapons-delivery systems, and space exploration hardware. When the project consists of separable units, such as a group of buildings or miles of roadway, contract provisions may provide for delivery in installments. In that case, the seller would bill the buyer and transfer title at stated stages of completion, such as the completion of each building unit or every 10 miles of road. The accounting records should record sales when installments are "delivered."[17]

Two distinctly different methods of accounting for long-term construction contracts are recognized.[18] They are:

- **Percentage-of-Completion Method.** Companies recognize revenues and gross profits each period based upon the progress of the construction—that is, the percentage of completion. The company accumulates construction costs **plus gross profit earned to date** in an inventory account (Construction in Process), and it accumulates progress billings in a contra inventory account (Billings on Construction in Progress).
- **Completed-Contract Method.** Companies recognize revenues and gross profit **only** when the contract is completed. The company accumulates construction costs in an inventory account (Construction in Process), and it accumulates progress billings in a contra inventory account (Billings on Construction in Process).

The rationale for using percentage-of-completion accounting is that under most of these contracts the buyer and seller have enforceable rights. The buyer has the legal right to require specific performance on the contract. The seller has the right to require progress payments that provide evidence of the buyer's ownership interest. As a result, a continuous sale occurs as the work progresses. Companies should recognize revenue according to that progression.

UNDERLYING CONCEPTS

The percentage-of-completion method recognizes revenue from long-term contracts in the periods in which the revenue is earned. The firm contract fixes the selling price. And, if costs are estimable and collection reasonably assured, the revenue recognition concept is not violated.

Companies *must* use the percentage-of-completion method when estimates of progress toward completion, revenues, and costs are reasonably dependable and **all of the following conditions** exist.[19]

1. The contract clearly specifies the enforceable rights regarding goods or services to be provided and received by the parties, the consideration to be exchanged, and the manner and terms of settlement.
2. The buyer can be expected to satisfy all obligations under the contract.
3. The contractor can be expected to perform the contractual obligations.

Companies should use the completed-contract method when one of the following conditions applies:

[17] *Statement of Financial Accounting Concepts No. 5*, par. 84, item c.

[18] *Accounting Trends and Techniques—2004* reports that of the 119 of its 600 sample companies that referred to long-term construction contracts, 110 used the percentage-of-completion method and 9 used the completed-contract method.

[19] "Accounting for Performance of Construction-Type and Certain Production-Type Contracts," *Statement of Position 81-1* (New York: AICPA, 1981), par. 23.

- when a company has primarily short-term contracts, *or*
- when a company cannot meet the conditions for using the percentage-of-completion method, *or*
- when there are inherent hazards in the contract beyond the normal, recurring business risks.

The presumption is that percentage-of-completion is the better method. Therefore, companies should use the completed-contract method only when the percentage-of-completion method is inappropriate. We discuss the two methods in more detail in the following sections.

Percentage-of-Completion Method

OBJECTIVE 3
Apply the percentage-of-completion method for long-term contracts.

The **percentage-of-completion method** recognizes revenues, costs, and gross profit as a company makes progress toward completion on a long-term contract. To defer recognition of these items until completion of the entire contract is to misrepresent the efforts (costs) and accomplishments (revenues) of the accounting periods during the contract. In order to apply the percentage-of-completion method, a company must have some basis or standard for measuring the progress toward completion at particular interim dates.

Measuring the Progress toward Completion

As one practicing accountant wrote, "The big problem in applying the percentage-of-completion method . . . has to do with the ability to make reasonably accurate estimates of completion and the final gross profit."[20] Companies use various methods to determine the **extent of progress toward completion**. The most common are the *cost-to-cost* and *units-of-delivery* methods.[21]

The objective of all these methods is to measure the extent of progress in terms of costs, units, or value added. Companies identify the various measures (costs incurred, labor hours worked, tons produced, floors completed, etc.) and classify them as input or output measures. **Input measures** (costs incurred, labor hours worked) are efforts devoted to a contract. **Output measures** (with units of delivery measured as tons produced, floors of a building completed, miles of a highway completed) track results. Neither are universally applicable to all long-term projects. Their use requires the exercise of judgment and careful tailoring to the circumstances.

Both input and output measures have certain disadvantages. The input measure is based on an established relationship between a unit of input and productivity. If inefficiencies cause the productivity relationship to change, inaccurate measurements result. Another potential problem is front-end loading, in which significant up-front costs result in higher estimates of completion. To avoid this problem, companies should disregard some early-stage construction costs—for example, costs of uninstalled materials or costs of subcontracts not yet performed—if they do not relate to contract performance.

Similarly, output measures can produce inaccurate results if the units used are not comparable in time, effort, or cost to complete. For example, using floors (stories) completed can be deceiving. Completing the first floor of an eight-story building may require more than one-eighth the total cost because of the substructure and foundation construction.

The most popular input measure used to determine the progress toward completion is the **cost-to-cost basis**. Under this basis, a company like **EDS** measures the percentage of completion by comparing costs incurred to date with the most recent estimate of the total costs required to complete the contract. Illustration 16-3 shows the formula for the cost-to-cost basis.

---

[20]Richard S. Hickok, "New Guidance for Construction Contractors: 'A Credit Plus,'" *The Journal of Accountancy* (March 1982), p. 46.

[21]R. K. Larson and K. L. Brown, "Where Are We with Long-Term Contract Accounting?" *Accounting Horizons* (September 2004), pp. 207–219.

ILLUSTRATION 16-3
Formula for Percentage of Completion, Cost-to-Cost Basis

$$\frac{\text{Costs incurred to date}}{\text{Most recent estimate of total costs}} = \text{Percent complete}$$

Once EDS knows the percentage that costs incurred bear to total estimated costs, it applies that percentage to the total revenue or the estimated total gross profit on the contract. The resulting amount is the revenue or the gross profit to be recognized to date. Illustration 16-4 shows this computation.

ILLUSTRATION 16-4
Formula for Total Revenue to Be Recognized to Date

Percent complete	×	Estimated total revenue (or gross profit)	=	Revenue (or gross profit) to be recognized to date

To find the amounts of revenue and gross profit recognized each period, EDS subtracts total revenue or gross profit recognized in prior periods, as shown in Illustration 16-5.

ILLUSTRATION 16-5
Formula for Amount of Current-Period Revenue, Cost-to-Cost Basis

Revenue (or gross profit) to be recognized to date	−	Revenue (or gross profit) recognized in prior periods	=	Current-period revenue (or gross profit)

Because **the cost-to-cost method is widely used** (without excluding other bases for measuring progress toward completion), we have adopted it for use in our examples.[22]

Example of Percentage-of-Completion Method—Cost-to-Cost Basis

To illustrate the percentage-of-completion method, assume that Hardhat Construction Company has a contract to construct a $4,500,000 bridge at an estimated cost of $4,000,000. The contract is to start in July 2007, and the bridge is to be completed in October 2009. The following data pertain to the construction period. (Note that by the end of 2008 Hardhat has revised the estimated total cost from $4,000,000 to $4,050,000.)

	2007	2008	2009
Costs to date	$1,000,000	$2,916,000	$4,050,000
Estimated costs to complete	3,000,000	1,134,000	—
Progress billings during the year	900,000	2,400,000	1,200,000
Cash collected during the year	750,000	1,750,000	2,000,000

Hardhat would compute the percentage complete as shown in Illustration 16-6.

ILLUSTRATION 16-6
Application of Percentage-of-Completion Method, Cost-to-Cost Basis

	2007	2008	2009
Contract price	$4,500,000	$4,500,000	$4,500,000
Less estimated cost:			
Costs to date	1,000,000	2,916,000	4,050,000
Estimated costs to complete	3,000,000	1,134,000	—
Estimated total costs	4,000,000	4,050,000	4,050,000
Estimated total gross profit	$ 500,000	$ 450,000	$ 450,000
Percent complete	25%	72%	100%
	$\left(\frac{\$1,000,000}{\$4,000,000}\right)$	$\left(\frac{\$2,916,000}{\$4,050,000}\right)$	$\left(\frac{\$4,050,000}{\$4,050,000}\right)$

[22]Committee on Accounting Procedure, "Long-Term Construction-Type Contracts," *Accounting Research Bulletin No. 45* (New York: AICPA, 1955), p. 7.

On the basis of the data above, Hardhat would make the following entries to record (1) the costs of construction, (2) progress billings, and (3) collections. These entries appear as summaries of the many transactions that would be entered individually as they occur during the year.

ILLUSTRATION 16-7
Journal Entries—Percentage-of-Completion Method, Cost-to-Cost Basis

	2007		2008		2009	
To record cost of construction:						
Construction in Process	1,000,000		1,916,000		1,134,000	
Materials, Cash, Payables, etc.		1,000,000		1,916,000		1,134,000
To record progress billings:						
Accounts Receivable	900,000		2,400,000		1,200,000	
Billings on Construction in Process		900,000		2,400,000		1,200,000
To record collections:						
Cash	750,000		1,750,000		2,000,000	
Accounts Receivable		750,000		1,750,000		2,000,000

In this example, the costs incurred to date are a measure of the extent of progress toward completion. To determine this, Hardhat evaluates the costs incurred to date as a proportion of the estimated total costs to be incurred on the project. The estimated revenue and gross profit that Hardhat will recognize for each year are calculated as shown in Illustration 16-8.

ILLUSTRATION 16-8
Percentage-of-Completion, Revenue and Gross Profit, by Year

	2007	2008	2009
Revenue recognized in:			
2007 $4,500,000 × 25%	$1,125,000		
2008 $4,500,000 × 72%		$3,240,000	
Less: Revenue recognized in 2007		1,125,000	
Revenue in 2008		$2,115,000	
2009 $4,500,000 × 100%			$4,500,000
Less: Revenue recognized in 2007 and 2008			3,240,000
Revenue in 2009			$1,260,000
Gross profit recognized in:			
2007 $500,000 × 25%	$ 125,000		
2008 $450,000 × 72%		$ 324,000	
Less: Gross profit recognized in 2007		125,000	
Gross profit in 2008		$ 199,000	
2009 $450,000 × 100%			$ 450,000
Less: Gross profit recognized in 2007 and 2008			324,000
Gross profit in 2009			$ 126,000

Illustration 16-9 shows Hardhat's entries to recognize revenue and gross profit each year and to record completion and final approval of the contract.

ILLUSTRATION 16-9
Journal Entries to Recognize Revenue and Gross Profit and to Record Contract Completion—Percentage-of-Completion Method, Cost-to-Cost Basis

	2007		2008		2009	
To recognize revenue and gross profit:						
Construction in Process (gross profit)	125,000		199,000		126,000	
Construction Expenses	1,000,000		1,916,000		1,134,000	
Revenue from Long-Term Contract		1,125,000		2,115,000		1,260,000
To record completion of the contract:						
Billings on Construction in Process					4,500,000	
Construction in Process						4,500,000

Note that Hardhat debits gross profit (as computed in Illustration 16-8) to Construction in Process. Similarly, it credits Revenue from Long-Term Contract for the amounts computed in Illustration 16-8. Hardhat then debits the difference between the amounts recognized each year for revenue and gross profit to a nominal account, Construction Expenses (similar to Cost of Goods Sold in a manufacturing company). It reports that amount in the income statement as the actual cost of construction incurred in that period. For example, Hardhat uses the actual costs of $1,000,000 to compute both the gross profit of $125,000 and the percent complete (25 percent).

Hardhat continues to accumulate costs in the Construction in Process account, in order to maintain a record of total costs incurred (plus recognized profit) to date. Although theoretically a series of "sales" takes place using the percentage-of-completion method, the selling company cannot remove the inventory cost until the construction is completed and transferred to the new owner. Hardhat's Construction in Process account for the bridge would include the following summarized entries over the term of the construction project.

ILLUSTRATION 16-10
Content of Construction in Process Account—Percentage-of-Completion Method

Construction in Process				
2007 construction costs	$1,000,000	12/31/09	to close completed project	$4,500,000
2007 recognized gross profit	125,000			
2008 construction costs	1,916,000			
2008 recognized gross profit	199,000			
2009 construction costs	1,134,000			
2009 recognized gross profit	126,000			
Total	$4,500,000	Total		$4,500,000

Recall that the Hardhat Construction Company example contained a **change in estimate**: In the second year, 2008, it increased the estimated total costs from $4,000,000 to $4,050,000. The change in estimate is accounted for in a **cumulative catch-up manner.** This is done by, first, adjusting the percent completed to the new estimate of total costs. Next, Hardhat deducts the amount of revenues and gross profit recognized in prior periods from revenues and gross profit computed for progress to date. That is, it accounts for the change in estimate in the period of change. That way, the balance sheet at the end of the period of change and the accounting in subsequent periods are as they would have been if the revised estimate had been the original estimate.

Financial Statement Presentation—Percentage-of-Completion

Generally when a company records a receivable from a sale, it reduces the Inventory account. Under the percentage-of-completion method, however, the company continues to carry both the receivable and the inventory. Subtracting the balance in the **Billings account** from Construction in Process avoids double-counting the inventory. During the life of the contract, Hardhat reports in the balance sheet the difference between the

Construction in Process and the Billings on Construction in Process accounts. If that amount is a debit, Hardhat reports it **as a current asset**; if it is a credit, it reports it **as a current liability**.

At times, the costs incurred plus the gross profit recognized to date (the balance in Construction in Process) exceed the billings. In that case, Hardhat reports this excess as a current asset entitled "Cost and recognized profit in excess of billings." Hardhat can at any time calculate the unbilled portion of revenue recognized to date by subtracting the billings to date from the revenue recognized to date, as illustrated for 2007 for Hardhat Construction in Illustration 16-11.

ILLUSTRATION 16-11
Computation of Unbilled Contract Price at 12/31/07

Contract revenue recognized to date: $\$4{,}500{,}000 \times \dfrac{\$1{,}000{,}000}{\$4{,}000{,}000}$	$1,125,000
Billings to date	900,000
Unbilled revenue	$ 225,000

At other times, the billings exceed costs incurred and gross profit to date. In that case, Hardhat reports this excess as a current liability entitled "Billings in excess of costs and recognized profit."

It probably has occurred to you that companies often have more than one project going at a time. When a company has a number of projects, costs exceed billings on some contracts and billings exceed costs on others. In such a case, the company segregates the contracts. The asset side includes only those contracts on which costs and recognized profit exceed billings. The liability side includes only those on which billings exceed costs and recognized profit. Separate disclosures of the dollar volume of billings and costs are preferable to a summary presentation of the net difference.

Using data from the bridge example, Hardhat Construction Company would report the status and results of its long-term construction activities under the perentage-of-completion method as shown in Illustration 16-12.

ILLUSTRATION 16-12
Financial Statement Presentation—Percentage-of-Completion Method

HARDHAT CONSTRUCTION COMPANY

		2007	2008	2009
Income Statement				
Revenue from long-term contracts		$1,125,000	$2,115,000	$1,260,000
Costs of construction		1,000,000	1,916,000	1,134,000
Gross profit		$ 125,000	$ 199,000	$ 126,000
Balance Sheet (12/31)				
Current assets				
Accounts receivable		$ 150,000	$ 800,000	
Inventories				
Construction in process	$1,125,000			
Less: Billings	900,000			
Costs and recognized profit in excess of billings		225,000		
Current liabilities				
Billings ($3,300,000) in excess of costs and recognized profit ($3,240,000)			$ 60,000	

Note 1. Summary of significant accounting policies.
Long-Term Construction Contracts. The company recognizes revenues and reports profits from long-term construction contracts, its principal business, under the percentage-of-completion method of accounting. These contracts generally extend for periods in excess of one year. The amounts of revenues and profits recognized each year are based on the ratio of costs incurred to the total estimated costs. Costs included in construction in process include direct materials, direct labor, and project-related overhead. Corporate general and administrative expenses are charged to the periods as incurred and are not allocated to construction contracts.

Completed-Contract Method

OBJECTIVE 4
Apply the completed-contract method for long-term contracts.

Under the **completed-contract method**, companies recognize revenue and gross profit only at point of sale—that is, when the contract is completed. Under this method, companies accumulate costs of long-term contracts in process, but they make no interim charges or credits to income statement accounts for revenues, costs, or gross profit.

The principal advantage of the completed-contract method is that reported revenue reflects final results rather than *estimates* of unperformed work. Its major disadvantage is that it does not reflect current performance when the period of a contract extends into more than one accounting period. Although operations may be fairly uniform during the period of the contract, the company will not report revenue until the year of completion, creating a distortion of earnings.

UNDERLYING CONCEPTS

The completed-contract method does not violate the *matching concept* because the costs are also deferred until the completion of the contract.

Under the completed-contract method, the company would make the same **annual entries** to record costs of construction, progress billings, and collections from customers as those illustrated under the percentage-of-completion method. The significant difference is that the company **would not make entries to recognize revenue and gross profit.**

For example, under the completed-contract method for the bridge project illustrated on the preceding pages, Hardhat Construction Company would make the following entries in 2009 to recognize revenue and costs and to close out the inventory and billing accounts.

Billings on Construction in Process	4,500,000	
Revenue from Long-Term Contracts		4,500,000
Costs of Construction	4,050,000	
Construction in Process		4,050,000

Illustration 16-13 compares the amount of gross profit that Hardhat Construction Company would recognize for the bridge project under the two revenue-recognition methods.

ILLUSTRATION 16-13
Comparison of Gross Profit Recognized under Different Methods

	Percentage-of-Completion	Completed-Contract
2007	$125,000	$ 0
2008	199,000	0
2009	126,000	450,000

Under the completed-contract method, Hardhat Construction would report its long-term construction activities as follows.

ILLUSTRATION 16-14
Financial Statement Presentation—Completed-Contract Method

HARDHAT CONSTRUCTION COMPANY

		2007	2008	2009
Income Statement				
Revenue from long-term contracts		—	—	$4,500,000
Costs of construction		—	—	4,050,000
Gross profit		—	—	$ 450,000

		2007	2008	2009
Balance Sheet (12/31)				
Current assets				
Accounts receivable		$150,000	$800,000	
Inventories				
Construction in process	$1,000,000			
Less: Billings	900,000			
Unbilled contract costs		100,000		
Current liabilities				
Billings ($3,300,000) in excess of contract costs ($2,916,000)			$384,000	

Note 1. Summary of significant accounting policies.
Long-Term Construction Contracts. The company recognizes revenues and reports profits from long-term construction contracts, its principal business, under the completed-contract method. These contracts generally extend for periods in excess of one year. Contract costs and billings are accumulated during the periods of construction, but no revenues or profits are recognized until completion of the contract. Costs included in construction in process include direct material, direct labor, and project-related overhead. Corporate general and administrative expenses are charged to the periods as incurred.

Long-Term Contract Losses

Two types of losses can become evident under long-term contracts:[23]

OBJECTIVE 5
Identify the proper accounting for losses on long-term contracts.

1. *Loss in the Current Period on a Profitable Contract.* This condition arises when, during construction, there is a significant increase in the estimated total contract costs but the increase does not eliminate all profit on the contract. Under the percentage-of-completion method only, the estimated cost increase requires a current-period adjustment of excess gross profit recognized on the project in prior periods. The company records this adjustment as a loss in the current period because it is a **change in accounting estimate** (discussed in Chapter 18).
2. *Loss on an Unprofitable Contract.* Cost estimates at the end of the current period may indicate that a loss will result on completion of the *entire* contract. Under both the percentage-of-completion and the completed-contract methods, the company must recognize in the current period the entire expected contract loss.

The treatment described for unprofitable contracts is consistent with the accounting custom of anticipating foreseeable losses to avoid overstatement of current and future income (conservatism).

UNDERLYING CONCEPTS

Conservatism justifies recognizing the losses immediately. Loss recognition does not require *realization;* it only requires evidence that an impairment of asset value has occurred.

Loss in Current Period

To illustrate a loss in the current period on a contract expected to be profitable upon completion, we'll continue with the Hardhat Construction Company bridge project. Assume that on December 31, 2008, Hardhat estimates the costs to complete the bridge contract at $1,468,962 instead of $1,134,000. Assuming all other data are the same as before, Hardhat would compute the percentage complete and recognize the loss as shown in Illustration 16-15. Compare these computations with those for 2008 in Illustration 16-6. The "percent complete" has dropped, from 72 percent to 66½ percent, due to the increase in estimated future costs to complete the contract.

ILLUSTRATION 16-15
Computation of Recognizable Loss, 2008—Loss in Current Period

Cost to date (12/31/08)	$2,916,000
Estimated costs to complete (revised)	1,468,962
Estimated total costs	$4,384,962
Percent complete ($2,916,000 ÷ $4,384,962)	66½%
Revenue recognized in 2008	
($4,500,000 × 66½%) − $1,125,000	$1,867,500
Costs incurred in 2008	1,916,000
Loss recognized in 2008	$ 48,500

The 2008 loss of $48,500 is a cumulative adjustment of the "excessive" gross profit recognized on the contract in 2007. Instead of restating the prior period, the company absorbs the prior period misstatement entirely in the current period. In this illustration, the adjustment was large enough to result in recognition of a loss.

Hardhat Construction would record the loss in 2008 as follows.

Construction Expenses	1,916,000	
Construction in Process (loss)		48,500
Revenue from Long-Term Contract		1,867,500

Hardhat will report the loss of $48,500 on the 2008 income statement as the difference between the reported revenues of $1,867,500 and the costs of $1,916,000.[24] **Under**

[23]Sak Bhamornsiri, "Losses from Construction Contracts," *The Journal of Accountancy* (April 1982), p. 26.

[24]In 2009 Hardhat Construction will recognize the remaining 33½ percent of the revenue ($1,507,500), with costs of $1,468,962 as expected, and will report a gross profit of $38,538. The total gross profit over the three years of the contract would be $115,038 [$125,000 (2007) − $48,500 (2008) + $38,538 (2009)]. This amount is the difference between the total contract revenue of $4,500,000 and the total contract costs of $4,384,962.

the completed-contract method, the company does not recognize a loss in 2008. Why not? Because the company still expects the contract **to result in a profit,** to be recognized in the year of completion.

Loss on an Unprofitable Contract

To illustrate the accounting for an **overall loss on a long-term contract,** assume that at December 31, 2008, Hardhat Construction Company estimates the costs to complete the bridge contract at $1,640,250 instead of $1,134,000. Revised estimates for the bridge contract are as follows.

	2007	2008
	Original Estimates	Revised Estimates
Contract price	$4,500,000	$4,500,000
Estimated total cost	4,000,000	4,556,250*
Estimated gross profit	$ 500,000	
Estimated loss		$ (56,250)

*($2,916,000 + $1,640,250)

Under the percentage-of-completion method, Hardhat recognized $125,000 of gross profit in 2007 (see Illustration 16-8). This amount must be offset in 2008 because it is no longer expected to be realized. In addition, since losses must be recognized as soon as estimable, the company must recognize the total estimated loss of $56,250 in 2008. Therefore, Hardhat must recognize a total loss of $181,250 ($125,000 + $56,250) in 2008.

Illustration 16-16 shows Hardhat's computation of the revenue to be recognized in 2008.

ILLUSTRATION 16-16
Computation of Revenue Recognizable, 2008—Unprofitable Contract

Revenue recognized in 2008:		
Contract price		$4,500,000
Percent complete		× 64%*
Revenue recognizable to date		2,880,000
Less: Revenue recognized prior to 2008		1,125,000
Revenue recognized in 2008		$1,755,000
*Cost to date (12/31/08)	$2,916,000	
Estimated cost to complete	1,640,250	
Estimated total costs	$4,556,250	
Percent complete: $2,916,000 ÷ $4,556,250 = 64%		

To compute the construction costs to be expensed in 2008, Hardhat adds the total loss to be recognized in 2008 ($125,000 + $56,250) to the revenue to be recognized in 2008. Illustration 16-17 shows this computation.

ILLUSTRATION 16-17
Computation of Construction Expense, 2008—Unprofitable Contract

Revenue recognized in 2008 (computed above)		$1,755,000
Total loss recognized in 2008:		
Reversal of 2007 gross profit	$125,000	
Total estimated loss on the contract	56,250	181,250
Construction cost expensed in 2008		$1,936,250

Hardhat Construction would record the long-term contract revenues, expenses, and loss in 2008 as follows.

Construction Expenses	1,936,250	
Construction in Process (Loss)		181,250
Revenue from Long-Term Contracts		1,755,000

At the end of 2008, Construction in Process has a balance of $2,859,750 as shown below.[25]

ILLUSTRATION 16-18
Content of Construction in Process Account at End of 2008—Unprofitable Contract

Construction in Process			
2007 Construction costs	1,000,000		
2007 Recognized gross profit	125,000		
2008 Construction costs	1,916,000	2008 Recognized loss	181,250
Balance	**2,859,750**		

Under the completed-contract method, Hardhat also would recognize the contract loss of $56,250, through the following entry in 2008 (the year in which the loss first became evident).

Loss from Long-Term Contracts	56,250	
Construction in Process (Loss)		56,250

Just as the Billings account balance cannot exceed the contract price, neither can the balance in Construction in Process exceed the contract price. In circumstances where the Construction in Process balance exceeds the billings the company can deduct the recognized loss from such accumulated costs on the balance sheet. That is, under both the percentage-of-completion and the completed-contract methods, the provision for the loss (the credit) may be combined with Construction in Process, thereby reducing the inventory balance. In those circumstances, however (as in the 2008 example above), where the billings exceed the accumulated costs, Hardhat must report separately on the balance sheet, as a current liability, the amount of the estimated loss. That is, under both the percentage-of-completion and the completed-contract methods, Hardhat would take the $56,250 loss, as estimated in 2008, from the Construction in Process account and report it separately as a current liability titled "Estimated liability from long-term contracts."[26]

Disclosures in Financial Statements

Construction contractors usually make some unique financial statement disclosures in addition to those required of all businesses. Generally these additional disclosures are made in the notes to the financial statements. For example, a construction contractor should disclose the following: the method of recognizing revenue,[27] the basis used to classify assets and liabilities as current (the nature and length of the operating cycle), the basis for recording inventory, the effects of any revision of estimates, the amount

[25]If the costs in 2009 are $1,640,250 as projected, at the end of 2009 the Construction in Process account will have a balance of $1,640,250 + $2,859,750, or $4,500,000, equal to the contract price. When the company matches the revenue remaining to be recognized in 2009 of $1,620,000 [$4,500,000 (total contract price) − $1,125,000 (2007) − $1,755,000 (2008)] with the construction expense to be recognized in 2009 of $1,620,000 [total costs of $4,556,250 less the total costs recognized in prior years of $2,936,250 (2007, $1,000,000; 2008, $1,936,250)], a zero profit results. Thus the total loss has been recognized in 2008, the year in which it first became evident.

[26]*Construction Contractors,* Audit and Accounting Guide (New York: AICPA, 1981), pp. 148–149.

[27]Ibid., p. 30.

of backlog on uncompleted contracts, and the details about receivables (billed and unbilled, maturity, interest rates, retainage provisions, and significant individual or group concentrations of credit risk).

WHAT DO THE NUMBERS MEAN?

LESS CONSERVATIVE

Halliburton provides engineering- and construction-related services, in jobs around the world. Much of the company's work is completed under contract over long periods of time. The company uses percentage-of-completion accounting. Recently the SEC started enforcement proceedings against the company related to its accounting for contract claims and disagreements with customers, including those arising from change orders and disputes about billable amounts and costs associated with a construction delay.

Prior to 1998 Halliburton took a very conservative approach to its accounting for disputed claims. As stated in the company's 1997 annual report, "Claims for additional compensation are recognized during the period such claims are resolved." That is, the company waited until all disputes were resolved before recognizing associated revenues. In contrast, in 1998 the company recognized revenue for disputed claims before their resolution, using estimates of amounts expected to be recovered. Such revenue and its related profit are more tentative and are subject to possible later adjustment than revenue and profit recognized when all claims have been resolved. As a case in point, the company noted that it incurred losses of $99 million in 1998 related to customer claims.

The accounting method put in place in 1998 is more aggressive than the company's former policy, but it is still within the boundaries of generally accepted accounting principles. However, the SEC noted that over six quarters, Halliburton failed to disclose its change in accounting practice. In the absence of any disclosure the SEC believed the investing public was misled about the precise nature of Halliburton's income in comparison to prior periods. The Halliburton situation illustrates the difficulty of using estimates in percentage-of-completion accounting and the impact of those estimates on the financial statements.

Source: "Failure to Disclose a 1998 Change in Accounting Practice," SEC (August 3, 2004), *www.sec.gov/news/press/2004-104.htm*. See also "Accounting Ace Charles Mulford Answers Accounting Questions," *Wall Street Journal Online* (June 7, 2002).

Completion-of-Production Basis

UNDERLYING CONCEPTS

This is not an exception to the revenue recognition principle. At the completion of production, realization is virtually assured and the earning process is substantially completed.

In certain cases companies recognize revenue at the completion of **production** even though no sale has been made. Examples of such situations involve precious metals or agricultural products with assured prices. Under the **completion-of-production basis**, companies recognize revenue when these metals are mined or agricultural crops harvested because the sales price is reasonably assured, the units are interchangeable, and no significant costs are involved in distributing the product.[28] (See discussion in Chapter 8, "Valuation at Net Realizable Value")

Likewise, when sale or cash receipt precedes production and delivery, as in the case of magazine subscriptions, companies recognize revenues as earned by production and delivery.[29]

[28]Such revenue satisfies the criteria of *Concepts Statement No. 5* since the assets are readily realizable and the earning process is virtually complete (see par. 84, item c).

[29]*Statement of Financial Accounting Concepts No. 5*, par. 84, item b.

REVENUE RECOGNITION AFTER DELIVERY

In some cases, the collection of the sales price is not reasonably assured and revenue recognition is deferred. One of two methods is generally employed to defer revenue recognition until the company receives cash: the **installment-sales method** or the **cost-recovery method**. A third method, the **deposit method**, applies in situations in which a company receives cash prior to delivery or transfer of the property; the company records that receipt as a deposit because the sale transaction is incomplete. This section examines these three methods.

Installment-Sales Accounting Method

OBJECTIVE 6
Describe the installment-sales method of accounting.

The **installment-sales method** recognizes income in the periods of collection rather than in the period of sale. The logic underlying this method is that when there is no reasonable approach for estimating the degree of collectibility, companies should not recognize revenue until cash is collected.

The expression "installment sales" generally describes any type of sale for which payment is required in periodic installments over an extended period of time. All types of farm and home equipment as well as home furnishings are sold on an installment basis. The heavy equipment industry also sometimes uses the method for machine installations paid for over a long period. Another application of the method is in land-development sales.

UNDERLYING CONCEPTS

Realization is a critical part of revenue recognition. Thus, if a high degree of uncertainty exists about collectibility, a company must defer revenue recognition.

Because payment is spread over a relatively long period, the risk of loss resulting from uncollectible accounts is greater in installment-sales transactions than in ordinary sales. Consequently, selling companies use various devices to protect themselves. Two common devices are: (1) the use of a *conditional sales contract*, which specifies that title to the item sold does not pass to the purchaser until all payments are made, and (2) use of notes secured by a *chattel* (personal property) *mortgage* on the article sold. Either of these permits the seller to "repossess" the goods sold if the purchaser defaults on one or more payments. The seller can then resell the repossessed merchandise at whatever price it will bring to compensate for the uncollected installments and the expense of repossession.

Under the installment-sales method of accounting, companies defer income recognition until the period of cash collection. They recognize both revenues and costs of sales in the period of sale, but defer the related gross profit to those periods in which they collect the cash. Thus, **instead of deferring the sale, along with related costs and expenses, to the future periods of anticipated collection, the company defers only the proportional gross profit.** This approach is equivalent to deferring both sales and cost of sales. Other expenses—that is, selling expense, administrative expense, and so on—are not deferred.

Thus, the installment-sales method matches cost and expenses against sales through the gross profit figure, but no further. Companies using the installment-sales method generally record operating expenses without regard to the fact that they will defer some portion of the year's gross profit. This practice is often justified on the basis that (1) these expenses do not follow sales as closely as does the cost of goods sold, and (2) accurate apportionment among periods would be so difficult that it could not be justified by the benefits gained.[30]

INTERNATIONAL INSIGHT

In Japan, installment method accounting is frequently used whenever the collection period exceeds two years, whether or not there is any uncertainty with regard to the collectibility of cash.

Acceptability of the Installment-Sales Method

The use of the installment-sales method for revenue recognition has fluctuated widely. At one time it was widely accepted for installment-sales transactions. Somewhat paradoxically, as installment-sales transactions increased in popularity, acceptance and

[30]In addition, other theoretical deficiencies of the installment-sales method could be cited. For example, see Richard A. Scott and Rita K. Scott, "Installment Accounting: Is It Inconsistent?" *The Journal of Accountancy* (November 1979).

use of the installment-sales method decreased. Finally the profession concluded that except in special circumstances, "the installment method of recognizing revenue is not acceptable."[31] The rationale for this position is simple: Because the installment method recognizes no income until cash is collected, it is not in accordance with the accrual accounting concept.

Use of the installment-sales method was often justified on the grounds that the risk of not collecting an account receivable may be so great that the sale itself is not sufficient evidence that recognition should occur. In some cases, this reasoning is valid, but not in a majority of cases. The general approach is that a company should recognize a completed sale. If the company expects bad debts, it should record this possibility as separate estimates of uncollectibles. Although collection expenses, repossession expenses, and bad debts are an unavoidable part of installment-sales activities, the incurrence of these costs and the collectibility of the receivables are reasonably predictable.

We study this topic in intermediate accounting because the method is acceptable in cases where a company believes there to be no reasonable basis of estimating the degree of collectibility. In addition, the sales method of revenue recognition has certain weaknesses when used for franchise and land-development operations. Application of the sales method to **franchise and license operations** has resulted in the abuse described earlier as "front-end loading." In some cases, franchisors recognized revenue prematurely, when they granted a franchise or issued a license, rather than when revenue was earned or the cash is received. Many **land-development** ventures were susceptible to the same abuses. As a result, the FASB prescribes application of the installment-sales method of accounting for sales of real estate under certain circumstances.[32]

Procedure for Deferring Revenue and Cost of Sales of Merchandise

One could work out a procedure that deferred both the uncollected portion of the sales price and the proportionate part of the cost of the goods sold. Instead of apportioning both sales price and cost over the period of collection, however, the installment-sales method defers **only the gross profit**. This procedure has exactly the same effect as deferring both sales and cost of sales, but it requires only one deferred account rather than two.

For the **sales in any one year**, the steps companies use to defer gross profit are as follows.

1. During the year, record both sales and cost of sales in the regular way, using the special accounts described later, and compute the rate of gross profit on installment-sales transactions.
2. At the end of the year, apply the rate of gross profit to the cash collections of the current year's installment sales, to arrive at the realized gross profit.
3. Defer to future years the gross profit not realized.

For **sales made in prior years**, companies apply the gross profit rate of each year's sales against cash collections of accounts receivable resulting from that year's sales, to arrive at the realized gross profit.

---

[31] "Omnibus Opinion," *Opinions of the Accounting Principles Board No. 10* (New York: AICPA, 1966), par. 12.

[32] "Accounting for Sales of Real Estate," *Statement of Financial Accounting Standards No. 66* (Norwalk, Conn.: FASB, 1982), pars. 45–47. The installment-sales method of accounting must be applied to a retail land sale that meets **all** of the following criteria: (1) the period of cancellation of the sale with refund of the down payment and any subsequent payments has expired; (2) cumulative cash payments equal or exceed 10 percent of the sales value; and (3) the seller is financially capable of providing all promised contract representations (e.g., land improvements, off-site facilities).

Special accounts must be used in the installment-sales method. These accounts provide certain special information required to determine the realized and unrealized gross profit in each year of operations. In computing net income under the installment-sales method as generally applied, the only peculiarity is the **deferral of gross profit until realized by accounts receivable collection.** We will use the following data to illustrate the installment-sales method in accounting for the sales of merchandise.

	2007	2008	2009
Installment sales	$200,000	$250,000	$240,000
Cost of installment sales	150,000	190,000	168,000
Gross profit	$ 50,000	$ 60,000	$ 72,000
Rate of gross profit on sales	25%[a]	24%[b]	30%[c]
Cash receipts			
2007 sales	$ 60,000	$100,000	$ 40,000
2008 sales		100,000	125,000
2009 sales			80,000

[a] $\frac{\$50,000}{\$200,000}$ [b] $\frac{\$60,000}{\$250,000}$ [c] $\frac{\$72,000}{\$240,000}$

To simplify this example, we have excluded interest charges. Summary entries in general journal form for the year 2007 are as follows.

2007

Installment Accounts Receivable, 2007	200,000	
Installment Sales		200,000
(To record sales made on installment in 2007)		
Cash	60,000	
Installment Accounts Receivable, 2007		60,000
(To record cash collected on installment receivables)		
Cost of Installment Sales	150,000	
Inventory (or Purchases)		150,000
(To record cost of goods sold on installment in 2007 on either a perpetual or a periodic inventory basis)		
Installment Sales	200,000	
Cost of Installment Sales		150,000
Deferred Gross Profit, 2007		50,000
(To close installment sales and cost of installment sales for the year)		
Deferred Gross Profit	15,000	
Realized Gross Profit on Installment Sales		15,000
(To remove from deferred gross profit the profit realized through cash collections; $60,000 × 25%)		
Realized Gross Profit on Installment Sales	15,000	
Income Summary		15,000
(To close profits realized by collections)		

Illustration 16-19 shows computation of the realized and deferred gross profit for the year 2007.

ILLUSTRATION 16-19
Computation of Realized and Deferred Gross Profit, 2007

2007

Rate of gross profit current year	25%
Cash collected on current year's sales	$60,000
Realized gross profit (25% of $60,000)	15,000
Gross profit to be deferred ($50,000 − $15,000)	35,000

Summary entries in journal form for year 2 (2008) are as follows.

2008		
Installment Accounts Receivable, 2008	250,000	
Installment Sales		250,000
(To record sales made on installment in 2008)		
Cash	200,000	
Installment Accounts Receivable, 2007		100,000
Installment Accounts Receivable, 2008		100,000
(To record cash collected on installment receivables)		
Cost of Installment Sales	190,000	
Inventory (or Purchases)		190,000
(To record cost of goods sold on installment in 2008)		
Installment Sales	250,000	
Cost of Installment Sales		190,000
Deferred Gross Profit, 2008		60,000
(To close installment sales and cost of installment sales for the year)		
Deferred Gross Profit, 2007 ($100,000 × 25%)	25,000	
Deferred Gross Profit, 2008 ($100,000 × 24%)	24,000	
Realized Gross Profit on Installment Sales		49,000
(To remove from deferred gross profit the profit realized through cash collections)		
Realized Gross Profit on Installment Sales	49,000	
Income Summary		49,000
(To close profits realized by collections)		

Illustration 16-20 shows computation of the realized and deferred gross profit for the year 2008.

ILLUSTRATION 16-20
Computation of Realized and Deferred Gross Profit, 2008

2008	
Current year's sales	
Rate of gross profit	24%
Cash collected on current year's sales	$100,000
Realized gross profit (24% of $100,000)	24,000
Gross profit to be deferred ($60,000 − $24,000)	36,000
Prior year's sales	
Rate of gross profit—2007	25%
Cash collected on 2007 sales	$100,000
Gross profit realized in 2008 on 2007 sales (25% of $100,000)	25,000
Total gross profit realized in 2008	
Realized on collections of 2007 sales	$ 25,000
Realized on collections of 2008 sales	24,000
Total	$ 49,000

The entries in 2009 would be similar to those of 2008, and the total gross profit taken up or realized would be $64,000, as shown by the computations in Illustration 16-21.

In summary, here are the basic concepts you should understand about accounting for installment sales:

1. How to compute a proper gross profit percentage.
2. How to record installment sales, cost of installment sales, and deferred gross profit.
3. How to compute realized gross profit on installment receivables.
4. How the deferred gross profit balance at the end of the year results from applying the gross profit rate to the installment accounts receivable.

2009	
Current year's sales	
Rate of gross profit	30%
Cash collected on current year's sales	$ 80,000
Gross profit realized on 2009 sales (30% of $80,000)	24,000
Gross profit to be deferred ($72,000 − $24,000)	48,000
Prior years' sales	
2007 sales	
Rate of gross profit	25%
Cash collected	$ 40,000
Gross profit realized in 2009 on 2007 sales (25% of $40,000)	10,000
2008 sales	
Rate of gross profit	24%
Cash collected	$125,000
Gross profit realized in 2009 on 2008 sales (24% of $125,000)	30,000
Total gross profit realized in 2009	
Realized on collections of 2007 sales	$ 10,000
Realized on collections of 2008 sales	30,000
Realized on collections of 2009 sales	24,000
Total	$ 64,000

ILLUSTRATION 16-21
Computation of Realized and Deferred Gross Profit, 2009

Additional Problems of Installment-Sales Accounting

In addition to computing realized and deferred gross profit currently, other problems are involved in accounting for installment-sales transactions. These problems are related to:

1. Interest on installment contracts.
2. Uncollectible accounts.
3. Defaults and repossessions.

Interest on Installment Contracts. Because the collection of installment receivables is spread over a long period, it is customary to charge the buyer interest on the unpaid balance. The seller and buyer set up a schedule of equal payments consisting of interest and principal. Each successive payment is attributable to a smaller amount of interest and a corresondingly larger amount of principal, as shown in Illustration 16-22. This illustration assumes that a company sells for $3,000 an asset costing $2,400 (rate of gross profit = 20%), with interest of 8 percent included in the three installments of $1,164.10.

Date	Cash (Debit)	Interest Earned (Credit)	Installment Receivables (Credit)	Installment Unpaid Balance	Realized Gross Profit (20%)
1/2/07	—	—	—	$3,000.00	—
1/2/08	$1,164.10[a]	$240.00[b]	$ 924.10[c]	2,075.90[d]	$184.82[e]
1/2/09	1,164.10	166.07	998.03	1,077.87	199.61
1/2/10	1,164.10	86.23	1,077.87	-0-	215.57
					$600.00

[a]Periodic payment = Original unpaid balance ÷ PV of an annuity of $1.00 for three periods at 8%; $1,164.10 = $3,000 ÷ 2.57710.
[b]$3,000.00 × .08 = $240.
[c]$1,164.10 − $240.00 = $924.10.
[d]$3,000.00 − $924.10 = $2,075.90.
[e]$924.10 × .20 = $184.82.

ILLUSTRATION 16-22
Installment Payment Schedule

The company accounts for interest separate from the gross profit recognized on the installment-sales collections during the period, by recognizing interest revenue at the time of its cash receipt.

Uncollectible Accounts. The problem of bad debts or uncollectible accounts receivable is somewhat different for concerns selling on an installment basis because of a repossession feature commonly incorporated in the sales agreement. This feature gives the selling company an opportunity to recoup an uncollectible account through repossession and resale of repossessed merchandise. If the experience of the company indicates that repossessions do not, as a rule, compensate for uncollecible balances, it may be advisable to provide for such losses through charges to a special bad debt expense account, just as is done for other credit sales.

Defaults and Repossessions. Depending on the terms of the sales contract and the policy of the credit department, the seller can repossess merchandise sold under an installment arrangement if the purchaser fails to meet payment requirements. The seller may then recondition repossessed merchandise before offering it for re-sale, for cash or installment payments.

The accounting for **repossessions** recognizes that the company is not likely to collect the related installment receivable and should write it off. Along with the installment account receivable, the company must remove the applicable deferred gross profit using the following entry:

Repossessed Merchandise (an inventory account)	xxx	
Deferred Gross Profit	xxx	
Installment Accounts Receivable		xxx

This entry assumes that the company will record the repossessed merchandise at exactly the amount of the uncollected account less the deferred gross profit applicable. This assumption may or may not be proper. To determine the correct amount, the company should consider the condition of the repossessed merchandise, the cost of reconditioning, and the market for second-hand merchandise of that particular type. The objective should be to put any asset acquired on the books at its fair value, or at the best possible approximation of fair value when fair value is not determinable. A loss can occur if the fair value of the repossessed merchandise is less than the uncollected balance less the deferred gross profit. In that case, the company should record a "loss on repossession" at the date of repossession.[33]

To illustrate the required entry, assume that Klein Brothers sells a refrigerator to Marilyn Hunt for $1,500 on September 1, 2007. Terms require a down payment of $600 and $60 on the first of every month for 15 months, starting October 1, 2007. It is further assumed that the refrigerator cost $900, and that Klein Brothers priced it to provide a 40 percent rate of gross profit on selling price. At the year-end, December 31, 2007, Klein Brothers should have collected a total of $180 in addition to the original down payment.

If Hunt makes her January and February payments in 2008 and then defaults, the account balances applicable to Hunt at time of default are as shown in Illustration 16-23.

ILLUSTRATION 16-23
Computation of Installment Receivable Balances

Installment accounts receivable (September 1, 2007)		$1,500
Less: Down payment:	$600	
Payments to date ($60 × 5)	300	900
Installment accounts receivable (March 1, 2008)		$ 600
Installment accounts receivable (March 1, 2008)		$600
Gross profit rate		× 40%
Deferred gross profit		$240

[33]Some contend that a company should record repossessed merchandise at a valuation that will permit the company to make its regular rate of gross profit on resale. If the company enters the value at its approximated cost to purchase, the regular rate of gross profit could be provided for upon its ultimate sale, but that is completely a secondary consideration. It is more important that the company record the repossessed asset at fair value. This accounting would be in accordance with the general practice of carrying assets at acquisition price, as represented by the fair market value at the date of acquisition.

As indicated, Klein Brothers compute the balance of deferred gross profit applicable to Hunt's account by applying the gross profit rate for the year of sale to the balance of Hunt's account receivable: 40 percent of $600, or $240. The account balances are therefore:

Installment Account Receivable, 2007	600 (dr.)
Deferred Gross Profit, 2007	240 (cr.)

Klein repossesses the refrigerator following Hunt's default. If Klein sets the estimated fair value of the repossessed article at $150, it would make the following entry to record the repossession.

Deferred Gross Profit, 2007	240	
Repossessed Merchandise	150	
Loss on Repossession	210	
Installment Accounts Receivable, 2007		600

Klein determines the amount of the loss in two steps: (1) It subtracts the deferred gross profit from the amount of the account receivable, to determine the unrecovered cost (or book value) of the merchandise repossessed. (2) It then subtracts the estimated fair value of the merchandise repossessed from the unrecovered cost, to get the amount of the loss on repossession. Klein Brothers computes the loss on the refrigerator as shown in Illustration 16-24.

ILLUSTRATION 16-24
Computation of Loss on Repossession

Balance of account receivable (representing uncollected selling price)	$600
Less: Deferred gross profit	240
Unrecovered cost	360
Less: Estimated fair value of merchandise repossessed	150
Loss (Gain) on repossession	$210

As pointed out earlier, the loss on repossession may be charged to Allowance for Doubtful Accounts if a company carries such an account.

Financial Statement Presentation of Installment-Sales Transactions

If installment-sales transactions represent a significant part of total sales, it is desirable to make full disclosure of installment sales, the cost of installment sales, and any expenses allocable to installment sales. However, if installment-sales transactions constitute an insignificant part of total sales, it may be satisfactory to include only the realized gross profit in the income statement as a special item following the gross profit on sales. Illustration 16-25 shows this simpler presentation.

ILLUSTRATION 16-25
Disclosure of Installment-Sales Transactions—Insignificant Amount

HEALTH MACHINE COMPANY
INCOME STATEMENT
FOR THE YEAR ENDED DECEMBER 31, 2008

Sales	$620,000
Cost of goods sold	490,000
Gross profit on sales	130,000
Gross profit realized on installment sales	51,000
Total gross profit on sales	$181,000

If a company wants more complete disclosure of installment-sales transactions, it would use a presentation similar to that shown in Illustration 16-26.

ILLUSTRATION 16-26
Disclosure of Installment-Sales Transactions—Significant Amount

HEALTH MACHINE COMPANY
INCOME STATEMENT
FOR THE YEAR ENDED DECEMBER 31, 2008

	Installment Sales	Other Sales	Total
Sales	$248,000	$620,000	$868,000
Cost of goods sold	182,000	490,000	672,000
Gross profit on sales	66,000	130,000	196,000
Less: Deferred gross profit on installment sales of this year	47,000		47,000
Realized gross profit on this year's sales	19,000	130,000	149,000
Add: Gross profit realized on installment sales of prior years	32,000		32,000
Gross profit realized this year	$ 51,000	$130,000	$181,000

The presentation in Illustration 16-26 is awkward. Yet the awkwardness of this method is difficult to avoid if a company wants to provide full disclosure of installment-sales transactions in the income statement. One solution, of course, is to prepare a separate schedule showing installment-sales transactions, with only the final figure carried into the income statement.

In the balance sheet it is generally considered desirable to classify installment accounts receivable by year of collectibility. There is some question as to whether companies should include in current assets installment accounts that are not collectible for two or more years. Yet if installment sales are **part of normal operations**, companies may consider them as current assets because they are collectible within the operating cycle of the business. Little confusion should result from this practice if the company fully discloses maturity dates, as illustrated in the following example.

ILLUSTRATION 16-27
Disclosure of Installment Accounts Receivable, by Year

Current assets		
Notes and accounts receivable		
Trade customers	$78,800	
Less: Allowance for doubtful accounts	3,700	
	75,100	
Installment accounts collectible in 2008	22,600	
Installment accounts collectible in 2009	47,200	$144,900

On the other hand, a company may have receivables from an installment contract, resulting from a transaction not related to normal operations. In that case, the company should report such receivable in the "Other assets" section if due beyond one year.

Repossessed merchandise is a part of inventory, and companies should report it as such in the "Current assets" section of the balance sheet. They should include any gain or loss on repossession in the income statement in the "Other revenues and gains" or "Other expenses and losses" section.

If a company has **deferred gross profit on installment sales**, it generally treats it as unearned revenue and classifies it as a current liability. Theoretically, deferred gross profit consists of three elements: (1) income tax liability to be paid when the sales are reported as realized revenue (current liability); (2) allowance for collection expense, bad debts, and repossession losses (deduction from installment accounts receivable); and (3) net income (retained earnings, restricted as to dividend availability). Because of the difficulty in allocating deferred gross profit among these three elements, however, companies frequently report the whole amount as unearned revenue.

In contrast, the FASB in *SFAC No. 6* states that "no matter how it is displayed in financial statements, deferred gross profit on installment sales is conceptually an asset valuation—that is, a reduction of an asset."[34] We support the FASB position, but we recognize that until an official standard on this topic is issued, financial statements will probably continue to report such deferred gross profit as a current liability.

Cost-Recovery Method

OBJECTIVE 7
Explain the cost-recovery method of accounting.

Under the **cost-recovery method,** a company recognizes no profit until cash payments by the buyer exceed the cost of the merchandise sold. After the seller has recovered all costs, it includes in income any additional cash collections. The seller's income statement for the period reports sales revenue, the cost of goods sold, and the gross profit—both the amount (if any) that is recognized during the period and the amount that is deferred. The deferred gross profit is offset against the related receivable—reduced by collections—on the balance sheet. Subsequent income statements report the gross profit as a separate item of revenue when the company recognizes it as earned.

APB Opinion No. 10 allows a seller to use the cost-recovery method to account for sales in which "there is no reasonable basis for estimating collectibility." In addition, *FASB Statements No. 45* (franchises) and *No. 66* (real estate) require use of this method where a high degree of uncertainty exists related to the collection of receivables.[35]

To illustrate the cost-recovery method, assume that early in 2007, Fesmire Manufacturing sells inventory with a cost of $25,000 to Higley Company for $36,000. Higley will make payments of $18,000 in 2007, $12,000 in 2008, and $6,000 in 2009. If the cost-recovery method applies to this transaction and Higley makes the payments as scheduled, Fesmire recognizes cash collections, revenue, cost, and gross profit as follows.[36]

ILLUSTRATION 16-28
Computation of Gross Profit—Cost-Recovery Method

	2007	2008	2009
Cash collected	$18,000	$12,000	$6,000
Revenue	$36,000	–0–	–0–
Cost of goods sold	25,000	–0–	–0–
Deferred gross profit	11,000	$11,000	$6,000
Recognized gross profit	–0–	5,000*	6,000
Deferred gross profit balance (end of period)	$11,000	$ 6,000	$ –0–

*$25,000 − $18,000 = $7,000 of unrecovered cost at the end of 2007; $12,000 − $7,000 = $5,000, the excess of cash received in 2008 over unrecovered cost.

Under the cost-recovery method, Fesmire reports total revenue and cost of goods sold in the period of sale, similar to the installment-sales method. However, unlike the installment-sales method, which recognizes income as cash is collected, Fesmire recognizes profit under the cost-recovery method **only when cash collections exceed the total cost of the goods sold.**

[34]*See Statement of Financial Accounting Concepts No. 6*, pars. 232–234.

[35]"Omnibus Opinion—1966," *Opinions of the Accounting Principles Board No. 10* (New York: AICPA, 1969), footnote 8, page 149; "Accounting for Franchise Fee Revenue," *Statement of Financial Accounting Standards No. 45* (Stamford, Conn.: FASB, 1981), par. 6; "Accounting for Sales of Real Estate," *Statement of Financial Accounting Standards No. 66*, pars. 62 and 63.

[36]An alternative format for computing the amount of gross profit recognized annually is shown below.

Year	Cash Received	Original Cost Recovered	Balance of Unrecovered Cost	Gross Profit Realized
Beginning balance	—	—	$25,000	—
12/31/07	$18,000	$18,000	7,000	$ -0-
12/31/08	12,000	7,000	-0-	5,000
12/31/09	6,000	-0-	-0-	6,000

Therefore, Fesmire's journal entry to record the deferred gross profit on the Higley sale transaction (after recording the sale and the cost of sale in the normal manner) at the end of 2007 is as follows.

2007		
Sales	36,000	
Cost of Sales		25,000
Deferred Gross Profit		11,000
(To close sales and cost of sales and to record deferred gross profit on sales accounted for under the cost-recovery method)		

In 2008 and 2009, the deferred gross profit becomes realized gross profit as the cumulative cash collections exceed the total costs, by recording the following entries.

2008		
Deferred Gross Profit	5,000	
Realized Gross Profit		5,000
(To recognize gross profit to the extent that cash collections in 2008 exceed costs)		
2009		
Deferred Gross Profit	6,000	
Realized Gross Profit		6,000
(To recognize gross profit to the extent that cash collections in 2009 exceed costs)		

LIABILITY OR REVENUE?

WHAT DO THE NUMBERS MEAN?

Suppose you purchased a gift card for spa services at Sundara Spa for $300. The gift card expires at the end of six months. When should Sundara record the revenue? Here are two choices:

1 At the time Sundara receives the cash for the gift card.

2 At the time Sundara provides the service to the gift-card holder.

If you answered number 2, you would be right. Companies should recognize revenue when the obligation is satisfied—which is when Sundara performs the service.

Now let's add a few more facts. Suppose that the gift-card holder fails to use the card in the six-month period. Statistics show that between 2 and 15 percent of gift-card holders never redeem their cards. So, do you still believe that Sundara should record the revenue at the expiration date?

If you say you are not sure, you are probably right. Here is why: Certain states (such as California) do not recognize expiration dates, and therefore the customer has the right to redeem an otherwise expired gift card at any time. Let's for the moment say we are in California. Because the card holder may never redeem, when can Sundara recognize the revenue? In that case Sundara would have to show statistically that after a certain period of time, the likelihood of redemption is remote. If it can make that case, it can recognize the revenue. Otherwise it may have to wait a long time.

Unfortunately Sundara may still have a problem. It may be required to turn over the value of the spa service to the state. The treatment for unclaimed gift cards may fall under the state abandoned-and-unclaimed-property laws. Most common unclaimed items are required to be remitted to the states after a five-year period. Failure to report and remit the property can result in additional fines and penalties. So if Sundara is in a state where unclaimed property must be sent to the state, Sundara should report a liability on its balance sheet.

Source: PricewaterhouseCoopers, "Issues Surrounding the Recognition of Gift Card Sales and Escheat Liabilities," *Quick Brief* (December 2004).

Deposit Method

In some cases, a company receives cash from the buyer before it transfers the goods or property. In such cases the seller has not performed under the contract and has no claim against the purchaser. There is not sufficient transfer of the risks and rewards of ownership for a sale to be recorded. The method of accounting for these incomplete transactions is the **deposit method**.

Under the **deposit method** the seller reports the cash received from the buyer as a deposit on the contract and classifies it on the balance sheet as a liability (refundable deposit or customer advance). The seller continues to report the property as an asset on its balance sheet, along with any related existing debt. Also, the seller continues to charge depreciation expense as a period cost for the property. **The seller does not recognize revenue or income until the sale is complete.**[37] At that time, it closes the deposit account and applies one of the revenue recognition methods discussed in this chapter to the sale.

The **major difference between the installment-sales and cost-recovery methods and the deposit method** relates to contract performance. In the installment-sales and cost-recovery methods it is assumed that the seller has performed on the contract, but cash collection is highly uncertain. In the deposit method, the seller has *not* performed and no legitimate claim exists. The deposit method postpones recognizing a sale until the company determines that a sale has occurred for accounting purposes. If there has not been sufficient transfer of risks and rewards of ownership, even if the selling company has received a deposit, the company postpones recognition of the sale until sufficient transfer has occurred. In that sense, the deposit method is not a revenue recognition method as are the installment-sales and cost-recovery methods.

Summary of Product Revenue Recognition Bases

Illustration 16-29 summarizes the revenue-recognition bases or methods, the criteria for their use, and the reasons for departing from the sale basis.[38]

ILLUSTRATION 16-29
Revenue Recognition Bases Other Than the Sale Basis for Products

Recognition Basis (or Method of Applying a Basis)	Criteria for Use	Reason(s) for Departing from Sale Basis
Percentage-of-completion method	Long-term construction of property; dependable estimates of extent of progress and cost to complete; reasonable assurance of collectibility of contract price; expectation that both contractor and buyer can meet obligations; and absence of inherent hazards that make estimates doubtful.	Availability of evidence of ultimate proceeds; better measure of periodic income; avoidance of fluctuations in revenues, expenses, and income; performance is a "continuous sale" and therefore not a departure from the sale basis.
Completed-contract method	Use on short-term contracts, and whenever percentage-of-completion cannot be used on long-term contracts.	Existence of inherent hazards in the contract beyond the normal, recurring business risks; conditions for using the percentage-of-completion method are absent.
Completion-of-production basis	Immediate marketability at quoted prices; unit interchangeability; and no significant distribution costs.	Known or determinable revenues; inability to determine costs and thereby defer expense recognition until sale.
Installment-sales method and cost-recovery method	Absence of reasonable basis for estimating degree of collectibility and costs of collection.	Collectibility of the receivable is so uncertain that gross profit (or income) is not recognized until cash is actually received.
Deposit method	Cash received before the sales transaction is completed.	No recognition of revenue and income because there is not sufficient transfer of the risks and rewards of ownership.

[37] *Statement of Financial Accounting Standards No. 66*, par. 65.

[38] Adapted from *Survey of Present Practices in Recognizing Revenues, Expenses, Gains, and Losses*, op. cit., pp. 12–13.

CONCLUDING REMARKS

INTERNATIONAL INSIGHT

There is no international enforcement body comparable to the U.S. SEC.

As indicated, revenue recognition principles are sometimes difficult to apply and often vary by industry. Recently the SEC has attempted to provide more guidance in this area because of concern that the revenue recognition principle is sometimes being incorrectly applied. Many cases of intentional misstatement of revenue to achieve better financial results have recently come to light. Such practices are fraudulent, and the SEC is vigorously prosecuting these situations.

For our capital markets to be efficient, investors must have confidence that the financial information provided is both relevant and reliable. As a result, it is imperative that the accounting profession, regulators, and companies eliminate aggressive revenue recognition practices. It is our hope that recent efforts by the SEC and the accounting profession will lead to higher-quality reporting in this area.

QUESTIONS

1. Explain the current environment regarding revenue recognition.

2. When is revenue conventionally recognized? What conditions should exist for the recognition at date of sale of all or part of the revenue and income of any sale transaction?

3. When is revenue recognized in the following situations: (a) Revenue from selling products? (b) Revenue from services rendered? (c) Revenue from permitting others to use enterprise assets? (d) Revenue from disposing of assets other than products?

4. Identify several types of sales transactions and indicate the types of business for which that type of transaction is common.

5. What are the three alternative accounting methods available to a seller that is exposed to continued risks of ownership through return of the product?

6. Under what conditions may a seller who is exposed to continued risks of a high rate of return of the product sold recognize sales transactions as current revenue?

7. What are the two basic methods of accounting for long-term construction contracts? Indicate the circumstances that determine when one or the other of these methods should be used.

8. F. Scott Fitzgerald Construction Co. has a $60 million contract to construct a highway overpass and cloverleaf. The total estimated cost for the project is $50 million. Costs incurred in the first year of the project are $9 million. F. Scott Fitzgerald Construction Co. appropriately uses the percentage-of-completion method. How much revenue and gross profit should F. Scott Fitzgerald recognize in the first year of the project?

9. For what reasons should the percentage-of-completion method be used over the completed-contract method whenever possible?

10. What methods are used in practice to determine the extent of progress toward completion? Identify some "input measures" and some "output measures" that might be used to determine the extent of progress.

11. What are the two types of losses that can become evident in accounting for long-term contracts? What is the nature of each type of loss? How is each type accounted for?

12. Under the percentage-of-completion method, how are the Construction in Process and the Billings on Construction in Process accounts reported in the balance sheet?

13. Explain the differences between the installment-sales method and the cost-recovery method.

14. Identify and briefly describe the two methods generally employed to account for the cash received in situations where the collection of the sales price is not reasonably assured.

15. What is the deposit method and when might it be applied?

16. What is the nature of an installment sale? How do installment sales differ from ordinary credit sales?

17. Describe the installment-sales method of accounting.

18. How are operating expenses (not included in cost of goods sold) handled under the installment-sales method of accounting? What is the justification for such treatment?

19. J. K. Rowling sold her condominium for $500,000 on September 14, 2006; she had paid $310,000 for it in 1998. Rowling collected the selling price as follows: 2006, $80,000; 2007, $320,000; and 2008, $100,000. Rowling appropriately uses the installment-sales method. Prepare a schedule to determine the gross profit for 2006, 2007, and 2008 from the installment sale.

20. When interest is involved in installment-sales transactions, how should it be treated for accounting purposes?

21. How should the results of installment sales be reported on the income statement?

22. At what time is it proper to recognize income in the following cases: (a) Installment sales with no reasonable basis for estimating the degree of collectibility? (b) Sales for future delivery? (c) Merchandise shipped on consignment? (d) Profit on incomplete construction contracts? (e) Subscriptions to publications?

23. When is revenue recognized under the cost-recovery method?

24. When is revenue recognized under the deposit method? How does the deposit method differ from the installment-sales and cost-recovery methods?

CHAPTER SEVENTEEN

ACCOUNTING FOR INCOME TAXES

Tax Uncertainty

One set of costs that companies manage are those related to taxes. In fact, in today's competitive markets, managers are expected to look for places in the tax code that a company can exploit to pay less tax to state and federal governments. By paying less in taxes, companies have more cash available to fund operations, finance expansion, and create new jobs. What happens, though, when companies push the tax saving envelop? Well, they may face a tax audit, the results of which could hurt their financial statements.

A notable example of corporate maneuvering to reduce taxable income involved **Limited Brands Inc.** It managed state-tax costs downward by locating part of its business in low-tax-rate states while operating retail outlets elsewhere. For example, by basing a subsidiary (which does nothing more than hold the trademarks for Bath and Body Works and Victoria's Secret) in Delaware, it is able to transfer hundreds of millions of dollars from Limited's retail outlets in high-tax states into Delaware, which has a state tax rate of zero.

However, the IRS and some states have been increasing their scrutiny of transactions that seem done only to avoid taxes and that do not serve a legitimate business purpose. In one case, an attorney for North Carolina alleged that Limited Brands Inc. ". . . engaged in hocus pocus bookkeeping and deceptive accounting," the sole purpose of which was to reduce its state-tax bill. The court agreed, and Limited Inc. had to pay millions of dollars in taxes dating back to 1994.

Limited Brands shareholders likely got an unpleasant surprise when they learned the company also had a big tax obligation from its "uncertain tax position" related to off-shore locations. The same can be said for many other companies that take tax deductions that may not hold up under the scrutiny of the tax court or an IRS audit. Current accounting rules are not very specific on when companies have to record an obligation for taxes that will be owed on uncertain tax positions. This is changing because the SEC and the FASB are concerned about non-recognition of significant tax obligations. As this text is being written, the FASB is working on a rule that would require companies to record loss contingencies for more uncertain tax provisions in their financial statements.[1]

[1]See Glenn Simpson, "A Tax Maneuver in Delaware Puts Squeeze on States," *Wall Street Journal* (August 9, 2002), p. A1; and FASB, "Uncertain Tax Positions: Recognition of Tax Benefits," (July 14, 2005), *www.fasb.org/project/uncertain_tax_positions.shtml.*

Learning Objectives

After studying this chapter, you should be able to:

1 Identify differences between pretax financial income and taxable income.

2 Describe a temporary difference that results in future taxable amounts.

3 Describe a temporary difference that results in future deductible amounts.

4 Explain the purpose of a deferred tax asset valuation allowance.

5 Describe the presentation of income tax expense in the income statement.

6 Describe various temporary and permanent differences.

7 Explain the effect of various tax rates and tax rate changes on deferred income taxes.

8 Apply accounting procedures for a loss carryback and a loss carryforward.

9 Describe the presentation of deferred income taxes in financial statements.

10 Indicate the basic principles of the asset-liability method.

PREVIEW OF CHAPTER 17

As our opening story indicates, companies spend a considerable amount of time and effort to minimize their income tax payments. And with good reason, as income taxes are a major cost of doing business for most corporations. Yet, at the same time, companies must present financial information to the investment community that provides a clear picture of present and potential tax obligations and tax benefits. In this chapter, we discuss the basic guidelines that companies must follow in reporting income taxes. The content and organization of the chapter are as follows.

ACCOUNTING FOR INCOME TAXES

FUNDAMENTALS OF ACCOUNTING FOR INCOME TAXES
- Future taxable amounts and deferred taxes
- Future deductible amounts and deferred taxes
- Income statement presentation
- Specific differences
- Rate considerations

ACCOUNTING FOR NET OPERATING LOSSES
- Loss carryback
- Loss carryforward
- Loss carryback example
- Loss carryforward example

FINANCIAL STATEMENT PRESENTATION
- Balance sheet
- Income statement

REVIEW OF ASSET-LIABILITY METHOD

FUNDAMENTALS OF ACCOUNTING FOR INCOME TAXES

OBJECTIVE 1
Identify differences between pretax financial income and taxable income.

Up to this point, you have learned the basic guidelines that corporations use to report information to investors and creditors. Corporations also must file income tax returns following the guidelines developed by the Internal Revenue Service (IRS). Because GAAP and tax regulations differ in a number of ways, so frequently do pretax financial income and taxable income. Consequently, the amount that a company reports as tax expense will differ from the amount of taxes payable to the IRS. Illustration 17-1 highlights these differences.

Pretax financial income is a *financial reporting* term. It also is often referred to as *income before taxes, income for financial reporting purposes*, or *income for book purposes*. Companies determine pretax financial income according to GAAP. They measure it with the objective of providing useful information to investors and creditors.

Taxable income (income for tax purposes) is a *tax accounting* term. It indicates the amount used to compute income tax payable. Companies determine taxable income according to the Internal Revenue Code (the tax code). Income taxes provide money to support government operations.

To illustrate how differences in GAAP and IRS rules affect financial reporting and taxable income, assume that Chelsea Inc. reported revenues of $130,000 and expenses of $60,000 in each of its first three years of operations. Illustration 17-2 shows the (partial) income statement over these three years.

For tax purposes (following the tax code), Chelsea reported the same expenses to the IRS in each of the years. But, as Illustration 17-3 shows, Chelsea reported taxable revenues of $100,000 in 2007, $150,000 in 2008, and $140,000 in 2009.

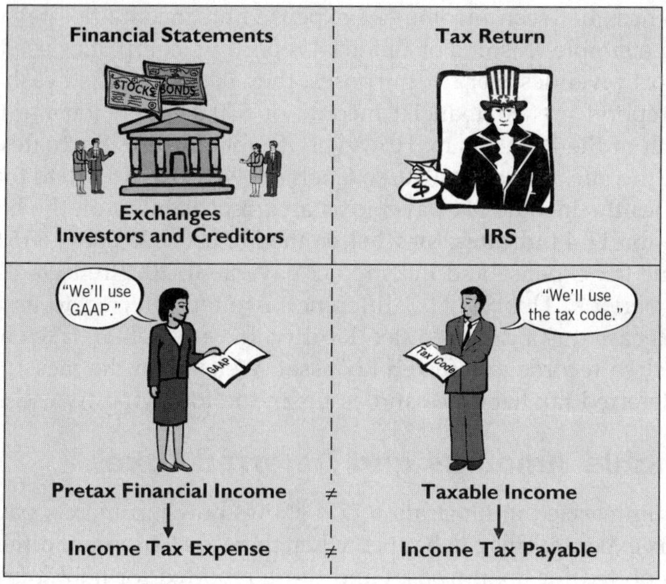

ILLUSTRATION 17-1
Fundamental Differences between Financial and Tax Reporting

CHELSEA INC.
GAAP Reporting

	2007	2008	2009	Total
Revenues	$130,000	$130,000	$130,000	
Expenses	60,000	60,000	60,000	
Pretax financial income	$ 70,000	$ 70,000	$ 70,000	$ 210,000
Income tax expense (40%)	$ 28,000	$ 28,000	$ 28,000	$ 84,000

ILLUSTRATION 17-2
Financial Reporting Income

CHELSEA INC.
Tax Reporting

	2007	2008	2009	Total
Revenues	$100,000	$150,000	$140,000	
Expenses	60,000	60,000	60,000	
Taxable income	$ 40,000	$ 90,000	$ 80,000	$ 210,000
Income tax payable (40%)	$ 16,000	$ 36,000	$ 32,000	$ 84,000

ILLUSTRATION 17-3
Tax Reporting Income

Income tax expense and income tax payable differed over the three years, but were equal **in total**, as Illustration 17-4 shows.

CHELSEA INC.
Income Tax Expense and Income Tax Payable

	2007	2008	2009	Total
Income tax expense	$28,000	$28,000	$28,000	$84,000
Income tax payable	16,000	36,000	32,000	84,000
Difference	$12,000	$ (8,000)	$ (4,000)	$ 0

ILLUSTRATION 17-4
Comparison of Income Tax Expense to Income Tax Payable

INTERNATIONAL INSIGHT

In some countries, taxable income equals pretax financial income. As a consequence, accounting for differences between tax and book income is insignificant.

The differences between income tax expense and income tax payable in this example arise for a simple reason. For financial reporting, companies use the full accrual method to report revenues. For tax purposes, they use a modified cash basis. As a result, Chelsea reports pretax financial income of $70,000 and income tax expense of $28,000 for each of the three years. However, taxable income fluctuates. For example, in 2007 taxable income is only $40,000, so Chelsea owes just $16,000 to the IRS that year. Chelsea classifies the income tax payable as a current liability on the balance sheet.

As Illustration 17-4 indicates, for Chelsea the $12,000 ($28,000 − $16,000) difference between income tax expense and income tax payable in 2007 reflects taxes that it will pay in future periods. This $12,000 difference is often referred to as a **deferred tax amount**. In this case it is a **deferred tax liability**. In cases where taxes will be lower in the future, Chelsea records a **deferred tax asset**. We explain the measurement and accounting for deferred tax liabilities and assets in the following two sections.

Future Taxable Amounts and Deferred Taxes

OBJECTIVE 2
Describe a temporary difference that results in future taxable amounts.

The example summarized in Illustration 17-4 shows how income tax payable can differ from income tax expense. This can happen when there are temporary differences between the amounts reported for tax purposes and those reported for book purposes. A **temporary difference** is the difference between the tax basis of an asset or liability and its reported (carrying or book) amount in the financial statements, which will result in taxable amounts or deductible amounts in future years. **Taxable amounts** increase taxable income in future years. **Deductible amounts** decrease taxable income in future years.

In Chelsea's situation, the only difference between the book basis and tax basis of the assets and liabilities relates to accounts receivable that arose from revenue recognized for book purposes. Illustration 17-5 indicates that Chelsea reports accounts receivable at $30,000 in the December 31, 2007, GAAP-basis balance sheet. However, the receivables have a zero tax basis.

ILLUSTRATION 17-5
Temporary Difference, Sales Revenue

Per Books	12/31/07	Per Tax Return	12/31/07
Accounts receivable	$30,000	Accounts receivable	$-0-

What will happen to the $30,000 temporary difference that originated in 2007 for Chelsea? Assuming that Chelsea expects to collect $20,000 of the receivables in 2008 and $10,000 in 2009, this collection results in future taxable amounts of $20,000 in 2008 and $10,000 in 2009. These future taxable amounts will cause taxable income to exceed pretax financial income in both 2008 and 2009.

An assumption inherent in a company's GAAP balance sheet is that companies recover and settle the assets and liabilities at their reported amounts (carrying amounts). This assumption creates a requirement under accrual accounting to recognize *currently* the deferred tax consequences of temporary differences. That is, companies recognize the amount of income taxes that are payable (or refundable) when they recover and settle the reported amounts of the assets and liabilities, respectively. Illustration 17-6 shows the reversal of the temporary difference described in Illustration 17-5 and the resulting taxable amounts in future periods.

ILLUSTRATION 17-6
Reversal of Temporary Difference, Chelsea Inc.

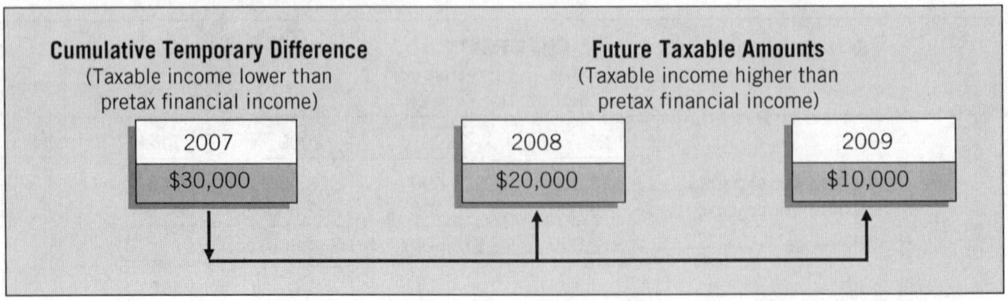

Chelsea assumes that it will collect the accounts receivable and report the $30,000 collection as taxable revenues in future tax returns. A payment of income tax in both 2008 and 2009 will occur. Chelsea should therefore record in its books in 2007 the deferred tax consequences of the revenue and related receivables reflected in the 2007 financial statements. Chelsea does this by recording a deferred tax liability.

Deferred Tax Liability

A **deferred tax liability** is the deferred tax consequences attributable to taxable temporary differences. In other words, **a deferred tax liability represents the increase in taxes payable in future years as a result of taxable temporary differences existing at the end of the current year.**

Recall from the Chelsea example that income tax payable is $16,000 ($40,000 × 40%) in 2007 (Illustration 17-4). In addition, a temporary difference exists at year-end because Chelsea reports the revenue and related accounts receivable differently for book and tax purposes. The book basis of accounts receivable is $30,000, and the tax basis is zero. Thus, the total deferred tax liability at the end of 2007 is $12,000, computed as shown in Illustration 17-7.

ILLUSTRATION 17-7
Computation of Deferred Tax Liability, End of 2007

Book basis of accounts receivable	$30,000
Tax basis of accounts receivable	–0–
Cumulative temporary difference at the end of 2004	30,000
Tax rate	40%
Deferred tax liability at the end of 2007	$12,000

Companies may also compute the deferred tax liability by preparing a schedule that indicates the future taxable amounts due to existing temporary differences. Such a schedule, as shown in Illustration 17-8, is particularly useful when the computations become more complex.

ILLUSTRATION 17-8
Schedule of Future Taxable Amounts

	Future Years		
	2008	2009	Total
Future taxable amounts	$20,000	$10,000	$30,000
Tax rate	40%	40%	
Deferred tax liability at the end of 2007	$ 8,000	$ 4,000	$12,000

Because it is the first year of operations for Chelsea, there is no deferred tax liability at the beginning of the year. Chelsea computes the income tax expense for 2007 as shown in Illustration 17-9.

ILLUSTRATION 17-9
Computation of Income Tax Expense, 2007

Deferred tax liability at end of 2007	$12,000
Deferred tax liability at beginning of 2007	–0–
Deferred tax expense for 2007	12,000
Current tax expense for 2007 (Income tax payable)	16,000
Income tax expense (total) for 2007	$28,000

This computation indicates that income tax expense has two components—**current tax expense** (the amount of income tax payable for the period) and deferred tax expense. **Deferred tax expense** is the increase in the deferred tax liability balance from the beginning to the end of the accounting period.

Companies credit taxes due and payable to Income Tax Payable, and credit the increase in deferred taxes to Deferred Tax Liability. They then debit the sum of those two items to Income Tax Expense. For Chelsea, it makes the following entry at the end of 2007.

Income Tax Expense	28,000	
Income Tax Payable		16,000
Deferred Tax Liability		12,000

At the end of 2008 (the second year), the difference between the book basis and the tax basis of the accounts receivable is $10,000. Chelsea multiplies this difference by the applicable tax rate to arrive at the deferred tax liability of $4,000 ($10,000 × 40%), which it reports at the end of 2008. Income tax payable for 2008 is $36,000 (Illustration 17-3), and the income tax expense for 2008 is as shown in Illustration 17-10.

ILLUSTRATION 17-10
Computation of Income Tax Expense, 2008

Deferred tax liability at end of 2008	$ 4,000
Deferred tax liability at beginning of 2008	12,000
Deferred tax expense (benefit) for 2008	(8,000)
Current tax expense for 2008 (Income tax payable)	36,000
Income tax expense (total) for 2008	$28,000

Chelsea records income tax expense, the change in the deferred tax liability, and income tax payable for 2008 as follows.

Income Tax Expense	28,000	
Deferred Tax Liability	8,000	
Income Tax Payable		36,000

The entry to record income taxes at the end of 2009 reduces the Deferred Tax Liability by $4,000. The Deferred Tax Liability account appears as follows at the end of 2009.

ILLUSTRATION 17-11
Deferred Tax Liability Account after Reversals

Deferred Tax Liability			
2008	8,000	2007	12,000
2009	4,000		

The Deferred Tax Liability account has a zero balance at the end of 2009.

WHAT DO THE NUMBERS MEAN?

"REAL LIABILITIES"

Some analysts dismiss deferred tax liabilities when assessing the financial strength of a company. But the FASB indicates that the deferred tax liability meets the definition of a liability established in *Statement of Financial Accounting Concepts No. 6,* "Elements of Financial Statements" because:

1. ***It results from a past transaction.*** In the Chelsea example, the company performed services for customers and recognized revenue in 2007 for financial reporting purposes but deferred it for tax purposes.
2. ***It is a present obligation.*** Taxable income in future periods will exceed pretax financial income as a result of this temporary difference. Thus, a present obligation exists.
3. ***It represents a future sacrifice.*** Taxable income and taxes due in future periods will result from past events. The payment of these taxes when they come due is the future sacrifice.

A study by B. Ayers indicates that the market views deferred tax assets and liabilities similarly to other assets and liabilities. Further, the study concludes that *SFAS No. 109* increased the usefulness of deferred tax amounts in financial statements.

Source: B. Ayers, "Deferred Tax Accounting Under *SFAS No. 109*: An Empirical Investigation of Its Incremental Value-Relevance Relative to *APB No. 11*," *The Accounting Review* (April 1998).

Summary of Income Tax Accounting Objectives

One objective of accounting for income taxes is to recognize the amount of taxes payable or refundable for the current year. In Chelsea's case, income tax payable is $16,000 for 2007.

A **second objective** is to recognize deferred tax liabilities and assets for the future tax consequences of events already recognized in the financial statements or tax returns. For example, Chelsea sold services to customers that resulted in accounts receivable of $30,000 in 2007. It reported that amount on the 2007 income statement, but not on the tax return as income. That amount will appear on future tax returns as income for the period **when collected**. As a result, a $30,000 temporary difference exists at the end of 2007, which will cause future taxable amounts. Chelsea reports a deferred tax liability of $12,000 on the balance sheet at the end of 2007, which represents the increase in taxes payable in future years ($8,000 in 2008 and $4,000 in 2009) as a result of a temporary difference existing at the end of the current year. The related deferred tax liability is reduced by $8,000 at the end of 2008 and by another $4,000 at the end of 2009.

In addition to affecting the balance sheet, deferred taxes impact income tax expense in each of the three years affected. In 2007, taxable income ($40,000) is less than pretax financial income ($70,000). Income tax payable for 2007 is therefore $16,000 (based on taxable income). Deferred tax expense of $12,000 results from the increase in the Deferred Tax Liability account on the balance sheet. Income tax expense is then $28,000 for 2007.

In 2008 and 2009, however, taxable income will exceed pretax financial income, due to the reversal of the temporary difference ($20,000 in 2008 and $10,000 in 2009). Income tax payable will therefore exceed income tax expense in 2008 and 2009. Chelsea will debit the Deferred Tax Liability account for $8,000 in 2008 and $4,000 in 2009. It records credits for these amounts in Income Tax Expense. These credits are often referred to as a **deferred tax benefit** (which we discuss again later on).

Future Deductible Amounts and Deferred Taxes

OBJECTIVE 3
Describe a temporary difference that results in future deductible amounts.

Assume that during 2007, Cunningham Inc. estimated its warranty costs related to the sale of microwave ovens to be $500,000, paid evenly over the next two years. For book purposes, in 2007 Cunningham reported warranty expense and a related estimated liability for warranties of $500,000 in its financial statements. For tax purposes, **the warranty tax deduction is not allowed until paid**. Therefore, Cunningham recognizes no warranty liability on a tax-basis balance sheet. Illustration 17-12 shows the balance sheet difference at the end of 2007.

ILLUSTRATION 17-12
Temporary Difference, Warranty Liability

Per Books	12/31/07	Per Tax Return	12/31/07
Estimated liability for warranties	$500,000	Estimated liability for warranties	$-0-

When Cunningham pays the warranty liability, it reports an expense (deductible amount) for tax purposes. Because of this temporary difference, Cunningham should recognize in 2007 the tax benefits (positive tax consequences) for the tax deductions that will result from the future settlement of the liability. Cunningham reports this future tax benefit in the December 31, 2007, balance sheet as a **deferred tax asset**.

We can think about this situation another way. Deductible amounts occur in future tax returns. These **future deductible amounts** cause taxable income to be less than pretax financial income in the future as a result of an existing temporary difference. Cunningham's temporary difference originates (arises) in one period (2007) and reverses over two periods (2008 and 2009). Illustration 17-13 diagrams this situation.

ILLUSTRATION 17-13
Reversal of Temporary Difference, Cunningham Inc.

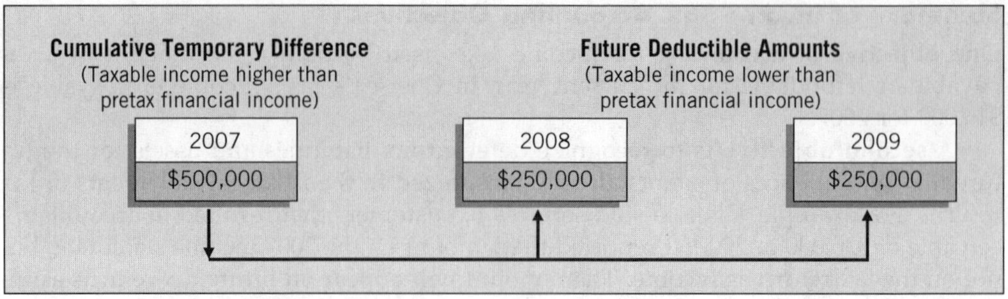

Deferred Tax Asset

A **deferred tax asset** is the deferred tax consequence attributable to deductible temporary differences. In other words, a **deferred tax asset represents the increase in taxes refundable (or saved) in future years as a result of deductible temporary differences existing at the end of the current year.**

To illustrate, assume that Hunt Co. accrues a loss and a related liability of $50,000 in 2007 for financial reporting purposes because of pending litigation. Hunt cannot deduct this amount for tax purposes until the period it pays the liability, expected in 2008. As a result, a deductible amount will occur in 2008 when Hunt settles the liability (Estimated Litigation Liability), causing taxable income to be lower than pretax financial income. Illustration 17-14 shows the computation of the deferred tax asset at the end of 2007 (assuming a 40 percent tax rate).

ILLUSTRATION 17-14
Computation of Deferred Tax Asset, End of 2007

Book basis of litigation liability	$50,000
Tax basis of litigation liability	–0–
Cumulative temporary difference at the end of 2007	50,000
Tax rate	40%
Deferred tax asset at the end of 2007	$20,000

Hunt can also compute the deferred tax asset by preparing a schedule that indicates the future deductible amounts due to deductible temporary differences. Illustration 17-15 shows this schedule.

ILLUSTRATION 17-15
Schedule of Future Deductible Amounts

	Future Years
Future deductible amounts	$50,000
Tax rate	40%
Deferred tax asset at the end of 2007	$20,000

Assuming that 2007 is Hunt's first year of operations, and income tax payable is $100,000, Hunt computes its income tax expense as follows.

ILLUSTRATION 17-16
Computation of Income Tax Expense, 2007

Deferred tax asset at end of 2007	$ 20,000
Deferred tax asset at beginning of 2007	–0–
Deferred tax expense (benefit) for 2007	(20,000)
Current tax expense for 2007 (Income tax payable)	100,000
Income tax expense (total) for 2007	$ 80,000

The **deferred tax benefit** results from the increase in the deferred tax asset from the beginning to the end of the accounting period (similar to the Chelsea example earlier). The deferred tax benefit is a negative component of income tax expense. The total income tax expense of $80,000 on the income statement for 2007 thus consists of two elements—current tax expense of $100,000 and a deferred tax benefit of $20,000. For Hunt, it makes the following journal entry at the end of 2007 to record income tax expense, deferred income taxes, and income tax payable.

Income Tax Expense	80,000	
Deferred Tax Asset	20,000	
Income Tax Payable		100,000

At the end of 2008 (the second year), the difference between the book value and the tax basis of the litigation liability is zero. Therefore, there is no deferred tax asset at this date. Assuming that income tax payable for 2008 is $140,000, Hunt computes income tax expense for 2008 as shown in Illustration 17-17.

Deferred tax asset at the end of 2008	$ -0-
Deferred tax asset at the beginning of 2008	20,000
Deferred tax expense (benefit) for 2008	20,000
Current tax expense for 2008 (Income tax payable)	140,000
Income tax expense (total) for 2008	$160,000

ILLUSTRATION 17-17
Computation of Income Tax Expense, 2008

The company records income taxes for 2008 as follows.

Income Tax Expense	160,000	
Deferred Tax Asset		20,000
Income Tax Payable		140,000

The total income tax expense of $160,000 on the income statement for 2008 thus consists of two elements—current tax expense of $140,000 and deferred tax expense of $20,000. Illustration 17-18 shows the Deferred Tax Asset account at the end of 2008.

Deferred Tax Asset			
2007	20,000	2008	20,000

ILLUSTRATION 17-18
Deferred Tax Asset Account after Reversals

"REAL ASSETS"

WHAT DO THE NUMBERS MEAN?

A key issue in accounting for income taxes is whether a company should recognize a deferred tax asset in the financial records. Based on the conceptual definition of an asset, a deferred tax asset meets the three main conditions for an item to be recognized as an asset:

1 ***It results from a past transaction.*** In the Hunt example, the accrual of the loss contingency is the past event that gives rise to a future deductible temporary difference.

2 ***It gives rise to a probable benefit in the future.*** Taxable income exceeds pretax financial income in the current year (2007). However, in the next year the exact opposite occurs. That is, taxable income is lower than pretax financial income. Because this deductible temporary difference reduces taxes payable in the future, a probable future benefit exists at the end of the current period.

3 ***The entity controls access to the benefits.*** Hunt can obtain the benefit of existing deductible temporary differences by reducing its taxes payable in the future. Hunt has the exclusive right to that benefit and can control others' access to it.

Market analysts' reaction to the **write-off** of deferred tax assets also supports their treatment as assets. When **Bethlehem Steel** reported a $1 billion charge in a recent year to write off a deferred tax asset, analysts believed that Bethlehem was signaling that it would not realize the future benefits of the tax deductions. Thus, Bethlehem should write down the asset like other assets.

Source: J. Weil and S. Liesman, "Stock Gurus Disregard Most Big Write-Offs But They Often Hold Vital Clues to Outlook," *Wall Street Journal Online* (December 31, 2001).

Deferred Tax Asset—Valuation Allowance

OBJECTIVE 4
Explain the purpose of a deferred tax asset valuation allowance.

Companies recognize a deferred tax asset for all deductible temporary differences. However, based on available evidence, a company should reduce a deferred tax asset by a **valuation allowance if it is more likely than not** that it **will not realize** some portion or all of the deferred tax asset. **"More likely than not"** means a level of likelihood of at least slightly more than 50 percent.

Assume that Jensen Co. has a deductible temporary difference of $1,000,000 at the end of its first year of operations. Its tax rate is 40 percent, which means it records a deferred tax asset of $400,000 ($1,000,000 × 40%). Assuming $900,000 of income taxes payable, Jensen records income tax expense, the deferred tax asset, and income tax payable as follows.

Income Tax Expense	500,000	
Deferred Tax Asset	400,000	
Income Tax Payable		900,000

After careful review of all available evidence, Jensen determines that it is more likely than not that it will not realize $100,000 of this deferred tax asset. Jensen records this reduction in asset value as follows.

Income Tax Expense	100,000	
Allowance to Reduce Deferred Tax Asset to Expected Realizable Value		100,000

This journal entry increases income tax expense in the current period because Jensen does not expect to realize a favorable tax benefit for a portion of the deductible temporary difference. Jensen **simultaneously establishes a valuation allowance to recognize the reduction in the carrying amount of the deferred tax asset.** This valuation account is a contra account. Jensen reports it on the financial statements in the following manner.

ILLUSTRATION 17-19
Balance Sheet Presentation of Valuation Allowance Account

Deferred tax asset	$400,000
Less: Allowance to reduce deferred tax asset to expected realizable value	100,000
Deferred tax asset (net)	$300,000

Jensen then evaluates this allowance account at the end of each accounting period. If, at the end of the next period, the deferred tax asset is still $400,000, but now it expects to realize $350,000 of this asset, Jensen makes the following entry to adjust the valuation account.

Allowance to Reduce Deferred Tax Asset to Expected Realizable Value	50,000	
Income Tax Expense		50,000

Jensen should consider all available evidence, both positive and negative, to determine whether, based on the weight of available evidence, it needs a valuation allowance. For example, if Jensen has been experiencing a series of loss years, it reasonably assumes that these losses will continue. Therefore, Jensen will lose the benefit of the future deductible amounts. We discuss the use of a valuation account under other conditions later in the chapter.

OBJECTIVE 5
Describe the presentation of income tax expense in the income statement.

Income Statement Presentation

Circumstances dictate whether a company should add or subtract the change in deferred income taxes to or from income tax payable in computing income tax expense. For example, a company adds an increase in a deferred tax liability to income tax payable. On the other hand, it subtracts an increase in a deferred tax asset from income tax payable. The formula in Illustration 17-20 is used to compute income tax expense (benefit).

ILLUSTRATION 17-20
Formula to Compute Income Tax Expense

Income Tax Payable or Refundable	±	Change in Deferred Income Taxes	=	Total Income Tax Expense or Benefit

In the income statement or in the notes to the financial statements, a company should disclose the significant components of income tax expense attributable to continuing operations. Given the information related to Chelsea, Chelsea reports its income statement as follows.

ILLUSTRATION 17-21
Income Statement Presentation of Income Tax Expense

CHELSEA INC.
INCOME STATEMENT
FOR THE YEAR ENDING DECEMBER 31, 2007

Revenues		$130,000
Expenses		60,000
Income before income taxes		70,000
Income tax expense		
Current	$16,000	
Deferred	12,000	28,000
Net income		$ 42,000

As illustrated, Chelsea reports both the current portion (amount of income tax payable for the period) and the deferred portion of income tax expense. Another option is to simply report the total income tax expense on the income statement, and then indicate in the notes to the financial statements the current and deferred portions. Income tax expense is often referred to as "Provision for income taxes." Using this terminology, the current provision is $16,000, and the provision for deferred taxes is $12,000.

Specific Differences

OBJECTIVE 6
Describe various temporary and permanent differences.

Numerous items create differences between pretax financial income and taxable income. For purposes of accounting recognition, these differences are of two types: (1) temporary, and (2) permanent.

Temporary Differences

Taxable temporary differences are temporary differences that will result in taxable amounts in future years when the related assets are recovered. **Deductible temporary differences** are temporary differences that will result in deductible amounts in future years, when the related book liabilities are settled. Taxable temporary differences give rise to recording deferred tax liabilities. Deductible temporary differences give rise to recording deferred tax assets. Illustration 17-22 provides examples of temporary differences.[2]

[2] *SFAS No. 109* gives more examples of temporary differences. We present the most common types in this chapter.

A. **Revenues or gains are taxable after they are recognized in financial income.**
An asset (e.g., accounts receivable or investment) may be recognized for revenues or gains that will result in **taxable amounts in future years** when the asset is recovered. Examples:
1. Sales accounted for on the accrual basis for financial reporting purposes and on the installment (cash) basis for tax purposes.
2. Contracts accounted for under the percentage-of-completion method for financial reporting purposes and a portion of related gross profit deferred for tax purposes.
3. Investments accounted for under the equity method for financial reporting purposes and under the cost method for tax purposes.
4. Gain on involuntary conversion of nonmonetary asset which is recognized for financial reporting purposes but deferred for tax purposes.

B. **Expenses or losses are deductible after they are recognized in financial income.**
A liability (or contra asset) may be recognized for expenses or losses that will result in **deductible amounts in future years** when the liability is settled. Examples:
1. Product warranty liabilities.
2. Estimated liabilities related to discontinued operations or restructurings.
3. Litigation accruals.
4. Bad debt expense recognized using the allowance method for financial reporting purposes; direct write-off method used for tax purposes.
5. Stock-based compensation expense.

C. **Revenues or gains are taxable before they are recognized in financial income.**
A liability may be recognized for an advance payment for goods or services to be provided in future years. For tax purposes, the advance payment is included in taxable income upon the receipt of cash. Future sacrifices to provide goods or services (or future refunds to those who cancel their orders) that settle the liability will result in **deductible amounts in future years**. Examples:
1. Subscriptions received in advance.
2. Advance rental receipts.
3. Sales and leasebacks for financial reporting purposes (income deferral) but reported as sales for tax purposes.
4. Prepaid contracts and royalties received in advance.

D. **Expenses or losses are deductible before they are recognized in financial income.**
The cost of an asset may have been deducted for tax purposes faster than it was expensed for financial reporting purposes. Amounts received upon future recovery of the amount of the asset for financial reporting (through use or sale) will exceed the remaining tax basis of the asset and thereby result in **taxable amounts in future years**. Examples:
1. Depreciable property, depletable resources, and intangibles.
2. Deductible pension funding exceeding expense.
3. Prepaid expenses that are deducted on the tax return in the period paid.

ILLUSTRATION 17-22
Examples of Temporary Differences

Determining a company's temporary differences may prove difficult. A company should prepare a balance sheet for tax purposes that it can compare with its GAAP balance sheet. Many of the differences between the two balance sheets are temporary differences.

Originating and Reversing Aspects of Temporary Differences. An **originating temporary difference** is the initial difference between the book basis and the tax basis of an asset or liability, regardless of whether the tax basis of the asset or liability exceeds or is exceeded by the book basis of the asset or liability. A **reversing difference**, on the other hand, occurs when eliminating a temporary difference that originated in prior periods and then removing the related tax effect from the deferred tax account.

For example, assume that Sharp Co. has tax depreciation in excess of book depreciation of $2,000 in 2003, 2004, and 2005. Further, it has an excess of book depreciation over tax depreciation of $3,000 in 2006 and 2007 for the same asset. Assuming a tax rate of 30 percent for all years involved, the Deferred Tax Liability account reflects the following.

ILLUSTRATION 17-23
Tax Effects of Originating and Reversing Differences

	Deferred Tax Liability				
Tax Effects of Reversing Differences	2006	900	2003	600	Tax Effects of Originating Differences
	2007	900	2004	600	
			2005	600	

The originating differences for Sharp in each of the first three years are $2,000. The related tax effect of each originating difference is $600. The reversing differences in 2006 and 2007 are each $3,000. The related tax effect of each is $900.

Permanent Differences

Some differences between taxable income and pretax financial income are permanent. **Permanent differences** result from items that (1) enter into pretax financial income but **never** into taxable income, or (2) enter into taxable income but **never** into pretax financial income.

Congress has enacted a variety of tax law provisions to attain certain political, economic, and social objectives. Some of these provisions exclude certain revenues from taxation, limit the deductibility of certain expenses, and permit the deduction of certain other expenses in excess of costs incurred. A corporation that has tax-free income, nondeductible expenses, or allowable deductions in excess of cost, has an effective tax rate that differs from its statutory (regular) tax rate.

Since permanent differences affect only the period in which they occur, they do not give rise to future taxable or deductible amounts. As a result, **companies recognize no deferred tax consequences**. Illustration 17-24 shows examples of permanent differences.

ILLUSTRATION 17-24
Examples of Permanent Differences

A. **Items are recognized for financial reporting purposes but not for tax purposes.**
Examples:
1. Interest received on state and municipal obligations.
2. Expenses incurred in obtaining tax-exempt income.
3. Proceeds from life insurance carried by the company on key officers or employees.
4. Premiums paid for life insurance carried by the company on key officers or employees (company is beneficiary).
5. Fines and expenses resulting from a violation of law.

B. **Items are recognized for tax purposes but not for financial reporting purposes.**
Examples:
1. "Percentage depletion" of natural resources in excess of their cost.
2. The deduction for dividends received from U.S. corporations, generally 70% or 80%.

Examples of Temporary and Permanent Differences

To illustrate the computations used when both temporary and permanent differences exist, assume that Bio-Tech Company reports pretax financial income of $200,000 in each of the years 2005, 2006, and 2007. The company is subject to a 30 percent tax rate, and has the following differences between pretax financial income and taxable income.

1 Bio-Tech reports an installment sale of $18,000 in 2005 for tax purposes over an 18-month period at a constant amount per month beginning January 1, 2006. It recognizes the entire sale for book purposes in 2005.

2 It pays life insurance premiums for its key officers of $5,000 in 2006 and 2007. Although not tax-deductible, Bio-Tech expenses the premiums for book purposes.

The installment sale is a temporary difference, whereas the life insurance premium is a permanent difference. Illustration 17-25 shows the reconciliation of Bio-Tech's pretax financial income to taxable income and the computation of income tax payable.

ILLUSTRATION 17-25
Reconciliation and Computation of Income Taxes Payable

	2005	2006	2007
Pretax financial income	$200,000	$200,000	$200,000
Permanent difference			
Nondeductible expense		5,000	5,000
Temporary difference			
Installment sale	(18,000)	12,000	6,000
Taxable income	182,000	217,000	211,000
Tax rate	30%	30%	30%
Income tax payable	$ 54,600	$ 65,100	$ 63,300

Note that Bio-Tech **deducts** the installment sales revenue from pretax financial income to arrive at taxable income. The reason: pretax financial income includes the installment sales revenue; taxable income does not. Conversely, it **adds** the $5,000 insurance premium to pretax financial income to arrive at taxable income. The reason: pretax financial income records an expense for this premium, but for tax purposes the premium is not deductible. As a result, pretax financial income is lower than taxable income. Therefore, the life insurance premium must be added back to pretax financial income to reconcile to taxable income.

Bio-Tech records income taxes for 2005, 2006, and 2007 as follows.

December 31, 2005		
Income Tax Expense ($54,600 + $5,400)	60,000	
Deferred Tax Liability ($18,000 × 30%)		5,400
Income Tax Payable ($182,000 × 30%)		54,600
December 31, 2006		
Income Tax Expense ($65,100 − $3,600)	61,500	
Deferred Tax Liability ($12,000 × 30%)	3,600	
Income Tax Payable ($217,000 × 30%)		65,100
December 31, 2007		
Income Tax Expense ($63,300 − $1,800)	61,500	
Deferred Tax Liability ($6,000 × 30%)	1,800	
Income Tax Payable ($211,000 × 30%)		63,300

Bio-Tech has one temporary difference, which originates in 2005 and reverses in 2006 and 2007. It recognizes a deferred tax liability at the end of 2005 because the temporary difference causes future taxable amounts. As the temporary difference reverses, Bio-Tech reduces the deferred tax liability. There is no deferred tax amount associated with the difference caused by the nondeductible insurance expense because it is a permanent difference.

Although an enacted tax rate of 30 percent applies for all three years, the effective rate differs from the enacted rate in 2006 and 2007. Bio-Tech computes the **effective tax rate** by dividing total income tax expense for the period by pretax financial income. The effective rate is 30 percent for 2005 ($60,000 ÷ $200,000 = 30%) and 30.75 percent for 2006 and 2007 ($61,500 ÷ $200,000 = 30.75%).

Tax Rate Considerations

OBJECTIVE 7
Explain the effect of various tax rates and tax rate changes on deferred income taxes.

In our previous illustrations, the enacted tax rate did not change from one year to the next. Thus, to compute the deferred income tax amount to report on the balance sheet, a company simply multiplies the cumulative temporary difference by the current tax rate. Using Bio-Tech as an example, it multiplies the cumulative temporary difference of $18,000 by the enacted tax rate, 30 percent in this case, to arrive at a deferred tax liability of $5,400 ($18,000 × 30%) at the end of 2005.

Future Tax Rates

What happens if tax rates are expected to change in the future? In this case, a company should use the **enacted tax rate** expected to apply. Therefore, a company must consider presently enacted changes in the tax rate that become effective for a particular future year(s) when determining the tax rate to apply to existing temporary differences. For example, assume that Warlen Co. at the end of 2004 has the following cumulative temporary difference of $300,000, computed as shown in Illustration 17-26.

ILLUSTRATION 17-26
Computation of Cumulative Temporary Difference

Book basis of depreciable assets	$1,000,000
Tax basis of depreciable assets	700,000
Cumulative temporary difference	$ 300,000

Furthermore, assume that the $300,000 will reverse and result in taxable amounts in the future, with the enacted tax rates shown in Illustration 17-27.

ILLUSTRATION 17-27
Deferred Tax Liability Based on Future Rates

	2005	2006	2007	2008	2009	Total
Future taxable amounts	$80,000	$70,000	$60,000	$50,000	$40,000	$300,000
Tax rate	40%	40%	35%	30%	30%	
Deferred tax liability	$32,000	$28,000	$21,000	$15,000	$12,000	$108,000

The total deferred tax liability at the end of 2004 is $108,000. Warlen may only use tax rates other than the current rate when the future tax rates have been enacted, as is the case in this example. **If new rates are not yet enacted for future years, Warlen should use the current rate.**

In determining the appropriate enacted tax rate for a given year, companies must use the **average tax rate**. The Internal Revenue Service and other taxing jurisdictions tax income on a graduated tax basis. For a U.S. corporation, the IRS taxes the first $50,000 of taxable income at 15 percent, the next $25,000 at 25 percent, with higher incremental levels of income at rates as high as 39 percent. In computing deferred income taxes, companies for which graduated tax rates are a significant factor must therefore **determine the average tax rate and use that rate.**

Revision of Future Tax Rates

When a change in the tax rate is enacted, companies should record its effect on the existing deferred income tax accounts immediately. **A company reports the effect as an adjustment to income tax expense in the period of the change.**

Assume that on December 10, 2004, a new income tax act is signed into law that lowers the corporate tax rate from 40 percent to 35 percent, effective January 1, 2006. If Hostel Co. has one temporary difference at the beginning of 2004 related to $3 million of excess tax depreciation, then it has a Deferred Tax Liability account with a balance of $1,200,000 ($3,000,000 × 40%) at January 1, 2004. If taxable amounts related to this difference are scheduled to occur equally in 2005, 2006, and 2007, the deferred tax liability at the end of 2004 is $1,100,000, computed as follows.

ILLUSTRATION 17-28
Schedule of Future Taxable Amounts and Related Tax Rates

	2005	2006	2007	Total
Future taxable amounts	$1,000,000	$1,000,000	$1,000,000	$3,000,000
Tax rate	40%	35%	35%	
Deferred tax liability	$ 400,000	$ 350,000	$ 350,000	$1,100,000

Hostel, therefore, recognizes the decrease of $100,000 ($1,200,000 − $1,100,000) at the end of 2004 in the deferred tax liability as follows.

Deferred Tax Liability	100,000	
Income Tax Expense		100,000

Corporate tax rates do not change often. Therefore, companies usually employ the current rate. However, state and foreign tax rates change more frequently, and they require adjustments in deferred income taxes accordingly.[3]

[3]Tax rate changes nearly always will substantially impact income numbers and the reporting of deferred income taxes on the balance sheet. As a result, you can expect to hear an economic consequences argument every time that Congress decides to change the tax rates. For example, when Congress raised the corporate rate from 34 percent to 35 percent in 1993, companies took an additional "hit" to earnings if they were in a deferred tax liability position.

WHAT DO THE NUMBERS MEAN?

SHELTERED

As mentioned in our opening story, companies employ various tax strategies to reduce their tax bills and their effective tax rates. The following table reports some recent high-profile cases in which profitable companies paid little income tax and, in some cases, got tax refunds.

Company	Pre-Tax Income ($ millions)	Federal Tax Paid (Refund) ($ millions)	Tax Rate (%)
Enron	$ 1,785	$(381)	(21.34)%
El Paso Energy	1,638	(254)	(15.51)
Goodyear	442	(23)	(5.20)
Navistar	1,368	28	2.05
General Motors	12,468	740	5.94

These companies used various tools to lower their tax bills, including off-shore tax shelters, tax deferrals, and hefty use of stock options, the cost of which reduce taxable income but do not affect pretax financial income. Thus, companies can use various provisions in the tax code to reduce their effective tax rate well below the statutory rate of 35 percent.

One IRS provision designed to curb excessive tax avoidance is the **alternative minimum tax (AMT)**. Companies compute their potential tax liability under the AMT, adjusting for various preference items that reduce their tax bills under the regular tax code. (Examples of such preference items are accelerated depreciation methods and the installment method for revenue recognition.) Companies must pay the higher of the two tax obligations computed under the AMT and the regular tax code. But, as indicated by the cases above, some profitable companies avoid high tax bills, even in the presence of the AMT. Many citizens and public-interest groups cite corporate avoidance of income taxes as a reason for more tax reform.

Source: H. Gleckman, D. Foust, M. Arndt, and K. Kerwin, "Tax Dodging: Enron Isn't Alone," *Business Week* (March 4, 2002), pp. 40–41.

ACCOUNTING FOR NET OPERATING LOSSES

OBJECTIVE 8
Apply accounting procedures for a loss carryback and a loss carryforward.

Every management hopes its company will be profitable. But hopes and profits may not materialize. For a start-up company, it is common to accumulate operating losses while expanding its customer base but before realizing economies of scale. For an established company, a major event such as a labor strike, rapidly changing regulatory and competitive forces, or a disaster such as 9/11 or Hurricane Katrina can cause expenses to exceed revenues—a net operating loss.

A **net operating loss (NOL)** occurs for tax purposes in a year when tax-deductible expenses exceed taxable revenues. An inequitable tax burden would result if companies were taxed during profitable periods without receiving any tax relief during periods of net operating losses. Under certain circumstances, therefore, the federal tax laws permit taxpayers to use the losses of one year to offset the profits of other years.

Companies accomplish this income-averaging provision through the **carryback and carryforward of net operating losses**. Under this provision, a company pays no income taxes for a year in which it incurs a net operating loss. In addition, it may select one of the two options discussed below and on the following pages.

Loss Carryback

Through use of a **loss carryback**, a company may carry the net operating loss back two years and receive refunds for income taxes paid in those years. The company must apply the loss to the earlier year first and then to the second year. It may **carry**

forward any loss remaining after the two-year carryback up to 20 years to offset future taxable income. Illustration 17-29 diagrams the loss carryback procedure, assuming a loss in 2007.

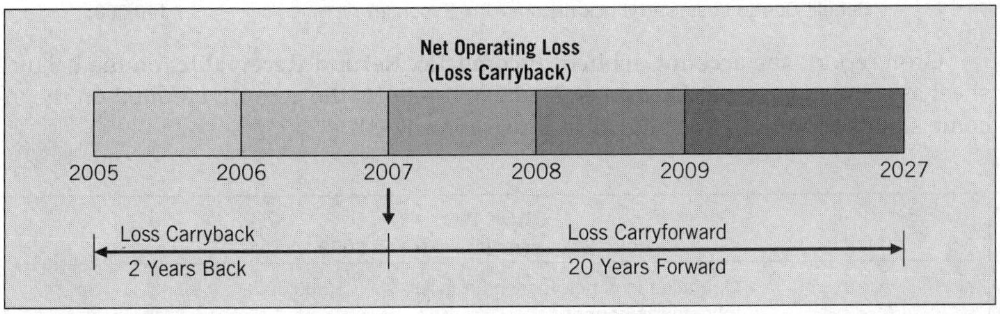

ILLUSTRATION 17-29
Loss Carryback Procedure

Loss Carryforward

A company may forgo the loss carryback and use only the **loss carryforward** option, offsetting future taxable income for up to 20 years. Illustration 17-30 shows this approach.

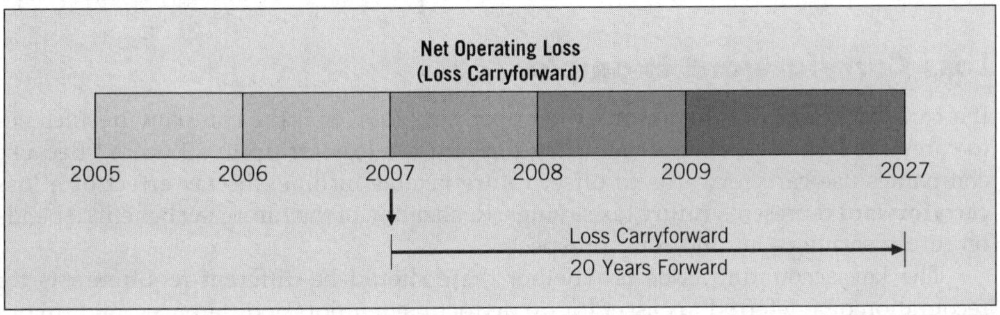

ILLUSTRATION 17-30
Loss Carryforward Procedure

Operating losses can be substantial. For example, **Yahoo** had net operating losses of approximately $5.4 billion at year-end 2004. That amount translates into tax savings of $1.4 billion if Yahoo is able to generate taxable income before the NOLs expire.

Loss Carryback Example

To illustrate the accounting procedures for a net operating loss carryback, assume that Groh Inc. has no temporary or permanent differences. Groh experiences the following.

Year	Taxable Income or Loss	Tax Rate	Tax Paid
2003	$ 50,000	35%	$17,500
2004	100,000	30%	30,000
2005	200,000	40%	80,000
2006	(500,000)	—	-0-

In 2006, Groh incurs a net operating loss that it decides to carry back. Under the law, Groh must apply the carryback first to the **second year preceding the loss year**. Therefore, it carries the loss back first to 2004. Then, Groh carries back any unused loss to 2005. Accordingly, Groh files amended tax returns for 2004 and 2005, receiving refunds for the $110,000 ($30,000 + $80,000) of taxes paid in those years.

For accounting as well as tax purposes, the $110,000 represents the **tax effect (tax benefit)** of the loss carryback. Groh should recognize this tax effect in 2006, the loss year. Since the tax loss gives rise to a refund that is both measurable and currently realizable, Groh should recognize the associated tax benefit in this loss period.

Groh makes the following journal entry for 2006.

Income Tax Refund Receivable	110,000	
Benefit Due to Loss Carryback (Income Tax Expense)		110,000

Groh reports the account debited, **Income Tax Refund Receivable,** on the balance sheet as a current asset at December 31, 2006. It reports the account credited on the income statement for 2006 as shown in Illustration 17-31.

ILLUSTRATION 17-31
Recognition of Benefit of the Loss Carryback in the Loss Year

GROH INC.
INCOME STATEMENT (PARTIAL) FOR 2006

Operating loss before income taxes	$(500,000)
Income tax benefit	
Benefit due to loss carryback	110,000
Net loss	$(390,000)

Since the $500,000 net operating loss for 2006 exceeds the $300,000 total taxable income from the 2 preceding years, Groh carries forward the remaining $200,000 loss.

Loss Carryforward Example

If a carryback fails to fully absorb a net operating loss, or if the company decides not to carry the loss back, then it can carry forward the loss for up to 20 years.[4] Because companies use carryforwards to offset future taxable income, the **tax effect of a loss carryforward** represents **future tax savings**. Realization of the future tax benefit depends on future earnings, an uncertain prospect.

The key accounting issue is whether there should be different requirements for recognition of a deferred tax asset for (a) deductible temporary differences, and (b) operating loss carryforwards. The FASB's position is that in substance these items are the same—both are tax-deductible amounts in future years. As a result, the Board concluded that there **should not be different requirements** for recognition of a deferred tax asset from deductible temporary differences and operating loss carryforwards.[5]

Carryforward Without Valuation Allowance

To illustrate the accounting for an operating loss carryforward, return to the Groh example from the preceding section. In 2006 the company records the tax effect of the $200,000 loss carryforward as a deferred tax asset of $80,000 ($200,000 × 40%), assuming that the enacted future tax rate is 40 percent. Groh records the benefits of the carryback and the carryforward in 2006 as follows.

To recognize benefit of loss carryback		
Income Tax Refund Receivable	110,000	
Benefit Due to Loss Carryback (Income Tax Expense)		110,000
To recognize benefit of loss carryforward		
Deferred Tax Asset	80,000	
Benefit Due to Loss Carryforward (Income Tax Expense)		80,000

[4]The length of the carryforward period has varied. It has increased from 7 years to 20 years over a period of time.

[5]This requirement is controversial because many believe it is inappropriate to recognize deferred tax assets except when assured beyond a reasonable doubt. Others argue that companies should never recognize deferred tax assets for loss carryforwards until realizing the income in the future.

Groh realizes the income tax refund receivable of $110,000 immediately as a refund of taxes paid in the past. It establishes a Deferred Tax Asset for the benefits of future tax savings. The two accounts credited are contra income tax expense items, which Groh presents on the 2006 income statement shown in Illustration 17-32.

ILLUSTRATION 17-32
Recognition of the Benefit of the Loss Carryback and Carryforward in the Loss Year

GROH INC. INCOME STATEMENT (PARTIAL) FOR 2006		
Operating loss before income taxes		$(500,000)
Income tax benefit		
Benefit due to loss carryback	$110,000	
Benefit due to loss carryforward	80,000	190,000
Net loss		$(310,000)

The **current tax benefit** of $110,000 is the income tax refundable for the year. Groh determines this amount by applying the carryback provisions of the tax law to the taxable loss for 2006. The $80,000 is the **deferred tax benefit** for the year, which results from an increase in the deferred tax asset.

For 2007, assume that Groh returns to profitable operations and has taxable income of $250,000 (prior to adjustment for the NOL carryforward), subject to a 40 percent tax rate. Groh then realizes the benefits of the carryforward for tax purposes in 2007, which it recognized for accounting purposes in 2006. Groh computes the income tax payable for 2007 as shown in Illustration 17-33.

ILLUSTRATION 17-33
Computation of Income Tax Payable with Realized Loss Carryforward

Taxable income prior to loss carryforward	$ 250,000
Loss carryforward deduction	(200,000)
Taxable income for 2007	50,000
Tax rate	40%
Income tax payable for 2007	$ 20,000

Groh records income taxes in 2007 as follows.

Income Tax Expense	100,000	
Deferred Tax Asset		80,000
Income Tax Payable		20,000

The benefits of the NOL carryforward, realized in 2007, reduce the Deferred Tax Asset account to zero.

The 2007 income statement that appears in Illustration 17-34 does **not report** the tax effects of either the loss carryback or the loss carryforward, because Groh had reported both previously.

ILLUSTRATION 17-34
Presentation of the Benefit of Loss Carryforward Realized in 2007, Recognized in 2006

GROH INC. INCOME STATEMENT (PARTIAL) FOR 2007		
Income before income taxes		$250,000
Income tax expense		
Current	$20,000	
Deferred	80,000	100,000
Net income		$150,000

Carryforward with Valuation Allowance

Let us return to the Groh example. Assume that it is more likely than not that Groh will *not* realize the entire NOL carryforward in future years. In this situation, Groh records the tax benefits of $110,000 associated with the $300,000 NOL carryback, as we previously described. In addition, it records a Deferred Tax Asset of $80,000 ($200,000 × 40%) for the potential benefits related to the loss carryforward, and an allowance to reduce the deferred tax asset by the same amount. Groh makes the following journal entries in 2006.

To recognize benefit of loss carryback

Income Tax Refund Receivable	110,000	
Benefit Due to Loss Carryback (Income Tax Expense)		110,000

To recognize benefit of loss carryforward

Deferred Tax Asset	80,000	
Benefit Due to Loss Carryforward (Income Tax Expense)		80,000

To record allowance amount

Benefit Due to Loss Carryforward (Income Tax Expense)	80,000	
Allowance to Reduce Deferred Tax Asset to Expected Realizable Value		80,000

The latter entry indicates that because positive evidence of sufficient quality and quantity is unavailable to counteract the negative evidence, Groh needs a valuation allowance.

Illustration 17-35 shows Groh's 2006 income statement presentation.

ILLUSTRATION 17-35
Recognition of Benefit of Loss Carryback Only

GROH INC.
INCOME STATEMENT (PARTIAL) FOR 2006

Operating loss before income taxes	$(500,000)
Income tax benefit	
Benefit due to loss carryback	110,000
Net loss	$(390,000)

In 2007, assuming that Groh has taxable income of $250,000 (before considering the carryforward), subject to a tax rate of 40 percent, it realizes the deferred tax asset. It thus no longer needs the allowance. Groh records the following entries.

To record current and deferred income taxes

Income Tax Expense	100,000	
Deferred Tax Asset		80,000
Income Tax Payable		20,000

To eliminate allowance and recognize loss carryforward

Allowance to Reduce Deferred Tax Asset to Expected Realizable Value	80,000	
Benefit Due to Loss Carryforward (Income Tax Expense)		80,000

Groh reports the $80,000 Benefit Due to the Loss Carryforward on the 2007 income statement. The company did not recognize it in 2006 because it was more likely than not that it would not be realized. Assuming that Groh derives the income for 2007 from continuing operations, it prepares the income statement as shown in Illustration 17-36.

ILLUSTRATION 17-36
Recognition of Benefit of Loss Carryforward When Realized

GROH INC.
INCOME STATEMENT (PARTIAL) FOR 2007

Income before income taxes		$250,000
Income tax expense		
Current	$ 20,000	
Deferred	80,000	
Benefit due to loss carryforward	(80,000)	20,000
Net income		$230,000

Another method is to report only one line for total income tax expense of $20,000 on the face of the income statement and disclose the components of income tax expense in the notes to the financial statements.

Valuation Allowance Revisited

A company should consider all positive and negative information in determining whether it needs a valuation allowance. Whether the company will realize a deferred tax asset depends on whether sufficient taxable income exists or will exist within the carryforward period available under tax law. Illustration 17-37 shows possible sources of taxable income that may be available under the tax law to realize a tax benefit for deductible temporary differences and carryforwards.

ILLUSTRATION 17-37
Possible Sources of Taxable Income

Taxable Income Sources

a. Future reversals of existing taxable temporary differences

b. Future taxable income exclusive of reversing temporary differences and carryforwards

c. Taxable income in prior carryback year(s) if carryback is permitted under the tax law

d. **Tax-planning strategies** that would, if necessary, be implemented to:
(1) Accelerate taxable amounts to utilize expiring carryforwards
(2) Change the character of taxable or deductible amounts from ordinary income or loss to capital gain or loss
(3) Switch from tax-exempt to taxable investments.[6]

If any one of these sources is sufficient to support a conclusion that a valuation allowance is unnecessary, a company need not consider other sources.

Forming a conclusion that a valuation allowance is not needed is difficult when there is negative evidence such as cumulative losses in recent years. Companies may also cite positive evidence indicating that a valuation allowance is not needed. Illustration 17-38 presents examples (not prerequisites) of evidence to consider when determining the need for a valuation allowance.

ILLUSTRATION 17-38
Evidence to Consider in Evaluating the Need for a Valuation Account

Negative Evidence

a. A history of operating loss or tax credit carryforwards expiring unused

b. Losses expected in early future years (by a presently profitable entity)

c. Unsettled circumstances that, if unfavorably resolved, would adversely affect future operations and profit levels on a continuing basis in future years

d. A carryback, carryforward period that is so brief that it would limit realization of tax benefits if (1) a significant deductible temporary difference is expected to reverse in a single year or (2) the enterprise operates in a traditionally cyclical business.

Positive Evidence

a. Existing contracts or firm sales backlog that will produce more than enough taxable income to realize the deferred tax asset based on existing sale prices and cost structures

b. An excess of appreciated asset value over the tax basis of the entity's net assets in an amount sufficient to realize the deferred tax asset

c. A strong earnings history exclusive of the loss that created the future deductible amount (tax loss carryforward or deductible temporary difference) coupled with evidence indicating that the loss is an aberration rather than a continuing condition (for example, the result of an unusual, infrequent, or extraordinary item).[7]

INTERNATIONAL INSIGHT

Under international accounting standards *(IAS 12)*, a company may not recognize a deferred tax asset unless realization is "probable." However, "probable" is not defined in the standard, leading to diversity in the recognition of deferred tax assets.

The use of a valuation allowance provides a company with an opportunity to manage its earnings. As one accounting expert notes, "The 'more likely than not' provision is perhaps the most judgmental clause in accounting." Some companies may set up a valuation account and then use it to increase income as needed. Others may take the income immediately to increase capital or to offset large negative charges to income.

[6]"Accounting for Income Taxes," *Statement of Financial Accounting Standards No. 109* (Norwalk, Conn.: FASB, 1992). Companies implement a tax-planning strategy to realize a tax benefit for an operating loss or tax credit carryforward before it expires. Companies consider tax-planning strategies when assessing the need for and amount of a valuation allowance for deferred tax assets.

[7]Ibid., pars. 23 and 24.

READ THOSE NOTES

WHAT DO THE NUMBERS MEAN?

A recent study of companies' valuation allowances indicates that the allowances are related to the factors identified as positive and negative evidence. And though there is little evidence that companies use the valuation allowance to manage earnings, the press sometimes understates the impact of reversing the deferred tax valuation allowance.

For example, in one year **Verity, Inc.** eliminated its entire valuation allowance of $18.9 million but focused on a net deferred tax gain of $2.9 million in its press release. Why the difference? As revealed in Verity's financial statement notes, other deferred tax expense amounts totaled over $16 million. Thus, the one-time valuation reversal gave an $18.9 million bump to income, not the net $2.9 million reported in the press.

The lesson: After you read the morning paper, read the financial statement notes.

Source: G. S Miller and D. J. Skinner, "Determinants of the Valuation Allowance for Deferred Tax Assets under *SFAS No. 109*," *The Accounting Review* (April 1998).

FINANCIAL STATEMENT PRESENTATION

Balance Sheet

OBJECTIVE 9
Describe the presentation of deferred income taxes in financial statements.

Deferred tax accounts are reported on the balance sheet as assets and liabilities. Companies should classify these accounts as a net current amount and a net noncurrent amount. **An individual deferred tax liability or asset is classified as current or noncurrent based on the classification of the related asset or liability for financial reporting purposes.**

A company considers a deferred tax asset or liability to be related to an asset or liability, if reduction of the asset or liability causes the temporary difference to reverse or turn around. A company should classify a deferred tax liability or asset that is unrelated to an asset or liability for financial reporting, including a deferred tax asset related to a loss carryforward, according to the expected reversal date of the temporary difference.

To illustrate, assume that Morgan Inc. records bad debt expense using the allowance method for accounting purposes and the direct write-off method for tax purposes. It currently has Accounts Receivable and Allowance for Doubtful Accounts balances of $2 million and $100,000, respectively. In addition, given a 40 percent tax rate, Morgan has a debit balance in the Deferred Tax Asset account of $40,000 (40% × $100,000). It considers the $40,000 debit balance in the Deferred Tax Asset account to be related to the Accounts Receivable and the Allowance for Doubtful Accounts balances because collection or write-off of the receivables will cause the temporary difference to reverse. Therefore, Morgan classifies the Deferred Tax Asset account as current, the same as the Accounts Receivable and Allowance for Doubtful Accounts balances.

In practice, most companies engage in a large number of transactions that give rise to deferred taxes. Companies should classify the balances in the deferred tax accounts on the balance sheet in two categories: one for the **net current amount**, and one for the **net noncurrent amount**. We summarize this procedure as follows.

1 *Classify the amounts as current or noncurrent.* If related to a specific asset or liability, classify the amounts in the same manner as the related asset or liability. If not related, classify them on the basis of the expected reversal date of the temporary difference.

2 *Determine the net current amount* by summing the various deferred tax assets and liabilities classified as current. If the net result is an asset, report it on the balance sheet as a current asset; if a liability, report it as a current liability.

3 *Determine the net noncurrent amount* by summing the various deferred tax assets and liabilities classified as noncurrent. If the net result is an asset, report it on the balance sheet as a noncurrent asset; if a liability, report it as a long-term liability.

To illustrate, assume that K. Scott Company has four deferred tax items at December 31, 2007. Illustration 17-39 shows an analysis of these four temporary differences as current or noncurrent.

ILLUSTRATION 17-39
Classification of Temporary Differences as Current or Noncurrent

Temporary Difference	Resulting Deferred Tax (Asset)	Resulting Deferred Tax Liability	Related Balance Sheet Account	Classification
1. Rent collected in advance: recognized when earned for accounting purposes and when received for tax purposes.	$(42,000)		Unearned Rent	Current
2. Use of straight-line depreciation for accounting purposes and accelerated depreciation for tax purposes.		$214,000	Equipment	Noncurrent
3. Recognition of profits on installment sales during period of sale for accounting purposes and during period of collection for tax purposes.		45,000	Installment Accounts Receivable	Current
4. Warranty liabilities: recognized for accounting purposes at time of sale; for tax purposes at time paid.	(12,000)		Estimated Liability under Warranties	Current
Totals	$(54,000)	$259,000		

K. Scott classifies as current a deferred tax asset of $9,000 ($42,000 + $12,000 − $45,000). It also reports as noncurrent a deferred tax liability of $214,000. Consequently, K. Scott's December 31, 2007, balance sheet reports deferred income taxes as shown in Illustration 17-40.

ILLUSTRATION 17-40
Balance Sheet Presentation of Deferred Income Taxes

Current assets	
Deferred tax asset	$ 9,000
Long-term liabilities	
Deferred tax liability	$214,000

As we indicated earlier, a deferred tax asset or liability **may not be related** to an asset or liability for financial reporting purposes. One example is an operating loss carryforward. In this case, a company records a deferred tax asset, but there is no related, identifiable asset or liability for financial reporting purposes. In these limited situations, deferred income taxes are classified according to the **expected reversal date** of the temporary difference. That is, a company should report the tax effect of any temporary difference reversing next year as current, and the remainder as noncurrent. If a deferred tax asset is noncurrent, a company should classify it in the "Other assets" section.

The total of all deferred tax liabilities, the total of all deferred tax assets, and the total valuation allowance should be disclosed. In addition, companies should disclose the following: (1) any net change during the year in the total valuation allowance, and (2) the types of temporary differences, carryforwards, or carrybacks that give rise to significant portions of deferred tax liabilities and assets.

Income tax payable is reported as a current liability on the balance sheet. Corporations make estimated tax payments to the Internal Revenue Service quarterly. They record these estimated payments by a debit to Prepaid Income Taxes. As a result, the balance of the Income Tax Payable offsets the balance of the Prepaid Income Taxes account when reporting income taxes on the balance sheet.

Income Statement

Companies should allocate income tax expense (or benefit) to continuing operations, discontinued operations, extraordinary items, and prior period adjustments. This approach is referred to as intraperiod tax allocation.

wiley.com/college/kieso

Expanded Discussion of Intraperiod Tax Allocation

In addition, companies should disclose the significant components of income tax expense attributable to continuing operations:

1. Current tax expense or benefit.
2. Deferred tax expense or benefit, exclusive of other components listed below.
3. Investment tax credits.
4. Government grants (if recognized as a reduction of income tax expense).
5. The benefits of operating loss carryforwards (resulting in a reduction of income tax expense).
6. Tax expense that results from allocating tax benefits either directly to paid-in capital or to reduce goodwill or other noncurrent intangible assets of an acquired entity.
7. Adjustments of a deferred tax liability or asset for enacted changes in tax laws or rates or a change in the tax status of a company.
8. Adjustments of the beginning-of-the-year balance of a valuation allowance because of a change in circumstances that causes a change in judgment about the realizability of the related deferred tax asset in future years.

In the notes, companies must also reconcile (using percentages or dollar amounts) income tax expense attributable to continuing operations with the amount that results from applying domestic federal statutory tax rates to pretax income from continuing operations. Companies should disclose the estimated amount and the nature of each significant reconciling item. Illustration 17-41 presents an example from the 2004 annual report of **PepsiCo, Inc.**.

These income tax disclosures are required for several reasons:

wiley.com/college/kieso

Additional Examples of Deferred Tax Disclosures

1. ***Assessing Quality of Earnings.*** Many investors seeking to assess the quality of a company's earnings are interested in the reconciliation of pretax financial income to taxable income. Analysts carefully examine earnings that are enhanced by a favorable tax effect, particularly if the tax effect is nonrecurring. For example, the tax disclosure in Illustration 17-41 indicates that **PepsiCo**'s effective tax rate declined from 28.5 percent in 2003 to 24.7 percent in 2004 (primarily due to settlement of a prior year's tax audit.) The decline translates into a tax savings of $38 million. These savings contributed to PepsiCo's increase in bottom-line income from 2003 to 2004.
2. ***Making Better Predictions of Future Cash Flows.*** Examination of the deferred portion of income tax expense provides information as to whether taxes payable are likely to be higher or lower in the future. In **PepsiCo**'s case, analysts expect significant future taxable amounts and higher tax payments, due to realization of gains on equity investments, lower depreciation in the future, and higher payments for pension expense. As a result, it may be possible to predict future reductions in deferred tax liabilities leading to a loss of liquidity. Why? Because actual tax payments will be higher than the tax expense reported on the income statement.[8]
3. ***Predicting Future Cash Flows from Operating Loss Carryforwards.*** Companies should disclose the amounts and expiration dates of any operating loss carryforwards for tax purposes. From this disclosure, analysts determine the amount of income that the company may recognize in the future on which it will pay no income tax. For example, the **PepsiCo** disclosure in Illustration 17-41 indicates that PepsiCo has $4.3 billion in net operating loss carryforwards that it can use to reduce future taxes up to the year 2024 and beyond. However, the valuation allowance indicates that $564 million of the deferred tax asset may not be realized in the future.

Loss carryforwards can be valuable to a potential acquirer. For example, as mentioned earlier, **Yahoo** has a substantial net operating loss carryforward. A potential acquirer would find Yahoo more valuable as a result of these carryforwards. That is, the

[8]An article by R. P. Weber and J. E. Wheeler, "Using Income Tax Disclosures to Explore Significant Economic Transactions," *Accounting Horizons* (September 1992), discusses how analysts use deferred tax disclosures to assess the quality of earnings and to predict future cash flows.

PEPSICO

ILLUSTRATION 17-41
Disclosure of Income Taxes—PepsiCo, Inc.

PepsiCo, Inc.
(in millions)

Note 13: Income Taxes	2004	2003
Income before income taxes—continuing operations		
U.S.	$2,946	$3,267
Foreign	2,600	1,725
	$5,546	$4,992
Provision for income taxes—continuing operations		
Current: U.S. Federal	$1,030	$1,326
Foreign	256	341
State	69	80
	1,355	1,747
Deferred: U.S. Federal	11	(274)
Foreign	5	(47)
State	1	(2)
	17	(323)
	$1,372	$1,424
Tax rate reconciliation—continuing operations		
U.S. Federal statutory tax rate	35.0%	35.0%
State income tax, net of U.S. Federal tax benefit	0.8	1.0
Lower taxes on foreign results	(5.4)	(5.5)
Settlement of prior years audit	(4.8)	(2.2)
Merger-related costs and impairment and restructuring charges	—	0.1
Other, net	(0.9)	0.1
Annual tax rate	24.7%	28.5%
Deferred tax liabilities		
Investments in noncontrolled affiliates	$ 850	$ 792
Property, plant and equipment	857	806
Pension benefits	669	563
Intangible assets other than nondeductible goodwill	153	146
Safe harbor leases	13	33
Zero coupon notes	46	53
Other	144	199
Gross deferred tax liabilities	2,732	2,592
Deferred tax assets		
Net carryforwards	666	535
Stock-based compensation	402	332
Retiree medical benefits	402	343
Other employee-related benefits	379	384
Various current and noncurrent liabilities	460	482
Gross deferred tax assets	2,309	2,076
Valuation allowances	(564)	(438)
Deferred tax assets, net	1,745	1,638
Net deferred tax liabilities	$ 987	$ 954
Deferred taxes included within:		
Prepaid expenses and other current assets	$ 229	$ 307
Deferred income taxes	$1,216	$1,261
Analysis of valuation allowances		
Balance, beginning of year	$ 438	$ 487
Provision/(benefit)	118	(52)
Other additions/(deductions)	8	3
Balance, end of year	$ 564	$ 438

Carryforwards, Credits and Allowances

Operating loss carryforwards totaling $4.3 billion at year-end 2004 are being carried forward in a number of foreign and state jurisdictions where we are permitted to use tax operating losses from prior periods to reduce future taxable income. These operating losses will expire as follows: $0.1 billion in 2005, $3.1 billion between 2006 and 2024 and $1.1 billion may be carried forward indefinitely. In addition, certain tax credits generated in prior periods of approximately $49.3 million are available to reduce certain foreign tax liabilities through 2011. We establish valuation allowances for our deferred tax assets when the amount of expected future taxable income is not likely to support the use of the deduction or credit.

Tax Benefit from Discontinued Operations

In the fourth quarter of 2004, we reached agreement with the taxing authorities for an open issue related to our discontinued restaurant operations which resulted in a tax benefit of $38 million or $0.02 per share.

acquirer may be able to use these carryforwards to shield future income. However the acquiring company has to be careful, because the structure of the deal may lead to a situation where the deductions will be severely limited.

Much the same issue arises in companies emerging from bankruptcy. In many cases these companies have large NOLs, but the value of the losses may be limited. This is because any gains related to the cancellation of liabilities in bankruptcy must be offset against the NOLs. For example, when **Kmart Holding Corp.** emerged from bankruptcy in early 2004, it disclosed NOL carryforwards approximating $3.8 billion. At the same time, Kmart disclosed cancellation of debt gains that reduced the value of the NOL carryforward. These reductions soured the merger between Kmart and **Sears Roebuck** because the cancellation of the indebtedness gains reduced the value of the Kmart carryforwards to the merged company by $3.74 billion.[9]

NOLs: GOOD NEWS OR BAD?

WHAT DO THE NUMBERS MEAN?

Here are some net operating loss numbers recently reported by several notable companies.

NOLs ($ in millions)

Company	2004 Income (Loss)	Operating Loss Carryforward	Tax Benefit (Deferred Tax Asset)	Comment
Delta Airlines, Inc.	($5,198.00)	$7,500.00	$2,848.00	Begins to expire in 2022. Valuation allowance recorded.
Goodyear	114.80	1,306.60*	457.30	Begins to expire in 2005. Full valuation allowance.
Kodak	556.00	509.00	234.00	Begins to expire in 2005. Valuation allowance on foreign credits only.
Krispy Kreme	57.09	26.40*	9.24	No valuation allowance.
Yahoo Inc.	42.82	5,400.00	1,443.50	State and federal carryforwards. Begins to expire in 2005. Valuation allowance recorded.

*Not reported; estimated as [(Tax benefit) ÷ 35%].

All of these companies are using the carryforward provisions of the tax code for their NOLs. For many of them, the NOL is an amount far exceeding their reported profits. Why carry forward the loss to get the tax deduction? First, the company may have already used up the carryback provision, which allows only a two-year carryback period. (Carryforwards can be claimed up to 20 years in the future.) In some cases, management expects the tax rates in the future to be higher. This difference in expected rates provides a bigger tax benefit if the losses are carried forward and matched against future income. Is there a downside? To realize the benefits of carryforwards, a company must have future taxable income in the carryforward period in order to claim the NOL deductions. As we learned, if it is more likely than not that a company will not have taxable income, it must record a valuation allowance (and increased tax expense). As the data above indicate, recording a valuation allowance to reflect the uncertainty of realizing the tax benefits has merit. But for some, the NOL benefits begin to expire in the following year, which may be not enough time to generate sufficient taxable income in order to claim the NOL deduction.

Source: Company annual reports.

[9]P. McConnell, J. Pegg, C. Senyak, and D. Mott, "The ABCs of NOLs," *Accounting Issues*, Bear Stearns Equity Research (June 2005). The IRS frowns on acquisitions done solely to obtain operating loss carryforwards. If it determines that the merger is solely tax motivated, the IRS disallows the deductions. But because it is very difficult to determine whether a merger is or is not tax-motivated, the "purchase of operating loss carryforwards" continues.

REVIEW OF THE ASSET-LIABILITY METHOD

OBJECTIVE 10
Indicate the basic principles of the asset-liability method.

The FASB believes that the **asset-liability method** (sometimes referred to as the **liability approach**) is the most consistent method for accounting for income taxes. One objective of this approach is to recognize the amount of taxes payable or refundable for the current year. A second objective is to recognize **deferred tax liabilities and assets** for the **future tax consequences** of events that have been recognized in the financial statements or tax returns.

To implement the objectives, companies apply some basic principles in accounting for income taxes at the date of the financial statements, as listed in Illustration 17-42.

ILLUSTRATION 17-42
Basic Principles of the Asset-Liability Method

Basic Principles

a. A current tax liability or asset is recognized for the estimated taxes payable or refundable on the tax return for the current year.
b. A deferred tax liability or asset is recognized for the estimated future tax effects attributable to temporary differences and carryforwards.
c. The measurement of current and deferred tax liabilities and assets is based on provisions of the enacted tax law; the effects of future changes in tax laws or rates are not anticipated.
d. The measurement of deferred tax assets is reduced, if necessary, by the amount of any tax benefits that, based on available evidence, are not expected to be realized.[10]

Discussion of Conceptual Approaches to Interperiod Tax Allocation

Illustration 17-43 diagrams the procedures for implementing the asset-liability method.

ILLUSTRATION 17-43
Procedures for Computing and Reporting Deferred Income Taxes

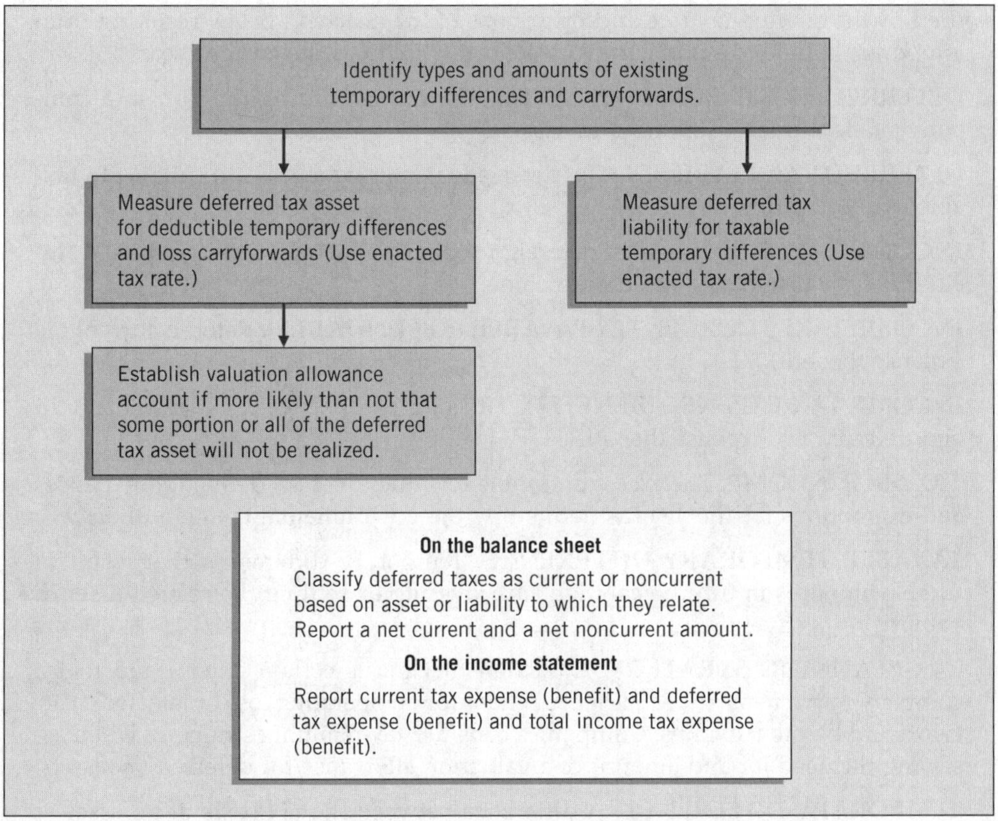

As an aid to understanding deferred income taxes, we provide the following glossary.[11]

[10]"Accounting for Income Taxes" (1992), pars. 6 and 8.

[11]"Accounting for Income Taxes," Appendix E.

INTERNATIONAL INSIGHT

The IFRS on income taxes is based on the same principles as the U.S. GAAP—comprehensive recognition of deferred tax assets and liabilities.

KEY DEFERRED INCOME TAX TERMS

CARRYBACKS. Deductions or credits that cannot be utilized on the tax return during a year and that may be carried back to reduce taxable income or taxes paid in a prior year. An **operating loss carryback** is an excess of tax deductions over gross income in a year. A **tax credit carryback** is the amount by which tax credits available for utilization exceed statutory limitations.

CARRYFORWARDS. Deductions or credits that cannot be utilized on the tax return during a year and that may be carried forward to reduce taxable income or taxes payable in a future year. An **operating loss carryforward** is an excess of tax deductions over gross income in a year. A **tax credit carryforward** is the amount by which tax credits available for utilization exceed statutory limitations.

CURRENT TAX EXPENSE (BENEFIT). The amount of income taxes paid or payable (or refundable) for a year as determined by applying the provisions of the enacted tax law to the taxable income or excess of deductions over revenues for that year.

DEDUCTIBLE TEMPORARY DIFFERENCE. Temporary differences that result in deductible amounts in future years when recovering or settling the related asset or liability, respectively.

DEFERRED TAX ASSET. The deferred tax consequences attributable to deductible temporary differences and carryforwards.

DEFERRED TAX CONSEQUENCES. The future effects on income taxes as measured by the enacted tax rate and provisions of the enacted tax law resulting from temporary differences and carryforwards at the end of the current year.

DEFERRED TAX EXPENSE (BENEFIT). The change during the year in a company's deferred tax liabilities and assets.

DEFERRED TAX LIABILITY. The deferred tax consequences attributable to taxable temporary differences.

INCOME TAXES. Domestic and foreign federal (national), state, and local (including franchise) taxes based on income.

INCOME TAXES CURRENTLY PAYABLE (REFUNDABLE). Refer to current tax expense (benefit).

INCOME TAX EXPENSE (BENEFIT). The sum of current tax expense (benefit) and deferred tax expense (benefit).

TAXABLE INCOME. The excess of taxable revenues over tax deductible expenses and exemptions for the year as defined by the governmental taxing authority.

TAXABLE TEMPORARY DIFFERENCE. Temporary differences that result in taxable amounts in future years when recovering or settling the related asset or liability, respectively.

TAX-PLANNING STRATEGY. An action that meets certain criteria and that a company implements to realize a tax benefit for an operating loss or tax credit carryforward before it expires. Companies consider tax-planning strategies when assessing the need for and amount of a valuation allowance for deferred tax assets.

TEMPORARY DIFFERENCE. A difference between the tax basis of an asset or liability and its reported amount in the financial statements that will result in taxable or deductible amounts in future years when recovering or settling the reported amount of the asset or liability, respectively.

VALUATION ALLOWANCE. The portion of a deferred tax asset for which it is more likely than not that a company will not realize a tax benefit.

QUESTIONS

1. Explain the difference between pretax financial income and taxable income.

2. What are the two objectives of accounting for income taxes?

3. Interest on municipal bonds is referred to as a permanent difference when determining the proper amount to report for deferred taxes. Explain the meaning of permanent differences, and give two other examples.

4. Explain the meaning of a temporary difference as it relates to deferred tax computations, and give three examples.

5. Differentiate between an originating temporary difference and a reversing difference.

6. The book basis of depreciable assets for Getty Co. is $900,000, and the tax basis is $700,000 at the end of 2007. The enacted tax rate is 34% for all periods. Determine the amount of deferred taxes to be reported on the balance sheet at the end of 2007.

7. Borg Inc. has a deferred tax liability of $68,000 at the beginning of 2007. At the end of 2007, it reports accounts receivable on the books at $80,000 and the tax basis at zero (its only temporary difference). If the enacted tax rate is 34% for all periods, and income tax payable for the period is $230,000, determine the amount of total income tax expense to report for 2007.

8. What is the difference between a future taxable amount and a future deductible amount? When is it appropriate to record a valuation account for a deferred tax asset?

9. Pretax financial income for Mott Inc. is $300,000, and its taxable income is $100,000 for 2007. Its only temporary difference at the end of the period relates to a $90,000 difference due to excess depreciation for tax purposes. If the tax rate is 40% for all periods, compute the amount of income tax expense to report in 2007. No deferred income taxes existed at the beginning of the year.

10. How are deferred tax assets and deferred tax liabilities reported on the balance sheet?

11. Describe the procedures involved in segregating various deferred tax amounts into current and noncurrent categories.

12. How is it determined whether deferred tax amounts are considered to be "related" to specific asset or liability amounts?

13. At the end of the year, North Carolina Co. has pretax financial income of $550,000. Included in the $550,000 is $70,000 interest income on municipal bonds, $30,000 fine for dumping hazardous waste, and depreciation of $60,000. Depreciation for tax purposes is $45,000. Compute income taxes payable, assuming the tax rate is 30% for all periods.

14. Raleigh Co. has one temporary difference at the beginning of 2007 of $500,000. The deferred tax liability established for this amount is $150,000, based on a tax rate of 30%. The temporary difference will provide the following taxable amounts: $100,000 in 2008; $200,000 in 2009, and $200,000 in 2010. If a new tax rate for 2010 of 25% is enacted into law at the end of 2007, what is the journal entry necessary in 2007 (if any) to adjust deferred taxes?

15. What are some of the reasons that the components of income tax expense should be disclosed and a reconciliation between the effective tax rate and the statutory tax rate be provided?

16. Differentiate between "loss carryback" and "loss carryforward." Which can be accounted for with the greater certainty when it arises? Why?

17. What are the possible treatments for tax purposes of a net operating loss? What are the circumstances that determine the option to be applied? What is the proper treatment of a net operating loss for financial reporting purposes?

18. What controversy relates to the accounting for net operating loss carryforwards?

C H A P T E R E I G H T E E N

ACCOUNTING CHANGES AND ERROR ANALYSIS

So Many Changes

The FASB's conceptual framework describes comparability (including consistency) as one of the qualitative characteristics that contribute to the usefulness of accounting information. Unfortunately, companies are finding it difficult to maintain comparability and consistency due to the numerous changes in accounting principles mandated by the FASB. In addition, a number of companies have faced restatements due to errors in their financial statements. For example, the table below shows types and numbers of accounting changes.

Consolidation of variable interest entities	200	Derivatives and hedging activities	158
Liability and equity financial instruments	188	Asset retirement obligations	125
Guarantees	172	Stock compensation	122
Cost of exit or disposal activities	171	Impairments	68

The following chart indicates an increasing trend in restatements.

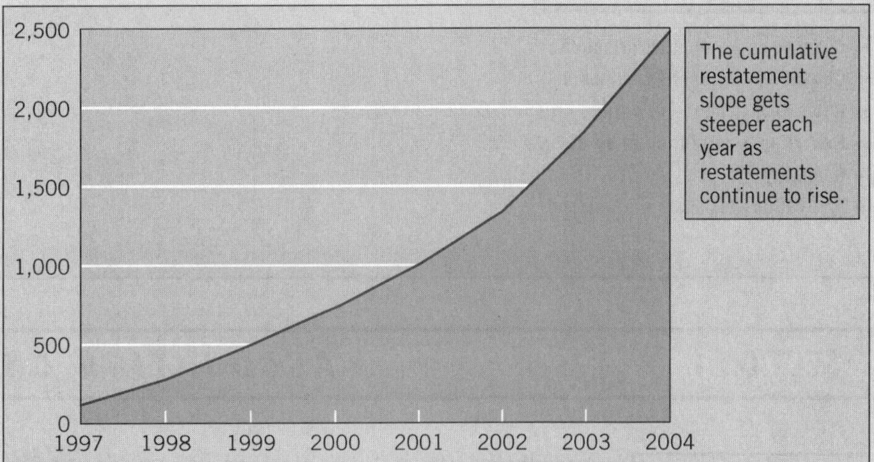

Source: Huron Consulting (1997 through 2002), Glass Lewis (2003 through 2004).

Although the percentage of companies reporting material changes or errors is small, you still must be careful. The reason: The amounts in the financial statements may have changed due to changing accounting principles and/or restatements.[1]

[1]Accounting change data from *Accounting Trends and Techniques—2004* (New York: AICPA, 2004). Restatement graph from T. Baldwin and D. Yoo, "Restatements—Traversing Shaky Ground," *Trend Alert* (June 2, 2005), Glass Lewis and Co., p. 7.

Learning Objectives

After studying this chapter, you should be able to:

1 Identify the types of accounting changes.

2 Describe the accounting for changes in accounting principles.

3 Understand how to account for retrospective accounting changes.

4 Understand how to account for impracticable changes.

5 Describe the accounting for changes in estimates.

6 Identify changes in a reporting entity.

7 Describe the accounting for correction of errors.

8 Identify economic motives for changing accounting methods.

9 Analyze the effect of errors.

PREVIEW OF CHAPTER 18

As our opening story indicates, changes in accounting principles and errors in financial information have increased substantially in recent years. When these changes occur, companies must follow specific accounting and reporting requirements. In addition, to ensure comparability among companies, the FASB has standardized reporting of accounting changes, accounting estimates, error corrections, and related earnings per share information. In this chapter, we discuss these reporting standards, which help investors better understand a company's financial condition. The content and organization of the chapter are as follows.

ACCOUNTING CHANGES AND ERROR ANALYSIS

ACCOUNTING CHANGES

- Changes in accounting principle
- Changes in accounting estimate
- Reporting a change in entity
- Reporting a correction of an error
- Summary
- Motivations for change of method

ERROR ANALYSIS

- Balance sheet errors
- Income statement errors
- Balance sheet and income statement effects
- Comprehensive example
- Preparation of statements with error corrections

SECTION 1 ACCOUNTING CHANGES

OBJECTIVE 1
Identify the types of accounting changes.

Accounting alternatives diminish the comparability of financial information between periods and between companies; they also obscure useful historical trend data. For example, if **Ford** revises its estimates for equipment useful lives, depreciation expense for the current year will not be comparable to depreciation expense reported by Ford in prior years. Similarly, if **Best Buy** changes to FIFO inventory pricing while **Circuit City** uses LIFO, it will be difficult to compare these companies' reported results. A reporting framework helps preserve comparability when there is an accounting change.

UNDERLYING CONCEPTS

While changes in accounting may enhance the qualitative characteristic of *usefulness*, these changes may adversely affect the characteristics of *comparability* and *consistency*.

The FASB has established a reporting framework, which involves three types of accounting changes.[2] The three types of accounting changes are:

1. ***Change in Accounting Principle.*** A change from one generally accepted accounting principle to another one. For example, a company may change its inventory valuation method from LIFO to average cost.
2. ***Change in Accounting Estimate.*** A change that occurs as the result of new information or additional experience. For example, a company may change its estimate of the useful lives of depreciable assets.
3. ***Change in Reporting Entity.*** A change from reporting as one type of entity to another type of entity. As an example, a company might change the subsidiaries for which it prepares consolidated financial statements.

A fourth category necessitates changes in accounting, though it is not classified as an accounting change.

[2] "Accounting Changes and Error Corrections," *Statement of Financial Accounting Standards No. 154* (Stamford, Conn.: FASB, 2005).

4 *Errors in Financial Statements.* Errors result from mathematical mistakes, mistakes in applying accounting principles, or oversight or misuse of facts that existed when preparing the financial statements. For example, a company may incorrectly apply the retail inventory method for determining its final inventory value.

The FASB classifies changes in these categories because each category involves different methods of recognizing changes in the financial statements. In this chapter we discuss these classifications. We also explain how to report each item in the accounts and how to disclose the information in comparative statements.

CHANGES IN ACCOUNTING PRINCIPLE

OBJECTIVE 2
Describe the accounting for changes in accounting principles.

By definition, a **change in accounting principle involves a change from one generally accepted accounting principle to another**. For example, a company might change the basis of inventory pricing from average cost to LIFO. Or it might change its method of revenue recognition for long-term construction contracts from the completed-contract to the percentage-of-completion method.

Companies must carefully examine each circumstance to ensure that a change in principle has actually occurred. **Adoption of a new principle** in recognition of events that have occurred for the first time or that were previously immaterial is not an accounting change. For example, a change in accounting principle has not occurred when a company adopts an inventory method (e.g., FIFO) for **newly** acquired items of inventory, even if FIFO differs from that used for **previously recorded** inventory. Another example is certain marketing expenditures that were previously immaterial and expensed in the period incurred. It would not be considered a change in accounting principle if they become material and so may be acceptably deferred and amortized.

Finally, what if a company previously followed an accounting principle that was not acceptable? Or what if the company applied a principle incorrectly? In such cases, the profession considers a change to a generally accepted accounting principle **a correction of an error**. For example, a switch from the cash (income tax) basis of accounting to the accrual basis is a correction of an error. Or, if a company deducted salvage value when computing double-declining depreciation on plant assets and later recomputed depreciation without deducting estimated salvage value, it has corrected an error.

There are three possible approaches for reporting changes in accounting principles:

Report changes currently. In this approach, companies report the cumulative effect of the change in the current year's income statement as an irregular item. The **cumulative effect** is the difference in prior years' income between the newly adopted and prior accounting method. Under this approach, the effect of the change on prior years' income appears only in the current-year income statement. The company does not change **prior-year financial statements.**

Advocates of this position argue that changing prior years' financial statements results in a loss of confidence in financial reports. How do investors react when told that the earnings computed three years ago are now entirely different? Changing prior periods, if permitted, also might upset contractual arrangements based on the old figures. For example, profit-sharing arrangements computed on the old basis might have to be recomputed and completely new distributions made, creating numerous legal problems. Many practical difficulties also exist: The cost of changing prior-period financial statements may be excessive, or determining the amount of the prior-period effect may be impossible on the basis of available data.

Report changes retrospectively. Retrospective application refers to the application of a different accounting principle to recast previously issued financial statements—**as if the new principle had always been used**. In other words, the company "goes back" and adjusts **prior years' statements** on a basis consistent with the newly adopted principle. The company shows any cumulative effect of the change as an adjustment to beginning retained earnings of the earliest year presented.

Advocates of this position argue that retrospective application ensures comparability. Think for a moment what happens if this approach is not used: The year *previous* to the change will be on the old method; the year *of the change* will report the entire cumulative adjustment; and the *following* year will present financial statements on the new basis without the cumulative effect of the change. Such lack of consistency fails to provide meaningful earnings-trend data and other financial relationships necessary to evaluate the business.

INTERNATIONAL INSIGHT

IAS 8 generally requires retrospective application to prior years for accounting changes. However, *IAS 8* permits the cumulative-effect method or prospective method if a company cannot reasonably determine the amounts to which to restate prior periods.

Report changes prospectively (in the future). In this approach, previously reported results remain. As a result, companies do not adjust opening balances to reflect the change in principle. Advocates of this position argue that once management presents financial statements based on acceptable accounting principles, they are final; management cannot change prior periods by adopting a new principle. According to this line of reasoning, the current-period cumulative adjustment is not appropriate, because that approach includes amounts that have little or no relationship to the current year's income or economic events.

Given these three possible approaches, which does the accounting profession prefer? The FASB **requires that companies use the retrospective approach.** Why? Because it provides financial statement users with more useful information than the cumulative-effect or prospective approaches.[3] The rationale is that changing the prior statements to be on the same basis as the newly adopted principle results in greater consistency across accounting periods. Users can then better compare results from one period to the next.[4]

QUITE A CHANGE

WHAT DO THE NUMBERS MEAN?

The cumulative-effect approach results in a loss of comparability. Also, reporting the cumulative adjustment in the period of the change can significantly affect net income, resulting in a misleading income figure. For example, at one time **Chrysler Corporation** (now **DaimlerChrysler**) changed its inventory accounting from LIFO to FIFO. If Chrysler had used the cumulative-effect approach, it would have reported a $53,500,000 adjustment to net income. That adjustment would have resulted in net income of $45,900,000, instead of a net loss of $7,600,000.

A second case: In the early 1980s the railroad industry switched from the retirement-replacement method of depreciating railroad equipment to more generally used methods such as straight-line depreciation. Using cumulative treatment, railroad companies would have made substantial adjustments to income in the period of change. Many in the industry argued that including such large cumulative-effect adjustments in the current year would distort the information and make it less useful.

Such situations lend support to retrospective application so that comparability is maintained.

Retrospective Accounting Change Approach

OBJECTIVE 3
Understand how to account for retrospective accounting changes.

A presumption exists that once a company adopts an accounting principle, it should not change. That presumption is understandable, given the idea that consistent use of

[3]"Accounting Changes and Error Corrections," *Statement of Financial Accounting Standards No. 154* (Stamford, Conn.: FASB, 2005). This recent standard carries forward many of the provisions in the previous accounting change standard (*APB Opinion No. 20*), including the accounting for errors, changes in estimates, and the disclosures related to accounting changes.

[4]Adoption of the retrospective approach contributes to international accounting convergence. The FASB and the IASB are collaborating on a project in which they have agreed to converge around high-quality solutions to resolve differences between U.S. GAAP and International Financial Reporting Standards (IFRS). By adopting the retrospective approach, which is the method used in IFRS, the FASB agreed that this approach is superior to the current approach.

an accounting principle enhances the usefulness of financial statements. However, the environment continually changes, and companies change in response. Recent standards on such subjects as stock options, exchanges of nonmonetary assets, derivatives, and so on indicate that changes in accounting principle will continue to occur.

When a company changes an accounting principle, it should report the change using retrospective application. In general terms, here is what it must do:

1. It adjusts its financial statements for each prior period presented. Thus, financial statement information about prior periods is on the same basis as the new accounting principle.
2. It adjusts the carrying amounts of assets and liabilities as of the beginning of the first year presented. By doing so, these accounts reflect the cumulative effect on periods prior to those presented of the change to the new accounting principle. The company also makes an offsetting adjustment to the opening balance of retained earnings or other appropriate component of stockholders' equity or net assets as of the beginning of the first year presented.

For example, assume that **Target** decides to change its inventory valuation method in 2007 from the retail inventory method (FIFO) to the retail inventory (average cost). It provides comparative information for 2005 and 2006 based on the new method. Target would adjust its assets, liabilities, and retained earnings for periods prior to 2005 and report these amounts in the 2005 financial statements, when it prepares comparative financial statements.

Example of Retrospective Accounting Change

To illustrate the retrospective approach, assume that Lancer Company has accounted for its inventory using the LIFO method. In 2007, the company changes to the FIFO method because management believes this approach provides a more appropriate measure of its inventory costs. Illustration 18-1 provides additional information related to Lancer Company.

ILLUSTRATION 18-1
Lancer Company Information

1. Lancer Company started its operations on January 1, 2005. At that time stockholders invested $100,000 in the business in exchange for common stock.
2. All sales, purchases, and operating expenses for the period 2005–2007 are cash transactions. Lancer's cash flows over this period are as follows.

	2005	2006	2007
Sales	$300,000	$300,000	$300,000
Purchases	90,000	110,000	125,000
Operating expenses	100,000	100,000	100,000
Cash flow from operations	$110,000	$ 90,000	$ 75,000

3. Lancer has used the LIFO method for financial reporting since its inception.
4. Inventory determined under LIFO and FIFO for the period 2005–2007 is as follows.

	LIFO Method	FIFO Method	Difference
January 1, 2005	$ 0	$ 0	$ 0
December 31, 2005	10,000	12,000	2,000
December 31, 2006	20,000	25,000	5,000
December 31, 2007	32,000	39,000	7,000

5. Cost of goods sold under LIFO and FIFO for the period 2005–2007 are as follows.

	Cost of Goods Sold LIFO	Cost of Goods Sold FIFO	Difference
January 1, 2005	$ 0	$ 0	$ 0
December 31, 2005	80,000	78,000	2,000
December 31, 2006	100,000	97,000	3,000
December 31, 2007	113,000	111,000	2,000

6. Earnings per share information is not required on the income statement.
7. All tax effects for this illustration should be ignored.

Given the information about Lancer Company, Illustration 18-2 shows its income statement, retained earnings statement, balance sheet, and statement of cash flows for 2005–2007 under LIFO.

ILLUSTRATION 18-2
Lancer Financial Statements (LIFO)

LANCER COMPANY
INCOME STATEMENT
FOR THE YEAR ENDED DECEMBER 31

	2005	2006	2007
Sales	$300,000	$300,000	$300,000
Cost of goods sold (LIFO)	80,000	100,000	113,000
Operating expenses	100,000	100,000	100,000
Net income	$120,000	$100,000	$ 87,000

LANCER COMPANY
RETAINED EARNINGS STATEMENT
FOR THE YEAR ENDED DECEMBER 31

	2005	2006	2007
Retained earnings (beginning)	$ 0	$120,000	$220,000
Add: Net income	120,000	100,000	87,000
Retained earnings (ending)	$120,000	$220,000	$307,000

LANCER COMPANY
BALANCE SHEET
AT DECEMBER 31

	2005	2006	2007
Cash	$210,000	$300,000	$375,000
Inventory (LIFO)	10,000	20,000	32,000
Total assets	$220,000	$320,000	$407,000
Common stock	$100,000	$100,000	$100,000
Retained earnings	120,000	220,000	307,000
Total liabilities and stockholder's equity	$220,000	$320,000	$407,000

LANCER COMPANY
STATEMENT OF CASH FLOWS
FOR THE YEAR ENDED DECEMBER 31

	2005	2006	2007
Cash flows from operating activities			
Sales	$300,000	$300,000	$300,000
Purchases	90,000	110,000	125,000
Operating expenses	100,000	100,000	100,000
Net cash provided by operating activities	110,000	90,000	75,000
Cash flows from financing activities			
Issuance of common stock	100,000	—	—
Net increase in cash	210,000	90,000	75,000
Cash at beginning of year	0	210,000	300,000
Cash at end of year	$210,000	$300,000	$375,000

As Illustration 18-2 indicates, under LIFO Lancer Company reports $120,000 net income in 2005, $100,000 net income in 2006, and $87,000 net income in 2007. The amount of inventory reported on Lancer's balance sheet reflects LIFO costing.

Illustration 18-3 shows Lancer's income statement, retained earnings statement, balance sheet, and statement of cash flows for 2005–2007 under **FIFO**. You can see that **the cash flow statement under FIFO is the same as under LIFO**. Although the net incomes are different in each period, there is no cash flow effect from these differences in net income. (If we considered income taxes, a cash flow effect would result.)

ILLUSTRATION 18-3
Lancer Financial Statements (FIFO)

LANCER COMPANY
INCOME STATEMENT
FOR THE YEAR ENDED DECEMBER 31

	2005	2006	2007
Sales	$300,000	$300,000	$300,000
Cost of goods sold (FIFO)	78,000	97,000	111,000
Operating expenses	100,000	100,000	100,000
Net income	$122,000	$103,000	$ 89,000

LANCER COMPANY
RETAINED EARNINGS STATEMENT
FOR THE YEAR ENDED DECEMBER 31

	2005	2006	2007
Retained earnings (beginning)	$ 0	$122,000	$225,000
Add: Net income	122,000	103,000	89,000
Retained earnings (ending)	$122,000	$225,000	$314,000

LANCER COMPANY
BALANCE SHEET
AT DECEMBER 31

	2005	2006	2007
Cash	$210,000	$300,000	$375,000
Inventory (FIFO)	12,000	25,000	39,000
Total assets	$222,000	$325,000	$414,000
Common stock	$100,000	$100,000	$100,000
Retained earnings	122,000	225,000	314,000
Total liabilities and stockholder's equity	$222,000	$325,000	$414,000

LANCER COMPANY
STATEMENT OF CASH FLOWS
FOR THE YEAR ENDED DECEMBER 31

	2005	2006	2007
Cash flows from operating activities			
Sales	$300,000	$300,000	$300,000
Purchases	90,000	110,000	125,000
Operating expenses	100,000	100,000	100,000
Net cash provided by operating activities	110,000	90,000	75,000
Cash flows from financing activities			
Issuance of common stock	100,000	—	—
Net increase in cash	210,000	90,000	75,000
Cast at beginning of year	0	210,000	300,000
Cash at end of year	$210,000	$300,000	$375,000

Compare the financial statements reported in Illustration 18-2 and Illustration 18-3. You can see that, under retrospective application, the change to FIFO inventory valuation affects reported inventories, cost of goods sold, net income, and retained earnings. In the following sections we discuss the accounting and reporting of Lancer's accounting change from LIFO to FIFO.

Accounting for and Reporting a Change in Principle

Given the information provided in Illustrations 18-1, 18-2, and 18-3, we now are ready to account for and report on the accounting change.

Accounting for a Change in Principle

Our first step is to adjust the financial records for the change from LIFO to FIFO. To do so, we perform the analysis in Illustration 18-4.

ILLUSTRATION 18-4
Data for Recording Change in Accounting Principle

	Net Income		Difference in Income
Year	LIFO	FIFO	
2005	$120,000	$122,000	$2,000
2006	100,000	103,000	3,000
Total at beginning of 2007	$220,000	$225,000	$5,000
Total in 2007	$ 87,000	$ 89,000	$2,000

The entry to record the change to the FIFO method at the beginning of 2007 is as follows.

Inventory	5,000	
Retained Earnings		5,000

The change increases the inventory account by $5,000. This amount represents the difference between the ending inventory at December 31, 2006, under LIFO ($20,000) and the ending inventory under FIFO ($25,000). The credit to Retained Earnings indicates the amount needed to change prior-year's income, assuming that Lancer had used FIFO in previous periods.

Reporting a Change in Principle

The disclosure of accounting changes is particularly important. Users of the financial statements want consistent information from one period to the next. Such consistency ensures the usefulness of financial statements. The major disclosure requirements are as follows.

1 The nature of and reason for the change in accounting principle. This must include an explanation of why the newly adopted accounting principle is preferable.

2 The method of applying the change, and:
   (a) A description of the prior-period information that has been retrospectively adjusted, if any.
   (b) The effect of the change on income from continuing operations, net income (or other appropriate captions of changes in net assets or performance indicators), any other affected line item, and any affected per-share amounts for the current period and for any prior periods retrospectively adjusted.
   (c) The cumulative effect of the change on retained earnings or other components of equity or net assets in the statement of financial position as of the beginning of the earliest period presented.[5]

Lancer Company will prepare comparative financial statements for 2006 and 2007 using FIFO (the new inventory method). Illustration 18-5 indicates how Lancer might present this information.

As Illustration 18-5 shows, Lancer Company reports net income under the newly adopted FIFO method for both 2006 and 2007. The company retrospectively adjusted the 2006 income statement to report the information on a FIFO basis. In addition, the note to the financial statements indicates the nature of the change, why the company made the change, and the years affected. The note also provides data on important differences between the amounts reported under LIFO versus FIFO. (When identifying

[5]Presentation of the effect on financial statement subtotals and totals other than income from continuing operations and net income (or other appropriate captions of changes in the applicable net assets or performance indicators) is not required *(SFAS No. 154,* par. 17.)

the significant differences, some companies show the *entire* financial statements and line-by-line differences between LIFO and FIFO.)

ILLUSTRATION 18-5
Comparative Information Related to Accounting Change (FIFO)

LANCER COMPANY
INCOME STATEMENT
FOR THE YEAR ENDED DECEMBER 31

	2007	2006
		As adjusted (Note A)
Sales	$300,000	$300,000
Cost of goods sold	111,000	97,000
Operating expenses	100,000	100,000
Net income	$ 89,000	$103,000

Note A

Change in Method of Accounting for Inventory Valuation On January 1, 2007, Lancer Company elected to change its method of valuing its inventory to the FIFO method; in all prior years inventory was valued using the LIFO method. The Company adopted the new method of accounting for inventory to better report cost of goods sold in the year incurred. Comparative financial statements of prior years have been adjusted to apply the new method retrospectively. The following financial statement line items for fiscal years 2007 and 2006 were affected by the change in accounting principle.

	2007			2006		
Balance Sheet	LIFO	FIFO	Difference	LIFO	FIFO	Difference
Inventory	$ 32,000	$ 39,000	$7,000	$ 20,000	$ 25,000	$5,000
Retained earnings	307,000	314,000	7,000	220,000	225,000	5,000
Income Statement						
Cost of goods sold	$113,000	$111,000	$2,000	$100,000	$ 97,000	$3,000
Net Income	87,000	89,000	2,000	100,000	103,000	3,000
Statement of Cash Flows						
(no effect)						

As a result of the accounting change, retained earnings as of January 1, 2006, increased from $120,000, as originally reported using the LIFO method, to $122,000 using the FIFO method.

Retained Earnings Adjustment

As indicated earlier, one of the disclosure requirements is to show the cumulative effect of the change on retained earnings as of the beginning of the earliest period presented. For Lancer Company, that date is January 1, 2006. Lancer disclosed that information by means of a narrative description (see Note A in Illustration 18-5). Lancer also would disclose this information in its retained earnings statement. Illustration 18-6 shows Lancer's retained earnings statement under LIFO—that is, before giving effect to the change in accounting principle. (This information comes from Illustration 18-2.)

ILLUSTRATION 18-6
Retained Earnings Statements (LIFO)

	2007	2006	2005
Retained earnings, January 1	$220,000	$120,000	$ 0
Net income	87,000	100,000	120,000
Retained earnings, December 31	$307,000	$220,000	$120,000

If Lancer presents comparative statements for 2006 and 2007 under FIFO, then it must change the beginning balance of retained earnings at January 1, 2006. The difference between the retained earnings balances under LIFO and FIFO is computed as shown on next page.

Retained earnings, January 1, 2006 (FIFO)	$122,000
Retained earnings, January 1, 2006 (LIFO)	120,000
Cumulative effect difference	$ 2,000

The $2,000 difference is the cumulative effect. Illustration 18-7 shows a comparative retained earnings statement for 2006 and 2007, giving effect to the change in accounting principle to FIFO.

ILLUSTRATION 18-7
Retained Earnings Statements after Retrospective Application

	2007	2006
Retained earnings, January 1, as reported		$120,000
Add: Adjustment for the cumulative effect on prior years of applying retrospectively the new method of accounting for inventory		2,000
Retained earnings, January 1, as adjusted	$225,000	122,000
Net income	89,000	103,000
Retained earnings, December 31	$314,000	$225,000

Lancer adjusted the beginning balance of retained earnings on January 1, 2006, for the excess of FIFO net income over LIFO net income in 2005. This comparative presentation indicates the type of adjustment that a company needs to make. It follows that the amount of this adjustment would be much larger if a number of prior periods were involved.

Direct and Indirect Effects of Changes

Are there other effects that a company should report when it makes a change in accounting principle? For example, what happens when a company like Lancer has a bonus plan based on net income and the prior year's net income changes when FIFO is retrospectively applied? Should Lancer change the reported amount of bonus expense also? Or what happens if we had not ignored income taxes in the Lancer example? Should Lancer adjust net income, given that taxes will be different under LIFO and FIFO in prior periods? The answers depend on whether the effects are direct or indirect.

Direct Effects

The FASB takes the position that companies should retrospectively apply the **direct effects of a change in accounting principle**. An example of a **direct effect** is an adjustment to an inventory balance as a result of a change in the inventory valuation method. For example, Lancer Company should change the inventory amounts in prior periods to indicate the change to the FIFO method of inventory valuation. Another inventory-related example would be an impairment adjustment resulting from applying the lower-of-cost-or-market test to the adjusted inventory balance. Related changes, such as deferred income tax effects of the impairment adjustment, are also considered direct effects.

To illustrate the impact of a direct effect on taxes, assume that Denson Construction has accounted for its income from long-term construction contracts using the completed-contract method. In 2007 the company changed to the percentage-of-completion method. Management believes this approach provides a more appropriate measure of the income earned. For tax purposes, the company uses the completed-contract method and plans to continue doing so in the future. (We assume a 40 percent enacted tax rate.)

Illustration 18-8 shows portions of income statements for 2005–2007—for both the completed-contract and percentage-of-completion methods.

ILLUSTRATION 18-8
Comparative Income Statements for Completed-Contract versus Percentage-of-Completion Methods

COMPLETED-CONTRACT METHOD
DENSON COMPANY
INCOME STATEMENT (PARTIAL)
FOR THE YEARS ENDED DECEMBER 31

	2005	2006	2007
Income before income tax	$400,000	$160,000	$190,000
Income tax (40%)	160,000	64,000	76,000
Net income	$240,000	$ 96,000	$114,000

PERCENTAGE-OF-COMPLETION METHOD
DENSON COMPANY
INCOME STATEMENT (PARTIAL)
FOR THE YEARS ENDED DECEMBER 31

	2005	2006	2007
Income before income tax	$600,000	$180,000	$200,000
Income tax (40%)	240,000	72,000	80,000
Net income	$360,000	$108,000	$120,000

To record a change from the completed-contract to the percentage-of-completion method, we analyze the various effects, as Illustration 18-9 shows.

ILLUSTRATION 18-9
Data for Indirect Effect Example

	Pretax Income from		Difference in Income		
Year	Percentage-of-Completion	Completed-Contract	Difference	Tax Effect 40%	Income Effect (net of tax)
Prior to 2006	$600,000	$400,000	$200,000	$80,000	$120,000
In 2006	180,000	160,000	20,000	8,000	12,000
Total at beginning of 2007	$780,000	$560,000	$220,000	$88,000	$132,000
Total in 2007	$200,000	$190,000	$ 10,000	$ 4,000	$ 6,000

The entry to record the change at the beginning of 2007 would be:

Construction in Process	220,000	
Deferred Tax Liability		88,000
Retained Earnings		132,000

The Construction in Process account increases by $220,000 (as indicated in the first column under "Difference in Income" in Illustration 18-9). The credit to Retained Earnings of $132,000 reflects the cumulative income effects prior to 2007 (third column under "Difference in Income" in Illustration 18-9). The company credits Retained Earnings because prior years' income is closed to this account each year. The credit to Deferred Tax Liability represents the adjustment to prior years' tax expense. The company now recognizes that amount, $88,000, as a tax liability for future taxable amounts. That is, in future periods, taxable income will be higher than book income as a result of current temporary differences; therefore Denson must report a deferred tax liability in the current year.

Denson reports the comparative financial statements, as shown in the lower half of Illustration 18-8. These include the new tax amounts. As indicated earlier, companies should record in the current year the direct effect of the change in taxes as a result of the change in accounting principle. They also should present information for prior periods, including changes in taxes, based on the new method.

Indirect Effects

In addition to direct effects, companies can have **indirect effects related to a change in accounting principle**. An **indirect effect** is any change to current or future cash flows of a company that result from making a change in accounting principle that is applied retrospectively. An example of an indirect effect is a change in profit-sharing or royalty payment that is based on a reported amount such as revenue or net income. **Indirect effects do not change prior-period amounts.**

For example, let's assume that Denson Construction has an employee profit-sharing plan based on net income. As Illustration 18-8 showed, Denson would report higher income in 2005 and 2006 if it used the percentage-of-completion method. In addition, let's assume that the profit-sharing plan requires that Denson pay the incremental amount due based on the percentage-of-completion income amounts. In this situation, Denson reports this additional expense **in the current period**; it would not change prior periods for this expense. If the company prepares comparative financial statements, it follows that it does not recast the prior periods for this additional expense.[6]

INTERNATIONAL INSIGHT

IFRS do not explicitly address the accounting and disclosure of indirect effects.

If the terms of the profit-sharing plan indicate that *no payment is necessary* in the current period due to this change, then the company need not recognize additional profit-sharing expense in the current period. Neither does it change amounts reported for prior periods.

When a company recognizes the indirect effects of a change in accounting principle, it includes in the financial statements a description of the indirect effects. In doing so, it discloses the amounts recognized in the current period and related per share information.

Impracticability

OBJECTIVE 4
Understand how to account for impracticable changes.

It is not always possible for companies to determine how they would have reported prior periods' financial information under retrospective application of an accounting principle change. Retrospective application is considered **impracticable** if a company cannot determine the prior-period effects using every reasonable effort to do so.

Companies should not use retrospective application if one of the following conditions exists:

1 The company cannot determine the effects of the retrospective application.

2 Retrospective application requires assumptions about management's intent in a prior period.

3 Retrospective application requires significant estimates for a prior period, and the company cannot objectively verify the necessary information to develop these estimates.

If any of the above conditions exists, it is deemed impracticable to apply the retrospective approach. In this case, the company **prospectively applies** the new accounting principle as of the earliest date it is practicable to do so.[7]

For example, assume that Williams Company changed its inventory method from FIFO to LIFO, effective January 1, 2008. Williams prepares statements on a calendar-year basis and has used the FIFO method since its inception. Williams judges it impracticable to retrospectively apply the new method. Determining prior-period effects would require subjective assumptions about the LIFO layers established in prior periods. These assumptions would ordinarily result in the computation of a number of different earnings figures.

As a result, the only adjustment necessary may be to restate the beginning inventory to a cost basis from a lower-of-cost-or-market approach. Williams must disclose only the effect of the change on the results of operations in the period of change. Also, the company should explain the reasons for omitting the computations of the cumulative

[6]The rationale for this approach is that companies should recognize, in the period the adoption occurs (not the prior period), the effect on the cash flows that is caused by the adoption of the new accounting principle. That is, the accounting change is a necessary "past event" in the definition of an asset or liability that gives rise to the accounting recognition of the indirect effect in the current period (*SFAS No. 154*, par. B19).

[7]*SFAS No. 154*, pars. 8–11.

effect for prior years. Finally, it should disclose the justification for the change to LIFO.[8] Illustration 18-10, from the annual report of **Quaker Oats Company**, shows the type of disclosure needed.

ILLUSTRATION 18-10
Disclosure of Change to LIFO

The Quaker Oats Company

Note 1 (In Part): Summary of Significant Accounting Policies

Inventories. Inventories are valued at the lower of cost or market, using various cost methods, and include the cost of raw materials, labor and overhead. The percentage of year-end inventories valued using each of the methods is as follows:

June 30	Current Year	Prior Year
Average quarterly cost	21%	54%
Last-in, first-out (LIFO)	65%	29%
First-in, first-out (FIFO)	14%	17%

Effective July 1, the Company adopted the LIFO cost flow assumption for valuing the majority of remaining U.S. Grocery Products inventories. The Company believes that the use of the LIFO method better matches current costs with current revenues. The cumulative effect of this change on retained earnings at the beginning of the year is not determinable, nor are the pro-forma effects of retroactive application of LIFO to prior years. The effect of this change on current-year fiscal results was to decrease net income by $16.0 million, or $.20 per share.

If the LIFO method of valuing certain inventories were not used, total inventories would have been $60.1 million higher in the current year, and $24.0 million higher in the prior year.

CHANGE MANAGEMENT

WHAT DO THE NUMBERS MEAN?

Halliburton offers a case study in the importance of good reporting of an accounting change. Recall from Chapter 16 that Halliburton uses percentage-of-completion accounting for its long-term construction-services contracts. Recently, the SEC questioned the company about its change in accounting for disputed claims.

Prior to 1998 Halliburton took a very conservative approach to its accounting for disputed claims. That is, the company waited until all disputes were resolved before recognizing associated revenues. In contrast, in 1998 the company recognized revenue for disputed claims *before* their resolution, using estimates of amounts expected to be recovered. Such revenue and its related profit are more tentative and subject to possible later adjustment. The accounting method adopted in 1998 is more aggressive than the company's former policy but is within the boundaries of GAAP.

It appears that the problem with Halliburton's accounting stems more from how the company handled its accounting change than from the new method itself. That is, Halliburton did not provide in its 1998 annual report an explicit reference to its change in accounting method. In fact, rather than stating its new policy, the company simply deleted the sentence that described how it accounted for disputed claims. Then later, in its 1999 annual report, the company stated its new accounting policy.

When companies make such changes in accounting, investors need to be informed about the change and about its effects on the financial results. With such information, investors and analysts can compare current results with those of prior periods and can make a more informed assessment about the company's future prospects.

Source: Adapted from "Accounting Ace Charles Mulford Answers Accounting Questions," *Wall Street Journal Online* (June 7, 2002).

[8]*SFAS No. 154*, par. 17. In practice, many companies defer the formal adoption of LIFO until year-end. Management thus has an opportunity to assess the impact that a change to LIFO will have on the financial statements and to evaluate the desirability of a change for tax purposes. As indicated in Chapter 7, many companies use LIFO because of the advantages of this inventory valuation method in a period of inflation.

CHANGES IN ACCOUNTING ESTIMATE

OBJECTIVE 5
Describe the accounting for changes in estimates.

To prepare financial statements, companies must estimate the effects of future conditions and events. For example, the following items require estimates.

1 Uncollectible receivables.
2 Inventory obsolescence.
3 Useful lives and salvage values of assets.
4 Periods benefited by deferred costs.
5 Liabilities for warranty costs and income taxes.
6 Recoverable mineral reserves.
7 Change in depreciation methods.

A company cannot perceive future conditions and events and their effects with certainty. Therefore, estimating requires the exercise of judgment. Accounting estimates will change as new events occur, as a company acquires more experience, or as it obtains additional information.

Companies report prospectively changes in accounting estimates. That is, companies should not adjust previously reported results for changes in estimates. Instead, they account for the effects of all changes in estimates in (1) the period of change if the change affects that period only, or (2) the period of change and future periods if the change affects both. The FASB views changes in estimates as **normal recurring corrections and adjustments**, the natural result of the accounting process. It prohibits retrospective treatment.

The circumstances related to a change in estimate differ from those for a change in accounting principle. If companies reported changes in estimates retrospectively, continual adjustments of prior years' income would occur. It seems proper to accept the view that, because new conditions or circumstances exist, the revision fits the new situation (not the old one). Companies should therefore handle such a revision in the current and future periods.

To illustrate, Underwriters Labs Inc. purchased for $300,000 a building that it originally estimated to have a useful life of 15 years and no salvage value. It recorded depreciation for 5 years on a straight-line basis. On January 1, 2007, Underwriters Labs revises the estimate of the useful life. It now considers the asset to have a total life of 25 years. (Assume that the useful life for financial reporting and tax purposes and depreciation method are the same.) Illustration 18-11 shows the accounts at the beginning of the sixth year.

ILLUSTRATION 18-11
Book Value after Five Years' Depreciation

Building	$300,000
Less: Accumulated depreciation—building (5 × $20,000)	100,000
Book value of building	$200,000

Underwriters Labs records depreciation for the year 2007 as follows:

Depreciation Expense	10,000	
Accumulated Depreciation—Building		10,000

The company computes the $10,000 depreciation charge as shown in Illustration 18-12.

ILLUSTRATION 18-12
Depreciation after Change in Estimate

$$\text{Depreciation charge} = \frac{\text{Book value of asset}}{\text{Remaining service live}} = \frac{\$200,000}{25\text{ years} - 5\text{ years}} = \$10,000$$

Companies sometime find it difficult to differentiate between a change in estimate and a change in accounting principle. Is it a change in principle or a change in estimate when a company changes from deferring and amortizing marketing costs to expensing them as incurred because future benefits of these costs have become doubtful? If it is impossible to determine whether a change in principle or a change in estimate has occurred, the rule is this: **Consider the change as a change in estimate.** This is often referred to as a **change in estimate effected by a change in accounting principle**.

Another example of a change in estimate effected by a change in principle is a change in depreciation (as well as amortization or depletion) methods. Because companies change depreciation methods based on changes in estimates about future benefits from long-lived assets, it is not possible to separate the effect of the accounting principle change from that of the estimates. **As a result, companies account for a change in depreciation methods as a change in estimate effected by a change in accounting principle.**[9]

A similar problem occurs in differentiating between a change in estimate and a correction of an error, although here the answer is more clear-cut. How does a company determine whether it overlooked the information in earlier periods (an error), or whether it obtained new information (a change in estimate)? Proper classification is important because the accounting treatment differs for corrections of errors versus changes in estimates. The general rule is this: **Companies should consider careful estimates that later prove to be incorrect as changes in estimate.** Only when a company obviously computed the estimate incorrectly because of lack of expertise or in bad faith should it consider the adjustment an error. There is no clear demarcation line here. Companies must use good judgment in light of all the circumstances.[10]

Disclosures

Illustration 18-13 shows disclosure of a change in estimated useful lives, which appeared in the annual report of **Ampco–Pittsburgh Corporation.**

ILLUSTRATION 18-13
Disclosure of Change in Estimated Useful Lives

Ampco–Pittsburgh Corporation

Note 11: Change in Accounting Estimate. The Corporation revised its estimate of the useful lives of certain machinery and equipment. Previously, all machinery and equipment, whether new when placed in use or not, were in one class and depreciated over 15 years. The change principally applies to assets purchased new when placed in use. Those lives are now extended to 20 years. These changes were made to better reflect the estimated periods during which such assets will remain in service. The change had the effect of reducing depreciation expense and increasing net income by approximately $991,000 ($.10 per share).

For the most part, companies need not disclose changes in accounting estimate made as part of normal operations, such as bad debt allowances or inventory obsolescence, unless such changes are material. However, for a change in estimate that affects

[9] *SFAS No. 154*, par. 20.

[10] In evaluating reasonableness, the auditor should use one or a combination of the following approaches.

(a) Review and test the process used by management to develop the estimate.

(b) Develop an independent expectation of the estimate to corroborate the reasonableness of management's estimate.

(c) Review subsequent events or transactions occurring prior to completion of fieldwork.

"Auditing Accounting Estimates," *Statement on Auditing Standards No. 57* (New York: AICPA, 1988).

several periods (such as a change in the service lives of depreciable assets), companies should disclose the effect on income from continuing operations and related per-share amounts of the current period. When a company has a change in estimate effected by a change in accounting principle, it must indicate why the new method is preferable. In addition, companies are subject to all other disclosure guidelines established for changes in accounting principle.

REPORTING A CHANGE IN ENTITY

OBJECTIVE 6
Identify changes in a reporting entity.

Occasionally companies make changes that result in different reporting entities. In such cases, companies report the change by **changing the financial statements of all prior periods presented**. The revised statements show the financial information for the **new reporting entity** for all periods.

Examples of a change in reporting entity are:

1. Presenting consolidated statements in place of statements of individual companies.
2. Changing specific subsidiaries that constitute the group of companies for which the entity presents consolidated financial statements.
3. Changing the companies included in combined financial statements.
4. Changing the cost, equity, or consolidation method of accounting for subsidiaries and investments.[11] In this case, a change in the reporting entity does not result from creation, cessation, purchase, or disposition of a subsidiary or other business unit.

In the year in which a company changes a reporting entity, it should disclose in the financial statements the nature of the change and the reason for it. It also should report, for all periods presented, the effect of the change on income before extraordinary items, net income, and earnings per share. These disclosures need not be repeated in subsequent periods' financial statements.

Illustration 18-14 shows a note disclosing a change in reporting entity, from the annual report of **Hewlett-Packard Company**.

ILLUSTRATION 18-14
Disclosure of Change in Reporting Entity

Hewlett-Packard Company

Note: Accounting and Reporting Changes (In Part)

Consolidation of Hewlett-Packard Finance Company. The company implemented *Statement of Financial Accounting Standards No. 94 (SFAS 94)*, "Consolidation of All Majority-owned Subsidiaries." With the adoption of *SFAS 94*, the company consolidated the accounts of Hewlett-Packard Finance Company (HPFC), a wholly owned subsidiary previously accounted for under the equity method, with those of the company. The change resulted in an increase in consolidated assets and liabilities but did not have a material effect on the company's financial position. Since HPFC was previously accounted for under the equity method, the change did not affect net earnings. Prior years' consolidated financial information has been restated to reflect this change for comparative purposes.

REPORTING A CORRECTION OF AN ERROR

OBJECTIVE 7
Describe the accounting for correction of errors.

No business, large or small, is immune from errors. Unfortunately, as the opening story discussed, the number of errors in financial statements has increased dramatically. Illustration 18-15 indicates significant restatements (error adjustments) for each quarter in 2003 and 2004.

[11] An exception to retrospective application occurs when changing from the equity method.

ILLUSTRATION 18-15
2003 and 2004
Restatements by Quarter

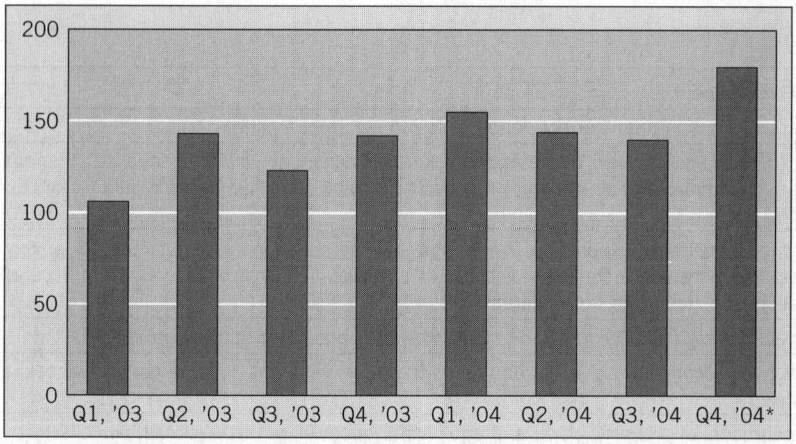

*Internal control audits mandated by Sarbanes-Oxley 404 resulted in a record number of 4th-quarter 2004 restatements.

SOURCE: T. Baldwin and D. Yoo, "Restatements—Traversing Shaky Ground," *Trend Alert*, Glass Lewis & Co. (June 2, 2005), p. 7.

Certain errors, such as misclassifications of balances within a financial statement, are not as significant to investors as other errors. Significant errors would be those resulting in overstating assets or income, for example. However, investors should know the potential impact of all errors. Even "harmless" misclassifications can affect important ratios. Also, some errors could signal important weaknesses in internal controls that could lead to more significant errors.

In general, accounting errors include the following types:

1. A change from an accounting principle that is **not** generally accepted to an accounting principle that is acceptable. The rationale is that the company incorrectly presented prior periods because of the application of an improper accounting principle. For example, a company may change from the cash (income tax) basis of accounting to the accrual basis.
2. Mathematical mistakes, such as incorrectly totaling the inventory count sheets when computing the inventory value.
3. Changes in estimates that occur because a company did not prepare the estimates in good faith. For example, a company may have adopted a clearly unrealistic depreciation rate.
4. An oversight, such as the failure to accrue or defer certain expenses and revenues at the end of the period.
5. A misuse of facts, such as the failure to use salvage value in computing the depreciation base for the straight-line approach.
6. The incorrect classification of a cost as an expense instead of an asset, and vice versa.

Accounting errors occur for a variety of reasons. Illustration 18-16 indicates 11 major categories of accounting errors that drive restatements.

As soon as a company discovers an error, it must correct the error. Companies record **corrections of errors** from prior periods as an adjustment to the beginning balance of retained earnings in the current period. Such corrections are called **prior period adjustments.**[12]

[12]"Prior Period Adjustments," *Statement of Financial Accounting Standards No. 16* (Stamford, Conn.: FASB, 1977), p. 5. See Mark L. DeFord and James Jiambalvo, "Incidence and Circumstances of Accounting Errors," *The Accounting Review* (July 1991) for examples of different types of errors and why these errors might have occurred.

ILLUSTRATION 18-16
Accounting-Error Types

Accounting Category	Type of Restatement
Expense recognition	Recording expenses in the incorrect period or for an incorrect amount
Revenue recognition	Improper revenue accounting. This category includes instances in which revenue was improperly recognized, questionable revenues were recognized, or any other number of related errors that led to misreported revenue.
Misclassification	Misclassifying significant accounting items on the balance sheet, income statement, or statement of cash flows. These include restatements due to misclassification of short- or long-term accounts or those that impact cash flows from operations
Equity—other	Improper accounting for EPS, restricted stock, warrants, and other equity instruments
Reserves/Contingencies	Errors involving accounts receivables bad debts, inventory reserves, income tax allowances, and loss contingencies
Long-lived assets	Asset impairments of property, plant, and equipment, goodwill, or other related items.
Taxes	Errors involving correction of tax provision, improper treatment of tax liabilities, and other tax-related items
Equity—other comprehensive income	Improper accounting for comprehensive income equity transactions including foreign currency items, minimum pension liability adjustments, unrealized gains and losses on certain investments in debt, equity securities, and derivatives.
Inventory	Inventory costing valuations, quantity issues, and cost of sales adjustments
Equity—stock options	Improper accounting for employee stock options
Other	Any restatement not covered by the listed categories including those related to improper accounting for acquisitions or mergers

SOURCE: T. Baldwin and D. Yoo, "Restatements—Traversing Shaky Ground," *Trend Alert*, Glass Lewis & Co. (June 2, 2005), p. 8.

If it presents comparative statements, a company should restate the prior statements affected, to correct for the error.[13] The company need not repeat the disclosures in the financial statements of subsequent periods.

Example

To illustrate, in 2008 the bookkeeper for Selectric Company discovered an error: In 2007 the company failed to record $20,000 of depreciation expense on a newly constructed building. This building is the only depreciable asset Selectric owns. The company correctly included the depreciation expense in its tax return and correctly reported its income taxes payable. Illustration 18-17 presents Selectric's income statement for 2007 (starting with income before depreciation expense) with and without the error.

ILLUSTRATION 18-17
Error Correction Comparison

SELECTRIC COMPANY
INCOME STATEMENT
FOR THE YEAR ENDED, DECEMBER 31, 2007

		Without Error		With Error
Income before depreciation expense		$100,000		$100,000
Depreciation expense		20,000		0
Income before income tax		80,000		100,000
Current	$32,000		$ 32,000	
Deferred	–0–	32,000	8,000	40,000
Net income		$ 48,000		$ 60,000

Illustration 18-18 shows the entries that Selectric should have made and did make for recording depreciation expense and income taxes.

[13]The term **"restatement"** is used for the process of revising previously issued financial statements to reflect the correction of an error. This distinguishes an error correction from a change in accounting principle (*SFAS No. 154*, par. 2, j).

ILLUSTRATION 18-18
Error Entries

Entries Company Should Have Made (Without Error)			Entries Company Did Make (With Error)		
Depreciation Expense	20,000		No entry made for depreciation		
Accumulated Depreciation—Buildings		20,000			
Income Tax Expense	32,000		Income Tax Expense	40,000	
Income Tax Payable		32,000	Deferred Tax Liability		8,000
			Income Tax Payable		32,000

As Illustration 18-18 indicates, the $20,000 omission error in 2007 results in the following effects.

Income Statement Effects

Depreciation expense (2007) is understated $20,000.

Income tax expense (2007) is overstated $8,000 ($20,000 × 40%).

Net income (2007) is overstated $12,000 ($20,000 − $8,000).

Balance Sheet Effects

Accumulated depreciation—buildings is understated $20,000.

Deferred tax liability is overstated $8,000 ($20,000 × 40%).

To make the proper correcting entry in 2008, Selectric should recognize that net income in 2007 is overstated by $12,000, the Deferred Tax Liability is overstated by $8,000, and Accumulated Depreciation—Buildings is understated by $20,000. The entry to correct this error in 2008 is as follows:

Retained Earnings	12,000	
Deferred Tax Liability	8,000	
Accumulated Depreciation—Buildings		20,000

The debit to Retained Earnings results because net income for 2007 is overstated. The debit to the Deferred Tax Liability is made to remove this account, which was caused by the error. The credit to Accumulated Depreciation—Buildings reduces the book value of the building to its proper amount. Selectric will make the same journal entry to record the correction of the error in 2008 whether it prepares single-period (noncomparative) or comparative financial statements.

Single-Period Statements

To demonstrate how to show this information in a single-period statement, assume that Selectric Company has a beginning retained earnings balance at January 1, 2008, of $350,000. The company reports net income of $400,000 in 2008. Illustration 18-19 shows Selectric's retained earnings statement for 2008.

ILLUSTRATION 18-19
Reporting an Error—Single-Period Financial Statement

SELECTRIC COMPANY
RETAINED EARNINGS STATEMENT
FOR THE YEAR ENDED DECEMBER 31, 2008

Retained earnings, January 1, as reported		$350,000
Correction of an error (depreciation)	$20,000	
Less: Applicable income tax reduction	8,000	(12,000)
Retained earnings, January 1, as adjusted		338,000
Add: Net income		400,000
Retained earnings, December 31		$738,000

The balance sheet in 2008 would not have any deferred tax liability related to the building, and Accumulated Depreciation—Buildings is now restated at a higher amount. The income statement would not be affected.

Comparative Statements

If preparing comparative financial statements, a company should make adjustments to correct the amounts for all affected accounts reported in the statements for **all periods** reported. The company should restate the data to the correct basis for each year presented. It should **show any catch-up adjustment as a prior period adjustment to retained earnings for the earliest period it reported.** These requirements are essentially the same as those for reporting a change in accounting principle.

For example, in the case of Selectric, the error of omitting the depreciation of $20,000 in 2007, discovered in 2008, results in the restatement of the 2007 financial statements. Illustration 18-20 shows the accounts that Selectric restates in the 2007 financial statements, presented in comparison with those of 2008.

ILLUSTRATION 18-20
Reporting an Error—Comparative Financial Statements

In the balance sheet:	
Accumulated depreciation—buildings	$20,000 increase
Deferred tax liability	$ 8,000 decrease
Retained earnings, ending balance	$12,000 decrease
In the income statement:	
Depreciation expense—buildings	$20,000 increase
Income tax expense	$ 8,000 decrease
Net income	$12,000 decrease
In the retained earnings statement:	
Retained earnings, ending balance (due to lower net income for the period)	$12,000 decrease

Selectric prepares the 2008 financial statements in comparative form with those of 2007 **as if the error had not occurred**. In addition, Selectric must disclose that it has restated its previously issued financial statements, and it describes the nature of the error. Selectric also must disclose the following:

1 The effect of the correction on each financial statement line item and any per-share amounts affected for each prior period presented.

2 The cumulative effect of the change on retained earnings or other appropriate components of equity or net assets in the statement of financial position, as of the beginning of the earliest period presented.[14]

SUMMARY OF ACCOUNTING CHANGES AND CORRECTIONS OF ERRORS

Having guidelines for reporting accounting changes and corrections has helped resolve several significant and long-standing accounting problems. Yet, because of diversity in situations and characteristics of the items encountered in practice, use of professional judgment is of paramount importance. In applying these guidelines, the primary objective is to serve the users of the financial statements. Achieving this objective requires accuracy, full disclosure, and an absence of misleading inferences.

Illustration 18-21 summarizes the main distinctions and treatments presented in the discussion in this chapter.

[14]*SFAS No. 154*, par. 26.

ILLUSTRATION 18-21
Summary of Guidelines for Accounting Changes and Errors

- **Changes in accounting principle**
  Employ the retrospective approach by:
  a. Changing the financial statements of all prior periods presented.
  b. Disclosing in the year of the change the effect on net income and earnings per share for all prior periods presented.
  c. Reporting an adjustment to the beginning retained earnings balance in the statement of retained earnings in the earliest year presented.
  If impracticable to determine the prior period effect (e.g., change to LIFO):
  a. Do not change prior years' income.
  b. Use opening inventory in the year the method is adopted as the base-year inventory for all subsequent LIFO computations.
  c. Disclose the effect of the change on the current year, and the reasons for omitting the computation of the cumulative effect and pro forma amounts for prior years.
- **Changes in accounting estimate.**
  Employ the current and prospective approach by:
  a. Reporting current and future financial statements on the new basis.
  b. Presenting prior period financial statements as previously reported.
  c. Making no adjustments to current-period opening balances for the effects in prior periods.
- **Changes in reporting entity.**
  Employ the retrospective approach by:
  a. Restating the financial statements of all prior periods presented.
  b. Disclosing in the year of change the effect on net income and earnings per share data for all prior periods presented.
- **Changes due to error.**
  Employ the restatement approach by:
  a. Correcting all prior period statements presented.
  b. Restating the beginning balance of retained earnings for the first period presented when the error effects occur in a period prior to that one.

Changes in accounting principle are appropriate **only** when a company demonstrates that the newly adopted generally accepted accounting principle is **preferable** to the existing one. Companies and accountants determine preferability on the basis of whether the new principle constitutes an **improvement in financial reporting**, not on the basis of the income tax effect alone.[15]

But it is not always easy to determine an improvement in financial reporting. **How does one measure preferability or improvement?** Such measurement varies from company to company. **Quaker Oats Company**, for example, argued that a change in accounting principle to LIFO inventory valuation "better matches current costs with current revenues" (see Illustration 18-10). Conversely, another company might change from LIFO to FIFO because it wishes to report a more realistic ending inventory. How do you determine which is the better of these two arguments? Determining the preferable method requires some "standard" or "objective." Because no universal standard or objective is generally accepted, the problem of determining preferability continues to be difficult.

UNDERLYING CONCEPTS

This is an example of two widely accepted concepts conflicting. Which is more important, matching (emphasis on the income statement) or qualitative characteristic of representational faithfulness (emphasis on the balance sheet)?

Initially the SEC took the position that the auditor should indicate whether a change in accounting principle was preferable. The SEC has since modified this approach, noting that greater reliance may be placed on management's judgment

[15]A change in accounting principle, a change in the reporting entity (special type of change in accounting principle), and a correction of an error require an explanatory paragraph in the auditor's report discussing lack of consistency from one period to the next. A change in accounting estimate does not affect the auditor's opinion relative to consistency; however, if the change in estimate has a material effect on the financial statements, disclosure may still be required. Error correction not involving a change in accounting principle does not require disclosure relative to consistency.

in assessing preferability. Even though the preferability criterion is difficult to apply, the general guidelines have acted as a deterrent to capricious changes in accounting principles.[16] **If an FASB standard creates a new principle, expresses preference for, or rejects a specific accounting principle, a change is considered clearly acceptable.**

WHAT DO THE NUMBERS MEAN?

CAN I GET MY MONEY BACK?

When companies report restatements, investors usually lose money. What should investors do if a company misleads them by misstating its financial results? Join other investors in a class-action suit against the company and in some cases, the auditor.

Class-action activity has picked up in recent years, and settlements can be large. To find out about class actions, investors can go online to see if they are eligible to join any class actions. Below are some recent examples.

Company	Settlement Amount	Contact for Claim
Quaker Oats	$ 10,400,000	*www.gilardi.com*
Smart Choice Automotive	$ 2,500,000	*www.gilardi.com*
Sunbeam	$110,000,000	*www.gilardi.com*

The amounts reported are *before* attorney's fees, which can range from 15 to 30 percent of the total. Also, investors may owe taxes if the settlement results in a capital gain on the investment. Thus, investors can get back some of the money they lost due to restatements, but they should be prepared to pay an attorney and the government first.

Source: Adapted from C. Coolidge, "Lost and Found," *Forbes* (October 1, 2001), pp. 124–125.

MOTIVATIONS FOR CHANGE OF ACCOUNTING METHOD

OBJECTIVE 8
Identify economic motives for changing accounting methods.

Difficult as it is to determine which accounting standards have the strongest conceptual support, other complications make the process even more complex. These complications stem from the fact that managers have self-interest in how the financial statements make the company look. They naturally wish to show their financial performance in the best light. A **favorable profit picture** can influence investors, and a strong liquidity position can influence creditors. **Too favorable a profit picture**, however, can provide union negotiators and government regulators with ammunition during bargaining talks. Hence, managers might have varying motives for reporting income numbers.

Research has provided additional insight into why companies may prefer certain accounting methods.[17] Some of these reasons are as follows:

1 *Political Costs.* As companies become larger and more politically visible, politicians and regulators devote more attention to them. The larger the firm, the more likely it is to become subject to regulation such as antitrust, and the more likely it

[16]If management has not provided reasonable justification for the change in accounting principle, the auditor should express a qualified opinion. Or, if the effect of the change is sufficiently material, the auditor should express an adverse opinion on the financial statements. "Reports on Audited Financial Statements," *Statement on Auditing Standards No. 58* (New York: AICPA, 1988).

[17]See Ross L. Watts and Jerold L. Zimmerman, "Positive Accounting Theory: A Ten-Year Perspective," *The Accounting Review* (January 1990) for an excellent review of research findings related to management incentives in selecting accounting methods.

is to be required to pay higher taxes. Therefore, companies that are politically visible may seek to report low income numbers, to avoid the scrutiny of regulators. In addition, other constituents, such as labor unions, may be less willing to ask for wage increases if reported income is low. Researchers have found that the larger the company, the more likely it is to adopt income-decreasing approaches in selecting accounting methods.

2 ***Capital Structure.*** A number of studies have indicated that the capital structure of the company can affect the selection of accounting methods. For example, a company with a high debt-to-equity ratio is more likely to be constrained by debt covenants. The debt covenant may indicate that the company cannot pay dividends if retained earnings fall below a certain level. As a result, such a company is more likely to select accounting methods that will increase net income.

3 ***Bonus Payments.*** Studies have found that if compensation plans tie managers' bonus payments to income, management will select accounting methods that maximize their bonus payments.

4 ***Smooth Earnings.*** Substantial earnings increases attract the attention of politicians, regulators, and competitors. In addition, large increases in income are difficult to achieve in following years. Further, executive compensation plans would use these higher numbers as a baseline and make it difficult for managers to earn bonuses in subsequent years. Conversely, investors and competitors might view large decreases in earnings as a signal that the company is in financial trouble. Also, substantial decreases in income raise concerns on the part of stockholders, lenders, and other interested parties about the competency of management. For all these reasons, companies have an incentive to "manage" or "smooth" earnings. In general, management tends to believe that a steady 10 percent growth a year is much better than a 30 percent growth one year and a 10 percent decline the next.[18] In other words, managers usually prefer a gradually increasing income report and sometimes change accounting methods to ensure such a result.

Management pays careful attention to the accounting it follows and often changes accounting methods, not for conceptual reasons, but for economic reasons. As indicated throughout this textbook, such arguments have come to be known as **economic consequences** arguments. These arguments focus on the supposed impact of the accounting method on the behavior of investors, creditors, competitors, governments, or managers of the reporting companies themselves.[19]

To counter these pressures, standard setters such as the FASB have declared, as part of their conceptual framework, that they will assess the merits of proposed standards from a position of **neutrality**. That is, they evaluate the soundness of standards on the basis of conceptual soundness, not on the grounds of possible impact on behavior. It is not the FASB's place to choose standards according to the kinds of behavior it wishes to promote and the kinds it wishes to discourage. At the same time, it must be admitted that some standards often **will have** the effect of influencing behavior. Yet their justification should be conceptual, and not viewed in terms of their economic impact.

[18] O. Douglas Moses, "Income Smoothing and Incentives: Empirical Tests Using Accounting Changes," *The Accounting Review* (April 1987). The findings provide evidence that earnings smoothing is associated with firm size, the existence of bonus plans, and the divergence of actual earnings from expectations.

[19] Lobbyists use economic consequences arguments—and there are many of them—to put pressure on standard setters. We have seen examples of these arguments in the oil and gas industry about successful efforts versus full cost, in the technology area with the issue of mandatory expensing of research and developmental costs and stock options.

SECTION 2 ERROR ANALYSIS

OBJECTIVE 9
Analyze the effect of errors.

In this section, we show some additional types of accounting errors. Companies generally do not correct for errors that do not have a significant effect on the presentation of the financial statements. For example, should a company with a total annual payroll of $1,750,000 and net income of $940,000 correct its financial statements if it finds it failed to record accrued wages of $5,000? No—it would not consider this error significant.

Obviously, defining materiality is difficult, and managers and auditors must use experience and judgment to determine whether adjustment is necessary for a given error. We assume **all errors discussed in this section to be material and to require adjustment.** (Also, we ignore all tax effects in this section.)

Companies must answer three questions in error analysis:

1. What type of error is involved?
2. What entries are needed to correct for the error?
3. After discovery of the error, how are financial statements to be restated?

As indicated earlier, companies treat errors **as prior-period adjustments and report them in the current year as adjustments to the beginning balance of Retained Earnings.** If a company presents comparative statements, it restates the prior affected statements to correct for the error.

BALANCE SHEET ERRORS

Balance sheet errors affect only the presentation of an asset, liability, or stockholders' equity account. Examples are the classification of a short-term receivable as part of the investment section, the classification of a note payable as an account payable, and the classification of plant assets as inventory.

When the error is discovered, the company reclassifies the item to its proper position. If the company prepares comparative statements that include the error year, it should correctly restate the balance sheet for the error year.

INCOME STATEMENT ERRORS

Income statement errors involve the improper classification of revenues or expenses. Examples include recording interest revenue as part of sales, purchases as bad debt expense, and depreciation expense as interest expense. An income statement classification error has no effect on the balance sheet and **no effect on net income.**

A company must make a reclassification entry when it discovers the error, if it makes the discovery in the same year in which the error occurs. If the error occurred in prior periods, the company does not need to make a reclassification entry at the date of discovery because the accounts for the current year are correctly stated. (Remember that the company has closed the income statement accounts from the prior period to retained earnings.) If the company prepares comparative statements that include the error year, it restates the income statement for the error year.

BALANCE SHEET AND INCOME STATEMENT ERRORS

The third type of error involves both the balance sheet and income statement. For example, assume that the bookkeeper overlooked accrued wages payable at the end of the accounting period. The effect of this error is to understate expenses, understate liabilities, and overstate net income for that period of time. This type of error affects both the balance sheet and the income statement. We classify this type of error in one of two ways—counterbalancing or noncounterbalancing.

Counterbalancing errors are those that will be offset or corrected over two periods. For example, the failure to record accrued wages is a counterbalancing error because over a two-year period the error will no longer be present. In other words, the failure to record accrued wages in the previous period means: (1) net income for the first period is overstated; (2) accrued wages payable (a liability) is understated, and (3) wages expense is understated. In the next period, net income is understated; accrued wages payable (a liability) is correctly stated; and wages expense is overstated. For the two **years combined**: (1) net income is correct; (2) wages expense is correct; and (3) accrued wages payable at the end of the second year is correct. Most errors in accounting that affect both the balance sheet and income statement are counterbalancing errors.

Noncounterbalancing errors are those that are not offset in the next accounting period. An example would be the failure to capitalize equipment that has a useful life of five years. If we expense this asset immediately, expenses will be overstated in the first period but understated in the next four periods. At the end of the second period, the effect of the error is not fully offset. Net income is correct in the aggregate only at the end of five years, because the asset is fully depreciated at this point. Thus, **noncounterbalancing errors are those that take longer than two periods to correct themselves.**

Only in rare instances is an error never reversed. An example would be if a company initially expenses land. Because land is not depreciable, theoretically the error is never offset, unless the land is sold.

Counterbalancing Errors

We illustrate the usual types of counterbalancing errors on the following pages. In studying these illustrations, keep in mind a couple of points, discussed below.

First, determine whether the company has closed the books for the period in which the error is found:

1 **If the company has closed the books in the current year:**
   - **(a)** If the error is already counterbalanced, no entry is necessary.
   - **(b)** If the error is not yet counterbalanced, make an entry to adjust the present balance of retained earnings.

2 **If the company has not closed the books in the current year:**
   - **(a)** If the error is already counterbalanced, make an entry to correct the error in the current period and to adjust the beginning balance of Retained Earnings.
   - **(b)** If the error is not yet counterbalanced, make an entry to adjust the beginning balance of Retained Earnings.

Second, if the company presents comparative statements, it must restate the amounts for comparative purposes. **Restatement is necessary even if a correcting journal entry is not required.**

To illustrate, assume that Sanford's Cement Co. failed to accrue revenue in 2005 when earned, but recorded the revenue in 2006 when received. The company discovered the error in 2008. It does not need to make an entry to correct for this error because the effects have been counterbalanced by the time Sanford discovered the error in 2008. However, if Sanford presents comparative financial statements for 2005 through 2008, it must **restate the accounts and related amounts for the years 2005 and 2006 for financial reporting purposes.**

The sections that follow demonstrate the accounting for the usual types of counterbalancing errors.

Failure to Record Accrued Wages

On December 31, 2007, Hurley Enterprises did not accrue wages in the amount of $1,500. The entry in 2008 to correct this error, assuming Hurley has not closed the books for 2008, is:

Retained Earnings	1,500	
Wages Expense		1,500

The rationale for this entry is as follows: (1) When Hurley pays the 2007 accrued wages in 2008, it makes an additional debit of $1,500 to 2008 Wages Expense. (2) Wages Expense—2008 is overstated by $1,500. (3) Because the company did not record 2007 accrued wages as Wages Expense in 2007, the net income for 2007 was overstated by $1,500. (4) Because 2007 net income is overstated by $1,500, the Retained Earnings account is overstated by $1,500 (because net income is closed to Retained Earnings).

If Hurley has closed the books for 2008, it makes no entry, because the error is counterbalanced.

Failure to Record Prepaid Expenses

In January 2007 Hurley Enterprises purchased a two-year insurance policy costing $1,000. It debited Insurance Expense, and credited Cash. The company made no adjusting entries at the end of 2007.

The entry on December 31, 2008, to correct this error, assuming Hurley has not closed the books for 2008, is:

Insurance Expense	500	
Retained Earnings		500

If Hurley has closed the books for 2008, it makes no entry, because the error is counterbalanced.

Understatement of Unearned Revenue

On December 31, 2007, Hurley Enterprises received $50,000 as a prepayment for renting certain office space for the following year. At the time of receipt of the rent payment, the company recorded a debit to Cash and a credit to Rent Revenue. It made no adjusting entry as of December 31, 2007. The entry on December 31, 2008, to correct for this error, assuming that Hurley has not closed the books for 2008, is:

Retained Earnings	50,000	
Rent Revenue		50,000

If Hurley has closed the books for 2008, it makes no entry, because the error is counterbalanced.

Overstatement of Accrued Revenue

On December 31, 2007, Hurley Enterprises accrued as interest revenue $8,000 that applied to 2008. On that date, the company recorded a debit Interest Receivable and a credit Interest Revenue. The entry on December 31, 2008, to correct for this error, assuming that Hurley has not closed the books for 2008, is:

Retained Earnings	8,000	
Interest Revenue		8,000

If Hurley has closed the books for 2008, it makes no entry, because the error is counterbalanced.

Overstatement of Purchases

Hurley's accountant recorded a purchase of merchandise for $9,000 in 2007 that applied to 2008. The physical inventory for 2007 was correctly stated. The company uses the periodic inventory method. The entry on December 31, 2008, to correct for this error, assuming that Harley has not closed the books for 2008, is:

Purchases	9,000	
Retained Earnings		9,000

If Hurley has closed the books for 2008, it makes no entry, because the error is counterbalanced.

Noncounterbalancing Errors

The entries for noncounterbalancing errors are more complex. Companies must make correcting entries, even if they have closed the books.

Failure to Record Depreciation

Assume that on January 1, 2007, Hurley Enterprises purchased a machine for $10,000 that had an estimated useful life of five years. The accountant incorrectly expensed this machine in 2007, but discovered the error in 2008. If we assume that Hurley uses straight-line depreciation on this asset, the entry on December 31, 2008, to correct for this error, given that Hurley has not closed the books, is:

Machinery	10,000	
Depreciation Expense	2,000	
Retained Earnings		8,000[a]
Accumulated Depreciation (20% × $10,000 × 2)		4,000

[a]Computations:

Retained Earnings	
Overstatement of expense in 2007	$10,000
Proper depreciation for 2007 (20% × $10,000)	(2,000)
Retained earnings understated as of Dec. 31, 2007	$ 8,000

If Hurley has closed the books for 2008, the entry is:

Machinery	10,000	
Retained Earnings		6,000[a]
Accumulated Depreciation		4,000

[a]Computations:

Retained Earnings	
Retained earnings understated as of Dec. 31, 2007	$ 8,000
Proper depreciation for 2008 (20% × $10,000)	(2,000)
Retained earnings understated as of Dec. 31, 2008	$ 6,000

Failure to Adjust for Bad Debts

Companies sometimes use a specific charge-off method in accounting for bad debt expense when a percentage of sales is more appropriate. They then make adjustments to change from the specific write-off to some type of allowance method. For example, assume that Hurley Enterprises has recognized bad debt expense when it has the following uncollectible debts.

	2007	2008
From 2007 sales	$550	$690
From 2008 sales		700

Hurley estimates that it will charge off an additional $1,400 in 2009, of which $300 is applicable to 2007 sales and $1,100 to 2008 sales. The entry on December 31, 2008, assuming that Hurley **has not closed the books for 2008**, is:

Bad Debt Expense	410[a]	
Retained Earnings	990[a]	
Allowance for Doubtful Accounts		1,400

[a]Computations to support the amounts in this entry are on the next page.

Allowance for doubtful accounts: Additional $300 for 2007 sales and $1,100 for 2008 sales.
Bad debts and retained earnings balance:

	2007	2008
Bad debts charged for	$1,240[b]	$ 700
Additional bad debts anticipated in 2009	300	1,100
Proper bad debt expense	1,540	1,800
Charges currently made to each period	(550)	(1,390)
Bad debt adjustment	$ 990	$ 410

[b]$550 + $690 = $1,240

If Hurley **has closed the books for 2008**, the entry is:

Retained Earnings	1,400	
Allowance for Doubtful Accounts		1,400

COMPREHENSIVE EXAMPLE: NUMEROUS ERRORS

In some circumstances a combination of errors occurs. The company therefore prepares a worksheet to facilitate the analysis. The following problem demonstrates use of the worksheet. The mechanics of its preparation should be obvious from the solution format. The income statements of Hudson Company for the years ended December 31, 2006, 2007, and 2008 indicate the following net incomes.

2006	$17,400
2007	20,200
2008	11,300

An examination of the accounting records for these years indicates that Hudson Company made several errors in arriving at the net income amounts reported:

1 The company consistently omitted from the records wages earned by workers but not paid at December 31. The amounts omitted were:

December 31, 2006	$1,000
December 31, 2007	$1,400
December 31, 2008	$1,600

When paid in the year following that in which they were earned, Hudson recorded these amounts as expenses.

2 The company overstated merchandise inventory on December 31, 2006, by $1,900 as the result of errors made in the footings and extensions on the inventory sheets.

3 On December 31, 2007, Hudson expensed unexpired insurance of $1,200, applicable to 2008.

4 The company did not record on December 31, 2007, interest receivable in the amount of $240.

5 On January 2, 2007, Hudson sold for $1,800 a piece of equipment costing $3,900. At the date of sale the equipment had accumulated depreciation of $2,400. The company recorded the cash received as Miscellaneous Income in 2007. In addition, it recorded depreciation for this equipment in both 2007 and 2008 at the rate of 10 percent of cost.

The first step in preparing the worksheet is to prepare a schedule showing the corrected net income amounts for the years ended December 31, 2006, 2007, and 2008. Each correction of the amount originally reported is clearly labeled. The next step is to indicate the balance sheet accounts affected as of December 31, 2008. Illustration 18-22 shows the completed worksheet for Hudson Company.

ILLUSTRATION 18-22
Worksheet to Correct Income and Balance Sheet Errors

HUDSON COMPANY
Worksheet to Correct Income and Balance Sheet Errors

	A	B	C	D	E	F	G	H
1		Worksheet Analysis of Changes in Net Income				Balance Sheet Correction at December 31, 2008		
2		2006	2007	2008	Totals	Debit	Credit	Account
3	Net income as reported	$17,400	$20,200	$11,300	$48,900			
4	Wages unpaid, 12/31/06	(1,000)	1,000		–0–			
5	Wages unpaid, 12/31/07		(1,400)	1,400	–0–			
6	Wages unpaid, 12/31/08			(1,600)	(1,600)		$1,600	Wages Payable
7	Inventory overstatement, 12/31/06	(1,900)	1,900		–0–			
8	Unexpired insurance, 12/31/07		1,200	(1,200)	–0–			
9	Interest receivable, 12/31/07		240	(240)	–0–			
10	Correction for entry made upon sale of equipment, 1/2/07[a]		(1,500)		(1,500)	$2,400	3,900	Accumulated Depreciation Machinery
11	Overcharge of depreciation, 2007		390		390	390		Accumulated Depreciation
12	Overcharge of depreciation, 2008			390	390	390		Accumulated Depreciation
13	Corrected net income	$14,500	$22,030	$10,050	$46,580			
14	[a]Cost	$ 3,900						
15	Accumulated depreciation	2,400						
16	Book value	1,500						
17	Proceeds from sale	1,800						
18	Gain on sale	300						
19	Income reported	(1,800)						
20	Adjustment	$(1,500)						

Sheet1 / Sheet2 / Sheet3

Assuming that Hudson Company **has not closed the books**, correcting entries on December 31, 2008, are:

Retained Earnings	1,400	
Wages Expense		1,400
(To correct improper charge to Wages Expense for 2008)		
Wages Expense	1,600	
Wages Payable		1,600
(To record proper wages expense for 2008)		
Insurance Expense	1,200	
Retained Earnings		1,200
(To record proper insurance expense for 2008)		
Interest Revenue	240	
Retained Earnings		240
(To correct improper credit to Interest Revenue in 2008)		
Retained Earnings	1,500	
Accumulated Depreciation	2,400	
Machinery		3,900
(To record write-off of machinery in 2007 and adjustment of Retained Earnings)		
Accumulated Depreciation	780	
Depreciation Expense		390
Retained Earnings		390
(To correct improper charge for depreciation expense in 2007 and 2008)		

If Hudson Company has closed the books for 2008, the correcting entries are:

Retained Earnings	1,600	
Wages Payable		1,600
(To record proper wage expense for 2008)		
Retained Earnings	1,500	
Accumulated Depreciation	2,400	
Machinery		3,900
(To record write-off of machinery in 2007 and adjustment of Retained Earnings)		
Accumulated Depreciation	780	
Retained Earnings		780
(To correct improper charge for depreciation expense in 2007 and 2008)		

PREPARATION OF FINANCIAL STATEMENTS WITH ERROR CORRECTIONS

Up to now, our discussion of error analysis has focused on identifying the type of error involved and accounting for its correction in the records. We have noted that companies must present the correction of the error on comparative financial statements.

The following example illustrates how a company would restate a typical year's financial statements, given many different errors.

Dick & Wally's Outlet is a small retail outlet in the town of Holiday. Lacking expertise in accounting, the company does not keep adequate records, and numerous errors occurred in recording accounting information.

1 The bookkeeper inadvertently failed to record a cash receipt of $1,000 on the sale of merchandise in 2008.

2 Accrued wages expense at the end of 2007 was $2,500; at the end of 2008, $3,200. The company does not accrue for wages; all wages are charged to Administrative Expenses.

3 The company had not set up an allowance for estimated uncollectible receivables. Dick and Wally decided to set up such an allowance for the estimated probable losses, as of December 31, 2008, for 2007 accounts of $700, and for 2008 accounts of $1,500. They also decided to correct the charge against each year so that it shows the losses (actual and estimated) relating to that year's sales. The company has written off accounts to bad debt expense (selling expense) as follows.

	In 2007	In 2008
2007 accounts	$400	$2,000
2008 accounts		1,600

4 Unexpired insurance not recorded at the end of 2007 was $600, and at the end of 2008, $400. All insurance is charged to Administrative Expenses.

5 An account payable of $6,000 should have been a note payable.

6 During 2007, the company sold for $7,000 an asset that cost $10,000 and had a book value of $4,000. At the time of sale Cash was debited, and Miscellaneous Income was credited for $7,000.

7 As a result of the last transaction, the company overstated depreciation expense (an administrative expense) in 2007 by $800 and in 2008 by $1,200.

Illustration 18-23 presents a worksheet that begins with the unadjusted trial balance of Dick & Wally's Outlet. You can determine the correcting entries and their effect on the financial statements by examining the worksheet.

ILLUSTRATION 18-23
Worksheet to Analyze Effect of Errors in Financial Statements

DICK & WALLY'S OUTLET
Worksheet Analysis to Adjust Financial Statements for the Year 2008

	A	B		C D		E F		G	H	I	J
1		Trial Balance Unadjusted		Adjustments				Income Statement Adjusted		Balance Sheet Adjusted	
2		Debit	Credit	Debit		Credit		Debit	Credit	Debit	Credit
3	Cash	3,100		(1)	1,000					4,100	
4	Accounts Receivable	17,600								17,600	
5	Notes Receivable	8,500								8,500	
6	Inventory	34,000								34,000	
7	Property, Plant, and Equipment	112,000				(6)	10,000[a]			102,000	
8	Accumulated Depreciation		83,500	(6)	6,000[a]						75,500
9				(7)	2,000						
10	Investments	24,300								24,300	
11	Accounts Payable		14,500	(5)	6,000						8,500
12	Notes Payable		10,000			(5)	6,000				16,000
13	Capital Stock		43,500								43,500
14	Retained Earnings		20,000	(3)	2,700[b]						
15				(6)	4,000[a]	(4)	600				
16				(2)	2,500	(7)	800				12,200
17	Sales		94,000			(1)	1,000		95,000		
18	Cost of Goods Sold	21,000						21,000			
19	Selling Expenses	22,000				(3)	500[b]	21,500			
20	Administrative Expenses	23,000		(2)	700	(4)	400	22,700			
21				(4)	600	(7)	1,200				
22	Totals	265,500	265,500								
23	Wages Payable					(2)	3,200				3,200
24	Allowance for Doubtful Accounts					(3)	2,200[b]				2,200
25	Unexpired Insurance			(4)	400					400	
26	Net Income							29,800			29,800
27	Totals				25,900		25,900	95,000	95,000	190,900	190,900

Sheet1 / Sheet2 / Sheet3

Computations:

[a]Machinery

Proceeds from sale	$7,000
Book value of machinery	4,000
Gain on sale	3,000
Income credited	7,000
Retained earnings adjustment	$4,000

[b]Bad Debts

	2007	2008
Bad debts charged for	$2,400	$1,600
Additional bad debts anticipated	700	1,500
	3,100	3,100
Charges currently made to each year	(400)	(3,600)
Bad debt adjustment	$2,700	$ (500)

QUESTIONS

1. In recent years, the *Wall Street Journal* has indicated that many companies have changed their accounting principles. What are the major reasons why companies change accounting methods?

2. State how each of the following items is reflected in the financial statements.

(a) Change from FIFO to LIFO method for inventory valuation purposes.

(b) Charge for failure to record depreciation in a previous period.

(c) Litigation won in current year, related to prior period.

(d) Change in the realizability of certain receivables.

(e) Writeoff of receivables.

(f) Change from the percentage-of-completion to the completed-contract method for reporting net income.

3. Discuss briefly the three approaches that have been suggested for reporting changes in accounting principles.

4. Identify and describe the approach the FASB requires for reporting changes in accounting principles.

5. What is the indirect effect of a change in accounting principle? Briefly describe the reporting of the indirect effects of a change in accounting principle.

6. Define a change in estimate and provide an illustration. When is a change in accounting estimate effected by a change in accounting principle?

7. Sandwich State Bank has followed the practice of capitalizing certain marketing costs and amortizing these costs over their expected life. In the current year, the bank determined that the future benefits from these costs were doubtful. Consequently, the bank adopted the policy of expensing these costs as incurred. How should the bank report this accounting change in the comparative financial statements?

8. Indicate how the following items are recorded in the accounting records in the current year of Tami Agler Co.

(a) Impairment of goodwill.

(b) A change in depreciating plant assets from accelerated to the straight-line method.

(c) Large writeoff of inventories because of obsolescence.

(d) Change from the cash basis to accrual basis of accounting.

(e) Change from LIFO to FIFO method for inventory valuation purposes.

(f) Change in the estimate of service lives for plant assets.

9. R. M. Andrews Construction Co. had followed the practice of expensing all materials assigned to a construction job without recognizing any salvage inventory. On December 31, 2007, it was determined that salvage inventory should be valued at $62,000. Of this amount, $29,000 arose during the current year. How does this information affect the financial statements to be prepared at the end of 2007?

10. E. A. Basler Inc. wishes to change from the completed-contract to the percentage-of-completion method for financial reporting purposes. The auditor indicates that a change would be permitted only if it is to a preferable method. What difficulties develop in assessing preferability?

11. Discuss how a change to the LIFO method of inventory valuation is handled when it is impracticable to determine previous LIFO inventory amounts.

12. How should consolidated financial statements be reported this year when statements of individual companies were presented last year?

13. Karen Beers controlled four domestic subsidiaries and one foreign subsidiary. Prior to the current year, Beers had excluded the foreign subsidiary from consolidation. During the current year, the foreign subsidiary was included in the financial statements. How should this change in accounting principle be reflected in the financial statements?

14. Distinguish between counterbalancing and noncounterbalancing errors. Give an example of each.

15. Discuss and illustrate how a correction of an error in previously issued financial statements should be handled.

16. Prior to 2008, Mary Boudreau Inc. excluded manufacturing overhead costs from work in process and finished goods inventory. These costs have been expensed as incurred. In 2008, the company decided to change its accounting methods for manufacturing inventories to full costing by including these costs as product costs. Assuming that these costs are material, how should this change be reflected in the financial statements for 2007 and 2008?

17. Lou Brady Corp. failed to record accrued salaries for 2005, $2,000; 2006, $2,100; and 2007, $3,900. What is the amount of the overstatement or understatement of Retained Earnings at December 31, 2008?

18. In January 2007, installation costs of $8,000 on new machinery were charged to Repair Expense. Other costs of this machinery of $30,000 were correctly recorded and have been depreciated using the straight-line method with an estimated life of 10 years and no salvage value. At December 31, 2008, it is decided that the machinery has a remaining useful life of 20 years, starting with January 1, 2008. What entry(ies) should be made in 2008 to correctly record transactions related to machinery, assuming the machinery has no salvage value? The books have not been closed for 2008 and depreciation expense has not yet been recorded for 2008.

19. On January 2, 2007, $100,000 of 11%, 20-year bonds were issued for $97,000. The $3,000 discount was charged to Interest Expense. The bookkeeper, John Castle, records interest only on the interest payment dates of January 1 and July 1. What is the effect on reported net income for 2007 of this error, assuming straight-line amortization of the discount? What entry is necessary to correct for this error, assuming that the books are not closed for 2007?

20. An account payable of $13,000 for merchandise purchased on December 23, 2007, was recorded in January 2008. This merchandise was not included in inventory at December 31, 2007. What effect does this error have on reported net income for 2007? What entry should be made to correct for this error, assuming that the books are not closed for 2007?

21. Equipment was purchased on January 2, 2007, for $18,000, but no portion of the cost has been charged to depreciation. The corporation wishes to use the straight-line method for these assets, which have been estimated to have a life of 10 years and no salvage value. What effect does this error have on net income in 2007. What entry is necessary to correct for this error, assuming that the books are not closed for 2007?

C H A P T E R N I N E T E E N

STATEMENT OF CASH FLOWS

Don't Take Cash Flow for Granted

Investors usually look to net income as a key indicator of a company's financial health and future prospects. The following graph shows the net income of one company over a seven-year period.

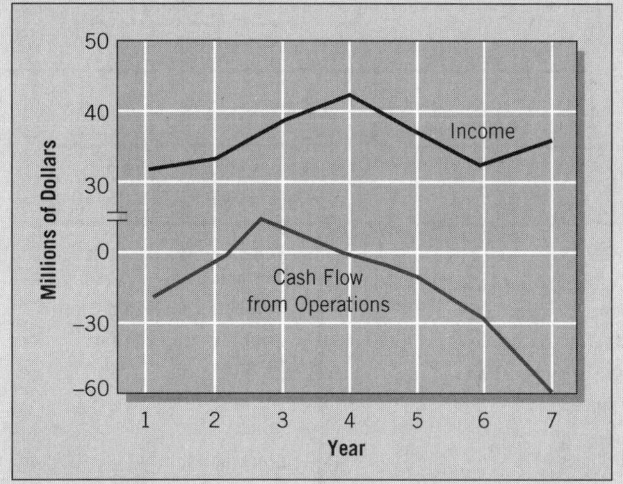

The company showed a pattern of consistent profitability and even some periods of income growth. Between years 1 and 4, net income for this company grew by 32 percent, from $31 million to $41 million. Would you expect its profitability to continue? The company had consistently paid dividends and interest. Would you expect it to continue to do so? Investors answered "yes" to these questions, by buying the company's stock. Eighteen months later, this company—**W. T. Grant**—filed for bankruptcy, in what was then the largest bankruptcy filing in the United States.

How could this happen? As indicated by the second line in the graph, the company had experienced several years of negative cash flow from its operations, even though it reported profits. How can a company have negative cash flows while reporting profits? The answer lay partly in the fact that W. T. Grant was having trouble collecting the receivables from its credit sales, causing cash flow to be less than the net income. Investors who analyzed the cash flows would have been likely to find an early warning signal of W. T. Grant's operating problems.[1]

[1]Adapted from James A. Largay III and Clyde P. Stickney, "Cash Flows, Ratio Analysis, and the W. T. Grant Company Bankruptcy," *Financial Analysts Journal* (July–August 1980), p. 51.

Learning Objectives

After studying this chapter, you should be able to:

1 Describe the purpose of the statement of cash flows.
2 Identify the major classifications of cash flows.
3 Differentiate between net income and net cash flows from operating activities.
4 Contrast the direct and indirect methods of calculating net cash flow from operating activities.
5 Determine net cash flows from investing and financing activities.
6 Prepare a statement of cash flows.
7 Identify sources of information for a statement of cash flows.
8 Discuss special problems in preparing a statement of cash flows.
9 Explain the use of a worksheet in preparing a statement of cash flows

PREVIEW OF CHAPTER 19

As the opening story indicates, examination of **W. T. Grant**'s cash flows from operations would have shown the financial inflexibility that eventually caused the company's bankruptcy. This chapter explains the main components of a statement of cash flows and the types of information it provides. The content and organization of the chapter are as follows.

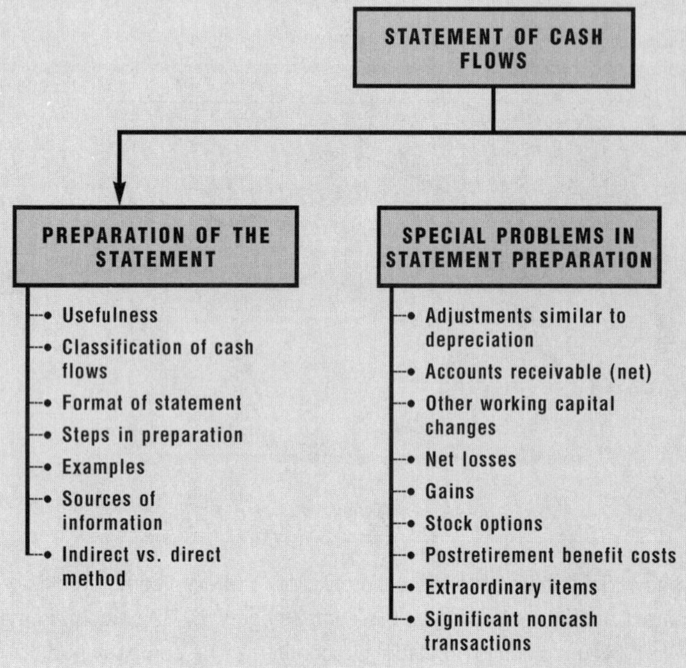

SECTION 1 — PREPARATION OF THE STATEMENT OF CASH FLOWS

OBJECTIVE 1
Describe the purpose of the statement of cash flows.

The primary purpose of the **statement of cash flows** is to provide information about a company's cash receipts and cash payments during a period. A secondary objective is to provide cash-basis information about the company's operating, investing, and financing activities. The statement of cash flows therefore reports cash receipts, cash payments, and net change in cash resulting from a company's operating, investing, and financing activities during a period. Its format reconciles the beginning and ending cash balances for the period.

USEFULNESS OF THE STATEMENT OF CASH FLOWS

The statement of cash flows provides information to help investors, creditors, and others assess the following:[2]

1 *The entity's ability to generate future cash flows.* A primary objective of financial reporting is to provide information with which to predict the amounts, timing, and

[2]"The Statement of Cash Flows," *Statement of Financial Accounting Standards No. 95* (Stamford, Conn.: FASB, 1987), pars. 4 and 5.

uncertainty of future cash flows. By examining relationships between items such as sales and net cash flow from operating activities, or net cash flow from operating activities and increases or decreases in cash, it is possible to better predict the future cash flows than is possible using accrual-basis data alone.

2 ***The entity's ability to pay dividends and meet obligations.*** Simply put, cash is essential. Without adequate cash, a company cannot pay employees, settle debts, pay out dividends, or acquire equipment. A statement of cash flows indicates where the company's cash comes from and how the company uses its cash. Employees, creditors, stockholders, and customers should be particularly interested in this statement, because it alone shows the flows of cash in a business.

3 ***The reasons for the difference between net income and net cash flow from operating activities.*** The net income number is important: It provides information on the performance of a company from one period to another. But some people are critical of accrual-basis net income because companies must make estimates to arrive at it. Such is not the case with cash. Thus, as the opening story showed, financial statement readers can benefit from knowing why a company's net income and net cash flow from operating activities differ, and can assess for themselves the reliability of the income number.

4 ***The cash and noncash investing and financing transactions during the period.*** Besides operating activities, companies undertake investing and financing transactions. *Investing* activities include the purchase and sale of assets other than a company's products or services. *Financing* activities include borrowings and repayments of borrowings, investments by owners, and distributions to owners. By examining a company's investing and financing activities, a financial statement reader can better understand why assets and liabilities increased or decreased during the period. For example, by reading the statement of cash flows, the reader might find answers to following questions:

Why did cash decrease for **Toys R Us** when it reported net income for the period?

How much did **Southwest Airlines** spend on property, plant, and equipment last year?

Did dividends paid by **Campbell's Soup** increase?

How much money did **Coca-Cola** borrow last year?

How much cash did **Hewlett-Packard** use to repurchase its common stock?

CLASSIFICATION OF CASH FLOWS

OBJECTIVE 2
Identify the major classifications of cash flows.

The statement of cash flows classifies cash receipts and cash payments by operating, investing, and financing activities.[3] Transactions and other events characteristic of each kind of activity is as follows.

1 **Operating activities** involve the cash effects of transactions that enter into the determination of net income, such as cash receipts from sales of goods and services, and cash payments to suppliers and employees for acquisitions of inventory and expenses.

[3]The basis recommended by the FASB for the statement of cash flows is actually "cash and cash equivalents." **Cash equivalents** are short-term, highly liquid investments that are both: (a) readily convertible to known amounts of cash, and (b) so near their maturity that they present insignificant risk of changes in interest rates. Generally, only investments with original maturities of three months or less qualify under this definition. Examples of cash equivalents are Treasury bills, commercial paper, and money market funds purchased with cash that is in excess of immediate needs.

Although we use the term "cash" throughout our discussion and illustrations, we mean cash and cash equivalents when reporting the cash flows and the net increase or decrease in cash.

2 **Investing activities** generally involve long-term assets and include (a) making and collecting loans, and (b) acquiring and disposing of investments and productive long-lived assets.

3 **Financing activities** involve liability and stockholders' equity items and include (a) obtaining cash from creditors and repaying the amounts borrowed, and (b) obtaining capital from owners and providing them with a return on, and a return of, their investment.

Illustration 19-1 classifies the typical cash receipts and payments of a company according to operating, investing, and financing activities. The operating activities category is the most important. It shows the cash provided by company operations. This source of cash is generally considered to be the best measure of a company's ability to generate enough cash to continue as a going concern.

ILLUSTRATION 19-1
Classification of Typical Cash Inflows and Outflows

Operating	**Income Statement Items**
Cash inflows	
From sales of goods or services.	
From returns on loans (interest) and on equity securities (dividends).	
Cash outflows	
To suppliers for inventory.	
To employees for services.	
To government for taxes.	
To lenders for interest.	
To others for expenses.	
Investing	**Generally Long-Term Asset Items**
Cash inflows	
From sale of property, plant, and equipment.	
From sale of debt or equity securities of other entities.	
From collection of principal on loans to other entities.	
Cash outflows	
To purchase property, plant, and equipment.	
To purchase debt or equity securities of other entities.	
To make loans to other entities.	
Financing	**Generally Long-Term Liability and Equity Items**
Cash inflows	
From sale of equity securities.	
From issuance of debt (bonds and notes).	
Cash outflows	
To stockholders as dividends.	
To redeem long-term debt or reacquire capital stock.	

INTERNATIONAL INSIGHT

According to International Accounting Standards, companies can define "cash and cash equivalents" as "net monetary assets"—that is, as "cash and demand deposits and highly liquid investments less short-term borrowings."

Note the following general guidelines about the classification of cash flows.

1 Operating activities involve income statement items.

2 Investing activities involve cash flows resulting from changes in investments and long-term asset items.

3 Financing activities involve cash flows resulting from changes in long-term liability and stockholders' equity items.

Companies classify some cash flows relating to investing or financing activities as operating activities.[4] For example, companies classify receipts of investment income (interest and dividends) and payments of interest to lenders as operating activities.

[4]For exceptions to the treatment of purchases and sales of loans and securities by banks and brokers, see *Statement of Financial Accounting Standards No. 102* (February 1989). Banks and brokers must classify cash flows from purchases and sales of loans and securities specifically for resale and carried at market value **as operating activities**. This requirement recognizes that for these firms these assets are similar to inventory in other businesses.

Why are these considered operating activities? Companies report these items in the income statement, where the results of operations are shown.

Conversely, companies classify some cash flows relating to operating activities as investing or financing activities. For example, a company classifies the cash received from the sale of property, plant, and equipment at a gain, although reported in the income statement, as an investing activity. It excludes the effects of the related gain in net cash flow from operating activities. Likewise, a gain or loss on the payment (extinguishment) of debt is generally part of the cash outflow related to the repayment of the amount borrowed. It therefore is a financing activity.

HOW'S MY CASH FLOW?

WHAT DO THE NUMBERS MEAN?

To evaluate overall cash flow, it is useful to understand where in the product life cycle a company is. Generally, companies move through several stages of development, which have implications for cash flow. As the graph below shows, the pattern of cash flows from operating, financing, and investing activities will vary depending on the stage of the product life cycle.

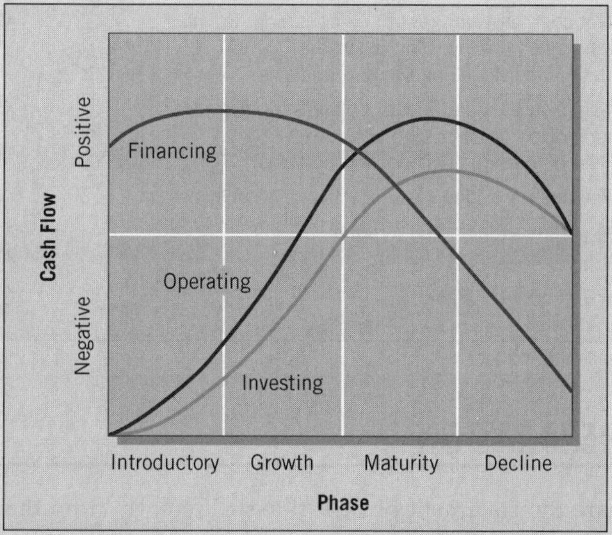

In the introductory phase, the product is likely not generating much revenue (operating cash flow is negative). Because the company is making heavy investments to get a product off the ground, cash flow from investment is negative, and financing cash flows are positive.

As the product moves to the growth and maturity phases, these cash flow relationships reverse. The product generates more cash flow from operations, which can be used to cover investments needed to support the product, and less cash is needed from financing. So is a negative operating cash flow bad? Not always. It depends on the product life cycle.

Source: Adapted from Paul D. Kimmel, Jerry J. Weygandt, and Donald E. Kieso, *Financial Accounting: Tools for Business Decision Making*, 4th ed. (New York: John Wiley & Sons, 2006), p. 591.

FORMAT OF THE STATEMENT OF CASH FLOWS

The three activities we discussed above constitute the general format of the statement of cash flows. The operating activities section always appears first. It is followed by the investing activities section and then the financing activities section.

A company reports the individual inflows and outflows from investing and financing activities separately. That is, a company reports them gross, not netted against one another. Thus, a cash outflow from the purchase of property is reported separately from the cash inflow from the sale of property. Similarly, a cash inflow from the issuance of debt is reported separately from the cash outflow from its retirement.

The net increase or decrease in cash reported during the period should reconcile the beginning and ending cash balances as reported in the comparative balance sheets. The general format of the statement of cash flows presents the results of the three activities discussed previously–operating, investing, and financing. Illustration 19-2 shows a widely used form of the statement of cash flows.

ILLUSTRATION 19-2
Format of the Statement of Cash Flows

COMPANY NAME STATEMENT OF CASH FLOWS PERIOD COVERED		
Cash flows from operating activities		
Net income		XXX
Adjustments to reconcile net income to net cash provided by operating activities:		
(List of individual items)	XX	XX
Net cash provided (used) by operating activities		XXX
Cash flows from investing activities		
(List of individual inflows and outflows)	XX	
Net cash provided (used) by investing activities		XXX
Cash flows from financing activities		
(List of individual inflows and outflows)	XX	
Net cash provided (used) by financing activities		XXX
Net increase (decrease) in cash		XXX
Cash at beginning of period		XXX
Cash at end of period		XXX

STEPS IN PREPARATION

Companies prepare the statement of cash flows differently from the three other basic financial statements. For one thing, it is not prepared from an adjusted trial balance. The cash flow statement requires detailed information concerning the changes in account balances that occurred between two points in time. An adjusted trial balance will not provide the necessary data. Second, the statement of cash flows deals with cash receipts and payments. As a result, the company must adjust the effects of the use of accrual accounting to determine cash flows. The information to prepare this statement usually comes from three sources:

1 **Comparative balance sheets** provide the amount of the changes in assets, liabilities, and equities from the beginning to the end of the period.

2 **Current income statement** data help determine the amount of cash provided by or used by operations during the period.

3 **Selected transaction data** from the general ledger provide additional detailed information needed to determine how the company provided or used cash during the period.

Preparing the statement of cash flows from the data sources above involves three major steps:

Step 1. Determine the change in cash. This procedure is straightforward. A company can easily compute the difference between the beginning and the ending cash balance from examining its comparative balance sheets.

Step 2. Determine the net cash flow from operating activities. This procedure is complex. It involves analyzing not only the current year's income statement but also comparative balance sheets as well as selected transaction data.

Step 3. Determine net cash flows from investing and financing activities. A company must analyze all other changes in the balance sheet accounts to determine their effects on cash.

On the following pages we work through these three steps in the process of preparing the statement of cash flows for Tax Consultants Inc. over several years.

FIRST EXAMPLE—2006

To illustrate a statement of cash flows, we use the **first year of operations** for Tax Consultants Inc. The company started on January 1, 2006, when it issued 60,000 shares of $1 par value common stock for $60,000 cash. The company rented its office space, furniture, and equipment, and performed tax consulting services throughout the first year. The comparative balance sheets at the beginning and end of the year 2006 appear in Illustration 19-3.

ILLUSTRATION 19-3
Comparative Balance Sheets, Tax Consultants Inc., Year 1

TAX CONSULTANTS INC.
COMPARATIVE BALANCE SHEETS

Assets	Dec. 31, 2006	Jan. 1, 2006	Change Increase/Decrease
Cash	$49,000	$-0-	$49,000 Increase
Accounts receivable	36,000	-0-	36,000 Increase
Total	$85,000	$-0-	
Liabilities and Stockholders' Equity			
Accounts payable	$ 5,000	$-0-	$ 5,000 Increase
Common stock ($1 par)	60,000	-0-	60,000 Increase
Retained earnings	20,000	-0-	20,000 Increase
Total	$85,000	$-0-	

Illustration 19-4 shows the income statement and additional information for Tax Consultants.

ILLUSTRATION 19-4
Income Statement, Tax Consultants Inc., Year 1

TAX CONSULTANTS INC.
INCOME STATEMENT
FOR THE YEAR ENDED DECEMBER 31, 2006

Revenues	$125,000
Operating expenses	85,000
Income before income taxes	40,000
Income tax expense	6,000
Net income	$ 34,000

Additional Information
Examination of selected data indicates that a dividend of $14,000 was declared and paid during the year.

Step 1: Determine the Change in Cash

To prepare a statement of cash flows, the first step is to **determine the change in cash.** This is a simple computation. Tax Consultants had no cash on hand at the beginning of the year 2006. It had $49,000 on hand at the end of 2006. Thus, cash changed (increased) in 2006 by $49,000.

Step 2: Determine Net Cash Flow from Operating Activities

OBJECTIVE 3
Differentiate between net income and net cash flows from operating activities.

To determine net cash flow from operating activities,[5] companies adjust net income in numerous ways. A useful starting point is to understand why net income must be converted to net cash provided by operating activities.

Under generally accepted accounting principles, most companies use the accrual basis of accounting. As you have learned, this basis requires that companies record revenue when earned and record expenses when incurred. Earned revenues may include credit sales for which the company has not yet collected cash. Expenses incurred may include some items that the company has not yet paid in cash. Thus, under the accrual basis of accounting, net income is not the same as net cash flow from operating activities.

To arrive at net cash flow from operating activities, a company must determine revenues and expenses on a **cash basis. It does this by eliminating the effects of income statement transactions that do not result in an increase or decrease in cash.** Illustration 19-5 shows the relationship between net income and net cash flow from operating activities.

ILLUSTRATION 19-5
Net Income versus Net Cash Flow from Operating Activities

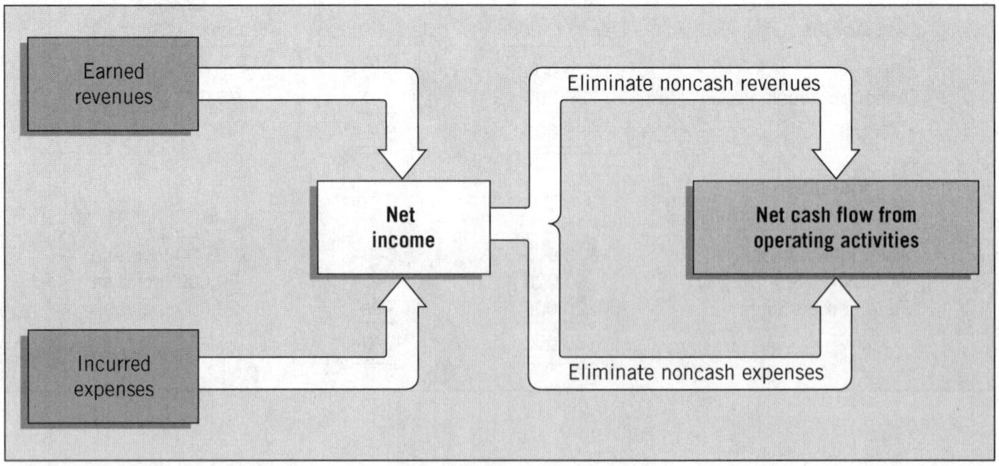

In this chapter, we use the term net income to refer to accrual-based net income. A company may convert net income to net cash flow from operating activities through either a direct method or an indirect method. We explain both methods in the following sections. The advantages and disadvantages of these two methods are discussed later in the chapter.

Direct Method

OBJECTIVE 4
Contrast the direct and indirect methods of calculating net cash flow from operating activities.

The **direct method** (also called the **income statement method**) reports cash receipts and cash disbursements from operating activities. The difference between these two amounts is the net cash flow from operating activities. In other words, the direct method deducts operating cash disbursements from operating cash receipts. The direct

[5]"Net cash flow from operating activities" is a generic phrase, replaced in the statement of cash flows with either "Net cash **provided by** operating activities" if operations increase cash, or "Net cash **used by** operating activities" if operations decrease cash.

method results in the presentation of a condensed cash receipts and cash disbursements statement.

As indicated from the accrual-based income statement, Tax Consultants reported revenues of $125,000. However, because the company's accounts receivable increased during 2006 by $36,000, the company collected only $89,000 ($125,000 − $36,000) in cash from these revenues. Similarly, Tax Consultants reported operating expenses of $85,000. However, accounts payable increased during the period by $5,000. Assuming that these payables relate to operating expenses, cash operating expenses were $80,000 ($85,000 − $5,000). Because no taxes payable exist at the end of the year, the company must have paid $6,000 income tax expense for 2006 in cash during the year. Tax Consultants computes net cash flow from operating activities as shown in Illustration 19-6.

ILLUSTRATION 19-6
Computation of Net Cash Flow from Operating Activities, Year 1—Direct Method

Cash collected from revenues	$89,000
Cash payments for expenses	80,000
Income before income taxes	9,000
Cash payments for income taxes	6,000
Net cash provided by operating activities	$ 3,000

"Net cash provided by operating activities" is the equivalent of cash basis net income. ("Net cash used by operating activities" is equivalent to cash basis net loss.)

Indirect Method

The **indirect method** (or **reconciliation method**) starts with net income and converts it to net cash flow from operating activities. In other words, **the indirect method adjusts net income for items that affected reported net income but did not affect cash.** To compute net cash flow from operating activities, a company adds back noncash charges in the income statement to net income and deducts noncash credits. We explain the two adjustments to net income for Tax Consultants, namely, the increases in accounts receivable and accounts payable, as follows.

Increase in Accounts Receivable—Indirect Method. Tax Consultant's accounts receivable increased by $36,000 (from $0 to $36,000) during the year. For Tax Consultants, this means that cash receipts were $36,000 lower than revenues. The Accounts Receivable account in Illustration 19-7 shows that Tax Consultants had $125,000 in revenues (as reported on the income statement), but it collected only $89,000 in cash.

ILLUSTRATION 19-7
Analysis of Accounts Receivable

Accounts Receivable				
1/1/06	Balance	–0–	Receipts from customer	89,000
	Revenues	125,000		
12/31/06	Balance	36,000		

As shown in Illustration 19-8, to adjust net income to net cash provided by operating activities, Tax Consultants must deduct the increase of $36,000 in accounts receivable from net income. When the Accounts Receivable balance *decreases*, cash receipts are higher than revenue earned under the accrual basis. Therefore, the company adds to net income the amount of the decrease in accounts receivable to arrive at net cash provided by operating activities.

Increase in Accounts Payable—Indirect Method. When accounts payable increase during the year, expenses on an accrual basis exceed those on a cash basis. Why? Because Tax Consultants incurred expenses, but some of the expenses are not yet paid. To convert net income to net cash flow from operating activities, Tax Consultants must add back the increase of $5,000 in accounts payable to net income.

As a result of the accounts receivable and accounts payable adjustments, Tax Consultants determines net cash provided by operating activities is $3,000 for the year 2006. Illustration 19-8 shows this computation.

ILLUSTRATION 19-8
Computation of Net Cash Flow from Operating Activities, Year 1—Indirect Method

Net income		$34,000
Adjustments to reconcile net income to net cash provided by operating activities:		
Increase in accounts receivable	$(36,000)	
Increase in accounts payable	5,000	(31,000)
Net cash provided by operating activities		$ 3,000

Note that net cash provided by operating activities is the same whether using the direct (Illustration 19-6) or the indirect method (Illustration 19-8).

WHAT DO THE NUMBERS MEAN?

PUMPING UP CASH

Due to recent concerns about a decline in quality of earnings, some investors have been focusing on cash flow. And management has an incentive to make operating cash flow look good, because Wall Street has paid a premium for companies that generate a lot of cash from operations, rather than through borrowings. However, similar to earnings, companies have ways to pump up cash flow from operations.

One way that companies boost their operating cash flow is by securitizing receivables—that is, turning their receivables into securities that can be sold. For example, at one time **Oxford Industries**, an apparel company, reported a $74 million dollar increase in cash flow from operations. This seems impressive until you read the fine print, which indicates that a big part of the increase was due to the sale of receivables. As discussed in the text, decreases in accounts receivable increase cash flow from operations. So while Oxford's core operations seemed to have improved, the company really did little more than accelerate collections of its receivables. In fact, without the cash flow boost from the securitizations, Oxford's operating cash flow would have been negative. Thus, just like earnings, cash flow can be of high or low quality.

Source: Adapted from Ann Tergesen, "Cash Flow Hocus Pocus," *Business Week* (July 16, 2002), pp. 130–131.

Step 3: Determine Net Cash Flows from Investing and Financing Activities

OBJECTIVE 5
Determine net cash flows from investing and financing activities.

After Tax Consultants has computed the net cash provided by operating activities, the next step is to determine whether any other changes in balance sheet accounts caused an increase or decrease in cash.

For example, an examination of the remaining balance sheet accounts for Tax Consultants shows increases in both common stock and retained earnings. The common stock increase of $60,000 resulted from the issuance of common stock for cash. The issuance of common stock is reported in the statement of cash flows as a receipt of cash from a financing activity.

Two items caused the retained earnings increase of $20,000:

1 Net income of $34,000 increased retained earnings.

2 Declaration of $14,000 of dividends decreased retained earnings.

Tax Consultants has converted net income into net cash flow from operating activities, as explained earlier. The additional data indicate that it paid the dividend. Thus, the company reports the dividend payment as a cash outflow, classified as a financing activity.

Statement of Cash Flows—2006

OBJECTIVE 6
Prepare a statement of cash flows.

We are now ready to prepare the statement of cash flows. The statement starts with the operating activities section. Tax Consultants may use either the direct or indirect method to report net cash flow from operating activities.

The FASB **encourages** the use of the direct method over the indirect method. If a company uses the direct method of reporting net cash flow from operating activities, the FASB **requires** that the company provide in a separate schedule a reconciliation of net income to net cash flow from operating activities. If a company uses the indirect method, it can either report the reconciliation within the statement of cash flows or can provide it in a separate schedule, with the statement of cash flows reporting only the **net** cash flow from operating activities.[6] Throughout this chapter we use the indirect method, which is also used more extensively in practice.[7] *In doing homework assignments, you should follow instructions for use of either the direct or indirect method.*

Illustration 19-9 shows the statement of cash flows for Tax Consultants Inc., for year 1 (2006).

ILLUSTRATION 19-9
Statement of Cash Flows, Tax Consultants Inc., Year 1

TAX CONSULTANTS INC.
STATEMENT OF CASH FLOWS
FOR THE YEAR ENDED DECEMBER 31, 2006
INCREASE (DECREASE) IN CASH

Cash flows from operating activities		
Net income		$34,000
Adjustments to reconcile net income to net cash provided by operating activities:		
Increase in accounts receivable	$(36,000)	
Increase in accounts payable	5,000	(31,000)
Net cash provided by operating activities		3,000
Cash flows from financing activities		
Issuance of common stock	60,000	
Payment of cash dividends	(14,000)	
Net cash provided by financing activities		46,000
Net increase in cash		49,000
Cash, January 1, 2006		-0-
Cash, December 31, 2006		$49,000

As indicated, the $60,000 increase in common stock results in a financing-activity cash inflow. The payment of $14,000 in cash dividends is a financing-activity outflow of cash. The $49,000 increase in cash reported in the statement of cash flows agrees with the increase of $49,000 shown in the comparative balance sheets as the change in the cash account.

SECOND EXAMPLE—2007

Tax Consultants Inc. continued to grow and prosper in its second year of operations. The company purchased land, building, and equipment, and revenues and net income increased substantially over the first year. Illustrations 19-10 and 19-11 present information related to the second year of operations for Tax Consultants Inc.

[6]"The Statement of Cash Flows," pars. 27 and 30.

[7]*Accounting Trends and Techniques—2004* reports that out of its 600 surveyed companies, 593 (approximately 99 percent) used the indirect method, and only 7 used the direct method.

ILLUSTRATION 19-10
Comparative Balance Sheets, Tax Consultants Inc., Year 2

TAX CONSULTANTS INC.
COMPARATIVE BALANCE SHEETS
AS OF DECEMBER 31

Assets	2007	2006	Change Increase/Decrease
Cash	$ 37,000	$49,000	$12,000 Decrease
Accounts receivable	26,000	36,000	10,000 Decrease
Prepaid expenses	6,000	-0-	6,000 Increase
Land	70,000	-0-	70,000 Increase
Building	200,000	-0-	200,000 Increase
Accumulated depreciation—building	(11,000)	-0-	11,000 Increase
Equipment	68,000	-0-	68,000 Increase
Accumulated depreciation—equipment	(10,000)	-0-	10,000 Increase
Total	$386,000	$85,000	
Liabilities and Stockholders' Equity			
Accounts payable	$ 40,000	$ 5,000	$ 35,000 Increase
Bonds payable	150,000	-0-	150,000 Increase
Common stock ($1 par)	60,000	60,000	-0-
Retained earnings	136,000	20,000	116,000 Increase
Total	$386,000	$85,000	

ILLUSTRATION 19-11
Income Statement, Tax Consultants Inc., Year 2

TAX CONSULTANTS INC.
INCOME STATEMENT
FOR THE YEAR ENDED DECEMBER 31, 2007

Revenues		$492,000
Operating expenses (excluding depreciation)	$269,000	
Depreciation expense	21,000	290,000
Income from operations		202,000
Income tax expense		68,000
Net income		$134,000

Additional Information
(a) The company declared and paid an $18,000 cash dividend.
(b) The company obtained $150,000 cash through the issuance of long-term bonds.
(c) Land, building, and equipment were acquired for cash.

Step 1: Determine the Change in Cash

To prepare a statement of cash flows from the available information, the first step is to determine the change in cash. As indicated from the information presented, cash decreased $12,000 ($49,000 − $37,000).

Step 2: Determine Net Cash Flow from Operating Activities—Indirect Method

Using the indirect method, we adjust net income of $134,000 on an accrual basis to arrive at net cash flow from operating activities. Explanations for the adjustments to net income follow.

Decrease in Accounts Receivable. Accounts receivable decreased during the period, because cash receipts (cash-basis revenues) are higher than revenues reported on an accrual basis. To convert net income to net cash flow from operating activities, the decrease of $10,000 in accounts receivable must be added to net income.

Increase in Prepaid Expenses. When prepaid expenses (assets) increase during a period, expenses on an accrual-basis income statement are lower than they are on a cash-basis income statement. The reason: Tax Consultants has made cash payments in the current period, but expenses (as charges to the income statement) have been deferred to future periods. To convert net income to net cash flow from operating activities, the company must deduct from net income the increase of $6,000 in prepaid expenses. An increase in prepaid expenses results in a decrease in cash during the period.

Increase in Accounts Payable. Like the increase in 2006, Tax Consultants must add the 2007 increase of $35,000 in accounts payable to net income, to convert to net cash flow from operating activities. The company incurred a greater amount of expense than the amount of cash it disbursed.

Depreciation Expense (Increase in Accumulated Depreciation). The purchase of depreciable assets is a use of cash, shown in the investing section in the year of acquisition. Tax Consultant's depreciation expense of $21,000 (also represented by the increase in accumulated depreciation) is a noncash charge; the company adds it back to net income, to arrive at net cash flow from operating activities. The $21,000 is the sum of the $11,000 depreciation on the building plus the $10,000 depreciation on the equipment.

Certain other periodic charges to expense do not require the use of cash. Examples are the amortization of intangible assets and depletion expense. Such charges are treated in the same manner as depreciation. Companies frequently list depreciation and similar noncash charges as the first adjustments to net income in the statement of cash flows.

As a result of the foregoing items, net cash provided by operating activities is $194,000 as shown in Illustration 19-12.

ILLUSTRATION 19-12
Computation of Net Cash Flow from Operating Activities, Year 2—Indirect Method

Net income		$134,000
Adjustments to reconcile net income to net cash provided by operating activities:		
Depreciation expense	$21,000	
Decrease in accounts receivable	10,000	
Increase in prepaid expenses	(6,000)	
Increase in accounts payable	35,000	60,000
Net cash provided by operating activities		$194,000

Step 3: Determine Net Cash Flows from Investing and Financing Activities

After you have determined the items affecting net cash provided by operating activities, the next step involves analyzing the remaining changes in balance sheet accounts. Tax Consultants Inc. analyzed the following accounts.

Increase in Land. As indicated from the change in the land account, the company purchased land of $70,000 during the period. This transaction is an investing activity, reported as a use of cash.

Increase in Building and Related Accumulated Depreciation. As indicated in the additional data, and from the change in the building account, Tax Consultants acquired an office building using $200,000 cash. This transaction is a cash outflow, reported in the investing section. The $11,000 increase in accumulated depreciation results from recording depreciation expense on the building. As indicated earlier, the reported depreciation expense has no effect on the amount of cash.

Increase in Equipment and Related Accumulated Depreciation. An increase in equipment of $68,000 resulted because the company used cash to purchase equipment. This transaction is an outflow of cash from an investing activity. The depreciation expense entry for the period explains the increase in Accumulated Depreciation—Equipment.

Increase in Bonds Payable. The bonds payable account increased $150,000. Cash received from the issuance of these bonds represents an inflow of cash from a financing activity.

Increase in Retained Earnings. Retained earnings increased $116,000 during the year. Two factors explain this increase: (1) Net income of $134,000 increased retained earnings, and (2) dividends of $18,000 decreased retained earnings. As indicated earlier, the company adjusts net income to net cash provided by operating activities in the operating activities section. Payment of the dividends is a financing activity that involves a cash outflow.

Statement of Cash Flows—2007

Combining the foregoing items, we get a statement of cash flows for 2007 for Tax Consultants Inc., using the indirect method to compute net cash flow from operating activities.

ILLUSTRATION 19-13
Statement of Cash Flows, Tax Consultants Inc., Year 2

TAX CONSULTANTS INC.
STATEMENT OF CASH FLOWS
FOR THE YEAR ENDED DECEMBER 31, 2007
INCREASE (DECREASE) IN CASH

Cash flows from operating activities		
Net income		$134,000
Adjustments to reconcile net income to net cash provided by operating activities:		
Depreciation expense	$ 21,000	
Decrease in accounts receivable	10,000	
Increase in prepaid expenses	(6,000)	
Increase in accounts payable	35,000	60,000
Net cash provided by operating activities		194,000
Cash flows from investing activities		
Purchase of land	(70,000)	
Purchase of building	(200,000)	
Purchase of equipment	(68,000)	
Net cash used by investing activities		(338,000)
Cash flows from financing activities		
Issuance of bonds	150,000	
Payment of cash dividends	(18,000)	
Net cash provided by financing activities		132,000
Net decrease in cash		(12,000)
Cash, January 1, 2007		49,000
Cash, December 31, 2007		$ 37,000

THIRD EXAMPLE—2008

Our third example, covering the 2008 operations of Tax Consultants Inc., is more complex. It again uses the indirect method to compute and present net cash flow from operating activities.

Tax Consultants Inc. experienced continued success in 2008 and expanded its operations to include the sale of computer software used in tax-return preparation and tax planning. Thus, inventory is a new asset appearing in the company's December 31, 2008, balance sheet. Illustrations 19-14 and 19-15 show the comparative balance sheets, income statements, and selected data for 2008.

ILLUSTRATION 19-14
Comparative Balance Sheets, Tax Consultants Inc., Year 3

TAX CONSULTANTS INC.
COMPARATIVE BALANCE SHEETS
AS OF DECEMBER 31

Assets	2008	2007	Change Increase/Decrease
Cash	$ 54,000	$ 37,000	$ 17,000 Increase
Accounts receivable	68,000	26,000	42,000 Increase
Inventories	54,000	–0–	54,000 Increase
Prepaid expenses	4,000	6,000	2,000 Decrease
Land	45,000	70,000	25,000 Decrease
Buildings	200,000	200,000	–0–
Accumulated depreciation—buildings	(21,000)	(11,000)	10,000 Increase
Equipment	193,000	68,000	125,000 Increase
Accumulated depreciation—equipment	(28,000)	(10,000)	18,000 Increase
Totals	$569,000	$386,000	
Liabilities and Stockholders' Equity			
Accounts payable	$ 33,000	$ 40,000	$ 7,000 Decrease
Bonds payable	110,000	150,000	40,000 Decrease
Common stock ($1 par)	220,000	60,000	160,000 Increase
Retained earnings	206,000	136,000	70,000 Increase
Totals	$569,000	$386,000	

ILLUSTRATION 19-15
Income Statement, Tax Consultants Inc., Year 3

TAX CONSULTANTS INC.
INCOME STATEMENT
FOR THE YEAR ENDED DECEMBER 31, 2008

Revenues		$890,000
Cost of goods sold	$465,000	
Operating expenses	221,000	
Interest expense	12,000	
Loss on sale of equipment	2,000	700,000
Income from operations		190,000
Income tax expense		65,000
Net income		$125,000

Additional Information
(a) Operating expenses include depreciation expense of $33,000 and amortization of prepaid expenses of $2,000.
(b) Land was sold at its book value for cash.
(c) Cash dividends of $55,000 were declared and paid.
(d) Interest expense of $12,000 was paid in cash.
(e) Equipment with a cost of $166,000 was purchased for cash. Equipment with a cost of $41,000 and a book value of $36,000 was sold for $34,000 cash.
(f) Bonds were redeemed at their book value for cash.
(g) Common stock ($1 par) was issued for cash.

Step 1: Determine the Change in Cash

The first step in the preparation of the statement of cash flows is to determine the change in cash. As the comparative balance sheets show, cash increased $17,000 in 2008.

Step 2: Determine Net Cash Flow from Operating Activities—Indirect Method

We explain the adjustments to net income of $125,000 as follows.

Increase in Accounts Receivable. The increase in accounts receivable of $42,000 represents recorded accrual-basis revenues in excess of cash collections in 2008. The company deducts this increase from net income to convert from the accrual basis to the cash basis.

Increase in Inventories. The $54,000 increase in inventories represents an operating use of cash, not an expense. Tax Consultants therefore deducts this amount from net income, to arrive at net cash flow from operations. In other words, when inventory purchased exceeds inventory sold during a period, cost of goods sold on an accrual basis is lower than on a cash basis.

Decrease in Prepaid Expenses. The $2,000 decrease in prepaid expenses represents a charge to the income statement for which Tax Consultants made no cash payment in the current period. The company adds back the decrease to net income, to arrive at net cash flow from operating activities.

Decrease in Accounts Payable. When accounts payable decrease during the year, cost of goods sold and expenses on a cash basis are higher than they are on an accrual basis. To convert net income to net cash flow from operating activities, the company must deduct the $7,000 in accounts payable from net income.

Depreciation Expense (Increase in Accumulated Depreciation). Accumulated Depreciation—Buildings increased $10,000 ($21,000 − $11,000). The Buildings account did not change during the period, which means that Tax Consultants recorded depreciation expense of $10,000 in 2008.

Accumulated Depreciation—Equipment increased by $18,000 ($28,000 − $10,000) during the year. But Accumulated Depreciation—Equipment decreased by $5,000 as a result of the sale during the year. Thus, depreciation for the year was $23,000. The company reconciled Accumulated Depreciation—Equipment as follows.

Beginning balance	$10,000
Add: Depreciation for 2008	23,000
	33,000
Deduct: Sale of equipment	5,000
Ending balance	$28,000

The company must add back to net income the total depreciation of $33,000 ($10,000 + $23,000) charged to the income statement, to determine net cash flow from operating activities.

Loss on Sale of Equipment. Tax Consultants Inc. sold for $34,000 equipment that cost $41,000 and had a book value of $36,000. As a result, the company reported a loss of $2,000 on its sale. To arrive at net cash flow from operating activities, it must add back to net income the loss on the sale of the equipment. The reason is that the loss is a noncash charge to the income statement. The loss did not reduce cash, but it did reduce net income.

From the foregoing items, the company prepares the operating activities section of the statement of cash flows, as shown in Illustration 19-16.

ILLUSTRATION 19-16
Operating Activities Section of Cash Flows Statement

Cash flows from operating activities		
Net income		$125,000
Adjustments to reconcile net income to net cash provided by operating activities:		
Depreciation expense	$33,000	
Loss on sale of equipment	2,000	
Increase in accounts receivable	(42,000)	
Increase in inventories	(54,000)	
Decrease in prepaid expenses	2,000	
Decrease in accounts payable	(7,000)	(66,000)
Net cash provided by operating activities		59,000

Step 3: Determine Net Cash Flows from Investing and Financing Activities

By analyzing the remaining changes in the balance sheet accounts, Tax Consultants identifies cash flows from investing and financing activities.

Land. Land decreased $25,000 during the period. As indicated from the information presented, the company sold land for cash at its book value. This transaction is an investing activity, reported as a $25,000 source of cash.

Equipment. An analysis of the equipment account indicates the following.

Beginning balance	$ 68,000
Purchase of equipment	166,000
	234,000
Sale of equipment	41,000
Ending balance	$193,000

The company used cash to purchase equipment with a fair value of $166,000—an investing transaction reported as a cash outflow. The sale of the equipment for $34,000 is also an investing activity, but one that generates a cash inflow.

Bonds Payable. Bonds payable decreased $40,000 during the year. As indicated from the additional information, the company redeemed the bonds at their book value. This financing transaction used $40,000 of cash.

Common Stock. The common stock account increased $160,000 during the year. As indicated from the additional information, Tax Consultants issued common stock of $160,000 at par. This financing transaction provided cash of $160,000.

Retained Earnings. Retained earnings changed $70,000 ($206,000 − $136,000) during the year. The $70,000 change in retained earnings results from net income of $125,000 from operations and the financing activity of paying cash dividends of $55,000.

Statement of Cash Flows—2008

Tax Consultants Inc. combines the foregoing items to prepare the statement of cash flows shown in Illustration 19-17.

ILLUSTRATION 19-17
Statement of Cash Flows, Tax Consultants Inc., Year 3

TAX CONSULTANTS INC.
STATEMENT OF CASH FLOWS
FOR THE YEAR ENDED DECEMBER 31, 2008
INCREASE (DECREASE) IN CASH

Cash flows from operating activities		
Net income		$125,000
Adjustments to reconcile net income to net cash provided by operating activities:		
Depreciation expense	$ 33,000	
Loss on sale of equipment	2,000	
Increase in accounts receivable	(42,000)	
Increase in inventories	(54,000)	
Decrease in prepaid expenses	2,000	
Decrease in accounts payable	(7,000)	(66,000)
Net cash provided by operating activities		59,000
Cash flows from investing activities		
Sale of land	25,000	
Sale of equipment	34,000	
Purchase of equipment	(166,000)	
Net cash used by investing activities		(107,000)
Cash flows from financing activities		
Redemption of bonds	(40,000)	
Sale of common stock	160,000	
Payment of dividends	(55,000)	
Net cash provided by financing activities		65,000
Net increase in cash		17,000
Cash, January 1, 2008		37,000
Cash, December 31, 2008		$ 54,000

SOURCES OF INFORMATION FOR THE STATEMENT OF CASH FLOWS

OBJECTIVE 7
Identify sources of information for a statement of cash flows.

Important points to remember in the preparation of the statement of cash flows are these:

1. Comparative balance sheets provide the basic information from which to prepare the report. Additional information obtained from analyses of specific accounts is also included.
2. An analysis of the Retained Earnings account is necessary. The net increase or decrease in Retained Earnings without any explanation is a meaningless amount in the statement. Without explanation, it might represent the effect of net income, dividends declared, or prior period adjustments.
3. The statement includes all changes that have passed through cash or have resulted in an increase or decrease in cash.
4. Writedowns, amortization charges, and similar "book" entries, such as depreciation of plant assets, represent neither inflows nor outflows of cash, because they have no effect on cash. To the extent that they have entered into the determination of net income, however, the company must add them back to or subtract them from net income, to arrive at net cash provided by operating activities.

NET CASH FLOW FROM OPERATING ACTIVITIES—INDIRECT VERSUS DIRECT METHOD

As we discussed previously, the two different methods available to adjust income from operations on an accrual basis to net cash flow from operating activities are the indirect (reconciliation) method and the direct (income statement) method.

The FASB encourages use of the direct method and permits use of the indirect method. Yet, if the direct method is used, the Board requires that companies provide in a separate schedule a reconciliation of net income to net cash flow from operating activities. Therefore, under either method, companies must prepare and report information from the indirect (reconciliation) method.

Indirect Method

For consistency and comparability and because it is the most widely used method in practice, we used the indirect method in the examples just presented. We determined net cash flows from operating activities by adding back to or deducting from net income those items that had no effect on cash. Illustration 19-18 presents more completely the common types of adjustments that companies make to net income to arrive at net cash flow from operating activities.

The additions and deductions listed on the next page reconcile net income to net cash flow from operating activities, illustrating why the indirect method is also called the reconciliation method.

Direct Method—An Example

Under the direct method the statement of cash flows reports net cash flow from operating activities as major classes of *operating cash receipts* (e.g., cash collected from customers and cash received from interest and dividends) and *cash disbursements* (e.g., cash paid to suppliers for goods, to employees for services, to creditors for interest, and to government authorities for taxes).

We illustrate the direct method here in more detail to help you understand the difference between accrual-based income and net cash flow from operating activities. This

ILLUSTRATION 19-18
Adjustments Needed to Determine Net Cash Flow from Operating Activities—Indirect Method

Net Income

Additions	Deductions
Depreciation expense	Amortization of bond premium
Amortization of intangibles and deferred charges	Decrease in deferred income tax liability
Amortization of bond discount	Income on investment in common stock using equity method
Increase in deferred income tax liability	Gain on sale of plant assets
Loss on investment in common stock using equity method	Increase in receivables
Loss on sale of plant assets	Increase in inventories
Loss on impairment of assets	Increase in prepaid expense
Decrease in receivables	Decrease in accounts payable
Decrease in inventories	Decrease in accrued liabilities
Decrease in prepaid expense	
Increase in accounts payable	
Increase in accrued liabilities	

→ = ←

Net Cash Flow from Operating Activities

example also illustrates the data needed to apply the direct method. Emig Company, which began business on January 1, 2008, has the following selected balance sheet information.

ILLUSTRATION 19-19
Balance Sheet Accounts, Emig Co.

	December 31	
	2008	2007
Cash	$159,000	–0–
Accounts receivable	15,000	–0–
Inventory	160,000	–0–
Prepaid expenses	8,000	–0–
Property, plant, and equipment (net)	90,000	–0–
Accounts payable	60,000	–0–
Accrued expenses payable	20,000	–0–

Emig Company's December 31, 2008, income statement and additional information are as follows.

ILLUSTRATION 19-20
Income Statement, Emig Co.

Revenues from sales		$780,000
Cost of goods sold		450,000
Gross profit		330,000
Operating expenses	$160,000	
Depreciation	10,000	170,000
Income before income taxes		160,000
Income tax expense		48,000
Net income		$112,000

Additional Information:
(a) Dividends of $70,000 were declared and paid in cash.
(b) The accounts payable increase resulted from the purchase of merchandise.
(c) Prepaid expenses and accrued expenses payable relate to operating expenses.

Under the **direct method**, companies compute net cash provided by operating activities by **adjusting each item in the income statement** from the accrual basis to the cash basis. To simplify and condense the operating activities section, only major classes of operating cash receipts and cash payments are reported. As Illustration 19-21 shows, the difference between these major classes of cash receipts and cash payments is the net cash provided by operating activities.

ILLUSTRATION 19-21
Major Classes of Cash Receipts and Payments

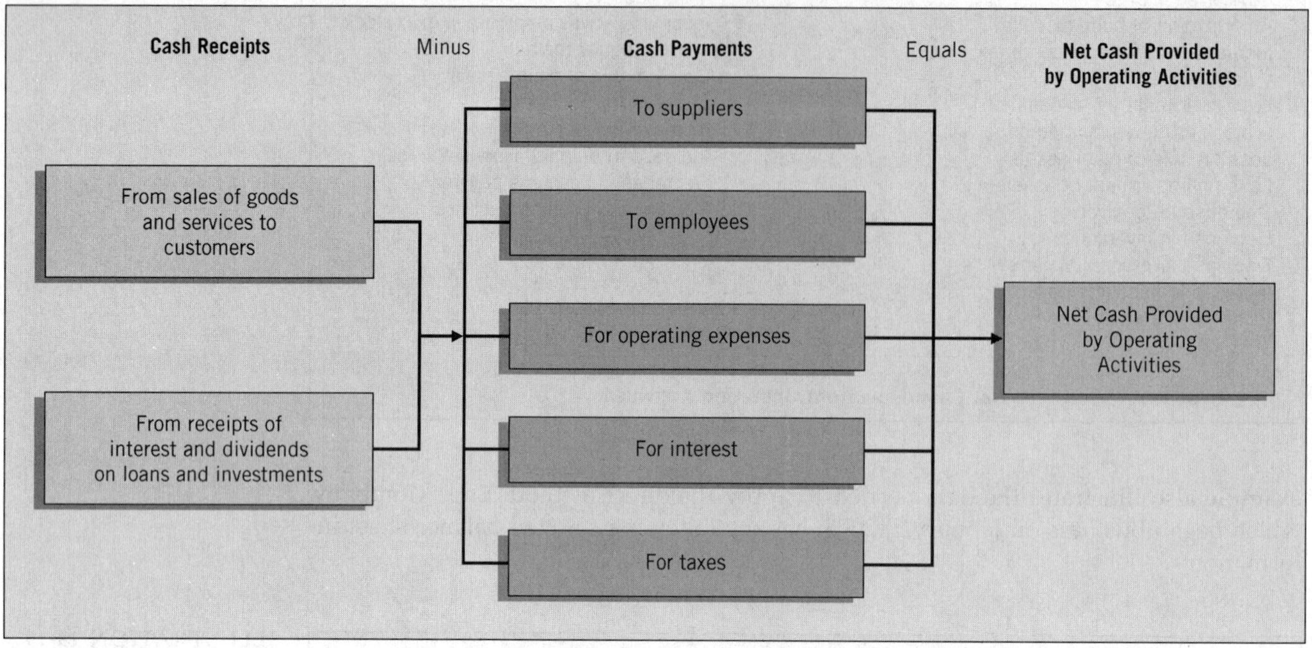

An efficient way to apply the direct method is to analyze the revenues and expenses reported in the income statement in the order in which they are listed. The company then determines cash receipts and cash payments related to these revenues and expenses. In the following sections, we present the direct method adjustments for Emig Company in 2008, to determine net cash provided by operating activities.

Cash Receipts from Customers. The income statement for Emig Company reported revenues from customers of $780,000. To determine cash receipts from customers, the company considers the change in accounts receivable during the year.

When accounts receivable increase during the year, revenues on an accrual basis are higher than cash receipts from customers. In other words, operations led to increased revenues, but not all of these revenues resulted in cash receipts. To determine the amount of increase in cash receipts, deduct the amount of the increase in accounts receivable from the total sales revenues. Conversely, a decrease in accounts receivable is added to sales revenues, because cash receipts from customers then exceed sales revenues.

For Emig Company, accounts receivable increased $15,000. Thus, cash receipts from customers were $765,000, computed as follows.

Revenues from sales	$780,000
Deduct: Increase in accounts receivable	15,000
Cash receipts from customers	$765,000

Emig could also determine cash receipts from customers by analyzing the Accounts Receivable account as shown below.

Accounts Receivable

1/1/08	Balance	–0–	Receipts from customers	765,000
	Revenue from sales	780,000		
12/31/08	Balance	15,000		

Illustration 19-22 shows the relationships between cash receipts from customers, revenues from sales, and changes in accounts receivable.

ILLUSTRATION 19-22
Formula to Compute Cash Receipts from Customers

Cash receipts from customers	=	Revenues from sales	+ Decrease in accounts receivable or − Increase in accounts receivable

Cash Payments to Suppliers. Emig Company reported cost of goods sold on its income statement of $450,000. To determine cash payments to suppliers, the company first finds purchases for the year, by adjusting cost of goods sold for the change in inventory. When inventory increases during the year, purchases this year exceed cost of goods sold. As a result, the company adds the increase in inventory to cost of goods sold, to arrive at purchases.

In 2008, Emig Company's inventory increased $160,000. The company computes purchases as follows.

Cost of goods sold	$450,000
Add: Increase in inventory	160,000
Purchases	$610,000

After computing purchases, Emig determines cash payments to suppliers by adjusting purchases for the change in accounts payable. When accounts payable increase during the year, purchases on an accrual basis are higher than they are on a cash basis. As a result, it deducts from purchases the increase in accounts payable to arrive at cash payments to suppliers. Conversely, if cash payments to suppliers exceed purchases, Emig adds to purchases the decrease in accounts payable. Cash payments to suppliers were $550,000, computed as follows.

Purchases	$610,000
Deduct: Increase in accounts payable	60,000
Cash payments to suppliers	$550,000

Emig also can determine cash payments to suppliers by analyzing Accounts Payable, as shown below.

Accounts Payable

Payments to suppliers	550,000	1/1/08	Balance	–0–
			Purchases	610,000
		12/31/08	Balance	60,000

Illustration 19-23 shows the relationships between cash payments to suppliers, cost of goods sold, changes in inventory, and changes in accounts payable.

ILLUSTRATION 19-23
Formula to Compute Cash Payments to Suppliers

Cash payments to suppliers	=	Cost of goods sold	+ Increase in inventory or − Decrease in inventory	+ Decrease in accounts payable or − Increase in accounts payable

Cash Payments for Operating Expenses. Emig reported operating expenses of $160,000 on its income statement. To determine the cash paid for operating expenses, it must adjust this amount for any changes in prepaid expenses and accrued expenses payable.

For example, when prepaid expenses increased $8,000 during the year, cash paid for operating expenses was $8,000 higher than operating expenses reported on the income statement. To convert operating expenses to cash payments for operating expenses, the company adds to operating expenses the increase of $8,000. Conversely, if prepaid expenses decrease during the year, it deducts from operating expenses the amount of the decrease.

Emig also must adjust operating expenses for changes in accrued expenses payable. When accrued expenses payable increase during the year, operating expenses on an accrual basis are higher than they are on a cash basis. As a result, the company deducts from operating expenses an increase in accrued expenses payable, to arrive at cash payments for operating expenses. Conversely, it adds to operating expenses a decrease in accrued expenses payable, because cash payments exceed operating expenses.

Emig Company's cash payments for operating expenses were $148,000, computed as follows.

Operating expenses	$160,000
Add: Increase in prepaid expenses	8,000
Deduct: Increase in accrued expenses payable	(20,000)
Cash payments for operating expenses	$148,000

The relationships among cash payments for operating expenses, changes in prepaid expenses, and changes in accrued expenses payable are shown in Illustration 19-24.

ILLUSTRATION 19-24
Formula to Compute Cash Payments for Operating Expenses

Cash payments for operating expenses	=	Operating expenses	+ Increase in prepaid expense or – Decrease in prepaid expense	+ Decrease in accrued expenses payable or – Increase in accrued expenses payable

Note that the company did not consider depreciation expense, because it is a noncash charge.

Cash Payments for Income Taxes. The income statement for Emig shows income tax expense of $48,000. This amount equals the cash paid. How do we know that? Because the comparative balance sheet indicated no income taxes payable at either the beginning or end of the year.

Summary of Net Cash Flow from Operating Activities—Direct Method

The following schedule summarizes the computations illustrated above.

ILLUSTRATION 19-25
Accrual Basis to Cash Basis

Accrual Basis			Adjustment	Add (Subtract)	Cash Basis
Revenues from sales	$780,000	–	Increase in accounts receivable	$(15,000)	$765,000
Cost of goods sold	450,000	+	Increase in inventory	160,000	
		–	Increase in accounts payable	(60,000)	550,000
Operating expenses	160,000	+	Increase in prepaid expenses	8,000	
		–	Increase in accrued expenses payable	(20,000)	148,000
Depreciation expense	10,000	–	Depreciation expense	(10,000)	–0–
Income tax expense	48,000				48,000
Total expense	668,000				746,000
Net income	$112,000		Net cash provided by operating activities		$ 19,000

Illustration 19-26 shows the presentation of the direct method for reporting net cash flow from operating activities for the Emig Company illustration.

ILLUSTRATION 19-26
Operating Activities Section—Direct Method, 2008

EMIG COMPANY
STATEMENT OF CASH FLOWS (PARTIAL)

Cash flows from operating activities		
Cash received from customers		$765,000
Cash payments:		
To suppliers	$ 550,000	
For operating expenses	148,000	
For income taxes	48,000	746,000
Net cash provided by operating activities		$ 19,000

If Emig Company uses the direct method to present the net cash flows from operating activities, it must provide in a separate schedule the reconciliation of net income to net cash provided by operating activities. The reconciliation assumes the identical form and content of the indirect method of presentation, as shown below.

ILLUSTRATION 19-27
Reconciliation of Net Income to Net Cash Provided by Operating Activities

EMIG COMPANY
RECONCILIATION

Net income		$112,000
Adjustments to reconcile net income to net cash provided by operating activities:		
Depreciation expense	$ 10,000	
Increase in accounts receivable	(15,000)	
Increase in inventory	(160,000)	
Increase in prepaid expenses	(8,000)	
Increase in accounts payable	60,000	
Increase in accrued expense payable	20,000	(93,000)
Net cash provided by operating activities		$ 19,000

When the direct method is used, the company may present this reconciliation at the bottom of the statement of cash flows or in a separate schedule.

Direct Versus Indirect Controversy

The most contentious decision that the FASB faced in issuing *Statement No. 95* was choosing between the direct method and the indirect method of determining net cash flow from operating activities. Companies lobbied *against* the direct method, urging adoption of the indirect method. Commercial lending officers expressed to the FASB a strong preference in favor of the direct method. In the next two sections, we consider the arguments in favor of each of the methods.

In Favor of the Direct Method

The principal advantage of the direct method is that **it shows operating cash receipts and payments.** Thus, it is more consistent with the objective of a statement of cash flows—to provide information about cash receipts and cash payments—than the indirect method, which does not report operating cash receipts and payments.

Supporters of the direct method contend that knowledge of the specific sources of operating cash receipts and the purposes for which operating cash payments were made in past periods is useful in estimating future operating cash flows. Furthermore, information about amounts of major classes of operating cash receipts and payments is more useful than information only about their arithmetic sum (the net cash flow from operating activities). Such information is more revealing of a company's ability (1) to generate sufficient cash from operating activities to pay its debts, (2) to reinvest in its operations, and (3) to make distributions to its owners.[8]

Many companies indicate that they do not currently collect information in a manner that allows them to determine amounts such as cash received from customers or cash paid to suppliers directly from their accounting systems. But supporters of the direct method contend that the incremental cost of determining operating cash receipts and payments is not significant.

In Favor of the Indirect Method

The principal advantage of the indirect method is that **it focuses on the differences between net income and net cash flow from operating activities**. That is, it provides a useful link between the statement of cash flows and the income statement and balance sheet.

Many companies contend that it is less costly to adjust net income to net cash flow from operating activities (indirect) than it is to report gross operating cash receipts and payments (direct). Supporters of the indirect method also state that the direct method, which effectively reports income statement information on a cash rather than an accrual basis, may erroneously suggest that net cash flow from operating activities is as good as, or better than, net income as a measure of performance.

Special Rules Applying to Direct and Indirect Methods

Companies that use the direct method are required, at a minimum, to report separately the following classes of operating cash receipts and payments:

Receipts

1 Cash collected from customers (including lessees, licensees, etc.).
2 Interest and dividends received.
3 Other operating cash receipts, if any.

INTERNATIONAL INSIGHT

Consolidated statements of cash flows may be of limited use to analysts evaluating multinational companies. Without disaggregation, users of such statements are not able to determine "where in the world" the funds are sourced and used.

Payments

1 Cash paid to employees and suppliers of goods or services (including suppliers of insurance, advertising, etc.).
2 Interest paid.
3 Income taxes paid.
4 Other operating cash payments, if any.

The FASB encourages companies to provide further breakdowns of operating cash receipts and payments that they consider meaningful.

Companies using the indirect method must disclose separately changes in inventory, receivables, and payables in order to reconcile net income to net cash flow from operating activities. In addition, they must disclose, elsewhere in the financial statements or in accompanying notes, interest paid (net of amount capitalized) and income taxes paid.[9] The FASB requires these separate and additional disclosures so that users may approximate the direct method. Also, an acceptable alternative presentation of the indirect method is to report net cash flow from operating activities as a single line item in the statement of cash flows and to present the reconciliation details elsewhere in the financial statements.

---

[8]"Statement of Cash Flows," pars. 107 and 111.

[9]*Accounting Trends and Techniques—2004* reports that of the 600 companies surveyed, 310 disclosed interest paid in notes to the financial statements, 264 disclosed interest paid at the bottom of the statement of cash flows, 9 disclosed interest paid within the statement of cash flows, and 17 reported no separate amount. Income taxes paid during the year were disclosed in a manner similar to interest payments.

NOT WHAT IT SEEMS

WHAT DO THE NUMBERS MEAN?

The controversy over direct and indirect methods highlights the importance that the market attributes to operating cash flow. By showing an improving cash flow, a company can give a favorable impression of its ongoing operations. For example, **WorldCom** concealed declines in its operations by capitalizing certain operating expenses—to the tune of $3.8 billion! This practice not only "juiced up" income but also made it possible to report the cash payments in the investing section of the cash flow statement rather than as a deduction from operating cash flow.

The SEC recently addressed a similar cash flow classification issue with automakers like **Ford**, **GM**, and **Daimler-Chrysler**. For years, automakers classified lease receivables and other dealer-financing arrangements as investment cash flows. Thus, they reported an increase in lease or loan receivables from cars sold as a use of cash in the investing section of the statement of cash flows. The SEC objected and now requires automakers to report these receivables as operating cash flows, since the leases and loans are used to facilitate car sales. At GM, these reclassifications reduced its operating cash flows from $7.6 billion to $3 billion in the year before the change. So while the overall cash flow—from operations, investing, and financing—remained the same, operating cash flow at these companies looked better than it really was.

Source: Peter Elstrom, "How to Hide $3.8 Billion in Expenses," *BusinessWeek Online* (July 8, 2002); and Judith Burns, "SEC Tells US Automakers to Retool Cash-Flow Accounting," *Wall Street Journal Online* (February 28, 2005).

SPECIAL PROBLEMS IN STATEMENT PREPARATION

SECTION 2

OBJECTIVE 8
Discuss special problems in preparing a statement of cash flows.

We discussed some of the special problems related to preparing the statement of cash flows in connection with the preceding illustrations. Other problems that arise with some frequency in the preparation of this statement include the following.

1 Adjustments similar to depreciation.
2 Accounts receivable (net).
3 Other working capital changes.
4 Net losses.
5 Gains.
6 Stock options.
7 Postretirement benefit cost.
8 Extraordinary items.
9 Significant noncash transactions.

ADJUSTMENTS SIMILAR TO DEPRECIATION

Depreciation expense is the most common adjustment to net income that companies make to arrive at net cash flow from operating activities. But there are numerous other noncash expense or revenue items. Examples of expense items that companies must add back to net income are the **amortization of limited-life intangible assets** such as patents, and the **amortization of deferred costs** such as bond issue costs. These charges to expense involve expenditures made in prior periods that a company amortizes currently. These charges reduce net income without affecting cash in the current period.

Also, **amortization of bond discount or premium** on long-term bonds payable affects the amount of interest expense. However, neither changes cash. As a result, a company should add back discount amortization and subtract premium amortization from net income to arrive at net cash flow from operating activities.

In a similar manner, **changes in deferred income taxes** affect net income but have no effect on cash. For example, **Delta Airlines** reported an increase in its liability for deferred taxes of approximately $1.2 billion. This change in the liability increased tax expense and decreased net income, but did not affect cash. Therefore, Delta added back $1.2 billion to net income on its statement of cash flows.

Another common adjustment to net income is **a change related to an investment in common stock** when recording income or loss under the equity method. Recall that under the equity method, the investor (1) debits the investment account and credits revenue for its share of the investee's net income, and (2) credits dividends received to the investment account. Therefore, the net increase in the investment account does not affect cash flow. A company must deduct the net increase from net income to arrive at net cash flow from operating activities.

Assume that Victor Co. owns 40 percent of Milo Inc. During the year Milo reports net income of $100,000 and pays a cash dividend of $30,000. Victor reports this in its statement of cash flows as a deduction from net income in the following manner—Equity in earnings of Milo, net of dividends, $28,000 [($100,000 − $30,000) × 40%].

If Victor Co. does not exercise significant influence over Milo, it cannot use the equity method. Instead, it uses the fair-value method. Under the fair-value method, Victor does not recognize any of Milo's net income. Further, it records any cash dividend received as revenue. As a result, the company makes no adjustment to net income in the statement of cash flows because cash dividends received are included in income.

ACCOUNTS RECEIVABLE (NET)

Up to this point, we assumed no allowance for doubtful accounts—a contra account—to offset accounts receivable. However, if a company needs an allowance for doubtful accounts, how does that allowance affect the company's determination of net cash flow from operating activities? For example, assume that Redmark Co. reports net income of $40,000. It has the accounts receivable balances as shown in Illustration 19-28.

ILLUSTRATION 19-28
Accounts Receivable Balances, Redmark Co.

	2008	2007	Change Increase/Decrease
Accounts receivable	$105,000	$90,000	$15,000 Increase
Allowance for doubtful accounts	(10,000)	(4,000)	6,000 Increase
Accounts receivable (net)	$ 95,000	$86,000	9,000 Increase

Indirect Method

Because an increase in the Allowance for Doubtful Accounts results from a charge to bad debts expense, a company should add back an increase in the Allowance for Doubtful Accounts to net income to arrive at net cash flow from operating activities. Illustration 19-29 shows one method for presenting this information in a statement of cash flows.

ILLUSTRATION 19-29
Presentation of Allowance for Doubtful Accounts—Indirect Method

REDMARK CO.
STATEMENT OF CASH FLOWS (PARTIAL)
FOR THE YEAR 2008

Cash flows from operating activities		
Net income		$40,000
Adjustments to reconcile net income to net cash provided by operating activities:		
Increase in accounts receivable	$(15,000)	
Increase in allowance for doubtful accounts	6,000	(9,000)
		$31,000

As we indicated, the increase in the Allowance for Doubtful Accounts balance results from a charge to bad debt expense for the year. Because bad debt expense is a noncash charge, a company must add it back to net income in arriving at net cash flow from operating activities.

Instead of separately analyzing the allowance account, a short-cut approach is to net the allowance balance against the receivable balance and compare the change in accounts receivable on a net basis. Illustration 19-30 shows this presentation.

ILLUSTRATION 19-30
Net Approach to Allowance for Doubtful Accounts—Indirect Method

REDMARK CO.
STATEMENT OF CASH FLOWS (PARTIAL)
FOR THE YEAR 2008

Cash flows from operating activities	
Net income	$40,000
Adjustments to reconcile net income to net cash provided by operating activities:	
Increase in accounts receivable (net)	(9,000)
	$31,000

This short-cut procedure works also if the change in the allowance account results from a writeoff of accounts receivable. This reduces both the Accounts Receivable and the Allowance for Doubtful Accounts. No effect on cash flows occurs. Because of its simplicity, *use the net approach for your homework assignments.*

Direct Method

If using the direct method, a company **should not net** the Allowance for Doubtful Accounts against Accounts Receivable. To illustrate, assume that Redmark Co.'s net income of $40,000 consisted of the following items.

ILLUSTRATION 19-31
Income Statement, Redmark Co.

REDMARK CO.
INCOME STATEMENT
FOR THE YEAR 2008

Sales		$100,000
Expenses		
Salaries	$46,000	
Utilities	8,000	
Bad debts	6,000	60,000
Net income		$ 40,000

If Redmark deducts the $9,000 increase in accounts receivable (net) from sales for the year, it would report cash sales at $91,000 ($100,000 − $9,000) and cash payments for operating expenses at $60,000. Both items would be misstated: Cash sales should be reported at $85,000 ($100,000 − $15,000), and total cash payments for operating expenses should be reported at $54,000 ($60,000 − $6,000). Illustration 19-32 shows the proper presentation.

ILLUSTRATION 19-32
Bad Debts—Direct Method

REDMARK CO.
STATEMENT OF CASH FLOWS (PARTIAL)
FOR THE YEAR 2008

Cash flows from operating activities		
Cash received from customers		$85,000
Salaries paid	$46,000	
Utilities paid	8,000	54,000
Net cash provided by operating activities		$31,000

An added complication develops when a company writes off accounts receivable. Simply adjusting sales for the change in accounts receivable will not provide the proper amount of cash sales. The reason is that the writeoff of the accounts receivable is not a cash collection. Thus an additional adjustment is necessary.

OTHER WORKING CAPITAL CHANGES

Up to this point, we showed how companies handled all of the changes in working capital items (current asset and current liability items) as adjustments to net income in determining net cash flow from operating activities. You must be careful, however, because **some changes in working capital, although they affect cash, do not affect net income**. Generally, these are investing or financing activities of a current nature.

One activity is the purchase of **short-term available-for-sale securities**. For example, the purchase of short-term available-for-sale securities for $50,000 cash has no effect on net income but it does cause a $50,000 decrease in cash.[10] A company reports this transaction as a cash flow from investing activities as follows.[11]

Cash flows from investing activities	
Purchase of short-term available-for-sale securities	$(50,000)

What about **trading securities**? Because companies hold these investments principally for the purpose of selling them in the near term, companies should classify the cash flows from purchases and sales of trading securities as cash flows from **operating activities.**[12]

Another example is the issuance of a **short-term nontrade note payable** for cash. This change in a working capital item has no effect on income from operations but it increases cash by the amount of the note payable. For example, a company reports the issuance of a $10,000 short-term note payable for cash in the statement of cash flows as follows.

Cash flows from financing activities	
Issuance of short-term note	$10,000

Another change in a working capital item that has no effect on income from operations or on cash is a **cash dividend payable**. Although a company will report the cash dividends when paid as a financing activity, it does not report the declared but unpaid dividend on the statement of cash flows.

NET LOSSES

If a company reports a net loss instead of a net income, it must adjust the net loss for those items that do not result in a cash inflow or outflow. The net loss, after adjusting for the charges or credits not affecting cash, may result in a negative or a positive cash flow from operating activities.

For example, if the net loss is $50,000 and the total amount of charges to add back is $60,000, then net cash provided by operating activities is $10,000. Illustration 19-33 shows this computation.

[10] If the basis of the statement of cash flows is **cash and cash equivalents** and the short-term investment is considered a cash equivalent, then a company reports nothing in the statement because the transaction does not affect the balance of cash and cash equivalents. The Board notes that cash purchases of short term investments generally are part of the company's cash management activities rather than part of its operating, investing, or financing activities.

[11] "Accounting for Certain Investments in Debt and Equity Securities," *Statement of Financial Accounting Standards No. 115* (Norwalk, Conn.: 1993), par. 118.

[12] Ibid., par. 118.

Net loss		$(50,000)
Adjustments to reconcile net income to net cash provided by operating activities:		
Depreciation of plant assets	$55,000	
Amortization of patents	5,000	60,000
Net cash provided by operating activities		$ 10,000

ILLUSTRATION 19-33
Computation of Net Cash Flow from Operating Activities—Cash Inflow

If the company experiences a net loss of $80,000 and the total amount of the charges to add back is $25,000, the presentation appears as follows.

Net loss	$(80,000)
Adjustments to reconcile net income to net cash used by operating activities:	
Depreciation of plant assets	25,000
Net cash used by operating activities	$(55,000)

ILLUSTRATION 19-34
Computation of Net Cash Flow from Operating Activities—Cash Outflow

Although not illustrated in this chapter, a negative cash flow may result even if the company reports a net income.

GAINS

In the illustration for Tax Consultants, the company experienced a loss of $2,000 from the sale of equipment. The company added this loss to net income to compute net cash flow from operating activities because **the loss is a noncash charge in the income statement.**

If Tax Consultants experiences a **gain** from a sale of equipment it too requires an adjustment to net income. Because a company reports the gain in the statement of cash flows as part of the cash proceeds from the sale of equipment under investing activities, **it deducts the gain from net income to avoid double counting**—once as part of net income, and again as part of the cash proceeds from the sale.

STOCK OPTIONS

Recall for share-based compensation plans that companies are required to use the fair value method to determine total compensation cost. The compensation cost is then recognized as an expense in the periods in which the employee provides services. When Compensation Expense is debited, Paid-in Capital—Stock Options is often credited. Cash is not affected by recording the expense. **Therefore, the company must increase net income by the amount of compensation expense from stock options in computing net cash flow from operating activities.**

To illustrate how this information should be reported on a statement of cash flows, assume that First Wave Inc. grants 5,000 options to its CEO, Ann Johnson. Each option entitles Johnson to purchase one share of First Wave's $1 par value common stock at $50 per share at any time in the next two years (the service period). The fair value of the options is $200,000. First Wave records compensation expense in the first year as follows:

Compensation Expense ($200,000 ÷ 2)	100,000	
Paid-in Capital—Stock Options		100,000

In addition, if we assume that First Wave has a 35 percent tax rate, it would recognize a deferred tax asset of $35,000 ($100,000 × 35%) in the first year as follows:

Deferred Tax Asset	35,000	
Income Tax Expense		35,000

Therefore on the statement of cash flows for the first year, First Wave reports the following (assuming a net income of $600,000).

Net income	$600,000
Adjustments to reconcile net income to net cash provided by operating activities:	
Share-based compensation expense	100,000
Increase in deferred tax asset	(35,000)

As shown in First Wave's statement of cash flows, it adds the share-based compensation expense to net income because it is a non-cash expense. The increase in the deferred tax asset and the related reduction in income tax expense increase net income. Although the negative income tax expense increases net income, it does not increase cash. Therefore it should be deducted.

Subsequently, if Ann Johnson exercises her options, Third Wave reports "Cash provided by exercise of stock options" in the financing section of the statement of cash flows.[13]

POSTRETIREMENT BENEFIT COSTS

If a company has postretirement costs such as an employee pension plan, chances are that the pension expense recorded during a period will either be higher or lower than the cash funded. It will be higher when there is an unfunded liability and will be lower when there is a prepaid pension cost. When the expense is higher or lower than the cash paid, **the company must adjust net income by the difference between cash paid and the expense reported** in computing net cash flow from operating activities.

EXTRAORDINARY ITEMS

Companies should report **either as investing activities or as financing activities** cash flows from extraordinary transactions and other events whose effects are included in net income, but which are not related to operations.

For example, assume that Tax Consultants had land with a carrying value of $200,000, which was condemned by the state of Maine for a highway project. The condemnation proceeds received were $205,000, resulting in a gain of $5,000 less $2,000 of taxes. In the statement of cash flows (indirect method), the company would deduct the $5,000 gain from net income in the operating activities section. It would report the $205,000 cash inflow from the condemnation as an investing activity, as follows.

Cash flows from investing activities	
Condemnation of land	$205,000

UNDERLYING CONCEPTS

By rejecting the requirement to allocate taxes to the various activities, the Board invoked the cost-benefit constraint. The information would be beneficial, but the cost of providing such information would exceed the benefits of providing it.

Note that Tax Consultants handles the gain at its **gross** amount ($5,000), not net of tax. The company reports the cash received in the condemnation as an investing activity at $205,000, also exclusive of the tax effect.

The FASB requires companies to classify **all income taxes paid as operating cash outflows.** Some suggested that income taxes paid be allocated to investing and financing transactions. But the Board decided that allocation of income taxes paid to

[13]Companies receive a tax deduction related to share-based compensation plans at the time employees exercise their options. The amount of the deduction is equal to the difference between the market price of the stock and the exercise price at the date the employee purchases the stock, which in most cases, is much larger than the total compensation expense recorded. When the tax deduction exceeds the total compensation recorded, this provides an additional cash inflow to the company. For example, in a recent year **Cisco Systems** reported an additional cash inflow related to its stock option plans equal to $537 million. Under the provisions of *SFAS No. 123(R)*, this tax-related cash inflow is reported in the financing section of the statement of cash flows. See "Share-Based Payment," *Statement of Financial Accounting Standard No. 123(R)* (Norwalk, Conn.: FASB, 2004) par. 68.

operating, investing, and financing activities would be so complex and arbitrary that the benefits, if any, would not justify the costs involved. Under both the direct method and the indirect method, companies must disclose the total amount of income taxes paid.[14]

SIGNIFICANT NONCASH TRANSACTIONS

Because the statement of cash flows reports only the effects of operating, investing, and financing activities in terms of cash flows, it omits some **significant noncash transactions** and other events that are investing or financing activities. Among the more common of these noncash transactions that a company should report or disclose in some manner are the following.

1 Acquisition of assets by assuming liabilities (including capital lease obligations) or by issuing equity securities.

2 Exchanges of nonmonetary assets.

3 Refinancing of long-term debt.

4 Conversion of debt or preferred stock to common stock.

5 Issuance of equity securities to retire debt.

Examples of Cash Flow Statements

A company does not incorporate these noncash items in the statement of cash flows. If material in amount, these disclosures may be either narrative or summarized in a separate schedule at the bottom of the statement, or they may appear in a separate note or supplementary schedule to the financial statements.[15] Illustration 19-35 shows the presentation of these significant noncash transactions or other events in a separate schedule at the bottom of the statement of cash flows.

ILLUSTRATION 19-35
Schedule Presentation of Noncash Investing and Financing Activities

Net increase in cash	$3,717,000
Cash at beginning of year	5,208,000
Cash at end of year	$8,925,000
Noncash investing and financing activities	
Purchase of land and building through issuance of 250,000 shares of common stock	$1,750,000
Exchange of Steadfast, NY, land for Bedford, PA, land	$2,000,000
Conversion of 12% bonds to 50,000 shares of common stock	$ 500,000

Or, companies may present these noncash transactions in a separate note, as shown in Illustration 19-36.

ILLUSTRATION 19-36
Note Presentation of Noncash Investing and Financing Activities

Note G: Significant noncash transactions. During the year the company engaged in the following significant noncash investing and financing transactions:

Issued 250,000 shares of common stock to purchase land and building	$1,750,000
Exchanged land in Steadfast, NY, for land in Bedford, PA	$2,000,000
Converted 12% bonds due 2007 to 50,000 shares of common stock	$ 500,000

[14]For an insightful article on some weaknesses and limitations in the statement of cash flows caused by implementation of *FASB Statement No. 95*, see Hugo Nurnberg, "Inconsistencies and Ambiguities in Cash Flow Statements Under *FASB Statement No. 95*," *Accounting Horizons* (June 1993), pp. 60–73. Nurnberg identifies the inconsistencies caused by the three-way classification of all cash receipts and cash payments, gross versus net of tax, the ambiguous disclosure requirements for noncash investing and financing transactions, and the ambiguous presentation of third-party financing transactions. See also Paul B. W. Miller, and Bruce P. Budge, "Nonarticulation in Cash Flow Statements and Implications for Education, Research, and Practice," *Accounting Horizons* (December 1996), pp. 1–15; and Charles Mulford and Michael Ely, "Calculating Sustainable Cash Flow: A Study of the S&P 100," *Georgia Tech Financial Analysis Lab* (October 2004).

[15]Some noncash investing and financing activities are part cash and part noncash. Companies should report only the cash portion on the statement of cash flows. The noncash component should be reported at the bottom of the statement or in a separate note.

Companies do not generally report certain other significant noncash transactions or other events in conjunction with the statement of cash flows. Examples of these types of transactions are **stock dividends, stock splits, and restrictions on retained earnings**. Companies generally report these items, neither financing nor investing activities, in conjunction with the statement of stockholders' equity or schedules and notes pertaining to changes in capital accounts.

CASH FLOW TOOL

WHAT DO THE NUMBERS MEAN?

By understanding the relationship between cash flow and income measures, analysts can gain better insights into company performance. Because earnings altered through creative accounting practices generally do not change operating cash flows, analysts can use the relationship between earnings and operating cash flow to detect suspicious accounting practices. Also, by monitoring the ratio between cash flow from operations and operating income, they can get a clearer picture of developing problems in a company.

For example, the chart below plots the ratio of operating cash flows to earnings for **Xerox Corp.** in the years leading up to the SEC singling it out in 2000 for aggressive revenue recognition practices on its leases.

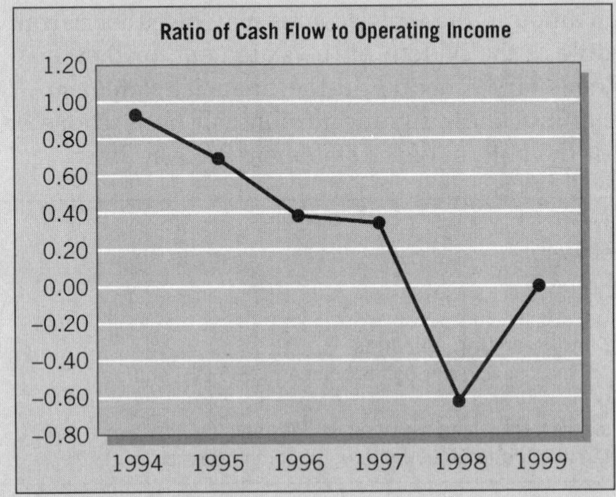

Similar to **W. T. Grant** in the chapter-opening story, Xerox was reporting earnings growth in the years leading up to its financial breakdown in 2000 but teetering near bankruptcy in 2001. However, Xerox's ratio of cash flow to earnings showed a declining trend and became negative well before its revenue recognition practices were revealed. The trend revealed in the graph should have given any analyst reason to investigate Xerox further. As one analyst noted, "Earnings growth that exceeds the growth in operating cash flow cannot continue for extended periods and should be investigated."

Source: Adapted from Charles Mulford and Eugene Comiskey, *The Financial Numbers Game: Detecting Creative Accounting Practices* (New York: John Wiley & Sons, 2002), Chapter 11, by permission.

SECTION 3 USE OF A WORKSHEET

OBJECTIVE 9
Explain the use of a worksheet in preparing a statement of cash flows.

When numerous adjustments are necessary or other complicating factors are present, companies often use **a worksheet to assemble and classify the data that will appear on the statement of cash flows.** The worksheet (a **spreadsheet** when using computer software) is merely a device that aids in the preparation of the statement. Its use is optional. Illustration 19-37 shows the skeleton format of the worksheet for preparation of the statement of cash flows using the indirect method.

XYZ COMPANY
Statement of Cash Flows For the Year Ended...

	A	B	C	D	E
1	Balance Sheet Accounts	End of Prior Year Balances	Reconciling Items Debits	Reconciling Items Credits	End of Current Year Balances
2	Debit balance accounts	XX	XX	XX	XX
3		XX	XX	XX	XX
4	Totals	XXX			XXX
5	Credit balance accounts	XX	XX	XX	XX
6		XX	XX	XX	XX
7	Totals	XXX			XXX
8	Statement of Cash Flows Effects				
9	Operating activities				
10	Net income		XX		
11	Adjustments		XX	XX	
12	Investing activities				
13	Receipts and payments		XX	XX	
14	Financing activities				
15	Receipts and payments		XX	XX	
16	Totals		XXX	XXX	
17	Increase (decrease) in cash		(XX)	XX	
18	Totals		XXX	XXX	

Sheet1 / Sheet2 / Sheet3

ILLUSTRATION 19-37
Format of Worksheet for Preparation of Statement of Cash Flows

The following guidelines are important in using a worksheet.

1 In the balance sheet accounts section, **list accounts with debit balances separately from those with credit balances.** This means, for example, that Accumulated Depreciation is listed under credit balances and not as a contra account under debit balances. Enter the beginning and ending balances of each account in the appropriate columns. Then, enter the transactions that caused the change in the account balance during the year as reconciling items in the two middle columns.

After all reconciling items have been entered, each line pertaining to a balance sheet account should foot across. That is, the beginning balance plus or minus the reconciling item(s) must equal the ending balance. When this agreement exists for all balance sheet accounts, all changes in account balances have been reconciled.

2 The bottom portion of the worksheet consists of the operating, investing, and financing activities sections. Accordingly, it provides the information necessary to prepare the formal statement of cash flows. **Enter inflows of cash as debits in the reconciling columns, and outflows of cash as credits in the reconciling columns.** Thus, in this section, a company would enter the sale of equipment for cash at book value as a debit under inflows of cash from investing activities. Similarly, it would enter the purchase of land for cash as a credit under outflows of cash from investing activities.

3 **Do not enter in any journal or post to any account the reconciling items shown in the worksheet.** These items do not represent either adjustments or corrections of the balance sheet accounts. They are used only to facilitate the preparation of the statement of cash flows.

PREPARATION OF THE WORKSHEET

The preparation of a worksheet involves the following steps.

Step 1. Enter the balance sheet accounts and their beginning and ending balances in the balance sheet accounts section.

Step 2. Enter the data that explain the changes in the balance sheet accounts (other than cash) and their effects on the statement of cash flows in the reconciling columns of the worksheet.

Step 3. Enter the increase or decrease in cash on the cash line and at the bottom of the worksheet. This entry should enable the totals of the reconciling columns to be in agreement.

To illustrate the preparation and use of a worksheet and to illustrate the reporting of some of the special problems discussed in the prior section, we present a comprehensive example for Satellite Corporation. Again, the indirect method serves as the basis for the computation of net cash provided by operating activities. Illustrations 19-38 and 19-39 present the balance sheet, combined statement of income and retained earnings,

ILLUSTRATION 19-38
Comparative Balance Sheet, Satellite Corporation

SATELLITE CORPORATION
Comparative Balance Sheet–December 31, 2008 and 2007

	A	B	C	D
1		2008	2007	Increase or (Decrease)
2	Assets			
3	Cash	$ 59,000	$ 66,000	$ (7,000)
4	Accounts receivable (net)	104,000	51,000	53,000
5	Inventories	493,000	341,000	152,000
6	Prepaid expenses	16,500	17,000	(500)
7	Investments in stock of Porter Co. (equity method)	18,500	15,000	3,500
8	Land	131,500	82,000	49,500
9	Equipment	187,000	142,000	45,000
10	Accumulated depreciation—equipment	(29,000)	(31,000)	(2,000)
11	Buildings	262,000	262,000	—
12	Accumulated depreciation—buildings	(74,100)	(71,000)	3,100
13	Trademark	7,600	10,000	(2,400)
14	Total assets	$1,176,000	$884,000	
15	Liabilities			
16	Accounts payable	$ 132,000	$ 131,000	1,000
17	Accrued liabilities	43,000	39,000	4,000
18	Income tax payable	3,000	16,000	(13,000)
19	Notes payable (long-term)	60,000	—	60,000
20	Bonds payable	100,000	100,000	—
21	Premium on bonds payable	7,000	8,000	(1,000)
22	Deferred tax liability (long-term)	9,000	6,000	3,000
23	Total liabilities	354,000	300,000	
24	Stockholders' Equity			
25	Common stock ($1 par)	60,000	50,000	10,000
26	Additional paid-in capital	187,000	38,000	149,000
27	Retained earnings	592,000	496,000	96,000
28	Treasury stock	(17,000)	—	17,000
29	Total stockholders' equity	822,000	584,000	
30	Total liabilities and stockholders' equity	$1,176,000	$884,000	

Sheet1 / Sheet2 / Sheet3

ILLUSTRATION 19-39
Income and Retained Earnings Statements, Satellite Corporation

SATELLITE CORPORATION
COMBINED STATEMENT OF INCOME AND RETAINED EARNINGS
FOR THE YEAR ENDED DECEMBER 31, 2008

Net sales		$526,500
Other revenue		3,500
Total revenues		530,000
Expense		
Cost of goods sold		310,000
Selling and administrative expenses		47,000
Other expenses and losses		12,000
Total expenses		369,000
Income before income tax and extraordinary item		161,000
Income tax		
Current	$47,000	
Deferred	3,000	50,000
Income before extraordinary item		111,000
Gain on condemnation of land (net of $2,000 tax)		6,000
Net income		117,000
Retained earnings, January 1		496,000
Less:		
Cash dividends	6,000	
Stock dividend	15,000	21,000
Retained earnings, December 31		$592,000
Per share:		
Income before extraordinary item		$2.02
Extraordinary item		.11
Net income		$2.13

Additional Information

(a) Other income of $3,500 represents Satellite's equity share in the net income of Porter Co., an equity investee. Satellite owns 22% of Porter Co.

(b) An analysis of the equipment account and related accumulated depreciation indicates the following:

	Equipment Dr./(Cr.)	Accum. Dep. Dr./(Cr.)	Gain or (Loss)
Balance at end of 2007	$142,000	$(31,000)	
Purchases of equipment	53,000		
Sale of equipment	(8,000)	2,500	$(1,500)
Depreciation for the period		(11,500)	
Major repair charged to accumulated depreciation		11,000	
Balance at end of 2008	$187,000	$(29,000)	

(c) Land in the amount of $60,000 was purchased through the issuance of a long-term note; in addition, certain parcels of land costing $10,500 were condemned. The state government paid Satellite $18,500, resulting in an $8,000 gain which has a $2,000 tax effect.

(d) The change in the accumulated depreciation—buildings, trademark, and premium on bonds payable accounts resulted from depreciation and amortization entries.

(e) An analysis of the paid-in capital accounts in stockholders' equity discloses the following:

	Common Stock	Additional Paid-In Capital
Balance at end of 2007	$50,000	$ 38,000
Issuance of 2% stock dividend	1,000	14,000
Sale of stock for cash	9,000	135,000
Balance at end of 2008	$60,000	$187,000

(f) Interest paid (net of amount capitalized) is $9,000; income taxes paid is $62,000.

and additional information for Satellite Corporation. The discussion that follows these financial statements provides additional explanations related to the preparation of the worksheet.

ANALYSIS OF TRANSACTIONS

The following discussion explains the individual adjustments that appear on the worksheet in Illustration 19-40. Because cash is the basis for the analysis, Satellite reconciles the cash account last. Because income is the first item that appears on the statement of cash flows, it is handled first.

Change in Retained Earnings

Net income for the period is $117,000. The entry for it on the worksheet is as follows.

(1)

Operating—Net Income	117,000	
Retained Earnings		117,000

Satellite reports net income on the bottom section of the worksheet. This **is the starting point for preparation of the statement of cash flows (under the indirect method).**

A stock dividend and a cash dividend also affected retained earnings. The retained earnings statement reports a stock dividend of $15,000. The worksheet entry for this transaction is as follows.

(2)

Retained Earnings	15,000	
Common Stock		1,000
Additional Paid-in Capital		14,000

The issuance of stock dividends is not a cash operating, investing, or financing item. Therefore, **although the company enters this transaction on the worksheet for reconciling purposes, it does not report it in the statement of cash flows.**

The $6,000 cash dividend paid represents a financing activity cash outflow. Satellite makes the following worksheet entry:

(3)

Retained Earnings	6,000	
Financing—Cash Dividends		6,000

The company reconciles the beginning and ending balances of retained earnings by entry of the three items above.

Accounts Receivable (Net)

The increase in accounts receivable (net) of $53,000 represents adjustments that did not result in cash inflows during 2008. As a result, the company would deduct from net income the increase of $53,000. Satellite makes the following worksheet entry.

(4)

Accounts Receivable (net)	53,000	
Operating—Increase in Accounts Receivable (net)		53,000

Inventories

The increase in inventories of $152,000 represents an operating use of cash. The incremental investment in inventories during the year reduces cash without increasing the cost of goods sold. Satellite makes the following worksheet entry.

(5)

Inventories	152,000	
Operating—Increase in Inventories		152,000

Prepaid Expense

The decrease in prepaid expenses of $500 represents a charge in the income statement for which there was no cash outflow in the current period. Satellite should add that amount back to net income through the following entry.

(6)

Operating—Decrease in Prepaid Expenses	500	
Prepaid Expenses		500

Investment in Stock

Satellite's investment in the stock of Porter Co. increased $3,500. This amount reflects Satellite's share of net income earned by Porter (its equity investee) during the current year. Although Satellite's revenue, and therefore its net income increased $3,500 by recording Satellite's share of Porter Co.'s net income, no cash (dividend) was provided. Satellite makes the following worksheet entry.

(7)

Investment in Stock of Porter Co.	3,500	
Operating—Equity in Earnings of Porter Co.		3,500

Land

Satellite purchased land in the amount of $60,000 through the issuance of a long-term note payable. This transaction did not affect cash. It is a significant noncash investing/financing transaction that the company would disclose either in a separate schedule below the statement of cash flows or in the accompanying notes. Satellite makes the following entry to reconcile the worksheet.

(8)

Land	60,000	
Notes Payable		60,000

In addition to the noncash transaction involving the issuance of a note to purchase land, the Land account was decreased by the condemnation proceedings. The following worksheet entry records the receipt of $18,500 for land having a book value of $10,500.

(9)

Investing—Proceeds from Condemnation of Land	18,500	
Land		10,500
Operating—Gain on Condemnation of Land		8,000

In reconciling net income to net cash flow from operating activities, Satellite deducts from net income the extraordinary gain of $8,000. The reason is that the transaction that gave rise to the gain is an item whose cash effect is already classified as an investing cash inflow. The Land account is now reconciled.

Equipment and Accumulated Depreciation

An analysis of Equipment and Accumulated Depreciation shows that a number of transactions have affected these accounts. The company purchased equipment in the amount of $53,000 during the year. Satellite records this transaction on the worksheet as follows.

(10)

Equipment	53,000	
Investing—Purchase of Equipment		53,000

In addition, Satellite sold at a loss of $1,500 equipment with a book value of $5,500. It records this transaction as follows.

(11)

Investing—Sale of Equipment	4,000	
Operating—Loss on Sale of Equipment	1,500	
Accumulated Depreciation—Equipment	2,500	
Equipment		8,000

The proceeds from the sale of the equipment provided cash of $4,000. In addition, the loss on the sale of the equipment has reduced net income, but did not affect cash. Therefore, the company adds back to net income the amount of the loss, in order to accurately report cash provided by operating activities.

Satellite reported depreciation on the equipment at $11,500 and recorded it on the worksheet as follows.

(12)

Operating—Depreciation Expense—Equipment	11,500	
Accumulated Depreciation—Equipment		11,500

The company adds depreciation expense back to net income because that expense reduced income but did not affect cash.

Finally, the company made a major repair to the equipment. It charged this expenditure, in the amount of $11,000, to Accumulated Depreciation—Equipment. This expenditure required cash, and so Satellite makes the following worksheet entry.

(13)

Accumulated Depreciation—Equipment	11,000	
Investing—Major Repairs of Equipment		11,000

After adjusting for the foregoing items, Satellite has reconciled the balances in the Equipment and related Accumulated Depreciation accounts.

Building Depreciation and Amortization of Trademark

Depreciation expense on the buildings of $3,100 and amortization of trademark of $2,400 are both expenses in the income statement that reduced net income but did not require cash outflows in the current period. Satellite makes the following worksheet entry.

(14)

Operating—Depreciation Expense—Buildings	3,100	
Operating—Amortization of Trademark	2,400	
Accumulated Depreciation—Buildings		3,100
Trademark		2,400

Other Noncash Charges or Credits

Analysis of the remaining accounts indicates that changes in the Accounts Payable, Accrued Liabilities, Income Tax Payable, Premium on Bonds Payable, and Deferred Tax Liability balances resulted from charges or credits to net income that did not affect cash. The company should individually analyze each of these items and enter them in the worksheet. The following compound entry summarizes these noncash, income-related items.

(15)

Income Tax Payable	13,000	
Premium on Bonds Payable	1,000	
Operating—Increase in Accounts Payable	1,000	
Operating—Increase in Accrued Liabilities	4,000	
Operating—Increase in Deferred Tax Liability	3,000	
Operating—Decrease in Income Tax Payable		13,000
Operating—Amortization of Bond Premium		1,000
Accounts Payable		1,000
Accrued Liabilities		4,000
Deferred Tax Liability		3,000

Common Stock and Related Accounts

Comparison of the common stock balances and the additional paid-in capital balances shows that transactions during the year affected these accounts. First, Satellite issues a stock dividend of 2 percent to stockholders. As the discussion of worksheet entry (2) indicated, no cash was provided or used by the stock dividend transaction. In addition to the shares issued via the stock dividend, Satellite sold shares of common stock at $16 per share. The company records this transaction as follows.

(16)

Financing—Sale of Common Stock	144,000	
Common Stock		9,000
Additional Paid-in Capital		135,000

Also, the company purchased shares of its common stock in the amount of $17,000. It records this transaction on the worksheet as follows.

(17)

Treasury Stock	17,000	
Financing—Purchase of Treasury Stock		17,000

Final Reconciling Entry

The final entry to reconcile the change in cash and to balance the worksheet is shown below. The $7,000 amount is the difference between the beginning and ending cash balance.

(18)

Decrease in Cash	7,000	
Cash		7,000

Once the company has determined that the differences between the beginning and ending balances per the worksheet columns have been accounted for, it can total the reconciling transactions columns, and they should balance. Satellite can prepare the statement of cash flows entirely from the items and amounts that appear at the bottom of the worksheet under "Statement of Cash Flows Effects," as shown in Illustration 19-40.

ILLUSTRATION 19-40
Completed Worksheet for Preparation of Statement of Cash Flows, Satellite Corporation

SATELLITE CORPORATION
Worksheet for Preparation of Statement of Cash Flows For the Year Ended December 31, 2008

	A	B	C	D	E	F	G
1		Balance 12/31/07	Reconciling Items–2008 Debits		Credits		Balance 12/31/08
2	Debits						
3	Cash	$ 66,000			(18)	7,000	$ 59,000
4	Accounts receivable (net)	51,000	(4)	$ 53,000			104,000
5	Inventories	341,000	(5)	152,000			493,000
6	Prepaid expenses	17,000			(6)	500	16,500
7	Investment (equity method)	15,000	(7)	3,500			18,500
8	Land	82,000	(8)	60,000	(9)	10,500	131,500
9	Equipment	142,000	(10)	53,000	(11)	8,000	187,000
10	Building	262,000					262,000
11	Trademark	10,000			(14)	2,400	7,600
12	Treasury stock		(17)	17,000			17,000
13	Total debits	$986,000					$1,296,100
14	Credits						
15	Accum. depr.–equipment	$ 31,000	(11)	2,500	(12)	11,500	
16			(13)	11,000			$ 29,000
17	Accum. depr.–building	71,000			(14)	3,100	74,100
18	Accounts payable	131,000			(15)	1,000	132,000
19	Accrued liabilities	39,000			(15)	4,000	43,000
20	Income tax payable	16,000	(15)	13,000			3,000
21	Notes payable	-0-			(8)	60,000	60,000
22	Bonds payable	100,000					100,000
23	Premium on bonds payable	8,000	(15)	1,000			7,000
24	Deferred tax liability	6,000			(15)	3,000	9,000
25	Common stock	50,000			(2)	1,000	
26					(16)	9,000	60,000
27	Additional paid-in capital	38,000			(2)	14,000	
28					(16)	135,000	187,000
29	Retained earnings	496,000	(2)	15,000	(1)	117,000	
30			(3)	6,000			592,000
31	Total credits	$986,000					$1,296,100
32	Statement of Cash Flows Effects						
33	Operating activities						
34	Net income		(1)	117,000			
35	Increase in accounts receivable (net)				(4)	53,000	
36	Increase in inventories				(5)	152,000	
37	Decrease in prepaid expenses		(6)	500			
38	Equity in earnings of Porter Co.				(7)	3,500	
39	Gain on condemnation of land				(9)	8,000	
40	Loss on sale of equipment		(11)	1,500			
41	Depr. expense–equipment		(12)	11,500			
42	Depr. expense–building		(14)	3,100			
43	Amortization of trademark		(14)	2,400			
44	Increase in accounts payable		(15)	1,000			
45	Increase in accrued liabilities		(15)	4,000			
46	Increase in deferred tax liability		(15)	3,000			
47	Decrease in income tax payable				(15)	13,000	
48	Amortization of bond premium				(15)	1,000	
49	Investing activities						
50	Proceeds from condemnation of land		(9)	18,500			
51	Purchase of equipment				(10)	53,000	
52	Sale of equipment		(11)	4,000			
53	Major repairs of equipment				(13)	11,000	
54	Financing activities						
55	Payment of cash dividend				(3)	6,000	
56	Issuance of common stock		(16)	144,000			
57	Purchase of treasury stock				(17)	17,000	
58	Totals			697,500		704,500	
59	Decrease in cash		(18)	7,000			
60	Totals			$704,500		$704,500	

Sheet1 / Sheet2 / Sheet3

PREPARATION OF FINAL STATEMENT

Illustration 19-41 presents a formal statement of cash flows prepared from the data compiled in the lower portion of the worksheet.

ILLUSTRATION 19-41
Statement of Cash Flows, Satellite Corporation

SATELLITE CORPORATION
STATEMENT OF CASH FLOWS
FOR THE YEAR ENDED DECEMBER 31, 2008
INCREASE (DECREASE) IN CASH

Cash flows from operating activities		
Net income		$117,000
Adjustments to reconcile net income to net cash used by operating activities:		
Depreciation expense	$ 14,600	
Amortization of trademark	2,400	
Amortization of bond premium	(1,000)	
Equity in earnings of Porter Co.	(3,500)	
Gain on condemnation of land	(8,000)	
Loss on sale of equipment	1,500	
Increase in deferred tax liability	3,000	
Increase in accounts receivable (net)	(53,000)	
Increase in inventories	(152,000)	
Decrease in prepaid expenses	500	
Increase in accounts payable	1,000	
Increase in accrued liabilities	4,000	
Decrease in income tax payable	(13,000)	(203,500)
Net cash used by operating activities		(86,500)
Cash flows from investing activities		
Proceeds from condemnation of land	18,500	
Purchase of equipment	(53,000)	
Sale of equipment	4,000	
Major repairs of equipment	(11,000)	
Net cash used by investing activities		(41,500)
Cash flows from financing activities		
Payment of cash dividend	(6,000)	
Issuance of common stock	144,000	
Purchase of treasury stock	(17,000)	
Net cash provided by financing activities		121,000
Net decrease in cash		(7,000)
Cash, January 1, 2008		66,000
Cash, December 31, 2008		$ 59,000

Supplemental Disclosures of Cash Flow Information:

Cash paid during the year for:	
Interest (net of amount capitalized)	$ 9,000
Income taxes	$ 62,000

Supplemental Schedule of Noncash Investing and Financing Activities:
Purchase of land for $60,000 in exchange for a $60,000 long-term note.

wiley.com/college/kieso

Discussion of the T-Account Approach to Preparation of the Statement of Cash Flows

QUESTIONS

1. What is the purpose of the statement of cash flows? What information does it provide?
2. Of what use is the statement of cash flows?
3. Differentiate between investing activities, financing activities, and operating activities.
4. What are the major sources of cash (inflows) in a statement of cash flows? What are the major uses (outflows) of cash?

5. Identify and explain the major steps involved in preparing the statement of cash flows.

6. Identify the following items as (1) operating, (2) investing, or (3) financing activities: purchase of land; payment of dividends; cash sales; and purchase of treasury stock.

7. Unlike the other major financial statements, the statement of cash flows is not prepared from the adjusted trial balance. From what sources does the information to prepare this statement come, and what information does each source provide?

8. Why is it necessary to convert accrual-based net income to a cash basis when preparing a statement of cash flows?

9. Differentiate between the direct method and the indirect method by discussing each method.

10. Bonnie Raitt Company reported net income of $3.5 million in 2008. Depreciation for the year was $520,000; accounts receivable increased $500,000; and accounts payable increased $350,000. Compute net cash flow from operating activities using the indirect method.

11. Sophie B. Hawkins Co. reported sales on an accrual basis of $100,000. If accounts receivable increased $30,000, and the allowance for doubtful accounts increased $9,000 after a writeoff of $4,000, compute cash sales.

12. Your roommate is puzzled. During the last year, the company in which she is a stockholder reported a net loss of $675,000, yet its cash increased $321,000 during the same period of time. Explain to your roommate how this situation could occur.

13. The board of directors of Kenny G Corp. declared cash dividends of $260,000 during the current year. If dividends payable was $85,000 at the beginning of the year and $70,000 at the end of the year, how much cash was paid in dividends during the year?

14. Explain how the amount of cash payments to suppliers is computed under the direct method.

15. The net income for Silverchair Company for 2008 was $320,000. During 2008, depreciation on plant assets was $114,000, amortization of patent was $40,000, and the company incurred a loss on sale of plant assets of $21,000. Compute net cash flow from operating activities.

16. Each of the following items must be considered in preparing a statement of cash flows for Frogstomp Inc. for the year ended December 31, 2008. State where each item is to be shown in the statement, if at all.

(a) Plant assets that had cost $20,000 6½ years before and were being depreciated on a straight-line basis over 10 years with no estimated scrap value were sold for $4,000.

(b) During the year, 10,000 shares of common stock with a stated value of $20 a share were issued for $41 a share.

(c) Uncollectible accounts receivable in the amount of $22,000 were written off against the Allowance for Doubtful Accounts.

(d) The company sustained a net loss for the year of $50,000. Depreciation amounted to $22,000, and a gain of $9,000 was realized on the sale of available-for-sale securities for $38,000 cash.

17. Classify the following items as (1) operating, (2) investing, (3) financing, or (4) significant noncash investing and financing activities, using the direct method.

(a) Purchase of equipment.

(b) Redemption of bonds payable.

(c) Sale of building.

(d) Cash payments to suppliers.

(e) Exchange of equipment for furniture.

(f) Issuance of preferred stock.

(g) Cash received from customers.

(h) Purchase of treasury stock.

(i) Issuance of bonds for land.

(j) Payment of dividends.

(k) Cash payments to employees.

(l) Cash payments for operating expenses.

18. Clay Walker and David Ball were discussing the presentation format of the statement of cash flows of McBride Co. At the bottom of McBride's statement of cash flows was a separate section entitled "Noncash investing and financing activities." Give three examples of significant noncash transactions that would be reported in this section.

19. During 2008, Adams Company redeemed $2,000,000 of bonds payable for $1,780,000 cash. Indicate how this transaction would be reported on a statement of cash flows, if at all.

20. What are some of the arguments in favor of using the indirect (reconciliation) method as opposed to the direct method for reporting a statement of cash flows?

21. Why is it desirable to use a worksheet when preparing a statement of cash flows? Is a worksheet required to prepare a statement of cash flows?

CHAPTER TWENTY

FULL DISCLOSURE IN FINANCIAL REPORTING

High-Quality Financial Reporting—It's a Necessity

Here are excerpts from leading experts regarding the importance of high-quality financial reporting:[1]

Warren E. Buffett, Chairman and Chief Executive Officer, **Berkshire Hathaway Inc.**:

Financial reporting for Berkshire Hathaway, and for me personally, is the beginning of every decision that we make around here in terms of capital. I'm punching out 10-Ks and 10-Qs every single day. We look at the numbers and try to evaluate the quality of the financial reporting, and then we try to figure out what that means for the bonds and stocks that we're looking at, and thinking of either buying or selling.

Judy Lewent, Executive Vice President and Chief Financial Officer, Merck & Co., Inc.

. . . Higher standards, when properly implemented, drive excellence. I can make a parallel to the pharmaceutical industry. If you look around the world at where innovations come from, economists have studied and seen that where regulatory standards are the highest is where innovation is also the highest.

Floyd Norris, Chief Financial Correspondent, the **New York Times**:

We are in a situation now in our society where the temptations to provide "bad" financial reporting are probably greater than they used to be. The need to get the stock price up, or to keep it up, is intense. So, the temptation to play games, the temptation to manage earnings—some of which can be legitimate and some of which cannot be—is probably greater than it used to be.

Abby Joseph Cohen, Chair, Investment Policy Committee, **Goldman, Sachs & Co.**:

High-quality financial reporting is perhaps the most important thing we can expect from companies. For investors to make good decisions—whether those investors are buying stocks or bonds or making private investments—they need to know the truth. And we think that when information is as clear as possible and is reported as frequently as makes sense, investors can do their jobs as best they can.

In short, these comments illustrate why high-quality financial reporting is important to companies, to investors, and to the capital markets. At the heart of high-quality financial reporting is full disclosure.

[1]Excerpts taken from video entitled "Financially Correct with Ben Stein," Financial Accounting Standards Board (Norwalk, Conn.: FASB, 2002). By permission.

Learning Objectives

After studying this chapter, you should be able to:

1 Review the full disclosure principle and describe implementation problems.
2 Explain the use of notes in financial statement preparation.
3 Discuss the disclosure requirements for major business segments.
4 Describe the accounting problems associated with interim reporting.
5 Identify the major disclosures in the auditor's report.
6 Understand management's responsibilities for financials.
7 Identify issues related to financial forecasts and projections.
8 Describe the profession's response to fraudulent financial reporting.

PREVIEW OF CHAPTER 20

As the opening story indicates, our markets will not function properly without transparent, complete, and truthful reporting of financial performance. Investors and other interested parties need to read and understand all aspects of financial reporting—the financial statements, the notes, the president's letter, and management's discussion and analysis. In this chapter, we cover the full disclosure principle in more detail and examine disclosures that must accompany financial statements so that they are not misleading. The content and organization of this chapter are as follows.

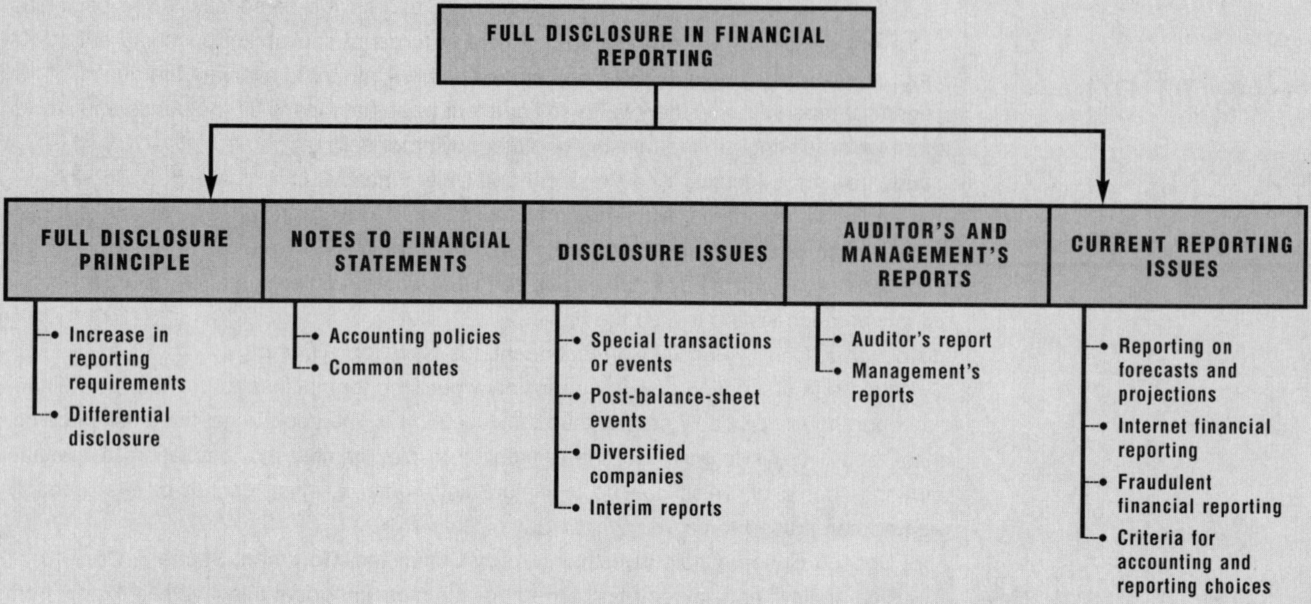

FULL DISCLOSURE PRINCIPLE

OBJECTIVE 1
Review the full disclosure principle and describe implementation problems.

FASB Concepts Statement No. 1 notes that some useful information is best provided in the financial statements, and some is best provided by means other than in financial statements. For example, earnings and cash flows are readily available in financial statements—but investors might do better to look at comparisons to other companies in the same industry, found in news articles or brokerage house reports.

FASB standards directly affect financial statements, notes to the financial statements, and supplementary information. Other types of information found in the annual report, such as management's discussion and analysis, are not subject to FASB standards. Illustration 20-1 indicates the various types of financial information.

As Chapter 2 indicated, the profession has adopted a **full disclosure principle**. The full disclosure principle calls for financial reporting of **any financial facts significant enough to influence the judgment of an informed reader**. In some situations, the benefits of disclosure may be apparent but the costs uncertain. In other instances, the costs may be certain but the benefits of disclosure not as apparent.

UNDERLYING CONCEPTS
Here is a good example of the trade-off between cost considerations and the benefits of full disclosure.

For example, recently, the SEC required companies to provide expanded disclosures about their contractual obligations. In light of the off-balance sheet accounting frauds at companies like **Enron**, the benefits of these expanded disclosures seem fairly obvious to the investing public. While no one has documented the exact costs of disclosure in these situations, they would appear to be relatively small.

On the other hand, the cost of disclosure can be substantial in some cases and the benefits difficult to assess. For example, at one time the *Wall Street Journal* reported that

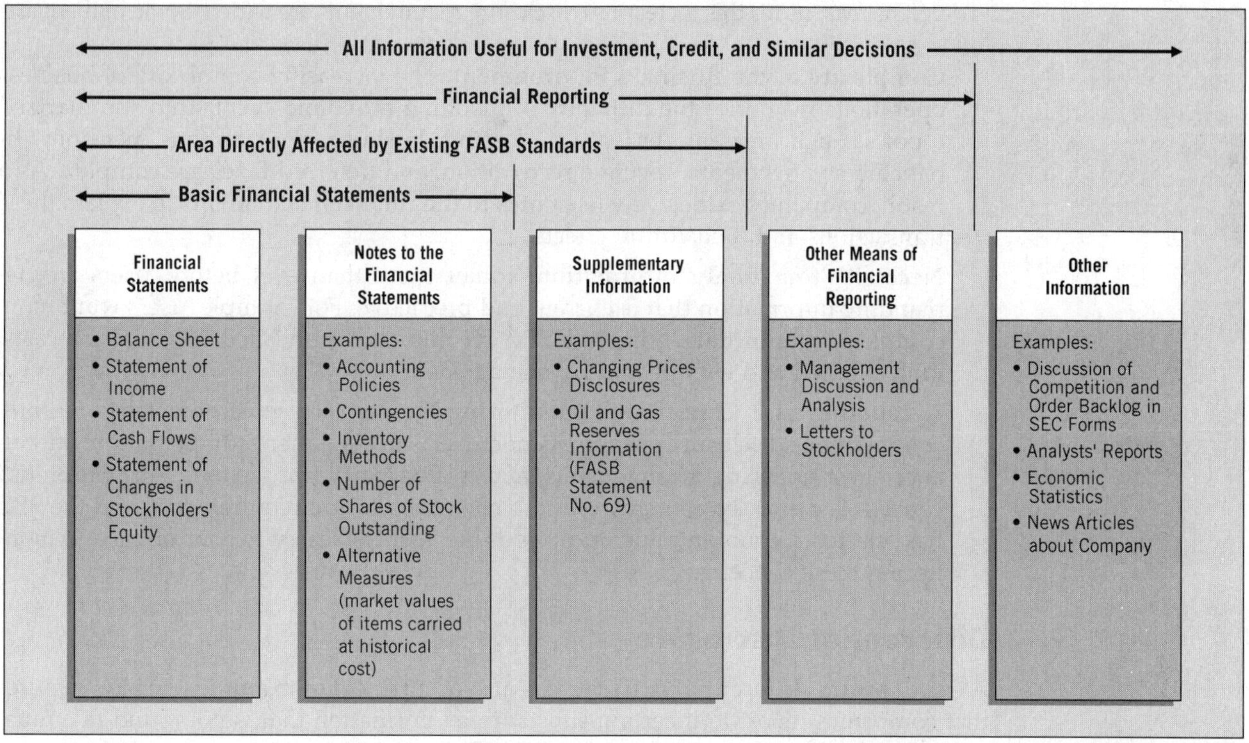

ILLUSTRATION 20-1
Types of Financial Information

if segment reporting were adopted, a company like **Fruehauf** would have had to increase its accounting staff 50 percent, from 300 to 450 individuals. In this case, the cost of disclosure can be measured, but the benefits are less well defined.

Some even argue that the reporting requirements are so detailed and substantial that users have a difficult time absorbing the information. These critics charge the profession with engaging in **information overload**.

Financial disasters at **Microstrategy**, **PharMor**, **WorldCom**, and **Global Crossing** highlight the difficulty of implementing the full disclosure principle. They raise the issue of why investors were not aware of potential problems: Was the information these companies presented not comprehensible? Was it buried? Was it too technical? Was it properly presented and fully disclosed as of the financial statement date, but the situation later deteriorated? Or was it simply not there? In the following sections, we describe the elements of high-quality disclosure that will enable companies to avoid these disclosure pitfalls.

UNDERLYING CONCEPTS

The AICPA's Special Committee on Financial Reporting notes that business reporting is not free, and improving it requires considering the relative costs and benefits of information. Undisciplined expansion of mandated reporting could result in large and needless costs.

Increase in Reporting Requirements

Disclosure requirements have increased substantially. One recent survey showed that the size of many companies' annual reports is growing in response to demands for increased transparency. For example, annual report page counts ranged from 70 pages for **Gateway** up to a whopping 244 pages in **Eastman Kodak**'s annual report. Compared to prior years' reports, the percentage increase in pages ranged from 17 percent at **IBM** to over 80 percent at **Siebel Systems.**[2] This result is not surprising; as illustrated throughout this textbook, the FASB has issued many standards in the last 10 years that have substantial disclosure provisions.

---

[2]Aliya Sternstein, "Heavy Lifting Required," *Forbes* (October 13, 2003) p. 58. Another earlier study documented annual report growth for a sample of 25 large, well-known companies over a recent 10-year period. The average number of pages of notes to the financial statements increased from 9 to 17 pages, and the average number of pages for management's discussion and analysis grew from 7 to 12 pages. See Ray J. Groves, "Financial Disclosure: When More Is Not Better," *Financial Executive* (May/June 1994).

The reasons for this increase in disclosure requirements are varied. Some of them are:

Complexity of the Business Environment. The increasing complexity of business operations magnifies the difficulty of distilling economic events into summarized reports. Such areas as derivatives, leasing, business combinations, pensions, financing arrangements, revenue recognition, and deferred taxes are complex. As a result, companies extensively use **notes to the financial statements** to explain these transactions and their future effects.

Necessity for Timely Information. Today, more than ever before, users are demanding information that is current and predictive. For example, users want more complete **interim data**. Also, the SEC recommends published financial forecasts, long avoided and even feared by management.

Accounting as a Control and Monitoring Device. The government has recently sought public disclosure of such phenomena as management compensation, off-balance-sheet financing arrangements, and related party transactions. An "Enronitis" concern is expressed in many of these newer disclosure requirements, and the SEC has selected accountants and auditors as the agents to assist in controlling and monitoring these concerns.

Differential Disclosure

A trend toward **differential disclosure** is also occurring. For example, the SEC requires that companies report to it certain substantive information that is not found in annual reports to stockholders. Likewise, the FASB, recognizing that certain disclosure requirements are costly and unnecessary for certain companies, has eliminated reporting requirements for nonpublic enterprises in such areas as fair value of financial instruments and segment reporting.[3]

WHAT DO THE NUMBERS MEAN?

"THE HEART OF THE MATTER"

As we discussed in the opening story, financial disclosure is one of a number of institutional features that contribute to vibrant security markets. In fact, a recent study of disclosure and other mechanisms (such as civil lawsuits and criminal sanctions) found that good disclosure is the most important contributor to a vibrant market.

The study, which compared disclosure and other legal and regulatory elements across 49 countries, found that countries with the best disclosure laws have the biggest stock markets. Countries with more successful market environments also tend to have regulations that make it relatively easy for private investors to sue corporations that provide bad information. That is, while criminal sanctions can be effective in some circumstances, disclosure and other legal and regulatory elements encouraging good disclosure are the most important determinants of highly liquid and deep securities markets.

These findings hold for nations in all stages of economic development, with particular importance for nations that are in the early stages of securities regulation. The lesson: Disclosure is good for your market.

Source: Rebecca Christie, "Study: Disclosure at Heart of Effective Securities Laws," *Wall Street Journal Online* (August 11, 2003).

[3]The FASB has had a disclosure-effectiveness project. The revised pension and postretirement benefit disclosures [*FASB Statement No. 132* and *FASB Statement No. 132(R)*] are one example of how disclosures can be streamlined and made more useful. However, as noted by one FASB member, the usefulness of expanded required disclosure also depends on users' ability to distinguish between disclosed versus recognized items in financial statements. Research to date is inconclusive on this matter. See Katherine Schipper, "Required Disclosures in Financial Reports," Presidential Address to the American Accounting Association Annual Meeting; San Francisco, CA (August 2005).

Some still complain that the FASB has not gone far enough. They note that certain types of companies (small or nonpublic) should not have to follow complex GAAP requirements such as those for deferred income taxes, leases, or pensions. This issue, often referred to as "**big GAAP versus little GAAP**," continues to be controversial. The FASB takes the position that there should be one set of GAAP, except in unusual situations.[4]

UNDERLYING CONCEPTS

The AICPA Special Committee on Financial Reporting indicated that users differ in their needs for information and that not all companies should report all elements of information. Rather, companies should report only information that users and preparers agree is needed in the particular circumstances.

NOTES TO THE FINANCIAL STATEMENTS

OBJECTIVE 2
Explain the use of notes in financial statement preparation.

As you know from your study of this textbook, notes are an integral part of the financial statements of a business enterprise. However, readers of financial statements often overlook them because they are highly technical and often appear in small print. **Notes are the means of amplifying or explaining the items presented in the main body of the statements.** They can explain in qualitative terms information pertinent to specific financial statement items. In addition, they can provide supplementary data of a quantitative nature to expand the information in the financial statements. Notes also can explain restrictions imposed by financial arrangements or basic contractual agreements. Although notes may be technical and difficult to understand, they provide meaningful information for the user of the financial statements.

Accounting Policies

Accounting policies are the specific accounting principles and methods a company currently uses and considers most appropriate to present fairly its financial statements. *APB Opinion No. 22,* "Disclosure of Accounting Policies," states that information about the accounting policies adopted by a reporting entity is essential for financial statement users in making economic decisions. It recommended that companies should present **as an integral part of the financial statements a statement identifying the accounting policies adopted and followed by the reporting entity**. Companies should present the disclosure as the first note or in a separate Summary of Significant Accounting Policies section preceding the notes to the financial statements.

The Summary of Significant Accounting Policies answers such questions as: What method of depreciation is used on plant assets? What valuation method is employed on inventories? What amortization policy is followed in regard to intangible assets? How are marketing costs handled for financial reporting purposes?

Illustration 20-2 shows another example, from **Tootsie Roll Industries.**

Analysts examine carefully the summary of accounting policies to determine whether a company is using conservative or liberal accounting practices. For example, depreciating plant assets over an unusually long period of time is considered liberal. Using LIFO inventory valuation in a period of inflation is generally viewed as conservative.

Companies that fail to adopt high-quality reporting policies may be heavily penalized by the market. For example, when **Microstrategy** disclosed that it would restate prior-year results due to use of aggressive revenue recognition policies, its share

UNDERLYING CONCEPTS

The AICPA's Special Committee on Financial Reporting states that to meet users' changing needs, business reporting must: (1) Provide more forward-looking information. (2) Focus more on the factors that create longer-term value, including nonfinancial measures. (3) Better align information reported externally with the information reported internally.

[4]In response to cost-benefit concerns, the SEC has exempted some small public companies from certain rules implemented in response to the Sarbanes-Oxley Act of 2002. For example, smaller companies have more time to comply with the internal control rules required by the Sarbanes-Oxley law and have more time to file annual and interim reports. Both the FASB and the AICPA are studying the big GAAP/little GAAP issue to ensure that any kind of differential reporting is conceptually sound and meets the needs of users. See Remarks of Robert H. Herz, Chairman, Financial Accounting Standards Board, 2004 AICPA National Conference on Current SEC and PCAOB Reporting Developments (December 7, 2004.)

price dropped over 60 percent in one day. Investors viewed Microstrategy's quality of earnings as low.

ILLUSTRATION 20-2
Note Disclosure of Accounting Policies

Tootsie Roll Industries, Inc. and Subsidiaries

(Dollars in thousands, except per share amounts)

Note 1—Significant Accounting Policies (in part)

Basis of consolidation:
The consolidated financial statements include the accounts of Tootsie Roll Industries, Inc. and its wholly-owned subsidiaries (the company), which are primarily engaged in the manufacture and sale of candy products. All significant intercompany transactions have been eliminated. . . .

Revenue recognition and other accounting pronouncements:
Products are sold to customers based on accepted purchase orders which include quantity, sales price and other relevant terms of sale. Revenues are recognized when products are delivered to customers and collectibility is reasonably assured. Shipping and handling costs of $31,795, $28,217 and $28,579 in 2004, 2003 and 2002, respectively, are included in selling, marketing and administrative expenses. Accounts receivable are unsecured. Revenues from a major customer aggregated approximately 20.8%, 20.6% and 19.6% of total net sales during the years ended December 31, 2004, 2003 and 2002, respectively. . . .

Cash and cash equivalents:
The company considers temporary cash investments with an original maturity of three months or less to be cash equivalents.

Investments:
Investments consist of various marketable securities with maturities of generally up to four years. The company classifies debt and equity securities as either held to maturity, available for sale or trading. Held to maturity securities represent those securities that the company has both the positive intent and ability to hold to maturity and are carried at amortized cost. Available for sale securities represent those securities that do not meet the classification of held to maturity, are not actively traded and are carried at fair value. Unrealized gains and losses on these securities are excluded from earnings and are reported as a separate component of shareholders equity, net of applicable taxes, until realized. Trading securities relate to deferred compensation arrangements and are carried at fair value.

Hedging activities:
From time to time, the company enters into commodities futures contracts that are intended and effective as hedges of market price risks associated with the anticipated purchase of certain raw materials (primarily sugar). To qualify as a hedge, the company evaluates a variety of characteristics of these transactions, including the probability that the anticipated transaction will occur. If the anticipated transaction were not to occur, the gain or loss would then be recognized in current earnings. The company does not engage in trading or other speculative use of derivative instruments. The company does assume the risk that counterparties may not be able to meet the terms of their contracts. The company does not expect any losses as a result of counterparty defaults.

The company's derivative instruments are being accounted for as cash flow hedges and are recorded on the balance sheet at fair value. Changes therein are recorded in other comprehensive earnings and are reclassified to earnings in the periods in which earnings are affected by the hedged item. Substantially all amounts reported in accumulated other comprehensive earnings (loss) are expected to be reclassified to cost of goods sold. During the years ended December 31, 2004, 2003 and 2002, ineffectiveness related to cash flow hedges was not material.

Inventories:
Inventories are stated at cost, not to exceed market. The cost of substantially all of the company's inventories ($54,794 and $42,735 at December 31, 2004 and 2003, respectively) has been determined by the last-in, first-out (LIFO) method. The excess of current cost over LIFO cost of inventories approximates $5,868 and $6,442 at December 31, 2004 and 2003, respectively. The cost of certain foreign inventories ($3,983 and $3,351 at December 31, 2004 and 2003, respectively) has been determined by the first-in, first-out (FIFO) method. Rebates, discounts and other cash consideration received from a vendor related to inventory purchases is reflected as a reduction in the cost of the related inventory item, and is therefore reflected in cost of sales when the related inventory item is sold.

Property, plant and equipment:
Depreciation is computed for financial reporting purposes by use of the straight-line method based on useful lives of 20 to 35 years for buildings and 5 to 20 years for machinery and equipment. Depreciation expense was $11,680, $11,379 and $12,354 in 2004, 2003 and 2002, respectively, including $744 relating to equipment disposals.

Carrying value of long-lived assets:
The company reviews long-lived assets to determine if there are events or circumstances indicating that the amount of the asset reflected in the company's balance sheet may not be recoverable. When such indicators are present, the company compares the carrying value of the long-lived asset, or asset group, to the future undiscounted cash flows of the underlying assets to determine if an impairment exists. If applicable, an impairment charge would be recorded to write down the carrying value to its fair value. The determination of fair value involves the use of estimates of future cash flows that involve considerable management judgment and are based upon assumptions about expected future operating performance. The actual cash flows could differ from management's estimates due to changes in business conditions, operating performance, and economic conditions. No impairment charges were recorded by the company during 2004, 2003 or 2002.

Postretirement health care and life insurance benefits:
The company provides certain postretirement health care and life insurance benefits. The cost of these postretirement benefits is accrued during employees' working careers. The company also provides split dollar life insurance benefits to certain executive officers. The company records an asset equal to the cumulative insurance premiums that will be recovered upon the death of a covered employee(s) or earlier under the terms of the plan. Split dollar premiums paid were $3,620, $4,237 and $6,890 in 2004, 2003 and 2002, respectively.

Intangible assets:
The company accounts for intangible assets in accordance with SFAS No. 142, "Goodwill and Other Intangible Assets," which was adopted by the company on January 1, 2002. In accordance with this statement, goodwill and intangible assets with indefinite lives are not amortized, but rather tested for impairment at least annually. All trademarks have been assessed by management to have indefinite lives because they are expected to generate cash flows indefinitely. The company has completed its annual impairment testing of its goodwill and trademarks during the fourth quarter of each of the years presented, and no impairment was found.

Income taxes:
Deferred income taxes are recorded and recognized for future tax effects of temporary differences between financial and income tax reporting. Federal income taxes are provided on the portion of income of foreign subsidiaries that is expected to be remitted to the U.S. and become taxable, but not on the portion that is considered to be permanently invested in the foreign subsidiary.

Foreign currency translation:
The company has determined the functional currency for each foreign subsidiary. The U.S. dollar is used as the functional currency where a substantial portion of the subsidiary's business is indexed to the U.S. dollar or where its manufactured products are principally sold in the U.S. All other foreign subsidiaries use the local currency as their functional currency. Where the U.S. dollar is used as the functional currency, foreign currency translation adjustments are recorded as a charge or credit to other income in the statement of earnings. Where the foreign currency is used as the functional currency, translation adjustments are recorded as a separate component of comprehensive earnings (loss).

Joint venture:
The company's 50% interest in two Spanish companies is accounted for using the equity method. The company records an increase in its investment in the joint venture to the extent of its share of the joint venture's earnings, and reduces its investment to the extent of dividends received. No dividends were received during 2004.

Comprehensive earnings:
Comprehensive earnings includes net earnings, foreign currency translation adjustments and unrealized gains/losses on commodity hedging contracts and marketable securities.

Earnings per share:
A dual presentation of basic and diluted earnings per share is not required due to the lack of potentially dilutive securities under the company's simple capital structure. Therefore, all earnings per share amounts represent basic earnings per share. . . .

Common Notes

We have discussed many of the **notes to the financial statements** throughout this textbook, and will discuss others more fully in this chapter. The more common are as shown on the next two pages.

MAJOR DISCLOSURES

Inventory. Companies should report the basis upon which inventory amounts are stated (lower of cost or market) and the method used in determining cost (LIFO, FIFO, average cost, etc.). Manufacturers should report, either in the balance sheet or in a separate schedule in the notes, the inventory composition (finished goods, work in process, raw materials). Unusual or significant financing arrangements relating to inventories that may require disclosure include transactions with related parties, product financing arrangements, firm purchase commitments, involuntary liquidation of LIFO inventories, and pledging of inventories as collateral. Chapter 8 illustrates these disclosures.

Property, Plant, and Equipment. Companies should state the basis of valuation for property, plant, and equipment. It is usually historical cost. Companies also should disclose pledges, liens, and other commitments related to these assets. In the presentation of depreciation, companies should disclose the following in the financial statements or in the notes: (1) depreciation expense for the period; (2) balances of major classes of depreciable assets, by nature and function, at the balance sheet date; (3) accumulated depreciation, either by major classes of depreciable assets or in total, at the balance sheet date; and (4) a general description of the method or methods used in computing depreciation with respect to major classes of depreciable assets. Finally, companies should explain any major impairments. Chapter 10 illustrates these disclosures.

Creditor Claims. Investors normally find it extremely useful to understand the nature and cost of creditor claims. However, the liabilities section in the balance sheet can provide the major types of liabilities only in the aggregate. Note schedules regarding such obligations provide additional information about how a company is financing its operations, the costs that it will bear in future periods, and the timing of future cash outflows. Financial statements must disclose for each of the five years following the date of the statements the aggregate amount of maturities and sinking fund requirements for all long-term borrowings. Chapter 13 illustrates these disclosures.

Equity Holders' Claims. Many companies present in the body of the balance sheet information about equity securities: the number of shares authorized, issued, and outstanding and the par value for each type of security. Or, companies may present such data in a note. Beyond that, a common equity note disclosure relates to contracts and senior securities outstanding that might affect the various claims of the residual equity holders. An example would be the existence of outstanding stock options, outstanding convertible debt, redeemable preferred stock, and convertible preferred stock. In addition, it is necessary to disclose certain types of restrictions currently in force. Generally, these types of restrictions involve the amount of earnings available for dividend distribution. Examples of these types of disclosures are illustrated in Chapter 14.

Contingencies and Commitments. A company may have gain or loss contingencies that are not disclosed in the body of the financial statements. These contingencies include litigation, debt and other guarantees, possible tax assessments, renegotiation of government contracts, and sales of receivables with recourse. In addition, companies should disclose in the notes commitments that relate to dividend restrictions, purchase agreements (through-put and take-or-pay), hedge contracts, and employment contracts. Disclosures of such items are illustrated in Chapter 6, Chapter 8, and Chapter 12.

Deferred Taxes, Pensions, and Leases. The FASB also requires extensive disclosure in the areas of deferred taxes, pensions, and leases. Chapter 17 discusses in detail

UNDERLYING CONCEPTS

The AICPA Special Committee on Financial Reporting notes that standard setters should address disclosures and accounting requirements for off-balance-sheet financial arrangements. The goal should be to report the risks, opportunities, resources, and obligations that result from those arrangements, consistent with users' needs for information.

each of these disclosures. Users of financial statements should carefully read notes to the financial statements for information about off-balance-sheet commitments, future financing needs, and the quality of a company's earnings.

Changes in Accounting Principles. The profession defines various types of accounting changes and establishes guides for reporting each type. Companies discuss, either in the summary of significant accounting policies or in the other notes, changes in accounting principles (as well as material changes in estimates and corrections of errors). See Chapter 18.

wiley.com/college/kieso

Additional Examples of Major Disclosures

In earlier chapters we discussed the disclosures listed above. The following sections of this chapter illustrate four additional disclosures of significance—special transactions or events, subsequent events, segment reporting, and interim reporting.

MORE PAGES, BUT BETTER?

WHAT DO THE NUMBERS MEAN?

The biggest overall change in annual reports recently is that companies are now disclosing debt-rating triggers buried in their financing arrangements. These triggers can require a company to pay off a loan immediately if the debt rating collapses; they are one of the reasons **Enron** crumbled so quickly. But few Enron stockholders knew about them until the gun had gone off. Companies are also telling more about their bank credit lines, liquidity, and any special purpose entities, which were major villains in the Enron drama.

Source: Gretchen Morgenson, "Annual Reports: More Pages, But Better?" *New York Times* (March 17, 2002).

DISCLOSURE ISSUES

Disclosure of Special Transactions or Events

Related-party transactions, errors and irregularities, and illegal acts pose especially sensitive and difficult problems. The accountant/auditor who has responsibility for reporting on these types of transactions must take care to properly balance the rights of the reporting company and the needs of users of the financial statements.

Related-party transactions arise when a company engages in transactions in which one of the parties has the ability to significantly influence the policies of the other. They may also occur when a nontransacting party has the ability to influence the policies of the two transacting parties.[5] Competitive, free-market dealings may not exist in related-party transactions, and so an "arm's-length" basis cannot be assumed. Transactions such as borrowing or lending money at abnormally low or high interest rates, real estate sales at amounts that differ significantly from appraised value, exchanges of nonmonetary assets, and transactions involving enterprises that have no economic substance ("shell corporations") suggest that related parties may be involved.

[5]Examples of related-party transactions include transactions between (a) a parent company and its subsidiaries; (b) subsidiaries of a common parent; (c) a company and trusts for the benefit of employees (controlled or managed by the enterprise); and (d) a company and its principal owners, management, or members of immediate families, and affiliates. Two classic cases of related-party transactions were **Enron**, with its misuse of special purpose entities, and **Tyco International**, which forgave loans to its management team.

In order to make adequate disclosure, companies should report the economic substance, rather than the legal form, of these transactions. *FASB Statement No. 57* requires the following disclosures of material related-party transactions.

1. The nature of the relationship(s) involved.
2. A description of the transactions (including transactions to which no amounts or nominal amounts were ascribed) for each of the periods for which income statements are presented.
3. The dollar amounts of transactions for each of the periods for which income statements are presented.
4. Amounts due from or to related parties as of the date of each balance sheet presented.

Illustration 20-3, from the annual report of **Knight-Ridder, Inc.**, shows disclosure of related-party transactions.

ILLUSTRATION 20-3
Disclosure of Related Party Transactions

Knight-Ridder, Inc.

Note 8 (in part): Related Party Transactions
We have ongoing purchase commitments with SP and Ponderay, our two newsprint mill partnership investments. These future commitments are for the purchase of a minimum of $42.5 million and $13.8 million of newsprint with SP and Ponderay, respectively, at current market prices. We also have a sales commitment with DN to supply them with 50% of their newsprint requirements, which will be approximately $27.4 million. We have the resources necessary to fulfill these commitments.

Many companies are involved in related-party transactions. Errors, irregularities, and illegal acts, however, are the exception rather than the rule. Accounting **errors** are *unintentional* mistakes, whereas **irregularities** are *intentional* distortions of financial statements.[6] As indicated earlier, companies should correct the financial statements when they discover errors. The same treatment should be given irregularities. The discovery of irregularities, however, gives rise to a different set of procedures and responsibilities for the accountant/auditor.[7]

Illegal acts encompass such items as illegal political contributions, bribes, kickbacks, and other violations of laws and regulations.[8] In these situations, the accountant/auditor must evaluate the adequacy of disclosure in the financial statements. For example, if a company derives revenue from an illegal act that is considered material in relation to the financial statements, this information should be disclosed. The Sarbanes-Oxley Act of 2002 is intended to deter these illegal acts. This law adds significant fines and longer jail time for those who improperly sign off on the correctness of financial statements that include willing and knowing misstatements.

Disclosure plays a very important role in these types of transactions because the events are more qualitative than quantitative and involve more subjective than objective evaluation. Users of the financial statements need some indication of the existence and nature of these transactions, through disclosures, modifications in the auditor's report, or reports of changes in auditors.

[6]"The Auditor's Responsibility to Detect and Report Errors and Irregularities," *Statement on Auditing Standards No. 53* (New York, AICPA, 1988). Since passage of the Sarbanes-Oxley Act of 2002, auditors of public companies are regulated by the Public Company Accounting Oversight Board (PCAOB). While the PCAOB has developed some new auditing standards, this Board has for the most part adopted the prior auditing standards issued by the Auditing Standards Board of the AICPA.

[7]The profession became so concerned with certain management frauds that affect financial statements that it established a National Commission on Fraudulent Financial Reporting. The major purpose of this organization was to determine how fraudulent reporting practices could be constrained. Fraudulent financial reporting is discussed later in this chapter.

[8]"Illegal Acts by Clients," *Statement on Auditing Standards No. 54* (New York, AICPA, 1988).

Post-Balance-Sheet Events (Subsequent Events)

Notes to the financial statements should explain any significant financial events that took place after the formal balance sheet date, but before the statement is issued. These events are referred to as **post-balance-sheet events**, or just plain **subsequent events**. Illustration 20-4 shows a time diagram of the subsequent events period.

ILLUSTRATION 20-4
Time Periods for Subsequent Events

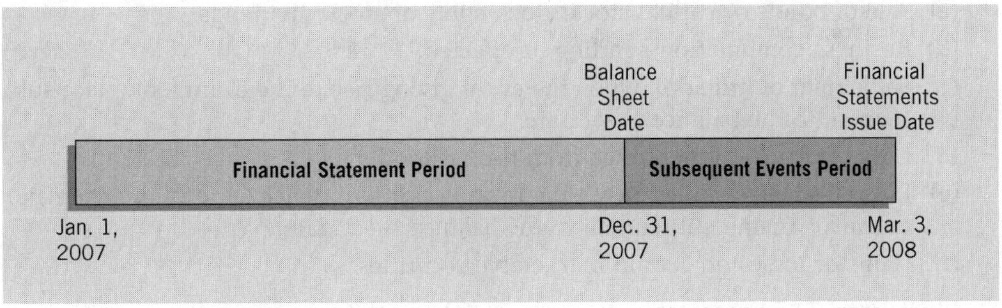

A period of several weeks, and sometimes months, may elapse after the end of the fiscal year but before the company issues financial statements. Various activities involved in closing the books for the period and issuing the statements all take time: taking and pricing the inventory, reconciling subsidiary ledgers with controlling accounts, preparing necessary adjusting entries, ensuring that all transactions for the period have been entered, obtaining an audit of the financial statements by independent certified public accountants, and printing the annual report. During the period between the balance sheet date and its distribution to stockholders and creditors, important transactions or other events may occur that materially affect the company's financial position or operating situation.

Many who read a balance sheet believe the balance sheet condition is constant, and they project it into the future. However, readers must be told if the company has experienced a significant change—e.g., sold one of its plants, acquired a subsidiary, suffered extraordinary losses, settled significant litigation, or experienced any other important event in the post-balance-sheet period. Without an explanation in a note, the reader might be misled and draw inappropriate conclusions.

Two types of events or transactions occurring after the balance sheet date may have a material effect on the financial statements or may need disclosure so that readers interpret these statements accurately:

UNDERLYING CONCEPTS

The periodicity or time period assumption implies that economic activities of an enterprise can be divided into artificial time periods for purpose of analysis.

1 Events that provide additional evidence about conditions that existed at the balance sheet date, that affect the estimates used in preparing financial statements, and that require adjustments to the financial statement. All information available prior to the issuance of the financial statements helps investors and creditors evaluate estimates previously made. To ignore these subsequent events is to pass up an opportunity to improve the accuracy of the financial statements. This first type of event encompasses information that an accountant would have recorded in the accounts had the information been known at the balance sheet date.

For example, if a loss on an account receivable results from a customer's bankruptcy subsequent to the balance sheet date, the company adjusts the financial statements before their issuance. The bankruptcy stems from the customer's poor financial health existing at the balance sheet date.

The same criterion applies to settlements of litigation. The company must adjust the financial statements if the events that gave rise to the litigation, such as personal injury or patent infringement, took place prior to the balance sheet date.

2 Events that provide evidence about conditions that did not exist at the balance sheet date but arise subsequent to that date, and that do not require adjustment of the financial statements. To illustrate, a loss resulting from a customer's fire or flood *after* the balance sheet date does not reflect conditions existing at that date. Thus, adjustment of the financial statements is not necessary. However, some of these events may have to be disclosed to keep the financial statements from being misleading. These disclosures take the form of notes, supplemental schedules, or even pro forma ("as if") financial data prepared as if the event had occurred on the balance sheet date. Examples of such events that require disclosure (but do not result in adjustment) are:

(a) Sale of bonds or capital stock; stock splits or stock dividends.

(b) Business combination pending or effected.

(c) Settlement of litigation when the event giving rise to the claim took place subsequent to the balance sheet date.

(d) Loss of plant or inventories from fire or flood.

(e) Losses on receivables resulting from conditions (such as customer's major casualty) arising subsequent to the balance sheet date.

(f) Gains or losses on certain marketable securities.[9]

Illustration 20-5 presents an example of subsequent events disclosure, excerpted from the annual report of **Goodrich Corporation**.

ILLUSTRATION 20-5
Disclosure of Subsequent Events

Goodrich Corporation

Note W. Subsequent Event

On February 16, 2004 the Company was notified by Pratt & Whitney, a United Technologies Company, that it will not meet the requirements for original equipment PW4000 engine components after the Company completes delivery of 45 shipsets (2 units per shipset) through early 2005. The Company had originally forecasted 90 shipsets to be delivered through 2009. As a result of this action, the total estimated revenue associated with this contract has been significantly reduced and anticipated cost reductions related to future deliveries under this contract will not occur.

The notice of termination is considered a Type 1 subsequent event under generally accepted accounting principles, the effects of which must be reflected in the Company's 2003 financial statements. As a result, the Company recorded a pre-tax charge of $15.1 million, as of December 31, 2003 related to this contract. The charge includes impairment of excess over average inventory of $7.0 million and $8.1 million for forward losses relating to the reduction in forecasted contract revenue and the increase in costs.

Many subsequent events or developments do not require adjustment of or disclosure in the financial statements. Typically, these are nonaccounting events or conditions that management normally communicates by other means. These events include legislation, product changes, management changes, strikes, unionization, marketing agreements, and loss of important customers.

Reporting for Diversified (Conglomerate) Companies

OBJECTIVE 3
Discuss the disclosure requirements for major business segments.

In certain business climates, companies have a tendency to diversify their operations. Take the case of conglomerate **General Electric (GE)**, whose products include locomotives and jet engines, credit card services, and water purification systems. Its

[9]"Subsequent Events," *Statement on Auditing Standards No. 1* (New York: AICPA, 1973), pp. 123–124. *Accounting Trends and Techniques—2004* listed the following types of subsequent events and their frequency of occurrence among the 600 companies surveyed: business combinations pending or effected, 83; debt incurred, reduced, or refinanced, 64; discontinued operations, 59; litigation, 29; and capital stock issued or repurchased, 27. The recent effects from hurricanes Katrina and Rita, which occurred after the year-end for companies with August fiscal years, require disclosure in order to keep the statements from being misleading. Some companies may have to consider whether these disasters affect their ability to continue as going concerns.

NBC Universal subsidiary owns **NBC TV**, **Vivendi Universal Entertainment**, and **Universal Pictures**. When businesses are so diversified, investors and investment analysts want more information about the details behind conglomerate financial statements. Particularly, they want income statement, balance sheet, and cash flow information on the **individual segments** that compose the total income figure.

Illustration 20-6 shows **segmented** (disaggregated) financial information of an office equipment and auto parts company.

ILLUSTRATION 20-6
Segmented Income Statement

OFFICE EQUIPMENT AND AUTO PARTS COMPANY
INCOME STATEMENT DATA
(IN MILLIONS)

	Consolidated	Office Equipment	Auto Parts
Net sales	$78.8	$18.0	$60.8
Manufacturing costs			
Inventories, beginning	12.3	4.0	8.3
Materials and services	38.9	10.8	28.1
Wages	12.9	3.8	9.1
Inventories, ending	(13.3)	(3.9)	(9.4)
	50.8	14.7	36.1
Selling and administrative expense	12.1	1.6	10.5
Total operating expenses	62.9	16.3	46.6
Income before taxes	15.9	1.7	14.2
Income taxes	(9.3)	(1.0)	(8.3)
Net income	$ 6.6	$ 0.7	$ 5.9

Much information is hidden in the aggregated totals. If the analyst has only the consolidated figures, he/she cannot tell the extent to which the differing product lines **contribute to the company's profitability, risk, and growth potential**. For example, in Illustration 20-6, the office equipment segment looks like a risky venture. Segmented reporting would provide useful information about the two business segments and would be useful for making an informed investment decision regarding the whole company.

A classic situation that demonstrates the need for segmented data involved **Caterpillar, Inc.** The SEC cited Caterpillar because it failed to tell investors that nearly a quarter of its income in one year came from a Brazilian unit and was nonrecurring in nature. The company knew that different economic policies in the next year would probably greatly affect earnings of the Brazilian unit. But Caterpillar presented its financial results on a consolidated basis, not disclosing the Brazilian operations. The SEC found that Caterpillar's failure to include information about Brazil left investors with an incomplete picture of the company's financial results and denied investors the opportunity to see the company "through the eyes of management."

Companies have always been somewhat hesitant to disclose segmented data for various reasons:

1. Without a thorough knowledge of the business and an understanding of such important factors as the competitive environment and capital investment requirements, the investor may find the segmented information meaningless or may even draw improper conclusions about the reported earnings of the segments.
2. Additional disclosure may be helpful to competitors, labor unions, suppliers, and certain government regulatory agencies, and thus harm the reporting company.
3. Additional disclosure may discourage management from taking intelligent business risks because segments reporting losses or unsatisfactory earnings may cause stockholder dissatisfaction with management.

4 The wide variation among companies in the choice of segments, cost allocation, and other accounting problems limits the usefulness of segmented information.

5 The investor is investing in the company as a whole and not in the particular segments, and it should not matter how any single segment is performing if the overall performance is satisfactory.

6 Certain technical problems, such as classification of segments and allocation of segment revenues and costs (especially "common costs"), are formidable.

On the other hand, the advocates of segmented disclosures offer these reasons in support of the practice:

1 Investors need segmented information to make an intelligent investment decision regarding a diversified company.

   (a) Sales and earnings of individual segments enable investors to evaluate the differences between segments in growth rate, risk, and profitability, and to forecast consolidated profits.

   (b) Segmented reports help investors evaluate the company's investment worth by disclosing the nature of a company's businesses and the relative size of the components.

2 The absence of segmented reporting by a diversified company may put its unsegmented, single product-line competitors at a competitive disadvantage because the conglomerate may obscure information that its competitors must disclose.

The advocates of segmented disclosures appear to have a much stronger case. Many users indicate that segmented data are the most useful financial information provided, aside from the basic financial statements. As a result, the FASB has issued extensive reporting guidelines in this area.

Objective of Reporting Segmented Information

The objective of reporting segmented financial data is to provide information about the **different types of business activities** in which an enterprise engages and the **different economic environments** in which it operates. Meeting this objective will help users of financial statements do the following.

(a) Better understand the enterprise's performance.

(b) Better assess its prospects for future net cash flows.

(c) Make more informed judgments about the enterprise as a whole.

Basic Principles

Financial statements can be disaggregated in several ways. For example, they can be disaggregated by products or services, by geography, by legal entity, or by type of customer. However, it is not feasible to provide all of that information in every set of financial statements. *FASB Statement No. 131* requires that general purpose financial statements include selected information on a single basis of segmentation. Thus, a company can meet the segmented reporting objective by providing financial statements segmented based on how the company's operations are managed. The method chosen is referred to as the **management approach.**[10] **The management approach reflects how management segments the company for making operating decisions.** The segments are evident from the components of the company's organization structure. These components are called **operating segments.**

Identifying Operating Segments

An **operating segment** is a component of an enterprise:

(a) That engages in business activities from which it earns revenues and incurs expenses.

[10]"Disclosures about Segments of an Enterprise and Related Information," *Statement of Financial Accounting Standards No. 131* (Norwalk, Conn.: FASB, 1997).

(b) Whose operating results are regularly reviewed by the company's chief operating decision maker to assess segment performance and allocate resources to the segment.
(c) For which discrete financial information is available that is generated by or based on the internal financial reporting system.

Companies may aggregate information about two or more operating segments only if the segments have the same basic characteristics in each of the following areas.

(a) The nature of the products and services provided.
(b) The nature of the production process.
(c) The type or class of customer.
(d) The methods of product or service distribution.
(e) If applicable, the nature of the regulatory environment.

After the company decides on the possible segments for disclosure, it makes a quantitative materiality test. This test determines whether the segment is significant enough to warrant actual disclosure. An operating segment is deemed significant, and therefore a reportable segment, if it satisfies **one or more** of the following quantitative thresholds.

1 Its **revenue** (including both sales to external customers and intersegment sales or transfers) is 10 percent or more of the combined revenue of all the company's operating segments.

2 The absolute amount of its **profit or loss** is 10 percent or more of the greater, in absolute amount, of **(a)** the combined operating profit of all operating segments that did not incur a loss, or **(b)** the combined loss of all operating segments that did report a loss.

3 Its **identifiable assets** are 10 percent or more of the combined assets of all operating segments.

In applying these tests, the company must consider two additional factors. First, segment data must explain a significant portion of the company's business. Specifically, the segmented results must equal or exceed 75 percent of the combined sales to unaffiliated customers for the entire company. This test prevents a company from providing limited information on only a few segments and lumping all the rest into one category.

Second, the profession recognizes that reporting too many segments may overwhelm users with detailed information. The FASB decided that 10 is a reasonable upper limit for the number of segments that a company must disclose.

To illustrate these requirements, assume a company has identified six possible reporting segments, as shown in Illustration 20-7 (000s omitted).

ILLUSTRATION 20-7
Data for Different Possible Reporting Segments

Segments	Total Revenue (Unaffiliated)	Operating Profit (Loss)	Identifiable Assets
A	$ 100	$10	$ 60
B	50	2	30
C	700	40	390
D	300	20	160
E	900	18	280
F	100	(5)	50
	$2,150	$85	$970

The company would apply the respective tests as follows:

Revenue test: 10% × $2,150 = $215; C, D, and E meet this test.
Operating profit (loss) test: 10% × $90 = $9 (note that the $5 loss is ignored, because the test is based on non-loss segments); A, C, D, and E meet this test.
Identifiable assets tests: 10% × $970 = $97; C, D, and E meet this test.

UNDERLYING CONCEPTS

The AICPA Special Committee on Financial Reporting notes that multi-segment companies operate diverse businesses that are subject to different opportunities and risks. Segment information provides additional insight about the opportunities and risks of investments and sharpens predictions. Because of its predictive value, providing segment information is of the highest priority.

The reporting segments are therefore A, C, D, and E, assuming that these four segments have enough sales to meet the 75 percent of combined sales test. The 75 percent test is computed as follows.

75% of combined sales test: 75% × \$2,150 = \$1,612.50. The sales of A, C, D, and E total \$2,000 (\$100 + \$700 + \$300 + \$900); therefore, the 75 percent test is met.

Measurement Principles

The accounting principles that companies use for segment disclosure need not be the same as the principles they use to prepare the consolidated statements. This flexibility may at first appear inconsistent. But, preparing segment information in accordance with generally accepted accounting principles would be difficult because some principles are not expected to apply at a segment level. Examples are accounting for the cost of company-wide employee benefit plans, accounting for income taxes in a company that files a consolidated tax return, and accounting for inventory on a LIFO basis if the pool includes items in more than one segment.

The FASB does not require allocations of joint, common, or company-wide costs solely for external reporting purposes. **Common costs** are those incurred for the benefit of more than one segment and whose interrelated nature prevents a completely objective division of costs among segments. For example, the company president's salary is difficult to allocate to various segments. Allocations of common costs are inherently arbitrary and may not be meaningful. There is a presumption that if companies allocate common costs to segments, these allocations are either directly attributable or reasonably allocable.

Segmented Information Reported

The FASB requires that an enterprise report the following.

1 *General information about its operating segments.* This includes factors that management considers most significant in determining the company's operating segments, and the types of products and services from which each operating segment derives its revenues.

2 *Segment profit and loss and related information.* Specifically, companies must report the following information about each operating segment if the amounts are included in determining segment profit or loss.

- **(a)** Revenues from transactions with external customers.
- **(b)** Revenues from transactions with other operating segments of the same enterprise.
- **(c)** Interest revenue.
- **(d)** Interest expense.
- **(e)** Depreciation, depletion, and amortization expense.
- **(f)** Unusual items.
- **(g)** Equity in the net income of investees accounted for by the equity method.
- **(h)** Income tax expense or benefit.
- **(i)** Extraordinary items.
- **(j)** Significant noncash items other than depreciation, depletion, and amortization expense.

3 *Segment assets.* A company must report each operating segment's total assets.

4 *Reconciliations.* A company must provide a reconciliation of the total of the segments' revenues to total revenues, a reconciliation of the total of the operating segments' profits and losses to its income before income taxes, and a reconciliation of the total of the operating segments' assets to total assets.

5 *Information about products and services and geographic areas.* For each operating segment not based on geography, the company must report (unless it is impracticable): (1) revenues from external customers, (2) long-lived assets, and (3) expenditures during the period for long-lived assets. This information, if material, must be reported (a) in the enterprise's country of domicile and (b) in each other country.

6 *Major customers.* If 10 percent or more of company revenue is derived from a single customer, the company must disclose the total amount of revenue from each such customer by segment.

Illustration of Disaggregated Information

Illustration 20-8 shows the segment disclosure for **Johnson & Johnson**.

ILLUSTRATION 20-8
Segment Disclosure

Johnson & Johnson
(Notes excluded)
Segments of Business and Geographic Areas

(dollars in millions)	Sales to Customers 2004	2003	2002
Consumer—United States	$ 4,224	$ 3,968	$ 3,605
International	4,109	3,463	2,959
Total	8,333	7,431	6,564
Pharmaceutical—United States	14,960	13,271	11,919
International	7,168	6,246	5,232
Total	22,128	19,517	17,151
Medical Devices and Diagnostics—United States	8,586	8,035	6,931
International	8,301	6,879	5,652
Total	16,887	14,914	12,583
Worldwide total	$47,348	$41,862	$36,298

	Operating Profit			Identifiable Assets		
(dollars in millions)	2004	2003	2002	2004	2003	2002
Consumer	$ 1,514	$1,393	$1,229	$ 6,142	$ 5,371	$ 5,056
Pharmaceutical	7,608	5,896	5,787	16,058	15,001	11,112
Medical Devices and Diagnostics	4,091	3,370	2,489	15,805	16,082	15,052
Segments total	13,213	10,659	9,505	38,005	36,454	31,220
Expenses not allocated to segments	(375)	(351)	(214)			
General corporate				15,312	11,809	9,336
Worldwide total	$12,838	$10,308	$9,291	$53,317	$ 48,263	$40,556

	Additions to Property, Plant & Equipment			Depreciation and Amortization		
(dollars in millions)	2004	2003	2002	2004	2003	2002
Consumer	$ 227	$ 229	$ 222	$ 222	$ 246	$ 244
Pharmaceutical	1,197	1,236	1,012	1,008	765	557
Medical Devices and Diagnostics	630	639	713	769	761	776
Segments total	2,054	2,104	1,947	1,999	1,772	1,577
General corporate	121	158	152	125	97	85
Worldwide total	$2,175	$2,262	$2,099	$2,124	$1,869	$1,662

	Sales to Customers			Long-Lived Assets		
(dollars in millions)	2004	2003	2002	2004	2003	2002
United States	$27,770	$25,274	$22,455	$14,324	$14,367	$11,822
Europe	11,151	9,483	7,636	6,142	5,193	4,613
Western Hemisphere excluding U.S.	2,589	2,236	2,018	748	772	583
Asia-Pacific, Africa	5,838	4,869	4,189	620	605	555
Segments total	47,348	41,862	36,298	21,834	20,937	17,573
General corporate				444	448	383
Other non long-lived assets				31,039	26,878	22,600
Worldwide total	$47,348	$41,862	$36,298	$53,317	$48,263	$40,556

Interim Reports

Another source of information for the investor is interim reports. As noted earlier, **interim reports** cover periods of less than one year. The stock exchanges, the SEC, and the accounting profession have an active interest in the presentation of interim information.

OBJECTIVE 4
Describe the accounting problems associated with interim reporting.

The SEC mandates that certain companies file a **Form 10-Q**, in which a company discloses quarterly data similar to that disclosed in the annual report. It also requires those companies to disclose selected quarterly information in notes to the annual financial statements. Illustration 20-9 presents the selected quarterly disclosure of **Tootsie Roll Industries, Inc.** In addition to Form 10-Q, the APB issued *Opinion No. 28*, which attempted to narrow the reporting alternatives related to interim reports.[11]

ILLUSTRATION 20-9
Disclosure of Selected Quarterly Data

Tootsie Roll Industries, Inc.
For the Year Ended December 31, 2004

(Thousands of dollars except per share data)

	First	Second	Third	Fourth	Total
Net sales	$80,046	$77,157	$156,971	$105,936	$420,110
Gross margin	34,730	34,992	64,804	41,083	175,609
Net earnings	11,493	11,828	26,976	13,877	64,174
Net earnings per share	.22	.22	.52	.27	1.23

	Stock Prices 2004 High	Stock Prices 2004 Low	Dividends 2004
1st Qtr	$37.86	$35.00	$.0681
2nd Qtr	$37.60	$32.41	$.0701
3rd Qtr	$32.60	$29.08	$.0700
4th Qtr	$34.63	$29.24	$.0700

UNDERLYING CONCEPTS
For information to be relevant, it must be available to decision makers before it loses its capacity to influence their decisions (timeliness). Interim reporting is an excellent example of this concept.

Because of the short-term nature of the information in these reports, there is considerable controversy as to the general approach companies should employ. One group, which favors the **discrete approach**, believes that companies should treat each interim period as a separate accounting period. Using that treatment, companies would follow the principles for deferrals and accruals used for annual reports. In this view, companies should report accounting transactions as they occur, and expense recognition should not change with the period of time covered.

Another group, which favors the **integral approach**, believes that the interim report is an integral part of the annual report and that deferrals and accruals should take into consideration what will happen for the entire year. In this approach, companies should assign estimated expenses to parts of a year on the basis of sales volume or some other activity base.

At present, many companies follow the discrete approach for certain types of expenses and the integral approach for others, because the standards currently employed in practice are vague and lead to differing interpretations.

Interim Reporting Requirements

Generally, companies should use the same accounting principles for interim reports and for annual reports. They should recognize revenues in interim periods on the same basis as they are for annual periods. For example, if Cedars Corp. uses the installment-sales method as the basis for recognizing revenue on an annual basis, then it should

[11]"Interim Financial Reporting," *Opinions of the Accounting Principles Board No. 28* (New York: AICPA, 1973).

use the installment basis for interim reports as well. Also, Cedars should treat costs directly associated with revenues (product costs, such as materials, labor and related fringe benefits, and manufacturing overhead) in the same manner for interim reports as for annual reports.

Companies should use the same inventory pricing methods (FIFO, LIFO, etc.) for interim reports and for annual reports. However, the following exceptions are appropriate at interim reporting periods.

1. Companies may use the gross profit method for interim inventory pricing. But they must disclose the method and adjustments to reconcile with annual inventory.
2. When a company liquidates LIFO inventories at an interim date and expects to replace them by year-end, cost of goods sold should include the expected cost of replacing the liquidated LIFO base, rather than give effect to the interim liquidation.
3. Companies should not defer inventory market declines beyond the interim period unless they are temporary and no loss is expected for the fiscal year.
4. Companies ordinarily should defer planned variances under a standard cost system; such variances are expected to be absorbed by year-end.

Companies often charge to the interim period, as incurred, costs and expenses other than product costs (often referred to as **period costs**). But companies may allocate these costs among interim periods on the basis of an estimate of time expired, benefit received, or activity associated with the periods. Companies display considerable latitude in accounting for these costs in interim periods, and many believe more definitive guidelines are needed.

Regarding disclosure, companies should report the following interim data at a minimum.

1. Sales or gross revenues, provision for income taxes, extraordinary items, and net income.
2. Basic and diluted earnings per share where appropriate.
3. Seasonal revenue, cost, or expenses.
4. Significant changes in estimates or provisions for income taxes.
5. Disposal of a component of a business and extraordinary, unusual, or infrequently occurring items.
6. Contingent items.
7. Changes in accounting principles or estimates.
8. Significant changes in financial position.

The FASB encourages, but does not require, companies to publish an interim balance sheet and statement of cash flows. If a company does not present this information, it should disclose significant changes in such items as liquid assets, net working capital, long-term liabilities, and stockholders' equity.

Unique Problems of Interim Reporting

In *APB Opinion No. 28*, the Board indicated that it favored the integral approach. However, within this broad guideline, a number of unique reporting problems develop related to the following items.

Advertising and Similar Costs. The general guidelines are that companies should defer in an interim period costs such as advertising if the benefits extend beyond that period; otherwise the company should expense those costs as incurred. But such a determination is difficult, and even if the company defers the costs, how should it allocate them between quarters?

Because of the vague guidelines in this area, accounting for advertising varies widely. At one time, some companies in the food industry, such as **RJR Nabisco** and **Pillsbury**, charged advertising costs as a percentage of sales and adjusted to actual at year-end, whereas **General Foods** and **Kellogg** expensed these costs as incurred.

The same type of problem relates to such items as Social Security taxes, research and development costs, and major repairs. For example, should the company expense Social Security costs (payroll taxes) on highly paid personnel early in the year, or allocate and spread them to subsequent quarters? Should a major repair that occurs later in the year be anticipated and allocated proportionately to earlier periods?

Expenses Subject to Year-End Adjustment. Companies often do not know with a great deal of certainty amounts of bad debts, executive bonuses, pension costs, and inventory shrinkage until year-end. **They should estimate these costs and allocate them to interim periods as best they can.** Companies use a variety of allocation techniques to accomplish this objective.

Income Taxes. Not every dollar of corporate taxable income is taxed at the same rate; the tax rate is progressive. This aspect of business income taxes poses a problem in preparing interim financial statements. Should the company use the **annualized approach**, which is to annualize income to date and accrue the proportionate income tax for the period to date? Or should it follow the **marginal principle approach,** which is to apply the lower rate of tax to the first amount of income earned? At one time, companies generally followed the latter approach and accrued the tax applicable to each additional dollar of income.

The profession now, however, uses the annualized approach. This requires that "at the end of each interim period the company should make its best estimate of the effective tax rate expected to be applicable for the full fiscal year. The rate so determined should be used in providing for income taxes on income for the quarter."[12]

Because businesses did not uniformly apply this guideline in accounting for similar situations, the FASB issued *Interpretation No. 18*. This interpretation requires that to compute the year-to-date tax, companies apply the **estimated annual effective tax rate** to the year-to-date "ordinary" income at the end of each interim period. Further, the **interim period tax** related to "ordinary" income shall be the difference between the amount so computed and the amounts reported for previous interim periods of the fiscal period.[13]

Extraordinary Items. Extraordinary items consist of unusual and nonrecurring material gains and losses. In the past, companies handled them in interim reports in one of three ways: (1) absorbed them entirely in the quarter in which they occurred; (2) prorated them over four quarters; or (3) disclosed them only by note. **The required approach now is to charge or credit the loss or gain in the quarter in which it occurs,** instead of attempting some arbitrary multiple-period allocation. This approach is consistent with the way in which companies must handle extraordinary items on an annual basis. No attempt is made to prorate the extraordinary items over several years.

Some favor the omission of extraordinary items from the quarterly net income. They believe that inclusion of extraordinary items that may be large in proportion to interim results distorts the predictive value of interim reports. Many, however, consider such an omission inappropriate because it deviates from actual results.

Earnings per Share. Interim reporting of earnings per share has all the problems inherent in computing and presenting annual earnings per share, and then some. If a company issues shares in the third period, EPS for the first two periods will not reflect

---

[12] "Interim Financial Reporting," *Opinions of the Accounting Principles Board No. 28* (New York: AICPA, 1973), par. 19. The estimated annual effective tax rate should reflect anticipated tax credits, foreign tax rates, percentage depletion, capital gains rates, and other available tax planning alternatives.

[13] "Accounting for Income Taxes in Interim Periods," *FASB Interpretation No. 18* (Stamford, Conn.: FASB, March 1977), par. 9. "Ordinary" income (or loss) refers to "income (or loss) from continuing operations before income taxes (or benefits)" excluding extraordinary items, discontinued operations, and cumulative effects of changes in accounting principles.

year-end EPS. If an extraordinary item is present in one period and the company sells new equity shares in another period, the EPS figure for the extraordinary item will change for the year. On an annual basis only one EPS figure can be associated with an extraordinary item and that figure does not change; the interim figure is subject to change.

For purposes of computing earnings per share and making the required disclosure determinations, each interim period should stand alone. That is, all applicable tests should be made for that single period.

Seasonality. **Seasonality** occurs when most of a company's sales occur in one short period of the year while certain costs are fairly evenly spread throughout the year. For example, the natural gas industry has its heavy sales in the winter months. In contrast, the beverage industry has its heavy sales in the summer months.

The problem of seasonality is related to the matching concept in accounting. Expenses should be matched against the revenues they create. In a seasonal business, wide fluctuations in profits occur because off-season sales do not absorb the company's fixed costs (for example, manufacturing, selling, and administrative costs that tend to remain fairly constant regardless of sales or production).

To illustrate why seasonality is a problem, assume the following information.

ILLUSTRATION 20-10
Data for Seasonality Example

Selling price per unit	$1
Annual sales for the period (projected and actual)	
100,000 units @ $1	$100,000
Manufacturing costs	
Variable	10¢ per unit
Fixed	20¢ per unit or $20,000 for the year
Nonmanufacturing costs	
Variable	10¢ per unit
Fixed	30¢ per unit or $30,000 for the year

Sales for four quarters and the year (projected and actual) were:

ILLUSTRATION 20-11
Sales Data for Seasonality Example

		Percent of Sales
1st Quarter	$ 20,000	20%
2nd Quarter	5,000	5
3rd Quarter	10,000	10
4th Quarter	65,000	65
Total for the year	$100,000	100%

Under the present accounting framework, the income statements for the quarters might be as shown in Illustration 20-12.

ILLUSTRATION 20-12
Interim Net Income for Seasonal Business—Discrete Approach

	1st Qtr	2nd Qtr	3rd Qtr	4th Qtr	Year
Sales	$20,000	$ 5,000	$10,000	$65,000	$100,000
Manufacturing costs					
Variable	(2,000)	(500)	(1,000)	(6,500)	(10,000)
Fixed[a]	(4,000)	(1,000)	(2,000)	(13,000)	(20,000)
	14,000	3,500	7,000	45,500	70,000
Nonmanufacturing costs					
Variable	(2,000)	(500)	(1,000)	(6,500)	(10,000)
Fixed[b]	(7,500)	(7,500)	(7,500)	(7,500)	(30,000)
Net income	$ 4,500	$(4,500)	$ (1,500)	$31,500	$ 30,000

[a]The fixed manufacturing costs are inventoried, so that equal amounts of fixed costs do not appear during each quarter.
[b]The fixed nonmanufacturing costs are not inventoried, so equal amounts of fixed costs appear during each quarter.

An investor who uses the first quarter's results might be misled. If the first quarter's earnings are $4,500, should this figure be multiplied by four to predict annual earnings of $18,000? Or, if first-quarter sales of $20,000 are 20 percent of the predicted sales for the year, would the net income for the year be $22,500 ($4,500 × 5)? Both figures are obviously wrong, and after the second quarter's results occur, the investor may become even more confused.

The problem with the conventional approach is that the fixed nonmanufacturing costs are not charged in proportion to sales. Some enterprises have adopted a way of avoiding this problem by making all fixed nonmanufacturing costs follow the sales pattern, as shown in Illustration 20-13.

ILLUSTRATION 20-13
Interim Net Income for Seasonal Business—Integral Approach

	1st Qtr	2nd Qtr	3rd Qtr	4th Qtr	Year
Sales	$20,000	$ 5,000	$10,000	$65,000	$100,000
Manufacturing costs					
Variable	(2,000)	(500)	(1,000)	(6,500)	(10,000)
Fixed	(4,000)	(1,000)	(2,000)	(13,000)	(20,000)
	14,000	3,500	7,000	45,500	70,000
Nonmanufacturing costs					
Variable	(2,000)	(500)	(1,000)	(6,500)	(10,000)
Fixed	(6,000)	(1,500)	(3,000)	(19,500)	(30,000)
Net income	$ 6,000	$ 1,500	$ 3,000	$19,500	$ 30,000

This approach solves some of the problems of interim reporting: Sales in the first quarter are 20 percent of total sales for the year, and net income in the first quarter is 20 percent of total income. In this case, as in the previous example, the investor cannot rely on multiplying any given quarter by four, but can use comparative data or rely on some estimate of sales in relation to income for a given period.

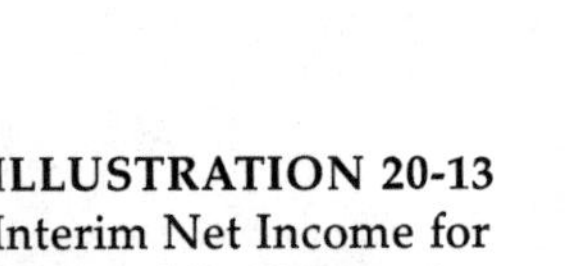

INTERNATIONAL INSIGHT

IFRS requires that interim financial statements use the discrete method, except for the tax expenses.

The greater the degree of seasonality experienced by a company, the greater the possibility of distortion. Because there are no definitive guidelines for handling such items as the fixed nonmanufacturing costs, variability in income can be substantial. To alleviate this problem, the profession recommends that companies subject to material seasonal variations disclose the seasonal nature of their business and consider supplementing their interim reports with information for 12-month periods ended at the interim date for the current and preceding years.

The two illustrations above highlight the difference between the **discrete** and **integral** approaches. Illustration 20-12 represents the discrete approach, in which the fixed nonmanufacturing expenses are expensed as incurred. Illustration 20-13 shows the integral approach, in which the manufacturing expenses are charged to expense on the basis of some measure of activity.

UNDERLYING CONCEPTS

The AICPA Special Committee on Financial Reporting indicates that users would benefit from separate fourth-quarter reporting, including management's analysis of fourth-quarter activities and events. Also, the Committee recommended quarterly segment reporting, which companies now provide under *FASB Statement No. 131.*

Continuing Controversy. The profession has developed some standards for interim reporting, but much still has to be done. As yet, it is unclear whether the discrete or the integral method, or some combination of the two, will be settled on.

Discussion also persists about the independent auditor's involvement in interim reports. Many auditors are reluctant to express an opinion on interim financial information, arguing that the data are too tentative and subjective. On the other hand, more people are advocating some examination of interim reports. A compromise may be a limited review of interim reports. Such a review would provide some assurance that an outside party has conducted an examination and that the published information appears to be in accord with generally accepted accounting principles.[14]

[14]The AICPA has been involved in developing guidelines for the review of interim reports. "Limited Review of Interim Financial Statements," *Statement on Auditing Standards No. 24* (New York: AICPA, 1979) sets standards for the review of interim reports.

Analysts and investors want financial information as soon as possible, before it's old news. We may not be far from a continuous database system in which corporate financial records can be accessed via the Internet. Investors might be able to access a company's financial records whenever they wish and put the information in the format they need. Thus, they could learn about sales slippage, cost increases, or earnings changes as they happen, rather than waiting until after the quarter has ended.[15]

A steady stream of information from the company to the investor could be very positive because it might alleviate management's continual concern with short-run interim numbers. Today many contend that U.S. management is too oriented to the short-term. The truth of this statement is echoed by the words of the president of a large company who decided to retire early: "I wanted to look forward to a year made up of four seasons rather than four quarters."

I WANT IT FASTER

WHAT DO THE NUMBERS MEAN?

The SEC has decided that timeliness of information is of extreme importance. First, the SEC has said that large public companies will have only 60 days to complete their annual reports, down from 90 days. Quarterly reports must be done within 40 days of the close of the quarter, instead of 45. In addition, corporate executives and shareholders with more than 10 percent of a company's outstanding stock now have two days to disclose their sale or purchase of stock.

Also, in a bid to increase Internet disclosure, the SEC encourages companies to post current, quarterly, and annual reports on their websites—or explain why they don't. The Internet postings would have to be made by the day the company submits the information to the SEC, rather than within 24 hours as current rules allow.

AUDITOR'S AND MANAGEMENT'S REPORTS

Auditor's Report

OBJECTIVE 5
Identify the major disclosures in the auditor's report.

Another important source of information, which is often overlooked, is the **auditor's report**. An **auditor** is an accounting professional who conducts an independent examination of a company's accounting data.

If satisfied that the financial statements present the financial position, results of operations, and cash flows fairly in accordance with generally accepted accounting principles, the auditor expresses an **unqualified opinion**. An example is shown in Illustration 20-14.[16]

In preparing the report, the auditor follows these reporting standards.

1. The report states whether the financial statements are in accordance with generally accepted accounting principles.
2. The report identifies those circumstances in which the company has not consistently observed such principles in the current period in relation to the preceding period.

[15]A step in this direction is the SEC's mandate for companies to file their financial statements electronically with the SEC. The system, called EDGAR (electronic data gathering and retrieval) provides interested parties with computer access to financial information such as periodic filings, corporate prospectuses, and proxy materials.

[16]This auditor's report is in exact conformance with the specifications contained in "Reports on Audited Financial Statements," *Statement on Auditing Standards No. 58* (New York: AICPA, 1988). The last paragraph refers to the assessment of the company's internal controls, as required by the PCAOB.

3 Users are to regard the informative disclosures in the financial statements as reasonably adequate unless the report states otherwise.

4 The report contains either an expression of opinion regarding the financial statements taken as a whole or an assertion to the effect that an opinion cannot be expressed. When the auditor cannot express an overall opinion, the report should state the reasons. In all cases where an auditor's name is associated with financial statements, the report should contain a clear-cut indication of the character of the auditor's examination, if any, and the degree of responsibility being taken.

ILLUSTRATION 20-14
Auditor's Report

Best Buy Co., Inc.

Report of Independent Registered Public Accounting Firm on Consolidated Financial Statements

Shareholders and Board of Directors

We have audited the accompanying consolidated balance sheets of Best Buy Co., Inc. and subsidiaries as of February 26, 2005, and February 28, 2004, and the related consolidated statements of earnings, changes in shareholders' equity, and cash flows for each of the three years in the period ended February 26, 2005. Our audits also included the financial statement schedule listed in Item 15(a). These financial statements and schedule are the responsibility of the Company's management. Our responsibility is to express an opinion on these financial statements and schedule based on our audits.

We conducted our audits in accordance with the standards of the Public Company Accounting Oversight Board (United States). Those standards require that we plan and perform the audit to obtain reasonable assurance about whether the financial statements are free of material misstatement. An audit includes examining, on a test basis, evidence supporting the amounts and disclosures in the financial statements. An audit also includes assessing the accounting principles used and significant estimates made by management, as well as evaluating the overall financial statement presentation. We believe that our audits provide a reasonable basis for our opinion.

In our opinion, the financial statements referred to above present fairly, in all material respects, the consolidated financial position of Best Buy Co., Inc. and subsidiaries of February 26, 2005, and February 28, 2004, and the consolidated results of their operations and their cash flows for each of the three years in the period ended February 26, 2005, in conformity with U.S. generally accepted accounting principles. Also, in our opinion, the related financial statement schedule, when considered in relation to the basic financial statements taken as a whole, presents fairly, in all material respects, the information set forth therein.

As discussed in Note 5 to the financial statements, effective February 26, 2005, Best Buy Co., Inc. and subsidiaries adopted EITF Issue No. 04-08, "The Effect of Contingently Convertible Instruments on Diluted Earnings per Share," and restated earnings per share for all prior periods.

We also have audited, in accordance with the standards of the Public Company Accounting Oversight Board (United States), the effectiveness of the Best Buy Co., Inc. and subsidiaries' internal control over financial reporting as of February 26, 2005, based on the criteria established in Internal Control — Integrated Framework issued by the Committee of Sponsoring Organizations of the Treadway Commission and our report dated May 5, 2005 expressed an unqualified opinion thereon.

Ernst + Young LLP

Minneapolis, Minnesota
May 5, 2005

In most cases, the auditor issues a standard **unqualified** or **clean opinion**. That is, the auditor expresses the opinion that the financial statements present fairly, in all material respects, the financial position, results of operations, and cash flows of the entity in conformity with generally accepted accounting principles.

Certain circumstances, although they do not affect the auditor's unqualified opinion, may require the auditor to add an explanatory paragraph to the audit report. Some of the more important circumstances are as follows.

1. *Uncertainties.* A matter involving an **uncertainty** is one that is expected to be resolved at a future date, at which time sufficient evidence concerning its outcome is expected to be available. In deciding whether an explanatory paragraph is needed, the auditor should consider the likelihood of a material loss resulting from the contingency. If, for example, the possibility that a loss due to the uncertainty is remote, then an explanatory paragraph is not warranted. If the loss is probable but not estimable, or is reasonably possible and material, then an explanatory paragraph is warranted.
2. *Lack of Consistency.* If a company has changed accounting principles or the method of their application in a way that has a material effect on the comparability of its financial statements, the auditor should refer to the change in an explanatory paragraph of the report. Such an explanatory paragraph should identify the nature of the change and refer readers to the note in the financial statements that discusses the change in detail. The auditor's concurrence with a change is implicit unless the auditor takes exception to the change in expressing an opinion as to fair presentation in conformity with generally accepted accounting principles.
3. *Emphasis of a Matter.* The auditor may wish to emphasize a matter regarding the financial statements, but nevertheless intends to express an unqualified opinion. For example, the auditor may wish to emphasize that the entity is a component of a larger business enterprise or that it has had significant transactions with related parties. The auditor presents such explanatory information in a separate paragraph of the report.

In some situations, however, the auditor is required to express (1) a **qualified** opinion or (2) an **adverse** opinion, or (3) to **disclaim** an opinion.

A **qualified opinion** contains an exception to the standard opinion. Ordinarily the exception is not of sufficient magnitude to invalidate the statements as a whole; if it were, an adverse opinion would be rendered. The usual circumstances in which the auditor may deviate from the standard unqualified short-form report on financial statements are as follows.

1. The scope of the examination is limited or affected by conditions or restrictions.
2. The statements do not fairly present financial position or results of operations because of:
   (a) Lack of conformity with generally accepted accounting principles and standards.
   (b) Inadequate disclosure.

If confronted with one of the situations noted above, the auditor must offer a qualified opinion. A qualified opinion states that, except for the effects of the matter to which the qualification relates, the financial statements present fairly, in all material respects, the financial position, results of operations, and cash flows in conformity with generally accepted accounting principles.

Illustration 20-15 shows an example of an auditor's report with a qualified opinion. The auditor qualified the opinion because the company used an accounting principle at variance with generally accepted accounting principles.

An **adverse opinion** is required in any report in which the exceptions to fair presentation are so material that in the independent auditor's judgment, a qualified opinion is not justified. In such a case, the financial statements taken as a whole are not presented in accordance with generally accepted accounting principles. Adverse opinions are rare, because most companies change their accounting to conform with GAAP. The SEC will not permit a company listed on an exchange to have an adverse opinion.

A **disclaimer of an opinion** is appropriate when the auditor has gathered so little information on the financial statements that no opinion can be expressed.

The profession also requires the auditor to evaluate whether there is substantial doubt about the entity's **ability to continue as a going concern** for a reasonable period of time. (This period is not to exceed one year beyond the date of the financial statements.) If substantial doubt exists about the company continuing as a going

ILLUSTRATION 20-15
Qualified Auditor's Report

Helio Company

Independent Auditor's Report

(Same first and second paragraphs as the standard report)

Helio Company has excluded, from property and debt in the accompanying balance sheets, certain lease obligations that, in our opinion, should be capitalized in order to conform with generally accepted accounting principles. If these lease obligations were capitalized, property would be increased by $1,500,000 and $1,300,000, long-term debt by $1,400,000 and $1,200,000, and retained earnings by $100,000 and $50,000 as of December 31, in the current and prior year, respectively. Additionally, net income would be decreased by $40,000 and $30,000 and earnings per share would be decreased by $.06 and $.04, respectively, for the years then ended.

In our opinion, except for the effects of not capitalizing certain lease obligations as discussed in the preceding paragraph, the financial statements referred to above present fairly, in all material respects, the financial position of Helio Company, and the results of its operations and its cash flows for the years then ended in conformity with generally accepted accounting principles.

concern, the auditor adds to the report an explanatory note describing the potential problem.[17]

The audit report should provide useful information to the investor. One investment banker noted, "Probably the first item to check is the auditor's opinion to see whether or not it is a clean one—'in conformity with generally accepted accounting principles'—or is qualified in regard to differences between the auditor and company management in the accounting treatment of some major item, or in the outcome of some major litigation."

Management's Reports

Management's Discussion and Analysis

The SEC mandates inclusion of **management's discussion and analysis (MD&A)**. This section covers three financial aspects of an enterprise's business—liquidity, capital resources, and results of operations. In it, management highlights favorable or unfavorable trends and identifies significant events and uncertainties that affect these three factors. This approach obviously involves subjective estimates, opinions, and soft data. However, the SEC believes that the relevance of this information exceeds the potential lack of reliability.

Illustration 20-16 presents an excerpt from the MD&A section (2004 "Business Risks" only) of **PepsiCo**'s annual report.

ILLUSTRATION 20-16
Management's Discussion and Analysis

PEPSICO

PepsiCo, Inc.

Our Business Risks
We are subject to risks in the normal course of business. We manage our risks through an integrated risk management framework.

Our Reputation
We have a longstanding history of maintaining a good reputation globally which is critical to selling our branded products. If we fail to maintain high standards for product quality and integrity, our reputation could be jeopardized. In addition, we must protect our reputation by maintaining high ethical, social and environmental standards for all of our operations and activities. Damage to our reputation might result in rejection of our products by consumers and a loss of brand equity, as well as require additional resources to rebuild our reputation.

[17]"The Auditor's Consideration of an Entity's Ability to Continue as a Going Concern," *Statement on Auditing Standards No. 59* (New York: AICPA, 1988).

Information Technology
Information technology is becoming increasingly important as an enabler to operating efficiently and interfacing with customers, as well as maintaining financial accuracy and efficiency. If we do not allocate, and effectively manage, the resources necessary to build and sustain the proper technology infrastructure, we could be subject to transaction errors, processing inefficiencies, the loss of customers, business disruptions, or the loss of or damage to intellectual property through security breach.

Product Demand and Retail Consolidation
We are a consumer products company operating in highly competitive markets and rely on continued demand for our products. To generate revenues and profits, we must sell products that appeal to our customers and to consumers. As our chairman notes, our continued success is dependent on our product innovation, including maintaining a strong pipeline of new products, effective sales incentives, appropriate advertising campaigns and marketing programs, and the ability to secure adequate shelf space at our retailers. In addition, our success depends on our responses to consumer trends, such as low carbohydrate diets, consumer health concerns, including obesity and the consumption of certain ingredients, and changes in product category consumption and consumer demographics, including the aging of the general population. Seasonal weather conditions, particularly for sports drinks and hot cereals, can also impact demand. Our top five retail customers now represent approximately 27% of our North American net revenue reflecting the continuing consolidation of the retail trade.

Global Economic and Environmental Conditions
Unforeseen global economic and environmental changes and political unrest may result in business interruption, supply constraints, foreign currency devaluation, inflation, deflation or decreased demand. Economic conditions in North America could also adversely impact growth. For example, rising fuel costs may impact the sales of our products in convenience stores where our products are generally sold in higher margin single serve packages.

Regulatory Environment
Changes in laws, regulations and the related interpretations may alter the environment in which we do business and, therefore, impact our results or increase our liabilities. Such regulatory environment changes include changes in food and drug laws, laws related to advertising and deceptive marketing practices, accounting standards, taxation requirements, competition laws and environmental laws, including the regulation of water consumption and treatment.

Workforce Retention
Our continued growth requires us to develop our leadership bench and to implement programs, such as our long-term incentive program, designed to retain talent. We also compete to hire new employees, and then must train them and develop their skills and competencies. We have in place human resource programs, including our diversity and inclusion focus mentioned by our chairman, aimed at hiring, developing and retaining our talented and motivated workforce which provides us with competitive advantage. However, unplanned turnover could deplete our institutional knowledge base and erode our competitive advantage.

Market Risks
We are exposed to the market risks arising from adverse changes in:
- commodity prices, affecting the cost of our raw materials and energy;
- foreign exchange rates;
- Interest rates;
- stock prices; and
- discount rates, affecting the measurement of our pension and retiree medical liabilities.

UNDERLYING CONCEPTS

FASB Concepts Statement No. 1 notes that management knows more about the company than users and therefore can increase the usefulness of financial information by identifying significant transactions that affect the company and by explaining their financial impact.

The MD&A section also must provide information about the effects of inflation and changing prices, if they are material to financial statement trends. The SEC has not required specific numerical computations, and companies have provided little analysis on changing prices.

Expanded Discussion of Accounting for Changing Prices

An additional voluntary disclosure provided in the MD&A of many companies is discussion of the company's critical accounting policies. This disclosure identifies accounting policies that require management to make subjective judgments regarding uncertainties, resulting in potentially significant effects on the financial results.[18] For

[18]See *Cautionary Advice Regarding Disclosure about Critical Accounting Policies,* Release Nos. 33-8040; 34-45149; FR-60 (Washington, D.C.: SEC); and *Proposed Rule: Disclosure in Management's Discussion and Analysis about the Application of Critical Accounting Policies,* Release Nos. 33-8098; 34-45907; International Series Release No. 1258; File No. S7-16-02 (Washington, D.C.: SEC).

example, in its critical accounting policy disclosure, **PepsiCo** showed the impact on stock-based compensation expense in response to changes in estimated interest rates and stock return volatility. Through this voluntary disclosure, companies can expand on the information contained in the notes to the financial statements to indicate the sensitivity of the financial results to accounting policy judgments.

OBJECTIVE 6
Understand management's responsibilities for financials.

Management's Responsibilities for Financial Statements

The Sarbanes-Oxley Act requires the SEC to develop guidelines for *all* publicly traded companies to report on management's responsibilities for, and assessment of, the internal control system. An example of the type of disclosure that public companies are now making is shown in Illustration 20-17.[19]

ILLUSTRATION 20-17
Report on Management's Responsibilities

Home Depot

Management's Responsibility for Financial Statements

The financial statements presented in this Annual Report have been prepared with integrity and objectivity and are the responsibility of the management of The Home Depot, Inc. These financial statements have been prepared in conformity with U.S. generally accepted accounting principles and properly reflect certain estimates and judgments based upon the best available information.

The financial statements of the Company have been audited by KPMG LLP, an independent registered public accounting firm. Their accompanying report is based upon an audit conducted in accordance with the standards of the Public Company Accounting Oversight Board (United States).

The Audit Committee of the Board of Directors, consisting solely of outside directors, meets five times a year with the independent registered public accounting firm, the internal auditors and representatives of management to discuss auditing and financial reporting matters. In addition, a telephonic meeting is held prior to each quarterly earnings release. The Audit Committee retains the independent registered public accounting firm and regularly reviews the internal accounting controls, the activities of the independent registered public accounting firm and internal auditors and the financial condition of the Company. Both the Company's independent registered public accounting firm and the internal auditors have free access to the Audit Committee.

Management's Report on Internal Control over Financial Reporting

Our management is responsible for establishing and maintaining adequate internal control over financial reporting, as such term is defined in Exchange Act Rules 13a–15(f). Under the supervision and with the participation of our management, including our principal executive officer and principal financial officer, we conducted an evaluation of the effectiveness of our internal control over financial reporting based on the framework in *Internal Control-Integrated Framework* issued by the Committee of Sponsoring Organizations of the Treadway Commission (COSO). Based on our evaluation, our management concluded that our internal control over financial reporting was effective as of January 30, 2005. Our management's assessment of the effectiveness of our internal control over financial reporting as of January 30, 2005 has been audited by KPMG LLP, an independent registered public accounting firm, as stated in its report which is included herein.

Robert L. Nardelli
Chairman, President &
Chief Executive Officer

Carol B. Tomé
Executive Vice President &
Chief Financial Officer

Kelly H. Barrett
Vice President
Corporate Controller

[19] As indicated in this disclosure, management is responsible for preparing the financial statements and establishing and maintaining an effective system of internal controls. The auditor provides an independent assessment of whether the financial statements are prepared in accordance with GAAP, and for public companies, whether the internal controls are effective (see the audit opinion in Illustration 20-14.)

CURRENT REPORTING ISSUES

Reporting on Financial Forecasts and Projections

In recent years, the investing public's demand for more and better information has focused on disclosure of corporate expectations for the future.[20] These disclosures take one of two forms:[21]

OBJECTIVE 7
Identify issues related to financial forecasts and projections.

Financial forecasts. A **financial forecast** is a set of prospective financial statements that present, to the best of the responsible party's knowledge and belief, a company's expected financial position, results of operations, and cash flows. The responsible party bases a financial forecast on conditions it expects to exist and the course of action it expects to take.

Financial projections. **Financial projections** are prospective financial statements that present, to the best of the responsible party's knowledge and belief, given one or more *hypothetical assumptions*, an entity's expected financial position, results of operations, and cash flows. The responsible party bases a financial projection on conditions it expects *would* exist and the course of action it expects *would* be taken, given one or more hypothetical assumptions.

The difference between a financial forecast and a financial projection is clearcut: A forecast provides information on what is **expected** to happen, whereas a projection provides information on what **might** take place, but is not necessarily expected to happen.

Whether companies should be required to provide financial forecasts is the subject of intensive discussion with journalists, corporate executives, the SEC, financial analysts, accountants, and others. Predictably, there are strong arguments on either side. Listed below are some of the arguments.

Arguments for requiring published forecasts:

1 Investment decisions are based on future expectations. Therefore information about the future facilitates better decisions.

2 Companies already circulate forecasts informally. This situation should be regulated to ensure that the forecasts are available to all investors.

3 Circumstances now change so rapidly that historical information is no longer adequate for prediction.

Arguments against requiring published forecasts:

1 No one can foretell the future. Therefore forecasts will inevitably be wrong. Worse, they may mislead, if they convey an impression of precision about the future,.

2 Companies may strive only to meet their published forecasts, thereby failing to produce results that are in the stockholders' best interest.

3 If forecasts prove inaccurate, there will be recriminations and probably legal actions.[22]

[20]Some areas in which companies are using financial information about the future are equipment lease-versus-buy analysis, analysis of a company's ability to successfully enter new markets, and examination of merger and acquisition opportunities. In addition, companies also prepare forecasts and projections for use by third parties in public offering documents (requiring financial forecasts), tax-oriented investments, and financial feasibility studies. Use of forward-looking data has been enhanced by the increased capability of microcomputers to analyze, compare, and manipulate large quantities of data.

[21]"Guide for Prospective Financial Information," *Audit and Accounting Guide* (New York: AICPA, May 1999), pars. 3.04 and 3.05.

[22]The issue is serious. Over a recent three-year period, 8 percent of the companies on the NYSE were sued because of an alleged lack of financial disclosure. Companies complain that they are subject to lawsuits whenever the stock price drops. And as one executive noted, "You can even be sued if the stock price goes up—because you did not disclose the good news fast enough."

4 Disclosure of forecasts will be detrimental to organizations, because forecasts will inform competitors (foreign and domestic), as well as investors.

UNDERLYING CONCEPTS

The AICPA's Special Committee on Financial Reporting indicates that the legal environment discourages companies from disclosing forward-looking information. Companies should not have to expand reporting of forward-looking information unless there are more effective deterrents to unwarranted litigation.

The AICPA has issued a statement on standards for accountants' services on prospective financial information. This statement establishes guidelines for the preparation and presentation of financial forecasts and projections.[23] It requires accountants to provide (1) a summary of significant assumptions used in the forecast or projection and (2) guidelines for minimum presentation.

To encourage management to disclose prospective financial information, the SEC has a **safe harbor rule**. It provides protection to a company that presents an erroneous forecast, as long as the company prepared the forecast on a reasonable basis and disclosed it in good faith.[24] However, many companies note that the safe harbor rule does not work in practice, since it does not cover oral statements, nor has it kept them from investor lawsuits.

Experience in Great Britain

Great Britain has permitted financial forecasts for years, and the results have been fairly successful. Some significant differences do exist between the English and the U.S. business and legal environments.[25] But such differences probably could be overcome if influential interests in this country cooperated to produce an atmosphere conducive to quality forecasting. A typical British forecast adapted from a construction company's report to support a public offering of stock is as follows.

ILLUSTRATION 20-18
Financial Forecast of a British Company

> Profits have grown substantially over the past 10 years and directors are confident of being able to continue this expansion. . . . While the rate of expansion will be dependent on the level of economic activity in Ireland and England, the group is well structured to avail itself of opportunities as they arise, particularly in the field of property development, which is expected to play an increasingly important role in the group's future expansion.
>
> Profits before taxation for the half year ended 30th June were 402,000 pounds. On the basis of trading experiences since that date and the present level of sales and completions, the directors expect that in the absence of unforeseen circumstances, the group's profits before taxation for the year to 31st December will be not less than 960,000 pounds.
>
> No dividends will be paid in respect of the current year. In a full financial year, on the basis of above forecasts (not including full year profits) it would be the intention of the board, assuming current rates of tax, to recommend dividends totaling 40% (of after-tax profits), which will be payable in the next two years.

A general narrative-type forecast issued by a U.S. corporation might appear as follows.

ILLUSTRATION 20-19
Financial Forecast for an American Company

> On the basis of promotions planned by the company for the second half of the fiscal year, net earnings for that period are expected to be approximately the same as those for the first half of the fiscal year, with net earnings for the third quarter expected to make the predominant contribution to net earnings for the second half of the year.

[23] "Guide for Prospective Financial Information," op. cit., par. 1.02.

[24] "Safe-Harbor Rule for Projections," *Release No. 5993* (Washington: SEC, 1979). The Private Securities Litigation Reform Act of 1995 recognizes that some information that is useful to investors is inherently subject to less certainty or reliability than other information. By providing safe harbor for forward-looking statements, Congress has sought to facilitate access to this information by investors.

[25] The British system, for example, does not permit litigation on forecasted information, and the solicitor (lawyer) is not permitted to work on a contingent fee basis. See "A Case for Forecasting—The British Have Tried It and Find That It Works," *World* (New York: Peat, Marwick, Mitchell & Co., Autumn 1978), pp. 10–13.

Questions of Liability

What happens if a company does not meet its forecasts? Can the company and the auditor be sued? If a company, for example, projects an earnings increase of 15 percent and achieves only 5 percent, should stockholders be permitted to have some judicial recourse against the company?

One court case involving **Monsanto Chemical Corporation** has set a precedent. In this case, Monsanto predicted that sales would increase 8 to 9 percent and that earnings would rise 4 to 5 percent. In the last part of the year, the demand for Monsanto's products dropped as a result of a business turndown. Instead of increasing, the company's earnings declined. Investors sued the company because the projected earnings figure was erroneous, but a judge dismissed the suit because the forecasts were the best estimates of qualified people whose intents were honest.

As indicated earlier, the SEC's safe harbor rules are intended to protect companies that provide good-faith projections. However, much concern exists as to how the SEC and the courts will interpret such terms as "good faith" and "reasonable assumptions" when erroneous forecasts mislead users of this information.

Internet Financial Reporting

Most companies now use the power and reach of the Internet to provide more useful information to financial statement readers. All large companies have Internet sites, and a large proportion of companies' websites contain links to their financial statements and other disclosures. The popularity of such reporting is not surprising, since companies can reduce the costs of printing and disseminating paper reports with the use of Internet reporting.

Does Internet financial reporting improve the usefulness of a company's financial reports? Yes, in several ways: First, dissemination of reports via the Web allows firms **to communicate more easily and quickly with users** than do traditional paper reports. In addition, **Internet reporting allows users to take advantage of tools** such as search engines and hyperlinks to quickly find information about the firm and, sometimes, to download the information for analysis, perhaps in computer spreadsheets. Finally, **Internet reporting can help make financial reports more relevant** by allowing companies to report expanded disaggregated data and more timely data than is possible through paper-based reporting. For example, some companies voluntarily report weekly sales data and segment operating data on their websites.

While there continue to be concerns about **equality of access** to electronic financial reporting as well as the **reliability** of the information distributed via the Internet, organizations are developing new technologies and standards to further enable Internet financial reporting. An example is increasing use of extensible business reporting language (XBRL). **XBRL** is a computer language adapted from the code of the Internet. The language "tags" accounting data to correspond to financial reporting items, which are reported in the balance sheet, income statement, and the cash flow statement. Once tagged, any company's XBRL data can be easily processed using spreadsheets and other computer programs. Users can more easily search a company's reports, extract and analyze data, and perform financial comparisons within industries. As more financial statement users get on the Web, armed with tools like XBRL, we expect Internet reporting to continue to grow in popularity.[26]

[26]Reuters, "Lifting the Lid: Tech Seen Easing Financial Analysis," *nytimes.com* (January 22, 2005). See *www.xbrl.org/us/us/BusinessCaseForXBRL.pdf* for additional information on XBRL. The FASB has issued a report on electronic dissemination of financial reports. This report summarizes current practice and research conducted on Internet financial reporting. See Business Reporting Research Project, "Electronic Distribution of Business Reporting Information" (Norwalk, Conn.: FASB, 2000).

Fraudulent Financial Reporting

OBJECTIVE 8
Describe the profession's response to fraudulent financial reporting.

Fraudulent financial reporting is defined as "intentional or reckless conduct, whether act or omission, that results in materially misleading financial statements."[27] Fraudulent reporting can involve gross and deliberate distortion of corporate records (such as inventory count tags), or misapplication of accounting principles (failure to disclose material transactions). Although frauds are unusual, recent events involving such well-known companies as **Enron**, **WorldCom**, **Adelphia**, and **Tyco** indicate that more must be done to address this issue.

HERE'S A FRAUD

WHAT DO THE NUMBERS MEAN?

The case of **ESM Government Securities, Inc. (ESM)** exemplifies the seriousness of financial reporting frauds. ESM was a Fort Lauderdale securities dealer entrusted with monies to invest by municipalities from Toledo, Ohio to Beaumont, Texas. The cities that provided funds thought, based on the company name, that ESM was collateralized with government securities.

Examination of ESM's balance sheet indicated that the company owed about as much as it expected to collect. Unfortunately, the amount it expected to collect was from insolvent affiliates which, in effect, meant that ESM was bankrupt. In fact, ESM had been bankrupt for more than six years, and the fraud was discovered only because a customer questioned a note to the balance sheet! ESM had disguised more than $300 million of losses.

Source: For an expanded discussion of this case, see Robert J. Sack and Robert Tangreti, "ESM: Implications for the Profession," *Journal of Accountancy* (April 1987).

Causes of Fraudulent Financial Reporting

Fraudulent financial reporting usually occurs because of conditions in a company's internal or external environment.[28] Influences in the **internal environment** relate to poor internal control systems, management's poor attitude toward ethics, or perhaps a company's liquidity or profitability. Those in the **external environment** may relate to industry conditions, overall business environment, or legal and regulatory considerations.

General incentives for fraudulent financial reporting vary. Common ones are the desire to obtain a higher stock price, to avoid default on a loan covenant, or to make a personal gain of some type (additional compensation, promotion). Situational pressures on the company or an individual manager also may lead to fraudulent financial reporting. Examples of these situational pressures include the following.

- ***Sudden decreases in revenue or market share*** for a single company or an entire industry.
- ***Unrealistic budget pressures*** may occur when headquarters arbitrarily determines profit objectives (particularly for short-term results) and budgets without taking actual conditions into account.
- ***Financial pressure resulting from bonus plans*** that depend on short-term economic performance. This pressure is particularly acute when the bonus is a significant component of the individual's total compensation.

[27]"Report of the National Commission on Fraudulent Financial Reporting" (Washington, D.C., 1987), page 2. Unintentional errors as well as corporate improprieties (such as tax fraud, employee embezzlements, and so on) which do not cause the financial statements to be misleading are excluded from the definition of fraudulent financial reporting.

[28]The discussion in this section is based on the Report of the National Commission on Fraudulent Financial Reporting, pp. 23–24. See "2004 Report to the Nation on Occupational Fraud and Abuse, Association of Certified Fraud Examiners," (*www.cfenet.com/pdfs/2004RttN.pdf*) for evidence that fraudulent financial reporting causes and consequences are much the same today.

Opportunities for fraudulent financial reporting are present in circumstances when the fraud is easy to commit and when detection is difficult. Frequently these opportunities arise from:

1 ***The absence of a board of directors or audit committee*** that vigilantly oversees the financial reporting process.

2 ***Weak or nonexistent internal accounting controls.*** This situation can occur, for example, when a company's revenue system is overloaded as a result of a rapid expansion of sales, an acquisition of a new division, or the entry into a new, unfamiliar line of business.

3 ***Unusual or complex transactions*** such as the consolidation of two companies, the divestiture or closing of a specific operation, and the purchase and sale of derivative instruments.

4 ***Accounting estimates requiring significant subjective judgment*** by company management, such as the allowance for loan losses and the estimated liability for warranty expense.

5 ***Ineffective internal audit staffs*** resulting from inadequate staff size and severely limited audit scope.

A weak corporate ethical climate contributes to these situations. Opportunities for fraudulent financial reporting also increase dramatically when the accounting principles followed in reporting transactions are nonexistent, evolving, or subject to varying interpretations.

The AICPA has issued numerous auditing standards in response to concerns of the accounting profession, the media, and the public.[29] For example, the most recent standard on fraudulent financial reporting "raises the bar" on the performance of financial statement audits by explicitly requiring auditors to assess the risk of material financial misstatement due to fraud.[30] As indicated earlier, the Sarbanes-Oxley Act now raises the penalty substantially for executives who are involved in fraudulent financial reporting.

Criteria for Making Accounting and Reporting Choices

Throughout this textbook, we have stressed the need to provide information that is useful to predict the amounts, timing, and uncertainty of future cash flows. To achieve this objective, companies must make judicious choices between alternative accounting concepts, methods, and means of disclosure. You are probably surprised by the large number of choices that exist among acceptable alternatives.

You should recognize, however, as indicated in Chapter 1, that accounting is greatly influenced by its environment. It does not exist in a vacuum. Therefore, it is unrealistic to assume that the profession can entirely eliminate alternative presentations of certain transactions and events. Nevertheless, we are hopeful that the profession, by adhering to the conceptual framework, will be able to focus on the needs of financial statement users and eliminate diversity where appropriate. The SEC's and FASB's projects on principle-based standards are directed at these very issues. They seek to develop standards and implementation guidance that will result in accounting and financial reporting that reflects the economic substance of the transactions, not the desired financial result of management. The profession must continue its efforts to develop a sound foundation upon which to build financial standards and practice. As Aristotle said, "The correct beginning is more than half the whole."

UNDERLYING CONCEPTS

The FASB concept statements on objectives of financial reporting, elements of financial statements, qualitative characteristics of accounting information, and recognition and measurement are important steps in the right direction.

[29]Because the profession believes that the role of the auditor is not well understood outside the profession, much attention has been focused on the expectation gap. The **expectation gap** is the gap between (1) the expectation of financial statement users concerning the level of assurance they believe the independent auditor provides, and (2) the assurance that the independent auditor actually does provide under generally accepted auditing standards.

[30]"Consideration of Fraud in a Financial Statement Audit," *Statement on Auditing Standards No. 99* (New York: AICPA, 2002).

QUESTIONS

1. What are the major advantages of notes to the financial statements? What types of items are usually reported in notes?

2. What is the full disclosure principle in accounting? Why has disclosure increased substantially in the last 10 years?

3. The FASB requires a reconciliation between the effective tax rate and the federal government's statutory rate. Of what benefit is such a disclosure requirement?

4. What type of disclosure or accounting do you believe is necessary for the following items?

(a) Because of a general increase in the number of labor disputes and strikes, both within and outside the industry, there is an increased likelihood that a company will suffer a costly strike in the near future.

(b) A company reports an extraordinary item (net of tax) correctly on the income statement. No other mention is made of this item in the annual report.

(c) A company expects to recover a substantial amount in connection with a pending refund claim for a prior year's taxes. Although the claim is being contested, counsel for the company has confirmed the client's expectation of recovery.

5. The following information was described in a note of Cebar Packing Co.

"During August, A. Belew Products Corporation purchased 311,003 shares of the Company's common stock which constitutes approximately 35% of the stock outstanding. A. Belew has since obtained representation on the Board of Directors."

"An affiliate of A. Belew Products Corporation acts as a food broker for Cedar Packing in the greater New York City marketing area. The commissions for such services after August amounted to approximately $20,000."

Why is this information disclosed?

6. What are the major types of subsequent events? Indicate how each of the following "subsequent events" would be reported.

(a) Collection of a note written off in a prior period.

(b) Issuance of a large preferred stock offering.

(c) Acquisition of a company in a different industry.

(d) Destruction of a major plant in a flood.

(e) Death of the company's chief executive officer (CEO).

(f) Additional wage costs associated with settlement of a four-week strike.

(g) Settlement of a federal income tax case at considerably more tax than anticipated at year-end.

(h) Change in the product mix from consumer goods to industrial goods.

7. What are diversified companies? What accounting problems are related to diversified companies?

8. What quantitative materiality test is applied to determine whether a segment is significant enough to warrant separate disclosure?

9. Identify the segment information that is required to be disclosed by *FASB Statement No. 131*.

10. What is an operating segment, and when can information about two operating segments be aggregated?

11. The controller for Chang Lee Inc. recently commented, "If I have to disclose our segments individually, the only people who will gain are our competitors and the only people that will lose are our present stockholders." Evaluate this comment.

12. An article in the financial press entitled "Important Information in Annual Reports This Year" noted that annual reports include a management discussion and analysis section. What would this section contain?

13. "The financial statements of a company are management's, not the accountant's." Discuss the implications of this statement.

14. Olga Conrad, a financial writer, noted recently, "There are substantial arguments for including earnings projections in annual reports and the like. The most compelling is that it would give anyone interested something now available to only a relatively select few—like large stockholders, creditors, and attentive bartenders." Identify some arguments against providing earnings projections.

15. The following comment appeared in the financial press: "Inadequate financial disclosure, particularly with respect to how management views the future and its role in the marketplace, has always been a stone in the shoe. After all, if you don't know how a company views the future, how can you judge the worth of its corporate strategy?" What are some arguments for reporting earnings forecasts?

16. What are interim reports? Why are balance sheets often not provided with interim data?

17. What are the accounting problems related to the presentation of interim data?

18. Mysteries Inc., a closely held corporation, has decided to go public. The controller, C. Keene, is concerned with presenting interim data when a LIFO inventory valuation is used. What problems are encountered with LIFO inventories when quarterly data are presented?

19. What approaches have been suggested to overcome the seasonality problem related to interim reporting?

20. What is the difference between a CPA's unqualified opinion or "clean" opinion and a qualified one?

21. Mary Beidler and Lee Pannebecker are discussing the recent fraud that occurred at LowRental Leasing, Inc. The fraud involved the improper reporting of revenue to ensure that the company would have income in excess of $1 million. What is fraudulent financial reporting, and how does it differ from an embezzlement of company funds?

图书在版编目（CIP）数据

中级会计学：第12版/基索等著；饶菁，崔学刚改编
北京：中国人民大学出版社，2007
（工商管理经典教材·会计与财务系列）
教育部高校工商管理类教学指导委员会双语教学推荐教材
ISBN 978-7-300-07949-3

Ⅰ. 中…
Ⅱ. ①基… ②饶… ③崔…
Ⅲ. 会计学-双语教学-高等学校-教材
Ⅳ. F230

中国版本图书馆CIP数据核字（2007）第032161号

Intermediate Accounting，12e/by Donald E. Kieso et al.
ISBN：0471749559

教育部高校工商管理类教学指导委员会双语教学推荐教材
工商管理经典教材·会计与财务系列

中级会计学（第12版）

唐纳德·E·基索
杰里·J·韦安特　　著
特里·D·沃菲尔德
饶菁　崔学刚　改编

出版发行	中国人民大学出版社		
社　址	北京中关村大街31号	**邮政编码**	100080
电　话	010－62511242（总编室）		010－62511770（质管部）
	010－82501766（邮购部）		010－62514148（门市部）
	010－62515195（发行公司）		010－62515275（盗版举报）
网　址	http：//www. crup. com. cn		
经　销	新华书店		
印　刷	北京七色印务有限公司		
规　格	215 mm×275 mm　16开本	**版　次**	2007年4月第1版
印　张	37.25 插页1	**印　次**	2020年7月第10次印刷
字　数	1 104 000	**定　价**	49.00元

教师教学服务说明

中国人民大学出版社财会出版分社以出版经典、高品质的会计、财务管理、审计等领域各层次教材为宗旨。

为了更好地为一线教师服务，近年来财会出版分社着力建设了一批数字化、立体化的网络教学资源。教师可以通过以下方式获得免费下载教学资源的权限：

在中国人民大学出版社网站 www. crup. com. cn 进行注册，注册后进入“会员中心”，在左侧点击“我的教师认证”，填写相关信息，提交后等待审核。我们将在一个工作日内为您开通相关资源的下载权限。

如您急需教学资源或需要其他帮助，请在工作时间与我们联络：

中国人民大学出版社　财会出版分社

联系电话：010-62515987，62511076

电子邮箱：ckcbfs@crup. com. cn

通讯地址：北京市海淀区中关村大街甲 59 号文化大厦 1501 室（100872）

WILEY

John Wiley 教学支持信息反馈表

www.wiley.com

老师您好，若您需要与 John Wiley 教材配套的教辅（免费），烦请填写本表并传真给我们。也可联络 John Wiley 北京代表处索取本表的电子文件，填好后 e-mail 给我们。

原书信息

原版 ISBN：
英文书名（Title）：
版次（Edition）：
作者（Author）：

配套教辅可能包含下列一项或多项

教师用书（或指导手册）/ 习题解答/ 习题库 /PPT 讲义/ 其他

教师信息(中英文信息均需填写)

- 学校名称(中文)：
- 学校名称(英文)：
- 学校地址（中文）：
- 学校地址（英文）：
- 学校邮编：
- 院 / 系名称(中文)：
- 院 / 系名称(英文) ：

课程名称（Course Name）：
年级 / 程度（Year / Level）： □ 大专 □ 本科 Grade: 1 2 3 4 □ 硕士 □ 博士 □ MBA □ EMBA
课程性质（多选项）： □ 必修课 □ 选修课 □ 国外合作办学项目 □ 指定的双语课程
学年（学期）：□ 春季 □ 秋季 □ 整学年使用 □ 其他（起止月份____________）
使用的教材版本： □ 中文版 □ 英文影印（改编）版 □ 进口英文原版（购买价格为____元）
学生：______个班共______人
授课教师姓名：
电话：
传真：
E-mail：

WILEY - 约翰威立商务服务（北京）有限公司
John Wiley & Sons Commercial Service (Beijing) Co Ltd
北京市朝阳区太阳宫中路12A号,太阳宫大厦8层 805-808室，邮政编码100028
Direct +86 10 8418 7869 Fax +86 10 8418 7810
Email: Alyssa Yang <ayang@wiley.com>